FIREFLY'S WORLD OF FACTS

RUSSELL ASH

FIREFLY'S
WORLD OF
FACTS

FIREFLY BOOKS

A FIREFLY BOOK

Published by Firefly Books Ltd. 2009

First printing

**Publisher Cataloging-in-Publication Data
(U.S.)**
  Ash, Russell, 1946-
  Firefly's world of facts / Russell Ash.
[320] p. : col. ill., photos. ;   cm.
Includes index.
Summary: Covers an encyclopedic range of
subjects, including time, space, science,
technology, history, countries, music, film
and sports, and includes links to websites.
ISBN-13: 978-1-55407-499-0
ISBN-10: 1-55407-499-1
1. Encyclopedias and dictionaries. 2.
Curiosities and wonders. I. Title.
031.02 dc22   AG106.A84   2009

**Library and Archives Canada Cataloguing
in Publication**
Ash, Russell
      Firefly's world of facts / Russell Ash. --
3rd ed.
Includes index.
ISBN-13: 978-1-55407-499-0
ISBN-10: 1-55407-499-1
      1. Curiosities and wonders. 2.
Handbooks, vade-mecums, etc.
I. Title. II. Title: World of facts.
AG106.A76 2009   031.02   C2009-900629-4

Published in the United States by
Firefly Books (U.S.) Inc.
P.O. Box 1338, Ellicott Station
Buffalo, New York 14205

Published in Canada by
Firefly Books Ltd.
66 Leek Crescent
Richmond Hill, Ontario L4B 1H1

Illustrators Alan Baker (Illustration),
Julian Baker, KJA-artists
Heraldry consultant
    Henry Bedingfeld, College of Arms
Religions consultant
    Martin Palmer, ICOREC
Sports consultant Ian Morrison

Printed in China

CONTENTS

This new edition of *Firefly's World of Facts* has been updated from cover to cover. Inside, you will find thousands of amazing facts and hundreds of exciting pictures. Keep up-to-date with the most recent world record-breakers, cutting-edge scientific and medical breakthroughs and gadgets and gizmos from the latest e-readers to the cleverest robots.

Facts and figures

Firefly's World of Facts is divided into 20 sections — Planet Earth, People, World History and Space to name but a few. It includes information on a huge range of subjects, with data from authoritative sources and specialists on every subject under the Sun — and beyond. Among the countless new entries are features on the world's tallest building and the biggest ship, miraculous rescues and grisly torture methods, child soldiers and child film stars, the smallest mobile phones and the smallest snakes, animal heroes and toilets in space as well as important anniversaries coming up in 2010.

Inside information

Detailed lists and charts show global comparisons, while **special features** and **fact disks** provide fast information, revealing everything from the countries with the most computers to the highest-earning animated films, from the greatest achievers to the most popular social networking websites. You will also discover an array of **oddities**, including a time-eating clock with no hands, a lord whose carriage was pulled by zebras, a flying friar and people who dine in mid-air!

A section on **countries** gives essential information, including population, capital city and currency for every country in the world, as well as the flag of each one.

Timelines on subjects such as communications, astronomy, wars and inventions give a see-at-a-glance overview and pinpoint important milestones up to the present day.

Useful maps, **tables and formulae** include conversions, mathematical symbols and scales, from Beaufort (weather) to Richter (earthquakes).

Other features

Web link boxes suggest useful websites to help you explore subjects further. **See also** boxes guide you to information on a particular subject elsewhere in the book. There is an extensive **index** at the back of the book, as well as a **list of sources**.

Whitaker's World Website

You can write to me with comments, suggestions and corrections at the publisher's address on page four.

Russell Ash

About this book

Colored bars identify each section of the book

Follow these web links for more information

One and Only boxes identify unique facts

Detailed lists and statistics show global comparisons

Find cross-references throughout the book in these boxes

Fact disks highlight key facts

Timelines give you all the key milestones up to the present day

Lists give you the latest facts and figures, dates and rankings for all kinds of subjects

MVNDVS TRANS

Time

Eating time

This innovative clock was unveiled in 2008 by Professor Stephen Hawking at Corpus Christi College, Cambridge, UK. The work of a large team of experts, from engineers to craftspeople, it incorporates a traditional "grasshopper" clockwork mechanism alongside a number of new manufacturing methods. The creature at the top, known as a "chronophage" or time-eater, devours time while flashing LED lights on the face indicate the hours, minutes and seconds.

The Universe in a year!

The American astronomer Carl Sagan (1934–96) first suggested a "cosmic calendar" as a way of helping people understand the history of the Universe. He put everything into the scale of a calendar year: the galaxies are formed over nine months and the Earth appears in September.

Human history is crowded into the last five minutes of the year. Recent time is divided into seconds and fractions of a second. So everything that happened in the last 475 years takes place in less than the last second of the last minute of the year.

The world in a single day

In one day (24 hours or 1,440 minutes or 86,400 seconds) the world turns once on its axis. During that time, on average:
371,163 people are born
152,505 people die

Earth's life in a year

Jan 1 (midnight) Big Bang — Universe forms
Mar 15 First stars and galaxies form
May 1 Milky Way galaxy forms
Sep 8 Sun forms
Sep 9 Solar System forms
Sep 12 Earth forms
Sep 13 Moon forms
Sep 20 Earth's atmosphere forms
Oct 1 Earliest known life on Earth
Oct 7 Earliest known fossils
Dec 18 First many-celled life forms
Dec 19 First fish
Dec 21 First land plants; first insects
Dec 23 First reptiles
Dec 24 First dinosaurs
Dec 26 First mammals
Dec 27 First birds
Dec 28 First flowering plants
Dec 28 Dinosaurs extinct
Dec 31 (11:55 p.m.)
Homo sapiens (modern humans)

The last day

11:59.50.487 p.m. Great Pyramid is built (2520 BC)
11:59.55.333 p.m. Great Wall of China is built (215 BC)
11:59.56.785 p.m. Roman Empire falls (AD 476)
11:59.58.026 p.m. Battle of Hastings (1066)
11:59.58.921 p.m. Columbus lands in America (1492)
11:59.59.128 p.m. Shakespeare writes his first plays (1588–90)
11:59.59.865 pm World War II ends (1945)
11:59.59.882 pm Mount Everest is climbed (1953)
11:59.59.916 pm Man lands on the Moon (1969)
11:59.59.998 pm President Barack Obama is elected (2008)
Midnight Today

Royal Observatory, Greenwich; the "time ball" on the roof falls daily at 1:00 p.m.

Timetellers   1500BC

The following are some landmarks in the history of telling the time.

1500–1300 BC Sundials are used in Egypt: as the Earth rotates, the gnomon — the upright part of the sundial — casts a shadow that moves to indicate the time.

c. 400 BC Water clocks are used in Greece: as water drains from a container, each level it reaches represents a period of time.

c. AD 890 In England people use candles marked with time intervals.

12th century The hourglass, familiar to us as an eggtimer, is used by monks to show times of prayer.

1325 The first clock with a dial is installed in Norwich Cathedral, England.

1335 The first clock to strike the hours is made in Milan, Italy.

1350 The oldest known surviving alarm clock is made in Würzburg, Germany.

1364 Clocks are first used in people's homes.

1386 The clock is installed in Salisbury Cathedral, England. This is the world's oldest clock in working order.

1462 The earliest description of a watch is written in Italy.

1641 The pendulum clock is proposed by Vincenzio Galilei, son of the astronomer Galileo.

1657 The first pendulum clocks are made in Holland.

Time zones

The Earth is constantly turning on its axis. If people everywhere set their clocks to the same time, midnight would be in the middle of the night on one side of the globe, but the middle of the day on the opposite side. To avoid this problem the Earth is divided into artificial time zones. These generally follow lines of longitude — imaginary lines running from the North to the South Pole. Some large countries, such as the United States, cover several time zones. Mainland U.S. is divided into Atlantic, Eastern, Central, Mountain, Pacific and Alaska zones, with Hawaii and other islands falling into further zones.

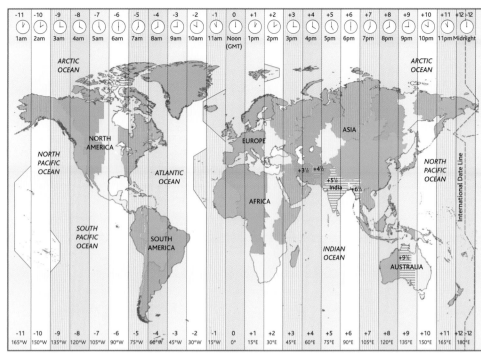

World time zones and the International Date Line

Since the Greenwich Prime Meridian (0°) was established in 1884, there have been 24 time zones, each of 15° longitude and an hour apart. Those to the east are ahead of Greenwich by one hour per zone.

Those to the west are behind by one hour each. Some countries, such as India, have chosen zones halfway between those on either side, so that the whole country can use the same time.

Two sides of the Earth

The International Date Line is an imaginary line between the North and South Poles. It marks the end of one day and the start of another. Countries to the east of the Date Line are always a day ahead of those to the west. Travelers who cross the line gain or lose a day, depending on which direction they are going.

The International Date Line

The Earth makes one complete turn in every 24 hours. In that time, each of the 360 degrees of longitude passes the Sun. This means that time progresses eastward by four minutes for every degree of longitude.

Most of the Date Line follows the 180° Meridian (on the opposite side of the globe from 0°, the Greenwich Meridian). The line generally passes through sea, but where it would pass through or near certain land areas, it is adjusted. It zigzags around islands, putting them either into the west or the east, and avoids dividing Siberia in northeast Asia into two time zones.

See also

Galileo Galilei: page 26

2010

c. 1665 The first watches with minute and second hands are made.
1759 John Harrison's marine chronometer is made. Accurate timekeeping at sea is important for calculating position, but previously the rolling of a ship had made it impossible.
1880 Greenwich Mean Time becomes the standard from which time around the world is set.

1880 The first practical wristwatches are made for the German navy.
1928 The first quartz crystal clock is made in the U.S.
1949 The first atomic clock is built in the U.S.
1957 The first battery watches are marketed in the U.S.
1969 Quartz wristwatches are first sold in Japan.

1970 Digital watches and displays become widely used worldwide and can be made and sold cheaply.
2007 Daylight Saving Time begins at 2:00 am on the second Sunday in March and reverts to Standard Time at 2:00 am on

the first Sunday of November in the United States. Previously it changed in April and October.
2010 Vancouver Winter Olympics countdown clock runs from 2007 until opening of 2010 games (February 12) and paralympics (March 12).

www.physics.nist.gov/GenInt/Time   search

Thor was the Scandinavian god of thunder and war. He is often shown brandishing a hammer. Thursday, or Thor's day, is named after him.

Names of months

The names of the months in English (as well as in many other languages) come from Latin words.

January
Januarius — this month was dedicated to Janus, the Roman god of doors. Janus had two faces, one looking back at the old year and the other looking forward to the new year.

February
Februarius — Februa was the Roman purification festival, which took place at this time of year.

March
Martius — from Mars, the Roman god of war.

April
Aprilis — from *aperire*, Latin for open, because plants begin to open during this month.

May
Maius — probably comes from Maia, the Roman goddess of growth and increase.

June
Junius — either from a Roman family name, Junius, which means young, or perhaps after the goddess Juno.

July
Julius — after Julius Caesar. This month was named in Caesar's honor by Mark Antony in 44 BC. Previously this month was called Quintilis from the word *quintus*, "five," as it was the fifth month in the Roman calendar.

August
Augustus — named in 8 BC in honor of Emperor Augustus.

September
September — from *septem*, "seven," because it was the seventh month in the Roman calendar.

October
October — from *octo*, "eight" (as in octopus, which has eight legs), the eighth month in the Roman calendar.

November
November — from *novem*, "nine," the ninth month in the Roman calendar.

December
December — from *decem*, "ten," the tenth month in the Roman calendar.

Leap seconds

The rotation of the Earth is slowing down. This means that a solar day (the time it takes Earth to make one complete revolution) and the time shown by atomic clocks would gradually diverge. This problem has been solved by adding "leap seconds." There have been 22 leap seconds since 1972. The last one was added on December 31, 2008, which delayed New Year's Day 2006 by one second!

Naming the days of the week

The ancient Babylonians, then the Romans, named the days of the week after planets and other bodies they saw in the sky. Some names we know today come from the names of Scandinavian gods.

Monday
Moon's day

Tuesday
Tiu's day — Mars, the Roman god of war, was adopted in Scandinavian mythology as the warrior Tiu or Tiw.

Wednesday
Woden's day — the Roman god Mercury became the Scandinavian god Woden.

Thursday
Thor's day — like the Roman god Jupiter, Thor was a thunder god.

Friday
Freyja's day — like Venus, Freyja or Frigg was the goddess of love.

Saturday
Saturn's day

Sunday
Sun's day

How long does it take?

One beat of a fly's wing (1/1,000 second) 0.001 seconds
Flash of lightning (1/1,000 second) 0.001 seconds
One beat of a hummingbird's wing (80 times a second) 0.0125 seconds
Mouse heartbeat (10.8 times a second) 0.09 seconds
Blink of a human eye 0.33 seconds
Human heartbeat 1.0 seconds
Land speed record: car *ThrustSSC* traveling 0.62 mi. (1 km) 2.9 seconds
Record-breaking Jamaican athlete Asafa Powell to run 328 ft (100 m) 9.77 seconds
Bullet train to travel 0.62 mi. (1 km) 13.75 seconds
Space Shuttle to travel 62 mi. (10 km) 15 seconds
Light reaching Earth from the Sun 497 seconds

Watches at sea

At sea, the 24-hour day is traditionally divided into seven watches, during which some of a ship's crew are on duty.

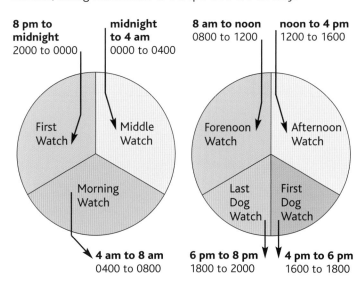

8 pm to midnight 2000 to 0000
midnight to 4 am 0000 to 0400
8 am to noon 0800 to 1200
noon to 4 pm 1200 to 1600

First Watch · Middle Watch · Morning Watch
Forenoon Watch · Afternoon Watch · Last Dog Watch · First Dog Watch

4 am to 8 am 0400 to 0800
6 pm to 8 pm 1800 to 2000
4 pm to 6 pm 1600 to 1800

www.physics.nist.gov/Genint/Time   **search**

Just a second

It will take you almost five seconds to read this sentence. During an average-length film more than 5,000 seconds will pass. In a lifetime of 80 years, there are more than 2.5 billion seconds — but you will spend more than 800 million of them asleep!

1 minute 60 seconds
1 hour 3,600 seconds
1 day 86,400 seconds
1 week 604,800 seconds
1 year 31,536,000 seconds

ThrustSCC set the first supersonic land-speed record, at 763,035 mph (1,227,986 km/h).

Time words

Here are some of the words used for units of time.

chronon
One-billionth of a trillionth of a second (the time a photon would take to cross the width of one electron at the speed of light)

femtosecond
0.000000000000001 of a second

picosecond
0.000000000001 (one-trillionth) of a second

nanosecond
0.000000001 (one-billionth) of a second

microsecond
0.000001 (one-millionth) of a second

millisecond
0.001 (one-thousandth) of a second; the blink of an eye takes 50–80 milliseconds

centisecond
0.01 (one-hundredth) of a second

second
1/60 of a minute

minute
60 seconds

hour
60 minutes

day
Sunrise to sunrise, or sunset to sunset, or midnight to midnight; 24 hours

week
Seven days; in Shakespeare's time, it was also called a sennight, or seven nights

fortnight
Two weeks (from the Old English for 14 nights)

month
Full Moon to full Moon; 1/12 of a year; 4 weeks, or 28, 29, 30 or 31 days, depending on month

bimester
Two months

trimester
A period of three months

year
365¼ days, 52 weeks, or 12 months

solar day
The time it takes for a place on the Earth directly facing the Sun to make one revolution and return to the same position (about 23 hours 56 minutes)

solar year
The time it takes for the Earth to make a complete revolution around the Sun, equal to 365.24219 solar days or 365 days, 5 hours 48 minutes, 45.51 seconds; also called a tropical year or astronomical year

leap year
366 days

decade
10 years; also called a decennium

century
100 years

millennium
1,000 years; also called a chiliad

bimillennium
2,000 years

era
A period of time measured from some important event

eon or aeon
A long period of time, usually thousands of years; in geology and astronomy it is one billion years

epoch
A geological era or very long period of time

See also

Geological time chart: page 34

THE CALENDAR

Gregorian calendar

The Gregorian calendar is the one most used nowadays. It is named after Pope Gregory XIII who introduced it in 1582. There is a leap year every four years (or more precisely, 97 leap years every 400 years). This means that the year corresponds closely with the astronomical year (365.24219 days) so that it gets just one day out of sync in every 3,300 years.

Calendar problems

Some non-Catholic countries such as Great Britain refused to adopt the Gregorian calendar at first. The Julian calendar previously used in Great Britain was based on a solar year, the time taken for the Earth to rotate around the Sun. This is 365.25 days, which is fractionally too long (it is actually 365.24219 days), so the calendar steadily fell out of line with the seasons. In 1752 Great Britain decided to correct this by abandoning the Julian calendar in favor of the Gregorian. By doing so, September 3 became September 14 — and, as a result, nothing whatsoever happened in British history between September 3 and 13, 1752. Many people believed their lives would be shortened. They protested in the streets, demanding, "Give us back our 11 days!"

1 January 31 days	**5 May** 31 days	**9 September** 30 days
2 February 28 days*	**6 June** 30 days	**10 October** 31 days
3 March 31 days	**7 July** 31 days	**11 November** 30 days
4 April 30 days	**8 August** 31 days	**12 December** 31 days

* In a leap year, February has 29 days.

Time pyramid

The Mayan pyramid at Chichén Itzá, Mexico, built around 1050, has four stairways, each with 91 steps and one platform. This makes a total of 365, the number of days in a year. The stairways also divide the nine terraces of each side of the pyramid into 18 segments, representing the 18 months of the Mayan calendar.

Mayan calendar

The Mayan people lived in the Yucatan area of present-day Mexico and the neighboring region. They built many amazing pyramids and temples, and had an astonishing knowledge of astronomy.

Mayan culture had declined by the time Spanish invaders occupied their territory in the 16th century, but we know something about it from the remains found. The Haab or civil calendar of the Maya had 18 months made up of 20 days each. Five extra days were added at the year's end, known as Uayeb, giving a year of 365 days.

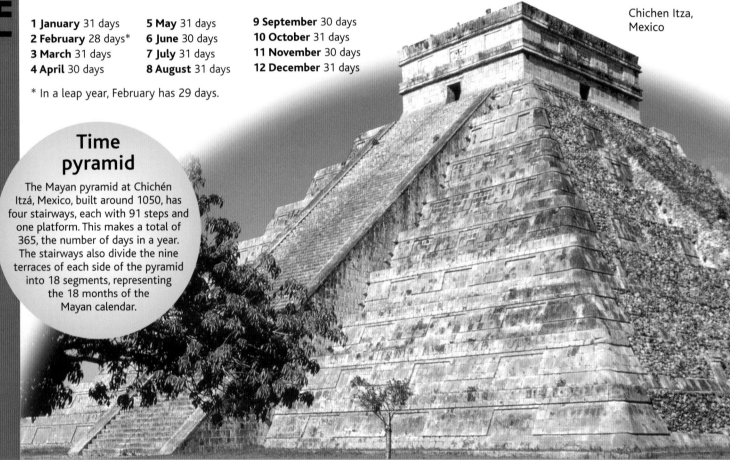

Chichen Itza, Mexico

Calendar timeline

Most of the world's countries and cultures use the Gregorian calendar, but some base their calendars on more ancient systems. Other countries have adopted an alternative calendar at some point in their history.

3761 BC Jewish calendar starts
2637 BC Original Chinese calendar starts
45 BC Julian calendar adopted by Roman Empire
AD 1 Christian calendar starts
AD 79 Hindu calendar starts
597 Julian calendar adopted in Great Britain
622 Islamic calendar starts

1582 Gregorian calendar introduced in Catholic countries
1752 Julian calendar abandoned, Gregorian calendar adopted in Britain and its colonies, including America
1873 Japan adopts the Gregorian calendar
1949 China adopts the Gregorian calendar

Mayan months

1 Pop	**10** Yax
2 Uo	**11** Zac
3 Zip	**12** Ceh
4 Zotz	**13** Mac
5 Tzec	**14** Kankin
6 Xul	**15** Muan
7 Yaxkin	**16** Pax
8 Mol	**17** Kayab
9 Chen	**18** Cumku

Chinese calendar

Present-day China uses the Gregorian calendar for most purposes, but traditional festivals, such as Chinese New Year, take place according to the ancient Chinese calendar. Legend has it that this was started during the reign of Emperor Huangdi in 2637 BC, and relates to the positions of the Moon and Sun.

The ancient Chinese calendar follows a 60-year cycle that combines a heavenly stem and earthly branch, represented by a zodiac animal. The first year of the cycle is jia-zi, the second yi-chou, and so on; the 11th year is jia-xu, 12th yi-hai and 13th bing-zi. This continues until the 60th year (gui-hai) and then starts again. Each earthly branch is believed to be linked with certain qualities.

Chinese dragon

Calendars meet

The Islamic year is about 11 days shorter than a year in the Gregorian calendar. The Islamic calendar started 622 years later than the Gregorian so its date is behind. But because the year is shorter, the Islamic calendar is gradually gaining on the Gregorian. The two will eventually coincide — in the year 20874.

 webexhibits.org/calendars   search

Hebrew and Islamic calendars

The Hebrew (Jewish) and Islamic (Muslim) calendars are based on the lunar (Moon) cycle. Every month starts approximately on the day of a new Moon, or when a crescent moon is first seen.

The visibility of the Moon varies according to the weather so the start date cannot be determined in advance. Printed calendars may vary by a few days. Tishri/Muharram corresponds approximately with September/October in the Gregorian calendar, Heshvan/Safar with October/November, and so on.

Hebrew	Islamic	Hebrew	Islamic
1 Tishri	Muharram* (30 days)	7 Nisan	Rajab* (30 days)
2 Heshvan	Safar (29 days)	8 Iyar	Sha'ban (29 days)
3 Kislev	Rabi'a I (30 days)	9 Sivan	Ramadan † (30 days)
4 Tevet	Rabi'a II (29 days)	10 Tammuz	Shawwal (29 days)
5 Shevat	Jumada I (30 days)	11 Av	Dhu al-Q'adah* (30 days)
6 Adar	Jumada II (29 days)	12 Elu	Dhu al-Hijjah (29 days)

* Holy months   † Month of fasting

Indian calendar

The Indian calendar is based on the motions of the Sun and Moon and is dated from the so-called Saka Era, equivalent to AD 79. It is used for dating religious and other festivals, but the Gregorian calendar is used for official dates.

Month	Length	Gregorian calendar
1 Caitra	30 days*	March 22
2 Vaisakha	31 days	April 21
3 Jyaistha	31 days	May 22
4 Asadha	31 days	June 22
5 Sravana	31 days	July 23
6 Bhadra	31 days	August 23
7 Asvina	30 days	September 23
8 Kartika	30 days	October 23
9 Agrahayana	30 days	November 22
10 Pausa	30 days	December 22
11 Magha	30 days	January 21
12 Phalguna	30 days	February 20

* In a leap year, Caitra has 31 days and 1 Caitra = March 21

Chinese calendar and Gregorian equivalents

HEAVENLY STEMS	EARTHLY BRANCHES			Zodiac animal	Gregorian calendar year beginning	Zodiac animal	Gregorian calendar year beginning
1 jia	1 zi (rat)	11 xu (dog)		Tiger	Jan 28, 1998	Rooster	Feb 9, 2005
2 yi	2 chou (ox)	12 hai (pig or boar)		Hare	Feb 16, 1999	Dog	Jan 29, 2006
3 bing	3 yin (tiger)			Dragon	Feb 5, 2000	Pig	Feb 18, 2007
4 ding	4 mao (hare or rabbit)			Snake	Jan 24, 2001	Rat	Feb 7, 2008
5 wu	5 chen (dragon)			Horse	Feb 12, 2002	Ox	Jan 26, 2009
6 ji	6 si (snake)			Sheep	Feb 1, 2003	Tiger	Feb 14, 2010
7 geng	7 wu (horse)			Monkey	Jan 22, 2004	Rabbit	Feb 3, 2011
8 zxin	8 wei (sheep or ram)						
9 ren	9 shen (monkey)						
10 gui	10 you (rooster)						

Space

Silhouette of the moon

The longest annular eclipse of the 21st century takes place on January 15, 2010. An annular eclipse is when the moon is in line with the sun, leaving only a small ring of the sun visible. The 2010 annular eclipse will be 11 minutes and 8 seconds long, creating a dramatic visual effect.

Twinkle twinkle little star...

Stars appear to twinkle because we see them through the layers of the Earth's atmosphere. Light is distorted as it passes through these layers, so that the amount we see changes constantly. Stars nearest the horizon seem to twinkle the most because the light is passing through a greater depth of atmosphere. Stars do not twinkle when viewed from space, so telescopes in space, such as the Hubble, give the best possible view of distant stars and galaxies.

Star facts

A star is a luminous body of gas, mostly hydrogen and helium. Stars generate light, which makes it possible for us to see them with a telescope or the naked eye.

Photographs all taken by the Hubble Space Telescope

Supergiant VY Canis Majoris

The Sun

● Brightest
Not counting the Sun, the brightest star as seen from Earth is Sirius, known as the dog star, in the constellation of Canis Major. It has a diameter of 92,955,900 mi. (149,598,020 km) and is more than 24 times brighter than the Sun. The star LBV 1806–20 in the constellation of Sagittarius may be 40 million times as bright as our Sun, but dust clouds make it almost invisible from Earth.

● Largest
The largest star is VY Canis Majoris, which has an estimated diameter of about 1,950 times greater than the Sun. For comparison, if it were a football, the Sun would be no bigger than a pinhead.

● Nearest
Proxima Centauri, discovered in 1915, is 4.22 light years from Earth. A spaceship moving at 25,000 mph (40,000 km/h) — which is faster than any human has yet traveled in space — would take more than 114,000 years to reach it.

● Supernovae
These are vast explosions in which a whole star blows up. They are extremely bright, rivaling for a few days the combined light output of all the stars in the galaxy. Supernovae are rare — the last one in our galaxy was seen in 1604 by the German astronomer Johannes Kepler.

● Quasars
These are extremely distant radio galaxies — galaxies giving out large amounts of radio energy — and the brightest objects in the Universe. Their radio emission is typically 1,000,000 to 100,000,000 times greater than that of a normal galaxy.

● Black holes
A black hole is a star that has collapsed into itself. It has a surface gravity so powerful that nothing can escape from within it.

Black Eye Galaxy

Swan Nebula

Monocerotis V838 (a red supergiant star surrounded by dust)

Traveling at the speed of light

In space, light travels at a speed of 186,282.4 mi. (299,792.46 km) a second, or 670,616,696 mi. (1,079,252,956 km) an hour. When we look at even the nearest star, we see light that left it more than four years ago. Here are the times it takes light to reach Earth from various bodies in space.

● Light years
A light year measures distance, not time. Distances in space are often described as light years, the distance light travels in a year.

Galaxy facts

Galaxies are groups of billions of stars held together by the force of gravity. Most are either spiral or elliptical, but some are irregular in shape.

● The Milky Way

This is the best-known galaxy. The word galaxy comes from the Greek for milk. Before telescopes were powerful enough to prove that they were made up of individual stars, galaxies looked like milky or cloudy areas in the sky. Our Solar System is only one of 100–200 billion stars in the Milky Way, which is 100,000 light years in diameter. The Sun and all the planets take about 200,000,000 years to complete one orbit around its center.

● Brightest

The Large Magellanic Cloud, which is visible only in the southern hemisphere, is 170,000 light years from Earth and 39,000 light years in diameter.

● Largest

The central galaxy of the Abell 2029 galaxy cluster was discovered in 1990. It is 1.07 billion light years distant and has a diameter of 5.6 million light years, 80 times the diameter of our own galaxy. It has a total light output equivalent to 2 trillion times that of the Sun.

● Nearest

Discovered in 1993, the Canis Major Dwarf galaxy is approximately 25,000 light years from the Solar System.

Constellations

Groups of stars form patterns in the night sky, which are called constellations. There are 88 known constellations. The Sumerians, a Middle Eastern civilization, probably named them, about 5,000 years ago.

The largest is Hydra, the sea serpent, and the smallest is Crux Australis, the Southern Cross. Centaurus, the Centaur, has the most stars that can be seen with the naked eye (94). Others include Aquila, the Eagle; Canis Major, the Great Dog; and Orion, the Hunter.

Small Magellanic Cloud

Canis Major — the Great Dog

Crux Australis — the Southern Cross

Orion — the Hunter

Aquila — the Eagle

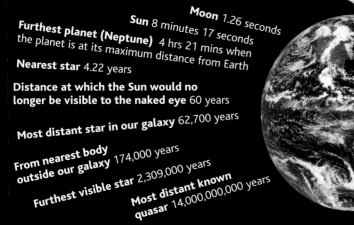

Moon 1.26 seconds

Sun 8 minutes 17 seconds

Furthest planet (Neptune) 4 hrs 21 mins when the planet is at its maximum distance from Earth

Nearest star 4.22 years

Distance at which the Sun would no longer be visible to the naked eye 60 years

Most distant star in our galaxy 62,700 years

From nearest body outside our galaxy 174,000 years

Furthest visible star 2,309,000 years

Most distant known quasar 14,000,000,000 years

www.astronautix.com | search

Solar System

The Solar System was formed about 4,560 million years ago. It is made up of the eight planets — Mercury, Venus, Earth, Mars, Jupiter, Saturn, Uranus and Neptune — as well as their moons, comets and other bodies. These all orbit our Sun, which they are attracted to by gravity.

Mercury

Mercury was named after the speedy messenger of the gods because it seemed to move more quickly than the other known planets. In 2004 NASA launched its MESSENGER probe, which is due to reach Mercury in 2011.

Diameter: 3,032 mi. (4,880 km)
Mass: 3.302 x 10^{23} kg (0.055 Earths)
Average distance from Sun: 35,983,093 mi. (57,909,175 km)
Rotation: 58.6462 days
Orbit: 87.969 days
Average temperature: 332.32˚F (166.86˚C)
Moons: 0

Venus

In size, mass, density and volume Venus is the planet most similar to Earth. Venus rotates backward, from east to west, so the Sun would appear to rise in the west and set in the east. In April 2006 the European Space Agency's *Venus Express* spacecraft reached Venus. Japan's Venus Climate Orbiter *PLANET-C* will be launched in 2010.

Diameter: 7,521 mi. (12,103.6 km)
Mass: 4.869 x 10^{24} kg (0.815 Earths)
Average distance from Sun: 67,237,912 mi. (108,208,930 km)
Rotation: 243.0187 days
Orbit: 224.701 days
Average temperature: 854.33˚F (456.85˚C)
Moons: 0

See also
Planets visited by spacecraft: page 29

Mars

Several space probes have flown past or landed on Mars, providing information on its atmosphere and features, such as the volcano Olympus Mons. This stands 17 mi. (27 km) high — more than three times the height of Mount Everest. The latest craft to visit the red planet are NASA's *Mars Reconnaissance Orbiter*, which began its four-year orbit in 2006, and the *Phoenix Mars* lander, which descended to the surface on May 25, 2008.

Diameter: 4,222 mi. (6,794 km)
Mass: 6.4185 x 10^{23} kg (0.107 Earths)
Average distance from Sun: 141,635,000 mi. (227,940,000 km)
Rotation: 1.025957 days
Orbit: 686.98 days
Average temperature: −81˚F(− 63˚C)
Moons: 2

Jupiter

Jupiter is the largest planet in the Solar System and is big enough to contain more than a thousand Earths. Four of its many moons were among the first ever astronomical discoveries made with a telescope, by Galileo in 1610. More were identified by later astronomers and in 1979 by the space probe *Voyager 2*. The NASA Juno mission to Jupiter is planned for launch in 2011.

Diameter: 88,846 mi. (142,984 km)
Mass: 1.8986 x 10^{27} kg (317.8 Earths)
Average distance from Sun: 483,682,799 mi. (778,412,010 km)
Rotation: 9 hours 50 minutes
Orbit: 11 years 314 days
Average temperature: −238˚F (−150˚C)
Moons: 63

Earth

Earth is a watery planet — 70 percent of its surface appears blue — and the only one that can support life. From space, astronauts have observed cities, forest fires, roads, airports, dams and other large structures, such as the Great Pyramid and the Great Wall of China.

Diameter: 7,926 mi. (12,756 km)
Mass: 5.972 x 10^{24} kg
Average distance from Sun: 92,957,130 mi. (149,600,000 km)
Rotation: 0.99727 days
Orbit: 365.256 days
Average temperature: 59˚F (15˚C)
Moons: 1

www.nineplanets.org   search

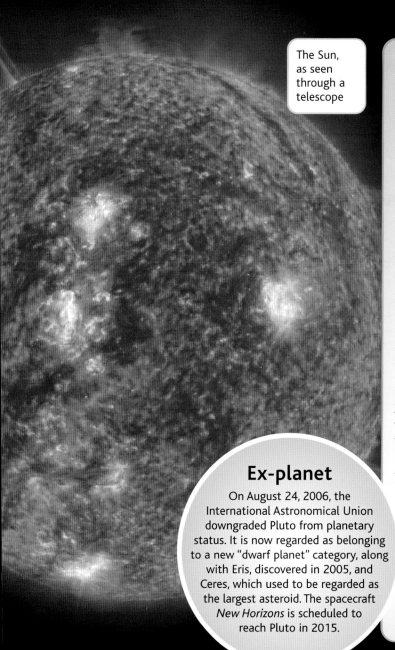

The Sun, as seen through a telescope

Sun facts

The Sun is 92,955,821 mi. (149,597,893 km) from Earth and has a diameter of 864,911 mi. (1,391,940 km). This is more than 100 times larger than Earth. Its mass is equivalent to 99.98 percent of the mass of the entire Solar System.

Elements

The Sun is mostly made up of two light gases, 75 percent hydrogen and 23 percent helium, with relatively small quantities of other elements — including metals such as gold. Helium was discovered in the Sun before it was detected on Earth. Its name comes from *helios*, the Greek word for sun.

Temperature

The Sun has a surface temperature of 5,880 K but it can be 56,000,000 K at its core. (K represents Kelvin, which is an astronomical temperature; it can be converted to Fahrenheit by subtracting 459.67.) At the Sun's center, nuclear fusion constantly changes hydrogen into helium, and the energy and heat released from this process rise to the surface. The yellow surface we see is called the photosphere.

The corona

The outermost layer of the Sun extends millions of miles into space but is visible only during eclipses. At a height of 46,600 mi. (75,000 km) in the corona, the temperature may reach 2,000,000 K.

Rotation

The Sun rotates once every 25.4 days, but because it is not solid, the poles spin at a different rate, taking as much as 36 days to complete a single revolution.

Solar eclipses

When the Moon is between Earth and the Sun, it blocks out the light causing a partial or total eclipse. At this time, astronomers are able to observe the corona in detail.

Ex-planet

On August 24, 2006, the International Astronomical Union downgraded Pluto from planetary status. It is now regarded as belonging to a new "dwarf planet" category, along with Eris, discovered in 2005, and Ceres, which used to be regarded as the largest asteroid. The spacecraft *New Horizons* is scheduled to reach Pluto in 2015.

Saturn

Saturn and its rings are being examined by NASA/European Space Agency's *Cassini* probe, which reached it in 2004. It released the *Huygens* probe to orbit Titan in 2005 and began flybys of Saturn's moons Lapetus in 2007 and Titan in 2008.

Diameter: 74,898 mi. (120,536 km)
Mass: 5.6846 x 10^{26} kg (95.15 Earths)
Average distance from Sun: 886,526,100 mi. (1,426,725,400 km)
Rotation: 10 hours 34 minutes
Orbit: 29 years 168 days
Average temperature: −219.1˚F (−139.5˚C)
Moons: 56

Uranus

All the satellites of Uranus are called after characters from either William Shakespeare's plays or Alexander Pope's poem *The Rape of the Lock*. Uranus has rings like those of Saturn, but they are visible only with a powerful telescope.

Diameter: 31,763 mi. (51,118 km)
Mass: 8.6832 x 10^{25} kg (14.54 Earths)
Average distance from Sun: 1,783,939,400 mi. (2,870,972,200 km)
Rotation: 17 hours 17 minutes
Orbit: 84 years 4 days
Average temperature: −322.87˚F (−197.15˚C)
Moons: 27

Neptune

Neptune is the furthest body from the Sun. Surface winds are the strongest of any planet at up to 2,000 km/h. Neptune's year is so long that it has not completed an orbit round the Sun since its discovery and will not do so until July 12, 2011.

Diameter: 30,772 mi. (49,522 km)
Mass: 10.247 x 10^{25} kg (17.15 Earths)
Average distance from Sun: 2,795,084,800 mi. (4,498,252,900 km)
Rotation: 16 hours 7 minutes
Orbit: 164 years 298 days
Average temperature: −328.27˚F (−200.15˚C)
Moons: 13

Buzz Aldrin, walking on the Moon

The Moon's near side

Our Moon's far side
The far side of our Moon always faces away from Earth, so it was unknown until October 1959, when the Soviet *Luna 3* probe sent pictures of it back to Earth.

Moon facts

Earth's Moon is the most familiar and also the largest satellite in relation to its planet in the Solar System. It is the first body in the Solar System on which vehicles from Earth landed, and the only one to be explored by humans.

Diameter: 2159.6 mi. (3,475.6 km)
Distance from Earth: 252,718 mi. (406,711 km)
— furthest 1912; to 221,441 mi. (356,375 km)
— closest, 1984; averaging 238,856 mi.
(384,403 km)
Mass: 7.3456×10^{23} kg (0.012 Earths)
809,709,000,000 tons; a person weighing 140 lb. (63.5 kg) on Earth would weigh 23.23 lb. (10.5 kg) on the Moon
Rotation: 27 days 7 hours 43 minutes 11.5 seconds
Surface temperature: −261°F to 243°F (−163°C to 117°C)
Largest crater: South Pole Aitken (far side) 1,305 mi. (2,100 km) diameter, 7.5 mi. (12 km) deep (largest in the Solar System)

Asteroid facts

Asteroids are often called minor planets. They are lumps of rock orbiting the Sun, mostly in the asteroid belt between the orbits of Mars and Jupiter.

● Ceres was once considered the largest asteroid but it has been recently reclassified as a dwarf planet. It is 582 mi. (936 km) in diameter and was found on New Year's Day, 1801. Since then thousands of asteroids have been found. Twelve of them are more than 155 mi. (250 km) wide and 26 are larger than 125 mi. (200 km) in diameter. As telescopes have improved, more and more small asteroids have been detected. Up to 2009, over 200,000 asteroids had been identified. There are probably more than one million asteroids larger than half a mile in diameter.

● Vesta, the fourth asteroid to be found (in 1807), is the only one bright enough to be seen without a telescope.

Part of the Bayeux Tapestry, showing Halley's comet, top left

Halley's comet   240BC   1450s

British astronomer Edmond Halley (1656–1742) was the first to prove that comets travel in orbits, making it possible to calculate when they will next be seen from Earth. He predicted that the comet he saw in 1682 would return in 1759. It did and was named in his honor. The regular orbit of Halley's comet means that we can find historical accounts of its appearances going back more than 2,000 years. They were often believed to foretell great events.

May 25, 240 BC Seen in China
October 10, 12 BC Believed to mark the death of Roman general Agrippa
June 28, AD 451 Believed to mark the defeat of Attila the Hun
March 20, 1066 William (later William the Conqueror) believed

the comet foretold victory over King Harold at the Battle of Hastings. The comet and battle are later depicted in the Bayeux Tapestry.
June 9, 1456 The defeat of the Turkish army by Papal forces was thought to be linked to the comet.

● Astronomers believe that, on average, one asteroid larger than 0.25 mi. (0.4 km) strikes Earth every 50,000 years. Some 65 million years ago a 6 mi. (10 km) diameter asteroid crashing to Earth may have been responsible for wiping out the dinosaurs. It would have caused a catastrophic explosion, affecting the climate and chemical composition of the atmosphere and destroying the plants and animals on which the dinosaurs fed. As recently as 1991 a small asteroid came within 106,000 mi. (170,600 km) of Earth, the closest recorded near miss. On Jan 30, 2052, an asteroid is predicted to pass as close as 74,364 mi. (119,678 km).

● Toutatis (asteroid 4,179) was discovered in 1989. It is named after the Celtic god Toutatis. Toutatis measures 2.9 by 1.5 by 1.2 mi. (4.6 by 2.4 by 1.9 km). It passes Earth every four years and is one of the largest space objects to come so close to us. On September 29, 2004, Toutatis came within 966,740 mi. (1,555,818 km) of Earth. It last visited on November 9, 2008, when it came within 4,675,677 mi. (7,524,773 km).

Titanic moon

Titan is the largest of Saturn's 34 moons. It is 3,200 mi. (5,150 km) in diameter — larger than the planet Mercury. Dutch astronomer Christiaan Huygens discovered Titan in 1655. We still have no idea what its surface looks like because Titan has a dense atmosphere containing nitrogen, ethane and other gases that shroud its surface — not unlike that of Earth four billion years ago.

Information sent back by the space probe *Voyager 1* during 1980 and recent radio telescope observations suggest that Titan may have ethane "oceans" and "continents" of ice or other solid matter. *Cassini*, a space probe launched by NASA and the European Space Agency, arrived in Saturn's orbit on July 1, 2004. On January 14, 2005, it launched the *Huygens* probe onto the surface of Titan and sent back scientific data.

Neptune's moon

Triton, discovered in 1846, is the only known large moon in the Solar System with a retrograde orbit. It revolves around its planet (Neptune) in the opposite direction to the planet's rotation.

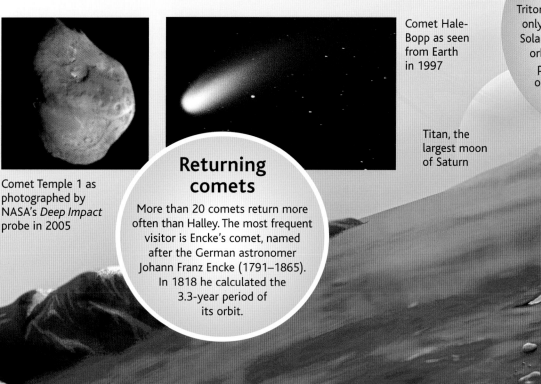

Comet Hale-Bopp as seen from Earth in 1997

Titan, the largest moon of Saturn

Comet Temple 1 as photographed by NASA's *Deep Impact* probe in 2005

Returning comets

More than 20 comets return more often than Halley. The most frequent visitor is Encke's comet, named after the German astronomer Johann Franz Encke (1791–1865). In 1818 he calculated the 3.3-year period of its orbit.

2000s

September 15, 1682 Observed by Edmond Halley, who predicted its return
March 13, 1759 The comet's first return, as predicted by Halley, proving his calculations correct
November 16, 1835 The American author Mark Twain is born. He always believed that his

fate was linked to that of the comet, and soon after it reappeared in 1910, he died.
April 10, 1910 There was panic as many believed the world would come to an end.
February 9, 1986 The Japanese *Suisei* probe, Soviet *Vega 1* and *Vega 2* and the European Space

Agency's *Giotto* passed close to Halley's comet. Astronomers concluded that the comet is made of dust held together by water and carbon dioxide ice.

July 28, 2061 Next due to appear. The orbit of Halley's comet is not exactly 76 years. Astronomers have to take into account the gravitational pull from planets when calculating its return.

Famous astronomers

John Couch Adams (UK, 1819–92) studied the Leonid meteor shower and predicted the existence of Neptune, which was discovered in 1846.

Edward Emerson Barnard (U.S., 1857–1923) discovered Barnard's Star and Amalthea, a moon of Jupiter.

Nicolaus Copernicus (Poland, 1473–1543) showed that the Sun was at the center of the Solar System.

Galileo Galilei (Italy, 1564–1642) made important discoveries concerning gravity and motion. He built some of the first telescopes used in astronomy and used them to discover many previously unknown space objects.

George Ellery Hale (U.S., 1868–1938) pioneered the astronomical study of the Sun and founded observatories, one with a major telescope named after him.

Edmond Halley (UK, 1656–1742) predicted the orbits of comets, including the one that bears his name.

William Herschel (Germany/U.K., 1738–1822) built huge telescopes, compiled catalogues of stars and discovered moons of Saturn and Uranus.

Edwin Hubble (U.S., 1889–1953) made important discoveries about galaxies. The Hubble Space Telescope was named in his honor.

Christiaan Huygens (Holland, 1629–95) discovered Saturn's rings and devised the wave theory of light.

Percival Lowell (U.S., 1855–1916) was founder of the Lowell Observatory, Arizona. He predicted that a planet would be found in the region where Pluto was later discovered.

Charles Messier (France, 1730–1817) studied comets and eclipses, but he is best known for his catalogue of stars first published in 1774.

Isaac Newton (England, 1643–1727) is considered one of the greatest of all astronomers. His theories of gravity and the motions of planets revolutionized the subject.

Telescopes and observatories

The following are some of the world's most famous telescopes and observatories.

Royal Observatory, Greenwich, London, England
Founded by King Charles II in 1675, but atmospheric and light pollution in London reduced its efficiency. In 1884 the Prime or Greenwich Meridian, 0°, which passes through the Observatory, was adopted as the basis for all mapping and measurements. Longitude measurements refer to west or east of the meridian.

Herschel's "Forty-foot" reflector, Slough, England
A giant telescope built in 1788 with a 48-in. (1.2 m) mirror.

Birr Castle, Co. Offaly, Ireland
The Earl of Rosse's 72 in. (1.8 m) reflecting telescope, built in 1845, was used to discover the spiral form of galaxies. It was the world's largest until the opening of Mount Wilson.

Yerkes Observatory, Williams Bay, Wisconsin
This 40 in. (1 m) telescope is the biggest refracting instrument made up to this time. It was completed in 1897.

Mount Wilson Observatory, California
The telescope was installed in 1917 with a mirror size of 100 in. (2.5 m). It was the world's largest until the Hale.

Hale Telescope, Palomar Observatory, California
The Hale's 200 in. (5 m) telescope was first used in 1949.

Jodrell Bank, Cheshire, England
Great Britain's first, and once the world's largest radio telescope, with a 250 ft. (76 m) dish, began operating in 1957.

Arecibo Observatory, Puerto Rico
Completed in 1963, this is the world's most powerful radio telescope. Its uses include searching for pulsars and quasars and the search for alien life forms under the SETI (Search for Extra-Terrestrial Intelligence) program. Its giant 1,000 ft. (305 m) dish is featured in the final scenes of the James Bond film *Golden Eye* (1995).

Yerkes Observatory, Wisconsin

Astronomy milestones

Astronomy is the scientific study of the Universe and the bodies it contains (excluding Earth). Astronomers are the scientists who study astronomy.

585 BC First prediction of eclipse of the Sun
130 BC Hipparchus calculates distance and size of Moon
AD 1543 Copernicus shows that the Sun is at the center of the Solar System
1609 Johannes Kepler describes laws of planetary motion
1610 Galileo Galilei discovers moons of Jupiter
1655 Christiaan Huygens discovers Titan, moon of Saturn

1600s

1668 Isaac Newton builds first reflecting telescope
1687 Isaac Newton publishes theories of motions of planets, etc.
1705 Edmond Halley predicts return of comet
1671–84 Giovanni Cassini discovers four moons of Saturn
1774 Charles Messier compiles star catalogue
1781 William Herschel discovers seventh planet, Uranus
1801 First asteroid, Ceres,

1800s

discovered by Giuseppe Piazzi
1846 Johann Galle and Urbain Le Verrier discover eight planet, Neptune
1787–89 Herschel finds two moons of Uranus and two of Saturn
1839–40 First photographs of the Moon
1894 Flagstaff Observatory, Arizona, founded
1905 Einstein's Special Theory of Relativity first proposed

Hubble Space Telescope

The HST was launched in 1990 and orbits 366 mi. (589 km) above Earth's atmosphere. It can photograph distant objects with 10 times the detail possible with ground-based telescopes.

Keck I & II Telescopes, Mauna Kea Observatory, Hawaii

The two Keck telescopes were opened in 1992–96. They are situated 13,600 ft. (4,145 m) up a Hawaiian mountain, so above 40 percent of the Earth's atmosphere. They are the world's most powerful ground-based instruments, with a 400 in. (10 m) total aperture made up of 36 hexagonal mirrors.

Hobby-Eberly Telescope, McDonald Observatory, Texas

This telescope is designed to collect light for spectrum analysis rather than for visual exploration. It has been in operation since 1999, and has an overall diameter of 360 in. (9.2 m), making it one of the largest ever optical telescopes.

Large Binocular Telescope, Arizona

The Large Binocular Telescope, completed in 2007, is the largest and most advanced optical telescope ever built. Sited at the Mount Graham International Observatory, it has two 331 in. (8.4 m) mirrors, giving a total area equal to one giant 450 in. (11.4 m) diameter mirror. It is expected to produce images as much as 10 times the resolution of those produced by the much smaller Hubble Space Telescope.

First telescopes

The first telescopes were made in 1608 by Dutchman Hans Lippershey. Galileo built his own soon after and used it to discover Jupiter's moons. The earliest type of telescope, known as a refracting telescope, produced a slight distortion of images (called aberration). Since about 1670, astronomers have used reflecting telescopes, which use mirrors that compensate for the distortion.

Hubble Space Telescope

1900s

1908 Giant and dwarf stars described
1923 Galaxies beyond the Milky Way proved
1927 Big Bang theory proposed
1930 Pluto discovered by Clyde Tombaugh
1959 First photographs of the far side of the Moon by Soviet satellite *Luna 3*
1961 First quasars discovered
1967 First pulsars identified
1971 Black hole first detected

1973 *Skylab* space laboratory launched
1976 Rings of Uranus are discovered
1977 *Voyager* deep space probes are launched
1971 *Mariner 9* spacecraft maps Mars
1980 *Voyager 1* explores Saturn
1978 Space probes *Pioneer 1* and *2* reach Venus
1985–89 *Voyager 2* discovers moons of Uranus and Neptune

2000s

1994 Comet Shoemaker-Levy observed crashing into Jupiter
1995 *Galileo* probe reaches Jupiter
1997 *Mars Pathfinder* lands
1997 *Cassini* probe launched to Saturn
1998 *International Space Station* construction starts
1999 Chandra X-Ray Observatory launched

2003 *Galileo* probe deliberately crash-landed on Jupiter
2006 *New Horizons* space probe launched to Pluto
2008 *Phoenix* mission to Mars landed on the planet.
2009 International Year of Astronomy celebrates 400th anniversary of Galileo's first telescope observations.

www.absoluteastronomy.com   search

SPACE EXPLORATION

Animal space pioneers

Before humans went into space animals were used to test equipment. The first animal to be sent up in a rocket — but not into space — was Albert 1, a male rhesus monkey, in 1948. He and his successor, Albert 2, died during the tests.

However, on September 20, 1951, a monkey and 11 mice were recovered after a launch in a U.S. *Aerobee* rocket. Many further animal experiments were carried out before the first manned space flight.

Space dogs, and a cat
Laika, a female Samoyed husky, became the first animal in orbit after being launched by the USSR in *Sputnik 2* in November 1957. There was no way to bring her down and she died after 10 days in space. Two female huskies, Belka and Strelka, orbited successfully in August 1960. Strelka later gave birth to puppies, one of which was given to U.S. President John F. Kennedy. In October 1963, a French *Veronique AGI* rocket put a cat called Félix into space and returned him safely to Earth by parachute.

Monkey business
Able, a female rhesus monkey, and Baker, a female squirrel monkey, were launched by the U.S. in May 1959. They did not orbit and successfully returned to Earth. In November 1961, Enos, a male chimpanzee, completed two orbits and survived. The USSR's first space primates were monkeys Abrek and Bion, who orbited in December 1983 in one of a series of Bion satellite experiments.

Flying frogs
In November 1970, the USA's Orbiting Frog Otolith satellite (OFO-A) launched two bullfrogs into orbit for a week. In December 1990, Toyohiro Akiyama, a Japanese journalist, took six green tree frogs to the Soviet *Mir* space station to conduct weightlessness experiments.

Worldwide web
Arabella, a garden spider, went to the U.S. *Skylab-3* in July 1973. She spent almost 60 days in orbit in an experiment to test the effect of weightlessness on her web-weaving skills.

A space menagerie
The *STS-90* mission of space shuttle *Columbia* (April/May 1998) contained the *Neurolab* — a space menagerie with 170 baby rats, 18 mice, 229 swordtail fish, 135 snails, four oyster toad fish and 1,514 cricket eggs and larvae.

In January 2006, an *Atlas V* rocket launched NASA's *New Horizons* probe on its 9-year journey to Pluto.

Space teddies
In 2008 a helium balloon carried four teddy bears to the edge of space, a height of 18.6 miles (30 km). An experiment by schoolchildren in Cambridge, UK, it was designed to test which spacesuit best protected the teddies at temperatures of −63°F (−53°C).

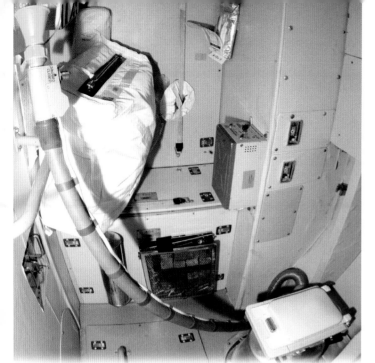

The toilet on the International Space Station was specially designed to operate in zero gravity.

Space toilets

Because the first space flights were short, no one had thought about what would happen if an astronaut needed to use a toilet, so on May 5, 1961, when Alan Shepard was kept waiting on the launchpad for four hours, he was given permission to relieve himself in his spacesuit.

● Diapers
As missions grew longer, the problem of zero gravity, where liquids and solids float around the cabin, had to be overcome. At first, astronauts used diapers and, on the Apollo Moon missions, plastic bags known as "Apollo bags" that were held on with sticky tape.

● Waste Collection System
Space toilets were first installed on the roomier space shuttle, with the Waste Collection System first used on shuttle mission STS-54 (1993) and an improved version on the International Space Station. This resembles an ordinary toilet, but with foot restraints, Velcro straps and handholds to prevent astronauts from floating around while they are using it. It features a fan-driven suction system and anti-bacteria filters to prevent odors. Solid waste is collected in removable plastic bags that are stored and returned to Earth, while liquids are either stored, recycled or vented into space in a "water dump": in the intense cold, they instantly form a cloud of ice crystals that reflect light and can be seen from Earth.

Artificial satellites

The USSR's *Sputnik 1* was the first artificial satellite to enter Earth's orbit. This 184 lb. (83.6 kg) metal sphere transmitted signals back to Earth for three weeks before its batteries failed.

In 1958 the U.S. began to launch its own satellites. Five went into orbit. All of the earliest satellites have since crashed back to Earth, except *Vanguard 1* (U.S., 1958) which is still in space — and likely to remain so for another 200 years.

Over the past 50 years, many more artificial satellites have been launched, with a greater range of uses.

Astronomy
The Hubble Space Telescope has been taking photographs of distant galaxies since 1990. In 2008 the Herschel Space Observatory is scheduled for launch. This new telescope will have the biggest mirror ever in space (138 in. [3.5 m] across).

Communications
Over 5,000 satellites have been launched to transmit telephone, radio and television signals around the world. Fewer than half are still orbiting, and many have stopped working.

Earth observation satellites
These transmit images of the weather and the Earth's environment. They helped to show the depletion of the ozone layer.

Military satellites
Governments use these "spies in the sky" for surveillance but their precise functions are secret.

Global Positioning System
This is a system of 24 linked satellites that allows people to pinpoint their exact position anywhere on Earth. The system is operated by the U.S. Department of Defense and is used by aircraft and ships. GPS systems are now common in cars, too.

Space rockets

Thrust is the force required to lift a vehicle such as an aircraft or rocket off the ground. Rockets often have several stages. Each one provides a proportion of the thrust required to carry a satellite, space shuttle or other vehicle into orbit or into space, dropping away as their propellant has been used so that their weight no longer needs to be carried.

Planets visited by spacecraft

No human has yet set foot on any space body other than Earth and the Moon. But unmanned spacecraft have taken photographs, made scientific readings and gathered data from all the planets in the Solar System, either by flying past or landing.

Venus *Mariner 2* (U.S.) flyby 1962; *Venera 4* (USSR) landed 1967; *MESSENGER* (U.S.) flybys 2006, 2007; *PLANET–C* (Japan), planned for 2010

Mars *Mariner 4* (U.S.) flyby 1965; *Mars Pathfinder* (U.S.) landed 1997; *MER-A* and *MER-B* landed 2004; *Mars Reconnaissance Orbiter* (U.S.) in orbit 2006– ; *Phoenix Mars* (U.S.) landed in 2008; *Dawn* (U.S.) flyby 2009

Jupiter *Pioneer 10* (U.S.) flyby 1973; *Galileo* (U.S.) landed* 2003; *New Horizons* (U.S.) flyby 2007

Mercury *Mariner 10* (U.S.) flyby 1974; *MESSENGER* (U.S.) flybys 2008 and 2009

Saturn *Pioneer 11* (U.S.) flyby 1979; *Cassini/Huygens* (U.S./ESA) orbiter/lander 2004/2005

Uranus *Voyager 2* (U.S.) flyby 1986

Neptune *Voyager 2* (U.S.) flyby 1989

* Deliberately destroyed entering Jupiter's atmosphere, rather than risk contaminating moon Europa with bacteria from Earth.

Manned space missions

During the 1950s, there was a "space race" between the U.S. and USSR to be the first country to send a human into space. NASA's *Mercury* missions were originally unmanned, or carried only animals. The USSR launched the first human into orbit in 1961.

Each country's subsequent space missions had different aims. The U.S. focused on Moon landings with their *Apollo* program and later the reusable space shuttle. The Soviets and later Russia concentrated on long-duration missions, with the *Mir* space station. The latest manned mission is the *International Space Station*, which is four times larger than *Mir*.

Mission	Country	Years
Mercury	U.S.	1959–63
Vostok	USSR	1961–63
Voskhod	USSR	1964–65
Gemini	U.S.	1965–66
Apollo	U.S.	1967–72
Soyuz	USSR	1967–76
Salyut	USSR	1971–82
Skylab	U.S.	1973
Apollo Soyuz	U.S./USSR	1975
Space shuttle	U.S.	1981
Mir space station	USSR/Russia	1986–2001
International Space Station	U.S., Canada, Japan, European Space Agency, Russia, Brazil	1998–
Shenzhou	China	2003–

International Space Station

STS-116 Patch design shows the names of the astronauts who went in *Discovery* to continue construction of the *International Space Station* in December 2006

Astronauts and cosmonauts

The word "astronaut" was first used in 1880 by the British writer Percy Greg. It was the name he gave to a spaceship in his novel *Across the Zodiac*. By the 1950s it was the word used for a space voyager. The Russian word is cosmonaut.

April 12, 1961, First person in space Soviet cosmonaut Yuri Gagarin made a single orbit of Earth in *Vostok 1*, a flight that lasted 1 hour 48 minutes.

May 5, 1961, First U.S. astronaut The U.S.'s first astronaut, Alan B. Shepard Jr., entered space aboard *Mercury 3* but did not orbit during his 15-minute 22-second mission.

August 6, 1961, First flight of over 24 hours Gherman S. Titov (USSR) in *Vostok 2* made the first flight of more than 24 hours. He was also the youngest ever astronaut at 25 years, 10 months, 25 days.

February 20, 1962, First U.S. orbit John H. Glenn Jr. in the *Friendship 7* capsule made the first U.S. orbit, completing three orbits in 4 hours, 55 minutes.

June 16, 1963, First woman in space Valentina V. Tereshkova (USSR) in *Vostok 6* was the first woman in space. She spent 2 days, 22 hours, 50 minutes, 8 seconds in space. She remains the youngest (26 years, 3 months, 10 days) woman in space.

March 18, 1965, First space walk Aleskei Leonov (USSR) made the first space walk, from *Voskhod 2*. It took 24 minutes and it almost ended in disaster when his spacesuit ballooned. He was unable to return through the airlock until he reduced the pressure in his suit to a dangerously low level.

March 23, 1965, First two-man U.S. mission John Young and Virgil "Gus" Grissom made the first two-man U.S. mission in *Gemini 3*.

June 3, 1965, First U.S. spacewalk Edward H. White II made a 36-minute spacewalk from *Gemini 4*.

April 24, 1967, First space death After 18 orbits in *Soyuz 1*, Vladimir M. Komarov (USSR) died when his parachute got tangled and his capsule crash-landed.

December 24, 1968, First manned spacecraft to orbit the Moon *Apollo 8* (followed in 1969 by *Apollo* missions 9 and 10) orbited the Moon but did not land.

All the men on the Moon

The human exploration of the Moon lasted just over three years and involved a total of six missions. In each, a pair of U.S. astronauts went down to the surface in a LEM (lunar excursion module) while a third orbited in a CSM (command service module). The missions provided scientists with a huge amount of information about the Moon.

Astronaut	Spacecraft	Total EVA* hr:min	Mission dates
1 Neil A. Armstrong	*Apollo 11*	2:32	Jul 16–24, 1969
2 Edwin E. "Buzz" Aldrin	*Apollo 11*	2:15	Jul 16–24, 1969
3 Charles Conrad Jr	*Apollo 12*	7:45	Nov 14–24, 1969
4 Alan L. Bean	*Apollo 12*	7:45	Nov 14–24, 1969
5 Alan B. Shepard	*Apollo 14*	9:23	Jan 31–Feb 9, 1971
6 Edgar D. Mitchell	*Apollo 14*	9:23	Jan 31–Feb 9, 1971
7 David R. Scott	*Apollo 15*	19:08	Jul 26–Aug 7, 1971
8 James B. Irwin	*Apollo 15*	18:35	Jul 26–Aug 7, 1971
9 John W. Young	*Apollo 16*	20:14	Apr 16–27, 1972
10 Charles M. Duke Jr	*Apollo 16*	20:14	Apr 16–27, 1972
11 Eugene A. Cernan	*Apollo 17*	22:04	Dec 7–19, 1972
12 Harrison H. Schmitt	*Apollo 17*	22:04	Dec 7–19, 1972

* Extra vehicular activity: time spent out of the lunar module on the Moon. The six *Apollo* missions above resulted in successful Moon landings. *Apollo 13*, April 11–17, 1970, was aborted and returned to Earth after an oxygen tank exploded.

Longest space walk

The record for the longest-ever spacewalk was broken from March 10–11, 2001, when mission specialists James Voss and Susan Helms stepped outside space shuttle *Discovery STS-102* to do construction work on the space station. Their EVA (extra vehicular activity) lasted 8 hours, 56 minutes.

Astronaut Christer Fuglesang resumes construction work on the *International Space Station*, December 2006

International Space Station

Work began on constructing the International Space Station (ISS) in 1998. It has been manned permanently since 2000 and is scheduled for completion in 2011. The project is a cooperative venture between the U.S., Russia, Japan, Canada and the European Space Agency.

For research
It is used for research in physics, astronomy and meteorology and the study of the effects on the human of long-duration stays in space. An understanding of these effects will be important as manned flights to planets are planned in the future.

Getting bigger
As each new mission arrives, further components are added, so the Space Station has steadily increased in size — it will weigh some 450 tons when complete and measures 306 x 240 ft (93 x 73 m). It orbits Earth over 15 times a day at a height of 217 miles (350 km). It is solar powered and has systems for generating oxygen and processing water, but relies on supply ships from Earth for food for the crew.

Most visited
Members of the crew are replaced, with previous personnel returning to Earth: it is the most-visited spacecraft ever, with over 160 people travelling to it since its launch.

July 20, 1969, First Moon landing Neil Armstrong and Edwin E. "Buzz" Aldrin became the first men on the Moon.

18 June 1983, First U.S. woman in space Sally Ride was launched in the space shuttle *Challenger STS-7*, which was the first reusable space vehicle.

October 5–13, 1984, First Canadian astronaut Quebec-born Marc Garneau traveled on the *STS-41G* space shuttle *Challenger*.

June 29, 1995, First space shuttle/space station docking Space shuttle *Atlantis STS-71* docked with the Soviet space station *Mir*.

September 26, 1996, U.S. endurance record On her 5th mission, U.S. astronaut Shannon Lucid completed 188 days aboard the Russian *Mir* station, setting a world record for women. Lucid was born in China. She flew more missions than any woman and at 53 was the oldest female in space.

December 4, 1998, International Space Station First stage of the *International Space Station* was established.

November 2, 2000, First crew on ISS An American and Russian crew began living aboard the *International Space Station*.

April 28–May 6, 2001 First space tourist U.S. millionaire Dennis Tito became the first space tourist, paying $20 million for his Russian *Soyuz TM-32* flight to the *International Space Station*.

October 15–16, 2003, First astronaut launched by China Chinese astronaut Lang Liwei made eight orbits of Earth in a *Shenzhou 5* spacecraft. China made its second flight, *Shenzhou 6*, with two astronauts on October 12–16, 2005.

2010 Virgin Galactic plans space tourism flights to over 62 miles (100 km) in *SpaceShipOne*, which carries six passengers at a cost of $200,000 per person.

2010 Last Space shuttle retires STS–133 *Endeavour* – probable last space shuttle flight. The Shuttle has been in use since 1981. It will be replaced by Orion spacecraft, planned for launch in 2014. The new vehicle will later be used, along with the Altair spacecraft, for Moon landings and journeys to Mars.

amazing-space.stsci.edu   search

Planet Earth

Forest fires

Australia was the focus of news stories in 2009 after devastating bushfires caused widespread damage and killed over 200 people in the state of Victoria. The hot, dry climate puts Australia at great risk of wildfires, and fire-management is failing to control the situation. It has been predicted that Australia will suffer from worse fires in 2010.

Layers of the Earth

The Earth is made up of a number of layers. At the top is the crust — the thinnest layer. Next is the mantle, then the outer and inner cores. The outer core is probably liquid and the inner core solid.

Ocean 2 mi. (3 km)

Crust 13 mi. (21 km)

Mantle 13–1,780 mi. (21–2,865 km)

Outer core 1,780–3,185 mi (2,865–5,125 km)

Inner core 3,185–3,959 mi. (5,125–6,371 km)

Inside the Earth showing the average depth of its layers

The largest meteorite craters

About 500 meteorites reach Earth every year. Many collision sites have been altered by weather over millions of years, and scientists are unsure whether some craters are actually the craters of extinct volcanoes. Those below are all agreed to be meteorite craters.

1 Vredefort, South Africa 185 mi. (300 km) in diameter
2 Sudbury, Ontario, Canada 155 mi. (250 km) in diameter
3 Chicxulub, Yucatan, Mexico 110 mi. (170 km) in diameter
4 Manicougan, Canada 60 mi. (100 km) in diameter
5 Popigai, Russia 60 mi. (100 km) in diameter

The 10 degrees of hardness

The Mohs scale, named after German mineralogist Friedrich Mohs (1773–1839), is used for comparing the relative hardness of minerals. Each mineral on the scale can be scratched by the harder ones below it.

Mohs scale No.	Substance	Mohs scale No.	Substance
1	Talc	6	Orthoclase
2	Gypsum	7	Quartz
3	Calcite	8	Topaz
4	Fluorite	9	Corundum
5	Apatite	10	Diamond

Meteor Crater, Arizona

Geological time   2010

CENOZOIC ERA
Quaternary period
Recent/Holocene epoch: 11,000 years ago (y.a.) to present day — modern humans
Pleistocene epoch: 1,800,000 to 11,000 y.a. — humans

Tertiary period
Pliocene epoch: 5 to 1.8 m.y.a (million years ago) — apelike human ancestors
Miocene epoch: 23 to 5 m.y.a. — apes and whales

Oligocene epoch: 38 to 23 m.y.a. — cats and dogs
Eocene epoch: 54 to 37 m.y.a. — grasslands
Paleocene epoch: 65 to 54 m.y.a. — large mammals

MESOZOIC ERA
Cretaceous period: 146 to 65 m.y.a. — flowering plants; dinosaurs became extinct
Jurassic period: 208 to 146 m.y.a. — birds and mammals
Triassic period: 245 to 208 m.y.a. — dinosaurs and flying reptiles

Uluru

The rock formerly known as Ayers Rock in Northern Territory, Australia, is believed to be the world's largest free-standing rock. It is made of sandstone and is 1,100 ft. (335 m) high, 2.2 mi. (3.6 km) long and 1.6 mi. (2 km) wide. It was originally named after South Australian premier Sir Henry Ayers, but it is now known by the name given to it by local Aborigines, to whom it is sacred.

Rocks

There are three categories of rocks — igneous, sedimentary and metamorphic.

● Igneous rocks originate deep in the Earth. They erupt from volcanoes as magma and cool or solidify as they rise to the upper layers. Basalt is an igneous rock and so is granite, a very hard rock often used in building. Pumice stone is a soft igneous rock that is ejected from volcanoes. As it cools, it often fills with so many air bubbles that it floats in water.

● Sedimentary rocks can be formed by deposits in water and occasionally by wind. Sandstone is a common example. Organic sedimentary rocks are formed by living plants and animals — coal comes from plant matter and limestone from the calcium from billions of plants and animals. Chemical sedimentary rocks occur when chemical processes take place and minerals are deposited.

● Metamorphic rocks are igneous or sedimentary rocks that have changed as a result of high temperatures or pressures. Slate used on roofs is a familiar example.

 www.webmineral.com   **search**

Minerals
Minerals are naturally occurring substances with a definite chemical composition. Most mineral names end in "ite." Many have a practical use or contain a chemical compound or element that can be extracted and used commercially. Bauxite, for instance, is the main source of aluminum. Gems are minerals that are highly prized for their rarity or appearance (e.g., diamonds, sapphires, emeralds and rubies).

Giant meteorites

Many meteorites land in the sea and in unpopulated areas so they are never seen. The Hoba meteorite, the largest in the world, was found in Namibia in 1920. It measures 9 x 8 ft. (2.73 x 2.43 m) and is 82 percent iron and 16 percent nickel. It weighs more than 66 tons (60 tonnes). Second largest is the Tent, found in Greenland in 1894 and now known by its original Eskimo name, Ahnighito. This meteorite weighs about 63.2 tons (57.3 tonnes) and is on display in the New York Museum of Natural History.

4,500,000,000 years ago

PALEOZOIC ERA
Permian period: 286 to 245 m.y.a. — deciduous plants
Carboniferous Pennsylvanian period: 325 to 286 m.y.a. — reptiles
Carboniferous Mississippian period: 360 to 325 m.y.a. — winged insects

Devonian period: 410 to 360 m.y.a. — amphibians
Silurian period: 440 to 410 m.y.a. — land plants and insects
Ordovician period: 500 to 440 m.y.a. — corals and mollusks
Cambrian period: 544 to 500 m.y.a. — fish and shelled creatures

PRECAMBRIAN ERA
Proterozoic period: 2,500 to 544 m.y.a. — earliest fossils; jellyfish
Archaic period: 3,800 to 2,500 m.y.a. — living cells

Hadean period: 4,500 to 3,800 m.y.a. — environment unable to support life; from 4,500 or earlier — the Earth was formed

Largest deserts

Deserts cover about a third of the world's land area. They range from extremely arid and barren sandy deserts (about 4 percent of the total land surface of the globe), through arid (15 percent) to semiarid (just under 15 percent).

Most deserts have features of all these, with one zone merging into the next, so the start and finish of any desert is not exact. Many of the world's largest deserts are broken down by geographers into smaller desert regions — the Australian Desert includes the Gibson, Great Sandy, Great Victoria and Simpson, for example.

1 Sahara, Northern Africa — 3,514,000 sq. mi. (9,100,000 sq km)

2 Australian, Australia (Includes Gibson, Great Sandy, Great Victoria and Simpson) — 1,313,000 sq. mi. (3,400,000 sq km)

3 Arabian Peninsula, Southwest Asia (Includes an-Nafud and Rub al Khali) — 1,004,000 sq. mi. (2,600,000 sq km)

4 Turkestan, Central Asia (Includes Kara-Kum and Kyzylkum) — 734,000 sq. mi. (1,900,000 sq km)

5 Gobi, Central Asia — 502,000 sq. mi. (1,300,000 sq km)

6 North American Desert, U.S./Mexico (Includes Great Basin, Mojave, Sonorah and Chihuahuan) — 502,000 sq. mi. (1,300,000 sq km)

The Devil's Marbles in the Australian desert

Mount Everest, the world's highest mountain

The highest mountain?

The height of mountains is usually measured from sea level. Mauna Kea in Hawaii is only 13,957 ft. (4,245 m) above sea level, but it rises a total of 33,474 ft. (10,203 m) from the floor of the Pacific Ocean, making its real height 4,439 ft. (1,353 m) greater than Mount Everest!

Everest (base moved to sea floor)

Mauna Kea

sea level

sea floor

Highest mountains

People used to think that Kangchenjunga in Nepal/India was the highest mountain. Then the Great Trigonometrical Survey of India measured all the country's land features. The survey was completed in 1852 and showed that Everest (then called Peak XV) was the world's highest mountain.

Everest's height was then reckoned to be 29,002 ft. (8,840 m). This has since been adjusted as improved measuring methods have been used. The mountain's name was suggested in 1865 as a tribute to Sir George Everest, the Surveyor General of India, who had led the survey.

Highest mountains

1 Everest, Nepal/China — 29,035 ft. (8,850 m)

2 K2 (Chogori), Pakistan/China — 28,238 ft. (8,607 m)

3 Kangchenjunga, Nepal/India — 28,208 ft. (8,598 m)

4 Lhotse, Nepal/China — 27,923 ft. (8,511 m)

5 Makalu I, Nepal/China — 27,824 ft. (8,481 m)

Largest island

An island is a piece of land surrounded by water. Australia is so large it is a continent, not an island; otherwise it would rank first. The smallest island with country status is Pitcairn, at 1.75 sq. mi. (4.53 sq km).

1 Greenland (Kalaatdlit Nunaat) — 840,070 sq. mi. (2,175,600 sq km)
2 New Guinea — 312,190 sq. mi. (789,900 sq km)
3 Borneo — 289,961 sq. mi. (751,000 sq km)
4 Madagascar (Malagasy Republic) — 226,674 sq. mi. (587,041 sq km)
5 Baffin Island, Canada — 195,926 sq. mi. (507,451 sq km)
6 Sumatra, Indonesia — 163,011 sq. mi. (422,200 sq km)
7 Honshu, Japan — 88,839 sq. mi. (230,092 sq km)
8 Great Britain — 84,185 sq. mi. (218,041 sq km)
9 Victoria Island, Canada — 83,896 sq. mi. (217,290 sq km)
10 Ellesmere Island, Canada — 75,767 sq. mi. (196,236 sq km)
11 Celebes, Indonesia — 69,100 sq. mi. (179,000 sq km)
12 South Island, New Zealand — 58,676 sq. mi. (151,971 sq km)
13 Java, Indonesia — 49,000 sq. mi. (126,900 sq km)
14 North Island, New Zealand — 44,204 sq. mi. (114,489 sq km)
15 Newfoundland, Canada — 42,031 sq. mi. (108,860 sq km)
16 Cuba — 40,519 sq. mi. (104,945 sq km)
17 Luzon, Philippines — 40,420 sq. mi. (104,688 sq km)
18 Iceland — 39,699 sq. mi. (102,819 sq km)
19 Mindanao, Philippines — 36,537 sq. mi. (94,630 sq km)
20 Ireland — 32,589 sq. mi. (84,406 sq km)
(Area excludes offshore islands)

Lowest places on land

Sea level is the average height of the sea at a point midway between high and low tides. The shore of the Dead Sea is the lowest exposed ground below sea level. Some land in Antarctica is 8,327 ft. (2,538 m) below sea level, but is covered by a 6,890-ft. (2,100 m) deep ice cap.

1 Dead Sea, Israel/Jordan — 1,312 ft. (400 m) below sea level
2 Lake Assa, Djibouti — 511 ft. (156 m) below sea level
3 Turfan Depression, China — 505 ft. (154 m) below sea level
4 Qattâra Depression, Egypt — 436 ft. (133 m) below sea level
5 Mangyshlak Peninsula, Kazakhstan — 433 ft. (132 m) below sea level

Geysers

Geysers are jets of boiling water and steam that erupt from beneath the ground where water is heated by volcanic activity. The name geyser comes from a hot spring called Geysir at Haukadalur, Iceland. Yellowstone National Park, Wyoming, has more geysers than anywhere else. There are 500 active ones including Steamboat, which erupts to a height of 375 ft. (120 m), and Old Faithful, which erupts about every 91 minutes.

Geyser erupting in Yellowstone National Park

The seven continents

The Americas are named after the explorer Amerigo Vespucci (1451–1512). Africa was perhaps originally a Berber tribal name. This was adopted by the Romans as the name of their province and later spread to the whole continent.

The name of Europe may simply mean mainland. Asia is probably from the Assyrian, *asu*, meaning sunrise or east. Australis is Latin for southern; Australia, with New Zealand and other islands, is also considered as part of Oceania, a name invented by the geographer Conrad Malte-Brun (1775–1826). Antarctica is Greek for opposite the Arctic. Arctic comes from the Greek for bear, because the region lies under the stars of the Great Bear constellation.

North America
Land area: 9,401,000 sq. mi. (24,349,000 sq km)
% of world total: 16.4

Europe
Land area: 4,053,000 sq. mi. (10,498,000 sq km)
% of world total: 7.1

Asia
Land area: 16,837,000 sq. mi. (43,608,000 sq km)
% of world total: 29.3

Africa
Land area: 11,712,000 sq. mi. (30,335,000 sq km)
% of world total: 20.4

Australasia
Land area: 3,445,000 sq. mi. (8,923,000 sq km)
% of world total: 6.0

South America
Land area: 6,800,000 sq. mi. (17,611,000 sq km)
% of world total: 11.8

Antarctica
Land area: 5,151,000 sq. mi. (13,340,000 sq km)
% of world total: 9.0

Niagara Falls

Longest river

The source of the Nile was discovered by Europeans in 1858 when British explorer John Hanning Speke reached Lake Victoria Nyanza, in what is now Burundi. About a hundred years later, in 1953, the source of the Amazon was identified as a stream called Huarco flowing from the Misuie glacier in the Peruvian Andes mountains.

By following the Amazon from its source and up the Rio Pará, it is possible to sail for 4,195 mi. (6,750 km), which is slightly more than the length of the Nile. But geographers do not consider the entire route to be part of the Amazon basin, so the Nile is considered the world's longest river.

1 Nile* flows through Burundi, Dem. Rep. of Congo, Egypt, Eritrea, Ethiopia, Kenya, Rwanda, Sudan, Tanzania, Uganda — 4,158 mi. (6,695 km)
2 Amazon flows through Peru and Brazil — 4,007 mi. (6,448 km)
3 Chang Jiang (Yangtze) flows through China — 3,964 mi. (6,378 km)
4 Huang He (Yellow) flows through China — 3,395 mi. (5,464 km)
5 Amur flows through China and Russia — 2,744 mi. (4,415 km)
* In 2006 the British and New Zealand Ascend the Nile team sailed from the mouth to the source of the river. Using Global Positioning, they measured their journey and came up with a total length 66.5 mi. (107 km) longer than the official figure.

Greatest waterfalls

The flow of many waterfalls varies according to the season, and some have been reduced by building dams to harness their power for hydroelectric plants.

The flow of the Boyoma waterfall is equivalent to 36 million gal. (17 million L) a second — enough to fill over 140,000 bathtubs per second, or for every person on Earth to have two baths a day!

1 Boyoma (Stanley), Democratic Republic of Congo — 22,235 cu. yd./sec (17,000 cu m/sec)
2 Khône, Laos † — 14,819 cu. yd./sec (11,330 cu m/sec)
3 Niagara (Horseshoe), Canada — 7,625 cu. yd./sec (5,830 cu m/sec)
4 Grande, Uruguay — 5,886 cu. yd./sec (4,500 cu m/sec)
5 Paulo Afonso, Brazil — 3,662 cu. yd./sec (2,800 cu m/sec)
(Based on volume of water)
† Also the widest waterfall at 6.7 mi. (10.8 km)

The Nile flowing through Cairo, Egypt

Highest waterfalls

Waterfalls form when a river or stream goes over a drop, often where softer rocks are eroded faster than harder ones. The drop is the distance from top to bottom of the waterfall.

1 Angel Falls, Carrao river, Venezuela — 3,212 ft. (979 m)*
2 Tugela Falls, Tugela river, South Africa — 3,110 ft. (948 m)
3 Ramnefjellsfossen, Jostedal Glacier, Nesdale, Norway — 2,625 ft. (800 m)
4 Mongefossen Falls, Monge river, Mongebekk, Norway — 2,540 ft. (774 m)
5 Gocta Falls, Cocahuayco river, Peru — 2,531 ft. (771 m)
6 Mutarazi Falls, Mutarazi river, Zimbabwe — 2,499 ft. (762 m)
7 Yosemite Falls, Yosemite Creek, California — 2,425 ft. (739 m)
8 Østre Mardøla Foss, Mardals river, Eikisdal, Norway — 2,152 ft. (656 m)
9 Tyssestrengane Falls, Tysso river, Hardanger, Norway — 2,120 ft.(646 m)
10 Cuquenán Falls, Arabopo river, Venezuela — 2,000 ft. (610 m)
* Longest single drop 2,648 ft. (807 m)

The Great Lakes

The Great Lakes are a group of five freshwater lakes in North America on the border between the U. S. and Canada. Superior is so called because it is higher upstream that the others. Huron takes its name from the name French settlers gave to a local Indian tribe (from *hure*, a boar's head). No one knows where the name Michigan comes from, but Erie and Ontario are both from the Iroquois language. Erie means cat, the animal the tribe used as its symbol. Ontario simply means beautiful lake.

1 Superior, Canada/U.S. — 31,820 sq. mi. (82,414 sq km)
2 Huron, Canada/U.S. — 23,010 sq. mi. (59,596 sq km)
3 Michigan, U.S. — 22,400 sq. mi. (58,016 sq km)
4 Erie, Canada/U.S. — 9,930 sq. mi. (25,719 sq km)
5 Ontario, Canada/U.S. — 7,520 sq. mi. (19,477 sq km)

Longest glaciers

During the last Ice Age, more than 30 percent of the Earth's surface was covered by glaciers — frozen rivers of ice that move very slowly. Today, as much as 10 percent is covered with glaciers.

The Lambert-Fisher Glacier is the longest in the world and was discovered (from the air) in 1956. The longest glacier in North America is the Hubbard Glacier, Alaska, which measures 91 mi. (146 km). The longest in Europe is the Aletsch Glacier, Switzerland, at 22 mi. (35 km).

1 Lambert-Fisher, Antarctica — 320 mi. (515 km)
2 Novaya Zemlya, Russia — 260 mi. (418 km)
3 Arctic Institute, Antarctica — 225 mi. (362 km)
4 Nimrod-Lennox-King, Antarctica — 180 mi. (290 km)
5 Denman, Antarctica — 150 mi. (241 km)

Glaciers

Glaciers hold about 75 percent of the world's fresh water. If all the glaciers melted, the world's sea level would rise about 230 ft. (70 m).

Greatest rivers

The volume of water flowing from the mouth of a river varies according to the season. The figures given are highest averages. The outflow of the Amazon would fill almost two million bathtubs every second.

1 Amazon flows into the South Atlantic, Brazil, at 286,441 cu. yd./sec (219,000 cu m/sec)
2 Ganges flows into the Bay of Bengal, Bangladesh, at 57,419 cu. yd./sec (43,900 cu m/sec)
3 Zaïre (Congo) flows into the South Atlantic, Angola/Congo, at 54,672 cu. yd./sec (41,800 cu m/sec)
4 Chang Jiang flows into the Yellow Sea, China, at 41,724 cu. yd./sec (31,900 cu m/sec)
5 Orinoco flows into the South Atlantic, Venezuela, at 41,724 cu. yd./sec (31,900 cu m/sec)
6 Plata-Paraná-Grande flows into the South Atlantic, Uruguay, at 33,614 cu. yd./sec (25,700 cu m/sec)
(Based on rate of discharge at mouth)

Lake fact file

● **Largest lake by volume and area**
The Caspian Sea (Russia, Kazakhstan, Turkmenistan, Azerbaijan and Iran) has a volume of 18,760 cu. mi. (78,200 cu km) and an area of 144,402 sq. mi. (374,000 sq km), making it the world's largest body of inland water. It would take 400 years for the entire contents of the Caspian to flow over Niagara Falls!

● **Largest freshwater lake by area**
Some geographers think that Lake Michigan and Lake Huron are one lake. They have a combined area of 45,410 sq. mi. (117,612 sq km) and have a larger area than half the world's countries.

● **Largest freshwater lake by volume and deepest lake**
Lake Baikal, Russia, contains 5,517 cu. mi. (22,995 cu km) of water. It has an average depth of 2,395 ft. (730 m) and is 5,712 ft. (1,741 m) at its deepest point — deep enough to cover more than four Empire State Buildings piled on top of one another.

● **Fastest-shrinking lake**
In 1960, The Aral Sea (Kazakhstan and Uzbekistan) was 24,904 sq. mi. (64,501 sq km). Since then, feeder rivers have been diverted for irrigation and the lake has shrunk to about 10,810 sq. mi. (28,000 sq km). It is now in danger of disappearing.

oceanexplorer.noaa.gov   search

Wave height scale

The wave height scale describes the sort of waves that sailors might meet at sea. Wave height varies according to wind speed. High waves can be very dangerous, especially to small boats which can be turned over and even smashed.

0 Glassy — 0 ft. (0 m)
1 Calm — 0–1 ft. (0 – 0.3 m)
2 Rippled — 1–2 ft. (0.3 – 0.6 m)
3 Choppy — 2–4 ft. (0.6 – 1.2 m)
4 Very choppy — 4 – 8 ft. (1.2–2.4 m)
5 Rough — 8–13 ft. (2.4 – 4 m)
6 Very rough — 13–20 ft. (4 – 6 m)
7 High — 20–30 ft. (6 – 9 m)
8 Very high — 30–45 ft. (9 – 4 m)
9 Ultra high — 45 + ft (14.0 + m)

Huge waves breaking over a lighthouse in Havana, Cuba during a hurricane

Tsunami

The word tsunami comes from the Japanese *tsu* (meaning port) and *nam i* (meaning wave). A tsunami is not a tidal wave, but a powerful surge of moving water caused by an earthquake or volcanic eruption beneath the sea bed.

There may be advance warning signs, such as bubbling water, a roaring noise and a sudden rise in water temperature. Tsunamis are rarely as high as tidal waves. However, powerful ones can cross huge distances, raising the sea level and destroying entire islands and coastal areas in their path. Lisbon, the capital of Portugal, was almost completely destroyed in 1755 by the combined effects of an earthquake, tsunami and fire. The worst recorded tsunami occurred in 2004 in Southeast Asia.

Animal survivors

Amazingly, few animals died in the tsunami that hit Sri Lanka and other areas in 2004. Elephants, buffalo and tigers, as well as smaller animals, moved to high ground in time. Scientists think that they sensed soundwaves and changes in air pressure in advance of the wave and this gave them time to escape.

Iceberg fact file

An iceberg is a large piece of ice that has broken away from a glacier or ice shelf. In the North Atlantic most came from Greenland glaciers, and in the South Atlantic from Antarctica.

● The word iceberg probably comes from the Dutch *ijsberg*, or ice hill.

● Icebergs float because they are made of fresh water, which is less dense than sea water.

● Seven-eighths of an iceberg is below the surface of the sea, hence the expression "the tip of the iceberg," which means that more is hidden than can be seen.

● The tallest iceberg measured was 551 ft. (168 m) high. It was seen in 1958 off Greenland and was as tall as a 50-storey skyscraper.

● Icebergs less than 3.25 ft. (1 m) high and 16.25 ft. (5 m) wide are known as growlers because of the noise they make.

● Icebergs larger than growlers are called bergy bits; then they are graded small, medium, large or very large. Very large icebergs are those measuring more than 245 ft. (75 m) high and 700 ft. (213 m) wide.

● One of the biggest icebergs of recent times, known as B-15, broke away from the Ross Ice Shelf, Antarctica, in March 2000. It had an average length of 183 mi. (295 km) and width of 23 mi. (37 km), making it about the size of Jamaica!

● About 10,000 to 15,000 new icebergs are formed every year. The process is called "calving."

● The air trapped in icebergs is "harvested" and sold for use in drinks. It may be 3,000 years old.

● At least 500 incidents have been recorded of ships striking icebergs. The worst disaster involving an iceberg happened when the *Titanic* struck one on April 14, 1912 and 1,503 people died.

Longest coastlines

The coastline of Canada, including all its islands, is more than six times as long as the distance round the Earth at the Equator (24,902 mi. [40,076 km]). Greenland (Kalaalit Nunaat) is not in this list as it is part of Denmark, not a separate country, but its coastline is 27,394 mi. (44,087 km) long.

1 Canada — 164,988 mi. (265,523 km)

2 U.S. — 82,836 mi. (133,312 km)

3 Russia — 68,543 mi. (110,310 km)

4 Indonesia — 59,143 mi. (95,181 km)

5 Chile — 48,817 mi. (78,563 km)

6 Australia — 41,340 mi. (66,530 km)

7 Norway — 33,056 mi. (53,199 km)

8 Philippines — 21,064 mi. (33,900 km)

9 Brazil — 20,741 mi. (33,379 km)

10 Finland — 19,336 mi. (31,119 km)

11 China — 18,652 mi. (30,017 km)

12 Japan — 18,032 mi. (29,020 km)

Deepest oceans and seas

The Pacific Ocean is the deepest ocean. Its greatest depth is 35,837 ft. (10,924 m) with an average depth of 13,215 ft. (4,028 m). The Indian Ocean is 24,460 ft. (7,455 m) at its deepest point and has an average depth of 13,002 ft. (3,963 m). The Atlantic Ocean is next with a greatest depth of 30,246 ft. (9,219 m) and an average depth of 12,880 ft. (3,926 m).

Giant feather stars live 650 ft. (200 m) deep in Cayman Trench, Caribbean.

Under the North Pole

On August 2, 2007 two Russian scientific research submersibles *MIR-1* and *MIR-2*, which had filmed the wreck of the *Titanic* for the 1997 film, descended to the seabed beneath the Geographic North Pole, a depth of 13,980 ft. (4,261 m). They took soil and water samples and *MIR-1* planted a titanium alloy Russian flag and a time capsule on the ocean floor.

Oceans and seas

Ocean is the term used for the world's sea water, except for landlocked seas such as the Caspian.

More than 70 percent of the planet's surface is occupied by oceans — the Pacific Ocean alone is more than 25 percent larger than the planet's entire land area. Smaller divisions of some oceans are separately named as seas.

Pacific Ocean — 64,185,629 sq. mi. (166,240,000 sq km)

Atlantic Ocean — 33,421,006 sq. mi. (86,560,000 sq km)

Indian Ocean — 28,351,484 sq. mi. (73,430,000 sq km)

Arctic Ocean — 5,108,132 sq. mi. (13,230,000 sq km)

South China Sea — 1,148,499 sq. mi. (2,974,600 sq km)

Caribbean Sea — 1,062,939 sq. mi. (2,753,000 sq km)

Mediterranean Sea — 969,116 sq. mi. (2,510,000 sq km)

Bering Sea — 872,977 sq. mi. (2,261,000 sq km)

Gulf of Mexico — 595,749 sq. mi. (1,542,985 sq km)

Sea of Okhotsk — 589,798 sq. mi. (1,527,570 sq km)

East China Sea — 482,299 sq. mi. (1,249,150 sq km)

Sea of Japan — 391,100 sq. mi. (1,012,945 sq km)

Andaman Sea — 307,993 sq. mi. (797,700 sq km)

Hudson Bay — 282,001 sq. mi. (730,380 sq km)

Russian *MIR* submersibles are used for deep-sea exploration.

● During World War II, Lord Mountbatten led a program to build artificial icebergs to use as aircraft carriers, but the project, codenamed Habbakuk, was abandoned.

● Cruise ship *MS Explorer* struck an iceberg in the Antarctic and sank on November 23, 2007. All 154 passengers and crew were rescued.

See also

Worst natural disasters: page 47

🔍 www.oceansatlas.org   search

ARCTIC
OCEAN

Beaufort Sea

Greenland

Baffin Bay

Bering Sea

Gulf of Alaska

Rocky Mountains

Hudson Bay

Labrador Sea

NORTH AMERICA

Great Basin

Mojave Desert

Sierra Madre

Gulf of Mexico

Caribbean Sea

ATLANTIC OCEAN

PACIFIC OCEAN

Andes

Atacama Desert

SOUTH AMERICA

Patagonian Desert

Climate

Weather and climate are not the same. Weather is how hot, cold or wet a place is at a particular time. Climate is the average weather of an area over time.

Several things decide the climate of an area, including how far it is from the Equator, how far from the sea, its height above sea level and its wind systems. The position of a place on an area of land and the size of that land area also affects the climate. Scientists divide the world into different climate regions: polar and tundra, temperate, tropical, desert and mountain.

Warm temperate

These areas have mild winters and warm to hot summers. There is rain all year round, but there are plenty of sunny days. This is an ideal climate for growing crops such as citrus fruits, grapes and olives.

Climate change

Climates have changed naturally throughout history. But scientists think that human activities, such as burning fossil fuels, are producing greenhouse gases such as carbon dioxide, and these are causing global warming. The effects include ocean currents altering, ice sheets melting, sea levels rising and severe weather, such as cyclones and floods, becoming more common.

The sea affects the climate of coastal regions, keeping them warmer than inland areas in winter and cooler in summer.

Key

	Polar and Tundra
	Cool temperate
	Desert
	Warm temperate
	Tropical
	Mountains

Mountain

The climates of mountain areas vary according to altitude. The higher the mountain, the colder it is. At a certain point, called the tree line, trees can no longer grow. The climate in mountain areas is usually wetter than in the lowlands around them.

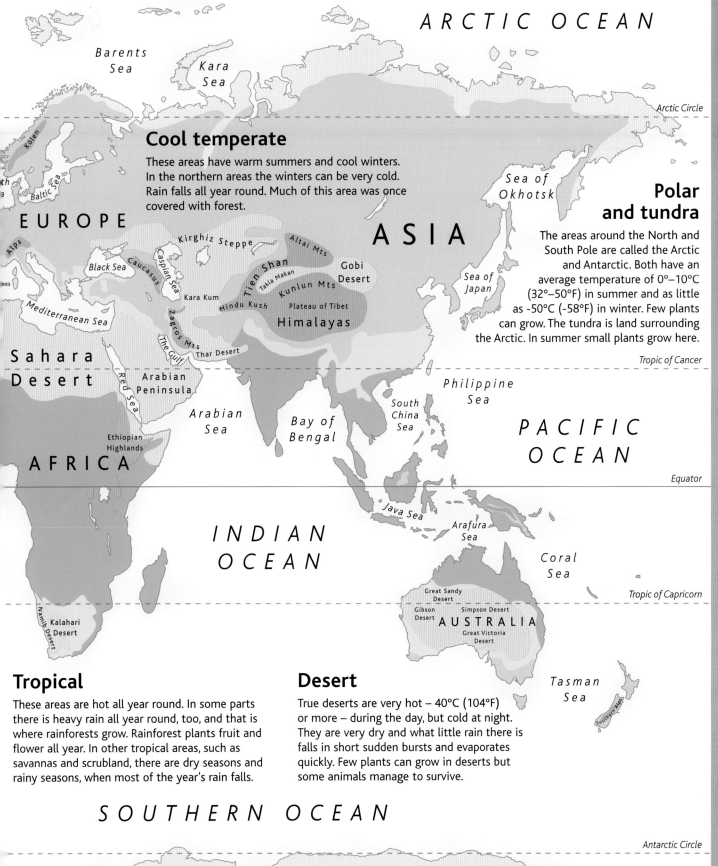

ARCTIC OCEAN

Barents Sea

Kara Sea

Arctic Circle

Cool temperate

These areas have warm summers and cool winters. In the northern areas the winters can be very cold. Rain falls all year round. Much of this area was once covered with forest.

Kölen

Baltic Sea

EUROPE

Alps

Black Sea

Caucasus

Caspian Sea

Mediterranean Sea

Kirghiz Steppe

Altai Mts

Tien Shan

Takla Makan

Gobi Desert

Kara Kum

Hindu Kush

Kunlun Mts

Plateau of Tibet

Zagros Mts

The Gulf

Thar Desert

Himalayas

ASIA

Sea of Okhotsk

Sea of Japan

Polar and tundra

The areas around the North and South Pole are called the Arctic and Antarctic. Both have an average temperature of 0°–10°C (32°–50°F) in summer and as little as -50°C (-58°F) in winter. Few plants can grow. The tundra is land surrounding the Arctic. In summer small plants grow here.

Tropic of Cancer

S a h a r a D e s e r t

Red Sea

Arabian Peninsula

Ethiopian Highlands

AFRICA

Arabian Sea

Bay of Bengal

South China Sea

Philippine Sea

PACIFIC OCEAN

Equator

INDIAN OCEAN

Java Sea

Arafura Sea

Coral Sea

Tropic of Capricorn

Namib Desert

Kalahari Desert

Great Sandy Desert

Gibson Desert

Simpson Desert

AUSTRALIA

Great Victoria Desert

Tasman Sea

Southern Alps

Tropical

These areas are hot all year round. In some parts there is heavy rain all year round, too, and that is where rainforests grow. Rainforest plants fruit and flower all year. In other tropical areas, such as savannas and scrubland, there are dry seasons and rainy seasons, when most of the year's rain falls.

Desert

True deserts are very hot – 40°C (104°F) or more – during the day, but cold at night. They are very dry and what little rain there is falls in short sudden bursts and evaporates quickly. Few plants can grow in deserts but some animals manage to survive.

SOUTHERN OCEAN

Antarctic Circle

ANTARCTICA

🔍 http://www.wmo.ch   search

The Beaufort scale

The Beaufort scale was introduced in 1806 by British Admiral Sir Francis Beaufort (1774–1857) to describe wind effects on a fully rigged man-of-war ship. It was later extended to describe how winds affect land features such as trees.

The Beaufort scale is divided into values from 0 for calm winds to 12 for hurricanes. Forecasters often describe winds by their force number — for example, a force 10 gale. Wind speed can also be measured in knots: 1 knot = 1.15 mph (1.85 km/h).

0 Calm: > 1 mph (0–2 km/h) Smoke rises vertically; the sea is mirror smooth
1 Light air: 1–3 mph (3–6 km/h) Smoke indicates the direction of the wind
2 Slight breeze: 4–7 mph (7–11 km/h) Wind felt on the face and leaves rustle in trees
3 Gentle breeze: 8–12 mph (12–19 km/h) Wind extends a light flag
4 Moderate breeze: 13–18 mph (20–28 km/h) Loose paper blows around; frequent whitecaps at sea
5 Fresh breeze: 19–24 mph (29–38 km/h) Small trees sway
6 Strong breeze: 25–31 mph (39–49 km/h) Wind whistles in telephone wires; some spray on the sea's surface
7 High wind: 32–38 mph (50–61 km/h) Large trees sway
8 Gale: 39–46 mph (62–74 km/h) Twigs break from trees; long streaks of foam on the sea
9 Strong gale: 47–54 mph (75–88 km/h) Branches break from trees
10 Whole gale: 55–63 mph (89–102 km/h) Trees uprooted; sea takes on a white appearance
11 Storm 64–72 mph (103–117 km/h) Widespread damage
12 Hurricane At speeds of more than 73 mph (118 km/h) Structural damage on land; storm waves at sea

A satellite image of Earth shows a hurricane over the Caribbean Sea.

Cloud layers
There are 10 types of clouds. Each has a characteristic shape and appears at certain levels in the sky. All types would not appear together as in this diagram.

Altocumulus 6,500–23,000 ft. (2,000–7,000 m)
Cirrocumulus 16,500–44,000 ft. (5,000–13,500 m)
Cirrus 16,500–44,000 ft. (5,000–13,500 m)
Cirrostratus 16,500–44,000 ft. (5,000–13,500 m)
Altostratus 6,500–23,00 ft. (2,000–7,000 m)
Cumulonimbus 1,500–6,500 ft. (450–2,000 m)
Stratus below 1,500 ft (450 m)
Stratocumulus 1,500–6,500 ft. (450–2,000 m)
Cumulus 1,500–6,500 ft. (450–2,000 m)
Nimbostratus 3,000–10,000 ft. (900–3,000 m)

Hottest and coldest
The hottest place where people live is Djibouti, in the Republic of Djibouti, Africa. The average temperature is 86°F (30°C). Next hottest are Timbuktu in Mali and Tirunelevi in India, both 84.7°F (29.3°C). The coldest place where people live is Norilsk, Russia, with an average temperature of 12.4°F (–10.9°C). Next coldest is Yakutsk in Russia, at 13.8°F (–10.1°C).

World extremes

Windiest place on Earth
Commonwealth Bay, Antarctica, has some consistently high wind speeds, occasionally reaching 200 mph (320 km/h). The highest individual gust of wind measured was 231 mph (371 km/h) at Mt. Washington, U.S., on April 12, 1934.

Tornado wind speed
Fastest: 280 mph (450 km/h) at Wichita Falls, Texas, U.S., on April 2, 1958.

Hurricane wind speed
The fastest sustained winds in a hurricane in the U.S. measured 200 mph (322 km/h), with 210 mph (338 km/h) gusts, on August 17–18, 1969, when Hurricane Camille hit the Mississippi/Alabama coast.

Hottest place on Earth
Dallol in Ethiopia had an average temperature of 94°F (34.4°C) during 1960–66.

Highest shade temperature recorded
Al'Aziziyah, Libyan desert, hit 136°F (57.8°C) on September 13, 1922. A temperature of 134°F (56.6°C) was recorded at Death Valley, California, on July 10, 1913.

Least sunshine
At the South Pole there is no sunshine for 182 days every year, and at the North Pole the same applies for 176 days.

Driest place
Atacama Desert, Chile, where average annual rainfall is officially nil (also longest drought — 400 years up to 1971). The average rainfall on the Pacific coast of Chile between Arica and Antofagasta is less than 0.04 in. (1 mm).

Coldest place
Vostok, Antarctica, –129°F (–89.2°C) on July 21, 1983.

Tornados

Tornadoes, or twisters, are columns of air that spin violently, reaching speeds of over 260 mph (420 km/h). They destroy crops and any houses or vehicles in their path. The United State's worst, the Tri-State Tornado of March 18, 1925, struck Missouri, Illinois and Indiana and left almost 700 people dead and over 2,000 injured. In the book and film of *The Wizard of Oz* (1939) Dorothy is carried by a tornado from her Kansas home to the magical land of Oz.

Tools of the trade

Weather forecasters use a range of instruments. Balloons, radar stations and orbiting satellites also provide increasingly accurate weather information, and computer programs are able to make detailed forecasts.

Anemometer

Wind speed is measured by a cup anemometer. This has three or four cups that rotate around a vertical rod. The speed at which the wind spins the cups around is recorded by a counter. A wind vane shows the direction of wind, and an anemograph records the speed on a chart.

Rain gauge

Rain gauges — containers that measure the amount of rain that has fallen — date from ancient China and India. In 1662, British architect Sir Christopher Wren invented a tipping bucket rain gauge, which emptied itself when full.

Thermometer

Galileo invented the thermsocope, a form of thermometer. Later, sealed thermometers using mercury, which expands in a narrow tube as the temperature rises, were developed. Gabriel Fahrenheit's scale dates from 1714, and that of Anders Celsius from 1742. The maximum and minimum thermometer, which records the highest and lowest temperatures reached over a period of time, was invented by James Six at Cambridge in 1780.

A tornado sets down in a field.

www.nws.noaa.gov   search

Greatest snowfall in 12 months
At Mt. Rainier, Washington, from February 19, 1971, to February 18, 1972 1,224 in. (3,110.2 cm) fell. This is an incredible 102 ft. (31 m), equivalent to 17 people standing on each other's heads!

Greatest depth of snow
At Tamarac, California, in March 1911: 38 ft. (11.46 m).

Freak snow storm
In the Sahara Desert, Algeria, February 18, 1979.

Heaviest hailstones
Coffeyville, Kansas, 1.65 lb. (0.75 kg), September 3, 1970. The largest hailstone — 7 in. (17.8 cm) diameter — fell in Aurora, Nebraska, on June 22, 2003.

Most rainfall in 24 hours
Cilaos, La Réunion, 74 in. (1,870 mm), March 15–16, 1952.

Greatest annual rainfall (extreme example)
Cherrapunji, Assam, India; 1,042 in. (26,461 mm) between August 1, 1860, and July 31, 1861. Also, at the same place, the greatest rainfall in one calendar month — 366 in. (9,300 mm) — fell in July 1861.

Greatest annual rainfall (annual average)
Mawsynram, India, with 467 in. (11,870 mm) a year; and Tutunendo, Colombia, 463 in. (11,770 mm).

Most rainy days in a year
Mt. Waialeale, Kauai, Hawaii, can have up to 350 days a year. The total rainfall is about 460 in. (11,684 mm), which approaches the annual record.

NATURAL DISASTERS

Volcanic eruptions

Santorini
The eruption of the Greek island of Santorini in c. 1450 BC is believed to have been one of the most powerful ever.

Vesuvius, Italy
On August 24, AD 79 Vesuvius erupted with little warning, engulfing the Roman city of Herculaneum in a mud flow. Nearby Pompeii was buried under a vast layer of pumice and volcanic ash. This preserved the city, including the bodies of many of its inhabitants, until it was excavated by archaeologists in the 19th and 20th centuries. As many as 20,000 people died. Vesuvius erupted again in 1631, killing up to 18,000 people.

Laki, Iceland
Iceland is one of the most volcanically active places on Earth, but the population is small so eruptions seldom cause many deaths. On June 11, 1783, the largest lava flow ever recorded engulfed many villages in a river of lava up to 50 mi. (80 km) long and 100 ft. (30 m) deep. It released poisonous gases that killed those who managed to escape the lava flow — up to 20,000 people.

Unsen, Japan
On April 1, 1793, the volcanic island of Unsen, or Unzen, completely disappeared, killing all 53,000 inhabitants.

Tambora, Indonesia
On the island of Sumbawa the eruption of Tambora between April 5 and 12, 1815, killed about 10,000 islanders immediately. A further 82,000 died later from disease and famine. This made it the worst-ever eruption for loss of human life.

Krakatoa, Sumatra/Java
The uninhabited island of Krakatoa exploded on August 27, 1883, with what may have been the biggest bang ever heard by humans. People heard it up to 3,000 mi. (4,800 km) away!

Mont Pelée, Martinique
Mont Pelée began to erupt in April 1902, after lying dormant for centuries. The 30,000 residents of the main city, St. Pierre, were told that they were not in danger, so stayed in their homes. They were there on May 8 when the volcano burst apart and showered the port with molten lava, ash and gas, destroying all buildings and killing as many as 40,000 people.

Nevado del Ruiz, Colombia
In 1985 this Andean volcano gave warning signs that it was about to erupt, but the local people were not evacuated soon enough. On November 13, the hot steam, rocks and ash ejected from Nevado del Ruiz melted its icecap, causing a mudslide. This completely engulfed the town of Armero, killing 22,940 people.

Earthquake detector
Chinese astronomer Chan Heng (AD 78–139) invented an earthquake detector made of a vase adorned with dragons' heads and surrounded by metal frogs. In each of the dragons' jaws was a carefully balanced ball. When the first tremors of an earthquake made the device vibrate, the balls fell into the frogs' mouths, making a noise to warn of the coming danger.

Mount St. Helens erupting in 1980

Avalanche!
An avalanche caused by the eruption of the Mount St. Helens volcano, Washington, on May 18, 1980, was believed to have travelled at 250 mph (400 km/h).

A volcano erupts on Réunion Island in the Indian Ocean. (Inset) Lava pouring from an erupting volcano.

www.earthquake.usgs.gov/4kids   search

The Richter scale

Seismic waves are vibrations from earthquakes that travel through the Earth. Sensitive instruments called seismographs can record the waves, even at great distances, and calculate their strength and location.

The Richter scale indicates the magnitude or strength of an earthquake based on the size of the seismic waves (the distance the ground moves). The biggest earthquake (9 on the Richter scale) is a billion times greater than the smallest.

0 Detected by sensitive seismographs (some can detect magnitudes of less than zero!)

1 Detected by instruments

2 Lowest felt by humans

3 Slight vibration; more than 100,000 a year around the world

4 Up to 15,000 a year; at 4.5, would be detected by seismographs worldwide, but cause little damage

5 About 3,000 a year; the 1960 earthquake in Agadir, Morocco, was 5.6

6 About 100 a year worldwide

7 About 20 a year; the 1995 earthquake in Kobe, Japan, was 7.2

8 Major destructive earthquakes; average two a year; the 1904 San Francisco earthquake was probably 8.25

9 No quake higher than 8.9 has been recorded, but 9.0 or even higher is theoretically possible

Earthquake

Earthquakes are movements of the Earth's surface, often as a result of a fault, or fracture, in the crust. They happen more often in some parts of the world than others. In heavily populated areas, they cause great damage to buildings and loss of life.

Worst ever
An earthquake affecting the Middle East and North Africa on May 20, 1202, may have been the worst in human history. Up to 1,000,000 people were killed, 110,000 in Cairo, Egypt, alone.

Most powerful
The worst earthquake affecting an inhabited area was in Assam, India, on June 12, 1897. It is believed to have reached 8.7, killing about 1,500. The Colombia/Ecuador earthquake of January 31, 1906, was 8.9 on the Richter scale. Fortunately, it was 200 mi. (300 km) off the coast, and so resulted in fewer than 1,000 deaths on land.

Worst modern earthquakes
An earthquake in Tang-shan, China, on July 28, 1976, killed 242,419. The Kashmir quake of October 8, 2005, officially killed 87,350 people, but it may have been more than 100,000.

Longest lasting
Most earthquakes last only a minute or two, but the Alaska earthquake of March 27, 1964, continued for at least five minutes and registered 8.6 on the Richter scale. It killed only 131 people but caused more than $450 million worth of damage.

Worst natural disasters

Drought
Serious droughts kill people and livestock and destroy crops. The drought in Australia in 1982 cost $6 billion, and one in Spain in 1995 cost $4.7 billion.

Flood
Floods caused by China's Huang He, or Yellow River, were first recorded in 2297 BC. The river has flooded at least 1,500 times since. In 1887 floods killed between 1.5 million and 7 million people, making it the worst flood ever.

Tsunami
On December 26, 2004, a tsunami created by an undersea earthquake caused catastrophic floods in Indonesia, Sri Lanka, Myanmar (formerly Burma), the Maldives, Malaysia, India and parts of Africa. More than 283,100 people died.

Cyclone
The worst cyclone of the 21st century has been Cyclone Nargis (2008) which killed an estimated 140,000 in Myanmar (Burma), with more than 2.5 million more gravely effected.

Life
Sciences

March of the penguins

Studies have found that melting sea ice in Antarctica is seriously threatening the future of the Emperor penguin. The penguins are being robbed of crucial nesting ground and mother penguins are forced to travel further in search of food. The changing conditions have caused a rapid decrease in the Emperor penguin population, and the situation is getting worse.

Top food plants

Every year the people of the world eat more than 2.4 billion tons of cereals, 995 million tons of vegetables and 579 million tons of fruit. These figures (in tons per year) come from the Food and Agriculture Organization of the United Nations, or FAO, which is based in Rome. The aim of the FAO is to help people around the world grow more food and eat a better diet.

Sugar cane	1,534,820,044
Corn/maize	766,357,997
Rice	699,533,077
Wheat	667,940,341
Potatoes	347,338,646
Beets	282,640,255
Cassava	249,494,272
Soybeans	244,162,989
Barley	152,827,262
Tomatoes	138,387,993
Sweet potatoes	136,146,218
Watermelons	110,895,155
Bananas	77,995,522
Cabbages	76,049,979
Grapes	76,007,444
Oranges	71,424,684
Apples	70,332,460
Onions	67,943,069
Sorghum	62,264,363
Coconuts	60,984,627

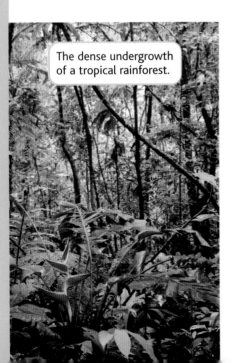

The dense undergrowth of a tropical rainforest.

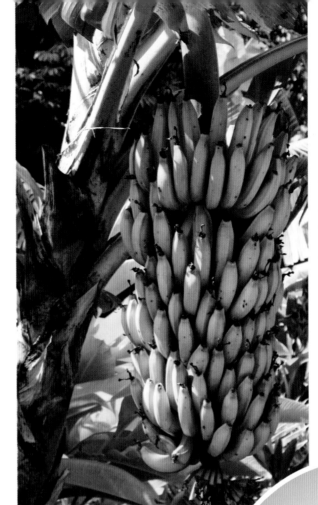

Bananas grow well in tropical climates.

Important crops

These are the most important crops grown for uses other than food.

Cotton (clothing, household items)
79,375,310 tons a year
Rubber (tires, shoes, balls, erasers)
10,933,544 tons a year
Tobacco (cigarettes, cigars)
7,406,775 tons a year
Jute (sacks, rope)
3,429,235 tons a year

Banana facts

● Although bananas grow on trees, botanically the banana is a herb.

● Bananas grow upwards, not down.

● A cluster of bananas is called a hand and consists of 10 to 20 bananas, which are known as fingers — the word *banan* is Arabic for finger.

● The first bananas grown in the Americas were planted in 1516 on the island of Hispañiola by Spanish missionary Tomás de Berlanga.

● India grows more bananas than any other country in the world, about 24 million tons a year, more than a quarter of the total world crop

● Worldwide, more than 88 million tons of bananas are eaten every year.

Going Bananas

● The phrase "going bananas" was first recorded in the 1930s, perhaps because of their connection with the wild behavior of monkeys.

● In 1987 Peter Dowdeswell (UK) set a record for eating 17 bananas in 1 minute 47 seconds.

● In an average year there are more than 300 banana-related accidents in Britain, most involving people slipping on skins.

● Billy Jones's recording of the song *Yes! We Have No Bananas* was U.S. No.1 for five weeks in 1923.

World forests

Forests cover 29.6 percent of Earth's land and almost a quarter of these are in Russia. There are three main types of forest, which grow in particular climates in different parts of the world.

● Tropical forests or rainforests grow near the Equator where it is always hot and wet. Here, temperatures are about 68–77°F (20–25°C) and there is more than 80 in. (200 cm) of rain a year.

● Temperate forests grow in places that have hot summers and cold winters. The summers can be as hot as 86°F (30°C) and winters as cold as −22°F (−30°C). Average rainfall is about 30–60 in. (75–150 cm) a year. Many trees are deciduous (drop their leaves in autumn).

● Boreal or taiga forests grow in Russia, Canada and elsewhere in the far north. Winters are long and very cold. There is rainfall of 16–40 in. (40–100 cm) a year, but most falls as snow. Most trees are evergreen conifers (cone-producing trees with needle-like leaves).

Dangerous plants

● Potatoes are safe to eat when cooked, but the stems and leaves of the plants contain a poison called solanine. If potatoes turn green, they may also contain solanine.

● Ricin is extracted from the seeds of the castor oil plant and is more poisonous than cyanide or snake venom. Even minute doses of ricin can be fatal.

● Opium is extracted from the juice of a poppy and contains morphine. Small quantities of both are used legally as painkillers and illegally as drugs. Both can easily cause death.

● The death cap is a highly poisonous mushroom. It is responsible for almost 90 percent of deaths from eating fungi. The poison causes severe diarrhea and vomiting.

● Curare is extracted from the bark of certain trees and is used by South American Native tribes to tip their poison arrows when they go hunting.

● Deadly nightshade is also known as belladonna. It contains a poison called atropine. Less than 0.0004 oz. (10 mg) could kill a child.

● Nicotine is a yellow oily liquid found in tobacco. About 0.002 oz. (50 mg) of nicotine would kill an adult within minutes.

● The leaves of the purple foxglove contain digitalis and eating just a few can be fatal. Digitalis is used in tiny doses to treat people suffering from heart disease.

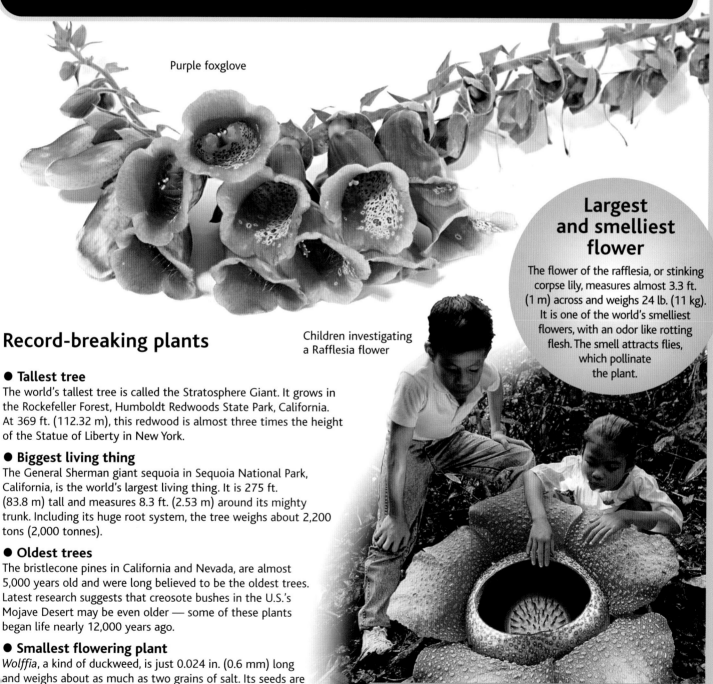

Purple foxglove

Children investigating a Rafflesia flower

Largest and smelliest flower

The flower of the rafflesia, or stinking corpse lily, measures almost 3.3 ft. (1 m) across and weighs 24 lb. (11 kg). It is one of the world's smelliest flowers, with an odor like rotting flesh. The smell attracts flies, which pollinate the plant.

Record-breaking plants

● **Tallest tree**
The world's tallest tree is called the Stratosphere Giant. It grows in the Rockefeller Forest, Humboldt Redwoods State Park, California. At 369 ft. (112.32 m), this redwood is almost three times the height of the Statue of Liberty in New York.

● **Biggest living thing**
The General Sherman giant sequoia in Sequoia National Park, California, is the world's largest living thing. It is 275 ft. (83.8 m) tall and measures 8.3 ft. (2.53 m) around its mighty trunk. Including its huge root system, the tree weighs about 2,200 tons (2,000 tonnes).

● **Oldest trees**
The bristlecone pines in California and Nevada, are almost 5,000 years old and were long believed to be the oldest trees. Latest research suggests that creosote bushes in the U.S.'s Mojave Desert may be even older — some of these plants began life nearly 12,000 years ago.

● **Smallest flowering plant**
Wolffia, a kind of duckweed, is just 0.024 in. (0.6 mm) long and weighs about as much as two grains of salt. Its seeds are also the tiniest known — they weigh only 70 micrograms, as much as a single grain of salt.

www.fao.org   search

Grouping living things

Living things are organized by scientists into five groups called kingdoms. These are: animals (Animalia); algae and protozoans (Protista); bacteria (Prokaryotae); mushrooms, molds and lichens (Fungi); plants (Plantae).

The animal kingdom alone has thousands of different species. A species is a type of animal, and animals of the same species can breed successfully with each other. Similar species are grouped in a genus. Genera are grouped into families, families into orders, right up to the level of phylum. The phylum Chordata contains all vertebrate animals — animals with a backbone. Here's how a human and a giant panda are classified.

	Human	Giant panda
Phylum	Chordata	Chordata
Class	Mammalia	Mammalia
Order	Primates	Carnivores
Family	Hominidae	Ursidae
Genus	*Homo*	*Ailuropoda*
Species	*sapiens*	*melanoleuca*

Animal species

Below is a list of the animals we know about. No one knows exactly how many species there may be altogether, but one recent estimate puts the total at 1,105,589. New species are often being found and there may be millions not yet discovered.

Some experts think there may be millions of species of insects and at least a million species of deep-sea fish that no one has ever seen. About half of all known creatures and plants live in tropical rainforests. In a study of just 19 trees in a tropical rainforest, 1,200 beetle species were found. About 80 percent of these had not been seen before.

- **Arachnids** 98,000 (spiders, scorpions, etc)
- **Molluscs** 81,000 (snails, clams, etc)
- **Nematodes** 80,000 (unsegmented worms)
- **Crustaceans** 40,000 (shrimps, crabs, etc)
- **Fish** 30,700
- **Flatworms** 25,000
- **Segmented worms** 15,000
- **Sponges** 10,000
- **Birds** 9,990
- **Jellyfish, coral, etc** 9,000
- **Reptiles** 8,734
- **Starfish** 7,000
- **Amphibians** 6,347
- **Mammals** 5,488

Insects
950,000

The first zoos

- As long ago as 2000 BC, the rulers of ancient Mesopotamia, Egypt and China had collections of animals. In medieval England King Henry I kept animals including a lion, leopard and camels at his palace at Woodstock, Oxford.

- Aztec ruler Montezuma II's animal collection in Tenochtitlán (modern Mexico City) contained many exotic creatures, such as jaguars, ocelots, snakes, monkeys and even human freaks.

- The imperial menagerie of Tiergarten Schönbrunn, Vienna, Austria, was built by Emperor Francis in 1752, and opened to the public in 1779. Its present-day inhabitants include giant pandas.

- London Zoo in Regent's Park was originally established in 1828 for the scientific study of animals, but was opened to the public in 1847. Officially called the Zoological Gardens, its name was shortened to "zoo," which became used worldwide.

- Melbourne Zoo, opened in 1862, was Australia's first.

- Traveling menageries toured the U.S. in the early 19th century. The first permanent zoo was established in Philadelphia in 1859, but the Civil War delayed its opening until 1874. Meanwhile, Central Park Zoo, New York, opened in 1864 and Lincoln Park, Chicago, in 1868.

A panda in captivity

Life on Earth　　　　3,900 million years ago

The first simple life forms began to appear on Earth almost four billion years ago. More familiar animals appeared about 500 million years ago, and humans only within the past two million. We know a little about extinct creatures and early humans from fossil remains found in rocks from each period.

3,900–2,500 m.y.a. Archaean period — the earliest marine life form (blue-green algae)

2,500–540 m.y.a. Proterozoic period — the first many-celled organisms evolve

540–490 m.y.a. Cambrian period — the first fossils of animals with shells and skeletons

490–443 m.y.a. Ordovician period — mollusks, some corals and fishlike vertebrates

443–417 m.y.a. Silurian period — fish develop jaws; first sharks

417–354 m.y.a. Devonian period—fish dominant; amphibians (the first land animals) evolve

354–290 m.y.a. Carboniferous period — insects; first reptiles

290–248 m.y.a. Permian period — insects evolve into modern types; reptiles evolve

248–206 m.y.a. Triassic period — early dinosaurs; marine reptiles

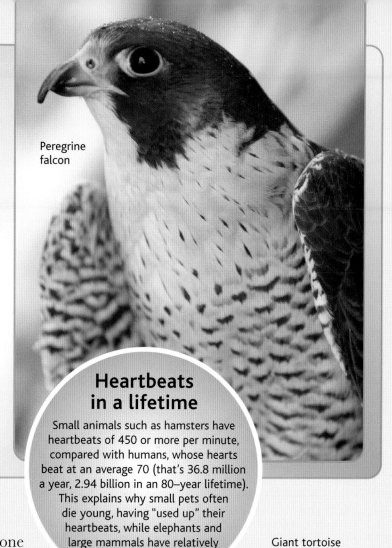

Peregrine falcon

How fast?

Most of the creatures in this list can keep up these speeds for only a short time — less than an hour. The peregrine falcon achieves its speed as it dives through the air to catch prey, not in level flight.

Peregrine falcon (diving speed) 185 mph (298 km/h)
Spine-tailed swift 106 mph (171 km/h)
Eider duck 70 mph (113 km/h)
Sailfish (fastest fish) 68 mph (110 km/h)
Cheetah (fastest on land) 65 mph (105 km/h)
Pronghorn antelope 55 mph (89 km/h)
Racing pigeon 50 mph (80 km/h)
Lion (charging) 50 mph (80 km/h)
Brown hare 45 mph (72 km/h)
Ostrich (fastest flightless bird) 45 mph (72 km/h)

Blue shark 43 mph (69 km/h)
Horse 43 mph (69 km/h)
Greyhound 42 mph (68 km/h)
Killer whale 35 mph (56 km/h)
Death's head hawkmoth (fastest flying insect) 33 mph (53 km/h)
Guano bat (fastest flying mammal) 32 mph (51 km/h)
Skipper butterfly 30 mph (48 km/h)
California sea lion 25 mph (40 km/h)
Dolphin 25 mph (40 km/h)
Fastest human over 328 ft (100 m) 23 mph (37km/h)

Heartbeats in a lifetime

Small animals such as hamsters have heartbeats of 450 or more per minute, compared with humans, whose hearts beat at an average 70 (that's 36.8 million a year, 2.94 billion in an 80–year lifetime). This explains why small pets often die young, having "used up" their heartbeats, while elephants and large mammals have relatively long lifespans.

Giant tortoise

How long do they live?

Who would have thought that a sea anemone could live for 80 years? All these figures are the longest ever recorded. Most of these animals have much shorter lives.

Marine clam 200
Giant tortoise 150
Human 122
Killer whale 90
Sea anemone 80
Asiatic elephant 78
American alligator 66
Blue macaw 64
Horse 62
Chimpanzee 56

Hippopotamus 54
Slow-worm 54
Beaver 50
Bactrian camel 50
Grizzly bear 50
Blue whale 45
Boa constrictor 40
Domestic cat 34
Lion 30
Pig 27

Common rabbit 18
Queen ant 18
Giant centipede 10
Millipede 7
House mouse 6
Bedbug 6 months
Common housefly (male) 2 weeks

2000s

206–144 m.y.a. Jurassic period — reptiles dominate land, sea and air; *Archaeopteryx* (first bird) appears; first mammals
144–65 m.y.a. Cretaceous period — dinosaurs become extinct; snakes and lizards appear

65–55 m.y.a. Paleocene period — first large land mammals
55–34 m.y.a. Eocene period — modern land mammals and whales appear
34–24 m.y.a. Oligocene period — modern mammals dominant

24–5 m.y.a. Miocene period — modern mammals, eg., primates; birds
5–1.8 m.y.a. Pliocene period — humanlike apes appear

1.8 m.y.a. to 10,000 years ago Pleistocene period — humans appear
10,000 years ago to present Holocene period — human civilization

🔍 animaldiversity.ummz.umich.edu   search

Types of mammal

A mammal is a warm-blooded vertebrate (animal with a backbone) with some hair on its body. Female mammals feed their young on milk from their mammary glands. Most mammals give birth to live young which develop inside the mother's body, but echidnas and the platypus lay eggs.

Marsupial mammals such as kangaroos give birth to live young, but they are very small and weak. They finish their development in a pouch on the mother's body. There are 21 main groups, or orders, of mammals. Listed below are the names of the main mammal groups, examples of the animals and the approximate number of known species. Common names are given where possible.

Rodents Beavers, squirrels, mice, rats, porcupines, voles, guinea pigs, chinchillas 2,052

Chiroptera Bats 977

Insectivores Shrews, moles, hedgehogs, tenrecs 440

Marsupials Opossums, koalas, bandicoots, kangaroos, wallabies, numbat 292

Primates Lemurs, lorises, tarsiers, marmosets, monkeys, gibbons, apes, humans 270

Carnivores Dogs, foxes, wolves, cats, bears, hyenas, raccoons, civets, mongooses, weasels, pandas 249

Even-toed ungulates Pigs, peccaries, giraffe, okapi, hippopotamuses, deer, camels, llamas, antelopes, cattle 225

Cetacea Whales, dolphins, porpoises 83

Lagomorphia Rabbits, hares, pikas 80

Pinnipedia Seals, sea-lions, walruses 34

Edentates Anteaters, sloths, armadillos 29

Odd-toed ungulates Horses, asses, zebras, rhinos, tapirs 19

Scandentia Tree shrews 19

Macroscelidea Elephant-shrews 15

Monotremes Duck-billed platypus, echidnas 5

Hyracoidea Hyraxes 8

Pholidota Pangolins 7

Sirenia Manatees, dugong 4

Proboscidea Elephants 3

Dermoptera Flying lemurs 2

Tubulidentata Aardvark 1

Big babies

The African elephant has the longest pregnancy of any mammal. She carries her baby for an average of 660 days. When the baby is born it weighs 200–265 lb. (90–120 kg). A baby blue whale is even bigger. It weighs 4,409 lb. (2,000 kg) and is 23 ft. (7 m) long. It puts on weight at the astonishing rate of 200 lb. (90 kg) a day.

African elephant

Biggest and smallest

The following are the biggest land mammals according to weight:

African elephant 14,400 lb. (7,000 kg)
White rhinoceros 7,900 lb. (3,600 kg)
Hippopotamus 5,500 lb. (2,500 kg)
Giraffe 3,520 lb. (1,600 kg)
American buffalo 2,200 lb. (1,000 kg)
Arabian camel (dromedary) 1,520 lb. (690 kg)
Polar bear 1,320 lb. (600 kg)

The following are the smallest land mammals, according to length:

Kitti's hog-nosed bat 1.1 in. (2.9 cm)
Pygmy shrew 1.4 in. (3.6 cm)
Pipistrelle bat 1.6 in. (4 cm)
Little brown bat 1.6 in. (4 cm)
Masked shrew 1.8 in. (4.5 cm)
Southern blossom bat 2 in. (5 cm)
Harvest mouse 2.3 in. (5.8 cm)

Big cats

Big cats like lions are perhaps the most powerful of all mammal predators. These measurements are from the nose to the tip of the tail. The length of tail varies — a leopard's tail can be as long as 43 in. (110 cm) and a jaguar's tail as short as 18 in. (45 cm).

Tiger (Asia) 130 in. (330 cm)
Leopard (Asia, Africa) 126 in. (320 cm)
Lion (Africa, Asia) 110 in. (280 cm)
Jaguar (North, Central and South America) 107 in. (271 cm)
Cougar (North, Central and South America) 96 in. (245 cm)
Snow leopard (Asia) 94 in. (240 cm)
Cheetah (Africa, Asia) 87 in. (220 cm)
Clouded leopard (Asia) 75 in. (197 cm)

Bears of the world

Scientists have long argued about whether the giant panda should be grouped with the raccoon family or the bears. DNA tests have now proved that it belongs with the bears. The koala, often called koala bear, is actually a marsupial not a bear.

Polar bear (Arctic) Length up to 101 in. (257cm); weight 440–1,760 lb. (200–800 kg)

Brown (grizzly) bear (North America, Europe, Asia) Length up to 114 in. (290 cm); weight 300–860 lb. (136–390 kg)

American black bear (North America) Length 50–75 in. (127–191 cm); weight 130–660 lb. (60–300 kg)

Asiatic black bear (Southern Asia) Length 50–74 in. (127–188 cm); weight 220–440 lb. (100–200 kg)

Sloth bear (Asia) Length 60–75 in. (152–191 cm); weight 175–310 lb. (80–140 kg)

Giant panda (China) Length 48–60 in. (122–152 cm); weight up to 275 lb. (125 kg)

Spectacled bear (South America) Length 60–72 in. (152–183 cm); weight 150–250 lb. (70–113 kg)

Sun bear (Asia) Length 48–60 in. (122–152 cm); weight 60–145 lb. (27–65 kg)

Champion divers

Lots of mammals can dive underwater, including humans, but whales are the champions. All have to hold their breath. These are average dives.

Northern bottlenose whale 120 min.

Sperm whale 112 min.

Greenland whale 60 min.

Seal 22 min.

Beaver 20 min.

Dugong 16 min.

Hippopotamus 15 min.

Porpoise 15 min.

Muskrat 12 min.

Duck-billed platypus 10 min.

Sea otter 5 min.

Human pearl diver 2.5 min.

Human 1 min

Western lowland gorilla

Intelligence

Edward O. Wilson, professor of zoology at Harvard, researched the intelligence of mammals. He defined intelligence on the basis of how fast and how well an animal can learn a wide range of tasks. He also took into account the size of the animal's brain compared with its body. His top 10 most intelligent mammals, in order are: human, chimpanzee, gorilla, orangutan, baboon, gibbon, monkey, small-toothed whale, dolphin and elephant.

Monkeys and apes

Monkeys and apes (and humans) belong to the group of mammals called primates. There are 256 known species of primate. The smallest is the pygmy mouse lemur, which weighs only 1 oz. (30 g). The largest is the gorilla, which weighs 485 lb. (220 kg). Humans comes next at an average 170 lb. (77 kg).

Siberian tiger cubs in the snow

Marine mammals

The biggest creatures in the sea are whales, which are mammals not fish. The blue whale is the largest creature that has ever lived. Whales spend all their lives in the sea, but there are other mammals that spend most of their time in water and some time on land. These include seals, sea lions and otters.

Smallest marine mammals

● The marine otter, which lives off the western coast of South America, is the smallest marine mammal. It weighs up to 10 lb. (4.5 kg) and is about 3.77 ft. (1.15 m) long. The sea otter of North American coasts is slightly larger.

● Small dolphins include Hector's dolphin, which lives off New Zealand. It is rarely more than 3.77 ft. (1.5 m) long and 126 lb. (57.2 kg) in weight.

Biggest marine mammals

● The blue whale is 110 ft. (33.5 m) long and weighs 145 tons (130 tonnes)

● The fin whale is 82 ft. (25 m) long and weighs 50 tons (45 tonnes)

● The right whale is 57.4 ft. (17.5 m) long and weighs 45 tons (40 tonnes)

● The sperm whale is 59 ft. (18 m) long and weighs 40 tons (36 tonnes)

Blue whales can be as long as three buses

Top food fish

Fish and shellfish are popular foods for people. The top catches are:

Type of fish	Total catch in 2006 (tons)
Carps, barbels, cyprinid	23,443,011
Herrings, sardines, anchovies	21,060, 428
Cod, hake, haddock	9,905,290
Tunas, bonitos, billfish	7,143,456
Shrimps, prawns	6,199,825
Clams, cockles, arkshell	5,565,937
Oysters	5,362,633
Squid, cuttlefish, octopus	4,688,181
Salmon, trouts, smelts	3,407,627
Tilapias, cichlids	3,364,264
Top 10 total	*90,140,652*
Aquaculture	*158,344,429*
Capture	*101,406,381*
World total caught for food	*259,750,810*

The most dangerous fish is the great white shark

Danger in the water

Most creatures living in the world's oceans and rivers are harmless to people, but there are a few that can be very dangerous if you encounter or provoke them.

● The tiny candiru fish lives in South American rivers. It can enter your body and kill you unless it is surgically removed.

● Cone-shells, found in the South Pacific and Indian Oceans, have poisonous barbs that cause paralysis and occasionally death if you touch them. The geographer cone is probably the most dangerous of all.

● Freshwater electric eels live in South America and are the most powerful of all the electric eels. They can release up to 650 volts, which is enough to kill a person. Fortunately, this rarely happens.

● Certain parts of the Japanese puffer fish, also known as the maki-maki or deadly death puffer fish, contain a powerful nerve poison that can kill you if you eat it. There is no known antidote. Despite the danger, puffer fish are eaten in Japan, where they are a very expensive delicacy. People are specially trained to prepare them because eating the wrong part causes death in about 60 percent of cases. About 50 people a year in Japan die after eating incorrectly prepared puffers.

Big fish

Whale sharks are probably the biggest fish in the world. They are usually up to 39 ft. (12 m) long, though one caught off Thailand in 1919 was believed to be 59 ft. (18 m) long.

Whale sharks eat only plankton — tiny plants and animals that float in water. Basking sharks also eat plankton, but most other big fish hunt.

Whale shark 48,500 lb. (22,000 kg)
Basking shark 35,200 lb. (16,000 kg)
Giant manta 6,600 lb. (3,000 kg)
Beluga 4,400 lb. (2,000 kg)
Great white shark 4,400 lb. (2,000 kg)
Sharptail mola 4,400 lb. (2,000 kg)
Greenland shark 2,200 lb. (1,000 kg)
Ocean sunfish 2,200 lb. (1,000 kg)

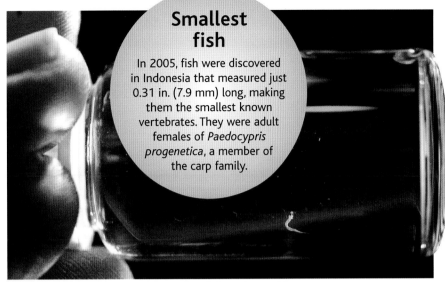

Smallest fish

In 2005, fish were discovered in Indonesia that measured just 0.31 in. (7.9 mm) long, making them the smallest known vertebrates. They were adult females of *Paedocypris progenetica*, a member of the carp family.

Paedocypris progenetica is the smallest fish in the world

Giant japanese spider crabs

Deep sea divers

● Emperor penguins sometimes dive to depths of 870 ft. (265 m).

● In 1987 a leatherback turtle fitted with a depth-gauge reached a depth of 3,900 ft. (1,200 m).

Leatherback turtle

● Sperm whales regularly dive to 3,900 ft. (1,200 m) and experts think they may sometimes go down to twice this depth.

● Fish called brotulids are the deepest living vertebrate animals. They have been found in deep-sea trenches at 27,230 ft. (8,300 m)— that is almost as deep as Mount Everest is high.

Amazing sea creatures

Most eggs
The black marlin fish lays as many as 226 million eggs.

Largest crustacean
The giant spider crab's body measures up to 12–14 in. (30.5–35.5 cm) across and it has a claw span of 7.8–8.8 ft. (2.4–2.7 m).

Smallest crustacean
Pea crabs measure only about 2.5 in. (6.5 cm) across the shell.

Heaviest crustacean
An Atlantic lobster weighing 42.44 lb. (19.25 kg) was caught off the Virginia State coast in 1934. It was nicknamed Mike.

Heaviest mollusk
A giant squid caught in 1878 had tentacles 35 ft. (10.7 m) long and weighed about 4,000 lb. (1,800 kg).

Largest clam
A clam known as *Tridacna derasa* measures up to 49 in. (124 cm) across and weighs 580 lb. (263 kg).

Largest gastropod
The gastropod group includes snails. The largest gastropod is the trumpet or baler conch. It lives off Australian coasts and weighs up to 40 lb. (18 kg). Its shell measures 30 in. (77 cm) long and 40 in. (101 cm) around.

Largest jellyfish
The lion's mane jellyfish (*Cyanea arctica*) is up to 7.5 ft. (2.3 m) long, with tentacles that add an extra 121 ft. (37 m).

Largest sponge
The barrel sponge of the Caribbean is up to 6–8 ft. (1.8–2.4 m) tall.

● Several species of octopus are dangerous. The sting of the blue-ringed octopus, which lives in the Australian seas, can cause paralysis and even death.

● Piranha are small but incredibly ferocious fish that live in rivers in parts of South America. They hunt in groups, attacking any creatures in the water — including humans unlucky enough to encounter them. They strip their prey to the bone in minutes.

● Sea wasps, also known as box jellyfish, live off the coast of Australia. They have tentacles up to 29 ft. (9 m) long and venom as powerful as that of a cobra. Australian lifeguards often wear nylon tights to protect them against stings, which can cause death within three minutes.

● Most sharks are harmless but a few species have been known to attack people. The great white, tiger and bull sharks are the most dangerous. Of the 631 attacks on humans recorded from 1508 to 2007, 135 resulted in death.

● Stonefish lie on the seabed where they resemble rocks encrusted with seaweed. Unsuspecting swimmers who tread on the fish receive a very painful sting from their spines. In severe cases, victims may die.

www.fishbase.org   search

Bird fact file

Birds are vertebrate animals with two legs and front limbs that have become adapted to form wings. All birds have feathers and most, but not all, can fly. Birds reproduce by laying eggs from which their young hatch.

Smallest bird
The smallest bird is the bee hummingbird, which is 2.2 in. (5.7 cm) long and weighs 0.056 oz. (1.6 g).

Longest beak
The bird with the longest beak in relation to its body is the sword-billed hummingbird — its beak is 4.1 in. (10.5 cm) long and its body is 5.3 in. (13.5 cm) long. The bird with the longest beak of all is the Australian pelican. Its beak is 18.5 in. (47 cm) long.

Highest flyer
Ruppell's griffon is the highestflying bird. In 1973 one was recorded at 37,000 ft. (11,300 m) above sea level — 7,900 ft. (2,400 m) higher than Mt. Everest — after colliding with an airliner.

Longest migration
The Arctic tern migrates farther than any other bird. Every year it flies from the Arctic to Antarctica and back again — a round trip of at least 25,000 mi. (40,000 km).

Largest flying birds

- **Great bustard**: wingspan 9 ft. (2.7 m); weight 46 lb. (20.9 kg)
- **Trumpeter swan**: wingspan 11 ft. (3.4 m); weight 37 lb. (16.8 kg)
- **Mute swan**: wingspan 10 ft. (3.1 m); weight 36 lb. (16.3 kg)
- **Albatross**: wingspan 12 ft. (3.7 m); weight 34.8 lb. (15.8 kg)
- **Whooper swan**: wingspan 10 ft. (3.1 m); weight 34.8 lb. (15.8 kg)

Arctic tern

One and only

The North American whippoorwill is the only bird that hibernates. In autumn the bird dozes off in a rock crevice or an old nest and sleeps through the winter. Its heart rate and breathing slow down and its body temperature drops from its normal 105°F (41°C) down to 55.4°F (13°C) so it uses as little energy as possible.

All about feathers

The body of a feather is called its vane, the shaft is known as the rachis and the individual tufts are known as barbs. The barbs have hooks called barbules that cling to the others like Velcro to make a smooth surface.

Peacock feather

- Feathers are made of keratin, the same material as our hair and nails.

- Birds shed their feathers at intervals and grow new ones. This process is called molting. Feathers fall in a set pattern and in pairs, one from each side, so that the bird's flight is not unbalanced. Birds that do not fly, such as penguins, molt all over.

- A songbird such as a sparrow has about 3,000 feathers in the summer but as many as 3,500 in the winter to keep it warm. A swan may have 25,200 or more — up to 20,000 of them on its head and neck. The bird with the fewest feathers is the ruby-throated hummingbird with only 940.

- Pens for writing were once made from the quills, or feathers, of geese, turkeys and other birds. The word pen comes from the Latin *penna*, a feather.

- Grebes eat their own feathers. They are thought to form pellets that help the birds regurgitate (bring up) the bones and scales of the fish they eat.

- The Japanese phoenix fowl is a domestic bird. It has tail feathers measuring up to 34.8 ft. (10.6 m), the longest of any bird. Various types of pheasant have tail feathers 6.6 ft. (2 m) long or more and a peacock's tail feathers can be 5 ft. (1.5 m) long.

- Each feather weighs very little, but together they make up a large part of the weight of a bird, especially as flying birds have very light skeletons. The skeleton of the frigate bird, a large bird with a 6.9 ft. (2.1 m) wingspan, weighs just 4 oz. (113 g), less than the weight of all its feathers.

Largest flightless birds

● **Ostrich**: height 9 ft. (2.7 m); weight 345 lb. (156.5 kg)
● **Emu**: height 5 ft. (1.5 m); weight 88 lb. (40 kg)
● **Cassowary**: height 5 ft. (1.5 m); weight 74 lb. (33.5 kg)
● **Rhea**: height 4.5 ft. (1.4 m); weight 55 lb. (25 kg)
● **Emperor penguin**: 4.3 ft. (1.3 m); weight 64.8 lb. (29.4 kg)

Birds' eggs

The biggest ostrich eggs weigh up to 5.2 lb. (2.35 kg), but they are not the largest eggs of all time. The extinct elephant bird (*Aepyornis maximus*) of Madagascar laid eggs that were up to 13 in. (33 cm) long.

This is larger than the eggs of any dinosaur, seven times bigger than an ostrich egg, 180 times bigger than a chicken egg and over 20,000 times the size of a hummingbird's egg!

Ostrich 56.4 oz. (1,600 g)
Albatross 21 oz. (595 g)
Kiwi 15.9 oz. (450 g)
Emperor penguin 15.9 oz. (450 g)
Mute swan 12 oz. (340 g)
Eagle 5.1 oz. (145 g)
Snowy owl 2.9 oz. (83 g)
Domestic hen 2.3 oz. (65 g)
Mallard 1.9 oz. (54 g)
Peregrine falcon 1.8 oz. (52 g)
Sparrow 0.106 oz. (3 g)
Vervain hummingbird 0.013 oz. (0.375 g)

Emperor penguins

The Emperor penguin is the largest penguin. It lives in Antarctica, where there are about 200,000 breeding pairs. The female lays one egg, then goes off to feed for about two months. The male keeps the egg warm on his feet, beneath his body. Chicks stay with their mothers for about seven weeks, then gather together in a group to keep warm.

Flying mammals

Bats are the only mammals capable of true flight. They belong to the order Chiroptera, which means hand-wing. Instead of front legs, bats have wings made of skin that are supported by the bones of the arms and hands.

● There are about 977 species of bats. Flying foxes are among the largest. These bats are 18 in. (45 cm) long, have wings that span 5.6 ft. (1.7 m) and weigh up to 3.5 lb. (1.6 kg). The Kitti's hog-nosed bat, which lives in Thailand, is the smallest. It weighs 0.07 oz. (2 g), which is less than a table tennis ball. It is only 1.1 in. (2.9 cm) long, making it the smallest of all mammals.

● Bats sleep during the day and wake up at night, when they go in search of food. Most bats are insect-eaters — a little brown bat can catch 1,200 insects in an hour—but others eat fruit or nectar from plants. Some larger species catch frogs, birds and fish.

● Many bats live in large groups called colonies. Bracken Cave in Texas, contains the world's largest bat colony, with about 20 million animals. This is one of the densest populations of any mammal and there can be as many as 450 newborn babies per square foot (0.09 sq m). These bats eat 1,102 tons (1,000 tonnes) of insects every night.

Emperor penguins and their young

www.bsc-eoc.org/avibase/avibase.jsp **search**

Tarantula

Shortest-lived
Male houseflies live for about 17 days and females for about 29 days. Mayflies may live for only a single day as adults, but for two or three years as larvae.

Distance fliers
Butterflies have been tracked flying for 3,000 mi. (4,800 km).

Fastest
Dragonflies can fly at speeds of 18–20 mph (29–32 km/h).

Amazing insects

Most abundant
Insects called springtails live in topsoil all over the world. There are probably as many as 1.5 billion per acre (600 million per hectare) . Together, they weigh more than the entire human race.

Longest
Stick insects have the longest bodies. Some measure up to 20.1 in. (51 cm) long, including their legs.

Heaviest
Goliath beetles can be 4.3 in. (11 cm) long and weigh 3.5 oz. (100 g).

Largest wingspan
The wings of the female Queen Alexandra birdwing butterfly of Papua New Guinea measure 11 in. (128 cm) across.

Smallest
The wings of a battledore wing fairy fly, which is a kind of parasitic wasp, measure only 0.008 in. (0.21 mm).

Longest lived
Jewel beetle larvae, or young, may live inside lumber for up to 30 years or more before emerging and turning into adult insects.

Spiders

Spiders are not insects. They belong to a separate group called arachnids, which also includes scorpions. A spider's body is divided into two parts linked by a narrow waist. It has four pairs of legs tipped with claws, but no wings. All spiders can make silk but not all spin webs.

There are at least 35,000 species of spiders. Most are harmless but a few can be deadly. The banana spider of Central and South America produces enough venom to kill six adult humans. Other deadly spiders are the funnel-web, which lives in Australia, and the wolf spider of Central and South America. The black widow and various tarantulas are also dangerous and can kill.

Biggest spider
The goliath bird-eating spider, which lives in South American rainforests, has legs up to 10 in. (25 cm) long.

Smallest spider
A species called *Patu marplesi* from Western Samoa is the smallest known spider. It is only 0.018 in (0.46 mm) long.

Types of insect

The body of most insects has three parts — head, thorax and abdomen. Insects have three pairs of legs and many have two pairs of wings. Listed here are the main groups, or orders, of insects. Numbers are just the species that we know about and have been named. There may be thousands more still to be discovered. Total numbers are huge. Together, all the insects in the world would weigh at least 12 times as much as all the people in the world.

Coleoptera meaning "hard wings": 370,000 species, e.g., beetles

Hymenoptera "membrane wings": 198,000 species, e.g., ants, bees, wasps

Lepidoptera "scaly wings": 165,000 species, e.g., butterflies and moths

Diptera "two-wings": 122,000 species, e.g., midges, mosquitoes, true flies

Hemiptera "half wings": 82,000 species, e.g., aphids and cicadas

Orthoptera "straight wings": 20,000 species, e.g., crickets and locusts

Trichoptera "hairy wings": 8,000 species, e.g., caddisflies

Collembola "sticky peg": 6,500 species, e.g., springtails

Phthiraptera "louse wings": 6,000 species, e.g., biting and sucking lice

Odonata "toothed flies": 5,500 species, e.g., dragonflies

Bee facts

There are about 20,000 types of bee. The best known is probably the honeybee, but not all bees live in colonies like the honeybee. Many live alone and build their own nests.

● Honeybees are the only insects that make food which humans eat. Bees make honey to feed the inhabitants of their hives during winter. The honey they do not eat is harvested by beekeepers. Bees also make beeswax which is used for making candles and furniture polish.

● Wallace's giant bees are the world's largest at up to 1.6 in (4 cm) long. They were first found in Indonesia in 1858 but were then thought to have become extinct. In 1981 the bees were rediscovered.

www.insectguide.net   search

Honey bee on a flower

Colony Collapse Disorder

Colony Collapse Disorder is the name given to a recent phenomenon where entire colonies of honey bees suddenly die. It may result from pollution, a virus or some other unknown cause. It is of worldwide concern because bees are vital for pollinating many important food crops.

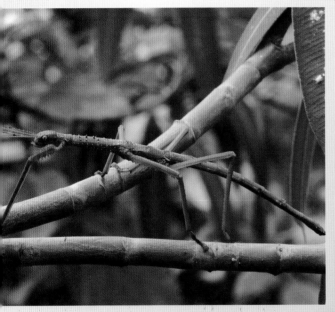

Some stick insects can be as long as a person's arm

● Honeybees visit up to five million flowers to make 2.2 lb (1 kg) of honey. In doing so, they fly a total distance equal to flying four times round the Earth.

● The smallest bee is the Brazilian *Trigona duckei* at 0.08–0.20 in (2–5 mm) long.

● One beehive may contain 50,000 worker bees — these are the bees which collect nectar from flowers to make honey.

● Honeybees' wings beat 11,400 times a minute. These wing movements make the bees' familiar buzz.

● Over 1.4 million tons of honey are produced worldwide every year. China is the main producer with 304,000 tons, followed by the U.S. with 90,000.

● Some people are allergic to bee stings, which can even be fatal. In 1962 in Rhodesia, Johanne Relleke was stung 2,243 times by wild bees, but survived!

● Queen bees can lay two or three thousand eggs a day — as many as 200,000 eggs a year. They may live as long as five years, so can produce a million eggs.

Thysanoptera "fringed wings": 5,000 species, e.g., thrips

Neuroptera "net-veined wings": 4,000 species, e.g., lacewings

Blattodea "insect avoiding light": 4,000 species, e.g., cockroaches

Pscoptera "milled wings": 3,500 species, e.g., hook lice

Isoptera "equal wings": 2,750 species, e.g., termites

Ephemeroptera "living for a day": 2,500 species, e.g., mayflies

Phasmatodea "like a ghost": 2,500 species, e.g., leaf insects

Mantodea "like a prophet": 2,000 species, e.g., mantids

Plecoptera "wickerwork wing": 2,000 species, e.g., stoneflies

Siphonaptera "tube without wings": 2,000 species, e.g., fleas

Dermaptera "leathery wings": 1,900 species, e.g., earwigs

Mecoptera "long wings": 550 species, e.g., hanging flies

Thysanura "fringed tail": 370 species, e.g., silverfish

Archaeognatha "ancient jaw": 350 species, e.g., bristletails

Embioptera "lively wings": 300 species, e.g., web-spinners

Megaloptera "large wings": 250 species, e.g., alderflies

Raphidioptera "embroidered wings": 150 species, e.g., snakeflies

Zoraptera "pure + wingless": 30 species, e.g., angel insects

Grylloblattodea "cricket cockroach": 25 species, e.g., rock crawlers

Reptiles

A reptile is a vertebrate animal with a body covered in tough scales. Most reptiles live on land, but turtles and some kinds of snakes live in water.

Crocodiles and their relatives spend time on land and in water. There are more than 8,000 species of reptiles, which are divided into the following groups.

Lizards 4,765 species
Snakes 2,978 species
Turtles and tortoises 307 species
Amphisbaenians (worm lizards) 165 species
Crocodiles, alligators, caimans 23 species
Tuataras 2 species

Deadly snakes

The coastal taipan of Australia injects the most venom per bite with 0.004 oz. (120 mg). Just 0.00004 oz. (1 mg) would be enough to kill a person. The common krait's venom is even more dangerous — only 0.00002 oz. (0.5 mg) can be fatal.

Alligators and crocodiles

The crocodile family contains 23 species, including alligators, caimans and gavials. All are large reptiles with long bodies and short legs. Most crocodiles have narrow V-shaped snouts, but alligators and caimans have wider, U-shaped snouts. The gavial has long slender jaws — just right for catching fish.

In alligators and caimans the teeth of the lower jaw fit into pits in the upper jaw and cannot be seen when the mouth is closed. In crocodiles the fourth tooth on each side of the lower jaw fits into a notch on the upper jaw, so they are always visible. Crocodiles are generally bigger and more aggressive than alligators.

Alligators
American alligator (southern U.S.) 13.1–14.8 ft. (4–4.5 m)
Chinese alligator (China) 6.6 ft. (2 m)
Spectacled caiman (South America) 6.6–8.2 ft. (2–2.5 m)
Broad-snouted caiman (South America) 6.6 ft. (2 m)
Yacaré caiman (South America) 8.2–9.8 ft. (2.5–3 m)
Black caiman (South America) 13.1–19.7 ft. (4–6 m)
Cuvier's dwarf caiman (South America) 4.9–5.2 ft. (1.5–1.6 m)
Schneider's or Smooth-fronted caiman (South America) 5.6–7.5 ft. (1.7–2.3 m)

Crocodiles
American crocodile (southern U.S., Mexico, Central and South America) 16.4 ft. (5 m)
Slender-snouted crocodile (West Africa) 8.2 ft. (2.5 m)
Orinoco crocodile (northern South America) 19.7 ft. (6 m)
Australian freshwater crocodile (Australia) 8.2–9.8 ft. (2.5–3 m)
Philippine crocodile (Philippines) 9.8 ft. (3 m)
Morelet's crocodile (Central America) 9.8 ft. (3 m)
Nile crocodile (Africa) 16.4 ft. (5 m)
New Guinea crocodile (New Guinea) 11.5 ft. (3.5 m)

Mugger or marsh crocodile (India, Sri Lanka) 13.1–16.4 ft. (4–5 m)
Estuarine or saltwater crocodile (Southeast Asia, Australia) 19.7–23 ft. (6–7 m)
Cuban crocodile (Cuba) 11.5 ft. (3.5 m)
Siamese crocodile (Southeast Asia, very rare) 9.8–13.1 ft. (3–4 m)
African dwarf crocodile (Central and West Africa) 6.2 ft. (1.9 m)
False gharial or gavial (Southeast Asia) 16.4 ft. (5 m)

Gavials
Indian gavial or gharial (India, Pakistan, Bangladesh, Nepal) 16.4–19.7 ft. (5–6 m)

Estuarine or saltwater crocodile

Amphibians

An amphibian is a vertebrate animal that spends at least some of its life in water. Its skin is not scaly. There are about 5,578 species of amphibian, divided into:

Frogs and toads 4,896 species
Newts and salamanders 517 species
Caecilians (legless amphibians) 165 species

Caecilian   Salamander

Snake facts

Largest snakes
Many people believe that the South American anaconda is the longest snake. There are reports of anacondas up to 120 ft. (36.5 m) long, but this has never been proven. The reticulated or royal python is probably the longest snake at up to 35 ft. (10.7 m), but the anaconda may be the heaviest at up to 500 lb. (230 kg).

Smallest snake
The thread snake is rarely longer than 4.3 in. (10.8 cm). The spotted dwarf adder is the smallest venomous snake at 9 in. (23 cm) long.

Actual size

Turtles and tortoises

These reptiles all have a hard shell that protects the body. There are about 250 species, some of which live in the sea, others in fresh water and the rest on land.

Biggest
● Fossils of the extinct turtle *Stupendemys geographicus* have been found with shells up to 10 ft. (3 m) long. They would have weighed more than 4,500 lb. (2,040 kg).

● The largest living turtle is the leatherback. A male washed up on the coast of Wales in 1988 holds the record — he was 113.5 in. (291 cm) long and weighed 2,019 lb. (916 kg).

● The Aldabra giant tortoise, which lives on an island in the Seychelles, weighs up to 670 lb. (304 kg) and is the largest land-living tortoise. It is also one of the slowest tortoises. It moves at an average speed of 0.17 mph (0.27 km/h).

Smallest
The smallest turtle or tortoise is the common musk turtle, which is 3 in. (7.6 cm) long and weighs 8 oz. (230 g).

Blue poison dart frog

Fantastic frogs and toads

Largest frogs and toads
● The world's largest known frog is the goliath frog, which lives in central Africa. It measures up to 34.5 in. (87.6 cm) long and weighs as much as 8.1 lb. (3.7 kg).

● The largest tree frog is *Hyla vasta*, which lives only on the island of Hispaniola. It is more than 4.7 in. (12 cm) long and has huge round finger and toe disks that grip like superglue.

● The world's largest toad is the South American marine toad. It can have a body length of over 9.1 in. (23 cm) and weigh up to 2.6 lb. (1.2 kg).

Smallest frog
The smallest frog and the world's smallest amphibian is the *Eleutherodactylus limbatus* frog, which measures only 0.3–0.5 in. (8.5–12 mm).

Newest frogs
In 2006, 20 previously unknown frog species were discovered in an expedition to Indonesia (see page 69) including a tiny microhylid frog that measures less than 0.6 in. (14 mm).

Egg laying
The marine toad lays 35,000 eggs a year, but the Cuban arrow-poison frog lays only one egg.

Highest and lowest homes
The green toad has been seen at 26,250 ft. (8,000 m) in the Himalayas and toads have been discovered more than 10,000 ft. (3,050 m) down a coal mine.

Most poisonous
The poison-arrow frogs of Central and South America are the most deadly. The world's most poisonous amphibian is the golden poison-arrow frog of western Colombia. One adult contains enough highly toxic poison in its skin to kill 1,000 people.

Smelliest
The smelliest frog is the Venezuela skunk frog, which was discovered in 1991. It warns off its enemies by releasing a bad-smelling chemical identical to the one produced by skunks.

Longest jumps
● On May 21, 1977, a female sharp-nosed frog leaped 33.5 ft. (10.2 m) in three consecutive jumps at a frog derby at Larula Natal Spa, Paulpietersburg, in South Africa.

● The cricket frog is only 1.4 in. (3.5 cm) and can jump 36 times its own length. If an adult human jumped 36 times his or her own length, the long-jump record could stand at 216 ft. (65.8 m)!

MAN AND BEAST

Life on man

As many as 100 trillion viruses and bacteria live on each of us. However much we wash, there are always 10 million or so bacteria on every square centimeter of our skin. There are also many tiny creatures called parasites, which can live inside or on the human body, feeding on our blood.

● Parasites such as roundworms, hookworms, flukes and tapeworms — which can grow as long as 32 ft. (9.8 m) — can live inside our bodies. They may cause such diseases as elephantiasis, in which the patient's limbs swell to gigantic sizes. Head lice live on human heads and feed on blood. The lice lay little white eggs, called nits, which cling to individual hairs.

● Follicle mites are in everyone's hair, even among our eyelashes. They were first described by 19th-century scientist Richard Owen (the man who first named dinosaurs), but are so tiny that few people have ever seen them or are even aware that they are there.

● Some of the tiny creatures that feed on us may also transmit diseases. Tsetse flies carry African sleeping sickness. Mosquitoes can infect humans with diseases such as malaria, dengue fever and yellow fever when they bite. Malaria has killed more people in human history than any other disease.

● Ticks can carry diseases such as encephalitis and Lyme disease. Mites and chiggers (baby mites) cause skin diseases and may transmit typhus.

See also

Black Death: page 104

Head louse
with egg

Animal heroes

St. Bernard
St. Bernard dogs have traditionally been used to aid mountain rescue crews. One of the most famous was Barry (1800–14), who lived at the monastery at the St. Bernard Pass, on the border of Switzerland and Italy, and rescued many travelers trapped in the snow. His body is preserved in the Natural History Museum, Berne, Switzerland.

Animal war heroes
In 2004, a statue was unveiled in Park Lane, London, with the inscription "Animals In War. This monument is dedicated to all the animals that served and died alongside British and allied forces in wars and campaigns throughout time." Since 1943, animal war heroes have been awarded the Dickin Medal, often described as the animals' Victoria Cross.

Gorilla
On August 16, 1996 a three-year-old boy fell into the gorilla enclosure at Brookfield Zoo, Chicago, and was knocked unconscious. Binti Jua, a female gorilla, protected the boy from another gorilla until he was rescued.

Counting sheep

There are about 1,084,979,126 sheep in the world — an average of one sheep for every six people. In some countries there are twice as many sheep as humans.

Falkland Islands 700,000 sheep, 2,483 people = 281.9 sheep per person
New Zealand 40,000,000 sheep, 4,169,496 people = 9.6 sheep per person
Mongolia 14,815,100 sheep, 2,677,720 people = 5.5 sheep per person
Australia 100,000,000 sheep, 20,442,256 people = 4.9 sheep per person
Uruguay 11,000,000 sheep, 3,416,603 people = 3.2 sheep per person
Mauritania 8,850,000 sheep, 3,085,331 people = 2.9 sheep per person

Plague carriers
Fleas are perhaps the most dangerous creatures of all — they were the carriers of the deadly bubonic plague that killed millions of people in medieval times.

Humans and animals

Since ancient times humans have used many types of animals for a vast range of different purposes.

Meat, milk and honey

Humans have always hunted and eaten wild animals. Milk from such animals as cows, goats, sheep, camels, buffalo, reindeer, llamas and yaks is drunk, used in cooking and made into butter and cheese. The eggs from birds such as hens, ducks, geese and quail are another important food. Honey has long been taken from the hives of wild bees, and now from domesticated bees kept in artificial hives.

Wool, fur and skin

Wool is shorn from live sheep, which then regrow their coats. The fur and leather of many other animals can be taken only after the animal has been killed. Cattle, goats, rabbits, mink, seals, wolves, foxes, kangaroos, big cats such as leopards, and alligators and snakes are among the many animals that have been used in this way. There are some very special uses for animal skin: for example, medieval manuscripts were written on vellum, made from calfskin.

Silk

Silk comes from the silkworm, the caterpillar of the silkmoth. Silkworms eat about a ton of mulberry leaves to make 11 lb. (5 kg) of silk.

Beasts of burden and transport

Strong animals such as horses, donkeys, camels, reindeer and buffalo are used to pull agricultural equipment and carts, and to carry people. Elephants drag heavy logs, pit ponies once drew trucks in coal mines, and dogs — usually huskies — pull sleds.

Security

Guard dogs (and even guard geese), police dogs and sniffer dogs (to detect drugs) are widely used.

Helpers

Sheepdogs, hunting hounds, retrievers and guide dogs for the blind are among the best known, but other animals, such as monkeys, can be trained to aid the disabled. Search and rescue dogs help to find missing people, lost walkers and climbers, and earthquake victims. Less well-known human helpers include pigs used to find truffles (edible fungi) and cats kept by the British Post Office to prevent mice from eating the mail! Animals kept as pets also provide millions of people with companionship.

Military

The warhorse is one of the most familiar of all military animals, but elephants have also been successfully used in battles. Many military organizations use dogs, goats and other animals as regimental mascots. Message-carrying dogs and carrier pigeons have been used by armies. During the Iraq war in 2004, dolphins were trained to find mines.

Maneater

A tigress known as the Champawat maneater, after the part of India in which she lived, killed a record 436 people over five years. She was shot in 1907 by British big-game hunter Colonel Jim Corbett (1875–1955).

Indian elephant carrying a log at a logging camp

Swine flu

Swine flu is a variety of influenza, also known as H1N1. In April 2009 it was discovered that an outbreak in Mexico had caused some deaths and spread by human-to-human transmission to a number of other countries. Global precautions have been put in place amid fears of a pandemic.

Top farm animals

These are the most popular farm animals worldwide (2007). They are kept for their meat, eggs and milk. The total number of these types of animal alone is three times that of the world's human population.

Chickens 17,251,899,000
Cattle 1,389,590,364
Sheep 1,112,520,621
Ducks 1,069,108,000
Pigs 989,884,170
Goats 850,219,925
Rabbits and hares 661,821,000

PET POWER

Countries with most pets

These totals include cats, dogs, birds, fish, small mammals (hamsters, guinea pigs, etc) and reptiles.

U.S. 368,118,200		**Turkey** 42,771,000	
China 276,370,000		**Philippines** 33,602,400	
Germany 77,795,000		**Netherlands** 30,644,000	
Brazil 76,333,100		**Mexico** 27,402,700	
France 68,135,000		**Canada** 25,912,400	
Japan 66,997,000		**Spain** 23,748,200	
Italy 59,852,000		**Argentina** 23,498,300	
Russia 59,680,000		**Australia** 22,070,000	
UK 50,261,000		**Ukraine** 21,728,000	

Top UK pets

Some 43% (11,180,000 households) in the UK own at least one pet, ranging from dogs, cats and rabbits to more exotic creatures such as snakes and spiders.

Dog 22% = 5,720,000 households (hh)
Cat 18% = 4,680,000 hh
Rabbit 2.8% = 728,000 hh
Indoor birds 2.4% = 624,000 hh
Hamster 1.7% = 442,000 hh
Horses/ponies 0.5% = 130,000 hh
Snakes 0.4% = 104,000 hh
Gerbils 0.3% = 78,000 hh
Tortoises/turtles 0.3% = 78,000 hh
Rats 0.3% = 78,000 hh
Lizards 0.2% = 52,000 hh
Insect groups 0.2% = 52,000 hh

Skye terrier

Faithful dog

After his owner, Edinburgh nightwatchman John Gray died in 1858, his faithful dog Bobby, a Skye terrier, stood guard over his grave in Greyfriars for almost 14 years until his own death. A statue was erected to him and he became the subject of books and films.

Cat-alogue

Heaviest
Himmy, owned by Thomas Vyse of Queensland, Australia, weighed 47 lb. (21.3 kg). He had a 15 in. (38.1 cm) neck and an 33 in. (84 cm) waist — similar to that of an adult human! He died in 1986 at the age of 10.

Smallest
Tinker Toy, a male Blue Point Himalayan owned by Katrina and Scott Forbes of Illinois, is 2.8 in. (7 cm) tall, 7.5 in. (19 cm) long and weighs 1.4 lb. (625 g).

Biggest breed
Maine Coons are a North American breed of muscular, big-boned cats. Males often reach 13–17.5 lb. (6–8 kg) in weight.

Oldest
There are several contenders for this title. The most reliable record is that of the French-born cat Grandpa Rex's Allen. This was a Sphynx cat owned by Jake Perry of Austin, Texas. The cat died in 1998 at the age of 34.

Largest litter
In 1970 Tarawood Antigone, a female Burmese owned by Valerie Gane of Kingham, Oxfordshire, England, gave birth to 19 kittens. Fifteen of the litter survived.

Racing greyhounds

The fastest dogs
Greyhound 41.72 mph (67.14 km/h)
Saluki 40+ mph (64+ km/h)
Ibizan hound 38–40 mph (60.8–64 km/h)
Whippet 36.52 mph (54.42 km/h)
Sloughi 36 mph (57.6 km/h)

Weird pets

Bear
Hercules, a grizzly bear owned by Scottish wrestler Andy Robin, appeared in TV adverts and in films including the James Bond film *Octopussy* (1983).

Dormouse
Xarifa, a dormouse owned by illustrator Beatrix Potter as a child, appears in her book *The Fairy Caravan* (1929).

Hippo
In 1927 Billy, a pygmy hippo, was given to U.S. President Calvin Coolidge, who also owned a wallaby, lion cubs and other animals. He gave it to a zoo rather than keep it at the White House.

Kinkajou
Paris Hilton kept a kinkajou or honey bear, called Baby Luv, until it bit her.

Pot-bellied pig
U.S. actor George Clooney owned a 300-lb (136-kg) pig called Max who died in 2006.

Tigers
American boxer Mike Tyson once kept four white Bengal tigers at his Texas home.

Wombats
At his London house Victorian painter and poet Dante Gabriel Rossetti kept two wombats as well as owls, kangaroos, wallabies, armadillos, parakeets, peacocks, a racoon, a Canadian marmot, a Japanese salamander, two laughing jackasses and a zebu.

Zebra
Lord Rothschild (1868–1937) was a famous zoologist — 239 animals were named after him. Among other animals he kept six zebra that he used to pull his carriage.

Pot-bellied pig

Dog-alogue

Largest dog
In 1989 Aicama Zorba of La-Susa, an Old English mastiff owned by Chris Eraclides of London, England, weighed 343 lb. (155.58 kg) and measured 8.25 ft. (2.5 m) nose to tail.

Smallest dog
A Yorkshire terrier owned by Arthur Marples of Blackburn, England, in the 1940s was just 2.5 in. (6.3 cm) tall and weighed 4 oz. (113 g).

Oldest dog
Bluey, an Australian cattledog owned by Les Hall of Victoria, Australia, died in 1938 at the age of 29 years, 5 months.

Largest litter
In 1944, Lena, an American foxhound, produced 23 puppies, all of which survived. Other dogs have equaled this record, but not all the pups have survived.

Longest jumper
Bang, a greyhound, jumped 30 ft. (9.2 m) while chasing a hare at Brecon Lodge in Gloucestershire, England.

Greatest climber
Tschingel, a beagle, climbed more than 50 peaks in the Alps, including the 13,664 ft. (4,165 m) Jungfrau and the 13,038 ft. (3,974 m) Eiger.

Famous dog lovers

Lee Duncan and Rin Tin Tin
Rescued as a puppy from a German trench in France at the end of World War I, the German shepherd Rin Tin Tin was taken to the United States where he became famous as an animal movie star.

J.M. Barrie and Luath
Luath, a Newfoundland dog, was the model for Nana in Barrie's book *Peter Pan*.

George Bush and Millie
Millie, the springer spaniel belonging to U.S. President George Bush (Sr.) had a best-selling "autobiography," *Millie's Book*, written by First Lady Barbara Bush.

William Wegman and Man Ray
American photographer Wegman named his Weimaraner after the famous photographer Man Ray, dressing him and other dogs in costumes and posing them in a variety of settings. Wegman's dogs appeared on TV in Sesame Street.

John Gray and Greyfriars Bobby
Bobby was a Skye terrier who faithfully guarded his master's grave at Greyfriars, Edinburgh, Scotland, for 14 years from 1858. The true story of the devoted dog has been the subject of books and films.

Charles Schulz and Spike
American cartoonist Charles Schulz based his comic character Snoopy on his family's basset hound Spike. In later strips a dog called Spike appears as Snoopy's brother.

Intelligent dogs
American psychology professor and pet trainer Stanley Coren ranked 133 breeds of dogs for intelligence. He studied their responses to a range of IQ tests, as well as the opinions of dog obedience judges. The five top breeds were the border collie, poodle, German shepherd, golden retriever and Doberman pinscher.

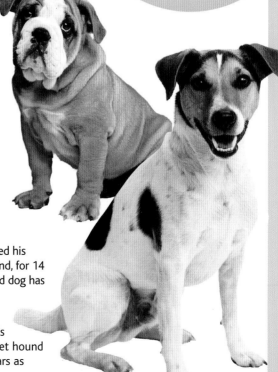

Tyrannosaurus rex skull and reconstruction (below)

Dinosaurs

Dinosaurs first appeared about 230 million years ago. These amazing reptiles then dominated life on Earth until they became extinct 65 million years ago. The first dinosaurs to be described were *Megalosaurus* (great lizard) by William Buckland in 1824 and *Iguanodon* (iguana tooth) by Gideon Mantell in 1825.

They were named before the word "dinosaur" had been invented. The name *dinosauria* (terrible lizards) was suggested by British scientist Richard Owen in July 1841. Since then 700 species have been identified. Not all dinosaurs were enormous — some measured less than 24 in. (60 cm) long, about the size of a chicken. Sizes of dinosaurs are mostly estimates worked out from the size of bones. The largest known complete skeleton is of a *Brachiosaurus* and is 73.2 ft. (22.3 m) long. The skeleton is in the Humboldt Museum, Berlin, Germany.

Biggest dinosaurs

Bruhathkayosaurus weight 153 tons; length 92–111 ft (28–34 m)

Amphicoelias weight 135 tons; length 131–198 ft (40–60 m)

Futalognkosaurus weight 80–97 tons; length 105–111 ft (32–34 m)

Argentinasaurus weight 80–97 tons; length 98 ft (30 m)

Supersaurus weight 38–44 tons; length 108–112 ft (33–34 m)

Diplodocus weight 41 tons; length 110 ft (33.5 m)

Dinosaur facts

● The biggest dinosaurs were all herbivores. *Tyrannosaurus rex*, one of the largest carnivorous dinosaurs, measured up to 49 ft. (15 m) long and weighed 132,000 lb. (60,000 kg) or more. Its huge jaws were packed with 60 teeth, the biggest of which were 9 in. (23 cm) long!

● A new type of tyrannosaur called *Guanlong wucaii* has recently been discovered in China. It lived 160 million years ago, measured about 10 ft. (3 m) long, and looked like a miniature version of *Tyrannosaurus rex*.

● The largest flying prehistoric creatures were pterosaurs. The wings of the biggest pterosaur, *Quetzalcoatlus*, measured 36 ft. (11 m) from tip to tip.

● The largest known dinosaur egg belonged to *Hypselosaurus*. The 100 million-year-old egg measures 10 by 12 in. (25 by 30 cm), about three times the volume of an ostrich egg.

● The fastest dinosaur, *Ornithomimus*, could probably run at a speed of up to 44 mph (70 km/h). The ostrich runs at a similar speed today.

● Dinosaurs have been in space! Fragments of bone and an eggshell of *Maiasaura peeblesorum* were taken into space by astronaut Loren Acton in 1985. A *Coelophysis* skull was taken into space by astronaut Bonnie Dunbar in 1998.

Coelacanth: a living fossil

Paleontologists discovered a large fish known as the coelacanth from fossil remains. They thought it had become extinct about 65 million years ago. But on December 22, 1938, one was caught alive off East London in South Africa. This strange-looking creature, about 5.6 ft. (1.7 m) long, snapped at the hand of Captain Henrik Goosen, but died soon afterward. Captain Goosen realized that he had found something unusual so took the fish to a local museum where scientists identified it as a "living fossil." Since then, more than 200 coelacanths, some measuring up to 6.2 ft. (1.9 m) long, have been caught, mostly off the Comoros islands.

Animals in danger

In the past 500 years, hundreds of species of animals have become extinct — they have disappeared from Earth forever. In many cases this is because of human actions. The animals have been hunted, or the areas where they lived have been destroyed.

Some creatures become extinct in the wild but have survived in artificial settings, such as zoos. If they can be successfully bred, they may be taken back to the wild. Przewalski's horse, for example, became extinct in the wild but has since been bred in captivity. Now there are herds of these wild horses in their old home around the Gobi Desert. Other species are defined as "threatened," or in danger of becoming extinct. According to the degree of threat they may be considered "critically endangered," "endangered" or "vulnerable."

Amphibians 6,199 known species; 1,808 threatened
Birds 9,956 known species; 1,217 threatened
Fish 30,000 known species; 1,201 threatened
Mammals 5,416 known species; 1,094 threatened
Mollusks 81,000 known species; 978 threatened
Insects 950,000 known species; 623 threatened
Crustaceans 40,000 known species; 460 threatened
Reptiles 8,240 known species; 422 threatened
Others 130,200 known species; 42 threatened

Dodo

Last seen alive

Saber-toothed tiger 12,000 years ago
Woolly mammoth 10,000 years ago
Moa 1,000 years ago
Aurochs (giant wild ox) 1627
Aepyornis (elephant bird) 1649
Dodo 1681
Steller's sea cow 1768
Great auk 1844
Tarpan (wild horse) 1851
Labrador duck 1875
Quagga (zebra-like creature) 1883
Pilori muskrat 1902
Badlands bighorn sheep 1905

Japanese gray wolf 1905
Passenger pigeon 1914
Carolina parakeet 1918
California grizzly bear 1922
Schomburgk's deer 1938
Arabian ostrich 1941
Euler's flycatcher 1955
Eskimo curlew 1963
Guam flying fox 1968
Pyrenean ibex 2000
Yangtze River dolphin 2006
Western black rhinoceros 2006
Madeiran large white butterfly 2007

🔍 www.dinodata.org   (search)

Lost world

In 2006 a team of 12 scientists returned from an area of rainforest in Indonesia where no humans had ever set foot before. It lies in the Foja Mountains on the island of New Guinea and it is so difficult to reach that the explorers had to be dropped in by helicopter. They discovered dozens of new animals and plants, including an orange-faced honeyeater, a golden-mantled tree kangaroo, 20 new species of frogs, four new species of butterflies, a giant rhododendron flower (about 6 in. [15 cm] across), and a species of bird that had been considered extinct for over 100 years.

The end of the tiger?

Some very familiar animals are under threat of extinction. They include the gorilla, African and Asian elephants, the black rhino, the giant panda and many species of whale, such as the blue, right and fin whales.

Tigers are also in serious danger. A century ago there were more than 100,000 tigers. Of the eight known subspecies of tiger, three — the Bali, Caspian and Javan — became extinct. There are now fewer than 5,000–7,500 tigers left in the wild because their habitats have been destroyed and they have been illegally hunted for their bones and other parts used in traditional Chinese medicines.

Numbers of the Amur or Siberian, the largest tiger, have recovered slightly to 600 in the wild, with fewer than 501 in wildlife parks and zoos. The Sumatran tiger is down to about 400–500, with 232 in captivity. The Bengal, including the rare white tiger, ranges from 3,176–4,556, with about 200 in zoos, and there are only an estimated 1,227–1,785 of the Indochinese, with 60 in zoos.

The rarest tiger of all is the South China tiger. Its population is down to only 20–30 individuals in the wild and 48 in zoos.

Siberian tiger

ENVIRONMENTAL CONCERNS

Pollution fact file

Pollution happens when unwanted gases and other materials escape into the environment. It causes waste, financial losses and damage to human, animal and plant health. Huge growth in industry and in the world's population in the last 100 years have led to more and more industrial processes and pollution. Deliberate dumping and accidents such as oil spills have seriously affected the Earth's air, land and water.

Loggers cutting down rainforest in Borneo

Air pollution

Most air pollution comes from burning fossil fuels (coal, oil and gas) and solid waste, or from gases released into the air. Carbon monoxide from vehicle exhausts is poisonous because it prevents the absorption of oxygen. Nitrogen oxide reacts with sunlight to produce smog (a combination of smoke and fog).

Acid rain

Acid rain is caused when nitrogen oxide, sulfur dioxide and other chemicals from volcanic eruptions and human sources combine with rain and fall as acid. It can damage buildings, kill fish and harm trees and other plants.

Land pollution

Soil can be damaged by the dumping of chemicals, toxic (poisonous), radioactive and other waste as well as the overuse of pesticides and fertilizers. Polluted land is unsafe for anything to live on.

Global warming

Greenhouse gases in Earth's atmosphere, such as carbon dioxide, nitrous oxide, water vapor and methane, help to trap heat and stop too much of it escaping into space. Without these gases, the Earth would not be warm enough for us to live on. But more and more greenhouse gases are being released into the atmosphere from human activities, and too much heat is being trapped. The Earth became 0.5°C (1°F) warmer during the 20th century and a further rise of even a couple of degrees will damage its natural balance.

Reversing pollution

Many countries have become more aware of pollution and the damage it causes and are taking action to reduce it. For example, since the 1990s, laws have been introduced in the United States to ban the use of lead-based paint and leaded gasoline. Clean air laws have reduced pollution in cities, and scientists are making vehicles that do not burn fossil fuels. People and businesses are heavily fined for dumping waste and chemicals. However, pollution is still a huge problem.

Destroying forests

About 35,000 sq. mi. (90,000 sq km) of forest are cut down every year worldwide to obtain lumber or to clear land so it can be used for farming. This is about the same area as the state of Indiana.

Cutting down forests increases the amount of carbon dioxide in the atmosphere, which can affect climate and destroy the homes of many animals and plants.

Country	Average annual forest loss 2000–2005
Brazil	13,382 sq. mi. (34,660 sq km)
Indonesia	5,578 sq. mi. (14,448 sq km)
Sudan	4,548 sq. mi. (11,780 sq km)
Zambia	2,055 sq. mi. (5,322 sq km)
Mexico	1,525 sq. mi. (3,950 sq km)

How much water?

People worldwide use 3,802,300,000,000,000 liters (8,035,600,000,000,000 pt) of water every year. On average everybody in the world uses 633,000 liters (1,337,767 pt) a year, or 1,734 liters (3,665 pt) a day. Of this, 9 percent (156 liters [330 pt]) a day is used in homes, 20 percent (347 liters [733 pt]) by industry and 71 percent (1,231 liters [2,602 pt]) by agriculture.

The United States uses 408 billion gallons of water a day (2000) — 1,450 gallons per person in total. Of this 48% is used in power generation, 34% in irrigation, 11% public supply, 5% industrial and less than 1% each for domestic, livestock and aquaculture

Household water usage
Brushing teeth (tap off) 2.5 liters (5.3 pt)
Brushing teeth (tap on) 5 liters (10.6 pt)
Toilet flush 5–20 liters (10.6–42.3 pt)
Shower (per minute) 22 liters (46.5 pt)
Washing machine 120 liters (253.6 pt)
Bath (full) 170 liters (359.3 pt)
Washing car 200 liters (422.7 pt)
Watering garden (1 hour) 600–1,500 liters (1,268–3,170 pt)

Worst polluters

Carbon dioxide (CO_2) pollution enters the atmosphere from three main sources — burning fossil fuel (coal and oil), cement manufacturing and gas burning.

These figures show the total amounts produced by some of the leading industrial countries in 2004 in tons (tonnes). CO_2 is produced naturally by animals, forest fires and other sources. But natural production has been overtaken by the amount produced by human activities. More carbon dioxide in the atmosphere increases the amount of heat absorbed, and this leads to global warming (see Pollution fact file).

China 1,986,289,988 (1,801,931,966)
Other 3,453,560,981 (3,133,017,821)
U.S. 1,748,500,057 (1,586,212,570)
Russia 476,733,712 (432,485,549)
India 473,554,097 (429,601,050)
Japan 371,879,656 (337,363,549)
Germany 231,071,429 (209,624,474)
Canada 159,546,558 (144,738,203)
UK 159,533,282 (144,726,159)
South Korea 143,379,784 (130,071,952)
Italy 133,469,710 (121,081,684)

Worst oil tanker spills

About two million tons of oil are spilled into the sea every year from oil tankers, mostly during collisions or other accidents. Most spills are small (tons or less), but some are much more serious. When huge quantities of oil are discharged into the sea and washed up on shorelines they harm many birds and other creatures.

The 1989 grounding of the *Exxon Valdez* in Prince William Sound, Alaska, caused the U.S.'s worst oil spill. The quantity spilled was smaller than the spills listed 38,500 tons (35,000 tonnes), but thousands of birds, fish, otters, seals and whales were killed.

Atlantic Empress and *Aegean Captain*, off Tobago, 1979, 316,000 tons (287,000 tonnes)
ABT Summer, off Angola, 1991, 286,000 tons (260,000 tonnes)
Castillio de Bellver, off Saldanha Bay, South Africa, 1983, 278,000 tons (252,000 tonnes)
Olympic Bravery, off Ushant, France, 1976, 276,000 tons (250,000 tonnes)
Amoco Cadiz, off Finistère, France, 1978, 246,000 tons (223,000 tonnes)

Water pollution

Increasing quantities of heavy metals such as mercury and lead, chemicals, sewage and oil spills are polluting lakes, rivers and oceans. Water in some places is now unsafe to drink or bathe in and animals are harmed or killed.

www.epa.gov   search

A brief history of garbage

The ancient world

In ancient times, nomadic peoples simply left their garbage and moved on. Once people settled in villages, they were faced with the problem of having to dispose of garbage where they lived. Often they just covered it with earth. This caused the ground level in ancient cities, such as Troy, to increase by over 3.3 ft. (1 m) a century. The first anti-dumping law was issued in Athens, Greece in 320 BC, when citizens were compelled to bury their garbage or put it in pits outside the city.

The Middle Ages

In medieval cities, people often threw their garbage into the street, causing the spread of rats, mice—and disease. Free-roaming pigs ate some of it, except in Paris where they were banned after King Louis VI's son was killed when his horse tripped over a pig in 1131. In London, kites and ravens scavenged among the garbage tips. The birds were so important that killing one was punishable by death.

The 19th century

Rag-and-bone men were a common sight in 19th-century streets. They went from house to house with a horse and cart, gathering anything that could be resold. Dustmen collected cinders from home fires to be used in brickmaking; human waste and horse manure were taken to farms for fertilizer; and dog droppings were used in the leather tanning trade. The first garbage-burning incinerator, called The Destructor, was built in Nottingham, England in 1874. The first garbage can appeared in Paris, France, in 1883. It was introduced by Eugène Poubelle, the Prefect of Police. To this day, the French call a garbage can a *poubelle*.

The 20th century

During the 20th century, thousands of new, disposable goods were invented and fewer people had open fires so more garbage was thrown away. Disused electronic equipment including TVs, computers, cell phones and fax machines began to join the growing garbage dumps.

Household waste

per person per year (OECD countries only)

Ireland 1,675 lb. (760 kg)	**Denmark** 1,475 lb. (670 kg)
U.S. 1,630 lb. (740 kg)	**Switzerland** 1,455 lb. (660 kg)
Iceland 1,610 lb. (730 kg)	**Germany, Luxembourg, Spain** 1,435 lb. (650 kg)
Norway 1,545 lb. (700 kg)	**U.K.** 1,345 lb. (610 kg)
Australia 1,520 lb. (690 kg)	**The Netherlands** 1,325 lb. (600 kg)

How much garbage is that?

In the contiguous United States (excluding Alaska and Hawaii), there are 1,654 landfill sites. The Fresh Kills Landfill on Staten Island, New York, closed in 2001 after operating for over 50 years.

It was the world's largest garbage dump, covering over 2,000 acres (810 ha) and receiving 29,000 tons (26,300 tonnes) of garbage every day. Following the events of 9/11, 1.8 million tons (1.6 million tonnes) of debris from the World Trade Center site was taken there to be searched for evidence, personal items and human remains. Puente Hills landfill in Whittier, California, is now the United States' largest dump in use.

How long to rot

Cotton rags 1–5 months
Paper 2–5 months
Orange peel up to 6 months
Wool socks 1–5 years
Cigarette butts 1–12 years
Plastic-coated drink cartons 5 years
Plastic bags 10–20 years
Photo film 20–30 years
Leather shoes 25–50 years
Artificial fiber clothes (nylon, etc.) 30–40 years
Metal cans 50–100 years

- Paper and cardboard 34.2%
- Yard waste 13.1%
- Food scraps 11.9%
- Plastics 11.8%
- Metals 7.6%
- Rubber, leather and textiles 7.3%
- Wood 5.7%
- Glass 5.2%
- Other 3.4%

Where does it go?

Landfills

Most waste ends up underground — in giant municipal pits, or landfill sites, where it can rot out of sight. These are usually lined to prevent dangerous chemicals seeping into the ground. However, many discarded objects take decades, even centuries to break down, and we are running out of suitable places to bury waste.

Incineration

Burning garbage is another solution. Burning gets rid of most kinds of waste and the heat can be converted into energy for other uses. The problem is that incineration releases harmful gases, some of which may contribute to global warming.

🔍 www.epa.gov/epaoswer/osw/kids ⬜ search

Compost is recycled organic waste

A mountain of junk

More than 1,000 people have climbed Mt. Everest since it was conquered in 1953. They, and their support teams, have dropped more than 50 tons (50 tonnes) of garbage, making Everest the world's highest garbage dump. In 2007, climbers recovered 1000 lbs (500 kg) of discarded tents, ladders, oxygen cylinders, food containers and other equipment left on the slopes. A garbage deposit of $4,000 is paid by each expedition, in addition to climbing fees of $10,000 to $25,000 per climber.

Recycling

Recycling uses old waste to make new products. It cuts down the amount of garbage and saves natural resources by reducing the need for new raw materials. Items most suitable for recycling are organic matter (plant and animal), which can be composted and used as fertilizer, metals (such as aluminum cans), glass and paper.

Reduce and reuse

The most sustainable solution is to reduce the amount of waste we create. Compared with 50 years ago, food cans are 50 percent lighter, yogurt containers are 60 percent lighter, glass bottles are 50 percent lighter and plastic shopping bags are half as thick. Shoppers can help by choosing not to buy goods with lots of packaging or disposable containers, as these make up 10–20 percent of all domestic garbage.

Aluminum cans that could be recycled

Ways to reduce waste

1. Use your own shopping bag and refuse unnecessary plastic bags
2. Buy refills
3. Buy fruits and vegetables loose, not prepacked
4. Buy recycled goods
5. Buy reusable diapers
6. Buy soft drinks in large bottles and pour into smaller bottles for daily use
7. Reuse wrapping paper, packing materials and envelopes
8. Pack your lunch in a reusable box rather than foil or plastic wrap
9. Choose durable products over disposable ones, e.g., rechargeable batteries
10. Donate unwanted clothes to charity or sell at yard sales
11. Donate unwanted furniture to a furniture recycling project
12. Buy drinks in glass bottles — they can be reused 20 times
13. If it's broken, mend it — don't throw it away!
14. Return clothes hangers to dry cleaners
15. Recycle glass, cans, paper and cardboard. If your community doesn't have a recycling program, propose one
16. Compost leftover food, yard waste and vacuum cleaner dust

Science & Technology

Robot games

BERTI is a robot designed to speak and mimic human gestures. Here, BERTI shows how he can play rock-paper-scissors. Scientists are working towards developing robots that will be capable of interacting naturally with humans. In the future, robots like BERTI may be used for developing artificial limbs.

How dense?

A cubic meter (equal to 35.3 cu. ft.) of pure water weighs 1,000 kg (2,205 lb.) or 1 metric tonne. Materials that have a density greater than water sink, and those that are less dense float.

Lightweight metals such as aluminum and titanium are important to engineers — for example, for building aircraft that need to be strong but light enough to fly. These are the average densities of some of the substances around us.

	kg/cu m	(lb/cu. ft.)		kg/cu m	(lb/cu. ft.)
Air at 32°F (0°C)	1.29	(0.08)	**Chalk**	2,300	(143.58)
Styrofoam	100	(6.24)	**China**	2,300	(143.58)
Balsa wood	150	(9.36)	**Concrete**	2,300	(143.58)
Cork	240	(14.98)	**Sand**	2,500	(156.07)
Steam	600	(37.46)	**Glass**	2,600	(162.31)
Gasoline	730	(45.57)	**Aluminum**	2,700	(168.56)
Oak	750	(46.82)	**Marble**	2,700	(168.56)
Butter	900	(56.19)	**Human tooth**		
Paper	900	(56.19)	**enamel**	2,900	(181.04)
Ice	920	(57.43)	**Diamonds**	3,500	(218.50)
Olive oil	920	(57.43)	**Titanium**	4,507	(281.36)
Rubber	940	(58.68)	**The Earth**		
Wax	950	(59.31)	**(average for**		
Pure water			**whole planet)**	5,520	(344.60)
at 32°F (0°C)	1,000	(62.43)	**Iron**	7,874	(491.56)
Milk	1,030	(64.30)	**Copper**	8,920	(556.86)
Sea water	1,030	(64.30)	**Silver**	10,490	(654.86)
Ebony	1,200	(74.91)	**Lead**	11,340	(707.93)
Spider silk	1,260	(78.66)	**Mercury**	13,570	(847.15)
Coal	1,400	(87.40)	**Tungsten**	19,250	(1,201.74)
Bone	1,800	(112.37)	**Gold**	19,300	(1,204.86)
Brick	2,100	(131.10)	**Platinum**	21,090	(1,316.61)
Salt	2,165	(135.16)	**Osmium**	22,610	(1,411.5)
Carbon	2,267	(141.52)			

Strange studies

Angelology Angels
Aphnology Wealth
Biometrology The effect of weather on people
Cereology Crop circles
Cryology Snow, ice and frozen ground
Cryptology Codes and ciphers
Draconology Dragons
Enigmatology Puzzles
Eremology Deserts
Fromology Cheese
Garbology Garbage
Gelotology Laughter
Googlology The Google search engine
Googology Large numbers
Hypnology Sleep
Kalology Beauty
Limacology Slugs
Loimology Plagues
Momilogy Mummies
Nanotechnology Very small objects
Nephology Clouds
Osmology Smells
Pharology Lighthouses
Polemology Wars
Pomology Fruit-growing
Rhinology Noses
Siphonapterology Fleas
Teratology Monsters
Toxicology Poisons
Tsiology Tea
Ufology Unidentified flying objects
Vermeology Worms
Xylology Wood

Cryology is the study of snow, ice and frozen ground

An iceberg is made of almost pure water. This is less dense than sea water, so the iceberg floats.

See also

Conversions: page 84

www.exploratorium.edu　　search

Acids and alkalis

The pH (potential Hydrogen) system was invented in 1909 by Danish chemist Søren Sørensen (1868–1939). In this, pH is a measure of the concentration of hydrogen ions, which shows whether something is acidic or base (also known as alkali).

Pure water has a pH of 7.0. Substances that have a pH of less are acidic. Substances with a pH of more than 7.0 are base (alkali). Acids make lemon juice and vinegar taste sharp, and acid rain harms trees and other plants. The traditional way of testing pH is by using litmus paper — acidic substances turn blue litmus red, while alkalis turn red litmus blue.

Substance	pH	Substance	pH
Hydrochloric acid	0	Orange juice	3.7
Car battery acid	1.0	Wine/beer	4.0
Gastric (digestive) juices	1–3	Tomato juice	4.3
Lime juice	2.3	Normal rainfall	5.6
Lemon juice	2.4	Saliva	6.4–6.9
Acid rain	2.4–3.6	Milk	6.6
Apple	3.0	Pure water	7.0
Vinegar	3.0	Human blood	7.4
Grapefruit	3.2	Sea water	7.8–8.3

A rainbow is created when sunlight passes through water droplets.

Spectrum colors

The electromagnetic spectrum includes all forms of light, from radio waves and microwaves at one end of the scale to X-rays and gamma rays at the other. In between is visible or white light, which is made up of a range of colors.

We can see the individual colors when they are split up by water droplets and form a rainbow, or by passing white light through a prism. The colors of the spectrum are red, orange, yellow, green, blue, indigo and violet.

Sound levels

The decibel (dB) is a way of measuring sound. Sounds of 80–90 dB or more can damage hearing and it is dangerous for people to work in sound levels of more than 90 dB.

Sounds above 130 dB become painful, and people should wear hearing protectors with sounds of more than 140 dB. A decibel level of more than 150 dB can cause permanent deafness.

Silence	0 dB
Rustle of leaves	10 dB
Quiet whisper at 16 ft. (5 m); library	20–30 dB
Normal conversation; soft music	30 dB
Sailing boat	35 dB
Quiet countryside; ticking watch	40 dB
Inside average home	45–50 dB
Restaurant; office; loud conversation	50–60 dB
Background music; motorboat	60 dB

Hairdryer	60–80 dB
Workshop	65 dB
Radio; telephone ring; busy traffic; orchestra; loud TV	70 dB
Inside car; underground train	80 dB
Pneumatic drill at 50 ft. (15 m); Niagara Falls; top level of comfort	85 dB
Very loud snore	88 dB
Heavy traffic at 50 ft. (15 m); roaring lion	90 dB
Loud shout at 50 ft. (15 m); lawnmower; chainsaw; blender	100 dB
Heavy truck 3 ft. (1 m) away; orchestra playing Beethoven's Ninth Symphony	105 dB

Circular saw at 3 ft. (1 m); car horn at 16 ft. (5 m)	110 dB
Shouting in someone's ear	114 dB
Personal stereo	115 dB
Loud scream; thunder; explosion; submarine engine room	120 dB
Loud rock music	120–130 dB
Racing car	125 dB
Motorbike (without silencer)	130 dB
Jumbo jet takeoff at 100 ft. (30 m)	140 dB
Rock music (peak at 16 ft. [5 m] from speaker)	150 dB
Level at ear of person firing powerful rifle	160 dB
Launch of *Saturn V* space rocket	172 dB
Blue whale call	188 dB
Volcanic eruption	272 dB

Brightness scale

A candela is a unit of light intensity. It was originally equivalent to the amount given out by a candle, but is now more precise.

Candelas per sq. ft. (sq m)	
Overcast sky	185 (2000)
Moon	232 (2,500)
Clear sky (average)	745 (8,000)
Candle (brightest spot)	930 (10,000)
Domestic light bulb	9,300 (100,000)
Sun at Equator	150,000 (1,600,000)
Flash of lightning	7,400,000 (80,000,000)
Atom bomb	185,000,000 (2,000,000,000)

A flash of lightning gives out 80,000,000 candelas

THE ELEMENTS

What is an element?

The elements are sometimes called the building blocks of the Universe because everything in the Universe — including ourselves — is made from them. The nucleus of each element consists of atoms with the same number of protons. Each element is unique, although elements can exist in different forms — for example, carbon may be soft graphite or hard diamond. Elements cannot usually be broken down into any other substance.

There are about 118 elements altogether, and 91 occur naturally on Earth. Others can be created in laboratories, but in minute quantities and they have very short lifespans of only thousandths of a second. Each element is also known by a one- or two-letter symbol as well as its name; for example, Fe is iron.

A chemical compound is a combination of two or more elements linked together, which can be broken down again into their constituent parts, but no further. Water, for example, is made up of two hydrogen atoms linked to one oxygen atom. Salt, or sodium chloride, is a compound of sodium and chlorine.

One and only

Element 98 was given the name Californium by the four scientists who discovered it in 1950. They were working at the University of California at Berkeley, and named the element for both the state and their university. One of them, Glen Theodore Seaborg (1912–99), received the Nobel Prize for Chemistry in 1951. The 106th element, Seaborgium, was named after him in 1994. It was the first to be named in honor of a living person.

Highest melting points

1 **Carbon** 6,381°F (3,527°C)
2 **Tungsten** 6,192°F (3,422°C)
3 **Rhenium** 5,767°F (3,186°C)
4 **Osmium** 5,491°F (3,033°C)
5 **Tantalum** 5,463°F (3,017°C)

The surface of the Sun reaches 10,121°F (5,605°C), so no element could approach it and remain solid.

See also

Air transport: pages 216–17

Various weights of gold in a gold refinery

The heaviest elements

● **Osmium**
Osmium is the heaviest element (13.07 oz./in.^{3} [22.61 g/cm^3]). It was discovered in 1803. It was named after the Greek word for smell because it smelled bad. Osmium is very hard, and is used to make hard-wearing points, such as the nibs of fountain pens.

● **Platinum**
Platinum was used before anyone realized that it was an element. It weighs almost as much as osmium (12.39 oz./in.^{3} [21.45 g/cm^3]) and is used to make jewelry. It is also used in catalytic converters in cars to reduce the pollution from exhaust gases.

● **Plutonium**
Plutonium was discovered in 1941 and is a heavy and highly radioactive metal. It is used as a nuclear fuel and in nuclear weapons — 1 lb. (0.45 kg) of plutonium produces an explosion equivalent to 10,000 tons (9,070 tonnes) of TNT.

● **Gold**
Gold is the best-known of all heavy metals—though at 11.15 oz./in.^{3} (19.29 g/cm^3) it is less heavy than the others here. Gold has been prized since ancient times and has many uses beyond coins and jewelry.

The lightest elements

● Hydrogen

Hydrogen is the simplest and lightest element, and the most common — 93 percent of all atoms in the universe are hydrogen atoms. On Earth, it is relatively rare in the atmosphere — only 10.6 of 211 million pints (5 of 100 million L) of air are hydrogen, but hydrogen combined with oxygen forms all the water in the world. Hydrogen is very light. This is why it was used in balloons carrying human passengers: the second-ever flight, in Paris on December 1, 1783, was in a hydrogen balloon. Hydrogen was also used in giant airships until May 6, 1937, when the giant German airship *Hindenburg* exploded, killing 36 people, at Lakehurst, New Jersey. Today, hydrogen fuel cells are used to power clean-energy cars.

● Helium

Helium is twice as heavy as hydrogen, but it is still only one-seventh the weight of air. Unlike hydrogen, helium does not burn, so it is used in modern airships.

● Lithium

Lithium was discovered in 1817 and takes its name from the Latin word for rock, although it is actually a metal. Lithium is so light and so soft that it can be easily cut with a knife. It floats because it is half as heavy as water and lighter than some types of wood. It is used to make lithium batteries.

● Potassium and sodium

Both were discovered in 1807. Both are metals that are lighter than water. In a laboratory, potassium and sodium are usually kept in paraffin wax because if they come into contact with water they will catch fire. Potassium is vital for plant growth and human well-being — our bodies contain about 5 oz. (140 g) of it. Sodium is relatively common as part of a compound: in combination with chlorine it is ordinary table salt.

Elements in sea water

Sea water is a treasure chest of elements, but sodium and chlorine, combined as sodium chloride, are the only two that are taken from it in large amounts.

Other elements, such as gold, are too expensive to extract, even though there may be as much as 4,595 pounds of gold in a cubic mile of sea water (4,595 lb/ml³)" with equivalent amount of gold in pounds in 1 cubic mile of sea water (500 kg/km³).

Elements in the sea

1 Oxygen* 114.43 oz./gal. (857,000 mg/l)
2 Hydrogen* 14.39 oz./gal. (107,800 mg/l)
3 Chlorine 2.65 oz./gal. (19,870 mg/l)
4 Sodium 1.48 oz./gal. (11,050 mg/l)
5 Magnesium 0.18 oz./gal. (1,326 mg/l)
* Combined as water

Elements on Earth

There is calcium in the Earth and ocean in the form of calcium carbonate. Sodium exists in the form of sodium chloride, the salt in the ocean and on our tables.

The quantities of both calcium and sodium are so vast that these elements are considered unlimited.

There are quite small amounts of some precious metals on Earth, which is why they are so valuable. For example, there are about 1.1 million tons (1 million tonnes) of silver and 16,500 tons (15,000 tonnes) of gold. Elements are constantly being taken from Earth, but new discoveries are being made.

The *Hindenburg*, a giant airship filled with hydrogen, bursts into flames.

www.webelements.com   search

Leonardo da Vinci

Italian Leonardo da Vinci (1452–1519) is best known as a painter, anatomist, sculptor and architect. *The Last Supper* and *Mona Lisa* are among the most famous paintings of all time.

But he is also hailed as one of the greatest inventors. Among his notebooks he left plans for countless advanced machines, often with descriptions written in secret mirror writing. Many of them were never built, but they anticipated modern inventions, often by hundreds of years. They include the following:

Air conditioner	Magnetic compass
Alarm clock	Mileometer
Crane	Multi-barreled machine gun
Diving suit and diving bell	Parachute
Double-hull ship	Revolving stage
Flying machine	Shrapnel bomb
Gas mask	Spectacles
Gears	Steam engine
Giant catapults and crossbows	Tank-like armored vehicle
Helicopter	Telescope
Lifebelt	Water turbine

Crazy inventions

Safety coffin

Frank Vester received a patent for this device in 1868, one of many similar inventions of the period — which allows anyone accidentally buried alive to summon help by means of a bell, or even to escape from his early grave via a ladder.

Dog scuba-diving apparatus

This 2001 invention by Dwane L. Folsom was designed for a performing dog called Shadow, but could be adapted for use by any animal.

What is a patent?

A patent is granted by a government to an inventor. It gives him or her the right for a limited period — usually 20 years — to stop others from making, using or selling the invention without the inventor's permission. The patent is territorial and protected only in the country in which it is patented. The first patent was granted to Filippo Brunelleschi in Florence in 1421, for a barge crane to transport marble.

Automatic haircutter

Patented by John J. Boax in 1951, it was designed to make hair stand on end by means of a vacuum attachment. It would then be trimmed off by mechanical cutters.

Scream muffler

Moira J. and Frank M. Figone patented this foam-insulated muffler in 1989. Users can shout and scream without disturbing their neighbours.

Thumb wrestling ring

Devised by Richard B. Hartman in 1991, players poke their thumbs into a miniature wrestling ring and fight with each other.

Over 100 years of everyday inventions   1900s

1903 the safety razor was invented by King Camp Gillette

1904 the ice cream cone was invented by Italo Marcioni

1906 the electric washing machine was invented by Alva J. Fisher

1907 vacuum cleaners with bags were invented by J. Murray Spangler

1913 the crossword puzzle was invented by Arthur Wynne

1913 the zipper was invented by Gideon Sundback

1920 the tea bag was invented by Joseph Krieger

1924 frozen food was invented by Clarence Birdseye

1926 the aerosol spray was invented by Erik Rotheim

1927 the pop-up toaster was invented by Charles Strite

1928 elastoplast was invented by Horatio Nelson Smith

1928 sliced bread was invented by Otto Rohwedder

1931 the electric razor was invented by Col. Jacob Schick

1934 the trampoline was invented by George Nissen and Larry Griswold

1938 the ballpoint pen was invented by László Biro

1938 instant coffee was invented by the Nestlé company

1945 the microwave oven was invented by Percy LeBaron Spencer

1945 Tupperware (food containers) was invented by Earl W. Tupper

1947 the long-playing record was invented by Goldmark

1950 the credit card was invented by Frank X. McNamara

The modern trampoline was invented by George Nissen when he was a student.

Brainchildren: young inventors

Horatio Adams
Adams was only 16 when he assisted his father, Thomas, in his experiments with chicle, the dried sap of a Mexican jungle tree. This led to the invention of chewing gum.

Charles Babbage
Babbage was 19 when he first thought of the idea of the mechanical computer.

Louis Braille
He invented Braille, the raised-dot writing used by blind people, at the age of 15. Louis himself was blind.

Peter Chilvers
Chilvers was 12 when he invented boardsailing (windsurfing) in 1958 off Hayling Island, UK.

Frank Epperson
The Popsicle was invented by 11-year-old Frank Epperson of San Francisco, California, in 1905. He had the idea when he left a fruit drink out during a freezing winter night and originally called it the Epsicle. He did not apply for a patent until 1923, by which time his son had renamed it Popsicle.

Chester Greenwood
Greenwood of Farmington, Maine, was aged 15 in 1873 when he invented earmuffs. He started Greenwood's Ear Protector Factory and made a fortune by supplying his product to U.S. soldiers in World War I.

Jeanie S. Low
At the age of 10 in 1992, Jeanie, of Houston, Texas, was granted a patent for a folding bathroom stool to enable small children to reach the bathroom sink.

George Nissen

George Nissen (born 1914), an American gymnast, came up with the idea of the trampoline when he was still at school. He built his first prototype in 1934 and started a company to manufacture them. Trampolining became so popular that in 2000 it was introduced as an Olympic sport.

John J. Stone-Parker
In 1989, when he was only 4 years old, John and his sister, Elaine W. Stone-Parker, invented a star-shaped gadget to prevent ice from slipping out of a drinking glass. He is the youngest-ever holder of a patent.

Austin Meggitt
U.S. schoolboy Meggitt was 9 when he invented a device for carrying a baseball bat, ball and glove safely on the handlebars of a bicycle. In 2000 he received US Patent No. 6,029,874.

See also

Computer timeline: page 86

2000s

1955 Lego was invented by Gotfried Kirk Christiansen
1956 Velcro was invented by Georges de Mestral
1958 videotape was invented by A.M. Poniatoff
1963 the pull-tab can was invented by Alcoa
1971 the digital watch was invented by George Theiss and Willy Crabtree

1971 E-mail was invented by Ray Tomlinson
1971 the pocket calculator was invented by the Sharp company
1974 the personal computer was invented by MITS
1975 the digital camera was invented by Steven Sasson and Kodak
1979 Post-it notes were invented by Spencer Silver and 3M

1979 the mobile phone was invented by NTT
1979 the Walkman was invented by Akio Morita
1981 the compact disc was invented by Philips
1982 the camcorder was invented by Sony
1989 the World Wide Web was invented by Tim Berners-Lee
1994 the GPS (completed) was

invented by I. Getting and B. Parkinson
2000 the iPod digital music player was invented by Apple Computer, Inc.
2001 Self-cleaning glass was invented by Kevin Sanderson
2005 YouTube video sharing website launched and becomes a global phenomenon
2008 MyVu launches personal media viewer (video glasses)

Roman numerals

Roman numerals use seven letters (I, V, X, L, C, D and M). A small numeral in front of a larger one is subtracted from it, so 90 is written as X (10) subtracted from C (100) — XC. A small number after a larger one is usually added to it — for example, XI (11).

Roman numerals are still in use today. You can find them in the introduction pages of books (i, ii, iii, iv, etc.), on traditional clock and watch faces, in film and TV credits (2007 will appear as MMVII), in serial film titles (such as *Star Wars: Episode III — Revenge of the Sith*). They are also used in the names of sporting events — the Beijing 2008 Olympics will be the XXIX (29th) Games.

Roman	Arabic	Roman	Arabic	Roman	Arabic
I	1	XX	20	CCC	300
II	2	XXX	30	CCCC	400
III	3	XL	40	D	500
IV	4	L	50	DC	600
V	5	LX	60	DCC	700
VI	6	LXX	70	DCCC	800
VII	7	LXXX	80	CM	900
VIII	8	XC	90	M	1,000
IX	9	C	100	MM	2,000
X	10	CC	200		

Mega multiples

Certain prefixes are used in the International System of Units (SI). The prefixes are the same whether describing weight, distance, or other measurements.

Prefix	Name	Value
exa-	quintillion	1,000,000,000,000,000,000
peta-	quadrillion	1,000,000,000,000,000
tera-	trillion	1,000,000,000,000
giga-	billion	1,000,000,000
mega-	million	1,000,000
kilo-	thousand	1,000
hecto-	hundred	100
deca-	ten	10
	one	1
deci-	tenth	0.1
centi-	hundredth	0.01
milli-	thousandth	0.001
micro-	millionth	0.000,001
nano-	billionth	0.000,000,001
pico-	trillionth	0.000,000,000,001
femto-	quadrillionth	0.000,000,000,000,001
atto-	quintillionth	0.000,000,000,000,000,001

Useful mathematical formulas

Area of a rectangle	length x height
Area of a triangle	½ length x height
Area of a circle	π x radius^2
Diameter of a circle	radius x 2
Circumference of a circle	π x diameter
Volume of a sphere	$^4/_3\pi$ x radius^3
Surface of a sphere	4 x π^2
Volume of a cylinder	π x radius^2 x height
Curved area of cylinder	2 x π x radius x height
Area of a cone	π x radius x length
Volume of a cone	$^1/_3\pi$ x radius^2 x height

π = pi, pi = 3.14159265

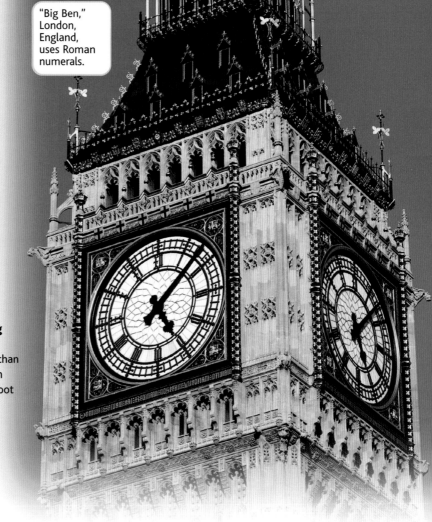

"Big Ben," London, England, uses Roman numerals.

Mathematical symbols

Symbol	Meaning	Symbol	Meaning
+	Plus or positive	%	Percent
−	Minus or negative	>	Greater than
±	Plus or minus, positive or negative	<	Less than
		√	Square root
x	Multiplied by	Σ	Sum of
÷ or /	Divided by	π	Pi
=	Equal to	°	Degree
≠	Not equal to	∞	Infinity
~	Of the order of, similar to		

Big numbers

The bigger the number, the more zeroes, so very large numbers such as a billion, are shown as 10^9, or 1.0×10^9, and so on.

Number	Equivalent to	Zeros	Written as
Thousand	100 hundreds	3	10^3
Million	1,000 thousand	6	10^6
Billion	1,000 million	9	10^9
Trillion	1,000 billion	12	10^{12}
Quadrillion	1,000 trillion	15	10^{15}
Quintillion	1,000 quadrillion	18	10^{18}
Sextillion	1,000 quintillion	21	10^{21}
Septillion	1,000 sextillion	24	10^{24}
Octillion	1,000 septillion	27	10^{27}
Nonillion	1,000 octillion	30	10^{30}
Decillion	1,000 nonillion	33	10^{33}
Undecillion	1,000 decillion	36	10^{36}
Duodecillion	1,000 undecillion	39	10^{39}
Tredecillion	1,000 duodecillion	42	10^{42}
Quattuordecillion	1,000 tredecillion	45	10^{45}
Quindecillion	1,000 quattuordecillion	48	10^{48}
Sexdecillion	1,000 quindecillion	51	10^{51}
Septendecillion	1,000 sexdecillion	54	10^{54}
Octodecillion	1,000 septendecillion	57	10^{57}
Novemdecillion	1,000 octodecillion	60	10^{60}
Vingtillion	1,000 novemdecillion	63	10^{63}

● There are names for even bigger numbers, including a centillion (303 zeros), a trigent-billillion (60,000,003 zeros) and a sextent-billillion (1,800,000,003 zeros).

● In 1938, 9-year-old Milton Sirotta came up with the word googol, which means a 1 followed by 100 zeros. Milton was the nephew of an American mathematician named Edward Kasner (1878–1955).

● A googolplex is an even bigger number — a 1 with a googol of zeros, or 10 to the googol power. This number is so vast that, as Kasner explained, "… there would not be enough room to write it, if one went to the furthest stars, touring all the nebulae in the Universe and putting down zeros every inch of the way."

● There is no such number as a zillion — the word just means a really huge amount.

www.factmonster.com/mathmoney.html   search

Prime numbers

A prime number is a whole number that can be divided only by 1 and itself, and not by any other number. Examples include 2, 3, 5, 7, 11 and 13. All prime numbers, except for 2, are also odd numbers. There are 168 prime numbers under 1,000.

Regular polygons

A polygon is a shape enclosed by straight lines. Regular polygons have sides of equal length and the inside angles are all the same. A regular polygon fits inside a circle with all its points touching the circumference. An irregular polygon does not.

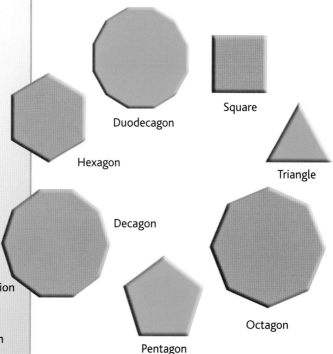

Duodecagon

Square

Hexagon

Triangle

Decagon

Octagon

Pentagon

Polygon	Number of sides	Each internal angle	Sum of internal angles
Triangle	3	60°	180°
Square (or quadrilateral)	4	90°	360°
Pentagon	5	108°	540°
Hexagon	6	120°	720°
Heptagon	7	128.57°	900°
Octagon	8	135°	1,080°
Nonagon	9	140°	1,260°
Decagon	10	144°	1,440°
Undecagon	11	147.27°	1,620°
Duodecagon (or dodecagon)	12	150°	1,800°
Quindecagon	15	156°	2,340°
Icosagon	20	162°	3,240°

Dodecahedron (12 sides)

Octahedron (8 sides)

Cube (6 sides)

Tetrahedron (4 sides)

Regular solids

There are five types of regular solid. All faces on a regular solid are exactly the same shape. If you put a regular solid inside a sphere, all its points will touch the surface of the sphere.

Isosahedron (20 sides)

Conversions

There are two systems of measuring length, area, weight, volume and so on — imperial and metric. Here's how to convert between the two different systems.

From	To	Multiply by
Area		
Square centimeters (cm²)	Square inches (in.²)	0.1550
Square inches (in.²)	Square centimeters (cm²)	6.4516
Square meters (m²)	Square feet (ft.²)	10.7639
Square feet (ft.²)	Square meters (m²)	0.0929
Square meters (m²)	Square yards (yd.²)	1.1960
Square yards (yd.²)	Square meters (m²)	0.8361
Square kilometers (km²)	Square miles (mi.²)	0.3861
Square miles (mi.²)	Square kilometers (km²)	2.5900
Hectares (ha)	Acres	2.4711
Acres	Hectares (ha)	0.4047
Speed		
Meters per second (m/s)	Feet per second (ft./s)	3.2808
Feet per second (ft./s)	Meters per second (m/s)	0.3048
Kilometers per hour (km/h)	Miles per hour (mph)	0.6214
Miles per hour (mph)	Kilometers per hour (km/h)	1.6093

From	To	Multiply by
Weight		
Grams (g)	Ounces (oz.)	0.0353
Ounces (oz.)	Grams (g)	28.3495
Kilograms (kg)	Pounds (lb.)	2.2046
Pounds (lb.)	Kilograms (kg)	0.4536
Tonnes (metric)	Tons (long)	0.9842
Tons (long)	Tonnes (metric)	1.0160
Tonnes (metric)	Tons (short)	1.1023
Tons (short)	Tonnes (metric)	0.9072
Length		
Centimeters (cm)	Inches (in.)	0.3937
Inches (in.)	Centimeters (cm)	2.5400
Meters (m)	Feet (ft.)	3.2808
Feet (ft.)	Meters (m)	0.3048
Meters (m)	Yards (yd.)	1.0936
Yards (yd.)	Meters (m)	0.9144
Kilometers (km)	Miles (mi.)	0.6214
Miles (mi.)	Kilometers (km)	1.6093

Namesakes

These measurements were named after the people who discovered them.

Ampere is a measure of electrical current. It was named after André-Marie Ampère (French, 1775–1836).

Beaufort scale measures wind speed and was named after Sir Francis Beaufort (British, 1774–1857).

Marie Curie in her laboratory

Bel/decibel is a measure of sound named after Alexander Graham Bell (Scottish/American, 1847–1922).

Celsius is a temperature measure. It was named for Anders Celsius (Swedish, 1701–44).

Curie is a measure of radiation named after Marie Curie (Polish/French, 1867–1934).

Fahrenheit is a measure of temperature named after Gabriel Fahrenheit (German, 1686–1736).

Joule is a measure of energy named after James Prescott Joule (British, 1818–89).

Kelvin is a temperature measure. It was named after William Thomson, Lord Kelvin (British, 1824–1907).

Mercalli scale measures earthquakes. It was named after Giuseppe Mercalli (Italian, 1850–1914).

Mohs' scale measures hardness and was named after Friedrich Mohs (German, 1773–1839).

Ohm/Mho measures electrical resistance. It was named after Georg Simon Ohm (German, 1787–1854).

Richter scale measures earthquakes and was named after Charles Richter (American, 1900–85).

Volt is a measure of electromagnetic force. It was named after Alessandro Volta (Italian, 1745–1827).

Watt is a measure of power and was named after James Watt (British, 1736–1819).

Volume conversions

From	To	Multiply by
Cubic centimeters (cc)	Cubic inches (in.³)	0.0610
Cubic inches (in.³)	Cubic centimeters (cc)	16.3871
Cubic feet (ft.³)	Cubic meters (m³)	0.0283
Cubic meters (m³)	Cubic feet (ft.³)	35.3147
Cubic yards (yd.³)	Cubic meters (m³)	1.3080
Cubic meters (m³)	Cubic yards (yd.³)	0.7646
Cubic kilometers (km³)	Cubic miles (mi.³)	0.2399
Cubic miles (mi.³)	Cubic kilometers (km³)	4.1682
Liters (l)	Pints (pt.)	1.7598
Pints (pt.)	Litres (l)	0.5683
Liters (l)	Quarts (qt.)	1.0567
Quarts (qt.)	Liters (l)	0.9464
Litres (l)	U.S. gallons (gal.)	0.2642
U.S. gallons (gal.)	Liters (l)	3.78532

Temperature conversions

Celsius (°C) to Fahrenheit (°F)
x 9 ÷ 5 + 32
Fahrenheit (°F) to Celsius (°C)
− 32 x 5 ÷ 9

The world's smallest

Aircraft The *Bumble Bee II* built by Robert H. Starr (U.S.) in 1988 measured only 8 ft 10 in (2.7 m) long with a wingspan of 5 ft 6 in (1.68 m). It was destroyed in a crash.

Book Malcolm Douglas Chaplin's 0.003 x 0.004 in (0.07 mm x 0.10 mm) *Teeny Ted from Turnip Town* (2007) was produced by the Nano Imaging Laboratory at Simon Fraser University, Canada. All 30 of its pages are etched onto a single crystal of silicon and require an electron microscope to read them.

Mobile phone Introduced in 2008, the Modu mobile phone is smaller than a credit card, measuring 2.8 x 1.5 x 0.3 in (72 x 37 x 8 mm) and weighing 1.4 oz (40 gm). It is designed to be slotted into other electronic devices and even incorporated into clothing.

Mini mobile

Weighty words

Acre
An acre describes an area of land and comes from the Old English word *aecer*, meaning a plowed field. It was the area a team of oxen could plow in one day. One acre is equivalent to 4,840 sq. yd.

Celsius
A temperature scale invented in 1742 by Swedish astronomer Anders Celsius. A Celsius degree is 1/100th of the difference between the freezing and boiling points of water (0°C and 100°C).

Fahrenheit
This temperature scale was devised by German physicist Gabriel Fahrenheit. On this scale the freezing point of water is 32°.

Foot
Foot originally meant the average length of an adult foot, and has been used since ancient times. Before France invented the metric system, the French foot was based on the length of the Emperor Charlemagne's foot.

Meter
The meter was introduced in France in June 1799. It was first set as one ten-millionth of a quarter of the circumference of the Earth. It was later set as the distance between two lines on a metal bar that was kept in Sèvres, France. The distance is now more precise. It is the distance light travels in a vacuum in 1/299792458th of a second. A centimeter is 1/100th of a meter. A millimeter is 1/1,000th of a meter and a kilometer is 1,000 meters.

Gram/kilogram
Gram comes from the same ancient Greek word that gave us grammar, and means a marked-off division. A kilogram is 1,000 grams. Kilo comes from the Greek *chilioi*, meaning one thousand.

Hectare
This is used for measuring land areas and comes from the ancient Greek *hekaton*, meaning one hundred. One hectare is equivalent to 10,000 square meters or 2.4711 acres.

Tons and tonnes
Tons are imperial weight measurements, whereas tonnes are metric — 1 short (U.S.) ton is equal to 2,000 lb. (907 kg), while 1 metric tonne (also simply called a tonne) is 2,204.6 lb. (1,000 kg).

Special measurements

Carat
The weight of diamonds and other valuable gems is measured in carats. The word comes from the carob bean, which has a consistent weight of 0.007 oz. (0.2 gram).

Hand
The height of horses is measured in hands. The measurement is taken from the ground to the highest point on the animal's shoulder. One hand is 4 in. (10.16 cm).

Knot
Speed at sea is measured in knots, which is the time it took a ship to travel the length of a knotted rope. A knot is now the same as a nautical mile, which is 6,076 ft. (1,852 m).

Point
This is used by typographers and printers and refers to the size of a letter such as an x. One point is equal to 0.0139 in. (0.3528 mm), so 6-point type is 0.083 in. (2.116 mm) high.

Troy ounce
This name comes from the city of Troyes, France, where dealers in precious stones and metals gathered in medieval times. Gold and other rare metals are still measured in troy ounces (1.1677 oz./31.1035 g).

Computer use worldwide

The personal computer and the Internet are two of the most important developments of the past 50 years. In that time, the world has gone from fewer than 10,000 computers to more than 740 million and Internet users can now visit over 100 million websites. From education and banking to online shopping and game-playing, countless aspects of all our lives have been changed by the computer revolution.

The computer mouse

The first computer mouse — so called because its size, shape and tail-like cable resemble a mouse — was patented by Douglas Engebart as early as 1968. Mice were not widely used until they were supplied with Apple Macintosh computers from 1984 onwards. Since then most desktop computers have used them. Leading manufacturer Logitech announced in 2008 that it had made its billionth mouse.

Computer countries

These are the countries with the most computers.

Country	% of world total	Computers in use, 2009 (million)
U.S.	22.19	264.1
China	8.29	98.67
Japan	7.24	86.22
Germany	5.21	61.96
UK	3.95	47.04
France	3.62	43.11
Russia	3.06	36.42
Italy	3.00	35.69
South Korea	2.93	34.87
Brazil	2.80	33.30
Total		741.38

Laptops

Although there were some early attempts at making laptops, the first successful model with a screen that folds inside the case was the British-designed Grid Compass 1110, launched in 1982 and used by astronauts on the Space Shuttle. Improvements in displays and battery life, Wi-Fi and the use of lightweight components have led to such advanced models as Apple's MacBook Air. In 2005 the OLPC — One Laptop Per Child — charity was set up to provide inexpensive laptops for people in developing countries. By 2009 over 1 million had been distributed, including the XO-1, specially designed for use by children.

Apple's MacBook Air, 2008

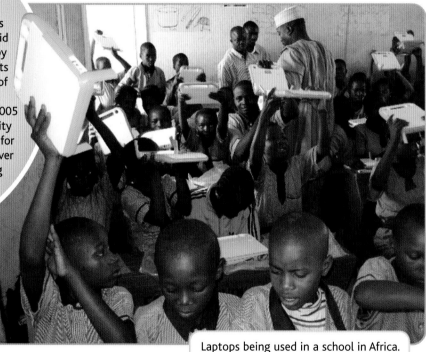

Laptops being used in a school in Africa.

Computer timeline 1600s

1642 Blaise Pascal, France, makes a numerical wheel calculator, an early mechanical adding machine

1694 Gottfried von Leibniz, Germany, makes a machine that can multiply numbers

1820 Charles Xavier de Colmar, France, makes an "Arithometer" that can add, subtract, multiply and divide

1822 Charles Babbage, England, devises his Difference Engine

1829 Charles Wheatstone uses punched paper tape to store data

1834 Babbage conceives the Analytical Engine

1889 Herman Hollerith's punch card machine used in U.S. Census

1928 IBM adopts 80-column punched card

1944 Harvard's Mark I, first digital computer

1952 Univac computer accurately predicts the U.S. presidential election winner

1953 First IBM electronic digital computer (IBM 701)

1956 First hard disk drive (IBM). Term "artificial intelligence" devised

1958 First chess game between computer and human

1960 U.S. has 6,000 computers

1963 ASCII (American Standard Code for Information Interchange) introduced

1967 IBM releases floppy disk

1970 Douglas Engelbart patents first computer mouse

1971 Intel builds the micro-processor, "computer on a chip."

Wang 1200, first word processor; E-mail invented by Ray Tomlinson.

1972 E-mail invented by Ray Tomlinson. First electronic video game, *PONG*

1975 Microsoft founded by Bill Gates, later to become the world's richest person

1976 First Apple computer. Cray-1, first supercomputer

1979 Compuserve launches first commercial Bulletin Board (BBN) service

1980 U.S. has more than one

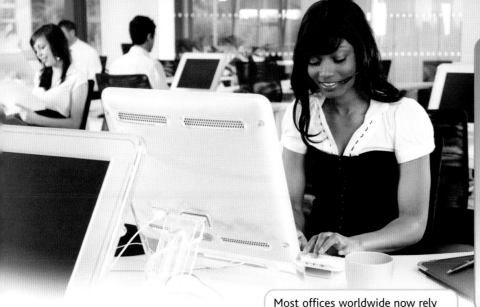

Internet users

Country	% of total population using Internet	Total users
China	19.0	253,000,000
U.S.	72.5	220,141,969
Japan	73.8	94,000,000
India	5.2	60,000,000
Germany	63.8	52,533,914
Brazil	26.1	50,000,000
UK	68.6	41,817,847
France	58.1	36,153,327
South Korea	70.7	34,820,000
Italy	59.7	34,708,144

Most offices worldwide now rely on computers to transact business.

Internet milestones

In little over 10 years, the Internet has become a global phenomenon. In 1995 it was used by about 45 million people around the world. By 2008 the figure had more than doubled to 1,463,632,361. By the time you read this, the figures will have increased again.

1960s
During the 1960s scientists in the U.S. began trying to work out how organizations could keep in touch with one another after a nuclear attack. In 1965 ARPA (Advanced Research Projects Agency) suggested linking computers. In 1969 computers at four U.S. universities were connected and could "talk" to each other for the first time.

1970s
The network was extended. At the same time, electronic mail (e-mail) was being used more and more to send messages between computers. In 1979 the first Usenet newsgroups (online discussion groups) began.

1980s
By 1981 the ARPA network had 213 hosts (sites to which users could connect). In 1982 a language called TCP/IP was invented which allowed all Internet computers to communicate with each other and the network was first called an Internet. The Internet began to be used commercially and by governments and universities.

1990s
In 1991 the World Wide Web (www) was created. By 1994 about 40 million people were connected to the Internet. They could exchange information, sell goods and work from any computer with a phone line. By 1996 users in almost 150 countries around the world were connected to the Internet.

2000s
High-speed broadband and Wi-Fi access is now widespread and many businesses offers goods and services on the Internet. The number of people using the Internet increased almost three times from 2000 to 2009, with the number of users in China and India growing by more than 1,000%. Almost 1.5 billion people use the Internet worldwide.

Most-visited websites

	Website	Launched*
1	Yahoo.com	18 Jan 1995
2	Google.com	15 Sep 1997
3	Youtube.com	23 Apr 2005
4	Live.com	1 Nov 2005
5	Msn.com	24 Aug 1995
6	Myspace.com	15 Aug 2003
7	Wikipedia.org	15 Jan 2001
8	Facebook.com	26 Sep 2006
9	Blogger.com	31 Jul 2000
10	Yahoo.co.jp	17 Nov 2000

*In some instances test versions started earlier

2000s

million computers. First laptop computers
1981 First Nintendo home video game. Commercial introduction of the computer mouse. Microsoft introduces software for IBM personal computers
1982 Worldwide, 200 computers connected to the Internet
1984 Apple Macintosh computers launched
1985 Microsoft ships Windows 1.0
1986 U.S. has more than

30 million computers
1988 4.7 million microcomputers, 120,000 minicomputers and 11,500 mainframe computers sold in U.S.
1989 World Wide Web invented by Tim Berners-Lee. 100,000 hosts on the net
1990 First palmtop computers
1991 First use of the phrase "surfing the net," by Jean Armour Polly
1993 Mosaic, the first graphical Internet browser, launched
1994 135 million PCs worldwide.

First ads on the World Wide Web (ad for *Wired* magazine claimed as first)
1995 Amazon.com Internet bookseller founded. Microsoft's Internet Explorer browser launched
1999 150 million people use Internet worldwide (more than half in U.S.)

2000 Dot-com crash
2002 iPod digital music players launched
2005 Nearly 200 million broadband lines worldwide
2007 Sales of iPods top 100 million
2008 More than 330 million broadband lines in use worldwide

computer.howstuffworks.com   search

The first telegraph message was sent by Morse code using a hand-operated key.

From fixed cables to satellites

In the early years of telecommunications, the only way of linking one telephone with another was by fixed cables. Links between continents relied on cables under the ocean. The invention of radio brought the first wireless communications, but because the surface of the Earth is curved these signals could not travel far.

Satellites changed everything. They sit at an exact height above the Earth's Equator (usually around 22,000 mi./35,000 km) and they rotate at the same speed as the Earth spins. This means that they stay in a fixed position. Telephone signals can be sent to the satellites and bounced back to Earth. Everywhere on the planet can be covered by only five or six satellites, except for the poles and surrounding areas, which are out of their range.

Cables under the sea

Soon after telegraph cables came into use in the 1840s, attempts were made to lay them across rivers and between islands and mainlands. Most didn't work. In 1850 the first cable was laid across the English Channel. It had to resist attack by salt water, ocean currents and water pressure, so had a thick, water-resistant, steel cover. Inside were copper wires that carried the power and signal.

Technical improvements and the demand for faster communications led to cables being laid over ever greater distances. Several attempts to lay them across the Atlantic failed when the cables snapped, but one was completed in 1858. To mark the occasion, Queen Victoria sent a telegraph message to President Buchanan in the U.S. It took almost 18 hours. Attempts were made to increase the pace by raising the voltage, but this burned out the cable. In 1865 the world's largest ship at the time, the *Great Eastern*, laid the first continuous cable across the Atlantic.

During the 20th century, telegraph cables, which transmitted Morse code, were steadily replaced by telephone cables, which could transmit voices. Hundreds of thousands of miles of underwater cables were laid across the world's oceans and seas. These have been replaced by fiber-optic cables, which offer faster transmission and many more connections.

Telecom timeline   1700s

1793 Word "telegraph" first used (in France)

1837 Charles Wheatstone and William Cooke set up first electric telegraph in London

1843 Morse code inventor Samuel Morse (U.S.) sends first telegraph message between Washington and Baltimore

1850 Telegraph cable laid between England and France across English Channel, but fails; 12,000 mi. (19,300 km) of telegraph line in U.S.

1852 First telegraph line in India; there are now 23,000 mi. (37,015 km) of telegraph line in U.S.

1854 First Australian telegraph line (Melbourne to Williamstown)

1858 First transatlantic telegraph cable laid, but fails

1861 First U.S. transcontinental telegraph

1862 32,000 mi. (51,500 km) of telegraph line and more than five million messages sent in U.S.

1867 First theory suggests using radio waves for telecommunication

1876 Alexander Graham Bell patents the telephone—beating his rival Elisha Gray by a matter of hours. He makes his historic first call to his assistant, Thomas Watson, who is in the next room: "Mr. Watson, come here, I want to see you." The invention is demonstrated at the Centennial Exposition, Philadelphia, where Emperor Don Pedro of Brazil hears Bell recite the "To be or not to be" speech from *Hamlet* over the phone.

1877 Bell makes the first long-distance call between Boston

and Salem, Massachusetts, 14 mi. (22.5 km) away

1878 Bell demonstrates his telephone to Queen Victoria at Osborne House on the Isle of Wight. She becomes the first European monarch to use a phone

1884 First telephone handset is launched

1889 First coin-in-the-slot public phone, U.S.

1894 Guglielmo Marconi invents wireless telegraphy

1897 There are seven phones per 1,000 people in the U.S.

Telephone Bell

Alexander Graham Bell (1847–1922) is often called the father of the telephone. He was born in Edinburgh, Scotland, moved to Canada in 1870, and later to the U.S. He became an expert on the science of speech, and his first inventions helped deaf people to hear sounds. During his research, Bell developed a method of transmitting voice messages along a wire. In 1876 he patented the device, which he called the harmonic telegraph. This was the first telephone.

Alexander Graham Bell making the first telephone call between New York and Chicago

Countries with most cell (mobile) phones

China 601,000,000
India 346,896,457
U.S. 260,000,000
Russia 172,000,000
Brazil 147,000,000
UK 69,675,000 (more phones than people!)
World total 3,665,000,000

In 2006, India joined the list of countries with more than 100 million cell phones, and has since risen rapidly to take second place on the world list.

2000s

1901 Marconi sends a radio signal across the Atlantic

1902 The trans-Pacific telephone cable connects Canada, New Zealand and Australia

1907 There are an estimated 1,027,348 mi. (1,653,356 km) of land telecommunications lines and 233,823 mi. (376,302 km) of submarine cable worldwide

1914 The first radio message is sent to an aircraft; the first transcontinental telephone call is made in the U.S.

1919 Rotary dial telephones are invented

1945 British writer Arthur C. Clarke proposes putting communications satellites in orbit above the Earth, which move at the same speed as the Earth spins; this means they stay in a fixed position, and communication with the ground is not interrupted

1956 The first transatlantic telephone cable is laid

1965 Intelsat I (*Early Bird*), the first commercial

telecommunications satellite, is launched

1967 The first cordless telephones go on sale

1975 The first handheld cell (mobile) phones are sold

1988 The first transatlantic fiber optic cable is laid

2004 There are 1.2 billion telephone lines around the world: 538,981,500 in Asia, 327,657,500 in Europe, 295,292,700 in North and South America, 25,929,800 in Africa and 13,773,000 in Oceania

2005 Cell phone users now

number more than two billion worldwide

2006 U.S. company Western Union ends its telegraph service after 150 years, as e-mails replace telegrams

2007 More than three billion worldwide use mobile phones. Apple's iPhone is launched

2008 The 3G iPhone has sold 14 million worldwide.

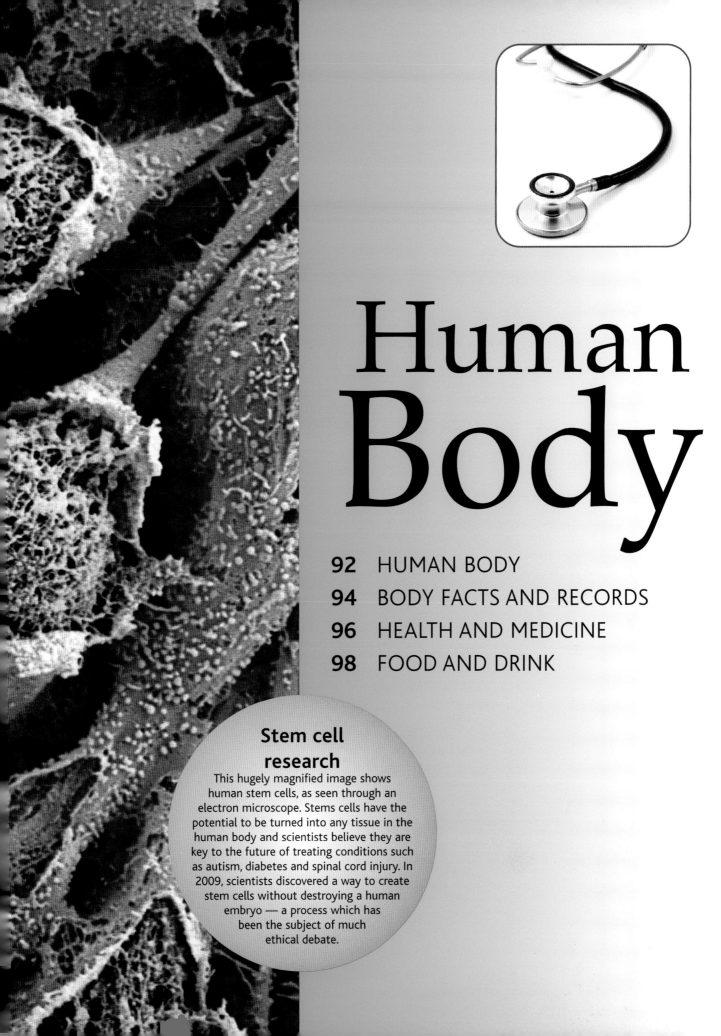

Human Body

Stem cell research

This hugely magnified image shows human stem cells, as seen through an electron microscope. Stems cells have the potential to be turned into any tissue in the human body and scientists believe they are key to the future of treating conditions such as autism, diabetes and spinal cord injury. In 2009, scientists discovered a way to create stem cells without destroying a human embryo — a process which has been the subject of much ethical debate.

Your amazing body

Blood
An adult man's body contains about 1.3 gal. (5 L) of blood. A woman's contains about 1.1 gal. (4.3 L). The blood travels along 62,000 mi. (100,000 km) of blood vessels. It contains 25 billion to 30 billion red cells. The life span of red cells is only about 120 days, and 1.2 million to 2 million of them are made every second.

Brain power
You lose 100,000 brain cells every day! Luckily you have 100 billion altogether. If the surface area of your brain could be ironed out it would measure 324 sq. in. (2,090 sq cm).

Breathing
The average person inhales 1.6 gal. (6 L) of air per minute, or 2,280 gal. (8,640 L) a day. You take 13 to 17 breaths a minute when sitting still and up to 80 during vigorous exercise.

Cells
There are 50 trillion cells in your body and 3 billion of them die every minute (4,320,000,000,000 a day). Most of these are replaced. You make 10 billion new white blood cells each day. You have a total of 1 trillion white cells, which help fight germs and infections.

Chemicals
There is enough carbon in your body to fill 900 pencils, enough fat to make 75 candles, enough phosphorus to make 220 match heads and enough iron to make a 3 in. (7.5 cm) nail.

Digestive system
Your stomach produces up to 0.5 gal. (2 L) of hydrochloric acid a day. It does not damage the stomach walls because 500,000 cells in your stomach lining are replaced every minute. The small intestine is about 16 ft. (5 m) long. The large intestine is thicker, but only about 5 ft. (1.5 m) long.

Eyes
You blink about 20,000 times a day.

Gas
On average, you release 0.5 gal. (2 L) of gases from your intestines as burps or farts.

Hair
Hair grows about 0.02 in. (0.5 mm) a day.

Heartbeats
Your heart pumps 3,600 gal. (13,640 L) of blood around your body in a day. An average heartbeat rate of 70 beats a minute adds up to more than 100,000 beats a day.

Mouth
You will produce 10,000 gal. (37,800 L) of saliva in your life.

Nerves
Your body has about 13 trillion nerve cells, transmitting messages at speeds of 180 mph (290 km/h).

Sweat
You lose about 0.5 qt. (0.5 L) of water a day through 3 million sweat glands. In hot climates you may lose as much as 3.6 gal. (13.5 L) a day.

Urine
You will pass 0.8 to 4.2 pt. (400 to 2,000 ml) of urine every day, depending on your age, your size and outside conditions, especially temperature.

Highly magnified image of red blood cells

Largest human organs

The weights listed below are all averages, but sometimes organs are much larger. Some brains have weighed more than 4.4 lb (2,000 g), but that doesn't mean the owners were super-intelligent!

Skin 384 oz. (10,886 g)
Liver 55 oz. (1,560 g)
Brain male 49.7 oz. (1,408 g)
Brain female 44.6 oz. (1,263 g)
Lungs right 20.5 oz. (580 g)
Lungs left 18 oz. (510 g)
Heart male 11.1 oz. (315 g)
Heart female 9.3 oz. (265 g)
Kidney left 5.3 oz. (150 g)
Kidney right 4.9 oz. (140 g)

Spleen 6 oz. (170 g)
Pancreas 3.5 oz. (98 g)
Thyroid 1.2 oz. (35 g)
Prostate (male only) 0.7 oz. (20 g)
Adrenals left 0.2 oz. (6 g)
Adrenals right 0.2 oz. (6 g)

One and only
The only bone in the human body that is not connected to another bone is the hyoid bone, a U-shaped bone at the base of the tongue. It is supported by the muscles in the neck, but it is not connected to any other bone.

What's your body made of?

Most of the human body is made up of water, or H_2O, which is a combination of hydrogen and oxygen. As much as 99 percent of the body is made up of oxygen, carbon, hydrogen, nitrogen, calcium and phosphorus. There are also small amounts of other elements.

Element	Avg. in 155 lb. (70 kg) person oz. (g)	Element	Avg. in 155 lb. (70 kg) person oz. (g)
Oxygen	1,1517 (43,000)	Potassium	4–5 (110–140)
Carbon	564 (16,000)	Sodium	3.5 (100)
Hydrogen	247 (7,000)	Chlorine	3.35 (95)
Nitrogen	64 (1,800)	Magnesium	0.8 (25)
Calcium	42 (1,200)	Iron	0.1 (4)
Phosphorus	28 (780)	Zinc	0.08 (2.3)
Sulphur	5 (140)	Silicon	0.03 (1)

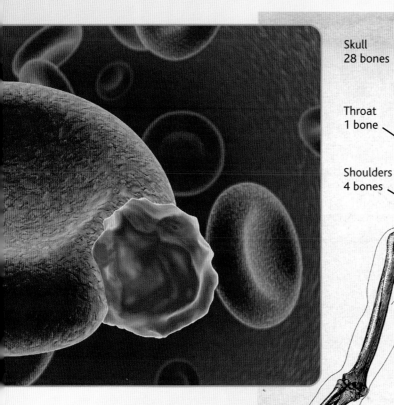

Skull
28 bones

Throat
1 bone

Shoulders
4 bones

The ear bones
are the smallest
in the body.

Sternum
(breastbone)
3 bones

Ribs
24 bones

Vertebrae
(backbone)
26 bones

Pelvis
2 bones

Arms and
hands
60 bones

Legs and feet
58 bones

Human skeleton

The skeleton is the body's framework. The bones of the skeleton support the body, protect the internal organs such as the heart and lungs, and allow you to move.

Longest bones in the body

These are the average measurements of the longest bones of an adult male. The same bones in the female skeleton are usually 6 to 13 percent smaller, except the breastbone, which is almost the same.

Femur (thighbone, upper leg)
19.88 in. (50.5 cm)
Tibia (shinbone, inner lower leg) 16.94 in. (43.03 cm)
Fibula (outer lower leg) 15.94 in. (40.5 cm)
Humerus (upper arm)
14.35 in. (36.46 cm)
Ulna (inner lower arm) 11.1 in. (28.20 cm)
Radius (outer lower arm) 10.4 in. (26.42 cm)
7th rib 9.45 in. (24 cm)
8th rib 9.06 in. (23 cm)
Hipbone (one half of pelvis)
7.28 in. (18.5 cm)
Sternum (breastbone) 6.69 in. (17 cm)

Nails

Your fingernails grow 0.02 in. (0.05 cm) a week — four times faster than your toenails.

Skin

Your skin weighs up to 8.8 lb. (4 kg) and covers up to 14–18.3 sq. ft. (1.3–1.7 sq m). Getting dressed and undressed, rubbing body parts together and even breathing cause microscopic flakes of skin to fall off at the rate of 50,000 flakes a minute. In a lifetime you will shed 40 lb. (18 kg) of skin.

How heavy?

The human skeleton makes up about one-fifth of a person's entire weight. An average adult weighing 155 lb. (70 kg) will have a skeleton that weighs 31 lb. (14 kg).

www.innerbody.com   search

Weighty wonder

Carol Yager (1960–94) of Beecher, Michigan, was claimed to have reached a peak weight of 1,600 lb (727 kg). If true, it would make her the heaviest person of all time. She was unable to stand or walk, and when taken out of her house through specially widened doorways, had to be lifted by a relay team of 20 strong firefighters.

Jon Minnoch (1941–83) of Bainbridge Island, Washington, was reportedly the world's heaviest man at approximately 1,400 lb (635 kg). At one point, he went on a strict diet and shed 952 lb (432 kg), the greatest weight loss ever recorded.

In comparison, the 727.5-lb (330-kg) **Daniel Lambert** (1770–1809) was almost a lightweight.

Daniel Lambert

Body records

Longest beard
Hans Langseth (1846–1927) had a beard that measured 17.5 ft. (5.33 m). It has been in the Smithsonian Institution, Washington DC, since 1967.

Longest nails
Shridhar Chillal of Pune, India (1937–) has not cut the nails on his left hand since 1952. By 2000 the total length of his nails on that hand was over 236 in. (600 cm).

Longest mustache
Kalyan Ramji Sain of Sundargath, India, holds the record. His mustache is 11 ft., 11.5 in. (3.29 m) from tip to tip.

Longest hair
Swami Pandarasannadhi was the head of a monastery in Madras, India. When his hair was measured in 1949 it was 26 ft. (7.9 m) long.

Longest sneezing bout
Donna Griffiths of Pershore, England, started sneezing on January 13, 1981, and continued for 978 days.

Math genius
When he was only 8 years old, American Zerah Colburn (1804–40) worked out how many seconds had elapsed since the birth of Christ. He did this in his head within

Hans Langseth

seconds. When Zerah was asked whether 4,294,967,297 was a prime number (one that cannot be divided evenly by another number), he instantly replied that it was not — it is equal to 641 times 6,700,417.

Longest hiccuping
Charles Osborne of Anthon, Iowa, hiccuped from 1922 to 1990.

Infant prodigy
By the age of 4, Kim Ung-Yong of Korea (1963–) could speak fluent Korean, English, Japanese and German, and could solve calculus problems.

Memory
Gon Yang-ling of Harbin, China, has memorized more than 15,000 telephone numbers.

World's oldest people

Below is a list of the world's longest living people, or supercentenarians. It includes only those for whom there are accurate records of their birth and death dates.

Although Christian Mortensen is ninth in the list, he is the world's oldest man. The others in the list are women.

Jeanne Calment (1875–1997), France: 122 years and 164 days
Sarah DeRemer Knauss (1880–1999), U.S.: 119 years and 97 days
Lucy Hannah (1875–1993), U.S.: 117 years and 248 days
Marie-Louise Meilleur (1880–1998), Canada: 117 years and 229 days
María Esther Heredia Lecaro de Capovilla (1889–2006) Ecuador: 116 years and 347 days
Tane Ikai (1879–1995), Japan: 116 years and 175 days
Elizabeth Bolden (1890–2006) U.S.: 116 years and 118 days
Maggie Barnes (1882–1998), U.S.: 115 years and 319 days
Christian Mortensen (1882–1998), Denmark/U.S.: 115 years and 252 days
Charlotte Hughes (1877–1993), UK: 115 years and 228 days

Oldest living person
Gertrude Baines (U.S.) was born on April 6, 1894 and celebrated her 115th birthday in 2009, making her the oldest person alive in the world.

Tom Thumb and friends

American showman P.T. Barnum first met Charles Sherwood Stratton (U.S., 1838–83) when he was 4 years old. He was 24 in. (61 cm) tall and weighed 15 lb. (6.8 kg). Barnum persuaded Charles's parents to allow him to exhibit their son for a fee of $3 a week. He was advertised as "General Tom Thumb, a dwarf 11 years of age, just arrived from England." By the time he died, he had grown to 3 ft. 3 in. (1 m) and weighed 70 lb. (32 kg). Lavinia Warren (U.S., 1841–1919) was 31 in. (79 cm) tall. Her first husband was Tom Thumb.

"Commodore" Nutt (U.S., 1844–81) was 29 in. (74 cm) tall. Like Tom Thumb, he was exhibited by P. T. Barnum.

Human endurance records

Under water
On August 5, 1926 escapologist Harry Houdini was lowered into the swimming pool of the Hotel Shelton, New York, inside a sealed iron coffin. Despite having no breathing apparatus, he survived being submerged for 1 hour 31 minutes before he escaped.

Without sleep
In 2007 Tony Wright of Penzance, UK, stayed awake for 266 hours to claim the record for the longest period anyone has stayed awake, However, some people believe Toimi Soini, of Hamina, Finland had already set a record of 276 hours in 1964, while others think Maureen Weston, of Peterborough, UK, stayed awake for an amazing 449 hours in a rocking chair marathon in 1977.

Swimming the Atlantic
In 2009 Jennifer Figge (U.S.) became the first woman to swim the Atlantic. She swam 2,000 miles (3,219 km) from the Cape Verde Islands to Trinidad inside a 19 x 14 ft (6 m x 4 m) cage to protect her from sharks. It took her 24 days.

Run-up records
In the annual Empire State Building Run-Up, runners race up the famous skyscraper's 1,576 steps. In 2006 Andrea Mayr of Austria set a new women's record of 11 minutes, 23 seconds. The overall record-holder is Australian athlete Paul Crake. In 2003, he got to the top in 9 minutes, 33 seconds. In 2008, Thomas Dodd (Germany) won the race for the third consecutive year.

Tallest real giants

These are the most reliable records. All are men, except Trijntje Keever and Jeng Jinlian.

Robert Pershing Wadlow (1918–40), U.S.: 8 ft., 11.1 in. (2.72 m)
John William Rogan (1868–1905), U.S.: 8 ft., 9.8 in. (2.68 m)
John Aasen (1887–1938), U.S.: 8 ft., 9.8 in. (2.67m)
John F. Carroll (1932–69), U.S.: 8 ft., 7.6 in. (2.64 m)
Al Tomaini (1918–62), U.S.: 8 ft., 4.4 in. (2.55 m)

Trijntje Keever (1616–33), Netherlands: 8 ft., 3.3 in. (2.54 m)
Edouard Beaupre (1881–1904), Canada: 8 ft., 2.5 in. (2.50 m)
Bernard Coyne (1897–1921), U.S.: 8 ft., 1.2 in. (2.49 m)
Don Koehler (1925–81), U.S.: 8 ft., 1.2 in. (2.49 m)
Jeng Jinlian (1964–82), China: 8 ft., 1.1 in. (2.48 m)
Väinö Myllyrinne (1909–63), Finland: 8 ft., 1.1 in. (2.48 m)
Louis Moilanen (1885–1913), Finland/U.S.: 8 ft., 1 in. (2.46 m)
Gabriel Estavo Monjane (1944–90), Mozambique: 8 ft., 0.75 in. (2.46 m)

Life expectancy

Life expectancy is the average number of years people in different countries are likely to live. Conditions can improve or sometimes get worse, so life expectancy can get higher or lower.

The country with the highest life expectancy is Andorra at 82.36 years. The country with the lowest life expectancy is Swaziland with 31.84 years. People who live in the UK and the U.S. have an average life expectancy of 79.16 years and 78.24 years respectively.

Robert Wadlow

Commodore Nutt, Miss Warren, normal-sized man and Tom Thumb

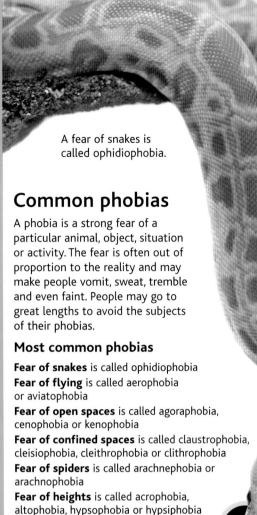

A fear of snakes is called ophidiophobia.

Common phobias

A phobia is a strong fear of a particular animal, object, situation or activity. The fear is often out of proportion to the reality and may make people vomit, sweat, tremble and even faint. People may go to great lengths to avoid the subjects of their phobias.

Most common phobias

Fear of snakes is called ophidiophobia

Fear of flying is called aerophobia or aviatophobia

Fear of open spaces is called agoraphobia, cenophobia or kenophobia

Fear of confined spaces is called claustrophobia, cleisiophobia, cleithrophobia or clithrophobia

Fear of spiders is called arachnephobia or arachnophobia

Fear of heights is called acrophobia, altophobia, hypsophobia or hypsiphobia

Unusual phobias

Fear of beards is called pogonophobia

Fear of chickens is called alektorophobia

Fear of dancing is called chorophobia

Fear of dolls is called pediophobia

Fear of fish is called ichthyophobia

Fear of frogs is called batrachophobia

Fear of hair is called chaetophobia

Fear of mirrors is called eisoptrophobia

Fear of the number 13 is called triskaidekaphobia

Fear of string is called linonophobia

Fear of teeth is called odontophobia

Calorie counts

A Calorie (with a capital C) is a unit that measures the amount of energy in foods. It is also known as a kilocalorie and is equal to 1,000 calories (with a small c). A calorie is the amount of heat needed to raise the temperature of 1 g (0.035 oz.) of water by 1°C (1.8°F).

An adult might eat up to 3,000 Calories a day. Eating too many Calories that the body does not use for energy may make you fat. The figures below are based on the average number of Calories a 155 lb. (70 kg) adult burns when doing an activity for one hour. A lighter person uses fewer Calories; a heavier person more.

Squash 844 Calories
Skipping, swimming 704 Calories
Basketball, cycling, running, walking upstairs 563 Calories
Canoeing or rowing 493 Calories
Football, ice skating, roller skating, skiing, tennis 493 Calories
Aerobics 422 Calories
Mowing lawn 387 Calories

Gardening, skateboarding 352 Calories
Dancing 317 Calories
Golf, table tennis 281 Calories
Housework, walking dog 246 Calories
Frisbee, surfing 211 Calories
Playing piano 176 calories
Standing 120 calories
Sitting 90 calories
Sleeping 65 calories

Causes of death worldwide

There are big differences between the causes of death in developing countries and in developed countries. In developing countries, many more deaths are caused by infectious diseases and illnesses spread by insects such as malaria.

In developed countries more people become ill from being overweight and eating rich diets. There are about 57,029,000 deaths a year worldwide.

Heart diseases 16,733,000 per year
Cancers 7,121,000 per year
Respiratory infections 3,963,000 per year
Lung diseases 3,702,000 per year
HIV/AIDS 2,777,000 per year
Digestive diseases 1,968,000 per year
Diarrheal diseases 1,798,000 per year
Tuberculosis 1,566,000 per year
Malaria 1,272,000 per year
Road traffic injuries 1,192,000 per year
Neuropsychiatric disorders 1,112,000 per year

Medical milestones   100 BC

c. 460 BC The first medical studies were carried out by Hippocrates (Greece)

AD 1543 Accurate anatomical drawings were made by Andreas Vesalius (Belgium)

1628 Blood circulation was discovered by William Harvey (UK)

1683 Bacteria were first described by Antonie van Leeuwenhoek (the Netherlands)

1796 The first smallpox vaccination was carried out by Edward Jenner (UK)

1805 Morphine was used as a painkiller by Friedrich Sertürner (Germany)

1810 Homeopathy was used by Samuel Hahnemann (Germany)

1816 The stethoscope was invented by René Laënnec (France)

1818 The first blood transfusion was carried out by Thomas Blundell (UK)

1842 Ether was administered as an anesthetic by Crawford Long (U.S.)

1844 Nitrous oxide (laughing gas) was used as an anesthetic by Horace Wells (U.S.)

1846 Ether vapor was used as an anesthetic by William Morton (U.S.)

1847 Chloroform was used as an anesthetic by John Bell/James Simpson (UK)

1864 The Red Cross was founded by Henri Dunant (Switzerland)

1867 Antiseptic was used before surgery by Joseph Lister (UK)

1885 Rabies vaccine was developed by Louis Pasteur (France)

1895 X-rays were discovered by William von Röntgen (Germany)

1895 Psychoanalysis was used by Sigmund Freud (Austria)

1898 Aspirin was made by Felix Hoffman (Germany)

1901 Blood groups were identified by Karl Landsteiner (Austria)

Dentistry

Some basic dentistry — treating and extracting decayed teeth and medicines to cure gum disease — was practiced in ancient times, but developed little until the early 19th century.

● False teeth were once made of animal teeth, hippopotamus or walrus ivory (U.S. president George Washington had teeth made of hippopotamus tusks, not wood as is commonly claimed).

● Sometimes false teeth were created using the teeth taken from dead people, often from soldiers killed in warfare, so they were sometimes called "Waterloo Teeth" after the battle fought there.

● In England in the 1820s, Claudius Ash began making dentures out of porcelain that looked natural and were set in gold, later vulcanite, a type of rubber.

● Since then new inventions such as the use of x-rays and anaesthetics and improved equipment, drills and filling and repairing materials have resulted in great advances in treating tooth and gum problems, preserving, whitening and straightening teeth.

Modern dentistry

The anopheles mosquito spreads malaria to humans.

Malaria

The word malaria comes from the medieval Italian for "bad air," but it is an infectious disease transmitted by the anopheles mosquitoes. This connection was proved in 1898 by Sir Ronald Ross, a British doctor in India, for which he received the second-ever Nobel Prize for Medicine, 1902.

● Worldwide, as many as 500 million people a year catch malaria, more than one million dying from it — in fact, in human history, malaria has probably killed more people than any other disease.

● Advances in anti-malarial drugs have reduced the number of cases, but a vaccine to combat and eradicate malaria remains the world's goal.

● To achieve this, the Bill and Melinda Gates Foundation have pledged $35 billion, the largest ever-donation to medical research.

2000s

1906 Vitamins were discovered by Frederick Hopkins (UK)

1922 Insulin was used to treat diabetes by Frederick Banting and John Macleod (Canada) and Charles Best (U.S.)

1927 Iron lung was invented by Philip Drinker (U.S.)

1928 Penicillin was discovered by Alexander Fleming (UK)

1940 Penicillin was first used by Howard Florey (Australia) and Ernest Chain (UK)

1952 The first artificial heart valve was used by Charles Hufnagel (U.S.)

1953 DNA structure was identified by Francis Crick (UK) and James Watson (U.S.)

1955 Kidney dialysis machine was invented by Willem J. Kolff (the Netherlands/U.S.)

1957 First heart pacemaker was used by Clarence Lillehie (U.S.)

1967 The first human heart transplant was performed by Christiaan Barnard (S. Africa)

1970 First artificial heart was used by Robert Jarvik (U.S.)

1971 CAT scanner was first used by Godfrey Hounsfield (UK)

1978 First test-tube baby (Louise Brown) was born after procedure perfomed by Patrick Steptoe (UK)

1980 Smallpox was eradicated by World Health Organization

1984 Genetic fingerprinting was invented by Alec Jeffreys (UK)

1984 AIDS virus was first identified by Centers for Disease Control (U.S.)

1996 First mammal was cloned (Dolly, a sheep) by Ian Wilmut, Roslin Institute (UK)

2000 Human DNA genome sequence was completed

2006 Robot heart surgery was performed by Carlo Pappone (Italy)

2008 DNA testing enables people to check for genetic disorders

2009 Stem cell research approved in U.S. offers hope that paralyzed people may walk.

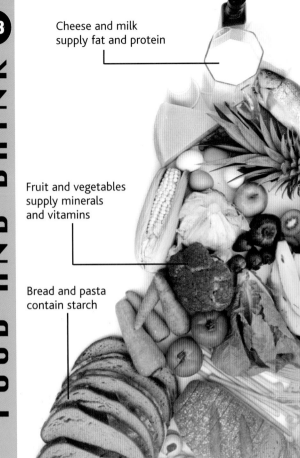

Cheese and milk supply fat and protein

Fish is rich in protein

Fruit and vegetables supply minerals and vitamins

Bread and pasta contain starch

Roadkill recipes

Eating roadkill (animals that have been killed on the road) has occurred ever since there have been cars. In the U.S., where deer and other large animals are common victims, a number of recipe books and websites have been devoted to the subject.

Britain's first "flattened fauna" (squashed animals) cookbook was announced in 2006 by Arthur Boyt of Davidstow, Cornwall, who has included badger, fox, weasel and bat among his meals over the past 50 years. His roadkill recipes include one for spaghetti with hedgehog.

Fish & chips

Fried fish became popular in England in the 19th century after being introduced by Jewish immigrants. Once the railways made it possible to transport fresh fish inland, it was teamed with chips (which probably originated in Belgium, despite the name "French fries"). The first fish and chip shop is claimed to have been been opened by John Lees in Oldham, Lancashire, in the 1860s.

What we eat

A family food survey is carried out in the UK every year. The latest figures for what we eat in the home (not including takeout and eating out) show that the average person will consume more than 50 tons of food and drink in an 80-year lifespan. These are some of the main items in the survey, and the amounts each of us can expect to eat in our lives:

Milk and cream (including yoghurt, etc) 18,195 lb (8,253 kg)
Soft drinks 15,463 lb (7,014 kg)
Vegetables 10,453 lb (4,742 kg)
Fresh fruit 7,842 lb (3,557 kg)
Potatoes 7,163 lb (3,249 kg)
Alcoholic drinks 7,079 lb (3,211 kg)
Bread 6,274 lb (2,816 kg)
Cereals and cereal products
4,916 lb (2,230 kg)
Fruit juice 3,117 lb (1,414 kg)
Poultry 2,302 lb (1,044 kg)
Fats 1,660 lb (753 kg)
Fish 1,512 lb (686 kg)
Biscuits 1,495 lb (678 kg)

Cakes and pastries 1,457 lb (661 kg)
Sweets 1,184 lb (537 kg)
Sugar and preserves (jam, etc)
1,146 lb (520 kg)
Cheese 1,091 lb (495 kg)
Bacon and ham 999 lb (453 kg)
Eggs 880 lb (399 kg)
Pasta 844 lb (383 kg)
Beverages (tea, coffee, etc)
514 lb (233 kg)
Mutton and lamb 505 lb (229 kg)
Flour 496 lb (225 kg)

Fish and chips

Extreme dining

A company called Dinner in the Sky offers diners in a number of countries the experience of eating a meal while suspended 164 ft (50 meters) above the ground. A table and chairs is lifted up by a crane and up to 22 guests — strapped in with seatbelts — are served by a chef and catering staff in the middle of the table. Musicians, including a grand piano, can also be winched up to provide entertainment.

Drinking chocolate

Chocolate was originally made by Aztecs and Mayas. When it was first imported to Europe it was very expensive and drunk only by wealthy people. London's first drinking chocolate house opened in Queen's Head Alley, Bishopsgate Street, in 1657. Quaker families led by Fry, Cadbury, and Rowntree promoted drinking chocolate as an alternative to alcohol to which they were opposed, establishing factories in the late 18th and early 19th centuries. It remained exclusively a drink until the mid-19th century when the first eating chocolate was made.

The drinks we drink

Soda water

Carbonated water — water with carbon dioxide forced into it to make it sparkling — was invented by Dr. William Brownrigg of Whitehaven, UK, in 1741. One of the most famous manufacturers was German-born scientist Jean Jacob Schweppe who moved to London in 1792. By the 1870s the company he founded was also making ginger ale and Indian Tonic Water, by adding quinine to sweetened soda water, after the style of the British in India who drank it as an antidote to malaria.

Bottled water

Drinking mineral water from natural springs has been done since Roman times and became fashionable in the 18th century when people went to spa towns to bathe and undergo medical treatments. It is claimed that water from Malvern, UK, was bottled as early as 1622, while French mineral water became especially popular, including Evian (1826), Badoit (1838), Vittel (1882) and Perrier (1898). Perrier's club-shaped bottles were designed to resemble the Indian clubs used for exercise by the spa's British owner William Albert St. John Harmsworth.

Carbonated drinks

The first Coca-Cola was served in Jacob's Pharmacy, in Atlanta, Georgia, on May 8, 1886. It was the creation of pharmacist Dr. John Stith Pemberton. It was first served in bottles in 1894 (although its distinctive bottle design was not introduced until 1915) and in cans in 1955. Its rival Pepsi dates from 1898, when it was named "Brad's Drink" after its inventor Caleb Bradham. It was trademarked as Pepsi-Cola in 1903.

World History

Barack Obama

On January 20, 2009, Barack Obama was sworn in as the 44th President of the United States of America. Obama has made history as the first African-American to hold the office, and his election as president has raised hopes around the world for a new era of international politics.

Prehistoric ages

Prehistory is the time before events were written down and recorded. Human prehistory is usually divided into three periods.

Stone Age
The period when stone was used for tools. It is divided into two parts: Paleolithic (Old Stone) from about 2 million to 10,000 BC and Neolithic (New Stone) from about 10,000 to 3300 BC.

Bronze Age (c. 3300–c. 2500 BC)
The period when people began to make things with bronze, which was more reliable and hardwearing than stone.

Iron Age (c. 1200 BC–c. AD 50–1000)
The period when iron was used for making tools. Bronze is a better material, but iron was more widely available, so cheaper.

Neolithic burial place, called a dolmen, in Portugal

Historical periods

History is usually divided into different periods to make it easier to study and talk about. The following are the main periods in the history of the Western world since the fall of the Roman empire.

The early Middle Ages (Dark Ages)
This period came after the fall of the Roman empire in AD 476, when so-called barbarians (Germanic tribes) took over areas that had been under Roman control. It became known as the Dark Ages because there was very little writing, science or culture during this time. The lack of writing also means that we do not know much about what happened. The early Middle Ages came to an end after the Norman Conquest when there was a revival in learning.

The Middle (Medieval) Ages
This was a very religious time. Most people believed in an all-powerful God, responsible for bringing order and prosperity. The Church was very influential and wealthy, and many great cathedrals and monasteries were built during this period. It was a great age of learning, and the first universities were founded in Parma and Bologna, then Paris and Oxford. Chartres Cathedral in France was built and the writings of Dante and Chaucer were published.

The Renaissance
The Renaissance began in Italy during the 14th century, and spread to northern Europe in the 16th century. The name Renaissance comes from the French word for rebirth; people looked back to Greek and Roman ideals in arts such as architecture and sculpture at this time. These ideas spread with the help of printing, which was invented by German Johannes Gutenberg in the mid-15th century. The Renaissance was marked by people's belief in progress and personal achievement. The playwright William Shakespeare and the artist Leonardo da Vinci lived and worked during this time.

The Reformation
In 16th-century Europe most people belonged to the Roman Catholic Church, which was headed by the Pope. Some were concerned that the Church was too involved with power and money. Leaders such as Erasmus and Martin Luther wanted people to reject the priests and return to the roots of Christianity and the Bible. This led to the start of Protestantism and its split from the Roman Catholic Church.

The age of colonialism
In 1492 Christopher Columbus discovered the Americas. This encouraged many European countries to invade and conquer other smaller or weaker countries so they could use their resources, trade with them or use them as stopping points for their ships. Portugal gained control of what is now Brazil, and Spain took most of Latin America, as well as large parts of what is now the U.S. The Dutch gained the Indonesian islands and the French took Canada. Great Britain was the most powerful colonizing power. It gained 13 colonies in North America, plus Australasia, some Caribbean islands and vast tracts of Africa and Asia, including India. European colonization continued throughout the 19th century and up to World War I (1914–18). After the War, the victors divided many of the territories of the losers.

See also
Inventions: pages 80–81

Extent of European colonialism 1815–1914

- Belgian
- British
- Dutch
- French
- German
- Italian
- Portuguese
- Russian
- Spanish

NORTH AMERICA

SOUTH AMERICA

The Industrial Revolution

The Industrial Revolution began with the invention of steam power and steam-driven machinery (mainly used in the textile industry) in 18th-century Great Britain. During the following century inventions such as steam-powered ships and railways spread throughout the world. This revolution led thousands of people to leave the countryside and move to crowded slum towns where there were large factories employing huge numbers of workers. The new industries needed better transportation to bring supplies and deliver finished goods, so a huge network of roads and canals was built during the 18th century, followed by railways in the 19th. The Industrial Revolution also led to a growth in child labor and a widening divide between rich and poor people.

The modern age

During the 20th century advances in technology led to great changes in society and global politics. New weapons and military techniques changed the way wars were fought. Huge numbers of people died during World Wars I and II. During the Cold War between the U.S. and the USSR there was no fighting, but both sides were afraid of the nuclear weapons they were developing.

Air travel, television and, most recently, the Internet have all enabled more people to experience the world beyond their own country. At the same time, cheap domestic appliances such as washing machines and dishwashers allow people more time to spend on activities such as entertainment and shopping.

Modern living

In the 20th century, factories began to mass-produce cars that ordinary people could afford. This allowed them to live further from their work places and led to the building of suburbs all over the Western world.

Working on a car production line

View down an elevator inside a shopping center

www.hyperhistory.com   search

Romulus and Remus, the founders of Rome, nursed by a she-wolf

The Statue of Liberty in New York has a tablet in her left hand that reads July 4, 1776.

753 BC Rome founded

According to legend, Rome was founded by Romulus and Remus, the twin sons of the god Mars and priestess Rhea Silvia. The city is named after Romulus, who killed his brother and ruled as Rome's first king. Rome was the capital of the Roman empire, which controlled the entire Mediterranean region and far beyond by 44 BC.

1789 French Revolution

The French people had many complaints against their system of government, especially the power of the monarchy and the land-owning aristocracy. These erupted in a revolution in which the Bastille prison was seized. The violent period that followed became known as the Reign of Terror, and King Louis XVI and many other members of the ruling class were executed.

Black Death

This epidemic was probably caused by bacteria that were passed on by fleabites and by contact with infected sufferers. It was known as the Black Death because victims suffered from black blotches on their skin before dying. The plague swept across Asia and Europe in the 14th century, killing as many as a third of the people.

1776 U.S. Independence

The Declaration of Independence was prepared after years of tension between Great Britain and the American colonies over matters such as taxation. It listed the colonies' complaints and expressed the determination of the people of America to separate themselves from their British rulers. The declaration was signed on July 4, 1776. The armed conflict that followed ended with the American victory in 1781. In 1783 the Treaty of Paris recognized the country's independence.

History timeline   1000s   1600s

753 BC Rome founded

221 BC Qin Shihuangdi becomes first Emperor of China

about AD 33 Jesus crucified

43 Emperor Claudius invades Britain

79 Pompeii, Italy, destroyed by the eruption of Vesuvius volcano

476 Roman empire ends when Goths invade

632 Death of Muhammad, founder of Islam

1066 Battle of Hastings; William the Conqueror becomes king of England

1096–99 First Crusade — European Christians attempt to

recover Jerusalem and the Holy Land from Muslim control

1215 King John signs Magna Carta, granting rights to English citizens

1347–80s Black Death kills 75 million in Asia and Europe

1337–1453 Hundred Years' War between England and France; France eventually wins

1415 Henry V of England defeats the French at Agincourt and goes on to conquer Normandy

1431 17-year-old French patriot Joan of Arc leads an army and defeats the English (1429), but is burned at the stake

1455–85 Wars of the Roses (civil war in England)

1476 Caxton begins printing in London

1478 Spanish Inquisition begins the persecution of non-Catholics

1492 Columbus sails from Palos, Spain, to Americas

1517 Reformation starts when Martin Luther publishes protests against Catholic Church

1519-22 Ferdinand Magellan's expedition circumnavigates the globe

1588 Spanish Armada defeated by the English fleet, fireships and storms

1618–48 Thirty Years' War (Catholic v. Protestant) in Europe

1620 The Pilgrim Fathers sail from Plymouth for America and found a new colony

1649 King Charles I executed

1660 Restoration of the monarchy; Charles II becomes king

1664–65 The Great Plague kills 70,000 in London

1666 Great Fire of London

1776 U.S. Declaration of Independence

1776–83 American War of Independence

Lenin addressing a crowd of workers

1917 Russian Revolution

The rule of the Russian royal family led by the tsar ended with the February Revolution in 1917. The revolution was triggered by problems such as food shortages and Russia's involvement in World War I. The October Revolution followed later that year, when Soviet forces seized control. They murdered the tsar and his family and attempted to create a Communist state under the leadership of Lenin. A civil war followed from 1918 to 1922. Soviet rule lasted until 1991.

1989 Fall of Berlin Wall

After World War II, control of the East German city of Berlin was split between West Germany (with U.S., British and French troops) and Soviet East Germany. In 1961 the East Germans built the Berlin Wall to stop its inhabitants fleeing to the West, and 192 people were shot while trying to defect. The wall was a symbol of the divide between the Soviet Union and the West. When the Soviet Union collapsed, the wall was torn down and East and West Germany were reunited, with Berlin as the new capital city.

2010 Centenaries

1510
The warship Mary Rose was completed. The pride of Henry VIII's navy, she sank in 1545, but was raised in 1982 and is now on display in Portsmouth.

1610
With his newly-invented telescope, Galileo discovered four moons of Jupiter.

British explorer Henry Hudson discovered Hudson Bay in what is now Canada.

1710
French king Louis XIV's palace at Versailles was completed.

1810
The Spanish colonies of Mexico and Colombia declared their independence. In North America, Spain's control of West Florida ended when it was annexed by the United States.

1910
Hungarian-American escapologist Harry Houdini became the first person to fly an aircraft (a *Voisin* biplane) in Australia.

King Edward VII died and George V became king of the United Kingdom. Edward's funeral was the first major news event filmed in colour.

Polish-French chemist Marie Curie first isolated radium.

See also

First telescopes: page 27
Famous artists: pages 242–43

2000s

1783 First balloon flight (Montgolfier brothers, France)
1788 First European settlers arrive in Australia
1789 French Revolution
1793 Louis XVI of France executed
1815 Battle of Waterloo; Wellington defeats Napoleon
1825 World's first public railway, Stockton to Darlington
1833 Slavery abolished in the British empire
1853–56 Crimean War
1860–65 American Civil War
1869 Suez Canal opens
1869 U.S. transcontinental railway completed

1876 Alexander Graham Bell invents telephone
1901–1910 Peak decade for immigration into U.S. (8.8 million immigrants)
1903 First airplane flights (Wright brothers, U.S.)
1903 Henry Ford begins mass production of cars
1914–18 World War I — 8,545,800 military deaths
1917 Russian Revolution establishes Soviet Union
1929–33 Great Depression (world economic crisis)
1939–45 World War II — 15,843,000 military deaths

1945 Atom bombs dropped on Hiroshima and Nagasaki, Japan
1945–90 Cold War between USSR and the West
1950–53 Korean War
1959–75 Vietnam War (U.S. involved 1961–73)
1961 First man in space (Yuri Gagarin, USSR)
1961 Berlin Wall built, separating East and West Germany
1963 U.S. President John F. Kennedy assassinated
1969 Neil Armstrong becomes first man on the Moon
1989 Fall of the Berlin Wall triggers the end of the Soviet Union

1994 Nelson Mandela becomes president of South Africa
2001 World Trade Center, New York, destroyed by terrorists; U.S. retaliates by invading Afghanistan
2003 Iraq War and Saddam Hussein overthrown; elections later held but violence continues
2006 Saddam Hussein executed
2008 Global financial crisis and recession begin with the collapse of banks and other businesses
2009 Barack Obama inaugurated as 44th U.S. President, watched by 1.8 million spectators

Mesopotamia/Sumeria

Mesopotamia was a region around the Tigris and Euphrates rivers, which is now part of Turkey, Syria and Iraq. The area was controlled by several different peoples, beginning with the Sumerians in around 3500 BC. They set up a number of city-states that constantly battled to control land and trade routes until they were united under one ruler in 2350 BC. They finally became absorbed into other races around 2000 BC.

Ancient Egypt

Egypt is an area in the Nile valley which was ruled as a single state from about 3200 BC. There were 30 dynasties, led by pharaohs who were both kings and gods. The pyramids were built during the fourth dynasty (2575–2467 BC) as tombs for the pharaohs of that time. The Great Pyramid of Giza was the world's tallest building for 4000 years, and it is the only wonder of the world that still stands. Like other powerful empires, ancient Egypt was weakened by invasions, until it was taken over by Alexander the Great in 332 BC.

Ancient Greece

Ancient Greece was called Hellas. The civilization was at its strongest in 500–400 BC, after Greece colonized Cyprus, parts of Italy, Ukraine and the South of France. This era was known as the Golden Age. Some city-states, such as Athens and Sparta, became great centers of art, learning and politics. Many famous thinkers lived in Athens during this period, including Aristotle,

Plato, Socrates and Aristophanes. The ancient Greeks also created the idea of democracy: its citizens were encouraged to debate and then vote on issues. The Golden Age ended in wars between the city-states, which paved the way for King Philip of Macedonia to invade Greece, followed later by his son Alexander.

Alexander the Great's empire

Alexander III of Macedonia lived for only 33 years, from 356 to 323 BC. In that short time he built an empire covering Persia (modern Iraq, Iran, Syria and Turkey), Egypt, Greece and Babylon. It was difficult to keep this huge empire together, and it collapsed soon after his death. Alexander ended the Achaemenid Persian Empire that had been established in 550 BC when Cyrus the Great conquered the Median Empire. Persia became part of the Selucid Empire but rose again as the Parthian Empire under Mithridates I and the Sassanid Empire that ruled for over 400 years, until the Islamic conquest of AD 651.

Chinese empire

China was one of the first places where people are known to have lived. From 1600 BC it was made up of many small kingdoms which all united in 221 BC under one leader or emperor. Various dynasties ruled the empire, starting with the Qin dynasty. During this time, the Great Wall of China was built to keep invaders out. China was an extremely learned civilization, ahead of Europe in the arts and sciences by up to 200 years. The empire finally fell apart under the Han dynasty in AD 220 as a result of corruption and poverty.

Roman empire

The Roman empire was formed in 31 BC under the leadership of Caesar Augustus, who ruled over every aspect of Roman life. Caesar Augustus brought peace, prosperity and culture. The empire expanded so much that by the 2nd century AD, Rome had colonies that stretched from the Middle East to Spain, and from Great Britain to North Africa. The sheer size of the empire brought problems. There was not enough money to pay for an army spread across the world, which made the empire vulnerable to enemies. Constant attacks by German barbarians eventually defeated the army, and the empire fell in AD 476. The influence of ancient Rome is staggering: Roman roads still cross Europe, the Roman legal system is still the model for countries in Europe and Latin America, and its language, Latin, is the basis of many languages spoken today.

Greek empires
- Colonies of the Ancient Greeks
- Empire of Alexander the Great

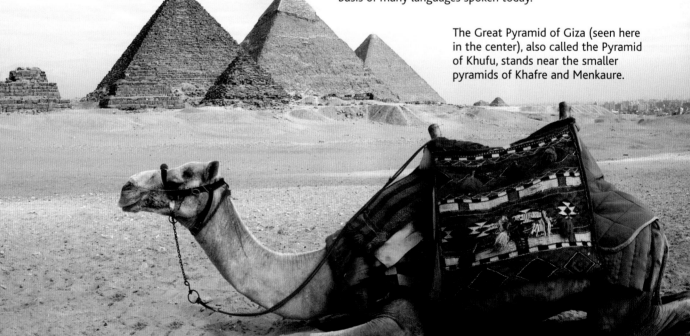

The Great Pyramid of Giza (seen here in the center), also called the Pyramid of Khufu, stands near the smaller pyramids of Khafre and Menkaure.

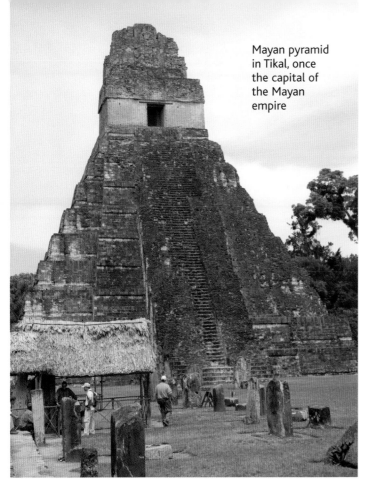

Mayan pyramid in Tikal, once the capital of the Mayan empire

The Taj Mahal in Agra, India

Mogul empire

The Mogul empire was founded in 1526 in northern India by a descendent of Genghis Khan. This was a hugely wealthy civilization and the Moguls greatly valued education, culture and art. The Taj Mahal was built by Moguls from 1632–53. This beautiful mausoleum was made for Emperor Shah Jahan's favorite wife, Mumtaz Mahal, and is built of marble with exquisite inlaid decoration. The empire's Muslim leaders wanted the people to keep Muslim ways, but many of its subjects were Hindu. In 1691 the empire was torn apart by bloody battles between Muslims and Hindus. The Mogul empire was finally overthrown by the British in 1857.

British empire

At the beginning of the 20th century, about a quarter of the world's people lived under British rule. The British had been expanding their empire since the 15th century, and by 1900 its lands included South Africa, Kenya, Egypt, Hong Kong, India, Iraq, Nepal, Singapore, Malta, Australia, New Zealand and Canada. Most of Great Britain's former colonies have now won or been granted independence. Many belong to the Commonwealth, which is a voluntary association of independent states founded in 1931 (see map on pages 102–3).

Mayan empire

The Mayan empire was made up of city-states that stretched across southern Mexico and northern Central America. There have been Mayan people since 2000 BC but their greatest period was from AD 300 to 900, when architectural wonders such as Palenque and Uxmal were built. These structures and many others show that the Mayans had an advanced knowledge of mathematics. The Mayan empire gradually declined after 900, and the Spanish invaded the area in the 15th century.

Inca empire

The Incas had a great empire that stretched 350,000 sq. mi. (900,000 sq km) across South America, including Colombia, Bolivia and Argentina, with a capital, Cuzco, in Peru. It lasted from around 1200 until 1533. Inca society was very organized: every person was told which job they had to do and where to do it. In return, they were looked after by the state. Like the Aztecs, the Incas were brutally repressed by Spanish conquistadors in the 15th century.

Aztec empire

The Aztecs arrived in Mexico in 1325 and founded the city of Tenochtitlán, home to about 90,000 people. It showed the Aztecs' skill in engineering and included a system of drainage that was far ahead of any in Europe. The Aztecs conquered neighboring city-states and extended their empire until it stretched from the Pacific to the Gulf of Mexico into Guatemala. The empire ended when the Spanish, led by Hernán Cortés, invaded between 1519 and 1522.

Ottoman empire

The Ottoman empire was an Islamic state from the 13th to 20th centuries and the most powerful empire in the world during the 1500s and 1600s. It covered Turkey, parts of southwest Asia, southeast Europe and North Africa. The capital was Constantinople (now Istanbul). The empire began to decline because its rulers refused to modernize and they lost lands in several wars. It allied with Germany in World War I. Defeated, its remaining lands were divided among the victors.

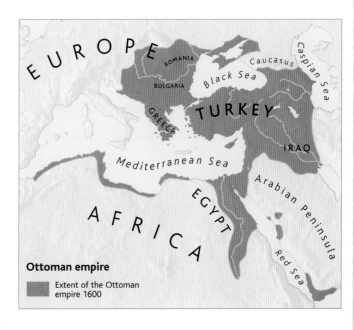

Ottoman empire

Extent of the Ottoman empire 1600

U.S. presidents

United States presidents are elected for a term of four years. George Washington was the first U.S. president and he served two terms. Only Franklin Delano Roosevelt served three terms. He died shortly after he was elected for a fourth term.

In 1951 the 22nd Amendment to the U.S. Constitution ruled that two terms are the most any president may serve. The two main political parties in the U.S. today are the Democratic Party and the Republican Party.

1 George Washington (Federalist Party) first elected 1789
2 John Adams (Federalist Party) first elected 1797
3 Thomas Jefferson (Dem-Rep Party) first elected 1801
4 James Madison (Dem-Rep Party) first elected 1809
5 James Monroe (Dem-Rep Party) first elected 1817
6 John Quincy Adams (Dem-Rep Party) first elected 1825
7 Andrew Jackson (Democratic Party) first elected 1829
8 Martin Van Buren (Democratic Party) first elected 1837
9 William Henry Harrison (Whig Party) first elected 1841
10 John Tyler (Whig Party) first elected 1841
11 James Knox Polk (Democratic Party) first elected 1845
12 Zachary Taylor (Whig Party) first elected 1849
13 Millard Fillmore (Whig Party) first elected 1850
14 Franklin Pierce (Democratic Party) first elected 1853
15 James Buchanan (Democratic Party) first elected 1857
16 Abraham Lincoln (Republican Party) first elected 1861
17 Andrew Johnson (Democratic Party) first elected 1865
18 Ulysses Simpson Grant (Republican Party) first elected 1869
19 Rutherford Birchard Hayes (Republican Party) first elected 1877
20 James Abram Garfield (Republican Party) first elected 1881
21 Chester Alan Arthur (Republican Party) first elected 1881
22 Grover Cleveland (Democratic Party) first elected 1885
23 Benjamin Harrison (Republican Party) first elected 1889
24 Grover Cleveland (Democratic Party) first elected 1893

The heads of presidents Washington, Jefferson, Lincoln and Roosevelt are carved into the face of Mt. Rushmore in South Dakota.

Abraham Lincoln on a U.S. 1-cent coin

25 William McKinley (Republican Party) first elected 1897
26 Theodore Roosevelt (Republican Party) first elected 1901
27 William Howard Taft (Republican Party) first elected 1909
28 Woodrow Wilson (Democratic Party) first elected 1913
29 Warren Gamaliel Harding (Republican Party) first elected 1921
30 Calvin Coolidge (Republican Party) first elected 1923
31 Herbert Clark Hoover (Republican Party) first elected 1929
32 Franklin Delano Roosevelt (Democratic Party) first elected 1933
33 Harry S. Truman (Democratic Party) first elected 1945
34 Dwight David Eisenhower (Republican Party) first elected 1953
35 John Fitzgerald Kennedy (Democratic Party) first elected 1961
36 Lyndon Baines Johnson (Democratic Party) first elected 1963
37 Richard Milhous Nixon (Republican Party) first elected 1969
38 Gerald Rudolph Ford (Republican Party) first elected 1974
39 Jimmy Carter (Democratic Party) first elected 1977
40 Ronald Reagan (Republican Party) first elected 1981
41 George Bush (Republican Party) first elected 1989
42 Bill Clinton (Democratic Party) first elected 1993
43 George W. Bush (Republican Party) first elected 2001
44 Barack Hussein Obama (Democratic party) 2009

World monarchies

A monarchy is a country where the head of state is a king, queen or other hereditary ruler — someone who inherits the throne from a family member. In some countries, such as Malaysia, the monarch is elected.

Bahrain Shaikh Hamad bin Isa al-Khalifa succeeded to the throne in 1999
Belgium King Albert II succeeded to the throne in 1993
Bhutan King Jigme Singye Wangchuck succeeded to the throne in 1972
Brunei Sultan Haji Hassanal Bolkiah succeeded to the throne in 1967

Cambodia King Norodom Sihamoni succeeded to the throne in 2004
Denmark Queen Margrethe II succeeded to the throne in 1972
Japan Emperor Akihito succeeded to the throne in 1989
Jordan King Abdullah II succeeded to the throne in 1999

Kuwait Shaikh Sabah al-Ahmad al-Sabah succeeded to the throne in 2006
Lesotho Letsie II became king in 1990 but stepped down in 1995. He succeeded to the throne again when his father was killed in 1996.
Liechtenstein Prince Hans Adam II succeeded to the throne in 1989

Amazing monarchs

Oldest monarch to ascend the British throne
William IV (ruled 1830–37) was 64 when he was crowned.

British monarchs with the most children
Edward I had 16 children (6 sons and 10 daughters). Both George III and James II had 15.

Most-married British monarch
Henry VIII had six wives who suffered various fates. They were: Catherine of Aragon (divorced), Anne Boleyn (beheaded), Jane Seymour (died 1537), Anne of Cleves (divorced), Catherine Howard (beheaded) and Catherine Parr, who survived Henry.

Youngest British monarchs
Henry VI was just 8 months old when he became king on September 1, 1422, after the death of his father, Henry V. When his grandfather, Charles VI, died 50 days later on October 21, 1422, Henry also became king of France.

Shortest reigning British monarchs
Queen Jane (Lady Jane Grey), ruled for only nine days in 1553, before being sent to the Tower of London. She was executed the following year. Edward V ruled for 75 days. He was one of the Princes in the Tower, who were allegedly murdered on the orders of their uncle, Richard III. Edward VIII abdicated (gave up the throne) on December 11, 1936, before his coronation. He had ruled for just 325 days.

Longest reigning world monarch
King Louis XIV of France became king at the age of 5. He ruled for 72 years, from 1643–1715.

Longest reigning British monarch
Queen Victoria was 18 years old when she became queen in 1837 and she ruled for 63 years.

Richest world ruler
Although no longer the richest man in the world, the Sultan of Brunei is estimated to have a fortune of $28 million.

Monarchies with the most rulers
Japan's monarchy dates from 40 BC. Since then, it has had 125 rulers.

Henry VIII

Oldest king to be crowned
The British crown usually passes to the next in line when the king or queen dies. Charles, Prince of Wales, is Queen Elizabeth II's oldest son and heir. If he becomes king on or after September 20, 2013, he will have overtaken William IV, who was crowned in 1830 at the age of 64 years, 10 months and 5 days, and currently holds the record as the oldest monarch to ascend the British throne. Queen Elizabeth II celebrated her 82th birthday on April 21, 2008.

Henry VII was the first Tudor. He devised the Tudor Rose to symbolize unity between the House of York (white rose) and the House of Lancaster (red rose).

See also
Types of government: pages 110–11

Malaysia Sultan Mizan Zainal Abidin succeeded to the throne in 2006

Monaco Prince Albert II succeeded to the throne in 2005

Morocco King Mohammed VI succeeded to the throne in 1999

Nepal King Gyanendra Bir Bikram Shah Dev succeeded to the throne in 2001

Netherlands Queen Beatrix succeeded to the throne in 1980

Norway King Harald V succeeded to the throne in 1991

Oman Sultan Qaboos Bin Said al-Said succeeded to the throne in 1970

Qatar Shaikh Hamad bin Kaalifa al-Thani succeeded to the throne in 1995

Samoa Tuiatua Tupua Tamasese Efi, a member of one of the country's ruling families, was elected head of state in 2007.

Saudi Arabia King Abdullah ibn Abdul Aziz al-Saud succeeded to the throne in 2005

Spain King Juan Carlos I succeeded to the throne in 1975

Swaziland King Mswati III succeeded to the throne in 1986

Sweden King Carl XVI Gustaf succeeded to the throne in 1973

Thailand King Bhumibol Adulyadej succeeded to the throne in 1946

Tonga George Tupou V succeeded to the throne in 2006

United Kingdom Queen Elizabeth II succeeded to the throne in 1952

Votes for women

The Isle of Man was the first place to give women the vote, in 1880, but the island is part of the UK and not a separate country. Until 1920 the only European countries that allowed women to vote were Sweden (1919) and Czechoslovakia (1920).

In the United States women were granted the vote in 1920, although some states allowed it earlier. Women could not vote in France or Italy until 1945, in Switzerland until 1971 or in Liechtenstein until 1984. Women were granted the right to vote in Kuwait for the first time in 2005, but they are still not allowed to vote in Brunei, Saudi Arabia and the United Arab Emirates. There are other countries where women have no vote — but neither do men.

1 The first country to give women the vote was New Zealand in 1893.

2 Australia followed suit in 1902 although women had the vote in South Australia in 1894 and in Western Australia in 1898 before the separate states were united in 1901.

3 Finland (then a Grand Duchy under the Russian Crown) granted women the vote in 1906.

4 Norway gave some women the vote in 1907. It was not until 1913 that all women over 25 could vote.

5 Denmark and Iceland (a Danish dependency until 1918) allowed women to vote in 1915.

6 The Netherlands and the USSR both gave women the vote in 1917.

8 Austria, Canada, Germany, Poland, Great Britain and Ireland all gave women the vote in 1918. (In Ireland, part of the U.K. until 1921, only women over 30 got the vote in 1918. This was lowered to 21 in 1928.)

www.rulers.org   search

British poster demanding votes for women

Types of government

There have been many different types of government around the world throughout history. Many of the names for them end in the term "-cracy," from a Greek word meaning power.

Aristocracy
Rule by a small group of members of a privileged class.

Autocracy
Government by one person with unrestricted power; also known as despotism and dictatorship.

Fidel Castro was President of Cuba for almost 50 years before handing power to his brother Raúl.

Communist
Government of a classless state in which private ownership is abolished and the state controls all means of production, as in China and Cuba.

Democracy
Government by the people directly or through elected representatives, as in the UK and U.S.

Roosevelt's Four Freedoms

On January 6, 1941, during World War II, U.S. President Roosevelt made a famous speech to Congress. He proclaimed that four freedoms are essential to a democracy: freedom of speech, freedom of worship, freedom from want, and freedom from fear. He looked forward to these freedoms being possible after the defeat of Hitler and the Axis powers. In 1997 a memorial park was opened in Washington DC, honoring Roosevelt. It contains the Four Freedoms fountain as a symbol of his ideas.

Major international organizations

A number of international organizations have been set up to deal with issues that concern the world in general, rather than the interests of individual countries. These organizations are not linked to political parties but often become involved in political matters.

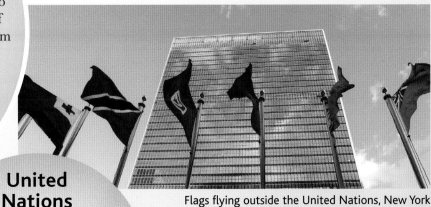

Flags flying outside the United Nations, New York

Women in parliament

There are 49 countries with at least 20 percent of their parliament made up of women — but a number of countries still do not have any women representatives at all.

Based on the most recent general election results, these countries have the highest percentages of women in parliament: Rwanda 56.3 percent, Sweden 47.0 percent, Cuba 43.2 percent, Finland 41.5 percent, Netherlands 41.3 percent, Argentina 40.0 percent.

Meritocracy
Government by leaders selected according to their ability.

Monarchy
Government in which power is held by a king (or queen, emperor or empress) who can pass power on to their heirs.

Oligarchy
Government by a small group of people.

Plutocracy
A government or state in which wealthy people rule.

Theocracy
Government ruled by or subject to religious authority.

United Nations

The UN was founded in 1945. Most countries of the world — a total of 192 — are members. The General Assembly of the UN makes decisions about peacekeeping and human rights.

Amnesty International (AI)
Amnesty International is a charitable organization set up in 1961. It campaigns for human rights throughout the world and against the detention of political prisoners.

International Monetary Fund (IMF)
The IMF was established in 1944 and promotes world trade. It has 184 member countries.

International Red Cross and Red Crescent Movement
These organizations help the victims of such events as warfare and natural disasters.

North Atlantic Treaty Organization (NATO)
Nato was founded in 1949. Ten countries signed a defense treaty that committed them to helping each other in the event of attack. There are now 26 country members, and the NATO headquarters are based in Belgium.

Organization for Economic Co-operation and Development (OECD)
The OECD was formed in 1961. It aims to encourage economic and social development in industrialized countries and provide aid to developing countries.

United Nations Children's Fund (UNICEF)
UNICEF was set up in 1947. It works to improve the health and welfare of children and mothers in developing countries.

United Nations Educational, Scientific and Cultural Organization (UNESCO)
UNESCO was set up in 1946. It encourages countries to get together on matters such as education, culture and science.

World Bank
The World Bank was founded in 1944 and has 184 member countries. It helps developing countries by giving loans.

World Health Organization (WHO)
The WHO is part of the UN. It promotes health matters worldwide and aims to raise medical standards and monitor diseases.

World Trade Organization (WTO)
The Swiss-based WTO encourages international trade by establishing trade agreements between countries.

World Wildlife Fund (WWF)
The WWF was set up in 1961 and is the world's largest conservation organization. Its main aims are to protect endangered animals and the places where they live.

G8

The Group of 8 (G8) is made up of the world's leading industrial countries (Canada, France, Germany, Italy, Japan, the UK, the U.S. and Russian Federation). The heads of the G8 countries meet each year to discuss global issues such as world poverty and security.

Countries
of the
World

Conflict in Gaza

In 2009, political disputes over the territory of the West Bank and Gaza led to further conflict between Israelis and Palestinians, creating a humanitarian crisis. The violence caused widespread destruction and fatalities, damaging hopes of peace.

ARCTIC OCEAN

Beaufort Sea

Greenland
(DENMARK)

Baffin
Bay

Arctic Circle

Alaska
(USA)

ICELAND

Hudson
Bay

Labrador
Sea

UNITED
KINGDOM

Bering
Sea

Gulf of
Alaska

CANADA

IRELAND

PACIFIC
OCEAN

UNITED STATES

ATLANTIC
OCEAN

PORTUGAL

Canary Islands
(SPAIN)

MOROCCO

MEXICO

Gulf of
Mexico

BAHAMAS

Western
Sahara
(MOROCCO)

Tropic of Cancer

Hawaii
(USA)

CUBA

DOMINICAN
REPUBLIC

HAITI

JAMAICA

Puerto Rico (USA)

ANTIGUA & BARBUDA

ST CHRISTOPHER
& NEVIS

DOMINICA

BELIZE

GUATEMALA

HONDURAS

Caribbean Sea

ST VINCENT & THE
GRENADINES

ST LUCIA

BARBADOS

CAPE
VERDE

MAURITANIA

MALI

GAMBIA

SENEGAL

EL SALVADOR

NICARAGUA

GRENADA

TRINIDAD &
TOBAGO

GUINEA-BISSAU

GUINEA

COSTA RICA

PANAMA

COLOMBIA

VENEZUELA

GUYANA

SURINAME

French Guiana
(FRANCE)

SIERRA
LEONE

LIBERIA

Equator

Galapagos Islands
(ECUADOR)

ECUADOR

PERU

BRAZIL

BOLIVIA

PACIFIC
OCEAN

Easter Island
(CHILE)

PARAGUAY

CHILE

ARGENTINA

URUGUAY

ATLANTIC
OCEAN

Falkland Islands
(UNITED KINGDOM)

Key to numbered countries

Europe
1 Netherlands
2 Luxembourg
3 Andorra
4 Monaco
5 Lichtenstein
6 Vatican City State
7 San Marino
8 Slovenia
9 Boznia-Herzegovina
10 Serbia
11 Macedonia
12 Montenegro
13 Kosovo

Africa
14 Republic of Congo

Asia
15 Singapore

Antarctica

ARCTIC OCEAN

Svalbard
(NORWAY)

Barents Sea

Kara
Sea

Arctic Circle

NORWAY

SWEDEN

FINLAND

Baltic Sea

ESTONIA

LATVIA

LITHUANIA

BELARUS

POLAND

UKRAINE

MOLDOVA

ROMANIA

BULGARIA

Black Sea

GEORGIA

ARMENIA

AZERBAIJAN

RUSSIA

KAZAKHSTAN

MONGOLIA

Sea of
Okhotsk

Sea of
Japan

NORTH
KOREA

SOUTH
KOREA

JAPAN

TURKEY

GREECE

Mediterranean Sea

MALTA

CYPRUS

LEBANON

ISRAEL

Corsica
(FRANCE)

Sardinia
(ITALY)

allorca
PAIN)

IRAQ

SYRIA

JORDAN

KUWAIT

IRAN

Caspian Sea

Aral
Sea

UZBEKISTAN

TURKMENISTAN

TAJIKISTAN

KYRGYZSTAN

AFGHANISTAN

PAKISTAN

NEPAL

BHUTAN

CHINA

INDIA

TAIWAN

Philippine
Sea

PHILIPPINES

PACIFIC
OCEAN

Tropic of Cancer

NMARK

NIGER

CHAD

LIBYA

EGYPT

SAUDI
ARABIA

QATAR

UNITED ARAB
EMIRATES

YEMEN

OMAN

BAHRAIN

Red Sea

TUNISIA

GERIA

NIGERIA

SUDAN

ERITREA

DJIBOUTI

ETHIOPIA

SOMALIA

Arabian
Sea

Bay of
Bengal

BANGLADESH

MYANMAR

LAOS

THAILAND

CAMBODIA

VIETNAM

South
China
Sea

MARSHALL
ISLANDS

MICRONESIA

PALAU

CAMEROON

CENTRAL AFRICAN
REPUBLIC

DEMOCRATIC
REPUBLIC OF
CONGO

UGANDA

KENYA

14

SRI LANKA

MALDIVES

MALAYSIA

15

Equator

NAURU

KIRIBATI

QUATORIAL
GUINEA

OME &
CIPÉ

GABON

RWANDA

BURUNDI

TANZANIA

SEYCHELLES

INDONESIA

PAPUA
NEW
GUINEA

EAST TIMOR

SOLOMON
ISLANDS

TUVALU

Angola

ANGOLA

ZAMBIA

MALAWI

MOZAMBIQUE

COMOROS

MADAGASCAR

MAURITIUS

INDIAN
OCEAN

Coral Sea

VANUATU

New Caledonia
(FRANCE)

FIJI

SAMOA

TONGA

NAMIBIA

ZIMBABWE

BOTSWANA

SWAZILAND

LESOTHO

SOUTH
AFRICA

AUSTRALIA

Tropic of Capricorn

Tasman Sea

NEW
ZEALAND

SOUTHERN OCEAN

Antarctic Circle

Antarctica

St. Peter's, Vatican City

Largest countries

These figures are based on total land area, including inland water, such as rivers and lakes. If the water area was not taken into account, China would be second largest, at 3,600,947 sq. mi. (9,326,410 sq km), the U.S. third with 3,537,439 sq. mi. (9,161,923 sq km) and Canada fourth at 3,511,023 sq. mi. (9,093,507 sq km).

Largest countries

Country	Area sq. mi.	(sq km)
Russia	6,592,770	(17,075,200)
Canada	3,855,105	(9,984,670)
U.S.	3,794,085	(9,826,630)
China	3,705,405	(9,596,960)
Brazil	3,286,490	(8,511,965)
Australia	2,967,910	(7,686,850)

Smallest countries

Country	Area sq. mi.	(sq km)
Vatican City	0.17	(0.44)
Monaco	0.77	(2)
Nauru	8	(21)
Tuvalu	10	(26)
Bermuda	20	(53)
San Marino	24	(61)
Liechtenstein	62	(160)

Biggest landlocked countries

A landlocked country has no coastline. This means that it has no direct access to the sea and fishing. Also, people and goods traveling to and from the country must go through another country. This may be difficult or expensive.

There are more than 40 landlocked countries in the world. The largest, Kazakhstan, has a coast on the Caspian Sea — which is a landlocked sea. The largest landlocked European country is Hungary (35,637 sq. mi. [92,300 sq km]). Europe also contains the world's smallest landlocked countries — Andorra, Liechtenstein, San Marino and Vatican City. All are less than 200 sq. mi. (518 sq km) in size. Liechtenstein and Uzbekistan are both double-landlocked. This means that they are surrounded by other landlocked countries.

Kazakhstan 1,049,155 sq. mi. (2,717,300 sq km)
Mongolia 603,908 sq. mi. (1,564,116 sq km)
Chad 495,755 sq. mi. (1,284,000 sq km)
Niger 489,190 sq. mi. (1,267,000 sq km)
Mali 478,765 sq. mi. (1,240,000 sq km)
Ethiopia 435,186 sq. mi. (1,127,127 sq km)
Bolivia 424,165 sq. mi. (1,098,580 sq km)

Longest and shortest frontiers

A country's frontier is made up of the combined length of all its land borders.

Longest
China 13,743 mi. (22,117 km)
Russia 12,488 mi. (20,097 km)
Brazil 10,488 mi. (16,885 km)
India 8,763 mi. (14,103 km)
U.S. 7,478 mi. (12,034 km)

Shortest
Vatican City 2.4 mi. (3.2 km)
Monaco 2.7 mi. (4.4 km)
Cuba 18 mi. (29.0 km)
San Marino 24 mi. (39.0 km)
Qatar 37 mi. (60 km)

Biggest and smallest populations

In most countries, more people are born every day than die, so population figures are going up all the time. China has the biggest population, but India is catching up fast.

Biggest population

Country	Population
China	1,321,359,943
India	1,169,733,970
U.S.	307,201,745
Indonesia	229,566,804
Brazil	194,747,347
Pakistan	155,360,000
Nigeria	151,030,462
Bangladesh	145,386,049
Russia	141,292,370
Japan	128,082,045

Smallest population

Country	Population
Vatican City	545
Tuvalu	9,971
Nauru	10,161
Palau	20,746
San Marino	30,475
Monaco	33,834
Liechtenstein	35,639
St. Christopher and Nevis	49,423
Marshall Islands	53,730
Dominica	70,545

Population density

In densely populated countries, lots of people live on a small amount of land, usually in cities. The least densely populated countries are usually difficult for people to live in. The climate may be very cold or very hot, or there may be large areas of mountain, desert or forest.

Most densely populated countries

Monaco 44,939 per sq mile (17,351 people per sq km)
Singapore 19,896 per sq mile (7,672 people per sq km)
Malta 3,326 per sq mile (1,284 people per sq km)
Vatican City 3,209 per sq mile (1,239 people per sq km)
Bahrain 2,985 per sq mile (1,164 people per sq km)

Least densely populated countries

Mongolia 4.43 per sq mile (1.71 people per sq km)
Namibia 6.81 per sq mile (2.63 people per sq km)
Australia 6.89 per sq mile (2.66 people per sq km)
Mauritania 7.72 per sq mile (2.98 people per sq km)
Iceland 8.13 per sq mile (3.14 people per sq km)

Crowded shopping street in Shanghai, China

Country development

These rankings from the United Nations are based on a range of factors, including how long people can expect to live, how much money they earn, education level and quality of life.

Most developed	Least developed
1 Iceland	1 Sierra Leone
2 Norway	2 Central African Republic
3 Canada	3 Democratic Republic of Congo
4 Australia	
5 Ireland	4 Liberia
15 U.S.	5 Mozambique
21 UK	6 Niger

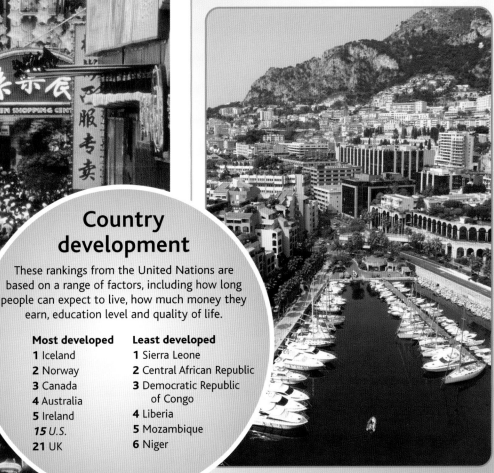

Monaco

Changing names

Many cities change their names after the countries they are in become independent. Others are renamed after political changes, such as those ending the former Soviet Union. Some changes come from variations in the way in which foreign languages are translated from one alphabet to another.

Was called/country	Now called (since)
Batavia, Indonesia	**Jakarta** (1949)
Bombay, India	**Mumbai** (1995)
Christiana, Norway	**Oslo** (1924)
Byzantium/Constantinople, Turkey	**Istanbul** (1930)
Danzig, Poland	**Gdansk** (1945)
Leningrad, USSR	**St. Petersburg**, Russia (1991)
Léopoldville, Belgian Congo	**Kinshasa**, Zaire (1960)
New Amsterdam, America	**New York**, U.S. (1664)
Pretoria, South Africa	**Tshwane** (2005)
Rangoon, Burma	**Yangon**, Myanmar (1989)
Saigon, Vietnam	**Ho Chi Minh City** (1975)
Salisbury, Rhodesia	**Harare**, Zimbabwe (1980)
Santa Isabel, Equatorial Guinea	**Malabo** (1973)
Tsaritsyn/Stalingrad, USSR	**Volgograd**, Russia (1961)

Cities with the most people*

1 Tokyo, Japan	37,468,203
2 Mexico City, Mexico	23,293,783
3 New York, U.S.	23,141,893
4 Seoul, South Korea	22,456,200
5 Mumbai (Bombay), India	21,347,412
6 São Paulo, Brazil	20,534,112
7 Manila, Philippines	19,888,419
8 Jakarta, Indonesia	18,924,470
9 Delhi, India	18,639,762
10 Los Angeles, U.S.	17,881,561

*Estimated figures for city and adjoining populated areas 2009. This calculation applies throughout this section. Source: World Gazetteer.

🔍 www.citypopulation.de/cities.html   **search**

Highest towns and cities

Some towns and cities are in surprisingly high places. The Chinese city of Wenchuan, founded in 1955, is at more than half the height of Mt. Everest. Even the towns and cities at the bottom of this list are at more than one-third the height of Everest.

1 Wenchuan, China — 16,729 ft. (5,099 m)
2 Potosí, Bolivia — 13,045 ft. (3,976 m)
3 Oruro, Bolivia — 12,146 ft. (3,702 m)
4 Lhasa, China — 12,087 ft. (3,684 m)
5 La Paz, Bolivia — 11,916 ft. (3,632 m)
6 Cuzco, Peru — 11,152 ft. (3,399 m)
7 Huancayo, Peru — 10,659 ft. (3,249 m)
8 Sucre, Bolivia — 9,301 ft. (2,835 m)
9 Tunja, Colombia — 9,252 ft. (2,820 m)
10 Quito, Ecuador — 9,249 ft. (2,819 m)

La Paz, the world's highest capital city

What is a city?

A city is a large town. In some countries, a city has a special status. In the United States it is an urban area with its own government.

A town is a densely populated area with a defined boundary and its own government. A town is smaller than a city and larger than a village.

A village is a small group of houses and other buildings in a country area.

A hamlet is a small village or a cluster of houses in a country area.

A settlement is a small group of inhabited buildings, or a small countryside community, such as a ranch or farm with a few dwellings.

The rediscovered city of Troy

Lost cities

There are some cities that were very famous in the past but have since been destroyed or abandoned.

Angkor, Cambodia
Angkor was once the largest city in the world and more than a million people lived there. The city had an area of more than 30 sq. mi. (78 sq km) and was surrounded by a water-filled moat. It was abandoned in about AD 1100. Frenchman Henri Mouhot was the first westerner to discover the city, in 1861.

Atlantis
Some people believe that there was a city and island of Atlantis, perhaps in the Mediterranean Sea, that was destroyed by an earthquake and flooding almost 12,000 years ago. No one knows exactly where it was or even whether it really existed.

Chichén Itzá, Mexico
Chichén Itzá was once the center of the Mayan empire. It was built in about AD 400 and had many buildings used in Mayan rituals. The city was abandoned in AD 1200.

Cliff Palace (Mesa Verde), Colorado, United States
This Native American city was built on a cliffside, but was abandoned during a long drought in the late 13th century. It lay unknown until December 18, 1888, when Richard Wetherill, a local farmer, spotted it while looking for stray cattle.

Machu Picchu, Peru
The fortified Inca city on top of a mountain was stumbled on in 1911 by American explorer Hiram Bingham. He was searching for Vilcabamba, another lost Inca city.

Pompeii, Italy
The entire city was buried by volcanic ash when Mt. Vesuvius erupted in AD 79. Nearby Herculaneum was buried at the same time. Excavations began in 1748, and many treasures have been uncovered, including beautifully preserved murals (wall paintings). Plaster casts have been made of the bodies of inhabitants who were buried beneath the debris.

Troy, Turkey
Troy was once thought to have existed only in legends, but its site was discovered in the 1870s.

Ur, Iraq
Ur was once one of the greatest cities in the world, but was abandoned in the 4th century BC. Its magnificent royal tombs and other sites were excavated by archaeologists in 1922–34 and many treasures were discovered.

One and only

The only city in two continents: Istanbul, Turkey, is partly in Europe and partly in Asia.

The only city center with no cars: Venice. Its only traffic is boats on the canals.

The only non-U.S. capital city named after a U.S. president: Monrovia, the capital of Liberia, in Africa, was named after U.S. president James Monroe.

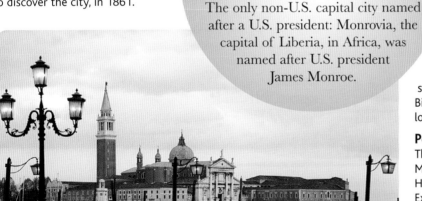

See also
World civilizations and empires: pages 106–107

Grand Canal, Venice

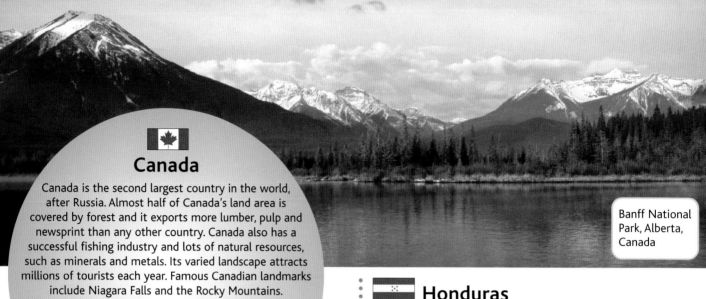

Banff National Park, Alberta, Canada

Canada

Canada is the second largest country in the world, after Russia. Almost half of Canada's land area is covered by forest and it exports more lumber, pulp and newsprint than any other country. Canada also has a successful fishing industry and lots of natural resources, such as minerals and metals. Its varied landscape attracts millions of tourists each year. Famous Canadian landmarks include Niagara Falls and the Rocky Mountains.

Area 3,855,105 sq. mi.
(9,984,670 sq km)
Country population 32,213,280
Capital city (pop)
Ottawa (1,152,721)
Official languages English/French
Currency
Canadian dollar

United States

The U.S. is made up of 50 states (including Alaska and Hawaii) and the District of Columbia, which contains the capital city, Washington. It includes a huge variety of landscapes, from hot deserts to snow-covered mountains. The country was once a colony under British rule but has been independent since 1776. It is now the world's wealthiest country and a great economic and military superpower.

Area 3,794,085 sq. mi. (9,826,630 sq km)
Country population 305,072,714
Capital city (pop) Washington, D.C. (8,281,142)
Official language English
Currency U.S. dollar

Mexico

Some of the world's oldest civilizations have lived in Mexico, such as the Aztecs and Mayans. Nowadays, many tourists visit and it has plenty of natural resources. However, almost half the people are very poor and many try to cross the border into the United States every year. Some of them are arrested by border patrols.

Area 761,605 sq. mi.
(1,972,550 sq km)
Country population
107,236,677
Capital city (pop) Mexico City (22,968,205)
Official language Spanish
Currency Peso

Guatemala

Guatemala is one of Central America's most beautiful countries, with a dramatic landscape of forests, lakes and volcanoes. It is also one of the poorest and most violent. The country is still suffering from the aftereffects of a long civil war (1960–96). Two-thirds of Guatemalan children live in poverty.

Area 42,045 sq. mi.
(108,890 sq km)
Country population 13,994,079
Capital city (pop) Guatemala City (3,293,168)
Official language Spanish
Currency Quetzal

Honduras

Honduras lies in Central America between the Caribbean Sea and the Atlantic Ocean. It is one of the world's poorest countries, although it has valuable stocks of lumber. In 1998 Hurricane Mitch caused $4 billion worth of damages.

Area 43,280 sq. mi. (112,090 sq km)
Country population 7,761,830
Capital city (pop) Tegucigalpa (2,063,368)
Official language Spanish
Currency Lempira

El Salvador

The tiny country of El Salvador is on Central America's Pacific coast. It often suffers hurricanes and earthquakes. Coffee is a major crop, but El Salvador relies heavily on aid money from other countries.

Area 8,125 sq. mi. (21,040 sq km)
Country population 7,218,048
Capital city (pop) San Salvador (1,912,758)
Official language Spanish
Currency U.S. dollar

Nicaragua

Nicaragua is the largest country in Central America. It is one of the poorest countries in the Western world and half its people are very poor indeed. In 1998, Hurricane Mitch caused great damage and left 20 percent of Nicaraguans homeless.

Area 50,000 sq. mi.
(129,494 sq km)
Country population
5,353,272
Capital city (pop)
Managua (1,752,912)
Official language
Spanish
Currency Córdoba

Panama

Panama is a narrow strip of land stretching between North and South America. It has coastlines on the Atlantic Ocean and the Pacific Ocean and has a canal, which connects the two oceans. Panama receives money from the many ships that use the canal each year and has other successful industries, but nearly 40 percent of the people are poor.

Area 30,195 sq. mi.
(78,200 sq km)
Country population
3,426,464
Capital city (pop)
Panama City
(1,242,192)
Official language
Spanish
Currency Balboa

Costa Rica

Costa Rica is one of the most successful Central American countries and has a good standard of living. Its landscape is beautiful, with many mountains and tropical forests, and tourism is increasing. However, the country is also becoming more and more involved in the illegal drug trade.

Area 19,730 sq. mi. (51,100 sq km)
Country population 4,572,364
Capital city (pop) San José (1,666,585)
Official language Spanish
Currency Costa Rican colón

St. Kitts and Nevis

The Caribbean islands of St. Kitts (also known as St. Christopher) and Nevis became independent of the UK in 1983. Most of the people are descended from slaves brought from West Africa to work on the islands. Sugar has always been the island's main crop, but tourism and financial services are now important industries.

Area 101 sq. mi. (261 sq km)
Country population 48,925
Capital city (pop) Basseterre (13,245)
Official language English
Currency East Caribbean dollar

The Bahamas

The Bahamas is made up of more than 700 islands, which lie southeast of Florida in the Atlantic Ocean. The islands were ruled by the British, but became independent in 1973. Queen Elizabeth II is still the head of state. About 40 percent of people work in tourism, but banking and finance are also important.

Area 5,380 sq. mi. (13,940 sq km)
Country population 335,187
Capital city (pop) Nassau (235,102)
Official language English
Currency Bahamian dollar

Jamaica

The Caribbean island of Jamaica became independent of the UK in 1962, but has remained in the Commonwealth. Tourism is its main industry, but many visitors are put off by the island's poverty and violence. Jamaica has one of the world's highest murder rates.

Area 4,244 sq. mi. (10,991 sq km)
Country population 2,687,852
Capital city (pop) Kingston (941,433)
Official language English
Currency Jamaican dollar

Dominican Republic

The Dominican Republic makes up the eastern two-thirds of the island of Hispaniola, sharing it with Haiti. It is the oldest European settlement in America. The Dominican Republic is one of the Caribbean's poorest countries, but it is now very popular with tourists.

Area 18,815 sq. mi. (48,730 sq km)
Country population 9,679,893
Capital city (pop) Santo Domingo (3,338,850)
Official language Spanish
Currency Dominican Republic peso

Belize

Belize was a British colony called British Honduras, but became independent in 1981. Queen Elizabeth II is still the head of state. The coral reef off the coast is the world's second largest after Australia's Great Barrier Reef. Belize is now popular with tourists.

Area 8,865 sq. mi. (22,966 sq km)
Country population 321,243
Capital city (pop) Belmopan (17,570)
Official language English
Currency Belize dollar

Antigua and Barbuda

The Caribbean islands of Antigua and Barbuda were settled by the Spanish, the French and the British before becoming independent in 1981. They are still part of the Commonwealth and Queen Elizabeth II is the head of state. The islands are popular with tourists.

Area 171 sq. mi. (443 sq km)
Country population 85,420
Capital city (pop) St. John's (22,077)
Official language English
Currency East Caribbean dollar

Haiti

Haiti shares the island of Hispaniola with the Dominican Republic. In 1804, Haiti was the first Caribbean state to become independent. Now Haiti is the poorest country in the Americas, after years of dictatorship and violence. Financial help from the EU and U.S. was stopped in 2000 after unfair elections, and drug-trafficking is a big problem.

Area 10,715 sq. mi. (27,750 sq km)
Country population 8,558,135
Capital city (pop) Port-au-Prince (1,720,655)
Official languages Haitian Creole/French
Currency Gourde

Cuba

Cuba is 93 mi. (150 km) south of Florida and is the largest island in the Caribbean. It has a Communist government, which has been led by Fidel Castro since 1959. Cuba attracts more and more tourists, but the collapse of the Soviet Union and trade restrictions put on Cuba by the U.S. have caused financial problems.

Area 42,805 sq. mi. (110,860 sq km)
Country population 11,237,171
Capital city (pop) Havana (2,599,655)
Official language Spanish
Currency Cuban peso

A street in Havana, Cuba

St. Vincent and the Grenadines

This Caribbean nation includes 33 small islands. It became independent from Britain in 1979, but it is still a member of the Commonwealth. Bananas are the main crop. Many tourists visit the islands.

Area 150 sq. mi.
(389 sq km)
Country population 102,133
Capital city (pop) Kingstown (16,610)
Official language English
Currency East Caribbean dollar

Boats docked near the island of St. Vincent

Dominica

This tropical, mountainous Caribbean island was once under British rule. It became independent in 1978. Dominica's main exports are bananas and fruit juices, but the crops are often destroyed by hurricanes.

Area 290 sq. mi. (750 sq km)
Country population 70,857
Capital city (pop) Roseau (13,803)
Official language English
Currency East Caribbean dollar

Barbados

This Caribbean island became an independent state in 1966, but it remains part of the Commonwealth. Queen Elizabeth II is the head of state. The main industries are tourism and sugar manufacturing.

Area 166 sq. mi. (431 sq km)
Country population 276,965
Capital city (pop) Bridgetown (92,467)
Official language English
Currency Barbados dollar

Grenada

Grenada lies between the Caribbean Sea and the Atlantic Ocean, north of Trinidad and Tobago. Nearly 400,000 tourists visit Grenada every year. The island exports spices, and about a quarter of the world's nutmeg comes from there.

Area 133 sq. mi. (344 sq km)
Country population 106,478
Capital city (pop) St. George's (5,159)
Official language English
Currency East Caribbean dollar

Trinidad and Tobago

The Caribbean islands of Trinidad and Tobago lie northwest of Venezuela. They have large reserves of oil and natural gas and are among the richest of all Caribbean nations. Tobago is quieter than Trinidad. Both islands are popular with tourists.

Area 1,980 sq. mi. (5,128 sq km)
Country population 1,339,932
Capital city (pop) Port of Spain (49,959)
Official language English
Currency Trinidad and Tobago dollar

South America

Argentina

Argentina was once ruled by Spain, but it became independent in 1816. This South American country is famous for its beef and has large mineral deposits.

Area 1,068,300 sq. mi. (2,766,890 sq km)
Country population 39,792,277
Capital city (pop) Buenos Aires (14,197,085)
Official language Spanish
Currency Peso

Venezuela

Venezuela is a land of great natural beauty in northern South America. Angel Falls is the world's highest waterfall, and Maracaibo is the largest lake in South America. Venezuela has large reserves of oil, coal and gold, but almost half of Venezuelans live in poverty.

Area 352,145 sq. mi. (912,050 sq km)
Country population 28,522,297
Capital city (pop) Caracas (4,259,737)
Official language Spanish
Currency Bolívar

Suriname

This is the smallest independent nation in South America. It was governed by the Netherlands but became independent in 1975. Suriname has large amounts of lumber as well as bauxite and gold, but 70 percent of the people are still very poor.

Area 63,040 sq. mi. (163,270 sq km)
Country population 439,117
Capital city (pop) Paramaribo (226,124)
Official language Dutch
Currency Suriname dollar

St. Lucia

This mountainous island lies between the Atlantic Ocean and the Caribbean Sea. It is famous for its two large, cone-shaped peaks known as the Pitons. Bananas are the island's main crop, but banking and tourism are also important.

Area 238 sq. mi. (616 sq km)
Country population 170,718
Capital city (pop) Castries (9,914)
Official language English
Currency East Caribbean dollar

Colombia

Colombia is in the northwest of South America. The main crops are coffee, bananas and sugar, and the country has oil and mineral reserves. Colombia is also the world's leading producer of cocaine.

Area 439,735 sq. mi. (1,138,910 sq km)
Country population 44,459,803
Capital city (pop) Bogotá (8,148,808)
Official language Spanish
Currency Colombian peso

 ## Uruguay

Uruguay is the second-smallest country in South America. It is wealthier than most South American nations because of its livestock, tourism and banking industries. It has a good welfare system and its people are well educated.

Area 68,040 sq. mi. (176,220 sq km)
Country population 3,383,284
Capital city (pop) Montevideo (1,843,196)
Official language Spanish
Currency Uruguayan peso

 ## Ecuador

Ecuador lies on the Equator and stretches across the Andes Mountains. The country's main exports are fish, bananas, cocoa and coffee. Oil was discovered there in 1972.

Area 109,485 sq. mi. (283,560 sq km)
Country population 835,076
Capital city (pop) Quito (1,594,883)
Official language Spanish
Currency U.S. dollar

 ## Bolivia

The Andes mountain range crosses Bolivia. The Bolivian capital La Paz is in the Andes and is the highest capital city in the world. Bolivia is one of only two landlocked countries in South America.

Area 424,165 sq. mi. (1,098,580 sq km)
Country population 10,300,696
Capital city (pop) La Paz (2,175,731)
Official language Spanish
Currency Boliviano

Peru

Peru lies on South America's Pacific coast. It has been home to famous ancient civilizations, including the Inca Empire. Peru has important natural resources, including gold and oil, but they have not yet been developed.

Area 496,225 sq. mi. (1,285,220 sq km)
Country population 26,901,638
Capital city (pop) Lima (8,057,397)
Official languages Spanish/Quechua
Currency New sol

 ## Paraguay

The Republic of Paraguay is landlocked. It has one of the smallest populations in South America. Alfredo Stroessner, the region's longest ruling dictator, was overthrown in 1989, but Paraguay is still struggling with political and financial problems.

Area 157,045 sq. mi. (406,750 sq km)
Country population 6,243,757
Capital city (pop) Asunción (2,014,725)
Official languages Spanish/Guaraní
Currency Guaraní

 ## Guyana

Guyana is the only country in South America where English is the official language. Its natural resources include gold and diamonds, but it is very poor and has political problems. The country has many fascinating animals and plants and is popular with tourists interested in nature.

Area 83,000 sq. mi. (214,970 sq km)
Country population 742,165
Capital city (pop) Georgetown (247,588)
Official language English
Currency Guyana dollar

Statue of Christ, Rio de Janeiro, Brazil

 ## Brazil

Area 3,286,490 sq. mi. (8,511,965 sq km)
Country population 192,047,523
Capital city (pop) Brasília (2,492,188)
Official language Portuguese
Currency Real

Brazil covers nearly half of South America. It contains the world's second-longest river, the Amazon, and vast tropical rainforests. About 82 percent of Brazil's population lives in cities, which are mostly on the coast in the south and southeast of the country. Brazil is the leading nation in South America but there are wide divisions between rich and poor.

 ## Chile

Chile is an extremely long, narrow country, which lies between the Andes Mountains and the Pacific Ocean. It is one of the most successful nations in South America and has many natural resources, including minerals and lumber, as well as thriving agriculture and fishing industries.

Area 292,260 sq. mi. (756,950 sq km)
Country population 16,998,021
Capital city (pop) Santiago (5,099,129)
Official language Spanish
Currency Chilean peso

Norway

Norway is famous for its fiords. The population is small and has a very good standard of living, thanks to the country's plentiful natural resources. Only Russia and Saudi Arabia export more oil than Norway, and it is the world's biggest exporter of seafood.

Area 125,021 sq. mi. (323,802 sq km)
Country population 4,714,633
Capital city (pop) Oslo (846,584)
Official language Norwegian
Currency Krone

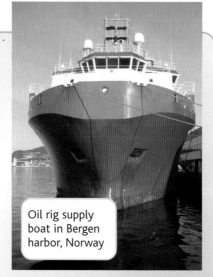

Oil rig supply boat in Bergen harbor, Norway

Ireland

Ireland was divided in the 1920s, when 26 counties in the south gained independence from the United Kingdom. Since then there has been conflict in Northern Ireland between those who want to remain part of the United Kingdom and those who want a united, independent Ireland. Since Ireland joined the European Community in 1973 it has become a modern, high-tech nation with successful industry. It began using the euro in January 1999, along with 10 other nations.

Area 27,135 sq. mi. (70,200 sq km)
Country population 4,364,523
Capital city (pop) Dublin (1,058,265)
Official languages Irish/English
Currency Euro

Denmark

Denmark shares a border with Germany and is the smallest, most southerly Scandinavian nation. It is a wealthy, high-tech country and has all the oil and natural gas it needs. The standard of living is high. Denmark is a monarchy and the kingdom includes the Faeroe Islands and Greenland.

Area 16,639 sq. mi. (43,094 sq km)
Country population 5,466,444
Capital city (pop) Copenhagen (1,082,884)
Official language Danish
Currency Danish krone

Finland

Since the end of World War II, Finland has changed from being a rural country covered with dense forest into a modern nation. It has very successful industries and an excellent welfare system. Finland joined the European Union in 1995 and adopted the euro as its currency in 2002.

Area 130,560 sq. mi. (338,145 sq km)
Country population 5,291,078
Capital city (pop) Helsinki (1,262,805)
Official languages Finnish/Swedish
Currency Euro

Luxembourg

Luxembourg is landlocked by Belgium, Germany and France. Its inhabitants have an amazingly high standard of living. Steel was once the main industry, but financial services have now become more important.

Area 999 sq. mi. (2,586 sq km)
Country population 463,129
Capital city (pop) Luxembourg (75,552)
Official languages French/German
Currency Euro

Window in Heidelberg Castle, Germany

Sweden

Sweden is a rich country with a high standard of living. Swedes have one of the world's longest life expectancies. The country has many natural resources including iron ore, lead, granite, zinc and forests. Forests cover about half the land and there are important lumber and paper industries.

Area 173,732 sq. mi. (449,964 sq km)
Country population 9,146,262
Capital city (pop) Stockholm (1,737,995)
Official language Swedish
Currency Swedish krona

Germany

Germany was divided after World War II. The Soviet Union and Poland claimed the East, and the U.S., UK and France controlled the West. The East became a Communist state and the West became a democracy. Thousands of East Germans fled to the West. The Berlin Wall was built in 1961 to close the border and stop the flow of people. The decline of the USSR led to the fall of the Berlin Wall in 1989 and Germany was reunited in 1990. Today, 80 percent of Germany's people live in the West, and the effects of Communism are still felt in the East.

Area 137,847 sq. mi. (357,021 sq km)
Country population 82,191,106
Capital city (pop) Berlin (4,040,690)
Official language German
Currency Euro

Iceland

Iceland is a volcanic island and is the most westerly country in Europe. Its capital city is the furthest north in the world. Iceland is a wealthy country with low unemployment and a good welfare system. Fishing provides 70 percent of its exports, which could cause problems as fish stocks decline.

Area 39,769 sq. mi. (103,000 sq km)
Country population 315,450
Capital city (pop) Reykjavíc (201,008)
Official language Icelandic
Currency Icelandic króna

People bathing in the Blue Lagoon, Iceland

The Netherlands

The Netherlands is a low-lying country and much of it has been reclaimed from the sea. Nearly a quarter of the land lies below sea level, which makes it vulnerable to flooding, despite coastal defences and a network of dikes and canals. Banking, shipping and fishing all are important industries. The Netherlands is the sixth-largest exporter in the world.

Area 16,033 sq. mi. (41,526 sq km)
Country population 16,409,082
Capital city (pop) Amsterdam (749,372)
Official language Dutch
Currency Euro

Belgium

Belgium is divided into Flanders (in the northwest) and Wallonia (in the southeast). Brussels is the headquarters of the European Union. This has brought wealth to the country as multinational companies have settled in the city. Belgium is well known for its fine chocolates and beer.

Area 11,787 sq. mi. (30,528 sq km)
Country population 10,629,889
Capital city (pop) Brussels (2,175,008)
Official languages Flemish/French/German
Currency Euro

France

France is the largest country in Western Europe and a key member of the European Union. It has a varied landscape ranging from coastal plains to the Alps in the southeast. Farms and forests cover a large proportion of the country, and agricultural products — particularly wine and liqueurs — are major exports. France once had one of the world's largest empires. Most of its former colonies are now independent, but French Guiana, Guadeloupe, Martinique, Réunion, Mayotte, St. Pierre and Miquelon, French Polynesia, New Caledonia, Wallis and Futuna and the Southern and Antarctic Territories all still have links with France.

Area 248,428 sq. mi. (643,427 sq km)
Country population 62,015,826
Capital city (pop) Paris (11,818,503)
Official language French
Currency Euro

United Kingdom

The United Kingdom is made up of Great Britain (England, Scotland and Wales) and Northern Ireland. Although it is a small country, the UK has had a huge influence on the world because of its cultural, military and industrial strengths. At one time, it controlled a vast empire of lands across the globe and was the world's leading industrial nation. Traditional manufacturing industries are now less important. In the 21st century the UK's main industries are technology, tourism and services such as banking, and it is still an important economic power.

Area 94,525 sq. mi. (244,820 sq km)
Country population 61,264,416
Capital city (pop) London (12,577,225)
Language English
Currency British pound

Monaco

Monaco is a principality — it is ruled by a prince. It is surrounded by France and is the second smallest independent state in the world. It has no income tax and low business taxes so rich people flock there to escape taxes.

Area 0.77 sq. mi. (2 sq km)
Country population 33,639
Capital city (pop) Monaco (955)
Official language French
Currency Euro

Plaza de España in Seville, Spain

Spain

Spain covers most of the Iberian peninsula. The country has many cultures. Basque, Catalan, Galician and Valencian are spoken in different regions, but Castilian Spanish is the official language. There are 19 regions with their own elected authorities. There is a campaign for independence by the Basque country in the north, which has caused ongoing problems for the government. Spain is the world's second most popular tourist destination (after France) and has more than 50 million visitors every year. The fishing industry is one of the biggest in Europe, but unemployment is high.

Area 194,897 sq. mi. (504,782 sq km)
Country population 4,113,018
Capital city (pop) Madrid (6,270,551)
Official language Castilian Spanish
Currency Euro

Portugal

Portugal lies to the west of Spain on the Iberian peninsula. It is one of the European Union's least developed countries and has the highest number of people working on the land. Portugal's economy has grown rapidly since it joined the European Union in 1986. Tourism is one of its fastest growing industries. Portugal once had a vast empire, stretching across the Americas, Africa and Asia. Over 177 million people worldwide speak Portuguese.

Area 35,672 sq. mi. (92,391 sq km)
Country population 10,634,138
Capital city (pop) Lisbon (2,634,878)
Official language Portuguese
Currency Euro

Malta

Malta, which includes the neighboring island of Gozo, used to be under British rule. It became independent in 1964, but remains a part of the Commonwealth. Malta became the European Union's smallest new member in 2004. Tourism is the island's most important industry and Malta has more than a million visitors every year.

Area 122 sq. mi. (316 sq km)
Country population 403,266
Capital city (pop) Valletta (255,377)
Official languages Maltese/English
Currency Maltese lira

Vatican City State

The Vatican City is the smallest country in the world, both in area and population. It is surrounded by the city of Rome. The Vatican is home to the Pope and it is the spiritual center of the Roman Catholic Church. It depends on contributions from Roman Catholics all over the world for its income, and the sale of souvenirs and publications.

Area 0.17 sq. mi. (0.44 sq km)
Country population 549
Capital city (pop) Vatican City (549)
Official languages Latin/Italian
Currency Euro

San Marino

San Marino is entirely surrounded by Italy and it is the third-smallest state in Europe. The tiny republic attracts about three million tourists every year. San Marino's inhabitants (known as Sammarinese) enjoy the world's sixth-highest income per person.

Area 24 sq. mi. (61 sq km)
Country population 30,684
Capital city (pop) San Marino (4,638)
Official language Italian
Currency Euro

Andorra

Andorra is a small principality (a state ruled by a prince), which dates from 1278. It lies in the mountains between France and Spain. Tourism is its main industry, but financial services are also becoming important.

Area 181 sq. mi. (468 sq km)
Country population 86,417
Capital city (pop) Andorra la Vella (25,204)
Official language Catalan
Currency Euro

Estonia

The small Baltic state of Estonia regained its independence in 1991 when the Soviet Union collapsed. It was one of the Eastern European nations that joined the European Union in 2004.

Area 17,462 sq. mi. (45,226 sq km)
Country population 1,339,330
Capital city (pop) Tallinn (394,898)
Official language Estonian
Currency Kroon

Italy

Italy is a long, narrow country reaching into the Mediterranean Sea. It includes the islands of Sicily and Sardinia among others. Italy can be divided into two: the wealthy, industrial north, and the poorer south, where most people work on the land and around 20 percent of the population is unemployed. About 40 million foreign tourists visit Italy every year, many of them to see its beautiful cities, which include Rome, Venice and Florence.

Area 116,305 sq. mi. (301,230 sq km)
Country population 59,279,992
Capital city (pop) Rome (3,858,111)
Official language Italian
Currency Euro

Austria

Austria is a small, mountainous country. It is landlocked by the Czech Republic, Slovakia, Italy, Slovenia, Hungary, Germany, Switzerland and Liechtenstein. It was once the center of the powerful Austro-Hungarian empire, until its defeat in World War I. It was occupied by Nazi Germany and then by the Allies after World War II. Since the war Austria has flourished, and it is now a popular vacation spot.

Area 32,380 sq. mi. (83,870 sq km)
Country population 8,370,759
Capital city (pop) Vienna (2,123,722)
Official language German
Currency Euro

Switzerland

Switzerland is the most mountainous country in Europe. The Alps occupy 60 percent of its land area. It has a very high income per person, low unemployment and its people have a long life expectancy. Switzerland was not involved in either world war and has not joined the European Union.

Area 15,940 sq. mi. (41,290 sq km)
Country population 7,555,082
Capital city (pop) Bern (121,837)
Official languages German/French/Italian/Romansch
Currency Swiss franc

Belarus

Belarus became independent when the Soviet Union collapsed in 1991. It continues to have close ties with Russia. The country still suffers from the effects of nuclear fallout from the 1986 Chernobyl accident, which took place in neighboring Ukraine.

Area 80,155 sq. mi. (207,600 sq km)
Country population 9,615,624
Capital city (pop) Minsk (1,753,547)
Official languages Belarusian/Russian
Currency Belarusian ruble

Czech Republic

The Czech Republic was part of Czechoslovakia until it split from Slovakia in 1993. It now attracts investment from other countries and has a thriving tourism industry. The country joined the European Union in 2004.

Area 30,450 sq. mi. (78,866 sq km)
Country population 10,310,957
Capital city (pop) Prague (1,406,142)
Official language Czech
Currency Koruna

Astronomical clock in Prague, Czech Republic

Poland

Poland is the largest nation in Central Europe and has the highest population. It was devastated by World War II, when more than six million people died — more than in any other country. In 1989 Poland was the first Eastern European nation to topple its Communist leaders. In May 2004 it joined the European Union.

Area 120,730 sq. mi. (312,685 sq km)
Country population 38,077,421
Capital city (pop) Warsaw (2,251,474)
Official language Polish
Currency Zloty

Latvia

Latvia is bounded by the Baltic Sea, Estonia, Lithuania, Belarus and Russia. It became independent of the Soviet Union in 1991 and in 2004 it was accepted into the European Union.

Area 24,938 sq. mi. (64,589 sq km)
Country population 2,268,001
Capital city (pop) Riga (808,248)
Official language Latvian
Currency Lats

Liechtenstein

Liechtenstein is the sixth-smallest country in the world. Its low taxes have encouraged extraordinary economic growth, and thousands of foreign companies have bank accounts there.

Area 62 sq. mi. (160 sq km)
Country population 35,406
Capital city (pop) Vaduz (5,088)
Official language German
Currency Swiss franc

Lithuania

Lithuania became independent of the Soviet Union in 1991. It used to depend on Russia, but more recently it has developed trade links with the West. It joined the European Union in 2004.

Area 25,174 sq. mi. (65,200 sq km)
Country population 3,366,913
Capital city (pop) Vilnius (543,642)
Official language Lithuanian
Currency Litas

Panoramic view of Florence, Italy

View of Rovinj, Croatia

Croatia

Croatia was one of Yugoslavia's most advanced and prosperous areas, and declared its independence in 1991. The country borders the Adriatic Sea and its coast was popular with tourists. The Yugoslavian conflict of 1991–95 threw the country into turmoil, but visitors are now returning.

Area 21,831 sq. mi. (55,542 sq km)
Country population 4,447,495
Capital city (pop) Zagreb (703,185)
Official language Croatian
Currency Kuna

Bulgaria

Bulgaria was Communist until 1990, when it became a democracy. It has now joined the European Union, despite organized crime, corruption, inflation and unemployment. Bulgaria is becoming popular with tourists, especially the historic capital city of Sofia.

Area 42,825 sq. mi. (110,910 sq km)
Country population 7,535,211
Capital city (pop) Sofia (1,205,048)
Official language Bulgarian
Currency Lev

Bosnia and Herzegovina

Bosnia and Herzegovina was recognized as an independent state in 1992 after Yugoslavia collapsed in 1991. Since then clashes between Bosnia's Croats, Serbs and Muslims have caused civil war, which is still not resolved. Despite this, more tourists are beginning to visit the country again.

Area 19,741 sq. mi. (51,129 sq km)
Country population 3,827,694
Capital city (pop) Sarajevo (424,354)
Official languages Bosnian/Croatian/Serbian
Currency Convertible marka

Slovakia

Slovakia is landlocked and mountainous. It became independent in 1993, when Czechoslovakia divided into the Czech Republic and Slovakia. It joined the European Union in 2004.

Area 18,859 sq. mi. (48,845 sq km)
Country population 5,395,346
Capital city (pop) Bratislava (419,211)
Official language Slovak
Currency Koruna

Moldova

Moldova is Europe's poorest country. It has no natural resources and imports all its energy supplies from Russia, from which it became independent in 1991.

Area 13,067 sq. mi. (33,843 sq km)
Country population 3,640,569
Capital city (pop) Chisinau (697,475)
Official language Moldovan
Currency Moldovan leu

Ukraine

Ukraine is a vast area between Poland and Russia. It became independent after the collapse of the Soviet Union. In 1986 it was the scene of the world's worst nuclear disaster, when a reactor at the Chernobyl nuclear plant exploded.

Area 233,090 sq. mi. (603,700 sq km)
Country population 46,396,212
Capital city (pop) Kiev (3,000,198)
Official language Ukrainian
Currency Hryvna

Albania

Albania depends mostly on farming, and its main crops are wheat, corn, beets, potatoes and fruit. It has borders with Serbia, Montenegro, Kosovo, Macedonia and Greece.

Area 11,100 sq. mi. (28,748 sq km)
Country population 3,175,119
Capital city (pop) Tirana (399,999)
Official language Albanian
Currency Lek

Georgia

Georgia lies in a key position east of the Black Sea between Russia and Turkey. It has coal deposits, but they have not yet been exploited. The country relies on farming — particularly grapes from which wine is made.

Area 26,910 sq. mi. (69,700 sq km)
Country population 4,658,143
Capital city (pop) Tbilisi (1,310,819)
Official language Georgian
Currency Lari

The Millennium Monument in Budapest, Hungary

Hungary

Hungary became Communist after World War II. In the 1990s, it defied the Soviet Union and began some free trade with the West. This central European country has flourished since the Soviet Union's collapse and it entered the European Union in 2004.

Area 35,919 sq. mi. (93,030 sq km)
Country population 9,981,334
Capital city (pop) Budapest (2,571,504)
Official language Hungarian
Currency Forint

Slovenia

About half of Slovenia is covered in forest, making it the third most forested country in Europe. Slovenia became independent from Yugoslavia in 1991 and joined the European Union in 2004. Its people now have a reasonably good standard of living.

Area 7,827 sq. mi. (20,273 sq km)
Country population 2,018,689
Capital city (pop) Ljubljana (258,810)
Official language Slovene
Currency Euro

 # Azerbaijan

Azerbaijan regained its independence from the Soviet Union in 1991. The country has rich mineral resources as well as oil and natural gas. However, conflict and corruption have kept it from developing a healthy economy.

Area 33,436 sq. mi. (86,600 sq km)
Country population 8,770,714
Capital city (pop) Baki/Baku (2,176,777)
Official language Azerbaijani
Currency Manat

 ## Greece

The ancient country of Greece lies in an important position between Europe, Asia and Africa. It includes about 2,000 islands as well as the mainland. About 14 million tourists visit Greece every year. However, it has few natural resources and relies on money from the European Union.

Area 131,940 sq km (50,942 sq miles)
Country population 11,205,946
Capital city (pop) Athens (3,829,018)
Official language Greek
Currency Euro

> Windmill on the Greek island of Santorini

 # Macedonia

Macedonia's full name is the Former Yugoslav Republic of Macedonia (FYROM), not to be confused with the Greek region of Macedonia. Macedonia became independent in 1991. Since then there have been clashes between the country's large Albanian minority and its Macedonian majority.

Area 9,781 sq. mi. (25,333 sq km)
Country population 9,047,846
Capital city (pop) Skopje (589,307)
Official languages Macedonian/Albanian
Currency Denar

 # Armenia

Armenia was the first country formally to adopt Christianity in AD 301. This mountainous country is bordered by Azerbaijan, Georgia, Iran and Turkey. Its key position between Europe and Asia led to invasions by the Persian, Ottoman, Roman and Byzantine empires, among others.

Area 11,506 sq. mi. (29,800 sq km)
Country population 3,237,660
Capital city (pop) Yerevan (1,414,740)
Official language Armenian
Currency Dram

 # Romania

The mountainous Republic of Romania is the largest Balkan nation. The Communist regime was overthrown in 1989 when the dictator Nicolae Ceausescu was executed. The country is still very poor, with almost half of Romanians living in poverty. It is now a member of the European Union.

Area 91,699 sq. mi. (237,500 sq km)
Country population 21,503,193
Capital city (pop) Bucharest (2,192,372)
Official language Romanian
Currency Leu

 ## Cyprus

The Mediterranean island of Cyprus has been divided since Turkey invaded the north of the island in 1974. The Turkish Republic of Northern Cyprus is recognized only by Turkey. Greek Cyprus attracts many tourists and was accepted into the European Union in 2004. The Turkish part depends heavily on loans from Turkey.

Area 3,571 sq. mi. (9,250 sq km)
Country population 1,099,421
Capital city (pop) Nicosia (213, 027)
Official languages Greek/Turkish
Currency Cyprus pound

 # Serbia

This landlocked country was formerly part of Yugoslavia but is now independent.

Area 34,116 sq. mi. (88,361 sq km)
Country population 9,567,484
Capital city (pop) Belgrade (1,818,237)
Official language Serbian
Currency Serbian dinar

 ## Kosovo

Area 4,203 sq. mi. (10,887 sq km)
Country population 2,130,008
Capital city (pop) Pristina (210,837)

Montenegro

Montenegro was a former part of Yugoslavia and became independent from Serbia in 2006. It is now a full member of the United Nations and, although not a member of the European Union, it has adopted the Euro as its national currency.

Area 5,415 sq. mi. (14,026 sq km)
Country population 625,536
Capital city (pop) Podgorica (143,718)
Official language Serbian
Currency Euro

Morocco

Morocco is in northwestern Africa. The country was divided between Spanish and French rule, but gained independence in 1956. It has rich mineral deposits and nearly three-quarters of the world's phosphate. Tourism is becoming increasingly important, but almost half the population work on the land.

Area 172,415 sq. mi. (446,550 sq km)
Country population 30,886,980
Capital city (pop) Rabat (1,754,425)
Official language Arabic
Currency Dirham

Algeria

Algeria became independent from France in 1962. Throughout the 1990s the country was torn apart by civil war, in which 100,000 people are thought to have died. Algeria is still struggling to control its religious militants.

Area 919,595 sq. mi. (2,381,740 sq km)
Country population 34,498,821
Capital city (pop) Algiers (6,253,265)
Official languages Arabic/Berber
Currency Algerian dinar

Tunisia

The North African country of Tunisia shares borders with Algeria and Libya and has a Mediterranean coastline. About one-fifth of the people live by farming and fishing.

Area 63,170 sq. mi. (163,610 sq km)
Country population 10,326,500
Capital city (pop) Tunis (2,050,434)
Official language Arabic
Currency Tunisian dinar

Cape Verde

Cape Verde is made up of the Windward Islands and the Leeward Islands in the Atlantic Ocean off the west coast of Africa. Their main exports are bananas and coffee.

Area 1,557 sq. mi. (4,033 sq km)
Country population 499,362
Capital city (pop) Praia (124,661)
Official language Portuguese
Currency Cape Verdean escudo

Ethiopia

Ethiopia is Africa's oldest independent country. It has suffered many droughts and famines. These, combined with civil war and a border dispute with Eritrea, have made Ethiopia one of Africa's poorest nations. Its natural resources are underdeveloped, and 85 percent of the people still depend upon the land for a living.

Area 435,186 sq. mi. (1,127,127 sq km)
Country population 79,183,659
Capital city (pop) Addis Ababa (3,144,918)
Official language There is no official language, but Amharic is the most widely used of the 70 languages
Currency Ethiopian birr

Libya

Libya has large oil reserves, but its economy has suffered from sanctions imposed by the United Nations. These were in response to the bombing of an airliner over Lockerbie in Scotland in 1988. Sanctions have now been lifted and Libya's leader, Colonel Gaddafi, has promised to bring his country back into the international community.

Area 679,360 sq. mi. (1,759,540 sq km)
Country population 6,455,346
Capital city (pop) Tripoli (1,943,454)
Official language Arabic
Currency Libyan dinar

Eritrea

Eritrea is in eastern Africa and has had violent border disputes with Ethiopia since 1998. The conflict has affected Eritrea's economy, but the government continues to improve the country's roads, schools and transport systems. Its Red Sea ports are an important source of income.

Area 46,840 sq. mi. (121,320 sq km)
Country population 4,936,403
Capital city (pop) Asmara (1,146,822)
Official languages No official language; Arabic, Tigrinya and English are the main working languages; Italian is also spoken.
Currency Nakfa

Camel and rider near the Great Pyramid in Egypt

Egypt

Egypt lies in a key position. It has a coastline on both the Mediterranean and Red seas, and borders with the Sudan, Libya, Israel and the Gaza Strip. Egypt also controls the vital Suez Canal. This allows about 15,000 ships each year to travel between the Mediterranean and the Indian Ocean without sailing around Africa. Famous landmarks include the pyramids.

Area 386,662 sq. mi. (1,001,450 sq km)
Country population 75,099,806
Capital city (pop) Cairo (16,078,877)
Official language Arabic
Currency Egyptian pound

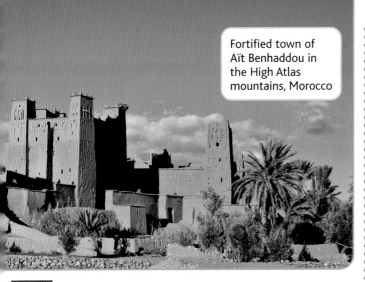

Fortified town of Aït Benhaddou in the High Atlas mountains, Morocco

Somalia

Somalia is one of the world's poorest countries and there has been conflict between different groups. The north declared independence under the name Somaliland, but is not recognized by any foreign government.

Area 246,201 sq. mi. (637,657 sq km)
Country population 12,692,376
Capital city (pop) Mogadishu (1,609,050)
Official languages Somali/Arabic
Currency Somali shilling

Mauritania

Mauritania is mainly desert. It became independent from France in 1960. There is conflict between the country's African and Arab peoples. Mauritania has rich mineral deposits, but these have not yet been exploited.

Area 397,955 sq. mi. (1,030,700 sq km)
Country population 3,022,150
Capital city (pop) Nouakchott (775,758)
Official language Arabic
Currency Ouguiya

Sudan

Sudan is the biggest country in Africa. It has large oil reserves, which have been exploited since 1999. However, the country has suffered from civil war since its independence in 1956. This war has been going on longer than any other war in Africa. Since 2003 fighting has been particularly severe in the western region of Darfur, which is one of the poorest parts of the country. The United Nations has described this as the world's worst humanitarian crisis.

Area 967,500 sq. mi. (2,505,810 sq km)
Country population 37,423,543
Capital city (pop) Khartoum (8,873,889)
Official language Arabic
Currency Sudanese dinar

Djibouti

Djibouti lies in a key position between Ethiopia and the Red Sea. The country provides refueling facilities for ships and operates a free port, which bring money into Djibouti.

Area 8,880 sq. mi. (23,000 sq km)
Country population 496,375
Capital city (pop) Djibouti (c. 400,000)
Official languages Arabic/French
Currency Djibouti franc

Senegal

Senegal is almost divided into two by The Gambia. It became independent from France in 1960. It is now popular with tourists, but has few natural resources, high unemployment and more than half its people live in poverty.

Area 75,749 sq. mi. (196,190 sq km)
Country population 11,291,344
Capital city (pop) Dakar (2,485,851)
Official language French
Currency CFA franc

Niger

Niger is the largest nation in West Africa. It is also one of the hottest and poorest countries in the world. Niger borders the Sahara Desert and droughts often kill much of the country's vital livestock. It has one of the world's lowest literacy rates.

Area 489,190 sq. mi. (1,267,000 sq km)
Country population 3,949,837
Capital city (pop) Niamey (931,928)
Official language French
Currency CFA franc

Guinea

Guinea has been placed under great strain by thousands of refugees from its war-torn neighbors, Liberia and Sierra Leone. Guinea has natural resources, including iron ore, gold and diamonds.

Area 94,926 sq. mi. (245,857 sq km)
Country population 10,174,655
Capital city (pop) Conakry (1,857,153)
Official language French
Currency Guinean franc

Gambia

The Gambia is a sliver of land and the smallest country in mainland Africa. About 80 percent of Gambians work on the land. It is becoming increasingly popular as a tourist destination.

Area 4,365 sq. mi. (11,300 sq km)
Country population 1,546,400
Capital city (pop) Banjul (33,820)
Official language English
Currency Dalasi

Dogon people from Mali dancing on stilts

Mali

Mali's first democratically elected government came to power in 1992 after more than 20 years of dictatorship. This West African nation is one of the world's poorest countries. About 80 percent of the people depend on farming for a living.

Area 478,765 sq. mi. (1,240,000 sq km)
Country population 12,781,404
Capital city (pop) Bamako (2,111,790)
Official language French
Currency CFA franc

Nigeria

Nigeria has the biggest population of any African country. It is the leading oil producer south of the Sahara. However, about 60 percent of Nigerians live in poverty because of corruption, unequal distribution of money and a rapidly growing population.

Area 356,668 sq. mi. (923,768 sq km)
Country population 147,357,690
Capital city (pop) Abuja (781,199)
Official language English
Currency Naira

Guinea-Bissau

Guinea-Bissau is one of the poorest countries in the world. A civil war in 1998 destroyed many of its roads, schools and hospitals, and ruined its economy. Most people live by fishing and farming. Cashew nuts are the main crop.

Area 13,945 sq. mi. (36,120 sq km)
Country population 1,403,569
Capital city (pop) Bissau (408,627)
Official language Portuguese
Currency CFA franc

Burkina Faso

Burkina Faso is an inland country in West Africa that was called Upper Volta. About 90 percent of people work on the land. It has the lowest literacy rate in the world.

Area 105,870 sq. mi. (274,200 sq km)
Country population 14,337,906
Capital city (pop) Ouagadougou (1,286,529)
Official language French
Currency CFA Franc

Ghana

Ghana was a British colony, but in 1957 it became the first African country to become independent. It contains Lake Volta, the world's largest artificial lake, and it is one of the world's top 10 gold producers.

Area 92,455 sq. mi. (239,460 sq km)
Country population 23,428,820
Capital city (pop) Accra (3,905,009)
Official language English
Currency Cedi

Liberia

The West African country of Liberia was founded by freed U.S. slaves. It has been independent since 1847. Its president is Africa's first elected female head of state.

Area 43,000 sq. mi. (111,370 sq km)
Country population 3,283,000
Capital city (pop) Monrovia (1,690,270)
Official language English
Currency Liberian dollar

Benin

The African country of Benin became fully independent from France in 1960. It now has a thriving tourist industry, which provides much-needed money.

Area 43,485 sq. mi. (112,620 sq km)
Country population 8,052,780
Capital city (pop) Porto Novo (250,262)
Official language French
Currency CFA Franc

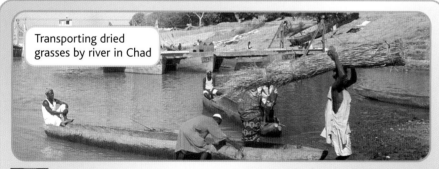
Transporting dried grasses by river in Chad

Chad

The Sahara desert covers much of Chad. Since gaining independence from France in 1960, it has suffered conflict with its neighbor Libya. Oil has been found in Chad and is now being exported. Most of its people work on the land.

Area 495,755 sq. mi. (1,284,000 sq km)
Country population 8,988,735
Capital city (pop) N'Djamena (1,518,988)
Official languages Arabic/French
Currency CFA Franc

Republic of Congo

The region of Middle Congo became independent from France in 1960 and was renamed the Republic of Congo. The country has large oil deposits and is one of Africa's largest producers of petroleum. It also produces zinc, lead, gold and diamonds.

Area 132,045 sq. mi. (342,000 sq km)
Country population 3,702,311
Capital city (pop) Brazzaville (1,180,176)
Official language French
Currency CFA franc

Cameroon

Cameroon in West Africa became an independent republic in 1972. It has good natural resources, including bauxite and aluminum, and grows crops such as cocoa, coffee and rubber.

Area 183,570 sq. mi. (475,440 sq km)
Country population 19,018,638
Capital city (pop) Yaoundé (2,075,562)
Official languages French/English
Currency CFA Franc

Côte d'Ivoire

Côte d'Ivoire became independent from France in 1960. It was a peaceful, prosperous African country until its first military coup in 1999. Trouble then began between rebels and the government, which is still going on.

Area 124,500 sq. mi. (322,460 sq km)
Country population 20,794,345
Capital city (pop) Yamoussoukro (226,994)
Official language French
Currency CFA Franc

Sierra Leone

Sierra Leone became independent from Britain in 1971. Between 1991–2002 the country was in a state of civil war. Many thousands of people were killed and thousands more were forced to move from their homes. Sierra Leone has diamond and gold deposits, but its political problems have made it one of the world's poorest countries, along with Somalia and East Timor. Unemployment is high and about three-quarters of its people live on less than U.S. $2 a day.

Area 27,700 sq. mi. (71,740 sq km)
Country population 5,226,221
Capital city (pop) Freetown (819,634)
Official language English
Currency Leone

Traditional woven baskets from the Republic of Congo

São Tomé and Príncipe

The islands of São Tomé and Príncipe lie on the Equator in the Gulf of Guinea and make up Africa's smallest country. Cocoa is the main crop, but São Tomé and Príncipe has other potential sources of income, such as newly discovered oil.

Area 387 sq. mi. (1,001 sq km)
Country population 157,847
Capital city (pop) São Tomé (62,531)
Official language Portuguese
Currency Dobra

Gabon

Gabon has a small population and good oil and mineral reserves. It is one of Africa's richest nations. However, many of its people are very poor because its wealth has been mismanaged and is unequally distributed.

Area 103,346 sq. mi. (267,667 sq km)
Country population 1,725,105
Capital city (pop) Libreville (713,167)
Official language French
Currency CFA franc

Central African Republic

The Central African Republic is a landlocked country in central Africa. It became independent from France in 1960. Since then there have been almost constant political problems and it is now a very poor country. It exports some lumber and diamonds, but most people work on the land.

Area 240,536 sq. mi. (622,984 sq km)
Country population 3,347,188
Capital city (pop) Bangui (752,914)
Official language French
Currency CFA Franc

Togo

Togo was the French territory of Togoland until it became independent in 1960. More than half the people work on the land. Cotton, coffee and cocoa are the main exports. Nearly one third of the people are very poor.

Area 21,924 sq. mi. (56,785 sq km)
Country population 5,582,583
Capital city (pop) Lomé (828,228)
Official language French
Currency CFA franc

Equatorial Guinea

Equatorial Guinea is made up of five islands and part of the African mainland. It became independent from Spain in 1968 and is one of the smallest countries in Africa. Many people work on the land, but gas and oil have been found and so the country is becoming wealthier.

Area 10,831 sq. mi. (28,051 sq km)
Country population 540,109
Capital city (pop) Malabo (170,964)
Official languages Spanish/French
Currency CFA franc

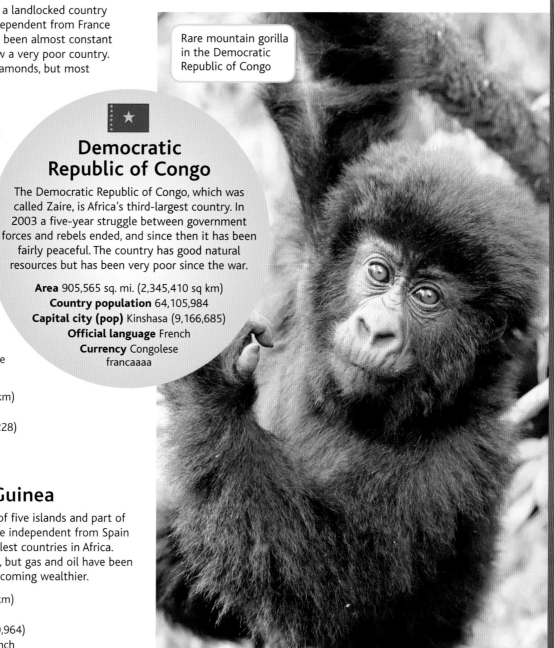

Rare mountain gorilla in the Democratic Republic of Congo

Democratic Republic of Congo

The Democratic Republic of Congo, which was called Zaire, is Africa's third-largest country. In 2003 a five-year struggle between government forces and rebels ended, and since then it has been fairly peaceful. The country has good natural resources but has been very poor since the war.

Area 905,565 sq. mi. (2,345,410 sq km)
Country population 64,105,984
Capital city (pop) Kinshasa (9,166,685)
Official language French
Currency Congolese francaaaa

Sand dune in the Namib desert

Namibia

Namibia became independent from South Africa in 1990. The country often suffers from drought so much of its food has to be imported from other countries. Namibia is an important producer of diamonds, but the wealth from this is unevenly distributed. Half of all Namibians are living in poverty.

Area 318,696 sq. mi. (825,418 sq km)
Country population 2,128,560
Capital city (pop) Windhoek (296,366)
Official language English
Currency Namibian dollar

Rwanda

Rwanda is a densely populated country in Central Africa. It is still suffering the effects of a civil war that began in 1990 and lasted for four years. At least 60 percent of the people live in poverty.

Area 10,169 sq. mi. (26,338 sq km)
Country population 8,995,038
Capital city (pop) Kigali (904,779)
Official languages Kinyarwanda/French/English
Currency Rwanda franc

Angola

Angola became independent from Portugal in 1975. Since then, there has been a civil war almost all the time. The country has valuable oil and diamond deposits, but has many financial problems.

Area 481,355 sq. mi. (1,246,700 sq km)
Country population 16,853,679
Capital city (pop) Luanda (2,524,459)
Official language Portuguese
Currency Kwanza

Uganda

Uganda is a landlocked West African nation on the shores of Lake Victoria. It is now a fairly peaceful country, after a devastating civil war and a military dictatorship. The land is fertile and it has natural resources, but Uganda is still being held back by a large international debt.

Area 91,135 sq. mi. (236,040 sq km)
Country population 29,395,836
Capital city (pop) Kampala (1,805,077)
Official language English
Currency Uganda shilling

Burundi

Burundi gained independence in the 1960s. Since then it has been devastated by fighting between the two main tribes, the Hutus and the Tutsis. Burundi lies between the politically troubled countries of Rwanda and the Democratic Republic of Congo, and is being held back by uncertainty over its future.

Area 10,745 sq. mi. (27,830 sq km)
Country population 8,731,814
Capital city (pop) Bujumbura (360,278)
Official languages Kirundi/French
Currency Burundi franc

Malawi

In 1964, the British territory of Nyasaland in southeastern Africa became Malawi, which is an independent republic. The country has had many natural disasters and depends on aid from other countries. About 15 percent of the adult population has HIV or AIDS, and Malawi now has one of the world's lowest life expectancies.

Area 45,745 sq. mi. (118,480 sq km)
Country population 13,444,359
Capital city (pop) Lilongwe (866,272)
Official languages Chichewa/English
Currency Kwacha

Zambia

The landlocked country of Zambia in Central Africa has a small population. Copper is its chief export, but demand for copper has fallen and Zambia is now one of the world's poorest countries. Almost 90 percent of its people live on less than U.S. $1 a day.

Area 290,586 sq. mi. (752,614 sq km)
Country population 12,450,229
Capital city (pop) Lusaka (2,679,083)
Official language English
Currency Kwacha

Swaziland

Swaziland is one of the world's few absolute monarchies — political parties were banned by the king in 1973. The country relies on South Africa for trade. About 40 percent of the people live on less than U.S. $1 a day. It has one of the highest levels of HIV/AIDS in the world and the world's lowest life expectancy.

Area 6,704 sq. mi. (17,363 sq km)
Country population 1,194,882
Capital city (pop) Mbabane (82,887)
Official languages English/Swazi
Currency Lilangeni

Lesotho

The Kingdom of Lesotho was once called Basutoland and became independent from the UK in 1966. It is entirely surrounded by South Africa. Lesotho has diamond mines but few other resources. Most people work on the land or in South African mines.

Area 11,720 sq. mi. (30,355 sq km)
Country population 1,884,897
Capital city (pop) Maseru (240,663)
Official languages Sotho/English
Currency Loti

Tanzania

Tanzania is made up of the country that used to be called Tanganyika on the eastern African mainland, and the island of Zanzibar, which is in the Indian Ocean just off the coast of Tanganyika. The two nations joined in 1964 after becoming independent. The country contains Lake Victoria, Mount Kilimanjaro and Serengeti National Park.

Area 364,900 sq. mi. (945,087 sq km)
Country population 40,120,715
Capital city (pop) Dodoma (203,999)
Official languages Swahili/English
Currency Tanzanian shilling

Botswana

Botswana used to be called the British Protectorate of Bechuanaland, but in 1966 it became an independent Commonwealth republic. It is now one of the wealthiest countries in Africa. Botswana has many natural resources and is one of the world's largest producers of diamonds. However, around one-third of the population has HIV/AIDS.

Area 231,805 sq. mi. (600,370 sq km)
Country population 1,914,815
Capital city (pop) Gaborone (224,990)
Official language English
Currency Pula

Zimbabwe

Zimbabwe was previously the British colony of Rhodesia. It used to be a fairly well-off country, but since 2000 has suffered a series of political problems and upsets. Zimbabweans now have an extremely low standard of living: one-third have HIV/AIDS and 70 percent live in poverty.

Area 150,805 sq. mi. (390,580 sq km)
Country population 12,352,402
Capital city (pop) Harare (2,999,481)
Official language English
Currency Zimbabwe dollar

Madagascar

Madagascar is in the Indian Ocean off the coast of Africa. It is the fourth-largest island in the world. More than 80 percent of people work on the land. The country has often suffered natural disasters. In 2000 most of its rice crop was destroyed by cyclones.

Area 226,655 sq. mi. (587,040 sq km)
Country population 18,622,208
Capital city (pop) Antananarivo (1,699,114)
Official languages Malagasy/French
Currency Malagasy franc

Mauritius

Mauritius is a group of islands in the Indian Ocean. It has a stable government, and Mauritians have high incomes. The country exports sugar cane and has a thriving tourist industry. It is home to some of the world's rarest plants and animals.

Area 790 sq. mi. (2,040 sq km)
Country population 1,261,926
Capital city (pop) Port Louis (637,324)
Official languages English/French
Currency Mauritius rupee

Women of the Samburu tribe in Kenya performing a traditional dance

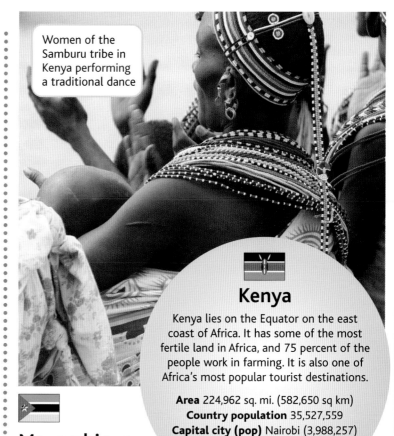

Kenya

Kenya lies on the Equator on the east coast of Africa. It has some of the most fertile land in Africa, and 75 percent of the people work in farming. It is also one of Africa's most popular tourist destinations.

Area 224,962 sq. mi. (582,650 sq km)
Country population 35,527,559
Capital city (pop) Nairobi (3,988,257)
Official languages Swahili/English
Currency Kenya shilling

Mozambique

Mozambique used to be a Portuguese colony. It gained independence in 1975, became a republic in 1990, and held its first free elections in 1994. About 70 percent of its people live in poverty. But since the beginning of the 21st century, things have begun to improve and other countries have started to invest in Mozambique.

Area 309,495 sq. mi. (801,590 sq km)
Country population 21,000,335
Capital city (pop) Maputo (1,994,900)
Official language Portuguese
Currency Metical

South Africa

South Africa lies on the southern tip of the continent. Until 1994 the country was ruled by its white minority and had an apartheid policy. This segregated the races — kept black and white apart — and denied black citizens the vote. Because of this many other countries refused to trade with South Africa. The African National Congress won South Africa's first inclusive elections in 1994, and it has been in power ever since.

Area 471,011 sq. mi. (1,219,912 sq km)
Country population 48,394,880
Capital city (pop) The seat of government is Tshwane (Pretoria) (2,253,260); the seat of the legislature is Cape Town (4,715,046); the seat of the judiciary is Bloemfontein (495,006)
Official languages There are 11 official languages: Afrikaans, English, Ndebele, Pedi, Sotho, Swazi, Tsonga, Tswana, Venda, Xhosa, Zulu
Currency Rand

Mount Kilimanjaro, Tanzania, is the highest mountain in Africa.

Yemen

In 1990 North and South Yemen were formally joined as the Republic of Yemen after years of conflict. Yemen is a poor country, affected by drought, political problems and a fast-growing population.

Area 203,850 sq. mi. (527,970 sq km)
Country population 21,175,675
Capital city (pop) Sana'a' (2,304,663)
Official language Arabic
Currency Riyal

Yemeni women in traditional veils

Turkey

Turkey is in a key position between Europe and Asia. The territory west of the Bosphorus strait is in Europe, while the much larger area to the east is in Asia. Turkey is popular with tourists, and between seven and ten million people every year visit its coastline and the historic city of Istanbul.

Area 301,385 sq. mi. (780,580 sq km)
Country population 76,375,182
Capital city (pop) Ankara (3,714,056)
Official language Turkish
Currency Turkish lir

Syria

Syria has been home to some of the world's oldest civilizations, and Damascus is probably the oldest city in the world. Syria became independent from France in 1946. Its people come from many different ethnic groups and religions, including Arabs, Kurds, Assyrians and Armenians, and Muslims, Christians and Jews.

Area 71,500 sq. mi. (185,180 sq km)
Country population 19,989,814
Capital city (pop) Damascus (2,688,278)
Official language Arabic
Currency Syrian pound

Kazakhstan

Kazakhstan is an enormous, landlocked nation almost four times the size of Texas. It was part of the former Soviet Union. Kazakhstan is rich in minerals and fossil fuels, including oil, coal, natural gas, gold, silver and lead.

Area 1,049,155 sq. mi. (2,717,300 sq km)
Country population 15,663,189
Capital city (pop) Astana (389,189)
Official language Kazakh
Currency Tenge

Israel

After World War II, Israel was created in Palestine as a homeland for Jews. When Great Britain left the area in 1948 the State of Israel was proclaimed, and there was immediate conflict between the Jewish settlers and the Arabs who were living there. The State of Israel gained a great deal of land in the conflict, and many Palestinians were made homeless. There have been many attempts to make peace between the two sides, but the conflict continues.

Area 8,020 sq. mi. (20,770 sq km)
Country population 7,325,999
Capital city (pop) Jerusalem (750,892) Jerusalem is the seat of government but is not recognized as the capital by the UN because East Jerusalem is part of the Occupied Territories captured in 1967. The UN considers Tel Aviv (1,117,842) to be the capital.
Official languages Hebrew/Arabic
Currency Shekel

United Arab Emirates

The UAE is a group of seven Middle Eastern states and is one of the wealthiest countries in the region. It used to be a very poor country where most people lived by fishing, but is now the Gulf's third-largest oil producer.

Area 32,280 sq. mi. (83,600 sq km)
Country population 5,402,375
Capital city (pop) Abu Dhabi (859,749)
Official language Arabic
Currency UAE dirham

The Burj Al Arab hotel in Dubai, United Arab Emirates

Kuwait

Kuwait has large oil reserves that make up more than 8 percent of the world's total. The country's economy was almost destroyed when Iraqi forces invaded in 1990 and burned oil wells as they retreated. The Kuwaiti government has spent billions of dollars on repairs, and oil production is now higher than it was before the invasion.

Area 6,880 sq. mi. (17,820 sq km)
Country population 2,906,764
Capital city (pop) Kuwait City (2,394,046)
Official language Arabic
Currency Kuwaiti dinar

Jordan

Jordan shares borders with Syria, Israel, the West Bank, Saudi Arabia and Iraq. Despite the problems of its neighbors the country is relatively peaceful. It doesn't have many natural resources, and its vital supplies of Iraqi oil were halted by the Iraq war of 2003.

Area 35,635 sq. mi. (92,300 sq km)
Country population 5,913,809
Capital city (pop) Amman (1,135,733)
Official language Arabic
Currency Jordanian dina

Saudi Arabia

Saudi Arabia is a monarchy. It is ruled by the sons and grandsons of Abdul Aziz ibn Saud, who founded the kingdom. Saudi Arabia is one of the richest countries in the Middle East. It has the largest reserves of petroleum in the world and exports more than any other country. It is about the same size as Western Europe and includes an area called the Empty Quarter, the world's largest sand desert. Saudi Arabia is a Muslim country and includes the city of Mecca (or Makkah). This was the birthplace of the Prophet Muhammad and millions of Muslims make a pilgrimage there every year.

Area 830,000 sq. mi. (2,149,690 sq km)
Country population 24,686,696
Capital city (pop) Riyadh (4,606,888)
Official language Arabic
Currency Saudi riyal

Iran

Iran is a mountainous Middle Eastern country. Until 1935 it was known as Persia. It shares borders with several of the world's most troubled nations, including Iraq, Afghanistan and Pakistan. This discourages investment from other countries and tourism, and Iran's economy depends on oil.

Area 636,295 sq. mi. (1,648,000 sq km)
Country population 71,028,973
Capital city (pop) Tehran (12,664,286)
Official language Farsi
Currency Rial

Iraq

Iraq has had a violent recent history. From 1979 to 2003, Iraq was controlled by the dictator President Saddam Hussein. The U.S., supported by countries including the UK, Spain, Australia, Poland and Denmark, removed Hussein from power in 2003. Hussein was executed in 2006, but conflict continues in Iraq.

Area 168,754 sq. mi. (437,072 sq km)
Country population 27,141,340
Capital city (pop) Baghdad (10,634,225)
Official language Arabic
Currency New Iraqi dinar

Lebanon

Lebanon is a small country bordering the Mediterranean Sea. It became independent from France in 1943. Since Lebanon's civil war of 1975–91 huge sums have been spent on rebuilding the country and it is heavily in debt.

Area 4,015 sq. mi. (10,400 sq km)
Country population 4,602,431
Capital city (pop) Beirut (1,987,173)
Official language Arabic
Currency Lebanese pound

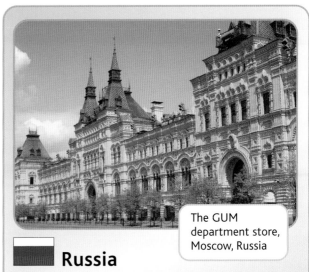

The GUM department store, Moscow, Russia

Russia

The Russian Federation is the largest country in the world, almost twice the size of the United States. It stretches from Europe to Asia and covers 13 percent of the world's total land area. Russia was the chief republic of the former Soviet Union, which in 1991 was split into 15 separate republics. Oil, natural gas, lumber and metals make up more than 80 percent of its exports. The country is still held back by poor transport and other systems. It also suffers from violent conflict in the Chechnya region.

Area 6,592,772 sq. mi. (17,075,200 sq km)
Country population 141,833,475
Capital city (pop) Moscow (14,744,150)
Official language Russian
Currency Ruble

Bahrain

The island state of Bahrain is 20 mi. (32 km) off the east coast of Saudi Arabia. Oil is its main source of income, but the country is also a center for offshore banking.

Area 257 sq. mi. (665 sq km)
Country population 788,873
Capital city (pop) Manama (668,089)
Official language Arabic
Currency Bahraini dinar

Qatar

Qatar became independent from Britain in 1971 and has changed from being a poor country dependent on pearl fishing to one of the Gulf's richest states. It has large reserves of oil and gas, which have brought great wealth.

Area 4,416 sq. mi. (11,437 sq km)
Country population 928,404
Capital city (pop) Doha (761,019)
Official language Arabic
Currency Qatar riyal

Oman

Oman borders Yemen, Saudi Arabia and the United Arab Emirates so is in a key position for the transportation of oil. Oil makes up more than 80 percent of Oman's exports, but the government wants to encourage tourism and information technology.

Area 82,030 sq. mi. (212,460 sq km)
Country population 2,721,576
Capital city (pop) Muscat (1,090,797)
Official language Arabic
Currency Omani rial

Kyrgyzstan

Kyrgyzstan is a picturesque country of mountains, glaciers and lakes. It became independent from the former Soviet Union in 1991. Since then it has seen many political changes.

Area 76,640 sq. mi. (198,500 sq km)
Country population 5,285,799
Capital city (pop) Bishkek (914,932)
Official languages Kyrgyz/Russian
Currency Som

Tajikistan

Tajikistan lies west of China in Central Asia. It was part of the former Soviet Union. About 50,000 people died in the civil war of 1992–97 and the country is still violent and unsettled.

Area 55,250 sq. mi. (143,100 sq km)
Country population 7,350,401
Capital city (pop) Dushanbe (937,445)
Official language Tajik
Currency Somoni

Bhutan

The mountainous kingdom of Bhutan lies between Tibet (China) and India in the eastern Himalayas. Its main exports are rice, machinery and diesel oil, but tourism is also important.

Area 18,145 sq. mi. (47,000 sq km)
Country population 2,671,887
Capital city (pop) Thimphu (79,185)
Official language Dzongkha
Currency Ngultrum

Afghanistan

Afghanistan is a mountainous country in Central Asia. It has been through more than 20 years of political upheaval. The country was controlled by the Taliban from 1996 until 2001, when the Taliban was overthrown by an alliance led by the U.S. military. At present many people are involved in the drug trade and over one million of the population may be close to starvation.

Area 250,000 sq. mi. (647,500 sq km)
Country population 23,725,835
Capital city (pop) Kabul (2,436,111)
Official languages Dari (Persian)/Pashto
Currency Afghani

Mongolia

Mongolia is a landlocked nation between Russia and China. It is three times the size of France and is a land of deserts, grasslands, forests and mountains. Temperatures range from summer highs of 104°F (40°C) in the Gobi Desert to −40°F (−40°C) during the winter. More than half the population are nomads — they move from place to place with their livestock. Gers (movable tentlike huts) are the most common form of shelter, even in cities.

Area 603,908 sq. mi. (1,564,116 sq km)
Country population 2,644,595
Capital city (pop) Ulaanbaatar (881,218)
Official language Khalkha Mongolian
Currency Tugrik

India

India is the largest democratic country in the world. It became independent from the U.K. in 1947 when it was divided into India and Pakistan. This division has led to three wars. India has the world's largest population, after China. In 1999 its population passed the one billion mark. Most people still live by farming and around 70 percent of the population live in rural areas. India has a booming information technology industry and one of the most successful film industries in the world.

Area 1,269,345 sq. mi. (3,287,590 sq km)
Country population 1,152,342,278
Capital city (pop) New Delhi (18,362,625)
Official languages Hindi/English
Currency Indian rupee

Turkmenistan

Turkmenistan borders the Caspian Sea in Central Asia. About 90 percent of its land is desert. It has the fifth-largest oil and natural gas reserves in the world, but is crippled by debt to other countries.

Area 188,455 sq. mi. (488,100 sq km)
Country population 7,193,046
Capital city (pop) Ashgabat (891,879)
Official languages Turkmen
Currency Manat

Pakistan

Pakistan was created in 1947 as a home for Indian Muslims. It was divided into Pakistan and Bangladesh in 1972. The country is in dispute with India over ownership of the state of Kashmir. This has led to fears of an arms race, as both countries are believed to have nuclear weapons.

Area 310,405 sq. mi. (803,940 sq km)
Country population 155,360,000
Capital city (pop) Islamabad (657,788)
Official language Urdu
(Punjabi is the most commonly used language, and English is used in business, government and higher education)
Currency Pakistan rupee

Sri Lanka

Sri Lanka was called Ceylon until 1948, when it became independent from the UK. It is a tropical island in the Indian Ocean, only 12 mi. (20 km) from the south coast of India. The country has textile, food processing and telecommunications industries. It is held back, however, by nearly 20 years of conflict between some of its people, the Tamils, who want independence, and the government.

Area 25,330 sq. mi. (65,610 sq km)
Country population 20,293,522
Capital city (pop) Colombo (2,588,148)
Official language Sinhala
Currency Sri Lankan rupee

Nepal

Nepal is home to Mt. Everest, the world's highest mountain, and tourism brings vital money into the country. In 2001, Nepal's Crown Prince murdered 10 members of the royal family before taking his own life.

Area 56,827 sq. mi. (147,181 sq km)
Country population 26,942,600
Capital city (pop) Kathmandu (1,611,647)
Official language Nepali
Currency Nepalese rupee

Yak train making its way over the Khumbu glacier, Nepal

 ## China

China is one of the oldest civilizations in the world and has the oldest continuously used language system. It also is home to the world's largest population. The economy of China is growing rapidly and it is now the world's fifth-largest exporter of goods. Tourism has also become a major industry.

Area 3,705,405 sq. mi. (9,596,960 sq km)
Country population 1,313,552,038
Capital city (pop) Beijing (11,941,418)
Official language Mandarin Chinese
Currency Renminbi (also known as the yuan)

Taiwan

The island of Taiwan lies 95 mi. (150 km) from mainland China. Taiwan has a thriving electronics industry. It is one of the world's leading producers of computer technology. Taiwan is home to the world's tallest building, the Taipei 101.

Area 13,890 sq. mi. (35,980 sq km)
Country population 23,195,487
Capital city (pop) Taipei (8,366,945)
Official language Chinese
Currency New Taiwan dollar

 ## Uzbekistan

Uzbekistan has the largest population in Central Asia. It has been independent of the Soviet Union since 1991. It is the second largest exporter of cotton in the world and has mineral deposits. However, its people are poor because the wealth is distributed unequally.

Area 172,740 sq. mi. (447,400 sq km)
Country population 27,363,389
Capital city (pop) Tashkent (3,247,012)
Official language Uzbek
Currency Som

 ## Bangladesh

Bangladesh won independence from Pakistan in 1971. About 70 percent of the people work in farming and the country produces all its own food. The main industries include cotton, tea, leather, sugar and natural gas, and its leading export is clothing.

Area 55,600 sq. mi. (144,000 sq km)
Country population 143,481,419
Capital city (pop) Dhaka (13,240,743)
Official language Bengali
Currency Taka

 ## North Korea

North Korea is one of the world's few remaining Communist states. As many as three million North Koreans have probably died of starvation because of famine and financial mishandling, while the regime spends money on military equipment. North Korea's nuclear program threatens the international food aid that keeps the population going at present.

Area 46,540 sq. mi. (120,540 sq km)
Country population 23,708,186
Capital city (pop) Pyongyang (3,128,617)
Official language Korean
Currency Won

 ## South Korea

During the three-year Korean War in 1953, North Korea attacked the South with Chinese support. The Korean Peninsula was then divided into two. South Korea is a democratic country and has a thriving, high-tech economy and a growing tourism industry.

Area 38,023 sq. mi. (98,480 sq km)
Country population 48,426,195
Capital city (pop) Seoul (22,254,620)
Official language Korean
Currency Won

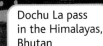

Dochu La pass in the Himalayas, Bhutan

Typical capsule hotel in Japan

Japan

Japan is made up of four large islands and many smaller islands. This mountainous and volcanic country is one of the world's most densely populated places, and there are more people in Tokyo than any other city in the world. Japan is a wealthy country and a world leader in the electronics, robotics and car production industries.

Area 145,880 sq. mi. (377,835 sq km)
Country population 127,939,307
Capital city (pop) Tokyo (37,203,122)
Official language Japanese
Currency Yen

The Philippines

The Philippines is made up of more than 7,000 islands in Southeast Asia. More than 80 percent of the population is Roman Catholic — the Philippines is the only Asian nation that is mainly Christian. It suffers from natural disasters, such as volcanic eruptions and typhoons, as well as a very high birth rate. Many Filipinos go to work abroad and their country depends on the U.S. $6 billion–7 billion they send home each year.

Area 115,830 sq. mi (.300,000 sq km)
Country population 90,317,981
Capital city (pop) Manila (19,195,048)
Official languages Filipino/English
Currency Philippine peso

Myanmar

Myanmar used to be called Burma. The country is ruled by an undemocratic military government and has been accused by foreign governments of severe human rights abuses. It may also be a major producer of heroin. These things have led the U.S. and the European Union to limit trade with the country.

Area 261,970 sq. mi. (678,500 sq km)
Country population 56,950,062
Capital city (pop) Rangoon (4,886,305)
Official language Burmese
Currency Kyat

Thailand

Until 1939, Thailand was called Siam. It is the only country in Southeast Asia never to have been under the control of a European power. About 10 million tourists visit Bangkok and the country's beautiful coasts each year. Farming is important and about half the people still work on the land.

Area 198,455 sq. mi. (514,000 sq km)
Country population 63,629,485
Capital city (pop) Bangkok (9,791,333)
Official language Thai
Currency Baht

Laos

Laos is a landlocked, mountainous country bordered by China, Vietnam, Cambodia, Thailand and Myanmar. It is one of the world's last remaining Communist states. Laos is popular with adventurous tourists, but it is extremely primitive. There are few paved roads and no railways.

Area 91,430 sq. mi. (236,800 sq km)
Country population 5,931,809
Capital city (pop) Vientiane (206,211)
Official language Lao
Currency Kip

Malaysia

Malaysia is made up of two regions, separated by about 640 mi. (1,030 km) of the South China Sea. The country used to rely on farming and exports of raw materials, but it is now a leading producer and exporter of high-tech electronic merchandise.

Area 127,315 sq. mi. (329,750 sq km)
Country population 27,737,693
Capital city (pop) Kuala Lumpur (7,239,871)
Official language Bahasa Malaysia (Malay)
Currency Malaysian dollar (Ringgit)

Singapore

The city state of Singapore in Southeast Asia is one of the richest nations in the world. Its people have one of the world's highest standards of living. Singapore's thriving manufacturing industry includes shipbuilding and electronics.

Area 267 sq. mi. (693 sq km)
Country population 4,974,232
Official languages Malay/Mandarin/Tamil/English
Currency Singapore dollar

 Vietnam

Vietnam

North and South Vietnam were rejoined in 1976 after 30 years of war. At first the war was between the Communists and the French colonialists, and later between the Communist North Vietnam and the South, which was supported by the U.S. Nearly four million people died and much of Vietnam's landscape was destroyed. There is now a Communist socialist government. Vietnam is now one of the world's leading rice exporters, and the country's oil production has increased.

Area 127,245 sq. mi. (329,560 sq km)
Country population 86,240,477
Capital city (pop) Hanoi (2,686,290)
Official language Vietnamese
Currency Dong

Villamendhoo Island in the Maldives

East Timor

East Timor became independent from Indonesia in 2002. It is Southeast Asia's youngest nation and the world's newest democracy. East Timor is a very poor country and often suffers floods.

Area 5,794 sq. mi. (15,007 sq km)
Country population 969,816

Capital city (pop) Dili (170,490)
Official languages Portuguese/Tetum
Currency U.S. dollar

Brunei

Brunei gained full independence from Great Britain in 1984. It is ruled by the Sultan, whose family have reigned for six centuries. Brunei is enormously wealthy because of its natural gas and oil fields.

Area 2,230 sq. mi. (5,770 sq km)
Country population 406,849

Capital city (pop) Bandar Seri Begawan (32,331)
Official language Malay
Currency Brunei dollar

The Comoros

Β The Comoros is a group of volcanic islands between Madagascar and Mozambique. It is one of the world's poorest countries. The Comoros has few natural resources. It exports vanilla, cloves and essential oils, but depends on aid from other countries.

Area 838 sq. mi. (2,170 sq km)
Country population 626,930
Capital city (pop) Moroni (47,040)
Official languages Arabic/French
Currency Comorian franc

Seychelles

The Seychelles is made up of 155 islands in the Indian Ocean, east of mainland Africa. It became independent from Great Britain in 1976. About 90 percent of the islands' people live on the main island of Mahé and are reasonably well off, thanks to successful tourism and tuna fishing industries.

Area 176 sq. mi. (455 sq km)
Country population 86,200
Capital city (pop) Victoria (22,198)
Official languages English/French/Creole
Currency Seychelles rupee

Traditional wayang golek wooden puppets from Indonesia

Indonesia

Indonesia includes more than 17,000 islands. The world's largest Muslim population lives on about 6,000 of these. Indonesia is rich in minerals, and it exports petroleum, textiles, lumber, natural gas and rubber. There are frequent natural disasters.

Area 741,100 sq. mi. (1,919,440 sq km)
Country population 227,070,492
Capital city (pop) Jakarta (18,588,548)
Official languages Indonesian/Bahasa
Currency Rupiah

Maldives

The Maldives are a chain of 1,190 coral islands, which are threatened by rising sea levels. The chief industries are fishing and tourism. Few crops can be grown there and almost all food must be imported.

Area 115 sq. mi. (300 sq km)
Country population 308,797
Capital city (pop) Malé (113,172)
Official language Dhivehi
Currency Rufiyaa

Cambodia

The year 1999 was Cambodia's first full year of peace after more than 20 years of conflict. In 1975 Phnom Penh was captured by Communist Khmer Rouge forces, who executed millions of Cambodians. The country is still very poor. Farming and fishing are the main occupations, but tourism has become more important.

Area 69,900 sq. mi. (181,040 sq km)
Country population 14,103,096
Capital city (pop) Phnom Penh (1,398,449)
Official language Khmer
Currency Riel

Papua New Guinea

Papua New Guinea is made up of many small islands and one half of New Guinea, the world's second-largest island. It has mineral deposits such as gold and copper, as well as oil and natural gas. It has been difficult to fully exploit these because the country lacks good roads and transport, and there are large areas of rainforest.

Area 178,705 sq. mi. (462,840 sq km)
Country population 6,315,896
Capital city (pop) Port Moresby (301,817)
Official language English
Currency Kina

Kiribati

Kiribati is made up of 33 islands in the Pacific Ocean, halfway between Hawaii and Australia. Kiribati's main exports are coconuts and fish.

Solomon Islands

The Solomon Islands include several densely forested volcanic islands in the South Pacific. People live by farming, forestry and fishing, but since 1998 there has been conflict between different groups in the population. Law and order has broken down, and the islanders' average income has been halved. A peacekeeping force led by Australia arrived in 2003.

Area 10,985 sq. mi. (28,450 sq km)
Country population 506,992
Capital city (pop) Honiara (57,456)
Official language English
Currency Solomon Islands dollar

Area 313 sq. mi. (811 sq km)
Country population 97,031
Capital city (pop) Tarawa (45,754)
Official language English
Currency Australian dollar

The Olgas, natural rock formations in Australia

Palau

The Republic of Palau is made up of 340 islands in the Pacific Ocean, southeast of the Philippines. It became independent in 1994 and is one of the world's youngest nations. The islands rely mainly on tourism. The waters around Palau are rich in marine life, and visitors come to snorkel and scubadive. The islands also export fish, shellfish and coconuts.

Area 177 sq. mi. (458 sq km)
Country population 20,548
Capital city (pop) Koror (10,650)
Official languages Palauan/English
Currency U.S. dollar

Micronesia

The Federated States of Micronesia is a group of more than 600 islands in the North Pacific Ocean. It gained independence from the U.S. in 1986, but the U.S. has kept the right to have military bases on the islands. This agreement brings Micronesia billions of dollars of financial aid.

Area 271 sq. mi. (702 sq km)
Country population 108,287
Capital city (pop) Palikir (7,321)
Official language English
Currency U.S. dollar

New Zealand

New Zealand lies in the Pacific Ocean, about 1,000 mi. (1,600 km) east of Australia. It is made up of two main islands and several smaller ones. The capital, Wellington, lies further south than any other capital city. New Zealand is mountainous and relatively unspoiled, and is becoming more and more popular with tourists from all over the world.

Area 103,740 sq. mi. (268,680 sq km)
Country population 4,121,662
Capital city (pop) Wellington (364,586)
Official languages English/Maori
Currency New Zealand dollar

A view of the city of Auckland in New Zealand

Australia

Australia was discovered by Captain James Cook in 1770. It became independent in 1931, but it is part of the British Commonwealth and Queen Elizabeth II is the head of state. Australia is the world's sixth-largest country. It has important mineral resources and vast areas are given over to sheep and cattle farming. Some famous landmarks include the Great Barrier Reef and Uluru.

Area 2,967,910 sq. mi. (7,686,850 sq km)
Country population 20,245,629
Capital city (pop) Canberra (329,200)
Official language English
Currency Australian dollar

 # Tonga

Tonga is a group of 169 islands in the southern Pacific Ocean. It is the only country in the Pacific ruled by a monarchy. The islands have no natural resources and people rely on farming. Tonga exports products such as coconuts, vanilla and yams. Around half of the Tongan people live abroad, particularly in the U.S. and Australasia.

Area 289 sq. mi. (748 sq km)
Country population 101,747
Capital city (pop) Nuku'alofa (23,164)
Official languages Tongan/English
Currency Pa'anga

Traditional Polynesian canoe on a beach in Tonga

 # Vanuatu

Vanuatu is a chain of 83 volcanic islands in the South Pacific Ocean, between Hawaii and Australia. About 65 percent of the people work on the land, but offshore banking and tourism are growing industries. However, the islands sometimes suffer earthquakes, tsunamis and cyclones, which may limit the growth of tourism.

Area 4,710 sq. mi. (12,200 sq km)
Country population 227,318
Capital city (pop) Port Vila (39,779)
Official languages Bislama/English/French
Currency Vatu

 # Fiji

Fiji is made up of more than 300 volcanic islands in the South Pacific Ocean, about 1,100 mi. (1,770 km) north of New Zealand. Fiji's main export is sugar cane, and it has a flourishing tourism industry. However, political problems from time to time have discouraged other countries from investing in the islands.

Area 7,055 sq. mi. (18,270 sq km)
Country population 832,390
Capital city (pop) Suva (86,061)
Official languages There is no official language, but the main languages are Fijian and Hindi
Currency Fiji dollar

 # Nauru

The island of Nauru lies 33 mi. (53 km) south of the Equator in the Pacific Ocean. It is the smallest independent republic in the world. At present, the people have one of the highest incomes per head in the world, thanks to the export of phosphates (fertilizer). However, Nauru's phosphate reserves are running low, and it has few other resources.

Area 8 sq. mi. (21 sq km)
Country population 10,147
Capital city (pop) no official capital
Official languages Nauruan/English
Currency Australian dollar

 # Samoa

Samoa is a group of islands in the South Pacific Ocean. Samoa's beaches and rainforests have led to a booming tourism industry. This now brings in one-quarter of the islands' income.

Area 1,137 sq. mi. (2,944 sq km)
Country population 188,359
Capital city (pop) Apia (42,141)
Official languages Samoan/English
Currency Tala

 # Tuvalu

Tuvalu was a British colony until 1975. It is a group of nine coral atolls in the South Pacific Ocean. It is the second-lowest country in the world and is under threat from rising sea levels. Tuvalu has the world's second-smallest population. The country has no known natural resources, and has fewer than 1,000 tourists a year. The islanders rely on exporting fish, stamps and handicrafts, as well as the money sent home from Tuvaluans working abroad.

Area 10 sq. mi. (26 sq km)
Country population 19,916
Capital city (pop) Funafuti (5,008)
Official languages Tuvaluan/English
Currency Australian dollar

 # Marshall Islands

The Marshall Islands lie in the central Pacific. The islands were occupied by the U.S. after World War II until 1986, and were used for nuclear weapons testing. About half the people work in farming. Coconut oil is the main export.

Area 4,576 sq. mi. (11,854 sq km)
Country population 53,236
Capital city (pop) Dalap-Uliga-Darrit (20,651)
Official languages Marshallese/English
Currency U.S. dollar

People

The global village

In 2009, it was announced that over half of the world's population now owns a mobile phone. The incredible increase in the use of mobile phones means that once remote places are now connected to the rest of the world, bringing fresh opportunities for development and communication.

http://www.behindthename.com   search

Princes Harry and William: Their names are now two of the favourite boys' names in England and Wales.

Surnames around the world

Surnames were not used in Great Britain until after the Norman Conquest in AD 1066. Until then, most people were known only by their first name. People started to add extra names in order to be able to tell one William from another.

Some surnames came from where a person lived or the person's father's name — so the son of someone called John was known as Johnson. Others were based on a person's occupation (a blacksmith would be called Smith) or their appearance (a brown-haired person might be called Brown). The origins of some surnames have been forgotten.

A very long name

Rhoshandiatellyneshiaunneveshenk Koyaanfsquatsiuty Williams, born Beaumont, Texas, September 12, 198. Soon afterwards, her father James Williams extended her first name to 1,019 letters and the middle name to 36.

Popular first names

First name fashions change — especially those for girls. Some traditional names remain popular but new names come into use. Olivia was not in the Top 10 in the United States until 2001, but has kept its popularity. These are the most popular boys and girls names now and 100 years ago in the U.S.

Girls (current)	Boys (current)	Girls (1910)	Boys (1910)
1 Emily	1 Jacob	1 Mary	1 John
2 Isabella	2 Michael	2 Helen	2 James
3 Emma	3 Ethan	3 Margaret	3 William
4 Ava	4 Joshua	4 Dorothy	4 Robert
5 Madison	5 Daniel	5 Ruth	5 George
6 Sophia	6 Christopher	6 Anna	6 Joseph
7 Olivia	7 Anthony	7 Elizabeth	7 Charles
8 Abigail	8 William	8 Mildred	8 Frank
9 Hannah	9 Matthew	9 Marie	9 Edward
10 Elizabeth	10 Andrew	10 Alice	10 Thomas

Most common surnames

U.S.	China	Denmark	Eng. & Wales	France	Germany	India	Ireland
1 Smith	1 Wáng	1 Jensen	1 Smith	1 Martin	1 Müller	1 Singh	1 Murphy
2 Johnson	2 Li	2 Nielsen	2 Jones	2 Bernard	2 Schmidt	2 Kumar	2 Kelly
3 Williams	3 Zhang	3 Hansen	3 Taylor	3 Dubois	3 Schneider	3 Sharma/Sarma	3 O'Sullivan
4 Brown	4 Liú	4 Pedersen	4 Williams	4 Thomas	4 Fischer	4 Patel	4 Walsh
5 Jones	5 Chén	5 Andersen	5 Brown	5 Robert	5 Meyer	5 Shah	5 Smith
6 Miller	6 Yáng	6 Christensen	6 Davies	6 Richard	6 Weber	6 Lal	6 O'Brien
7 Davis	7 Huáng	7 Larsen	7 Evans	7 Petit	7 Schulz	7 Gupta	7 Byrne
8 Garcia	8 Zhào	8 Sørensen	8 Wilson	8 Durand	8 Wagner	8 Bhat	8 Ryan
9 Rodríguez	9 Zhou	9 Rasmussen	9 Thomas	9 Leroy	9 Becker	9 Rao	9 Fitzgerald
10 Wilson	10 Wú	10 Jørgensen	10 Roberts	10 Moreau	10 Hoffmann	10 Reddy	10 O'Connor

Known by one name

Some people are so famous they are instantly recognizable by just one name.

Aaliyah U.S. singer/actress Aaliyah Haughton, 1979–2001

Barbie U.S. doll Barbara Millicent Roberts, 1959–

Beyoncé U.S. singer Beyoncé Knowles, 1981–

Björk Icelandic singer/actress Björk Gudmundsdóttir, 1965–

Bono Irish rock band U2 singer Paul Hewson, 1960–

Canaletto Italian painter Giovanni Antonio Canale, 1697–1768

Cher U.S. singer Cherilyn Sarkasian, 1946–

Colette French writer Sidonie-Gabrielle Colette, 1873–1954

Dido UK singer Dido Armstrong, 1971–

Eminem U.S. rap singer Marshall Mathers, 1972–

Enya Irish singer Eithne ní Bhraonáin, 1961–

Evita Argentinean politician Eva Peron, 1919–52

Flea U.S. Red Hot Chili Peppers bass guitarist Michael Peter Balzary, 1962–

Hergé Belgian Tintin cartoonist Georges Rémi, 1907–83

Houdini U.S. magician Erich Weiss, 1874–1926

Lulu UK singer Marie McDonald McLaughlin, 1948–

Madonna U.S. singer Madonna Louise Ciccone, 1958–

Meatloaf U.S. singer Marvin/Michael Lee Aday, 1947–

Michelangelo Italian painter Michelangelo Buonarroti, 1475–1564

Moby U.S. musician Richard Melville Hall, 1965–

Nelly Cornell Haynes Jr, U.S. rapper, 1974–

Pelé Brazilian footballer Edson Arantes Nascimento, 1940–

Pink U.S. singer Alecia Moore, 1979–

Ronaldo Brazilian footballer Ronaldo Luiz Nazario de Lima, 1976–

Shaggy Jamaican singer Orville Richard Burrell, 1968–

Sting UK singer Gordon Matthew Sumner, 1951–

Twiggy Lesley Hornby, British model, 1949–

Usher Usher Raymond IV, U.S. singer-songwriter, 1978–

Another long name!

In the late 19th century, the Reverend Ralph William Lyonel Tollemache of Grantham, Lincolnshire, England, gave his 15 children very long names. These included Lyulph Ydwallo Odin Nestor Egbert Lyonel Toedmag Hugh Erchenwyne Saxon Esa Cromwell Orma Nevill Dysart Plantagenet Tollemache-Tollemache (1876–1961). The initial letters of his first names spell "Lyonel the Second."

Initial impressions

These famous people are known by their initials and surnames, rather than their full first names.

W.H. (Wystan Hugh) Auden was a poet

Rev. W. (Wilbert) Awdry wrote *Thomas the Tank Engine*

P.T. (Phineas Taylor) Barnum was a circus proprietor

J.M. (James Matthew) Barrie was the author of *Peter Pan*

T.S. (Thomas Stearns) Eliot wrote the book on which the musical *Cats* was based

W.C. (William Claude) Fields was a film actor

H.J. (Henry John) Heinz manufactured food

k.d. (Kathryn Dawn) Lang is a singer

D.H. (David Herbert) Lawrence was a writer

T.E. (Thomas Edward) Lawrence was a soldier/writer (Lawrence of Arabia)

C.S. (Clive Staples) Lewis wrote *The Lion, the Witch and the Wardrobe*

A.A. (Alan Alexander) Milne wrote *Winnie the Pooh*

E. (Edith) Nesbit wrote *The Phoenix and the Carpet*

J.K. (Joanne Kathleen) Rowling is the author of *Harry Potter*

O.J. (Orenthal James) Simpson was a football player

R.L. (Robert Lawrence) Stine wrote the *Goosebumps* series

J.R.R. (John Roland Ruel) Tolkien wrote *Lord of the Rings*

J.M.W. (Joseph Mallord William) Turner was a painter

Early Heinz wagon from about 1900

H.G. (Herbert George) Wells was a science-fiction author

E.B. (Elwyn Brooks) White wrote *Charlotte's Web* and *Stuart Little*

F. W. (Frank Winfield) Woolworth was a retailer

Japan	Norway	Russia	Scotland	Spain	Sweden
1 Sato	1 Hansen	1 Smirnov	1 Smith	1 García	1 Johansson
2 Suzuki	2 Olsen	2 Ivanov	2 Brown	2 Fernández	2 Andersson
3 Takahashi	3 Johansen	3 Kuznetsov	3 Wilson	3 González	3 Karlsson
4 Tanaka	4 Larsen	4 Popov	4 Campbell	4 Rodríguez	4 Nilsson
5 Watanabe	5 Andersen	5 Sokolov	5 Stewart	5 López	5 Eriksson
6 Ito	6 Nilsen	6 Lebedev	6 Thomson	6 Martínez	6 Larsson
7 Yamamoto	7 Pedersen	7 Kozlov	7 Robertson	7 Sánchez	7 Olsson
8 Nakamura	8 Kristiansen	8 Novikov	8 Anderson	8 Pérez	8 Persson
9 Kobayashi	9 Jensen	9 Morozov	9 Macdonald	9 Martín	9 Svensson
10 Saito	10 Karlsen	10 Petrov	10 Scott	10 Gómez	10 Gustafsson

Even longer!

Louis Jullien (1812–60) was a French conductor and composer, born in Sisteron, France. His parents were persuaded by the 36 members of the local Philharmonic Society that they should all be godfathers, and Louis received all their names.

Who's who in the family?

We all know who's who in our immediate family — our mothers, fathers, grandparents, aunts and uncles, sisters and brothers. But who is a second cousin or a cousin once removed?

Nephew
Son of your sister or brother

Niece
Daughter of your sister or brother

Cousin, or first cousin
Child of your aunt and uncle

Second cousin
Child of your first cousin. Second cousins have the same great-grandparents as you, but not the same grandparents. Third cousins have the same great-great-grandparents, and so on.

Removed
A child of your first cousin is called "once removed." Removed means a different generation. Once removed is one generation, twice removed is two generations, and so on.

Step
Stepmother, stepfather, stepsister, stepbrother, stepson or stepdaughter is a person who is related to you only by the remarriage of someone in your immediate family after death or divorce. For example, if a woman marries again, her new husband will be her children's stepfather but he has no blood relationship with them.

Half
A half-sister or half-brother has either the same mother or father as you, but not both.

In-law
A relative by marriage — so the wife of your son is your daughter-in-law or the wife of your brother is your sister-in-law. It refers only to immediate members of your family (your own marriage, that of your brothers and sisters, and your children).

Weddings and divorces around the world

The number of people marrying every year varies from country to country. Some are tropical islands and countries that are popular with tourists who travel there for a romantic wedding.

Others have cultures that place a specially high value on marriage. The number of divorces varies greatly from country to country, according to the legal system and religion.

Number of marriages per 1,000 per year*	Number of divorces per 1,000 per year*
High rates	**High rates**
China 35.9	Russia 5.30
Cook Islands 32.8	Aruba 5.27
Barbados 13.1	U.S. 4.19
Cyprus 12.9	Ukraine 3.79
Medium rates	**Medium rates**
U.S. 7.8	Australia 2.85
Australia 5.4	U.K. 2.58
UK 5.1	Canada 2.24
Canada 4.7	
	Low rates
Low rates	Guatemala 0.12
Venezuela 3.3	Belize 0.17
Argentina 3.2	Mongolia 0.28
Armenia 3.2	
Saudi Arabia 3.2	* In those countries for which data are available

Wedding on a Pacific island beach

www.theheraldrysociety.com   search

Till death do us part...

Longest marriages
● Sir Temulji Bhicaji Nariman and Lady Nariman of Mumbai (Bombay), India were married in 1853 at 5 years old. They stayed married for 86 years until Sir Temulji's death in 1940.

● Lazarus Rowe and Molly Weber were allegedly married in Greenland, New Hampshire, in 1743. They remained married for 86 years until 1829 when Lazarus died.

According to the Bible, King Solomon had 700 wives as well as 300 concubines.

Most marriages
● King Mongkut of Siam (1804–68) had 39 wives and 82 children. His life inspired the musical *The King and I* and the film *Anna and the King* (1999).

● American Glynn "Scotty" de Moss Wolfe (1908–97) was married 29 times, which is a U.S. record. His 29th and last wedding was on June 20, 1996, to Linda Essex. It was her 23rd wedding — another U.S. record.

Tommy Manville (1894–1967), a wealthy resident of New York City, the heir to a fortune made from asbestos, married 13 times to 11 different women (he remarried two of them).

Family history is increasingly popular

Family history

Genealogy is the study of family connections, while family history includes additional information about family members, such as their education, work and homes. Both have long been popular pastimes among people keen to discover more about their ancestors and to locate living relatives. The Internet has enabled anyone to carry out online research and contact family members around the world and share information. Special computer software now makes it easy to organize records and create family trees.

● In the past, families often kept records of births, marriages and deaths in their family bibles. Sometimes it was the only book in the household, and was treasured and passed on through generations, along with other information such as photographs and diaries.

● The main official sources are records of births, marriages and deaths. In England and Wales these have been compulsory since Queen Victoria came to the throne in 1837, and from 1855 in Scotland. In the U.S. and Canada they are kept by individual states. For earlier years, back to the 16th century in some places, the registers of churches that recorded baptisms, marriages and burials are valuable to researchers, alongside a wide range of other sources such as wills, professional and military archives and immigration and emigration records.

● Censuses have been held in the UK every 10 years since 1841. Those up to 1911 are available online to researchers who can gain valuable information about family members, their birthplaces, occupations and addresses. A U.S. census has been held every 10 years since 1790 — those up to 1930 are available online.

● In recent years, genetic genealogy — the use of DNA tests — has become a useful way of establishing an individual's relationship to other family members.

Anniversary gifts

There is a very old tradition of celebrating wedding anniversaries by presenting special types of gift. For example, for a 25th anniversary people give gifts made of silver. In the U.S. and Canada most people celebrate only the milestone anniversaries: the 25th, 30th, 40th, 50th and 60th.

The 75th anniversary was traditionally the diamond but few married couples live long enough to celebrate it. Since Queen Victoria's Diamond Jubilee was held to mark her 60 years on the throne, the 60th wedding anniversary has become the diamond celebration.

1st paper	**11th** Steel	**45th** Sapphire
2nd Cotton	**12th** Silk	**50th** Gold
3rd Leather	**13th** Lace	**55th** Emerald
4th Linen	**14th** Ivory	**60th** Diamond
5th Wood	**15th** Crystal	**70th** Platinum
6th Iron	**20th** China	**75th** Diamond (again)
7th Wool	**25th** Silver	
8th Bronze	**30th** Pearl	
9th Pottery	**35th** Coral	
10th Tin	**40th** Ruby	

Christopher Columbus landing in the New World

Karl Marx
(1818–83) German
Karl Marx's ideas on economic history and sociology changed the world. Marx was a social philosopher who attacked the state and predicted a future in which everyone was equal. He explained his theories in the *Communist Manifesto* (compiled with Friedrich Engels and published in 1848) and *Das Kapital* (1867–94). His ideas eventually led to the Russian Revolution and communism. By 1950 almost half of the world's people lived under communist regimes.

Christopher Columbus
(1451–1506) Italian
Christopher Columbus is one of the most famous of all explorers. He believed he could reach Asia by sailing west across the Atlantic Ocean and in 1492 he set sail in the *Santa Maria* to prove his theory. Instead, he landed on the islands now known as the West Indies. His discoveries led to the European exploration and settlement of the Americas.

William Shakespeare
(1564–1616) English
William Shakespeare is generally agreed to be the greatest playwright in the English language. He began as an actor and wrote at least 154 love poems and 37 plays, including *King Lear*, *Hamlet*, *Romeo and Juliet* and *Macbeth*. Shakespeare also probably introduced more than 1,700 new words to the English language.

A 1964 U.S. stamp commemorating the 400th anniversary of Shakespeare's birth

Charles Darwin
(1809–82) English
Naturalist Charles Darwin established the theory of evolution. He began forming his ideas when he served as official naturalist on a world voyage on *HMS Beagle* (1831–36) and spent the rest of his life back in England developing them. When his famous book *The Origin of Species by Means of Natural Selection* was published in 1859 there were violent reactions against it. Darwin challenged the Bible's account of creation, and explained that human beings are descended from an apelike ancestor. Another English naturalist, Alfred Russel Wallace, independently developed very similar ideas at the same time as Darwin.

Emmeline Pankhurst
(1858–1928) English
Emmeline Pankhurst was the most famous of the women who campaigned for the right to vote in the UK From 1905 she fought for the vote by any means possible and was frequently arrested and imprisoned. She died in 1928 shortly before her aims were realized and every woman over 21 years old was granted the vote.

Mahatma Gandhi
(1869–1948) Indian
Gandhi began his career as a lawyer but became a great political and spiritual leader. He led the peaceful civil disobedience of Indians against British rule in India and negotiated with the British government until 1947, when India was granted independence. Gandhi became the first icon of a people's struggle against oppression. His simple lifestyle and his belief in religious tolerance have made him a symbol of decency and peace ever since.

Emmeline Pankhurst, 1914

Albert Einstein
(1879–1955) German/American
Einstein was one of the greatest of all physicists and his name has become a symbol of genius. When his most famous work, *The General Theory of Relativity*, was proven in 1919, Einstein became the most celebrated scientist in the world, and he won the Nobel Prize for Physics in 1921. Einstein was a firm believer in pacifism, but his scientific theories helped his adopted country, the U.S., to develop the atomic bomb. A week before he died Einstein wrote to Bertrand Russell, a British philosopher and leading anti-nuclear campaigner, asking to put his name to a manifesto urging all countries to give up their nuclear weapons.

Adolf Hitler

(1889–1945) Austrian

Adolf Hitler was Germany's leader from 1933 to 1945, during which time he led the world into the most devastating war in history. Hitler's hatred of Jewish people and his desire for a blue-eyed, blond-haired master race led to the murder of six million people during World War II; most died in concentration camps in Eastern Europe.

Nelson Mandela

(1918–) South African

Nelson Mandela dedicated his life to the fight against apartheid — a policy that kept black and white South Africans apart and denied black citizens the vote. He was imprisoned in 1964 for his aggressive opposition to South Africa's racist government and was held for 26 years. In 1990, after his release, Mandela was elected president of the African National Congress. In 1993 he won the Nobel Peace Prize for his work to end apartheid.

See also

History timeline: page 104

Bill Gates

(1955–) American

Bill Gates created his first computer program while still at high school, co-founded Microsoft in 1977, and by 1993 was the richest man on Earth. In 2000 Gates and his wife formed the Bill & Melinda Gates Foundation, which is the largest charity in the world. One of its aims is to rid the developing world of polio and other deadly diseases.

James Watson (1928–) American and Francis Crick

(1916–2004) English

American biologist James Watson and English scientist Francis Crick discovered the molecular structure of DNA, using theories already written by Maurice Wilkins. Their theory helps to explain how DNA carries hereditary information and their discoveries have revolutionized our understanding of genetics and the study of disease.

Martin Luther King, Jr.

(1929–68) American

Martin Luther King was a Baptist minister who campaigned against the segregation of blacks in the southern states of the U.S. He was influenced by Gandhi and believed in peaceful protest. He won the Nobel Peace Prize in 1964. King was assassinated in 1968, but will always be remembered for his dignified, passive resistance to an unjust society.

Mao Zedong/Mao Tse-tung/ Chairman Mao

(1893–1976) Chinese

Mao Zedong was one of the founders of the Chinese Communist Party and the first chairman of the People's Republic of China in 1949. He had an enormous influence on his country and was greatly admired for founding the Chinese republic and for changes in the early years of his rule. During his rule, Mao's image was displayed everywhere — in every school, home, factory and workplace.

The charity co-founded by Bill Gates (right) supports important medical research

Women adventurers

These are just some of the intrepid women who went where no other woman — in some cases, no man — had gone before.

Amelia Earhart in the cockpit of her plane

● French novelist Jules Verne's novel *Around the World in 80 Days* inspired American journalist Nellie Bly (real name Elizabeth Cochrane, 1864–1922) to beat this time. She set out in 1889, and returned to New York on January 25, 1890 — a record round-the-world trip of 72 days, 6 hours, 11 minutes and 14 seconds.

● Amelia Earhart (U.S. 1898–1937) became the first woman to fly solo across the Atlantic in 1932.

● Cosmonaut Valentina Tereshkova (USSR, 1937–) was the first woman in space. She went into orbit on June 16, 1963.

● Sheila Scott (UK 1927–88) was the first woman to fly around the world solo, in 1971. She was also the first woman to pilot a plane over the North Pole.

● Harriet Quimby (U.S. 1875–1912) was the first American woman to gain a pilot's license, and in 1912 became the first woman to fly across the English Channel.

● Jacqueline Cochran (U.S. 1906–80) raced aircraft in the 1930s and set more aviation records than any woman — in 1953 becoming the first to break the sound barrier.

Polar exploration firsts

The North and South Poles are two of the most difficult places on Earth to reach and so have been great challenges for explorers. These are some of the people who reached the poles by one means or another.

First to reach the North Pole
American adventurer Frederick Cook (1865–1940) claimed that he and two Inuit reached the North Pole on 21 April 1908, but he probably faked his journey. Another American, Robert Edwin Peary (1856–1920), his companion Matthew Alexander Henson (1866–1955) and four Inuit were said to have first reached the pole on April 9, 1909. The first corroborated overland journey was that of a team led by Wally Herbert (UK) that arrived at the pole on April 6, 1969 — 60 years after Peary's claimed expedition.

First to reach the South Pole
Norwegian explorer Roald Amundsen (1872–1928) and four companions reached the South Pole on December 14, 1911. They just beat British explorer Robert Falcon Scott and his team, who got there on January 17, 1912 but died on their return journey.

First pole-to-pole journey
British explorer Sir Ranulph Fiennes and his partner Charles Burton were the first people to walk from pole to pole. They crossed the South Pole on December 15, 1980 and reached the North Pole on April 10, 1982.

First solo overland journey to the North Pole
Japanese explorer Naomi Uemura reached the North Pole on May 1, 1978. He traveled by dog sled, but was then picked up by an aircraft. Frenchman Jean-Louis Etienne made the first solo journey without dogs, reaching the pole on May 11, 1986.

First woman to reach the South Pole solo
Norwegian Liv Arnesen trekked to the South Pole unaided in 50 days, arriving at the pole on December 25, 1994.

First swim at the North Pole
British swimmer Lewis Gordon Pugh swam 1 km in gaps between ice at the North Pole, July 15, 2007.

First manned descent to North Pole seabed
On August 2, 2007, two Russian *MIR* submarines placed a Russian flag on the seabed beneath the North Pole.

First cat to sail around the world
Trim the cat was born on board *HMS Reliance* in 1799 on the way to Australia. The following year he sailed to England and back to Australia.

First round the world

Since the first voyage around the world, almost 500 years ago, people have been looking for different ways of circumnavigating (traveling right around) the planet by land, sea or air.

First circumnavigation
Juan Sebastian de Elcano and his crew of 17 on *Vittoria* sailed from Spain in 1519 and returned 1,079 days later. The expedition was led by Ferdinand Magellan, but he was murdered in the Philippines on April 27, 1521.

First British circumnavigation
Sir Francis Drake and a crew of 50 left Plymouth, England, in 1577 on the *Golden Hind* and returned on September 26, 1580.

First solo sailing
Canadian-born sailor Captain Joshua Slocum (1844–1910) sailed around the world alone in *Spray*, an oyster boat he built himself. He left the U.S. on April 24, 1895, and returned on June 27, 1898.

First walk
George Matthew Schilling (U.S.) claimed to have walked around the world between 1897 and 1904, but his journey has not been verified. David Kunst (U.S.) made the first confirmed journey from June 20, 1970, to October 5, 1974. He wore out 21 pairs of shoes during his 14,445-mi. (23,250 km) walk.

Explorers and travelers

Today there are few places that have not been explored, but this was not always the case. The Americas were unknown to Europeans until a little over 500 years ago, and Australia was scarcely known by the rest of the world until the late 18th century. These are some of the people who made Europeans aware of the rest of the world.

Marco Polo (c. 1254–1324)
Italian traveler Marco Polo was one of the first Europeans to visit China and other Far Eastern territories. His reports were not believed, but he encouraged the idea of trading with the East.

John Cabot (1450–98)
Italian-born explorer John and his son Sebastian Cabot were employed by British merchants to seek a western route to Asia. During their travels they discovered parts of the northeast coast of North America.

Christopher Columbus (1451–1506)
Italian explorer Christopher Columbus discovered North, Central and South America and the islands of the West Indies.

Vasco da Gama (c. 1460–1524)
Portuguese explorer Vasco da Gama traveled around the Cape of Good Hope and up the East coast of Africa. He discovered a trade route to India.

Ferdinand Magellan (1480–1521)
Magellan was a Portuguese explorer who led the first voyage around the world. He discovered the Strait of Magellan, near the tip of South America.

Abel Tasman (1603–59)
Abel Tasman, a Dutchman, explored Australia. In 1642 he discovered Van Diemans Land (later called Tasmania) and New Zealand.

Henry Hudson (c. 1550–1611)
Henry Hudson was an English navigator who searched for a Northwest Passage (a route to the East by traveling north of North America). He discovered Hudson Bay.

James Cook (1728–79)
British Captain James Cook led several major expeditions. He explored the coasts of Australia, New Zealand and North America.

David Livingstone (1813–73)
Livingstone was a Scottish missionary and explorer of Africa. He discovered and named the Victoria Falls after Queen Victoria.

Sir Richard Burton (1821–90)
Burton was one of the first Europeans to travel to Arabia. With John Hanning Speke he discovered Lake Tanganyika in Africa.

John Hanning Speke (1827–64)
Speke discoverered Lake Tanganyika with Burton. He also discovered Lake Victoria, believed to be the source of the River Nile.

Sir Henry Morton Stanley (1841–1904)
Stanley was a British explorer of Africa and was involved in the search for Livingstone.

Top of the world
The first people to succeed in climbing Everest, the world's highest mountain, were Edmund Hillary from New Zealand and Tenzing Norgay from Nepal. They reached the summit on May 29, 1953.

Steve Fossett in *Virgin Atlantic Global Flyer*

First nonstop flight
USAF B-50A bomber *Lucky Lady II* piloted by Capt. James Gallagher flew from Fort Worth, Texas, on February 26, 1949. The journey took 94 hours, 1 minute, and the plane was refueled four times in mid-air.

First underwater
U.S. Navy nuclear submarine *Triton* traveled around the world underwater between February 16, and April 25, 1960.

First nonstop solo voyage
British yachtsman Robin Knox-Johnston sailed from and returned to Falmouth, UK, in *Suhali* between June 14, 1968, and April 22, 1969.

First in a wheelchair
Rick Hansen (Canada) went around the world in a wheelchair between March 21, 1985, and May 22, 1987. He traveled through 34 countries.

First balloon flight
Brian Jones (UK) and Bertrand Piccard (Switzerland) made a round-the-world voyage in the *Breitling Orbiter 3*. They left on March 1, 1999, and their journey took three weeks.

First solo flight
On March 7, 2005, Steve Fossett (U.S.) achieved the first solo round-the-world flight without refueling in *Virgin Atlantic Global Flyer*. He covered

22,878 mi. (36,818 km) in a flight time of 67 hours, 2 minutes and 38 seconds. On February 1, 2006 he once again took off from the U.S. to fly around the world. This time he carried on to Bournemouth, UK, making this voyage the longest ever solo, nonstop, round-the-world flight. He traveled a distance of 22,936.5 mi. (36,912.68 km) in 76 hours, 42 minutes, and 55 seconds.

Apollo 8 astronauts James Lovell, William Anders and Frank Borman, 1968 "people of the year"

Late success

As people live longer, many continue to work well into what was once thought of as extreme old age. These are all people who made great achievements in their eighties and beyond.

Alice Porlock, British writer, published her first book at 102 years old.

Ichijirou Araya, Japanese climber, climbed Mount Fuji aged 100 years.

George Burns, U.S. actor, appeared in *Radioland Murders* (1994) at 98.

Dimitrion Yornanidis, Greek athlete, ran a marathon at 98.

Pablo Casals, Spanish musician, conducted the Israel Festival Youth Orchestra when he was 96.

Michelangelo, Italian artist, produced his Rondandini *Pietà* sculpture at the age of 88.

Claude Monet, French painter, completed his waterlily paintings when he was 84 years old.

Against the odds

All these people triumphed over disability or illness to achieve fame.

Lance Armstrong (1971–) U.S. cyclist, contracted cancer that affected his brain and lungs. He recovered and went on to win the gruelling Tour de France cycle race a record seven times in a row, 1999–2005.

Ludwig van Beethoven (1770–1827) was one of the world's greatest composers. He continued to compose music even after he became totally deaf in 1817.

Lord Horatio Nelson

(1758–1805) was a British admiral. He lost an arm and an eye in battle, but won many naval victories, including the Battle of Trafalgar in 1805.

Stephen Hawking

(1942–) a British physicist and celebrated author of *A Brief History of Time*, suffers from motor neuron disease. He is confined to a wheelchair and speaks with the aid of a voice synthesizer.

In the news

Every year the editors of *Time* magazine nominate a person of the year — the individual or group who has most influenced world events during the year. The winner may not always have had a good influence — Adolf Hitler was nominated in 1938.

Nominees may be a man, a couple (Chinese leaders General and Madame Chiang Kai-shek in 1937), a woman (Queen Elizabeth II in 1952), a group of people (three astronauts in 1968), even a machine (a computer in 1982). Here are just some of the winners.

2008 Barack Obama (incoming U.S. President)

2007 Vladimir Putin (Russian president)

2006 You

2005 Bill and Melinda Gates/Bono

2003 The American Soldier

2000/04 George W. Bush (US president)

1999 Jeff Bezos (founder of Amazon.com)

1994 Pope John Paul II

1992/98 Bill Clinton (US president)

1987/89 Mikhail Gorbachev (Soviet leader)

1966 Young people

1963 Martin Luther King, Jr (civil rights campaigner)

1961 John F. Kennedy (US president)

1949 Winston Churchill (British prime minister)

1930 Mohandas Gandhi (Indian leader)

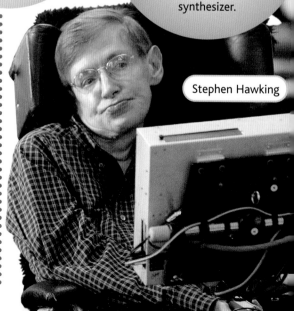

Stephen Hawking

🔍 s9.com   search

William Gladstone, British politician, became prime minister for the fourth time when he was 82 years old.

Benjamin Franklin, American statesman, helped write the U.S. Constitution when he was 81 years old.

George Cukor, U.S. film director, directed *Rich and Famous* (1981) at 81 years old.

One and only

At the age of 82, Irish playwright George Bernard Shaw won an Oscar for Best Screenplay for *Pygmalion* (1938). He had already won the Nobel Prize for Literature in 1925, so became the only person ever to win both a Nobel and an Oscar.

Sarah Bernhardt
(1844–1923) French actress, lost a leg in 1914 but continued acting.

Andrea Bocelli
(1958–) an Italian opera singer who was blinded at the age of 12. He went on to achieve international singing success.

Louis Braille
(1809–1852) was blind and invented the Braille system of printing with raised dots to enable blind people to read.

Terry Fox
(1958–81) Canadian athlete, lost a leg to cancer. He took up long-distance running, and through this he raised money for a cancer charity.

Mark Inglis
(1959–) In 2006, the New Zealander became the first double amputee to reach the top of Everest.

Helen Keller
(1880–1968) was a famed author and lecturer despite being blind and deaf.

Joseph Pulitzer
(1847–1911) U.S. publisher and founder of the prestigious Pulitzer Prizes, was blind from the age of 40.

Christopher Reeve
(1952–2004) American actor, star of four Superman movies, was paralyzed after a horse riding accident in 1995, but devoted his life to campaigning for disabled people.

Maria Runyan
(1969–) U.S. athlete, who despite being blind competed in the 2000 Olympic Games and in the 2002 New York City Marathon, achieving the second-fastest time by a woman.

Awards

Awards are presented in almost every area of achievement. The ones that receive the most attention in newspapers and on television are those given to famous film stars, writers, artists and singers. Among the best known are the following.

Academy Awards (Oscars®)
These are the most famous of all film awards. The Oscar® presentations are watched on television by more than a billion people worldwide. The Academy Awards — also called the Oscars® after the statuette that winners receive — were first presented in 1929. In 2009 *Slumdog Millionaire* won eight Oscars.

Booker Prize
This British book prize was set up in 1968 and is awarded each year for a novel published in the previous 12 months. It is now known as the Man Booker Prize.

Cannes Film Festival
This annual international film festival is held in Cannes in the South of France. Its most important award is the Palme d'Or (Golden Palm), which dates back to 1955.

Emmy Awards
Emmys have been awarded since 1949 for excellence in television (either daytime or primtime). In 2008, *30 Rock* won the Best Comedy Series category.

Golden Globe Awards
These U.S. film awards began in 1943. Julia Roberts has been nominated six times and won three awards, and Tom Hanks has won four of the six awards for which he was nominated.

Grammy Awards
The U.S. music awards have been presented since 1959. The classical awards have been dominated by conductor Sir Georg Solti, who won 38 Grammys. U2 has won more awards than any other band, a total of 22, while Robert Plant and Alison Krauss won five awards in 2009.

MTV Video Music Awards
The music television channel MTV established its awards in 1984. Madonna is the most successful MTV artist, with 70 nominations and 21 awards.

Nobel Prize
These international awards are named after Alfred Nobel, the inventor of dynamite, and were first presented in 1901. There are now six categories — Physics, Chemistry, Medicine, Literature, Peace and Economics.

Famous winners include Winston Churchill (Literature, 1953) and Mother Theresa (Peace, 1979).

Pulitzer Prizes
These U.S. awards are given for achievements in journalism, writing (fiction, non fiction and poetry) and music. They are named after publisher Joseph Pulitzer and began in 1917.

Sundance Film Festival Award
Sundance is the largest independent film festival in the U.S. In 2009, *Precious: Based on the Novel Push by Sapphire* won both the Grand Jury Prize and Audience Award in drama.

Turner Prize
This British art prize is named after landscape painter J.M.W. Turner and was established in 1984. The winning works are often controversial, and usually not conventional paintings. Damien Hirst is a notorious winner.

Golden Raspberry awards

The Golden Raspberries, founded in 1980, are joke awards presented to the worst films and actors! Madonna was a notable winner. She also received the Razzies award for worst actress of the 20th century. In 2009 Paris Hilton was voted worst actress and worst supporting actress, while *The Love Guru* won three awards: worst picture, worst screenplay and worst actor (Mike Myers).

"Oscar®"

Where are the children?

In countries such as India, where people have large families and relatively short lives, there are more children than older people. In North America there are more middle-aged and older people than children. Most people have smaller families so there are fewer young people. In the UK there are 10,132,365 children.

No. of children aged 0–14 yrs*

India	363,957,568
China	263,766,206
Indonesia	67,370,982
Pakistan	65,787,125
Nigeria	62,721,801
U.S.	62,380,610
Bangladesh	53,876,193
Brazil	53,305,222
Ethiopia	40,663,147

* Estimated for 2010

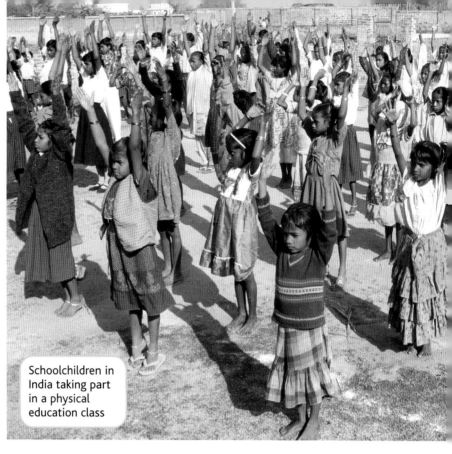

Schoolchildren in India taking part in a physical education class

Early success

Wolfgang Amadeus Mozart (Austria, 1756–91) began composing music at the age of 5, and a year later began a concert tour across Europe.
William James Sidis (U.S., 1898–1944) went to Harvard University to study mathematics at the age of 11.
Balamurali Ambati (U.S., 1977–) graduated from university at 13 and from medical school at the age of 17, becoming the world's youngest qualified doctor.

Young populations

Countries with a lot of people under 15 usually have high birth rates and high death rates. In countries where families have many children who are too young to work and adults die relatively young, there are not enough people of working age to earn money to feed and take care of the families. As a result, these countries tend to be among the world's poorest.

Population under 15 years old*

1 Uganda 50.0 percent
2 Niger 49.7 percent
3 Mali 48.3 percent
4 Democratic Republic of Congo 46.7 percent
5 São Tomé and Príncipe 46.6 percent
6 Chad 46.4 percent
7 Republic of Congo 45.8 percent
World average 26.9 percent

The U.S., UK and Canada have a lower than average proportion of children.

U.S. 20.1 percent
UK 16.5 percent
Canada 15.9 percent

* Estimated for 2010

Young fame

Miley Cyrus, the daughter of country singer Billy Ray Cyrus, was born on November 23, 1992.

At the age of 14 she became the star of the TV series *Hannah Montana* in 2006, appearing in the dual role of the pop star title character and Miley Stewart. By the time she was 16 she had released U.S. No.1 albums, earning a reputed $25 million in 2008, and appeared in films, including *Hannah Montana: The Movie* (released in 2009).

Hollywood star Angelina Jolie visiting a refugee camp in her role as Goodwill Ambassador for the United Nations High Commissioner for Refugees

The UN Convention on the Rights of the Child

The United Nations issued its Declaration on the Rights of the Child in 1959 to try to relieve the suffering of children in poor and war-torn countries. It came into force as a convention in 1990. One hundred and ninety three countries are parties to the Convention: Somalia and the United States are not.

All the signatories agree to make sure that children under 18 have certain basic rights, such as housing and medical care. Recent optional additions include one that children will not have to serve in military action.

The Convention on the Rights of the Child states that all children have the right to:

- a name and nationality
- affection, love, understanding and material security
- adequate nutrition, housing and medical services
- special care if disabled — physically, mentally or socially
- be among the first to receive protection and relief in all circumstances
- be protected against all forms of neglect, cruelty and exploitation
- full opportunity for play and recreation and equal opportunity
- to free and compulsory education, to enable the child to develop his/her individual abilities and to become a useful member of society
- develop his/her full potential in conditions of freedom and dignity
- be brought up in a spirit of understanding, tolerance, friendship among peoples, peace and universal brotherhood
- enjoy these rights regardless of race, color, sex, religion, political or other opinion, national or social origin and property, birth or other status.

International youth organizations

Scouts and Cub Scouts

Sir Robert Baden-Powell (1857–1941), a former general in the British army, launched the scouting movement in 1907. Today there are scouts in almost every country in the world — a total of 28 million. More than six million are in the U.S., but the leading scouting country is Indonesia, with almost nine million members. Scouting is forbidden in some countries, including Cuba and North Korea. The junior division for boys under 11 is called the Cub Scouts and was founded in 1930.

Girl Guides/Girl Scouts and Brownies

The Girl Guide Movement was started in 1910 by Sir Robert Baden-Powell and his younger sister Agnes (1858–1945). From then on, Girl Guides and Girl Scouts organizations were established around the world — the Girl Scouts of the United States of America dates from 1912 and the junior group, the Brownies, was set up in 1914. A century after the foundation, of the movement, there are Guides in 145 countries, with a total worldwide membership of more than 10 million.

YMCA and YWCA

The YMCA (Young Men's Christian Association) was founded by George Williams in the U.K. in 1844 and in the U.S. in 1851. Its aim was to provide shelter and other support for young men who came into cities to find work. The YMCA now has branches in 122 countries. The YWCA (Young Women's Christian Association), was founded in the UK in 1855 and in the U.S. in 1858.

www.unicef.org/crc/crc.htm   search

Beliefs & Ideas

Theory of evolution

2009 was the bicentenary of the birth of Charles Darwin, a man whose revoloutionary ideas have changed our understanding of the world. The incredible biodiversity of the Galápagos Islands was key to shaping Darwin's theory of evolution and the islands are now a world heritage site. Many of the unique species that live there are now endangered.

The Galápagos giant tortoise (pictured here) — fully grown adults weigh over 660 lb (300 kg) and measure over 4 ft (1.2 m) long.

Gods and goddesses

In most of the world's major religions today only one god is worshiped. But in many ancient religions, followers worshiped a group of gods. Each god had special characteristics and responsibilities, and some could appear in a variety of forms.

The myths and legends of ancient cultures and the range of gods worshiped often changed over thousands of years as different gods and goddesses rose or fell in importance. Those listed on these pages are a selection of the most revered and long-standing gods of some of the world's ancient cultures.

Chinese gods

The Chinese worshiped a large range of gods for more than 4,000 years, up to the coming of Chinese communism in the 20th century. Some Chinese people continue to worship these gods — often in secret — today.

Dragon Kings Ao-shin (North), Ao-chin (South), Ao-kuang (East) and Ao-jun (West), the gods of rain, rivers and seas
Fu-xi god of arts and creativity
Guan-yin god and goddess of compassion
Guan-yu god of war
Meng-po goddess of the underworld
Nu-guawas serpent goddess of creation
Pan-gu giant creator god
Qi-yu god of the rain (half bull, half giant)
Three Pure Ones supreme trinity of Yuan-shi-tian-zong, Ling-bao-tian-song and Lao-jun
Xi-he goddess of light
Xi-wangmu goddess of immortality
Yi-di god of wine
Zao-jun god of the household

Ancient Egyptian gods

Egyptian religion dates back about 5,000 years and lasted until the coming of Christianity and Islam. Its huge range of gods and goddesses were believed to control almost every aspect of people's lives.

Amun-Ra king of the gods
Anubis jackal god of death and Egyptian mummies
Aten god of the sun-disk
Bast/Bastet cat goddess of fertility
Bes lion-like domestic god
Hathor cow-headed goddess of happiness
Horus falcon-headed sky god
Isis wife of Osiris, mother of Horus, goddess of motherhood and royalty
Month falcon-headed god of war

Nefertum god of the sacred blue lotus and the rising sun
Osiris god of the underworld and agriculture
Ptah creator god and patron of craftsmen
Ra Sun god, ancient Egypt's most important god
Reshef god of war and thunder
Sekhmet/Sakhmet lion-headed goddess of war and destruction
Seth god of storms and violence
Thoth ibis-headed god of the Moon, arts and sciences

See also
World civilizations and empires: pages 106–107
Time: pages 14–16

Ancient Egyptian falcon-headed god Horus depicted on a mummy mask

Greek and Roman gods

The ancient Greeks had 12 major gods and goddesses. They believed the gods all lived on Mount Olympus and influenced the well-being of all humans. As the Greek civilization declined and the Roman empire grew, the Romans renamed the Greek gods and took them as their own.

Greek/Roman
Hera/Juno chief goddess — marriage
Aphrodite/Venus goddess of beauty
Artemis/Diana goddess of hunting
Athena/Minerva goddess of wisdom

Demeter/Ceres goddess of the harvest, nature
Hestia/Vesta goddess of the hearth
Zeus/Jupiter chief god — sky and air
Apollon/Apollo god of poetry, music, Sun

Ares/Mars god of war
Hephaistos/Vulcan god of blacksmiths
Hermes/Mercury messenger of the gods
Poseidon/Neptune god of the sea

Aztec gods

The Aztecs were based in central Mexico. They flourished from the 14th century until their conquest by Spanish invaders in 1522. They sacrificed humans to the gods, who were believed to control daily life and agriculture.

Chalchiuhtlicue goddess of lakes and streams, youth and beauty
Cinteotl god of maize
Coyolxauhqui goddess of the Moon
Ehecatl god of the wind and weather
Huehueteotl god of the hearth, the fire of life
Huitzilopochtli war god
Ilamatecuhtli goddess of the Earth, death and the Milky Way
Itztlacoliuhqui god of stone and the Morning Star
Mayahuel goddess of alcohol and the maguey plant (from which alcoholic drinks were made)
Mictlantecuhtli god of death
Quetzalcoatl creator god — and bringer of chocolate!
Tepeyollotl god of caves and earthquakes
Tezcatlipoca god of night and death
Tlahuizcalpantecuhtli god of dawn
Tonacatecuhtli god of food
Xipe-totec god of spring and agriculture, patron of goldsmiths
Xochipilli god of love, flowers, singing and dancing
Xochiquetzal goddess of love

Statue of the Aztec god Xochipilli, made between the 14th and 16th centuries

The 12 Norse gods

The Norse people lived in ancient and medieval Scandinavia (modern Norway, Sweden, Finland, Iceland and Denmark).

The 12 Norse, or Scandinavian, gods were together called the Aesir, and their homeland was Asgard. There was also a second group of gods called the Vanir, who fought the Aesir. Later some Vanir gods, including Frey and his sister Freya, became Aesir.

● Odin, or Woden, chief god in Norse mythology

● Thor, red-haired and bearded son of Odin and Jord, god of war (his name gave us Thursday — Thor's day)

● Tyr, Tiu or Tiw, another son of Odin, god of warfare and battle (his name is commemorated in Tuesday)

● Balder or Baldur, god of sunlight

● Brag or Bragi, god of poetry

● Vidar, god of silence, stealth and revenge

● Hoder the blind

● Hermód or Hermoder the Brave, Odin's son and his messenger

● Hönir or Hoenir, a minor god

● Odnir, husband of Freya

● Loki, god of strife or mischief, capable of changing shape and performing tricks

● Vali, Odin's youngest son by Rind, a giantess. He slew Hod, who had murdered his brother Balder

Inca gods

The Inca people lived in the part of South America that is now Peru from about 1200 to 1533. Inca gods were thought to influence natural events.

Apocatequil god of lightning
Apu Illapu god of thunder
Ilyap'a weather god
Inti Sun god
Kon god of rain and the southern wind
Mama Oello mother goddess, daughter of Inti and Mama Quilla

Mama Quilla Moon goddess, daughter of Viracocha and wife of Inti
Manco Capac creator god, Sun and fire
Pachacamac Earth god
Punchau Sun god
Vichaama god of death
Viracocha god of creation

Mayan gods

The Mayan civilization and neighboring Olmec culture date back 3,000 years. Descendants of the Mayans still live in southern Mexico, Belize and Guatemala.

Bacabs gods of the four directions — Mulac (North), Cauac (South), Kan (East) and Ix (West)
Balu-chabtan god of war and sacrifice
Chak god of rain, fertility and agriculture
Hunahau god of death

Itzamna reptile creator god
Ix-chel Moon goddess
Kinichi-ahau Sun god
Kukulcan feathered serpent god
Xbalanque god of the jaguar
Yum-kaax corn god

The five pillars of Islam

The following are the five most important aspects of the Muslim faith.

1 ash-Shahada — profession of faith in Allah and his prophet Muhammad
2 salat — prayer five times a day, facing Mecca
3 zakat — giving alms to the poor and needy
4 sawm — fasting between dawn and dusk during Ramadan
5 hajj — pilgrimage to Mecca, at least once in one's lifetime

Jihad, meaning holy war, is sometimes added as an extra pillar.

Major religions*

Christianity 2,173,816,023
Islam 1,358,290,337
Hinduism 872,921,745
Chinese folk-religions 379,843,528
Buddhism 378,724,109
Ethnic religions 259,917,388
Sikkhism 22,782,827

* followers worldwide

Religious buildings

- Abbey — a building occupied by monks or nuns and run by an abbot or abbess
- Basilica — a type of early Christian church
- Cathedral — the main church in an area and the seat of the bishop
- Chapel — a place of worship within a larger building, or a nonconformist Christian religious building
- Church — a building used for public worship by Christians
- Convent or nunnery — the home of a community of nuns
- Dagoba — a Buddhist shrine
- Friary — home to friars, members of a religious order
- Meeting house — a place where certain religious groups, such as Quakers, gather
- Monastery — the home to a religious community of monks
- Mosque — a Muslim place of worship
- Pagoda — an Eastern temple
- Priory — a religious house run by a prior; it may be under the control of an abbey

The Golden Temple, Amritsar, India

Holy places

A holy place is somewhere that is especially revered by the followers of a religion. Examples include the birthplace of the founder of a religion, shrines and places of pilgrimage. There has been conflict in some of these holy places when members of other religions have claimed or attacked the sites.

Amritsar, India
This city is the Sikh religion's spiritual center. The Golden Temple is the main shrine.

Athos, Greece
This is a holy mountain for the Greek Orthodox Church where there are many monasteries. Women are forbidden to go on to the mountain.

Benares, India
This Hindu holy city is dedicated to the god Shiva.

Bethlehem, Israel
The birthplace of Jesus

Canterbury, U.K.
The city was once England's most important pilgrimage center.

Ganges, India
The Ganges River is sacred to Hindus, who bathe here and scatter the ashes of their dead in its waters.

Jerusalem, Israel
A holy city for Christians, Muslims and Jews. Sites include the Western Wall, Dome of the Rock and Church of the Holy Sepulchre.

Karbala, Iraq
This city is the center of Shia Islam and contains the shrine of the Prophet Muhammad's grandson al-Husain.

- Shrine — a place of worship connected with a sacred person or saint. It may contain sacred objects or relics
- Synagogue — a building for Jewish religious services
- Tabernacle — a house or tent used for worship, named after the tent used by the Israelites to cover the Ark of the Covenant
- Temple — a place of worship dedicated to a particular god or gods. Also sometimes used instead of synagogue

Gate of a Shinto shrine in Miyajima, Japan

Holy cows

Visitors to India are often amazed by the number of cows wandering in the streets (one theory as to why they congregate in busy traffic is that the exhaust fumes kill the flies). Gau Mata, or Mother Cow, has long been an important part of the Indian economy, its milk providing nourishment and its dung used for fuel, but it is also the most revered animal in the Hindu religion and features in many myths and legends; the phrase "sacred cow" is even used in non-Hindu cultures. Gaudan, the act of presenting cows to Brahmin priests, is highly regarded, while killing a cow is prohibited and beef is never eaten (McDonalds restaurants in India serve vegetarian burgers). Once a cow has ceased to produce milk, it is often released to roam freely in the certain knowledge that devout Hindus will not let it starve.

The cow is revered in India

Gods of the Vedas (sacred books)

Indra is the thunder god of battle.
Varuna is the guardian of order.
Agni is the god of fire.
Surya is the sun deity.

Other Hindu gods
Brahma is the creator.
Vishnu is the preserver, who has 10 incarnations:
  Matsya, the fish
  Kurma, the tortoise
  Varah, the boar
  Nrisinha, half-man, half-lion
  Vamana, the dwarf
  Parasurama, Rama with the axe

Ramachandra, Rama with bow and arrows
Krishna, god of the Bhagavad-Gita
Buddha, teacher
Kalki, "the one to come."
Shiva is the god of destruction.
Ganesh is the elephant-headed god.
Hanuman is the monkey warrior god.

Hindu goddesses
Durga or Amba is the warrior god.
Parvati is the wife of Shiva.
Kali is the goddess of destruction.
Lakshmi is the wife of Vishnu, goddess of beauty, wealth and fortune.
Saraswati is the goddess of learning, arts and music.

Lhasa, Tibet (China)
The center of Tibetan Buddhism. The monastery here was once the home of the Dalai Lama.

Lourdes, France
In 1858 Bernadette Soubirous (later St. Bernadette) saw visions of the Virgin Mary in a grotto at Lourdes. Since then Catholics have made pilgrimages there, seeking cures for their illnesses.

Mecca (Makkah), Saudi Arabia
Every year, millions of Muslims go on pilgrimage to this city. They also turn to face Mecca when they pray.

Medina, Saudi Arabia
This is the site of the tomb of the prophet Muhammad.

Olympus, Greece
The ancient Greeks believed the mountain to be the home of Zeus and other gods.

Salt Lake City, Utah
The headquarters of the Church of Latter-Day Saints (Mormons)

Santiago de Compostela, Spain
In the 9th century a tomb believed to belong to the apostle James the Greater was discovered here. Christians make pilgrimages to a shrine made on the site.

Mount Shasta, California
A dormant volcano and a sacred site for Native Americans

Vatican City
The city-state in Rome, Italy, is the center of the Roman Catholic faith.

www.adherents.com   search

The Koran

Allah is the Islamic name for God. Muslims believe that He revealed His wishes for the world to a man called Muhammad. These messages were later collected together as the Koran (also written Qur'an). Muslims believe that the words of the Koran are the exact words of Allah. It is said that it has not been altered since it first appeared in AD 632. The Koran is written in Arabic, the language that Muhammad spoke, and it contains the main teachings of Islam.

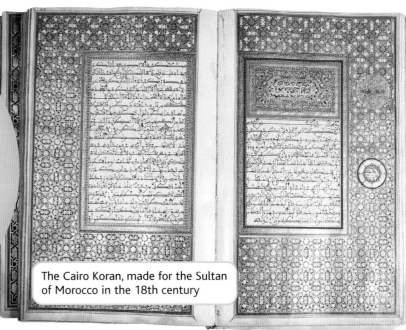

The Cairo Koran, made for the Sultan of Morocco in the 18th century

Boy reading from the Torah at a bar mitzvah ceremony

The Torah

The Torah is Judaism's most sacred text. It includes the first five books of the Bible, also known as the Pentateuch. These include the laws that God revealed to Moses on Mount Sinai. The Jewish scriptures also include the books of the prophets, historical writings and the Talmud. The Talmud contains instructions for following a Jewish way of life and understanding Jewish laws.

Sacred books

The Vedas

The four books of the Vedas contain the earliest Hindu beliefs and they have also influenced Buddhism, Sikhism and Jainism. The Rig-Veda is the oldest of the Vedas. It was composed about 1500 BC, although it was not written down until around 300 BC. The Vedas include rituals and hymns that give us a glimpse of life in ancient India. Another important Hindu text is the Bhagavad-Gita, or Song of the Lord. This is one section of a very long epic poem called the Mahabharata. The Bhagavad-Gita is about 700 verses long and sets out Hindu philosophy, explaining the importance of selflessness, duty, devotion and meditation.

The Pali Canon

The Pali Canon is a collection of sacred texts followed by the Theravada school of Buddhism. The teachings of the Buddha were first passed on through the spoken word and were not written down until the 1st century BC. The Pali Canon is written in the Pali language, and is also known as the Tripitaka, meaning three baskets. The texts are divided into three sections that were originally written on palm leaf scrolls and kept in three different baskets. They include rules for Buddhist monks and nuns, tales of the Buddha's life and teachings, stories and philosophical arguments.

Guru Granth Sahib

Sikhs believe that the Guru Granth Sahib is the supreme spiritual authority and head of the Sikh religion, rather than any living person. The original version was compiled by Guru Arjan Dev, the fifth Sikh guru, in 1604. He collected the compositions of previous gurus over a number of years. The text includes almost 6,000 hymns and poems composed at different times and in different languages, which makes it very difficult to translate. It also includes Hindu and Muslim writings, reflecting the religious tolerance of the gurus.

The Bible

The Christian sacred book is called the Bible. It is made up of two parts — the Old Testament and the New Testament. The Old Testament describes the history of the Israelites and contains books of history, law, poetry and wisdom. It was written by different people, probably between 1100 and 200 BC. The New Testament describes the story of Jesus' life and his importance for Christians, and also contains writings by some important early Christians. It was probably written between AD 50 and 150. Passages from the Bible are read at Christian church services, and Christians also see the Bible as containing a code to live by and guidance in following their faith.

The original 12 disciples

1 Andrew: a fisherman and brother of Simon Peter; crucifed in Achaia, Greece; the patron saint of Scotland and Russia (November 30)

2 Bartholomew (August 24)

3 James the Great: son of Zebedee and brother of John; martyred by Herod Agrippa (July 25)

4 James the Less (May 3)

5 John: son of Zebedee and younger brother of James the Great; also known as John the Evangelist; said to have written the Gospel that bears his name (December 27)

6 Judas Iscariot: the disciple who betrayed Jesus in return for 30 pieces of silver; he later hung himself

7 Jude: known as Judas, son of James; said to have been martyred in Persia with Simon (October 28)

8 Matthew: originally a tax collector before he became a disciple; author of the first Gospel (September 21)

9 Peter: a fisherman from Capernaeum; according to tradition he was crucified upside down; usually depicted holding the keys to heaven; considered to have been the first pope (June 29)

10 Philip (May 3)

11 Simon: also called Peter; a Galilee fisherman (October 28)

12 Thomas: known as Didymus, "the twin"; the patron saint of Portugal (December 21)

See also

Bestsellers: page 230

The Last Supper, painted by Pomponio Amalteo in 1574

The Last Supper

The Last Supper is an event described in the New Testament, which took place the day before Jesus was crucified. Jesus' 12 followers, called disciples, were all there. Following his crucifixion, they elected Matthias and Paul of Tarsus to join them, making a total of 14. Together they are known as the apostles and are regarded as the original Christians who acted as missionaries, spreading Jesus' teachings. All except Judas Iscariot later became saints in the Catholic church and have feast days devoted to them, listed above (some dates differ in other church traditions). The historical accounts of their lives contain many conflicting legends and details of their martyrdoms.

The Ten Commandments

The commandments are the divine law handed down to Moses by God on Mount Sinai.

They are key to both Christian and Jewish religions. The commandments appear in the books of Exodus and Deuteronomy in the Old Testament of the Bible, but are also described by Jesus in Matthew's Gospel in the New Testament, where he shortens them to just two — Love God, Love your neighbor.

1 Thou shalt have no other gods before me
2 Thou shalt not make unto thee any graven image
3 Thou shalt not take the name of the Lord thy God in vain
4 Remember the sabbath day, to keep it holy
5 Honor thy father and thy mother
6 Thou shalt not kill
7 Thou shalt not commit adultery
8 Thou shalt not steal
9 Thou shalt not bear false witness against thy neighbor
10 Thou shalt not covet thy neighbor's house, thou shalt not covet thy neighbor's wife, nor his manservant, nor his maidservant, nor his ox, nor his ass, nor any thing that is thy neighbor's

Animals in the Bible

There are many animals mentioned in the Bible. Sheep and lambs are referred to most often, probably because they were important for their meat and wool.

The lion appears because it is a symbol of power, strength and wisdom.

Animal	OT*	NT*	Total
1 Sheep	155	45	200
2 Lamb	153	35	188
3 Lion	167	9	176
4 Ox	156	10	166
5 Ram	165	0	165
6 Horse	137	27	164

* Occurrences in verses in the King James Bible
OT: Old Testament, NT: New Testament

Longest serving popes

Popes are usually chosen from among senior cardinals. They rarely live long enough to serve more than about 20 years. However, Pope Benedict IX is said to have been only 12 years old when he was elected in 1033!

Pius IX was the longest serving pope. He was 85 years old when he died. Leo XIII was even older at 93. The shortest serving pope was Urban VII, who died of malaria 12 days after his election in 1590.

Pius IX was in office for 31 years (June 16, 1846, to February 7, 1878).
John Paul II was in office for 26 years (October 16, 1978, to April 2, 2005).
Leo XIII was in office for 25 years (February 20, 1878, to July 20, 1903).
Pius VI was in office for 24 years (February 15, 1775, to August 29, 1799).
Adrian I was in office for 23 years (February 1, 772, to December 25, 795).
Pius VII was in office for 23 years (March 14, 1800, to August 20, 1823).
Alexander III was in office for 21 years (September 7, 1159, to August 30, 1181).

The Holy Grail

The Holy Grail was the cup that Jesus used at the Last Supper. According to legend, it was taken to England by Joseph of Arimathea but was lost, and King Arthur and his Knights of the Round Table went on a quest to find it. The cup was said to have magical powers — but only for those with a pure heart. The legend featured in many 19th-century paintings, as well as modern films, including *Monty Python and the Holy Grail* (1975), *Indiana Jones and the Last Crusade* (1989) and *The Da Vinci Code* (2006), based on the novel by Dan Brown.

Knights of the Round Table, a painting in the church of Trehorenteuc, France

Largest Christian populations

1 **U.S.** 245,930,675
2 **Brazil** 170,597,790
3 **Russia** 114,513,145
4 **China** 110,666,028
5 **Mexico** 99,945,687
6 **Philippines** 75,520,618
7 **India** 65,962,801

Christianity timeline

300s

1000s

c. 6 – 4 BC Birth of Jesus Christ, Bethlehem
AD c. 33 Christ crucified
c. 60 – 100 Gospels written
c. 64 Persecution of Christians by Roman Emperor Nero
312 Emperor Constantine converts to Christianity, leading to it becoming sole religion in the Roman Empire

324 Building of St. Peter's Basilica, Vatican, Rome, begun on site of Circus of Nero
c. 380 Final agreement on which books should be in the Christian Bible
635 Jerusalem and most of Middle East conquered by Muslims
999 Most of Europe converted to Christianity

1054 Christian church splits into Western (Catholic) and Eastern (Orthodox)
1095–1272 Crusades (series of wars by Christians to take holy sites in Middle East away from Muslim control)
1187 Jerusalem captured by Saladin
1209 Franciscan order of monks started

1382 John Wycliffe translates Bible into English
1456 First printed Bible (Johannes Gutenberg, Germany)
1479 Spanish Inquisition begins to persecute heretics
1517 Martin Luther begins Protestant Reformation, Germany

Patron saints

A patron saint is a saint chosen to be the protector of a particular person or group of people, or associated with a particular problem or situation.

Many more saints are called upon for help with problems than are linked with pleasant events. For example, at least 26 saints are connected with difficult marriages, but only one (St. Valentine) with happy marriages.

Patron saints for special problems

Appendicitis Erasmus
Arthritis/rheumatism James the Greater
Broken bones Drogo+
Cold weather Sebaldus
Coughs Blaise+
Dog bites Vitus

Earache Cornelius+
Famine Walburga
Floods Christopher+
Headaches Acacius+
Insect bites Felix+
Knee problems Roch+
Lost articles Anne+
Natural disasters Agatha

Poisoning Benedict+
Shipwreck Anthony of Padua
Snake bites Hilary of Poitiers+
Storms Scholastica+
Toothache Apollonia+
+ More than one saint

Patron saints of professions and groups

Accountants Matthew the Apostle
Actors Genesius of Rome+
Air travelers Joseph of Cupertino
Ambulance drivers Michael the Archangel
Architects Barbara+
Artists Luke the Apostle+
Astronauts Joseph of Cupertino
Athletes Sebastian
Authors Francis de Sales
Bakers Elizabeth of Hungary+
Beekeepers Ambrose of Milan+
Booksellers John of God+
Boys John Bosco+
Bricklayers Stephen of Hungary
Broadcasters Gabriel the Archangel
Cab drivers Christopher+
Carpenters Joseph+
Children Nicholas of Myra+
Comedians Vitus+
Cooks Martha+
Dentists Apollonia
Doctors Cosmas+
Farmers Isidore the Farmer+
Fathers Joseph

Firefighters Florian+
Fishermen Andrew the Apostle+
Gardeners Adelard
Girls Agnes of Rome+
Hairdressers Cosmas+
Librarians Jerome+
Mathematicians Barbara
Mothers Monica+
Motorcyclists Our Lady of Grace
Musicians Cecilia+
Nurses Agatha+
Plumbers Vincent Ferrer
Poets David+
Police officers Michael the Archangel+
Postal workers Gabriel the Archangel
Printers Augustine of Hippo+
Prisoners Dismas
Sailors Francis of Paola+
Scientists Albertus Magnus+
Sculptors Claude de la Columbiere+
Soldiers George+
Teachers Catherine of Alexandria+
+ More than one saint

The Flying Friar

Many Christian saints are claimed to have been able to fly, but Saint Joseph of Copertino (1603–63) is the most famous of them. The Italian Franciscan friar is said to have first levitated (risen into the air) in 1630, often hovering over people during religious ceremonies, including once in an audience with Pope Urban VIII, and even carrying fellow friars on his back during more than 100 flights. He became known as the "Flying Friar" and was canonized (officially declared a saint) in 1767. In the 20th century he became the patron saint of pilots, astronauts and air travelers.

1800s 1900s

1534 Henry VIII breaks with Rome; leads to the founding of the Church of England
1610–1795 Baptist, Congregationalist, Presbyterian, Quaker (Society of Friends) and Methodist Churches founded
1611 King James Bible published

1800–1900 The Age of the Mission. Western Churches send missionaries to every country in the world. Number of Christians doubles by the end of the century
1830 Church of the Latter-Day Saints (Mormons) founded, Fayette, New York, U.S.
1872 Jehovah's Witnesses founded by Charles Taze Russell, U.S.

1878 Salvation Army founded by William Booth, U.K.
1910 International Missionary Conference marks first attempt in nearly 1,000 years to reunite churches
1948 World Council of Churches founded
1962–65 Second Vatican Council radically reforms the Catholic Church worldwide

2005 Pope John Paul II dies; Pope Benedict XVI elected
2007 Boris Yeltsin's Russian Orthodox funeral is the first of a head of state in Russia since 1894

See also

History timeline: page 104

Buddhist festivals

There are a number of Buddhist traditions, and Buddhists in different countries have their own festivals on different dates. These are the most important Buddhist festivals.

● Wesak, held on the full moon in May, is the most important Buddhist festival and celebrates the birth of Buddha.

● Dharma Day celebrates Buddha's teaching and is held on the full moon of July. On Dharma Day there are readings from Buddhist scriptures, and people spend time reflecting on what they mean.

● Sangha Day is held on the full moon in November and celebrates the spiritual Buddhist community. Buddhists traditionally give presents on this day.

● Parinirvana Day, also known as Nirvana Day, marks the death of Buddha. Celebrations vary from place to place, but generally Buddhists go to temples or monasteries on this day, or meditate.

Losar

Losar is a Tibetan Buddhist festival. It is held in February and marks the New Year. The festival lasts for three days, when people go to monasteries, visit friends and family and exchange gifts.

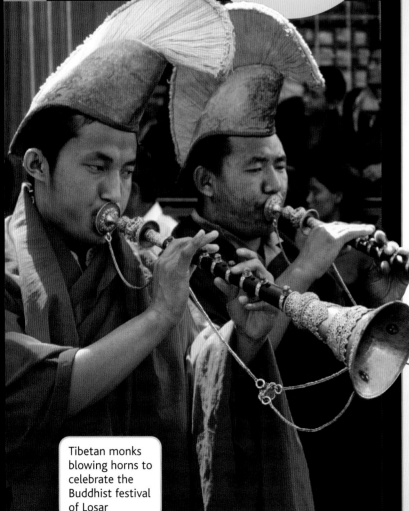

Tibetan monks blowing horns to celebrate the Buddhist festival of Losar

Christian festivals

Epiphany (also known as Twelfth Night)
January 6 (January 18 in Russia; February 1 in Ethiopia). The Epiphany (*Epiphaneia:* Greek for manifestation) celebrates three events that are all thought to have happened on this day: Jesus' appearance as a newborn to the Magi (three wise men); Jesus' baptism, when God acknowledged his son; Jesus' first public miracle, when he turned water to wine in Galilee.

Ash Wednesday
The first day of Lent (see below). Ash Wednesday is a day of repentance for Christians, when they make amends for the year's sins before the fasting of Lent. Anglican and Roman Catholic churches hold ceremonies at which churchgoers' foreheads are marked with crosses using ash.

Lent
The 44 days before Good Friday (including Sundays). Lent is a period of fasting when Christians identify with Jesus Christ's suffering. The day before the start of Lent is known as Shrove Tuesday or "Fat Tuesday" (Mardi Gras), when Christians traditionally eat up any leftover animal products (often in the form of pancakes), as these cannot be eaten during Lent.

Palm Sunday
The Sunday before Easter Sunday and the first day of Holy Week. Palm Sunday commemorates Jesus' arrival in Jerusalem, when the crowd threw palm leaves in front of his donkey. Later that week, many in the cheering crowd were calling for Christ's execution.

Maundy (or Holy) Thursday
The Thursday before Easter Sunday. Maundy Thursday commemorates the Last Supper, which established the ceremony of Holy Communion, when bread and wine became identified with Jesus' body and blood. It was also the day when Jesus washed the feet of his disciples. At Roman Catholic church services on Maundy Thursday the priest ceremonially washes 12 people's feet.

Good Friday
The Friday before Easter Sunday. Good Friday ("good" meant "holy" in Early Modern English) commemorates the day when Jesus Christ was crucified. The symbol of the cross is an important part of church services on Good Friday, and churchgoers read the psalms and the gospels to remember Christ's experience.

Easter Sunday
The Sunday that follows the first full moon after March 21 (the spring equinox). Easter always falls between March 22 and April 25 in the Western calendar. Easter is up to two weeks later in Orthodox churches. Easter Sunday is the most important day in the Christian calendar, as it celebrates Jesus' resurrection from the dead. Easter Sunday is a day of joy for Christians.

Pentecost/Whitsunday
Fifty days after Easter Sunday. Pentecost celebrates the day the Holy Spirit entered the Apostles, enabling them to speak many new languages and spread the word of God. This event is considered by most Christians to mark the birth of the Church.

Christmas
Christmas is the celebration of the birth of Jesus on December 25 (January 6 in Russia and January 17 in Ethiopia). It comes in midwinter, a time of the year when many faiths hold festivities.

Jewish festivals

The main Jewish festivals celebrate the great events in the history of the people of Israel. The Jewish month in which they fall is given here, with an approximate equivalent in the Gregorian calendar.

Tishri (September/October)
Rosh Hashana: New Year
Yom Kippur: Day of Atonement
Sukkoth: Feast of Tabernacles
Shemini Atzeret: 8th Day of the Solemn Assembly
Simhat Torah: Rejoicing of the Law
Kislev (November/December)
Hanukkah: Feast of Dedication
Adar (February/March)
Tanrit Esther: Fast of Esther
Purim: Feast of Lots

Nisan (March/April)
Pesach (Passover)
Holocaust Remembrance Day
Iyar (April/May)
Lag B'Omer: Counting Day of Barley Sheaves
Sivan (May/June)
Shavuoth: Feast of Weeks
Tammuz (June/July)
Shiva Asar be-Tammuz: Fast of 17th Tammuz
Av (July/August)
Tisha be-Av: Fast of 9th Av

Muslims at the Grand Mosque in Makkah before pilgrimage (Hajj) month

Islamic festivals

Most Islamic festivals (see below) commemorate events in the life of the Prophet Muhammad. New Year's Day, for example, marks the day on which he set out from Mecca to Medina in the year 622. The month of the Islamic calendar in which the festival falls is given.

Every month starts approximately on the day of a new moon, or when a crescent is first seen after a new moon, so the calendar shifts and these festivals fall at different times every year according to the Gregorian calendar.

> Sky lanterns lit up in India for the Divali festival

Islamic festival dates

New Year's Day 1 Muharram
Birthday of Muhammad, AD 572 12 Rabi I
Night of Ascent (of Muhammad to Heaven) 27 Rajab
Month of fasting during daylight hours 1 Ramadan
Night of Power (sending down the Koran to Muhammad) 27 Ramadan
Feast of Breaking of the Fast (Eid Ul Fitr) 1 Shawwal (end of Ramadan)
Pilgrimage (Hajj) **month** 8–13 Dhu-al-Hijja ceremonies at Makkah
Feast of the Sacrifice 10 Dhu-al-Hijja

Hindu festivals

These are the main Hindu festivals, held in honor of gods as well as to celebrate important events in mythology and in the heavens. The Hindu month in which they fall is given, with an approximate equivalent in the Gregorian calendar.

Chaitra (March/April)
Ramanavami: Birthday of Lord Rama
Asadha (June/July)
Rathayatra: Pilgrimage of the Chariot at Jaggannath
Sravana (July/August)
Jhulanayatra: Swinging the Lord Krishna
Rakshabandhana: Tying on Lucky Threads
Bhadrapada (August/September)
Janamashtami: Birthday of Lord Krishna
Asvina (September/October)
Durga-puja: Homage to Goddess Durga

Navaratri: Festival of Nine Nights
Lakshmi-puja: Homage to Goddess Lakshmi
Diwali, Dipavali: String of Lights
Magha (January/February)
Sarasvati-puja: Homage to Goddess Sarasvati
Maha-sivaratri: Great Night of Lord Shiva
Phalguna (February/March)
Holi: Festival of Fire
Dolayatra: Swing Festival

Q www.interfaithcalendar.org   search

The Labors of Hercules

The Greek hero Hercules killed his wife Megara and some of their children after being driven mad by his stepmother, the goddess Hera.

As a punishment he had to perform 12 dangerous tasks or labors. When he succeeded in all of them, he was granted immortality.

1 Slay the Nemean lion (its skin resisted weapons, so he strangled it)
2 Kill the Hydra (a many-headed monster) of Lerna
3 Catch the Arcadian stag
4 Destroy the giant Erymanthian boar
5 Clean the Augean stables
6 Destroy the cannibal birds of the Lake Stymphalis
7 Capture the fire-breathing Cretan bull
8 Catch the horses of the Thracian king Diomedes
9 Seize the girdle of Hippolyta, Queen of the Amazons
10 Capture the oxen of the monster Geryon
11 Obtain the golden apples of the Hesperides
12 Bring Cerberus from Hades (hell)

Unicorns

A unicorn has the body of a horse, a lion's tail, a goat's beard, an antelope's legs and a single, often twisted, horn growing from its forehead. The unicorn is a popular subject in medieval stories; it is ferocious but good, and can purify water — or neutralize poison — by dipping its horn into it. The way to catch a unicorn is to use a young girl as bait, as a unicorn will lie down peacefully next to a maiden.

Figurehead of *The Unicorn*, a former warship

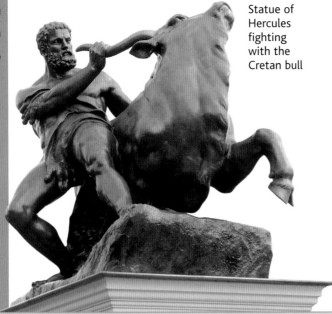

Statue of Hercules fighting with the Cretan bull

Mythical creatures

Almost every culture on Earth has legends of imaginary beasts. Some are like humans with supernatural powers; some are part human, part animal; while others are unlike anything we know.

Giants

Giants or ogres are enormous human-shaped creatures. They are usually seen as fearsome but stupid monsters that feed on human flesh. Famous giants include Goliath in the Bible, and Cyclops, Atlas and the Titans in Greek mythology.

Leprechauns

Leprechauns are small Irish fairies who bring good luck. They are helpful creatures, usually shown wearing green clothes, with an apron, buckled shoes and a red cap. Their fun-loving nature means that leprechauns are fond of alcohol, music and sports, but they are also mischievous and love practical jokes. Other "little people," including elves, dwarfs, gnomes and pixies, appear in many European fairy stories.

Centaurs

A centaur is half-horse and half-man, with the head and arms of a man and the body of a horse. It is one of the best known of all Greek mythological creatures and is said to have come from Thessaly in northern Greece. The myth may have arisen because of the skillful horsemanship of the people there.

Fairies

Fairies also feature in many tales. They are usually sweet, kindly creatures. In the Middle Ages, however, people believed that fairies stole children and replaced them with fairy beings known as changelings.

Heroes of legend

King Arthur

Legend says that Arthur, king of the Britons, won the throne by pulling a sword — the famous Excalibur — from a stone. This was a feat that only the true king was able to achieve. Arthur ruled during a period of peace and prosperity in Great Britain. Some folk tales say that if Great Britain is in danger, Arthur will return with his knights to defend the nation.

Beowulf

Beowulf was a Scandinavian warrior and the hero of *Beowulf*, the oldest poem in the English language. Beowulf was loyal to his king and also extremely brave. He killed Grendel the ogre, Grendel's mother and finally a fearsome dragon, which cost him his own life.

Paul Bunyan

The lumberjack Paul Bunyan is a famous character in American folklore. It is said that he was so enormous, he created the Grand Canyon by dragging his pick behind him, and his giant footsteps formed the lakes of Minnesota. The legend came from stories told by the lumberjacks of the northern United States.

El Cid

El Cid really did exist and many legends have grown up around him. He was also known as El Cid Campeador (meaning my lord, the champion). His real name was Rodrigo Díaz de Vivar and he was a Spanish nobleman who was born in about 1040 and died in 1099. El Cid is a national hero in Spain because he is seen as a brave and accomplished warrior who fought to take control of

Mermaids

Mermaids are beautiful creatures with the head and body of a woman and the tail of a fish. The first mermaid legend is thought to have been the story of Atargatis, a Syrian moon goddess of about 1000 BC. Atargatis had a child with a human. She then killed her lover, abandoned the child and jumped into a lake, where she took the form of a mermaid.

Vampires

Vampires are the "undead" who drink the blood of the living to survive. Ideas about vampires include the belief that plunging a wooden stake through a vampire's heart can destroy it. Some people also think that you can protect yourself against vampires with garlic, holy water, crosses and bibles, and that a vampire cannot enter a home unless invited.

Werewolves

Werewolves, or lycanthropes, are mythical creatures in the folk tales of many cultures. They usually appear as men by day, but may turn into wolves on the night of a full moon. The werewolf is bloodthirsty and ruthless. It devours its prey and shows none of the remorse that it might have felt in human form.

Trolls

Trolls are grotesque, malicious, rather dim-witted creatures in Scandinavian folklore. They are said to steal sleeping children, sometimes replacing them with one of their own. Trolls have poor eyesight, and are active only at night because sunlight turns them to stone.

Dragon at the end of the Dragon Bridge in Ljubljana, Slovenia

See also

Movie monsters: page 272

Dragons

Dragons appear in the myths of many cultures, especially China, where the dragon was a symbol of the emperor. A typical dragon has a serpent-like body covered with scales, large wings, and can breathe fire. In legends, dragons often guard a cave of treasure.

Spain from the Muslims. Legend suggests that El Cid fought for both sides at different times.

St. George

St. George was a soldier for the Roman Empire who refused to take part in the Empire's persecution of Christians. He was executed for treachery and became a Christian martyr. Later, King Edward III made him the patron saint of England.

St. George is the hero of a legend in which he slays a man-eating dragon that was guarding a city's water supply. The city's inhabitants were so grateful that they converted from paganism to George's Christianity.

Hercules/Heracles

According to Greek and Roman mythology, Hercules was born with superhuman strength. By the time he reached adulthood

he had killed a lion. Hercules had a jealous stepmother who drove him to madness. While in this state, Hercules killed his wife and children. In order to regain his honor, Hercules had to perform 12 difficult tasks (see p. 170).

Robin Hood

The Robin Hood of folklore was an English nobleman whose land was seized while King Richard the Lionheart was away fighting in

the Crusades (1188–92). He became an outlaw in Sherwood Forest and led a band of Merry Men (and Maid Marian, his true love). They robbed the nobility who traveled through the forest and passed on the valuables they stole to the poor and needy. Robin Hood was a master of disguise and many stories describe how he dressed as somebody else in order to trick his enemies or rescue his friends.

Good and bad luck signs

Black cats

Whether you find black cats to be good luck or bad depends on where you live. In the United States and Canada, a black cat is seen as a very bad omen, whereas in the UK, for instance, people think black cats are lucky, particularly if they cross your path. On the other hand, in the U.S. a white cat is very good luck, while in the UK, it is a sign of bad luck.

Horseshoes

A horseshoe is a piece of metal fixed to a horse's foot. Some people think that if you find a horseshoe and the open space is facing you it will bring you luck. Traditionally, people also hang horseshoes above the doorway of their home to bring good luck. In some countries, the horseshoe is hung downward — that's believed to let the luck flow out into the house. In others, the shoe must be hung with the opening at the top to keep the good fortune.

Aquarius Capricorn Sagittarius

Pisces

Aries

Taurus

Scorpio

Libra

Virgo

Gemini Leo

Cancer

Lucky horseshoe

See also
Constellations: page 21

Clovers

Four-leaf clovers are very rare. Anyone who finds one is said to be able to recognize evil influences and avoid them.

Ladders

A ladder leaning against a wall forms a triangle. Some believe it is disrespectful, and unlucky, to walk underneath one because triangles symbolize the Holy Trinity. The bad luck is warded off by crossing the fingers or making a wish while under the ladder.

Magpies

Magpies are generally thought to be unlucky. This belief is said to come from the Bible, as the magpie was the only bird that refused to enter Noah's Ark. In China, however, the magpie is a good omen, and should never be killed.

Mirrors

Breaking a mirror is said to bring seven years' bad luck. This idea may come from the old belief that your reflection is an image of your soul, so anything that changes the reflection may bring evil. The length of the period of bad luck may come from the Roman belief that life renews itself every seven years.

Spilling salt

Salt was once valuable and spilling it was thought to cause bad luck, unless the person who spills it throws a pinch over their left shoulder. In his painting of the Last Supper, Leonardo da Vinci shows Jesus' betrayer Judas knocking over the salt shaker.

The signs of the zodiac

In Western astrology the zodiac has 12 parts. Each is named after a constellation and corresponds to a different time of year. Astrologers believe that the movements of the planets influence what happens on Earth, and that people born under the different signs have certain characteristics.

Aries, the ram
March 21–April 19
Creative, impatient, masculine, competitive, warrior-like, independent, outspoken

Taurus, the bull
April 20–May 20
Determined, resourceful, materialistic, touchy, ruthless, entrepreneurial

Gemini, the twins
May 21–June 21
Intellectual, shallow, inquisitive, selfish, talkative, witty, indecisive, irritable

Cancer, the crab
June 22–July 22
Emotional, sympathetic, moody, sensitive, home-loving, romantic, loyal, tactless

Leo, the lion
July 23–August 22
Generous, creative, broad-minded, patronizing, bossy, extroverted, idealistic, arrogant

Virgo, the virgin
August 23–September 23
Diligent, intelligent, modest, conservative, overcritical, pedantic, affectionate, methodical

Libra, the scales
September 24–October 23
Charming, sociable, gullible, flirtatious, attractive, objective, artistic

Scorpio, the scorpion
October 24 –November 22
Forceful, passionate, jealous, obsessive, secretive, intense, outspoken, extreme, rebellious

Sagittarius, the archer
November 23–December 21
Optimistic, honest, philosophical, careless, irresponsible, energetic, adventurous

Capricorn, the goat
December 22–January 20
Disciplined, economical, patient, reserved, pessimistic, serious, organized, rational

Aquarius, the water bearer
January 1–February 19
Inventive, friendly, independent, unpredictable, serious, intelligent, eccentric

Pisces, the fishes
February 20–March 20
Imaginative, compassionate, vague, gentle, sensitive, creative, spiritual, easygoing

Number 13

The belief that the number 13 is unlucky is very ancient. The Romans believed the number 13 was a symbol of death and destruction. Norse legends claimed that the 13th guest at a banquet is the spirit of evil.

The Christian belief that the number brings bad luck is often said to come from the Last Supper, when Christ sat down with his 12 disciples — making 13 people. Some people think that the first person to leave a dinner table at which there are 13 diners will die before the end of the year.

Unlucky for some?

● The 13th *Apollo* space mission was known as *Apollo 13*. On April 13, 1970, there was an explosion on board and the spacecraft began to leak oxygen. This happened two days after it took off at 13:13 (1:13 pm). The spacecraft only just made it back to Earth.

● On Friday, September 13, 1928, a hurricane killed 2,000 people in Puerto Rico, Florida and the Virgin Islands, and caused approximately $25 million in damage.

● In some countries, high-rise buildings do not have a 13th floor. The floor numbering may skip directly from 12 to 14, or what would be the 13th is given another name, for example, "12A," or as in the Radisson Hotel, Winnipeg, Manitoba, where the 13th floor is called the "Pool Floor."

● The 13th of the month costs the U.S. about $1 billion a year through cancellations on trains and planes, absenteeism from work, and reduced business activity.

Lucky for others?

● The number 13 was sacred for the Mayans and Aztecs of Central America, and it is traditionally a lucky number in China.

● Buddhists pay homage to 13 Buddhas, and the orthodox Jewish prayerbook holds 13 principles of faith.

See also

The Last Supper: page 165

Crystal balls

Magicians traditionally claimed they could see into the future by gazing or "scrying" into crystal balls. Queen Elizabeth I's astrologer Dr. John Dee used a crystal ball that can still be seen in the British Museum, London, which also has his scrying mirror. It is made of obsidian, a hard black crystal, and had been used by Aztec sorcerers. It is claimed that in 1605 Dee's magic mirror foretold the Gunpowder Plot.

Heart line

Head line

Life line

Palmistry

Palmistry is the art of telling the future from the lines on the palms of your hands. The lines are unique to each person and are said to show the person's character and what will happen in the future. Palmistry began in India thousands of years ago as a form of counseling.

The heart, head and life lines are especially important. They are judged by their length and strength. The life line shows how healthy you are and how much you enjoy life. The head line shows how intelligent you are, and the heart line reveals the physical condition of the heart, as well as a person's sexual and emotional nature.

Mysterious places

The Nazca Lines

The Nazca Lines are enormous drawings on the ground (called geoglyphs) that stretch across the Nazca Desert in southern Peru. They show more than 300 geometric patterns, spirals and animals. The lines are so vast (one extends 40 mi. [65 km]) that they can only be seen properly from a height of about 1,000 ft. (300 m). Most experts agree that they were made by the Nazca Indians who lived in the region between 300 BC and AD 800, but there are many questions yet to be answered about them. For example, why were the pictures made and how are they so precise if their makers had no means to view them from the sky?

Stonehenge

Stonehenge is a circle of 17 upright stones called sarsens that stand on Salisbury Plain in southwest England. The stones weigh up to 55 tons (50 tonnes) and have other stones, called lintels, laid across the top. There is also an inner circle of smaller bluestones weighing up to 4.5 tons (4 tonnes) each. Stonehenge is the only stone circle in the world with lintels across the top of the stones, and experts think it was completed in about 1500 BC. They believe that the sarsen stones were transported from 20 mi. (32 km) away and the bluestones came from an incredible 155 mi. (250 km) away. At least 600 men would have been needed to move each sarsen stone on some of the steepest parts of the journey. Nobody knows exactly why Stonehenge was built, but it may have been a druids' temple or even a kind of astronomical calendar.

Teotihuacán

In AD 600 Teotihuacán in Mexico was the sixth-largest city in the world and about 200,000 people lived there. Just 150 years later, Teotihuacán was almost deserted, and plants had begun to grow over the city's huge pyramids. Nobody knows why Teotihuacán was abandoned, but it may have been devastated by a huge fire in AD 650.

Easter Island

Easter Island (or Rapa Nui) lies in the South Pacific between Chile and Tahiti, and is one of the most isolated islands in the world. By the 16th century, Easter Island had nearly 10,000 inhabitants, who made huge statues known as *moai*. The 887 *moai* were carved from the island's volcanic rock and have long, angular faces. Some have eyes made from coral. The average *moai* was about 13 ft. (4 m) tall and weighed over 15 tons (14 tonnes), so they would have been extremely difficult for the islanders to transport. Archaeologists believe that the statues symbolize the spirits of Easter Island's most important inhabitants.

The Bermuda Triangle

The Bermuda Triangle is an area of the Atlantic Ocean off the coast of Florida. It is famous for being the supposed site of many unexplained disappearances. The points of the triangle are Miami, Bermuda and San Juan in Puerto Rico. In the 15th century, Christopher Columbus claimed to have seen a "great flame of fire" falling into the ocean in the area. The Bermuda Triangle first began to attract attention in 1945, when Flight 19, a training mission of five U.S. bombers, vanished off the Florida coast. The plane that was sent to find them also disappeared, and around 100 boats and aircraft have been lost there. Explanations include magnetic fields, sea monsters and abduction by aliens, but most experts agree the disappearances are due to bad navigation and/or extreme weather conditions.

Teotihuacán

See also

Aztec empire: page 107

Four of the huge moai figures on Easter Island

Crop circles

Crop circles are complicated geometric patterns, usually in wheat fields. Some people believe that the patterns are left by the imprint of an extraterrestrial craft, or that they are a message from extraterrestrials themselves.

Another theory is that natural forces such as tornadoes, heat or strong winds create the patterns by flattening the crops, but the regular shapes of most crop circles makes this unlikely. The most likely explanation is that the circles are made by people as a hoax. They gradually build up a design by flattening the wheat, using very basic equipment such as rope and planks of wood.

Crop circles in Slovenia

Mysterious monsters

The Loch Ness Monster

The Loch Ness Monster, nicknamed Nessie, is said to live in Loch Ness in Scotland. The monster is generally thought to be a long-necked creature with flippers, like a prehistoric reptile. Many people have reported seeing Nessie, and in 2006 it was claimed that it might have been a circus elephant swimming in the Loch! However, there is no real evidence that the creature exists.

Yeti

The Yeti, also called the Abominable Snowman, is believed to live in the Himalayan mountains. People say this legendary creature measures up to 8 ft. (1.4 m), is covered in long brown hair, and walks upright like a human being. Everest mountaineers, including Sir Edmund Hillary and Sherpa Tenzing Norgay, have reported seeing mysterious footprints in the snow.

Bigfoot

Another legendary creature is said to live in the northwest of North America. People who claim to have seen Bigfoot say it is a large, hairy creature that walks upright like the Yeti. There is no firm evidence that Bigfoot exists, but there are some fuzzy photos and videos that are supposed to show this mystery monster.

On the Moon, or is this photo a fake?

Conspiracy theories

Many people believe that certain well-known historical events have been manipulated by governments and other secret organizations to conceal the truth. Some of the better-known beliefs are:

● A secret society called the Illuminati controls the world. This shadowy organization features in Dan Brown's novel *Angels and Demons*. Other powerful secret societies, including Opus Dei and the Priory of Sion, feature in his bestselling *The Da Vinci Code*.

● Sinister groups were responsible for plotting the deaths of U.S. President Abraham Lincoln, civil rights leader Martin Luther King Jr., musician John Lennon and Princess Diana. Some people claim that the Mafia were responsible for assassinating U.S. President John F. Kennedy. Others believe it was the work of Russian spies.

● Inventions have been hushed up by big businesses and oil companies who fear loss of income if new technologies become available. These include light bulbs that last for ever and ways of running cars on water.

● Aliens from other planets have crashed on Earth at Roswell, New Mexico. Their bodies and spacecraft have been secretly examined in a place in Nevada, known as Area 51, and the U.S. government has acquired advanced weapon and space travel technology from them.

● Photographs of the *Apollo* Moon landings (July 20, 1969) were faked by NASA in a TV studio. Conspiracy theorists have produced "evidence" such as the wrong sort of shadows and a lack of stars in the photographs, which were supposedly taken on the Moon's surface. They have even suggested that some astronauts were killed as part of the coverup.

Faking their own deaths

Many people find it so hard to believe that a famous person has died that it is often claimed that they faked their deaths so that they could continue to live without the media spotlight. Among those who are said to be still alive are a number of musicians including Elvis Presley (1977), Beatle John Lennon (1980), hip hop musician Tupac Shakur (1996) and Doors lead singer Jim Morrison (1971).

Conflict & Crime

Closing Guantánamo

Since 2001, the United States have used Guantánamo Bay Detention Camp, Cuba, to detain and try prisoners captured since the U.S. invasion of Afghanistan. The camp was not subject to U.S. law and it has been the focus of many human rights protests. One of President Obama's first acts as president was to order that the Guantánamo Bay camp be closed within a year.

Weapons named after people

● Big Bertha
Big Bertha was a 161 tons (144 tonne) cannon used by the German army to shell Paris from a distance of 76 mi. (122 km) during World War I. The name came from Bertha Krupp von Bohlen und Halbach (1886–1957), who inherited the German Krupp armaments business from her father.

● Browning pistol
Invented in the United States in 1896 by John Moses Browning (1855–1926), the Browning was an automatic pistol used by both civilians and military.

● Gatling gun
In 1862, Dr. Richard Jordan Gatling (1818–1903) patented the hand-cranked machine gun with a fire rate of up to 350 rounds per minute. It appeared too late to be widely used in the U.S. Civil War, and it was soon overtaken by more efficient weapons.
The slang term "gat" for any gun derives from the name.

● Kalashnikov
This machine gun is named after its inventor, Russian Mikhail Kalashnikov (1919–). More than 70 million have been made.

● Lüger
Gunmaker Georg Lüger (1849–1923) pioneered the P-08 pistol that bears his name in 1898. It was adopted by the German army and was widely used during both world wars.

● Mauser
The Mauser bolt-action rifle was developed in 1898 by German brothers Wilhelm (1834–82) and Peter Paul Mauser (1838–1914). They also invented an automatic pistol.

● Maxim gun
U.S. (later British) inventor Sir Hiram Maxim (1840–1916), who was also an aviation pioneer, made this machine gun in 1884.

● Molotov cocktail
This was a crude but effective bomb made with a gasoline-filled bottle and fuse. It was given its name by the Finns in about 1940 who used it during the war against Russia. They called it a cocktail for Molotov. Vyacheslav Mikhailovich Molotov (1890–1986) was the Soviet prime minister at the time.

● Shrapnel
This name was given to exploding shells invented by British officer Henry Shrapnel (1761–1842). Fragments of bombs are now also called shrapnel.

● Tommy gun
The Thompson submachine gun was invented by American army general John Taliaferro Thompson and U.S. Navy commander John N. Blish. It became known as the Tommy gun and was popular with gangsters during the 1920s.

Nuclear explosion

Weird weapons

Combined gun and plow
This was patented by C.M. French and W.H. Fancher of Waterloo, New York, in 1862. It was designed to be used by farmers so they could quickly turn their plows into powerful guns if they were attacked while plowing.

Hard cheese
In 1865 during a war between Uruguay and Brazil, a Uruguayan ship ran out of cannon balls. Instead they fired stale Dutch cheeses, one of which dismasted an enemy vessel and killed two sailors.

Boomerang bullets
These bullets were invented in the United States in 1870, and were designed to fire in a curved line. The danger was that if they traveled in a complete circle, they could kill the person who fired them.

Countries with nuclear weapons

The world's arsenal of nuclear warheads peaked at about 65,000 in 1985, and has been declining ever since. Precise figures are secret, but these are the best estimates and ranges:

Russia: 14,237–17,237
U.S.: approx 9,914
France: approx 350
Israel: 75–200
China: 100–200
UK: fewer than 160
India: up to 100
Pakistan: up to 60

World total: up to 28,221

Weapons milestones   1500s

500,000 BC Spears
250,000 BC Stone axes
25,000 BC Boomerang-like weapons (Poland) and knives
15,000 BC Spear-throwers
3000 BC Bows and arrows, shields and war chariots; Galleys (Crete)
2000 BC Armor and swords
865 BC Battering rams and other siege engines (Assyria)
397 BC Catapults propelling darts
332 BC Catapults throwing stones

AD 7th century Gunpowder (China)
8th century Viking longships
11th century Chain mail and crossbows
1150 Longbows
1221 Bombs (China)
1242 English monk Roger Bacon first describes gunpowder
1288 First guns (China)
1324 Cannon used at Battle of Metz
1346 Cannon (siege of Calais)
1370s Arbalests (crossbows)

1492 Leonardo da Vinci invents giant siege crossbows
1514 Man-of-war
1515 Wheel-lock muskets
1590 Bayonets made at Bayonne, France
1776 Submarine torpedoes
1784 Shrapnel shells
1835 Revolvers, Samuel Colt (U.S.)
1838 Breech-loading rifles
1847 Guncotton, invented by Christian Friedrick Schönbein
1847 Nitroglycerin (explosive) invented by Ascanio Solaro

1850 Battleships
1860 Repeating rifle invented by Christopher Spencer (U.S.)
1861 Metal gun cartridges and sea mines
1862 Gatling machine guns and Winchester repeating rifles
1866 Dynamite invented by Alfred Nobel (Sweden)
1872 Automatic pistols
1884 Maxim machine guns
1897 Dum-dum bullets (banned 1908)
1898 Lüger pistols

Largest armed forces

The number of personnel in the armed forces listed below are all active forces, but some countries have many reserves who can be called for service if needed. South Korea may have as many as 4.5 million reserve forces, Vietnam may have 5 million and China 800,000.

1 China 1,600,000 army, 255,000 navy and 400,000 air force personnel. Total: 2,255,000

2 U.S. 593,327 army, 341,588 navy and 336,081 air force personnel. Total: 1,498,157

3 India 1,100,000 army, 55,000 navy and 125,000 air force personnel. Total: 1,288,000

4 North Korea 950,000 army, 46,000 navy and 110,000 air force personnel. Total: 1,106,000

5 Russia 360,000 army, 142,000 navy and 195,000 air force personnel. Total: 1,027,000

Some totals include other forces.

Gunner on a U.S. army Black Hawk helicopter

Biological warfare

The aim of biological warfare is to infect enemies with deadly diseases. It is a modern form of warfare. However, in the Middle Ages the rotting carcasses of animals were catapulted into enemy castles to infect the inhabitants. In 1500 Leonardo da Vinci suggested using bombs containing saliva from mad dogs or pigs, or the venom of animals such as toads and spiders.

2000s

1901 Modern submarines
1902 Armored cars
1911 Aircraft carriers and bombers
1914 Zeppelin airships and large multi-engined aircraft able to carry heavy bombs used in aerial warfare
1914 Flechéttes first used — steel darts, designed to be dropped from aircraft on the enemy beneath
1915 Aircraft machine gun invented by German manufacturer Anthony Fokker

1915 Poisonous gases, such as mustard gas, chlorine and tear gas, first used by German army at Ypres. Gas masks invented to combat them
1915 Rifles with periscopic sights (allowing users to remain hidden) invented by an Australian soldier
1917 Water-cooled Browning machine guns invented by John Browning. Tanks introduced as a way of getting through enemy barbed wire, and increasingly as a battlefield weapon

1936 Nerve gas (Tabun) and Spitfire fighter aircraft
1939 Military helicopters
1940 Bazookas and radar
1942 Napalm and V2 rockets
1942 Dam-buster bombs
1943 Jet bombers and fighters
1945 Atomic bomb
1952 Hydrogen bomb
1955 Nuclear submarines
1960 Harrier jump jets
1970 Exocet missiles
1982 Air-launched cruise missiles

1984 Stun guns
1988 Stealth bombers
1988 IMINT (Imagery Intelligence) satellites
2001 Heckler and Koch MP7 submachine guns
2003 Multiple JDAM (Joint Direct Attack Munition) air-launched smart bombs
2009 Boeing YAL-1 Airborne Laser (ABL) system, capable of shooting down missiles, tested

World War I

World War I (1914–18) was the worst conflict the world had ever known, with a total of about 16 million civilian and military deaths and a further 21 million wounded.

World War I firsts

The war saw the introduction of many new weapons, among them:

First heavy bomber
On December 10, 1914 the Imperial Russian Air Force formed the first ever bomber squadron with a fleet of Ilya Muromets aircraft, the world's first four-engined bomber.

First aerial bombardment
The first time civilians were bombed from the air was on January 19, 1915 when German Zeppelin airships dropped bombs on Great Yarmouth and other East Coast UK towns. The first air raid on London occurred on May 31, 1915. A total of 558 people in the UK were killed by bombing in World War I.

First use of gas in battle
The German army used chlorine gas on April 22, 1915, during the Second Battle of Ypres.

First tank
The first tank used in battle was a British Mark I D1 at Delville Wood, France, on September 15, 1916. For secrecy, the new weapon was described as a "water tank," hence its name.

Countries suffering the most casualties

	Country	Mobilized*	Wounded	Missing/PoW#	Dead
1	Germany	11,000,000	4,216,058	1,152,800	1,773,700
2	Russia	12,000,000	4,950,000	2,500,000	1,700,000
3	France	8,410,000	4,266,000	537,000	1,375,800
4	Austria-Hungary	7,800,000	3,620,000	2,200,000	1,200,000
5	British Empire	8,904,467	2,090,212	191,652	908,371
6	Italy	5,615,000	947,000	600,000	650,000
7	Rumania	750,000	120,000	80,000	335,706
8	Turkey	2,850,000	400,000	250,000	325,000
9	U.S.	4,355,000	234,300	4,526	126,000
10	Bulgaria	1,200,000	152,390	27,029	87,500

* Total at peak strength
\# Prisoner of war

Medical advance

During World War I, many soldiers who received wounds to their faces received the first plastic surgery. Facial reconstruction methods were pioneered especially by Sir Harold Gillies, a New Zealand-born surgeon whose work continued in World War II, when it was also used to treat aircrew who had suffered severe burns.

Gas victims in World War I

Major wars

1600s

431–404 BC Peloponnesian War
Sparta vs Athens
264–146 BC Punic Wars
Rome vs Carthage
1095–1291 Crusades
Christians vs Muslims
1337–1543 Hundred Years' War
England vs France
1455–85 Wars of the Roses
York vs Lancaster

1618–48 Thirty Years' War
Catholic vs Protestant forces in Europe
1642–51 English Civil War
Crown vs Parliament
1701–1s4 War of the Spanish Succession
France vs Grand Alliance (of other European countries)

1740–48 War of the Austrian Succession
France, Spain, Bavaria, Prussia vs Great Britain, Netherlands, Savoy
1756–63 Seven Years' War
Austria, Russia, France, Sweden, Poland vs Prussia, Great Britain, Portugal
1775–83 American War of Independence
America vs Great Britain

1792–1815 Napoleonic Wars
Great Britain, Austria, Russia, Sweden, Naples vs France
1812–15 War of 1812
U.S. vs Great Britain
1846–48 Mexico-American War
Mexico vs U.S.
1853–56 Crimean War
Russia vs Turkey, Great Britain, France, Sardinia

www.militaryhistoryonline.com · search

Trafalgar

On October 21, 1805, during the Napoleonic Wars, the British fleet under Lord Nelson won this sea battle against the French, although Nelson was killed.

The Battle of Trafalgar, painted by John Callow, 1875

Great sea battles

Salamis, October 20, 480 BC (Greco-Persian Wars)
The Greeks overcame a Persian fleet, saving Greece from conquest.

Aegosopotami, 405 BC (Peloponnesian War)
In this battle 180 Athenian triremes were faced with 170 Peloponnesian ships. The Athenians were conquered, and the Peloponnesian War ended.

Actium, September 2, 31 BC (Wars of the Second Triumvirate)
Mark Antony and the Egyptian fleet were defeated by the Romans during this battle.

Lepanto, October 7, 1571 (Cyprus War)
The Spanish force defeated the Turkish fleet, which lost 25,000 sailors in 250 galleys.

Spanish Armada, July 29, 1588 (Anglo-Spanish War)
In July 1588, 130 Spanish ships with 2,500 guns and 30,000 troops set out to attack England. The English fleet badly damaged the Spanish ships with their guns, and the rest of the fleet was destroyed by bad weather.

Jutland, May 31, 1916 (World War I)
During this engagement the Royal Navy took on the German fleet, which withdrew.

Guadalcanal, August 9–November 30, 1942 (World War II)
This series of six naval engagements between the U.S. and Japanese resulted in heavy losses on both sides.

Coral Sea, May 8, 1942 (World War II)
The U.S. Navy took on the Japanese in the first major battle fought using aircraft from carriers.

Leyte Gulf, October 22–27, 1944 (World War II)
The U.S. defeated Japan in this battle. The Japanese lost three battleships, four aircraft carriers, 10 cruisers and nine destroyers.

Child soldiers

"Red Hand Day," commemorated around the world on February 12 each year, is part of a global campaign to eradicate the use of child soldiers. Although expressly forbidden under the Optional Protocol to the Convention on the Rights of the Child, which has been signed by 126 countries, Organizations such as the United Nations and Human Rights Watch report that some 15 countries and territories continue to use children as soldiers.

1900s

2000s

1861–65 American Civil War
North vs Confederate (Southern) states
1870–71 Franco-Prussian War
France vs Germany
1894–95 Chinese-Japanese War
China vs Japan
1898 Spanish-American War
Spain vs U.S.
1899–1902 Boer War
Boers (South Africa) vs Great Britain

1904–1905 Russo-Japanese War
Russia vs Japan
1914–18 World War I
Allies vs Germany and others
1931–33 Chinese-Japanese War
China vs Japan
1936–39 Spanish Civil War
Nationalists vs Republicans
1937–45 Chinese-Japanese War
China vs Japan

1939–45 World War II
Allies vs Germany and others (Axis powers)
1950–53 Korean War
North Korea (with Chinese aid) vs South Korea (supported by U.S.)
1957–75 Vietnam War
North Vietnam vs South Vietnam (with U.S. aid)

1982 Falklands War
Argentina vs Great Britain
1991 Gulf War
Iraq vs Allied forces
2001 "War on Terror"
U.S. and allies vs al-Qaeda, Taliban in Afghanistan
2003 Iraq War
U.S. and allies vs Iraq

Legal language

Accessory — someone who assists a criminal

Accomplice — a criminal's partner in crime

Acquit — to free or release from a charge, find not guilty

Affidavit — a written statement

Arson — deliberately setting a building on fire

Assault — inflicting harm on another person

Bail — a sum of money paid to ensure a person appears in court. The money is forfeited if they fail to appear

Battery — unlawful assault

Blackmail — attempting to obtain money by threats

Burglary — breaking into a building to commit theft

Capital crime — a crime for which the penalty is death

Civil cases — disputes between individuals

Criminal case — deals with acts considered harmful to the community

Damages — money paid as compensation for injury or loss

Defamation — harming a person's reputation by libel or slander

Evidence — information presented to a court to prove or disprove a legal issue, such as a defendant's guilt or innocence

Fraud — deception to gain money, etc.

Homicide — the unlawful killing of another person

Indictment — a written accusation

Kidnap — illegally carrying off a person, for example, to obtain ransom payment

Libel — defamation in writing, such as in a newspaper article

Manslaughter — taking another person's life without deliberate intent

Misdemeanor — United States law distinguishes between serious crimes, or felonies, and less serious, or petty (from the French word for "little") crimes or misdemeanors. The maximum penalty for a person convicted of a misdemeanor is 12 months in prison, but probation or community service are the more usual punishments.

Murder — the deliberate killing of another person

Oath — a promise to tell the truth in court, often sworn on a holy book such as the Bible

Perjury — a false statement made while under oath in a court

Probation — placing an offender under the supervision of a probation officer

Robbery — theft with force or threat of violence

Slander — defamation of a person in spoken language

Sue — to bring legal proceedings against a person, organization, etc.

Summons — an official order to attend court

Trespass — illegal entry of another person's property

Trial — the examination of a case in a court of law

Vandalism — deliberate damage to another's property

Verdict — the outcome of a trial, i.e., whether the accused is guilty or not guilty

Warrant — a legal document allowing for someone's arrest, the search of their property, etc.

Law courts

This is the court system in the United States. In many court rooms there is an image of justice as a woman, which dates from Roman times. It traditionally shows her holding scales in one hand, to show that she is impartial, and a sword to represent the power of the law. Sometimes she is blindfolded to show that justice cannot be influenced.

Juvenile Court
These courts deal with cases involving people under the age of 18, except in New York and North Carolina, where the maximum age is 16.

District Court
These courts deal with civil and criminal cases. There is at least one District Court in each state

Court of Appeals
The United States has thirteen Courts of Appeals that rank between District Courts and the Supreme Court. They try cases where a person who has been convicted can appeal against the lower court's verdict.

Federal Court
This is the name given to all courts acting under the United States Constitution, whether at District or Appeal level.

Supreme Court
The highest court in the United States sits in Washington, DC, and hears cases previously tried in a federal court whose decision is disputed.

A statue of justice holding scales and sword on the roof of the Old Bailey, the Central Criminal Court in London, UK

Canadian Law
Criminal law in Canada differs from that in the Unites States in that it is applied nationally with no differences between provinces and territories. Canada's legal system is based on the British common law system, except that of Québec, which comes from the French Code Napoléon. The court structure consists of Provincial and Territorial Courts, each with a court of appeal, with the Supreme Court of Canada as the final court of appeal.

Execution methods

Capital punishment is the legal killing of a person, usually those found guilty of murder or other serious crimes, although execution for minor offences or for political motives has occurred throughout history. These are some of the most common methods.

Hanging
Hanging has been used in Britain since the Saxon period. The bodies of highwaymen and other criminals were often hung in iron frames called gibbets to warn other would-be criminals. The last public hanging on mainland Britain was in 1868 and the last within a prison in 1964. Capital punishment was abolished in the UK in 1965. Hanging is still used in some countries and as an alternative to lethal injection in two U.S. states.

Burning at the stake
Many famous people were burned at the stake, including the French patriot Joan of Arc in 1431 and Protestant martyrs in England. In Germany up to 100,000 people accused of witchcraft and other crimes were burned during the 16th, 17th and 18th centuries. In 1589 133 people were burned in a single day. Witches were rarely burned in England, and never in America, where hanging was the usual punishment.

Beheading
Capital punishment literally means removing the head. In the UK it was the main execution method for aristocrats and members of the royal family. Heads of victims were often placed on spikes on the entrances to London as a warning. Beheading is still used in some countries, such as Saudi Arabia.

Firing squad
Execution by firing squad is common in warfare and for heads of state such as Emperor of Mexico Maximilian I, who was shot in 1867. In England, traitors and spies were shot at the Tower of London, the last in 1941. The firing squad is an optional method in three U.S. states.

Electric chair
The electric chair's first victim was William Kemmler at Auburn Prison, New York, on August 6, 1890. The chair remains an optional method in nine U.S. states.

Gas chamber
Introduced in Nevada, in 1924, the gas chamber is optional in five U.S. states, with lethal injection an alternative.

Lethal injection
Texas was the first U.S. state to use lethal injection with the execution of Charles Brooks Jr. on December 7, 1982. It is now authorized in 35 of the 50 U.S. states.

French Queen Marie Antoinette beheaded by guillotine, 1793

Guillotine
Devices for beheading people with a machine rather than an axe or sword were known in England (the Halifax Gibbet) as early as 1286 and in Ireland in 1307. The guillotine became used in France during the French Revolution after Dr. Joseph-Ignace Guillotin invented an improved version which was used to execute King Louis XVI and Queen Marie Antoinette. It was last used in public in 1939.

Strange laws

● Members of parliament are not allowed to wear suits of armour in the House of Commons.

● A law passed by Oliver Cromwell banning the eating of mince pies on Christmas Day has not yet been repealed.

● A law in Alderson, West Virginia, says that "No lions shall be allowed to run wild on the streets."

● Wyoming State Legislature banned the photographing of rabbits during January, February, March and April without an official permit.

● Anyone detonating a nuclear weapon within the city limits of Chico, California, is liable to a $500 fine.

● Owners of monkeys in Indonesia must have an identity card for the animal, complete with a photo of the monkey.

● No one may eat a rattlesnake in public on a Sunday in Kansas.

● In Spades, Indiana, you may not open a can with a revolver.

● In England it is illegal to impersonate a Chelsea Pensioner.

● In France, no pig may be called Napoleon.

● It is illegal to sell a teddy bear or play with a yo-yo on a Sunday in Memphis, Tennessee.

usdoj.gov/usao/eousa/kidspage/index.html   search

Punishments

In most countries people who break the law are either fined or imprisoned, but through the ages there have been many other forms of punishment.

Flogging

Whipping or flogging was once common: mutinous sailors were whipped with a cat-o'-nine-tails or keelhauled (dragged beneath a ship on the end of a rope). Flogging was widely used in the U.S. The last state to abolish it was Delaware — but not until 1972!

Stoning

Even today, some countries punish people by pelting them with stones, usually resulting in the victim's death.

Alcatraz, in the Bay of San Francisco, is no longer used as a prison.

Mid-19th-century ball and chain used as restraints when transporting prisoners

Stocks and pillory

Stocks were wooden structures that held the seated victim by the ankles. People threw things at them and ridiculed them — they were literally made a laughing stock. The pillory held victims in place by the neck and wrists. It was worse than the stocks as people could not use their hands to protect their faces from things thrown at them, and could be blinded or even killed.

Ducking stool

This punishment was used in the United States and England. The victims were usually women. They were strapped into a special chair and plunged into a river or pond.

Chain gang

Chain gangs, in which prisoners were chained together as they did heavy labor, such as breaking rocks, were used across the U.S. until 1955. In recent years they have been reintroduced in some prisons.

Branding

In some countries criminals were branded with a hot iron as a combined punishment, a sign that a person was guilty, and to warn other would-be offenders.

The rack

Although it is often used for comical effect in films, stretching on the rack was one of the most gruesome tortures ever devised. Victims' arms and legs were strapped to a machine that gradually pulled them out of their sockets. Accused of attempting to blow up the Houses of Parliament in 1605, Guy Fawkes was subjected to the rack and revealed the names of his accomplices and details of the plot.

Great robberies

Mona Lisa
Leonardo da Vinci's famous painting was stolen from the Louvre Museum, Paris, on August 21, 1911, by Vicenzo Peruggia. He kept it for two years, but when he tried to sell it he was caught and jailed.

Art theft
On March 18, 1990, two thieves disguised as policemen stole 12 works of art by Rembrandt, Degas, Vermeer and others from the Isabella Stewart Gardner Museum, Boston. The paintings were valued at $300 million and have never been recovered.

Dunbar Armored robbery
Believed to be the U.S.'s biggest cash robbery, an estimated $8.9 million was stolen in an armed holdup at the Dunbar Armored facility in Los Angeles, California, on the night of September 13, 1997. The gang leader was caught and jailed for 24 years, but most of the money has not been found.

Iraq Central Bank
In March 2003, just before the U.S.-led invasion of Iraq, President Saddam Hussein removed almost $1 billion in cash from the Iraq Central Bank. About $650 million was later discovered in his palace, but the rest has never been located.

Securitas depot robbery
On February 22, 2006, Great Britain's biggest ever robbery took place at the Securitas depot. The gang kidnaped the family of the depot manager and got away with over $105 million in cash. Following a series of police raids, some of the cash was recovered and several people were arrested.

Science and crime detection

Modern detectives use a wide range of scientific techniques to help them identify and catch criminals.

Fingerprinting
Fingerprints have been used for more than 100 years to prove whether someone was at a crime scene or held a weapon. Experts dust areas for hidden prints, which can also be revealed under special lights or on contact with certain chemicals. Faint prints can be improved by laser image enhancement.

DNA testing
Now forensic scientists use DNA testing or genetic fingerprinting to prove or disprove a suspect's connection with a crime. Everyone's DNA is unique and even the smallest samples — a single hair or a trace of saliva — can provide evidence.

Psychological profiling
Experts prepare profiles that suggest certain features of the killer, based on the nature of their murders. The profile may give likely age, background and habits. This builds a portrait of the criminal and helps detectives track him or her down.

Ballistics
All guns have a unique "fingerprint" — the marks made on a bullet as it leaves the barrel. Ballistics specialists examine these with microscopes and compare bullets used in crimes with those fired from a suspect's gun to find out whether they are identical.

Identikit
The Identikit system, which was developed in the United States in the 1940s, used transparent layers to build up a picture of a suspect's face. Witnesses' descriptions of eye color, hair styles, etc. were laid over a basic face shape. Modern developments include Photofit and computerized E-fit (Electronic Facial Identification Technique).

Surveillance
Crime fighters increasingly use electronic methods to spy on suspects. They can plant bugs (hidden microphones and video cameras) and intercept telephone calls and computer data.

Prison fact file

Longest jail sentence
In Thailand on July 27, 1989, fraudster Chamoy Thipyaso and her seven accomplices were each sentenced to 141,078 years.

Longest in jail
Paul Geidel, a New York State prisoner, was sentenced for murder on September 5, 1911, at the age of 17. He came out on May 7, 1980, at the age of 85, having served 68 years, 245 days.

Famous prisons

Alcatraz
This island in San Francisco Bay, California, is often known as The Rock, but was originally called Isla de los Alcatraces (Isle of the Pelicans). It was first used as a military prison, but then became a prison for the country's most dangerous criminals, among them Al Capone. Robert Stroud, a bird expert who became famous as the Birdman of Alcatraz, spent many years there.

Sing Sing
This New York prison was named after the Sin Sinck Native Americans who originally lived there. It was built from 1825 to 1828, and from 1891 onward many murderers were electrocuted in the electric chair at Sing Sing. In 1969 the prison was renamed Ossining Correctional Facility.

Guantánamo Bay
Since 2002, the detention camp on the U.S. Navy base at Guantánamo Bay, Cuba, has held hundreds of suspected al-Qaeda and other prisoners captured in Afghanistan and elsewhere. Following his inauguration in 2009, President Obama announced that the camp would be closed within the year.

Newgate
This was once London England's most notorious prison. Public hangings took place outside its gates, and it features in several of Charles Dickens' novels. Newgate was rebuilt several times, and finally demolished in 1902. The Central Criminal Court (Old Bailey) was built on the site of the prison.

Dartmoor
Dartmoor was first used for prisoners of war during the Napoleonic Wars and has served as a high-security, long-term prison ever since. The prison is miles from anywhere on a bleak English moor so if prisoners escape, they are usually recaptured quickly.

Most wanted
Since 1950, the FBI (Federal Bureau of Investigation) in the United States has issued a list of its "10 most wanted" criminals. Osama bin Laden, the international terrorist and Al-Qaeda leader, is currently at the top of the list. There is a $50 million reward to anyone who provides information that leads to his capture.

www.bop.gov search

Work & Home

World financial crisis

Starting in 2008, a series of events sent the world into a recession which will have repercussions for many years to come. Beginning in the U.S. and escalating to an international level, major banks collapsed, property prices fell, shares lost their value and millions of workers lost their jobs.

The first vacuum cleaner

In 1901, Englishman Hubert Cecil Booth invented the first successful vacuum cleaner. The machine worked well and was popular with rich people. It was also used in places such as Westminster Abbey, Buckingham Palace and Windsor Castle. Booth's cleaner was so large that it had to be pulled along by a horse, and six people were needed to operate it. The machines were only rented out, never sold.

The upright vacuum cleaner was invented in the United States by James Murray Spangler in 1907. Spangler realized that his asthma was made worse by dust, and wanted to find a more effective way of sweeping. He made the first upright vacuum cleaner with the help of a pillowcase tied to a broom handle and an electrical pump. Spangler sold the patent to his cousin William H. Hoover, who improved the invention and started a very successful business selling vacuum cleaners.

Washing up

Before the introduction of mass-produced china in the 18th century, people ate off wooden or metal platters that were wiped clean with straw or bread. All plates, dishes and cutlery had to be cleaned by hand until the first domestic hand-operated dishwasher was invented in the U.S. in 1886 by Josephine Cochran to prevent her precious china from being broken by clumsy servants. The first electric dishwashers date from 1922.

WHITE MOUNTAIN

WHITE MOUNTAIN GRAND

REFRIGERATORS
· 1903 ·

MAINE MANUFACTURING COMPANY
NASHUA · N·H · U·S·A·
ESTABLISHED - 1874 ·

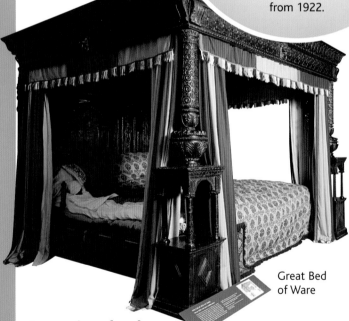

Great Bed
of Ware

Amazing beds

One of the largest beds in the world is the Great Bed of Ware. It is 10 ft., 8.5 in. (3.26 m) wide, 11 ft., 1 in. (3.38 m) long and was made in about 1580. The bed is mentioned by Shakespeare in *Twelfth Night*. It is now in the Victoria and Albert Museum in London, England.

In 1882 an Indian maharajah had a bed made of solid silver. At each corner there was a life-sized statue of a naked woman holding a fan. When the maharajah lay on the bed, his weight started a mechanism that made the women wave their fans.

Toilet paper

● Before the invention of toilet paper, people improvized with many different things. The rich used wool or lace, but the poor used anything they could find, including wood shavings, grass, stone, sand, leaves, corn cobs, moss, seashells, water or snow, as well as their hands. Later people began to use newspapers or telephone directories as toilet paper.

In the kitchen

The first washing machine

A washing machine was made in about 1677 by an Englishman named John Hoskin. Fellow English inventor William Bailey made a more efficient version in 1758. The first mass-produced washing machine was invented by American Alva J. Fisher in 1907, and was called the Thor.

The first microwave oven

The Raytheon Company in the United States began using microwave ovens in 1947 to cook food commercially. The idea came from one of their scientists, Percy Spencer. He had been standing near a microwave tube and noticed that a chocolate bar in his pocket had melted, although he had not felt any heat. The first home microwave appeared in 1952 and cost $1,295.

The first refrigerator

People used to pickle, smoke, dry and salt food so they could store it. During the 19th century some households began to use large boxes filled with blocks of ice, and the first electric fridge was made in 1913. It was called the Domelre (Domestic Electric Refrigerator) and was for home use, although it was very bulky. Refrigerators did not really become popular until after World War II, when the design was improved.

The first pop-up toaster

Charles Strite, a U.S. mechanic, invented the pop-up toaster in 1919. There were toasting machines before then, but they had to be watched carefully all the time so the toast didn't burn. Strite worked out a way to put a timer and springs into the design. His first toasters were large machines, used by restaurants, but in 1926 he launched a smaller version called the Toastmaster.

1903 advertisement for refrigerators

● Chinese emperors used toilet paper in the 14th century, but the first commercial toilet paper was produced in 1857 by Joseph Gayetty, a U.S. businessman. Gayetty's paper was sold as individual sheets with his name on them.

● Each person in the U.S. spends an average of $22.30 on toilet paper every year, compared with the average Brit's $28.70. The world average is $4.30 per person.

Home accidents

We think of our homes and gardens as safe places, but a surprising number of accidents are caused by everyday things. These figures record the number of people in a year who needed hospital treatment after accidents at home.

Estimated injuries

Home
Stairs 2,324,938
Beds and pillows 560,129
Chairs and sofas 476,109
Bathroom 330,102
Tables 309,252
Desks, shelves, etc 262,171
Clothing 245,129
Ladders, stools 227,769
Glass doors, windows, panels 155,269
Carpets, rugs 128,361

Gardens
Fences 109,181
Power saws 83,747
Garden equipment 80,970
Lawn mowers 78,773
Windows, door frames 69,427
Hand garden tools 57,556
Electric fixtures, lamps and equipment 55,662
Wheelbarrows and carts 51,427

Sports
Bicycles 515,871
Basketball 481,011
Football 455,193
ATVs, etc 278,671
Baseball 277,702
Exercise equipment 264,921
Toys 224,827
Playground equipment 219,625
Soccer 198,679
Swimming 155,322
Skateboards 143,682

Toilet fact file

● In medieval Europe people used chamber pots, which they emptied out of the window. In castles there would be a garderobe — a small cupboard with a hole that let waste out into the moat.

● Throwing waste out of the windows into the street, or rivers that provided drinking water, spread disease. The worst epidemic was the Black Death in the 14th century, which killed about one quarter of the people in Europe.

Estimated U.S. injuries in 2005 involving sports and recreation

Basketball 512,213
Bicycle 494,712
Football 418,260
Baseball, softball 262,529
All-terrain vehicles, mopeds, etc. 250,553
Exercise and exercise equipment 243,751
Playground equipment 218,506
Toys 196,052
Soccer 174,686
Swimming 150,553

The right path

During the 16th and 17th centuries it was good manners for a gentleman to walk closest to the street when escorting a lady. This meant that he was more likely to be in the path of sewage as it was thrown into the street!

● In London, England a gigantic cesspit was built under 200,000 houses and it often overflowed into them. Cesspits in London were abolished in 1847 and every home had to have a toilet. However, sewage was still diverted into the River Thames, which resulted in the "Great Stink" in the summer of 1858 — the worst smell in the city's history.

● The biggest cities in the U.S. and Europe's major cities started building sewers in the 19th century. Many of these early systems are still in use today. "Sewer tours" are popular in Paris, France, and in Brighton, UK. The systems are such amazing works of engineering that people travel to these cities just to visit them!

● Today, Japan makes the most advanced toilets. Known as "washlets," they have control panels, water jets, heated seats, dryers and telephones. More improvements are being developed, including voice-activated toilets and some that can do medical tests.

www.geffrye-museum.org.uk/kidszone   search

Valuable toys

Some wealthy collectors prize rare toys, especially those that are in good condition — in their original box, and never played with. These are just some of the toys that may have cost very little when they were made, but now sell for high prices.

● The GI Joe prototype was sold by Heritage Galleries & Auctioneers of Dallas, Texas, for $200,000 in 2003.

● A Kämmer and Reinhardt doll was sold at Sotheby's, in London, UK on February 8, 1994, for $277,981.

● Titania's Palace, a doll's house with 2,000 items of furniture, was sold at Christie's, London, in 1978 for $258,728.

● Dingley Hall, a doll's house dating from 1877, was sold at Christie's, London, in 2003 for $211,938.

● A 1906 train set made by German toymaker Märklin was sold at Christie's, London, in 2001 for £113,750 ($165,290).

● "Teddy Girl," a teddy bear made by the German manufacturer Steiff in 1904, was sold at Christie's, London, on December 5, 1994 for a record $171,600. Yoshiro Sekiguchi, a Japanese collector bought the bear for his teddy bear museum near Tokyo.

● A black mohair Steiff teddy bear, made in about 1912, was sold at Christie's, London, in 2000 for $132,157. It was one of only 494 black Steiff bears made as a mark of respect after the sinking of the *Titanic*. They are known as "mourning teddies."

● A tinplate clockwork motorcycle with Mickey Mouse and Minnie from about 1930, was sold at Christie's, London, in 1997 for $83,650.

● In 2007 the Stephen and Marilyn Steckbeck collection of nearly 500 mechanical banks (toy money boxes) was sold in the U.S. for a record total of $7.7 million. One, a whale from which the Biblical Jonah emerges when money is inserted, made $414,000.

● In 2008 a box of six Dinky toy vans was sold by Vectis of Stockton-on-Tees, UK, for $56,000 and a rare single van for $32,000.

The first Barbie dolls, in the Barbie Museum, Palo Alto, California

Birth of Barbie

The first Barbie doll appeared in February 1959. It was made by Ruth and Elliot Handler, co-founders of U.S. toy manufacturer Mattel, and they named the doll after their daughter Barbara. The doll was dressed in a black and white striped swimsuit, with sunglasses, high heels and gold hoop earrings. In the first year a total of 351,000 Barbies were sold at $3 each. The doll went on to become one of the bestselling toys of all time.

Toy-buying countries

Forecast sales of traditional toys (e.g., construction toys, model vehicles, indoor games, dolls and teddy bears) and video games in 2008 are estimated to average $15.20 for every person on the planet. There are huge differences between countries: North Americans spend the most and people in African countries the least per child.

G.I. Joe

A prototype G.I. Joe action figure was hand-carved in 1963 by Don Levine (U.S.). It went on to become one of the most popular boys' toys, with over 375 million sold in its first 40 years. As well as producing a range of designs and kit, manufacturers Hasbro have honoured a number of real people with G.I. Joe figures, including astronaut Buzz Aldrin and President Eisenhower.

Toys world total
$141,533,300

Other
$58,619,000

U.S.
$46,104,800

UK
$11,283,900

France
$9,098,300

China
$8,224,200

Japan
$8,203,100

Wii

Wii, a 7th generation games console made by Japanese manufacturer Nintendo, was launched in 2006. Originally codenamed "Revolution," the name "Wii" was chosen because it is easy to remember and pronounce in most languages, in English it sounds like "we," suggesting that it is for all. The two lowercase "i" characters standing side by side are said to represent two players.

In addition to buttons, the controller, the Wii Remote, allows users to point at the screen and make hand and arm movements to control the on-screen action. Many of the games available for the Wii, especially those involving sports and keep-fit, appeal to a wider age group than traditional computer game players. It has been one of the most successful entertainment products of the 21st century, with worldwide sales of over 50 million.

The Wii Series of games includes:

● Wii Sports — baseball, bowling, boxing, golf and tennis; over 40.5 million have been sold.

● Wii Play — includes billiards, laser hockey, shooting range and table tennis; over 21 million have been sold.

● Wii Fit — aerobics, balance games, strength training and yoga, used in conjunction with the Wii Balance Board; over 14 million have been sold.

● Wii Chess — as with other games, it offers the ability to play online.

● Wii Music — launched in 2008; 66 different instruments can be played.

● Wii Sports Resort — launched in 2009, it is used with the Wii MotionPlus accessory.

Nintendo also produces games such as Mario Kart Wii, played with the Wii Wheel, over 13.7 million of which have been sold. A large range of software has been produced by other manufacturers. Total world sales of Wii games to the end of 2008 was estimated at 312.22 million.

Scrabble

Scrabble was invented in the U.S. during the 1930s by an architect named Alfred Mosher Butts. First he called it Lexiko, then It and Criss-Cross, before hitting on the name Scrabble. Well over 100 million sets have been sold in more than 130 countries. The numbers of letters included vary according to the language. In Dutch, for example, there are 18 Es, 10 Ns and two Js. The Slovak version has 41 different letters — more than any other version.

Monopoly®

Monopoly was invented in 1934 by an unemployed engineer named Charles Darrow, who lived in Philadelphia, Pennsylvania. In his first version of the game he used street names from Atlantic City in New Jersey because he dreamed of going there, but could not afford the fare. The game was so successful that Darrow became a millionaire and spent the rest of his life traveling and growing rare orchids.

There are many national and local versions around the world, as well as specialised versions including those for animal lovers (Birdopoly, Dogopoly and Horse-opoly), those based on films such as James Bond and Shrek, as well as Bible-opoly and Elvis Monopoly. Parker Brothers, the U.S. manufacturer of the game, print more Monopoly money than the U.S. Treasury prints dollars.

Monopoly around the world

Country	City*	Boardwalk becomes
Australia	Canberra + state capitals	Kings Avenue
Canada	Vancouver, etc.	Robson Street
China	Hong Kong	Victoria Peak
Egypt	Cairo	Shari Qasr El Nil
France	Paris	Rue de la Paix
Germany	Munich	Schlossallee
Ireland	Dublin	Shrewsbury Road
Netherlands	Amsterdam	Kalverstraat
New Zealand	Auckland	Queen Street
Portugal	Lisbon	Rossio
Russia	Moscow	Arbat
Singapore	Singapore	Queen Astrid Park
South Africa	Johannesburg	Eloff Street/Eloffstraat
Spain	Madrid	Paseo Del Prado
Switzerland	Zurich, etc.	Paradeplatz
UK	London	Mayfair

* Some feature streets from more than one city

Russian Monopoly board

Jobs then and now

At the time of the 1911 UK Census the most common occupations in were domestic service (1.3 million people), agriculture (1.2 million), coal mining (1 million) and building (800,000). The most recent estimates show that 22.4 million people are now employed in service trades (shop and office work and other businesses), including 3.4 million in health and social work, 2.4 million in education and 1.68 million in hotels and restaurants. There are 2.9 million in manufacturing, 1.3 million in construction, 240,000 in agriculture and fishing and 60,000 in mining and quarrying.

Dirty work

Many unpleasant jobs of the past no longer exist. Among these are:

Climbing boy

Small boys were employed by chimney sweeps to climb inside with brushes. It was extremely dangerous and they were often trapped or injured. Even though it was banned in 1840, many boys continued in this work well into the 19th century.

Countries with the most workers

Less than half the world's population (about 3.167 billion people) are in paid employment. The rest are too young, students, retired or too old, unemployed or unable to work, or stay at home to look after children. Based on the number of people aged 15 to 64 who are currently employed, these countries have the most workers:

Country	% unemployed	Workers (2008)
1 China	4–9	807,700,000
2 India	6.8	523,500,000
3 U.S.	7.2	155,200,000
4 Indonesia	8.2	112,000,000
5 Brazil	8.0	100,900,000
6 Russia	6.2	75,700,000
7 Bangladesh	2.5	70,860,000
8 Japan	4.2	66,150,000
9 Nigeria	n/a	51,040,000
10 Pakistan	7.4	50,580,000

Oakum picker

Oakum is tarry old rope used from ships. Picking it apart by hand was an early recycling process. The strands were sent back to shipyards for sealing gaps in ships' planks. This messy job was carried out by inmates of workhouses — places where unemployed people were put to work in return for a small amount of food and a bed for the night.

Burlak

Before they were motorized, barges on canals and rivers in England and other countries were drawn by horses, but in Russia human haulers called burlaks were employed in this backbreaking task.

Gong farmer

Gong farmers or gong scourers were the men who took away the contents of toilets and cesspits, usually at night. They were often killed by the fumes.

Pure collector

"Pure" was the name given to dog droppings. They were collected from the streets by young girls or old women for use in the leather tanning industry.

State-owned Indian Railways is one of the world's largest employers

Biggest employers

WalMart employs some 1.8 million workers worldwide, while Indian Railways has about 1.6 million employees and China National Petroleum, the country's state-owned energy company, over 1 million. Various state organizations, such as the British National Health Service and the military forces of large countries also employ hundreds of thousands of people.

Money facts

The first coins Coins made from gold and silver were used in Lydia, an ancient Middle Eastern kingdom, in about 687–652 BC.

Smallest coins The silver quarter-jawa was made in Nepal in about 1740 and weighed 0.00007 oz. (0.002 g).

Largest coins Swedish 10-daler copper coins (made in 1644) weighed 43.45 lb. (19.71 kg).

U.S. coins made The U.S. mint issued more than 10 billion coins in 2008, more than half of them 1 cent coins.

Banknotes Paper money was first made in China in the 13th century. The first European notes were made in Sweden in 1548. Banknotes were issued in 1690 in America and 1695 in England.

Smallest banknotes Romanian 10-bani notes of 1917 had a printed area of just 1.08 x 1.5 in. (27.5 x 38 mm) — not much bigger than a postage stamp.

Largest banknotes One-guan Chinese notes from the late 14th century measured 9 x 13 in. (22.8 x 33 cm) — bigger than a page of this book.

Checks The first check was issued in London, England on April 22, 1659. It was for £10 ($20) and made payable to the bearer by Nicholas Vanacker. It was drawn on the bank of

Film stuntmen and women are in one of the riskiest professions

Dangerous jobs

There are many jobs that have a higher than average risk of being killed at work, including:
Bomb disposal and mine clearance expert
Deep sea diver
Deep sea fisherman
Construction worker
Oil platform worker
Professional stuntman
Steeplejack

Unemployment

In countries with economic problems, unemployment tends to increase. In turn, more people become dependant on the state and the output and demand for goods and services fall, so the economy worsens. These are the countries in which more than half the people who are available to work do not have paid jobs:

	Country	% of labor force unemployed
1	Nauru	90.0
2	Liberia	85.0
3	Zimbabwe	80.0
4	Burkina Faso	77.0
5	Turkmenistan	60.0
6	Djibouti	59.0
7=	East Timor	50.0
=	Zambia	50.0

Countries with most children who work

In many countries children traditionally work to help their families in agriculture. In some countries children are employed to work in often dangerous conditions in factories and mines, for example. They are paid low wages and the work prevents them from attending school. The United Nations and International Labor Organization are attempting to eradicate child labour around the world. More than half the children aged 7–14 work in some African countries:

	Country	% of children who work
1	Mali	70.9
2	Guinea-Bissau	67.5
3	Sierra Leone	65.0
4	Ethiopia	56.0
5	Burkina Faso	50.0

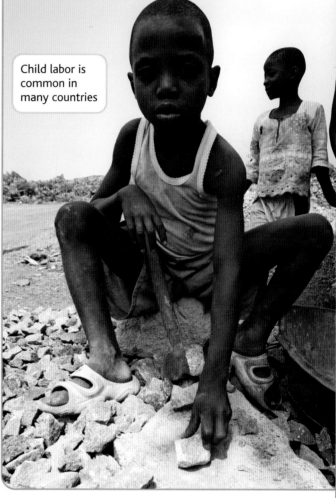

Child labor is common in many countries

Clayton & Morris. The original check was sold for $2,160 at Sotheby's, London, in 1976.
Credit cards The first credit card was invented by Frank X. McNamara in the U.S. and issued in 1950 by Diner's Club.
Holograms were first used for security on Visa cards in the U.S. in 1984. Smart cards (cards with built-in microchips) were introduced in France in 1975. There are about 142.8 million credit and debit cards in the UK. There are more than 1 billion credit cards in use in the U.S.
ATM The world's first ATM (Automated Teller Machine, or cashpoint) began operation on June 27, 1967 at Barclays Bank, Enfield, London.

Euro The new European currency was introduced in 1999 and was taken up by most European Union countries on January 1, 2002.

Lewes Pound In 2008, Lewes, the county town of East Sussex, issued its own currency, the Lewes Pound. It is designed to encourage people to pay for goods and services within the town and encourage local businesses.

 www.royalmint.com   search

Top energy users

These countries guzzle more energy than any others in the world. The figures below show the amount of gas, coal or other power needed to produce the same amount of energy as a tonne of oil. This is the standard way of comparing energy produced and consumed from different sources.

Country	Oil	Gas	Coal	Nuclear	HEP	Total
1 U.S.	943.1	595.7	573.7	192.1	56.8	2,361.4
2 China†	384.9	63.3	1,318.4	14.2	109.3	1,890.1
3 Russia	125.9	394.9	94.5	36.2	40.5	692.0
4 Japan	228.9	81.2	125.3	63.1	18.9	517.4
5 India	128.5	36.2	208.0	4.0	27.7	404.4
6 Canada	102.3	84.6	30.4	21.1	83.3	321.7
7 Germany	112.5	74.5	86.0	31.8	6.2	311.0
8 France	91.3	37.7	12.0	99.7	14.4	255.1
9 South Korea	107.6	33.3	59.7	32.3	1.1	234.0
10 Brazil	96.5	19.8	13.6	2.8	84.1	216.8

**Energy consumption
2006 World total**
Oil *3,952.8* Gas *2,637.7* Coal *3,177.5* Nuclear *622.0* HEP* *709.2* Total *11,099.2*
* Hydroelectric power

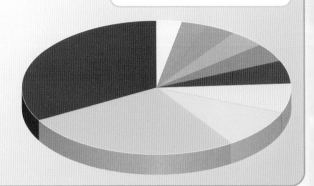

Peak oil

● The world uses over 85 million barrels of oil a day, 31 billion a year. Increased usage by countries such as China has led to some experts predicting that consumption will rise to 100 million or more barrels a day.

How much oil is left?

Oil is the world's single most important source of energy. It is used for the production of electricity and most motor vehicles run on gas or diesel that are refined from oil. The world's estimated reserves — the amount that is left under ground or under the sea — are:

Country	2009 reserves (barrels*)
1 Saudi Arabia	266,710,000,000
2 Iran	126,150,000,000
3 Iraq	115,000,000,000
4 Kuwait	104,000,000,000
5 Venezuela	99,377,000,000
6 United Arab Emirates	97,800,000,000
7 Russia	60,000,000,000
8 Libya	43,660,000,000
9 Nigeria	36,220,000,000
10 Kazakhstan	30,000,000,000
U.S.	21,317,000,000
UK	3,410,000,000
World total	1,342,207,000,000

* A barrel of crude oil is equivalent to 40 gallons (159 liters).

● If we continue to use oil at the current rate, a point will come when world output will reach a peak, then decline until it is completely exhausted. Around the world, this is occurring at different rates according to the size and production of oilfields: some counties have passed their peak — the U.S. in 1970 and UK in 1999 — while some, such as Saudi Arabia, Kuwait and Iraq, have not yet reached theirs.

● At the same time, new discoveries of oil and improved extraction methods mean that, despite increasing global consumption, total world reserves have actually increased and are now more than one-third greater than the trillion barrels identified in the early 1990s.

● As many of the world's economies shrink and people consume less energy or use it with greater efficiency — such as insulating homes, using energy efficient lightbulbs and not leaving electronic equipment on standby — and as car manufacturers become more fuel-conscious and the use of renewable energy sources increases, both peak oil and its final exhaustion may be more distant than has been predicted.

An oil and natural gas drilling platform

See also
Pollution fact file: page 70

Wind farm in California

Wind energy

Windmills were used in Persia (now Iran) in the 7th century, and in Europe since the 12th century, but they were first used for making electricity in the late 19th century. Today, the state of California is the world's leading area for wind-generated electricity. Tehachapi Wind Resource, California, produces as much wind energy as the rest of the U.S. combined.

The world's energy sources

A century ago, few homes had electricity and cars were a rare sight. Today, much of the world's energy is turned into electricity for homes, to power equipment in factories and to fuel our cars, buses, aircraft and other transportation. These are some of the main sources of this energy.

Oil

The first oil wells were drilled less than 150 years ago but oil, and petroleum that comes from it, has become the most important energy source. Almost 36 percent of the world's energy supply comes from oil. Most oil is found in the Middle East and has to be taken by tankers or pipelines to places where it is used around the world.

Coal

Coal is the world's second most important source of energy. It makes up over 28 percent of the total. Coal is a fossil fuel and is made from plants that lived and died 300 million years ago. The world's coal reserves will last about another 133 years. This is more than twice as long as gas (60 years) and more than three times as long as oil (41 years).

Natural gas

The third main source of power comes from gas that occurs naturally beneath the Earth's surface. It accounts for 24 percent of the world total. The gas is mainly methane, with some ethane, propane and other gases. It is collected and taken to where it is needed by pipelines.

Hydroelectric power

Flowing water has been used as a power source since the Middle Ages. Modern hydroelectric power uses water flowing through turbines in dams to produce electricity.

Nuclear power

The ifth most important power source (just under 6% of the world total) is nuclear power. A nuclear reaction releases huge amounts of heat which in turn heats water or other liquids and drives a turbine to produce electricity. The first nuclear power station to produce electricity for public use was Calder Hall, UK, which opened in 1956.

Solar energy

The Sun's warmth can be stored to produce energy. Mirrors and glass were used to collect heat in ancient times, but the first houses to use solar heating were not built until 1955. Solar energy is becoming more popular and the technology is getting better all the time. The world's largest solar energy generating plants are in the Mohave Desert, California. They are designed to use the Sun's rays to heat oil, which drives a generator. Each produces enough electricity to power a small town.

Tidal energy

Using waves and marine currents to release energy is expensive and as yet small-scale. The first and largest tidal power station on the Rance River, St. Malo, France, was completed in 1967. It can produce enough energy every year to supply power to 120,000 households.

Solar energy collectors concentrate the sun's rays

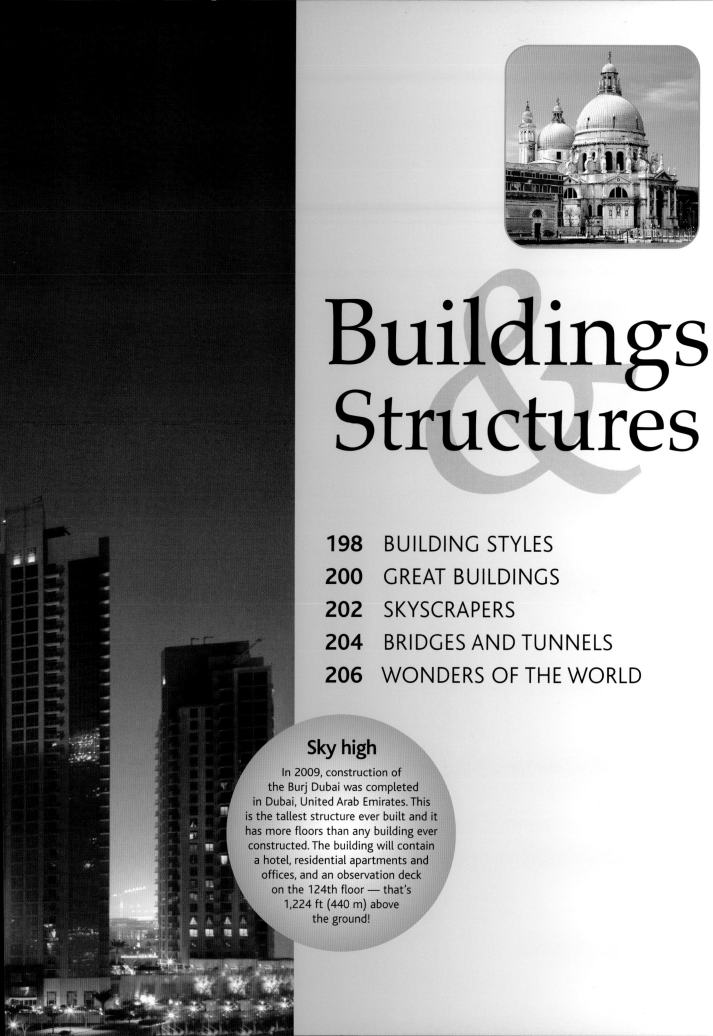

Buildings & Structures

Sky high

In 2009, construction of the Burj Dubai was completed in Dubai, United Arab Emirates. This is the tallest structure ever built and it has more floors than any building ever constructed. The building will contain a hotel, residential apartments and offices, and an observation deck on the 124th floor — that's 1,224 ft (440 m) above the ground!

BUILDING STYLES

Western architecture

Below are the main styles of Western architecture, from prehistory to the present day and famous examples of each. Styles did not stop and start abruptly; one style blended into another, so all dates are approximate.

Before the Renaissance most buildings had several architects or the architect's name was not recorded. The names of the architects of more recent buildings are given in brackets.

Prehistoric
Wooden post buildings, simple stone buildings, stone circles
Stonehenge, Wiltshire, UK

Ancient 3000–337 BC
Ancient Egyptian pyramids, tombs and temples
Great Pyramid, Giza, Egypt

Etruscan 700–200 BC
Alatri Temple, Villa Giulia, Rome, Italy

Greek 600–100 BC
Parthenon, Athens, Greece

Roman 100 BC–AD 370
The Baths of Caracalla, Rome, Italy
The Pantheon, Rome, Italy
The Colosseum, Rome, Italy
Maison Carrée, Nîmes, France

Byzantine 330–1450
Hagia Sophia, Istanbul, Turkey
St Mark's, Venice, Italy

Pre-Columbian 300–1540
Mayan, Aztec, Inca South and Central American
Mayan temples at Tikal, Guatemala

Carolingian 751–987
Chapel Palatine (now part of cathedral), Aachen, Germany

Romanesque 800 to 1200
St. James, Santiago de Compostela, Spain
Tournai Cathedral, Belgium

Moorish/Islamic from 8th century
Great Mosque, Cordoba, Spain

Norman 1045–1180
Durham Cathedral, Durham, UK
Ely Cathedral, Ely, UK

Gothic 1140–1534
Cologne Cathedral, Cologne, Germany
Notre Dame Cathedral, Paris, France
Chartres Cathedral, Chartres, France
Salisbury Cathedral, Salisbury, UK

Renaissance 1400–1600
Hampton Court Palace, London, UK
Little Moreton Hall, Cheshire, UK
Florence Cathedral, Florence, Italy (Filippo Brunelleschi)
Ducal Palace, Urbino, Italy (Luciano Laurana)
Château de Chambord, France (Domenico da Cortona)

Baroque 1585–1750
St. Paul's Cathedral, London, UK (Sir Christopher Wren)
Versailles Palace, France (Louis Le Vau and Jules Hardouin Mansart)
Greenwich Hospital (Royal Naval College), London, UK (Inigo Jones and Sir Christopher Wren)
Blenheim Palace, Oxfordshire, UK (Sir John Vanbrugh)

American Colonial 1600–1780
Governor's Palace, Williamsburg, Virginia (rebuilt 1930)

Jacobean 1618–25
Ham House, Twickenham, Middlesex, UK
Blickling Hall, Norfolk, UK

Rococo 1650–1790
Vierzehnheiligen Church, Banz, Germany (Johann Balthasar Neumann)

Georgian 1714–1837
The Circus, Bath, UK (John Wood, Sr. and Jr.)
Charlotte Square, Edinburgh, UK (Robert Adam)

Neoclassical/Federalist U.S. 1750–1880
Panthéon, Paris, France (Germain Soufflot)
Brighton Pavilion, Brighton, UK (John Nash)
University of Virginia, Charlottesville, Virginia (Thomas Jefferson)

See also
Mysterious places: page 174

The Parthenon

Greek
The Parthenon, Athens, Greece, 447–438 BC.
Doric is the first and simplest classical Greek building style and this is the finest Doric building still standing. When it was first built, the Parthenon was decorated with marble sculptures painted in bright colours. Some of these, known as the Elgin Marbles, were removed and are now in the British Museum, London.

www.greatbuildings.com **search**

Skyline of Chicago, with skyscrapers and other modern buildings

Victorian 1837–1901
Houses of Parliament, London, UK (Sir Charles Barry and A.W.N. Pugin)
Crystal Palace, London, UK (Joseph Paxton)
American Surety Building, New York (Bruce Price)

Arts and crafts 1860–1900
The Red House, Kent, UK (Philip Webb)

Art Nouveau 1890–1905
Glasgow Art School, Glasgow, UK (Charles Rennie Macintosh)
Paris Metro stations (Hector Guimard)
La Sagrada Familia, Barcelona, Spain (Antonio Gaudí)
Secession Building, Vienna, Austria (Joseph Maria Olbrich)

Art Deco 1925–35
Chrysler Building, New York (William Van Alen)

Bauhaus 1919–37
Bauhaus, Dessau, Germany (Walter Gropius)

International modernism 1920–50
Fallingwater, Pennsylvania (Frank Lloyd Wright)

Brutalism 1950s
Unité d'Habitation, Marseilles, France (Le Corbusier)
Seagram Building, New York (Mies van der Rohe)

High-tech 1970s–
Centre Georges Pompidou, Paris, France (Richard Rogers and Renzo Piano)
Swiss Re Building (The Gherkin), London, UK (Norman Foster)

Post-modern 1970s
Staatsgalerie, Stuttgart, Germany (James Stirling)

Deconstruction 1990s–
Guggenheim Museum, Bilbao, Spain (Frank Gehry)

Art Deco
Chrysler Building, New York, 1930.
The Chrysler is one of the best-known Art Deco buildings. The gleaming metal spire was based on the Chrysler cars of the time and skyscrapers are still a key feature of the New York skyline.

High-tech
Swiss Re Building (The Gherkin), London, 2004.
This building is London's first eco-friendly skyscraper. Its shape allows maximum natural light and ventilation inside so it uses only half the amount of energy consumed by a normal office block.

Japanese architecture

Eastern countries, such as Japan, had their own strong traditions of architecture. The Katsura Palace in Kyoto was built in the early 17th century, at the time of baroque and Jacobean architecture in Europe. It is a simple, elegant building and one of the most perfect examples of traditional Japanese architecture.

American Colonial
Governor's Palace, Williamsburg, Virginia, 1722
European settlers in the New World used architectural ideas from their home countries. The historic district of Williamsburg in Virginia has some of the most famous colonial buildings, dating from before the War of American Independence. The Governor's Palace is one of the finest.

Great religious buildings

The world's major religions, including Christianity, Islam, Judaism, Buddhism, Hinduism and Sikhism, have inspired many of the world's greatest buildings. Some are shrines to the religion's founders. Others are places of pilgrimage. Several are among the world's largest structures. These are the tallest churches.

1 The Chicago Methodist Temple * Chicago, Illinois, built 1924, 568 ft. (173 m)

2 Ulm Cathedral Ulm, Germany, built 1890, 528 ft. (161 m)

3 Notre Dame de la Paix Yamoussoukro, Côte d'Ivoire, built 1989, 519 ft. (158 m)

4 Cologne Cathedral Cologne, Germany, built 1880, 513 ft. (156 m)

5 Rouen Cathedral Rouen, France, built 1876, 485 ft. (148 m)

* Built on top of a 25-story, 330 ft. (100 m) building

Sagrada Familia

Spanish architect Antonio Gaudí's Sagrada Familia Cathedral in Barcelona, Spain, was begun in 1883, but it is still not finished. Its tallest spires are planned to be 558 ft. (170 m).

Sagrada Familia Cathedral, Barcelona

Largest churches

Salt Lake Temple, Utah, (1893) has a floor area of 253,015 sq. ft. (23,506 sq m). St Peter's in the Vatican (1612), the center of the Roman Catholic Church, is 717.5 ft. (218.7 m) long and covers an area of 247,570 sq. ft. (23,000 sq m). It was the largest Christian cathedral in the world until 1989, when it was overtaken by the 322,920 sq. ft. (30,000 sq m) basilica in Yamoussoukro, Côte d'Ivoire.

Tallest mosques

The Great Hassan II Mosque, Casablanca, Morocco (1993) is the tallest mosque at 689 ft. (210 m). The Saddam Mosque, Baghdad, Iraq was designed to be the largest in the Middle East, with a record-breaking 919 ft. (280 m) minaret, but it has not been completed.

Largest mosque

The Masjid al Haram is the holy mosque of Mecca (Makkah), the birthplace of the Prophet Muhammad. Millions of Muslim pilgrims visit the mosque every year. The mosque covers 882,640 sq. ft. (82,000 sq m) and the surrounding yards cover another 10,602,440 sq. ft. (985,000 sq m). Together they can accommodate up to 1.2 million worshipers.

Largest Buddhist temple

The largest Buddhist temple in the world is Borobudur (Many Buddhas), near Yogyakarta, Java, Indonesia. It was built between AD 750 and 842. The temple covers 645,835 sq. ft. (60,000 sq m) and contains 2 million cu. ft. (56,634 cu m) of stone.

Largest Hindu temple

Angkor Wat, Cambodia, built between AD 879 and 1191, is the largest religious structure in the world. The complex of buildings inside its walls and moat covers 894,590 sq. ft. (83,110 sq m).

Largest synagogue

The world's largest synagogue is Temple Emanu-El, New York City. It opened in 1929 and occupies an area of 37,921 sq. ft. (3,523 sq m).

Lighthouses

Tallest in the world

The biggest lighthouse ever built was the Pharos of Alexandria, which stood 407 ft. (124 m) tall. It was one of the Seven Wonders of the World. The world's tallest lighthouse today is in Yamashita Park, Yokohama, Japan, and is 348 ft. (106 m) tall.

Tallest in Canada

Built in 1858, the Cap des Rosiers Lighthouse, Northeast Gaspé Peninsula, Quebec, is situated near the mouth of the St. Lawrence River and stands 112 ft. (34 m) high. Its light can be seen from a distance of 24 nautical miles. It is open to the public from June to September.

Tallest in the U.S.

The Cape Hatteras lighthouse in North Carolina was built in 1870. It is the tallest in the U.S. at 196 ft (59.7 m). The lighthouse was being eroded by the sea so between 1999 and 2000 the entire 2,800-ton (2,540-tonne) building was moved 2,900 ft. (884 m) inland, very slowly, on tracks.

See also

Holy places: page 162

The O₂ (formerly the Millennium Dome), London, UK

Biggest domes and roofs

In 1434, the Duomo Cathedral in Florence, Italy, had the largest dome in the world. It was 149.3 ft (45.5 m) across and was still the world's largest dome 400 years later.

The diameter of the O₂ is almost eight times greater, thanks to modern building techniques and materials. Some of the domes in the list below are supported by struts and cables, others are free-standing. Some can even be opened.

The O₂ (formerly the Millennium Dome), London, UK, was completed in 1999. It measures 1,175 ft. (358 m) in diameter. The span is supported by steel masts that project through the dome.

Wembley Stadium, London, UK, was completed in 2007. It has the largest single-span roof in the world (supported only at the sides). It measures 1,033 ft. (315 m) in diameter.

The Georgia Superdome, Atlanta, Georgia, was completed in 1992 with a diameter of 840 ft. (256 m). It has the world's largest cable-supported fabric roof.

The Fantasy Entertainment Complex, Kyosho, Japan, was completed in 2002. It has a diameter of 710 ft. (216 m).

The Houston Astrodome, Houston, Texas, was completed in 1966. It measures 710 ft. (216 m) in diameter.

The Louisiana Superdome, New Orleans, Louisiana, was completed in 1975. It measures 680 ft. (207 m) in diameter.

The Rogers Centre (formerly the SkyDome) Toronto, Ontario, Canada, was completed in 1989 with a diameter of 674 ft. (205 m). It has the world's largest retractable roof.

The Multi-Purpose Arena, Nagoya, Japan, was completed in 1997. It measures 614 ft. (187 m) in diameter.

Tacoma Dome, Tacoma, Washington, was completed in 1983 with a diameter of 532 ft. (162 m).

The Superior Dome, Marquette, Michigan, was completed in 1991 and has a diameter of 523 ft. (160 m).

Obelisks and columns

Obelisks are stone columns made in ancient Egypt almost 4,000 years ago. Some were taken as trophies by invading armies and are now in cities such as Istanbul, Rome, London, Paris and New York. More recently, people have built memorials based on the design of obelisks.

● A column commemorating the battle of San Jacinto (1836) near Houston, Texas, is the world's tallest monument at 570 ft. (174 m). It was completed in 1939.

● The Washington Monument, Washington DC, was completed in 1884. It is 555 ft. (169 m) tall, made of 36,491 stone blocks on an iron frame and weighs 90,854 tons (82,421 tonnes). It was the world's tallest structure for five years until it was overtaken by the Eiffel Tower in 1889.

● The Wellington Monument in Dublin, Ireland, is a stone obelisk made to celebrate the victories of the Duke of Wellington. It was completed in 1861 and is Europe's tallest obelisk at 206 ft. (63 m).

● The Monument in London commemorates the Great Fire of London in 1666. It was built in 1667 and is 202 ft. (62 m) tall.

● Nelson's Column in Trafalgar Square, London, UK, was completed in 1842 to celebrate Great Britain's naval commander. The column is 145 ft. (44m) high and has a 17 ft. (5 m) statue of Nelson on top.

● The tallest Egyptian obelisk is in the Piazza San Giovanni in Laterano, Rome, Italy. It measures 106 ft. (32 m). The tallest still in Egypt is in Karnak and is 97 ft. (30 m) tall. The ancient Egyptian obelisk in New York is 73 ft. (22 m) and the London obelisk, Cleopatra's Needle, is 69 ft. (21 m).

Modern pyramids

The ancient Egyptian pyramids are the best known, but this style of building has also been used in modern times.

"Mad Jack" Fuller's tomb, Brightling, UK
Jack Fuller, an eccentric landowner and Member of Parliament, had his own 25 ft (8 m) pyramid tomb built in 1811. It is said that his body is inside, wearing a top hat!

Louvre Museum Pyramid, Paris, France
The architect I.M. Pei designed the 71 ft (22 m) glass pyramid which was built in 1989 as the main entrance to the Louvre Museum, Paris, France.

Christa McAuliffe Planetarium, Concord, New Hampshire
Christa McAuliffe was killed in the *Challenger* space shuttle disaster. The pyramid-shaped planetarium named after her opened in 1990.

Luxor Hotel and Casino, Las Vegas, Nevada
This was opened in 1993. It is 350 ft (107m)-tall and at its entrance is a sphinx that shoots laser beams from its eyes.

Rainforest Pyramid, Galveston, Texas
This 125 ft (38 m)-tall pyramid, finished in 1993, houses one of the world's largest indoor rainforests.

SKYSCRAPERS

Tallest skyscrapers over the last 100 years

New York's 391 ft. (119.2 m) Park Row Building was the tallest office or apartment building in the world when it was completed in 1899. Since then it has been overtaken many times by the progressively taller skyscrapers on this list. The latest world record-holder, the Burj Dubai, is almost seven times as tall as the Park Row Building.

	Building	Year completed	Floors	Height ft/m*	
1	Burj Dubai, Dubai, UAE	2009	162	2,684.0	818.0
2	Taipei 101, Taipei, Taiwan	2004	101	1,670.6	509.2
3	Petronas Tower, Kuala Lumpur, Malaysia	1996	88	1,482.6	451.9
4	Sears Tower, Chicago, USA	1974	108	1,450.1	442.0
5	One World Trade Center, New York, USA#	1972	110	1,368.1	417.0
6	Empire State Building, New York, USA	1931	102	1,250.0	381.0
7	Chrysler Building, New York, USA	1930	77	1,045.9	318.8
8	The Trump Building, New York, USA	1929	71	926.8	282.5
9	Woolworth Building, New York, USA	1913	59	792.0	241.4
10	Metropolitan Life, New York, USA	1909	50	700.1	213.4

* Excluding masts, etc
# Destroyed in terrorist attack of September 11, 2001

See also

Art Deco: page 199

Buildings that never were

Architects have often come up with exciting plans for fantasy buildings that in reality were too big, too difficult, too expensive, or often just too crazy ever to be built.

● In 1829 Thomas Willson announced his plans for a giant Pyramid to be built in London. It was to be taller than St. Paul's' cathedral and bigger than the Great Pyramid in Egypt, but it was to contain not one, but 5,167,104 tombs, to relieve the pressure on London's cemeteries. It was never built.

● In 1956 American architect Frank Lloyd Wright designed The Illinois, a mile-high (5,680 ft/1,731.1 m) skyscraper with 528 floors to be built in Chicago.

● In the 1980s, Domino's Pizza commissioned a design for a 30-storey office skyscraper that deliberately sloped at 15 degrees. It was never built, but was immediately nicknamed "The Leaning Tower of Pizza."

● X-Seed 4000 designed in Tokyo, Japan, in 1995, was a single building shaped like a volcano and bigger than Mount Fuji, at 13,123 ft (4,000 m) high, with 800 floors rising from the sea. It was so large that it would function as a city of up to a million people.

Chrysler Building

The Chrysler Building in New York held the record as the world's tallest for just 338 days, from May 28, 1930 to May 1, 1931, when the Empire State Building overtook it. Since the destruction of the twin towers of the World Trade Center in 2001, the two buildings were again the city's tallest and second tallest, but in 2009 the Chrysler Building was pushed into third place with the completion of the 1,200 ft (366-m) Bank of America Tower.

Cities with most skyscrapers*

1 Hong Kong, China 204
2 New York City, N.Y. 200
3 Chicago, Illinois 100
4 Tokyo, Japan 81
5 Shanghai, China 77
6 Dubai 68

* Habitable buildings of more than 500 ft (152 m) built or under construction

A view of the skyscrapers of Hong Kong from Victoria's Peak

The Empire State Building

New York's tallest building is the Empire State Building, which stands on Fifth Avenue, New York, between 33rd Street and 34th Street. It was built on the site of the Waldorf-Astoria Hotel and took 410 days at a rate of 4½ floors a week to complete. The building was opened on May 1, 1931, by remote control, when President Herbert Hoover pressed a button in Washington DC.

Tallest masts and towers

The world's tallest mast (a metal antenna supported by steel guy ropes, rather than a freestanding structure like a skyscraper) is the 2,063-ft (629-m) KVLY-TV mast in Blanchard, North Dakota, which has stood since 1963. In 1974, it was overtaken by the Warsaw, Poland, radio mast which was the world's tallest structure at 2,121 ft (646 m) until it collapsed on August 8, 1991, since when the KVLY-TV mast has once again held the record. The tallest tower (a self-supporting structure, but not habitable) is the 1,815-ft (553-m) CN Tower in Toronto, Canada, completed in 1976 and with an observation deck at 1,122 ft (342 m). While it was being built, it overtook the 1,772 ft (540m) (1,772 ft) Ostankino Tower, Moscow, Russia, which had held the record from 1967–75.

The Empire State Building towers 1,250 ft. (381 m) above ground, and measures 1,454.1 ft. (443.2 m) to the top of the TV tower. A further 54.8 ft. (16.7 m) is below ground. The spire on top was designed as an airship mooring mast, but after a German airship, the *Hindenburg*, burned at its mooring mast in New Jersey in 1937, the mast was never used. For more than 40 years, the Empire State held the record as the world's tallest office or apartment building, until the twin towers of the World Trade Center were completed. Since their destruction in 2001, it is once again New York's tallest. More than 2.5 million tourists a year go up to the observatories on the 86th and 102nd floors.

● The workforce — 3,400 at its peak — took seven million man-hours to complete the building.

● The cost was $40,948,900 including the land (the building cost only $24,718,000).

● It weighs 365,000 tons (331,120 tonnes), including a 60,000-ton (54,430 tonne) steel frame, 10 million bricks and 730 tons (662 tonnes) of aluminum and stainless steel.

● The Empire State is served by 73 elevators and contains 3,194,547 light bulbs, 50 mi. (80 km) of radiator pipes and 70 mi. (113 km) of water pipes.

● The lightning conductor was struck 68 times in the building's first 10 years.

● In 2003 Australian runner Paul Crake broke his own record for racing up the 1,575 steps to the 86th floor in 9 min., 33 sec.

● On July 28, 1945, a B-25 bomber crashed in fog between the building's 78th and 79th floors, killing the pilot and 13 other people. It happened on a Saturday so most offices were empty, or the casualties would have been higher.

● On St. Valentine's Day, couples can marry on the 80th floor.

● The building's colored lights are changed for seasonal celebrations. They are red, white and blue on Independence Day and green on St. Patrick's Day. The lights are turned off when birds are migrating to avoid confusing them.

Bridge types

Arch An arch bridge is a very strong curved structure made of stone, concrete or steel. It is firmly supported on both sides.

Bascule A bascule bridge has a central section that opens to allow tall ships to pass. London's Tower Bridge is one of the most famous bascule bridges.

Beam A beam bridge is supported by the shore at both ends. This is the simplest and oldest type of bridge – a log across a stream is a very simple beam bridge. It is not very strong and may need to be strengthened by supports underneath.

Cantilever This type of bridge has two long arms held in place at the ends by anchors. Some can swing to let large ships through. Cantilever bridges are closest in length to suspension bridges.

Suspension This bridge is supported by steel cables fixed to high towers on the banks. All the world's longest bridges are suspension bridges because they are very strong.

Swing A swing bridge can be swung to one side to allow ships through. The Gateshead Millennium Bridge across the Tyne is a unique swing bridge, which rotates upwards to allow boats to pass beneath.

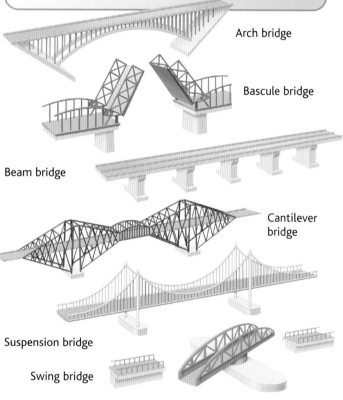

Arch bridge

Bascule bridge

Beam bridge

Cantilever bridge

Suspension bridge

Swing bridge

Famous bridges

Pont d'Avignon, France
This bridge was built in the 12th century. It was made famous by the song "Sur le Pont d'Avignon" (On Avignon Bridge).

Bridge of Sighs, Venice, Italy
The Bridge of Sighs was designed in 1560. It connects the Doge's Palace with the city jail, and prisoners who had been sentenced to death had to cross the bridge to reach the jail. Its name is said to come from their sighs of despair.

Pont Neuf, Paris, France
Pont Neuf was completed in 1604. The bridge is in two halves and links the Right and Left Banks of the River Seine to Ile de la Cité, the island on which Notre Dame Cathedral stands.

Kintai-Kyo Bridge, Iwakuni, Japan
This wooden arch bridge was built across the Nishiki River in 1673. It has been damaged and rebuilt many times.

Iron Bridge, Shropshire
The Iron Bridge was completed in 1781 and was the first bridge built of iron.

Longest bridges 200 BC

All these bridges were the world's longest when they were built. Today's longest, the Akashi Kaikyo in Japan, is nearly 54 times longer than the Martorell bridge in Spain.

† No longer standing

217 BC Martorell, Spain
A stone arch bridge with a span of 121 ft. (37 m)

27 BC Augustus, Narni, Italy
A stone arch bridge with a span of 142 ft. (43 m)

AD 104 Trajan, Danube, Romania
A timber arch bridge with stone piers and a span of 170 ft. (52 m)

1371 Trezzo, Adda, Italy †
A stone arch bridge with a span of 236 ft. (72 m)

1757 Schaffhausen, Switzerland †
A timber bridge with a span of 390 ft. (119 m)

1816 Schuylkill Falls, Philadelphia, Pennsylvania †
A suspension bridge with a span of 407 ft. (124 m)

1820 Union/Tweed, Berwick, UK
An iron chain suspension bridge with a span of 449 ft. (137 m)

1826 Menai Strait, Anglesey, UK
A chain suspension bridge with a span of 580 ft. (177 m)

1834 Fribourg, Switzerland †
Wire-cable suspension bridge with a span of 896 ft. (273 m)

1849 Wheeling, West Virginia,
A suspension bridge with a span of 1,010 ft. (308 m)

1851 Lewiston-Queenston, Niagara, U.S./Canada
A suspension bridge with a span of 1,043 ft. (318 m)

The Millau Viaduct, France, is the world's tallest bridge

Road and rail tunnels

The first tunnel built especially for passenger trains was the 2,513 ft. (766 m) Tyler Hill Tunnel in Kent, United Kingdom. It opened on May 4, 1830. The first underwater rail tunnel was the Thames Tunnel, London, UK, which opened in 1869.

Some of the most amazing tunnels are made under the sea. The Seikan tunnel was built to link the Japanese islands of Honshu and Hokkaido and is 14.5 mi. (23.3 km) below the sea bed. The Channel Tunnel has 23.6 mi. (38 km) under the sea. The tunnels listed are all for railways.

Longest tunnels

1 Gotthard Base Tunnel (Alp Transit Link) Switzerland, 2018*, will be 35.46 mi. (57.07 km)

2 Seikan Japan, 1988 is 33.46 mi. (53.85 km)

3 Channel Tunnel France/England, 1994 is 31.35 mi. (50.45 km)

4 Moscow Metro (Serpukhovsko-Timiryazevskaya line) Russia, 1983, is 24.17 mi. (38.9 km)

5 Lötschberg Base Tunnel Switzerland, 2007, will be 21.49 mi. (34.58 km)

6 Guadarrama Spain, 2007, will be 17.63 mi. (28.38 km)

7 Taihang China, 2008 is 17.4 mi. (27.9 km)

8 London Underground (East Finchley/Mordern, Northern Line) UK, 1939 is 17.29mi. (27.84 km)

9 Hakkoda Japan, 2010* will be 16.44 mi. (26.46 km)

10 Iwate Japan, 2002 is 16.04 mi. (25.81 km)

* Still being built

One and only

London Bridge was taken from the UK to the U.S. The five-arched stone bridge was made between 1823 and 1831. In the 20th century, London Bridge needed to be replaced by one better suited to modern traffic. U.S. businessman Robert P. McCulloch bought it for $2,460,000. The bridge was shipped out stone by stone. It was rebuilt in Lake Havasu City in Arizona and completed in 1971. It is the largest structure ever moved and the largest antique ever sold!

Tower Bridge, London
Tower Bridge was completed in 1894. It opens and lifts in the middle to allow tall ships to pass underneath.

Brooklyn Bridge, New York, USA
After many setbacks, Brooklyn Bridge was finally opened in 1883. For a short time it was the world's longest bridge.

Sydney Harbour Bridge, Sydney, Australia
Sydney Harbour Bridge was built in 1932 to carry road and rail traffic across the harbour. It is a famous feature of the Sydney harbour skyline.

London Bridge was transported and rebuilt as a tourist attraction in Arizona

1990s

1867 The Cincinnati-Ohio River, Covington
A suspension bridge with a span of 1,057 ft. (322 m)

1869 Niagara-Clifton, Niagara, U.S./Canada †
A suspension bridge with a span of 1,268 ft. (387 m)

1883 Brooklyn, New York
A suspension bridge with a span of 1,596 ft. (486 m)

1890 Firth of Forth Rail, Scotland
A cantilever bridge with a span of 1,710 ft. (521 m)

1917 Quebec Rail, Canada
A cantilever bridge with a span of 1,800 ft. (549 m)

1929 Ambassador, Detroit, U.S./Windsor, Canada
A suspension bridge with a span of 1,850 ft. (564 m)

1931 George Washington, New York
A suspension bridge with a span of 3,500 ft. (1,067 m)

1937 Golden Gate, San Francisco, California
A suspension bridge with a span of 4,200 ft. (1,280 m)

1964 Verazzano Narrows, New York, N.Y.
A suspension bridge with a span of 4,260 ft. (1,298 m)

1980 Humber Estuary, Hull, UK
A suspension bridge with a span of 4,626 ft. (1,410 m)

1997 East Bridge, Denmark
A suspension bridge with a span of 5,328 ft. (1,624 m)

1998 Akashi Kaikyo, Japan
A suspension bridge with a span of 6,529 ft. (1,990 m)

See also
Rail Transport: pages 214–15

The Seven Wonders of the Ancient World

Early Greek writers drew up lists of the most important buildings in the world they knew. Of these only the Great Pyramid survives, but we know about the others from writers' accounts and archaeologists.

The Great Pyramid of Giza

The Great Pyramid of Giza, Egypt, is the oldest, and the only one of the Seven Wonders to survive. It was made as a tomb for King Khufu, who ruled Egypt from about 2551–2528 BC, and it is the largest stone structure ever built. Its sides are 754 ft. (230 m) long and it covers an area the size of 200 tennis courts.

The Hanging Gardens of Babylon

The legendary gardens of King Nebuchadnezzar II may not have existed. Some people believe they were created in about 600 BC in Babylon, 55 mi. (88 km) south of present-day Baghdad, the capital of Iraq. "Hanging" suggests that they were a series of terraces made of bricks, some glazed and brightly colored.

The Statue of Zeus at Olympia

This was an enormous statue of the Greek god, carved by the sculptor Phidias. It was inside the Temple of Zeus, built about 466–456 BC. The statue was 43 ft. (13 m) high and one of the largest indoor sculptures ever made. Today little remains of the temple and nothing of the statue.

The Temple of Artemis

The Temple of Artemis at Ephesus, Turkey, was built to honor the Greek goddess of hunting and nature. The temple was completed in 550 BC. It was the largest of all ancient Greek buildings and measured 180 x 375 ft. (55 x 114 m). Archaeologists have found the foundations and some columns of this ancient wonder.

The Mausoleum at Halicarnassus

This was the tomb of Persian ruler Mausolus, who ruled part of the Persian empire in 377–353 BC. Halicarnassus (modern-day Bodrum) in Turkey was his capital. After his death his widow built this magnificent tomb, which measured 344 x 794 ft. (105 x 242 m) and was 140 ft. (43 m) high. It was damaged by an earthquake and demolished in 1522. The word mausoleum has come to mean any great tomb.

The Colossus of Rhodes

The huge statue of Sun god Helios stood in Rhodes harbor, Greece. In 305–304 BC warrior king Demetrius Poliorcetes attacked the city of Rhodes. When he abandoned his siege, the people built the giant statue as an offering to the god Helios. It took 12 years to build and stood 110 ft. (33 m) high, but in 226 BC it was destroyed by an earthquake.

See also
Chinese Empire:
page 106

The Great Wall of China can be seen from space.

The Great Pyramid of Giza and the Sphinx

The Pharos of Alexandria

This was a lighthouse off the coast of the city of Alexandria. Work started on it in about 299 BC and it took about 20 years to build. It was 407 ft. (124 m) tall—the tallest lighthouse ever made. It was damaged by earthquakes and toppled into the sea in 1375. A few remains have been found.

Seven modern wonders

There are many candidates for this list and here is a selection.

Hoover Dam, U.S.

When it was built in 1936, the 725 ft. (221 m) high Hoover Dam was the largest in the world. A record 128.19 million ft.^{3} (3.63 million m^3) of concrete were used to make the structure, which controls the flooding of the Colorado River.

Deltawerken flood barrier, Netherlands

After a disastrous flood in 1953, engineer Johan van Veen designed the Delta Project, or Deltawerken. This is a series of interconnected dams that forms a movable sea barrier while preserving the habitat and sea life within it.

Kansai International Airport, Japan

This airport was opened in 1994. It stands on a 0.75 x 2.5 mi. (1.2 x 4 km) island which is entirely humanmade. It was built with 48,000 huge blocks, made from earth excavated by flattening three mountains, and designed to withstand typhoons and earthquakes. Its terminal building was designed by Italian architect Renzo Piano.

Channel Tunnel, England/France

Work on the second longest underwater rail tunnel in the world began in 1987. It took seven years and 15,000 workers to create the 31.35 mi. (50.45 km) tunnel (23.6 mi. [38 km] under sea), which opened in 1994. The tunnel links Folkestone in England to Sangatte, France.

Guggenheim Museum, Bilbao, Spain

The Guggenheim was built in 1997 to the design of Canadian-born architect Frank Gehry. It houses a collection of modern art in a striking, ultramodern setting. The structure combines limestone blocks of varied shapes, curved sections covered in panels of titanium (a light, strong metal) and large areas of glass.

The Eden Project, Cornwall, UK

About 2 million tons (1.8 million tonnes) of earth were moved to make the foundations for the world's largest greenhouses. These are a series of domes, each devoted to a particular type of climate, and housing 100,000 plants. The Eden Project was designed by Nicholas Grimshaw and opened in 2001. It is one of the UK's most popular tourist attractions.

Panama Canal, Panama

It took 34 years, from 1880 to 1914, to build the ship canal that connects the Atlantic and Pacific Oceans. The 48-mi. (77 km) canal was a remarkable feat of engineering, but cost the lives of up to 27,500 workers.

Leaning Tower of Pisa

The Seven Wonders of the medieval world

People have never been able to agree on the Seven Wonders of the medieval world, and this is just one of several lists that have been made. It includes the Leaning Tower of Pisa (pictured right). In 2007, an organisation compiled a new list of Seven Wonders according to a voting system that included the Colossuem, Italy, and the Great Wall of China, along with the Taj Mahal, India, Chichén Itzà, Mexico, Macchu Picchu, Peru, Jordan and the statue of Christ the Redeemer, Rio do Janiero, which was completed as recently as 1931.

Stonehenge

The circle of huge stones was built in stages from about 3000 BC. The origin of the stones, how they were transported and the purpose of the site remain a mystery. It was possibly some sort of ancient observatory.

The Great Wall of China

This was a defensive wall designed to protect China from its warlike neighbors to the north. It was built in stages after 220 BC, using a huge labor force of as many as 300,000 workers. The main part is 2,150 mi. (3,460 km) long and wide enough for an army to march along it ten abreast.

The Colosseum, Rome, Italy

This amphitheater was opened in AD 80 with a huge spectacle lasting 100 days. It is oval and measures 157 ft. (48 m) high, 617 ft. (188 m) long and 512 ft. (156 m) wide. It could hold up to 50,000 spectators and could be flooded for re-enactments of sea battles.

The Catacombs of Alexandria (Kom El Shoqafa), Egypt

These Roman tombs beneath the city of Alexandria, Egypt, were discovered in 1900 when a donkey fell into them. The beautifully preserved, carved catacombs had been made in solid rock during the 2nd century AD.

Hagia Sophia, Istanbul, Turkey

Hagia Sophia (Holy Wisdom), Istanbul, Turkey, was originally built in AD 360 by the Emperor Constantius. It was later rebuilt as one of the world's finest churches, with many mosaics and ornate details. In 1453 the church was converted into an Islamic mosque.

The Porcelain Pagoda of Nanking, China

The Porcelain Pagoda was built in about 1412 by Emperor Yung-lo. It was an eight-sided structure covered in glazed tiles, and soared to 260 ft. (79 m). It was destroyed during a rebellion in 1853.

Leaning Tower of Pisa

Building began on the bell tower of Pisa Cathedral, Italy, in 1173. Soon the foundations began to sink on one side. The design was adjusted, but by the time the tower had reached its full height of 179 ft. (55 m) it was leaning sharply. The tilt increased over the centuries and it is amazing that the 15,400-ton (14,000-tonne) structure is still standing.

Transport & Travel

Flying car

Once the dream of science-fiction writers, the flying car has become a reality. Built by U.S. company Terrafugia, it made its first successful flight in 2009 and will be available to buy in 2011. It carries a driver/pilot and one passenger and can travel on the road at up to 80 mph (129 km/h) and fly at 115 mph (185 km/h). Its wings fold so it will fit in a standard car garage.

Types of ship

There are many different types of passenger and commercial ships:

Barge
This name is used for various types of ships, ranging from a slow canal boat to a small sailing cargo boat or a decorated rowing boat used by royalty.

Catamaran
A boat with two hulls side by side. There are different types of catamarans, including ferries and yachts.

Container ship
A cargo ship designed to carry standard-sized containers, making it easy to load and unload.

Ferry
A ship that takes passengers and vehicles from one port to another.

Galleon
A medieval sailing ship. The word was first used in 1529.

Galley
An ancient warship driven by oars. Biremes have oars on two levels, and triremes on three.

Hydrofoil
A boat with a special device to lift its hull out of the water, thus increasing speed.

Junk
A high-sterned (the stern is the aft, or back end), flat-bottomed, Chinese or Japanese sailing ship with two or three masts.

Liner or cruise ship
An ocean-going ship once used to take passengers on long journeys, such as across the Atlantic. Cruise ships are luxury liners designed to take people on pleasure cruises.

Oil tanker
A large vessel that carries oil from oil fields to refineries in other countries.

Yacht
A sailing or engine-powered ship used for pleasure cruises or racing.

Sailors racing a catamaran at top speed

Skyscraper?

During the 18th century, a skyscraper was a small triangular flag flown from the tip of a sailing ship's main mast. In the 19th century, the word began to be used to describe a tall horse or even an exceptionally tall person. And when the first very tall buildings were constructed in the 1890s people called them skyscrapers.

See also
The World's Oceans:
pages 40–41

Top speeds

Go-fast boat
These high-speed boats are used by the United States Coast Guard to intercept smugglers, who also use them. They have powerful engines and can travel at up to 80 knots (95 mph [150 km/h]).

Aircraft carrier
The U.S. Navy's Nimitz class nuclear-powered aircraft carriers can travel at more than 35 mph (56 km/h).

Submarine (submerged)
Russian Alfa class nuclear submarines could probably travel at 52 mph (83 km/h), but these are no longer in use. U.S. Navy Los Angeles class subs are said to achieve 46 mph (74 km/h), but the precise figures are military secrets.

Sailing vessel
During the 19th century, clippers could average 23 mph (37 km/h). The modern sailing yacht record is held by Simon McKeon and Tim Daddo of Australia. On October 26, 1993, they sailed their yacht *Yellow Pages Endeavour* at 53.57 mph (86.21 km/h).

Car ferry
The Spanish-built Australian catamaran *Luciano Federico L* can carry 52 cars and 450 passengers at a top speed of 67 mph (107 km/h).

Hovercraft
On January 25, 1980, a U.S. Navy Bell SES-1008 experimental vehicle achieved a speed of 106 mph (170 km/h).

Hydroplane
These super-fast racing motor boats are capable of great speeds: Dave Villwock set a record average speed of 213.4 mph (343.5 km/h) in *Miss Budweiser* at Oroville, California, on March 13, 2004.

Ocean liners
Steam ships began carrying passengers across the Atlantic between Europe and the U.S. in 1838. In the early years, the journey (about 3,000 miles/4,800 km) could take 18 days or longer. Shipping companies competed with each other and the fastest ship carried a blue flag, or Blue Riband. There were separate Blue Ribands for westbound and eastbound crossings, and after 1934 an award, the Hales Trophy, was presented to the ship with the fastest average speed. In 1952 the newly launched liner SS *United States* won both the westbound and eastbound Blue Riband with a time of 3 days, 10 hours, 40 minutes, and the Hales Trophy with an average speed of 40.95 mph (65.9 km/h). *Cat-Link V*, a Danish catamaran ferry, is the current Blue Riband and Hales Trophy holder. In 1998, it set a new transatlantic record of just 2 days, 20 hours and 9 minutes, and an average speed of 47.5 mph (76.5 km/h).

Warships

Aircraft carrier A warship from which aircraft can take off and land.

Cruiser A medium-sized, fast, long-range warship.

Battleship A large armored warship.

Destroyer A small, fast warship.

Frigate A warship that escorted cargo convoys to protect them from attack by submarines, introduced during World War II.

Minesweeper A naval ship designed to find and destroy mines.

Submarine Military submarines can travel long distances under water to avoid detection, and can fire torpedoes and missiles. Special civilian submarines are used for undersea research.

Biggest ships

All the ships listed here held the record as the biggest ship in the world when they were launched. The first, the *Great Western*, was a giant in its time but was less than $\frac{1}{100}$ the size of the current record holder *Queen Mary 2*, which is 1,132 ft. (345 m) long. The *Great Eastern* measured 692 ft. (211 m) and the *Titanic* was 882 ft. (269 m) long.

Some of these ships are still sailing, but many have been scrapped. The *Titanic* and *Lusitania* sank with the loss of many lives.

Great Western (launched in1838) gross tonnage*: 1,340
President (1840) gross tonnage: 2,360
Great Britain (1845) gross tonnage: 3,448
Great Eastern (1858) gross tonnage: 18,914
Oceanic (1899) gross tonnage: 17,274
Baltic (1904) gross tonnage: 23,884
Lusitania (1907) gross tonnage: 31,550
Mauretania (1907) gross tonnage: 31,938
Titanic (1912) gross tonnage: 46,232
Bismarck/Majestic/Caledonia†, (1922) gross tonnage: 56,621
Normandie/Lafayette† (1935) gross tonnage: 79,301
Queen Elizabeth (1938) gross tonnage: 83,673
Voyager of the Seas (1999) gross tonnage: 137,276
Explorer of the Seas (2000) gross tonnage: 137,308
Navigator of the Seas (2002) gross tonnage: 138,279
Queen Mary 2 (2003) gross tonnage: 142,200
Liberty of the Seas (2007) gross tonnage: 160,000
Oasis class (2009–) gross tonnage: 220,000

* Weights given are the weight of the ship when empty, without cargo, crew, supplies or passengers.
† Renamed

World's biggest ship

Twin *Oasis* class ships *Oasis of the Seas* (launched 2008, maiden voyage 2009) and *Allure of the Seas* (scheduled for completion in 2010) are the biggest cruise ships ever. Built in Finland, they are 16 decks high and 1,181 ft (360 m) long. They carry 5,400 passengers and have such facilities as gardens, four swimming pools, a basketball court and a golf course.

Oasis of the Seas is the largest cruise ship afloat

Famous ships

Some ships, such as the *Titanic*, are famous because they sank, but here are some famous ships that are celebrated for a variety of other reasons.

Niña, Pinta and Santa Maria
The three ships on Christopher Columbus' voyage to America in 1492.

Mayflower
The ship that took the settlers known as the Pilgrim Fathers from Plymouth to America in 1620.

Endeavour
Captain James Cook's ship on his exploration of Australia and New Zealand in 1768–71.

Bounty
The crew of this British ship mutinied against Captain William Bligh in 1789.

Victory
Captain Horatio Nelson's flagship at the Battle of Trafalgar, 1805. It is now on display in Portsmouth, England.

Beagle
The research ship on which British scientist Charles Darwin visited the Galápagos Islands in 1835.

Cutty Sark
A tea clipper (a sailing ship designed to bring tea from China as fast as possible) launched in 1869. The ship is preserved in dry dock at Greenwich, London.

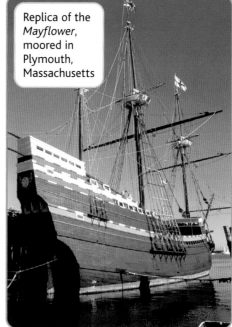

Replica of the *Mayflower*, moored in Plymouth, Massachusetts

Great Eastern
This ship was designed by Isambard Kingdom Brunel and launched in 1858. It laid the first transatlantic cable in 1866, but was scrapped in 1888.

Mary Celeste
A U.S. ship found abandoned in the Atlantic in 1872. The fate of its crew remains a mystery.

Kon-Tiki
A balsawood raft on which Norwegian anthropologist Thor Heyerdahl sailed from South America across the Pacific to Polynesia in 1947. He made the voyage to prove his theory that Polynesian people came from South America.

Famous cars

● Mercedes
The German luxury car, which has been made since 1901, took its name from Mercédès, the daughter of Daimler car company director Emil Jellinek.

● Rolls-Royce
British car enthusiasts Henry Royce and Charles Rolls joined forces to form Rolls-Royce in 1906 and set new standards for a luxury vehicle. The company's engines are also used in many of the world's aircraft.

● Model T Ford
The first Model T Ford, nicknamed the Tin Lizzie, was made in the U.S. in 1908 by the Ford Motor Company, which was founded in 1903 by Henry Ford. By 1927, when production finished, a total of 16,536,075 had been built. At one point, more than half the new cars in the world were Model Ts.

James Bond's Aston Martin

● Aston Martin
This luxury sports car has been made in the UK since the 1920s. It became one of the most featured and gadget-laden cars in the James Bond films.

● Bugatti Royale
Only six Bugatti Royales (1926) were ever made. The Royale was designed by Italian Ettore Bugatti and was one of the largest

vehicles of all time. It was 22 ft. (6.7 m) long with a 12.7 litre engine originally designed for aircraft. In 1980 one of these rare vehicles set a new world record price when it was sold for $15 million.

● Volkswagen Beetle
The Volkswagen Beetle was designed by Ferdinand Porsche and first manufactured in Germany in 1937. When production

Top vehicle-owning countries

There are so many cars today that there is one car for every 10.3 people in the world. In the U.S. there are 2.2 people per car and in the UK 2.0, but in some countries the ratio is amazingly high. In Myanmar, for example, there are more than 5,800 people per car!

Germany
Cars 46,569,657
Commercial vehicles 3,172,042

Italy
Cars 35,297,600
Commercial vehicles 4,579,600

France
Cars 30,400,000
Commercial vehicles 6,261,000

China
Cars 11,000,000
Commercial vehicles 24,000,000

Japan
Cars 57,521,043
Commercial vehicles 16,731,091

U.S.
Cars 135,046,706
Commercial vehicles 108,975,048

World total
Cars 635,284,155
Commercial vehicles 255,477,307

Rest of the world
Cars 319,449,149
Commercial vehicles 91,758,526

Car timeline

1800s

1883 First experimental gas-driven car (France)
1886 Karl Benz and Gottlieb Daimler (Germany) build first cars
1892 First U.S. car built by Charles and Frank Duryea
1893 Rudolf Diesel patents engine
1893 First electric car in Canada made for F.B. Featherstonhaugh of Toronto, Ontario
1895 First car race, Paris-Bordeaux-Paris, France, 732 miles (1,178 km)

1895 Michelin (France) makes first pneumatic car tires
1896 First car theft (France)
1896 First motoring death (UK)
1897 First gas-driven car in Canada built by George Foote Foss of Sherbrooke, Quebec
1898 First woman driver in U.S., Genevra Mudge
1899 Jacob German arrested for speeding in New York (12 mph/ 19 km/h)

1900s

1900 8,000 vehicles on the road in the U.S.
1902 First Canadian production car, the LeRoy, was built in Berlin (now Kitchener), Ontario
1903 First driving licenses issued, Paris, France
1903 Registration plates in UK
1904 There are 535 vehicles in Canada
1907 First Rolls-Royce made, the Silver Ghost (UK)
1908 First Model T Ford made

1910 468,500 vehicles in U.S.
1912 First gas station built (U.S.)
1912 Thomas Wilby and F.V. "Jack" Haney are the first to drive across Canada; it took them 51 days to travel from Halifax to Victoria
1915 Headlamp dipping and stoplights introduced (U.S.)
1919 Mechanical windscreen wipers developed (U.S.)
1919 There are 9,158 vehicles in Canada

ended in 2003 a total of 21,529,464 Beetles had been made, the last of them in Brazil and Mexico. A new version of the Beetle was introduced in 1998. Over 1 million of the new Beetle, introduced in 1998, were sold by 2008.

● MINI

The MINI was launched in the UK in August 1959, when it cost just under ($1,400). It was designed by Alec Issigonis (1906–88). More than 5.3 million MINIs had been made by 2000. The new MINI was launched in 2001. By 2009 over 1.3 million had been produced.

Fastest car

ThrustSSC is the most powerful car ever built. It uses two Rolls-Royce engines from Phantom fighter aircraft. In 1997, driven by Royal Air Force fighter pilot Andy Green, *Thrust* set a new land speed record of 763.035 mph (1,227.986 km/h). It was also the first road vehicle to break the sound barrier.

See also
ThrustSSC: page 15

Driving on the left

People in most countries drive on the right. But about one-third of the world's drivers in 75 countries and territories drive on the left. These include the UK, Japan, Australia, South Africa, Thailand, Ireland, Malaysia, Indonesia, India, New Zealand and Pakistan. The tradition of keeping to the left dates back to the time when most road users were on horseback. One explanation is that as most people are right-handed, riding on the left allowed them to use a sword to defend themselves against approaching riders.

Amazing vehicles

● **Biggest dumper trucks**
The General Motors Terex Titan 33-19 mine truck, first made in 1974, can carry 350 tons (317.5 tonnes). An average truck carries about 5.5 tons (5 tonnes).

● **Biggest fire engines**
Fire trucks made by the Oshkosh Truck Corporation of Wisconsin for airports have eight wheels, 860-hp engines and weigh 66 tons (60 tonnes).

● **Longest limos**
The current record-holder, built by Jay Ohrberg of California, measures 100 ft. (30.5 m) and has 26 wheels. It is so long that it has to be hinged in the middle to enable it to turn corners.

● **Biggest bus**
The articulated Super City Train Buses used in the Democratic Republic of Congo are 105.7 ft. (32.2 m) long. They can carry 110 seated passengers and 140 standing in the first part, and 60 seated and 40 standing in the second— a total of 350 people.

● **Fastest electric car**
The *White Lightning Electric Streamliner* holds the official record for the fastest electric vehicle. In 1999, driven by Patrick Rummerfield (U.S.), it went at a speed of 245.524 mph (395.133 km/h). It is powered by two 200 horse-power motors and a 420 volt battery pack.

● **Biggest tires**
The largest road vehicle tires are 12.5 ft. (3.82 m) in diameter. They are made by the Bridgestone Corporation, Tokyo, Japan, for giant dumper trucks. Normal car tires are about 24 in. (60 cm) in diameter..

White Lightning

2000s

1921 First autobahn (high speed road or motorway) built in Germany
1922 A survey shows there are 12,588,949 motor vehicles in the world, of which 10,506,660 (83%) are in the U.S.
1930 First traffic light installed in New York
1933 First drive-in theater built (U.S.)
1935 First parking meters installed in Oklahoma City

1940 There are 1,500,829 vehicles in Canada
1940 32,453,200 vehicles in U.S.
1955 Highway code issued in UK
1960 There are 5,256,341 vehicles in Canada
1960 73,868,600 vehicles in U.S.
1962 200 millionth car produced in U.S.
1969 Czechoslovakia first country to make seat belts compulsory
1970 Unleaded fuel introduced in the U.S.

1978 Bosch (Germany) patents first satellite navigation
1980 155,796,000 vehicles in the U.S.
1985 Seat belts made compulsory in New York
2005 The Bugatti Veyron 16.4 is the fastest, most powerful and most expensive car ever built

2007 Tesla Roadster electric cars capable of 250 miles (400 km) on a single charge
2009 The Tata Nano, the world's cheapest car ($2,500) goes on sale in India
2009 World motor vehicle production is cut and sales fall as a result of economic downturn

www.beaulieu.co.uk/motormuseum   search

Types of train

Not all trains are the same: these are just some of the variations around the world.

Rubber-tired metro

These electric trains run along a tracked roadway. They are quiet, can accelerate quickly and tackle slopes. They first ran in Paris, France, in the 1950s, and are now used in other urban centers, including Montreal, Quebec, and Mexico City.

Funicular

Funiculars (from the Latin *funiculus*, a thin rope) are designed to go up and down steep hills or mountains. Cars are drawn up by cables and descend by gravity. Funiculars are used in mountain and other resorts, and in hilly parts of cities, such as Montmartre in Paris, France. The steepest passenger funicular is the Katoomba Scenic Railway in New South Wales, Australia.

Cog railway

Cog or rack-and-pinion railways are used in mountains. The train has a rotating cog wheel that meshes with a rack rail, so the train can climb steep slopes. The highest one in the U.S. is Manitou and Pike's Peak Railway, Colorado, operating since 1891. The peak is 14,110 ft. (4,300 m) high.

Maglev

The name Maglev comes from the words magnetic and levitation. These trains do not run on a track, but float above it by means of magnetic repulsion. They can travel very smoothly at high speeds (up to 400 mph [650 km/h]) — and use little energy. A new 100-mi. (160 km) Maglev line is being built between Shanghai and Hangzhou, China — the first inter-city Maglev service.

Monorail

A monorail train runs on a single rail, instead of on a track or two rails. It is either suspended from the rail or straddles it. The Tokyo Monorail in Japan carries 100 million passengers a year. There are also monorails in the U.S., Malaysia, Australia.

A Maglev train in Germany

One and only

The only time a train has been powered by fish was during a coal shortage in Turkestan in 1919. Dried fish, caught in the Aral Sea, were used as fuel. Almost 9,900 tons (9,000 tonnes) were used to stoke the train's boilers.

The Ghan on its first journey across Australia

Famous trains

Orient Express

The Orient Express began trips from Paris, France, to Bulgaria on October 5, 1883, and from 1889 went as far as Constantinople (now Istanbul), Turkey. It was the first trans-European train and traveled a total of 1,700 mi. (2,735 km) across six countries. It stopped running in 1977, but was relaunched five years later.

20th Century Limited

The luxurious 20th Century Limited ran between New York and Chicago from 1902 to 1967.

Trans-Siberian Express

The Trans-Siberian Express travels 5,777 mi. (9,297 km) between Moscow and Vladivostok. The line opened in 1914 and is the world's longest continuous rail line.

The Canadian

The streamlined stainless steel transcontinental train originally operated by Canadian Pacific (now VIA Rail Canada) has run between Toronto, Ontario, and Vancouver, B.C., since 1955.

Golden Arrow

From 1929 to 1971, the Golden Arrow ran from Victoria, London, to Dover on the south coast of England.

From there passengers could sail across the Channel and then take the French Flèche d'Or to Paris.

Blue Train

This is one of the world's most luxurious trains and it has operated between Cape Town and Tshwane (Pretoria), South Africa, since 1939. The train, carriages and decor are mainly blue — hence the name.

Subimarks

Subways

A subway, or underground railway, is an urban train line that runs mostly, or completely, underground. The world's first subway system was the London Metropolitan Line in London, England.

Although New York had a short pneumatic (air-powered) system running down part of Broadway as early as 1868, the main New York City Subway opened to the public on October 27, 1904. On its first day, 111,881 people paid 5 cents each for a ticket to ride. It was the Unites State's second (after Boston) and the world's seventh underground railway to be opened.

First subways

London, England opened January 10, 1863
Budapest, Hungary opened May 2, 1896
Glasgow, Scotland opened December 14, 1896
Boston, Massachusetts opened September 1, 1897
Paris, France opened July 19, 1900

Longest underground rail networks

City (stations)	Total track length mi. (km)
London, UK (268)	254 (408)
New York, N.Y. (468)	229 (368)
Madrid, Spain (231)	183 (294)
Moscow, Russia (177)	182 (293)
Seoul, South Korea (266)	179 (287)
Shanghai, China (162)	142 (142228)
Paris, France (300)	133 (214)

Busiest subway systems
Annual passengers
Tokyo 2,916,000,000
Moscow 2,529,000,000
Seoul 1,654,000,000
New York 1,563,000,000
Mexico City 1,417,000,000
Paris 1,336,000,000
London 976,000,000

Longest rail networks

These countries all have more than 10,000 km (6,214 miles) of railway. At the other end of the scale, Puerto Rico, Saint Christopher and Nevis, Paraguay and Nicaragua have less than 100 km (62 miles). Some countries have none at all.

USA: 226,612 km (140,810 miles)
Russia: 87,157 km (54,157 miles)
China: 75,438 km (46,875 miles)
India: 63,221 km (39,284 miles)
Germany: 48,215 km (29,959 miles)
Canada: 48,068 km (29,868 miles)

Australia: 38,550 km (23,954 miles)
Argentina: 31,902 km (19,823 miles)
France: 29,370 km (18,250 miles)
Brazil: 29,295 km (18,203 miles)
Japan: 23,474 km (14,586 miles)
Poland: 23,072 km (14,336 miles)

Ukraine: 22,473 km (13,964 miles)
South Africa: 20,872 km (12,969 miles)
Italy: 19,460 km (12,092 miles)
Mexico: 17,665 km (10,977 miles)
UK: 16,567 km (10,294 miles)
Spain: 14,974 km (9,304 miles)

Kazakhstan: 13,700 km (8,513 miles)
Sweden: 11,528 km (7,163 miles)
Romania: 11,385 km (7,074 miles)
World total: 1,370,782 km (851,764 miles)

Bullet Train
Japanese bullet trains (shinkansen) are the world's fastest scheduled rail services. They were introduced in 1964 to coincide with the Tokyo Olympic Games.
TGV
The French TGV (Train à Grande Vitesse, or high speed train) was launched in 1981 and is an electric train service between Paris and Lyon. A specially modified TGV, the Atlantique, set a world speed record of 320.2 mph (515.3 km/h) on May 18, 1990.
Eurostar
The Eurostar service was launched on November 14, 1994 to carry passengers between London, Paris and Brussels through the Channel Tunnel. It can reach speeds of 186 mph (300 km/h). In its first 10 years it carried a total of 59 million passengers.
Ghan
The Ghan is the first rail service from Adelaide to Darwin on the north–south route across Australia. It was named after the camel trains that were once the only way to cross the desert. The first train ran in 2004. It had 43 carriages, measured more than 0.6 mi. (1 km) in length, and carried 330 passengers.

Aviation firsts

First flight
Orville Wright (U.S., 1871–1948) made the first ever flight, a distance of approximately 121 ft (37 m) at Kitty Hawk, North Carolina, on December 17, 1903.

First Channel crossing
On July 25, 1909 Louis Blériot (France, 1872–1936) became the first person to fly across the English Channel, in a time of 37 minutes.

First Channel crossing by jetpack
On September 26, 2008 Yves Rossy (Swiss, 1959–) crossed the Channel in 9 minutes 7 seconds using a jet-powered wing.

First non-stop Transatlantic flight
On June 14–15, 1919 John Alcock (UK, 1892–1919) and Arthur Whitten Brown (1886–1948) completed the first ever non-stop flight across the Atlantic, from Newfoundland to Ireland.

First solo Transatlantic flight
In his aircraft, *The Spirit of St Louis*, Charles Lindbergh (U.S., 1902–74) became the first pilot to fly solo across the Atlantic, from New York to Paris, on May 20–21, 1927.

First non-stop U.S. coast-to-coast flight
U.S. pilots Oakley G. Kelly and John A. Macready flew a Fokker T-2 monoplane from New York to California, landing on May 3, 1923 after a 2,521-mile (4,034-km) flight lasting 26 hours 50 minutes.

First to fly over Mount Everest
In an expedition led by Douglas Douglas-Hamilton (then Lord Clydesdale, UK, 1903–73), two open-cockpit Westland biplanes flew over Everest on April 3, 1933.

First non-stop round-the-world
Dick Rutan (U.S., 1938–) and Jeana Yeager (U.S., 1952–) flew the *Voyager* aircraft round the world, a distance of 24,986 miles (40,211 km), on December 14–23, 1986.

Concorde

Concorde fact file

Concorde, the only passenger aircraft ever to fly faster than the speed of sound, was first named in a speech by General de Gaulle on January 13, 1963. The England-France project began the following year.

- The first prototype Concorde was shown at the Toulouse Air Show on December 11, 1967.

- The first French flight took place on March 2, 1969.

- The first British flight took place on April 9, 1969.

- The first landing at London Heathrow was on September 13, 1970.

- The first Concorde landing in the U.S. was at Dallas-Fort Worth on September 20, 1973.

- The only Concorde crash was near Paris, on July 25, 2000, when 109 passengers and crew and four people on the ground died.

- Concorde's last flight took place on October 24, 2004. All surviving British Airways and Air France Concordes are on public display in museums and airports in the U.S., UK, France, Germany and Barbados.

The Wright brothers demonstrate their Wright Model A plane

See also
Steve Fossett: page 153

The Wright brothers

Orville Wright was the first person to fly a powered aircraft. He also became the first to fly a plane for more than one hour, on September 9, 1908, at Fort Meyer, Virginia. His brother Wilbur became the first to fly for more than two hours, on December 31, 1908, at Auvours, France. On May 20, 1909, French pilot Paul Tissandier became the first person other than the Wrights to fly for more than an hour.

Breaking the sound barrier

Charles "Chuck" Yeager became the first person to break the sound barrier on October 14, 1947. His Bell X-1 rocket plane was dropped from a carrier aircraft above Muroc Dry Lake, California. At 42,000 ft. (12,800 m) he reached a speed of 670 mph (1,078 km/h). He did not break the air-speed record because only aircraft that take off and land under their own power are eligible. The speed of sound is not fixed and varies according to height and air conditions. In dry air at sea level the speed of sound is 763 mph (1,227 km/h), but at high altitudes, where air density is less, it is lower.

One and only

The only flight of the Hercules H-4 aircraft, known as the "Spruce Goose," took place on November 2, 1947. It was the largest flying boat ever built. It had the greatest wingspan (320 ft./97.54 m) of any aircraft and eight engines. Millionaire aviator Howard Hughes built and flew it himself, just 65.6 ft. (20 m) above the water off Long Beach, California,. It traveled only 1 mi. (1.6 km). The flight is recreated in the film *The Aviator* (2004).

First manned balloon flights

The first balloons worked on the principle that when air is heated, it rises. They were filled with hot air by burning things under them, such as paper, straw and wool — and even old shoes and rotten meat!

The balloons often caught fire, and once the air cooled they quickly came down. Soon after the first hot-air flights, people realized that the gas hydrogen could be used instead. Hydrogen is the lightest of all elements — almost 15 times lighter than air. Gas balloons can also be filled with helium, which is not as light as hydrogen but does not catch fire so easily. Most balloons today use hot air made by burning propane gas.

www.flyingmachines.org   search

The first hot-air balloon flight
The Montgolfier brothers, Joseph and Etienne, tested their first unmanned hot-air balloon on June 5, 1783. On November 21, 1783, François Laurent, Marquis d'Arlandes and Jean-François Pilâtre de Rozier took off from the Bois de Boulogne, Paris, in a Montgolfier hot-air balloon. They traveled about 5.5 mi. (9 km) in 23 minutes.

First hydrogen balloon flight
On December 1, 1783, Jacques Alexandre César Charles and Nicholas-Louis Robert made the first flight in a hydrogen balloon. They took off from the Tuileries, Paris, watched by a crowd of 400,000, and traveled 43 km (27 miles) north to Nesle in about two hours. Charles then took off again alone, so was the first ever solo pilot.

First Channel crossing
On January 7, 1785 Jean-Pierre Blanchard made the first Channel crossing in a balloon with Dr. John Jeffries (the first American to fly). They also carried the first airmail letter. As they lost height, they had to reduce weight, so they threw almost everything overboard — including their clothes!

First flight in the U.S.
On January 9, 1793, in Philadelphia, Pennsylvania, Blanchard made the first balloon flight in the United States. He took a small black dog with him as a passenger. The flight was watched by President George Washington, who gave Blanchard a passport permitting his flight, which was the first pilot's license and the United States first airmail document in the United States.

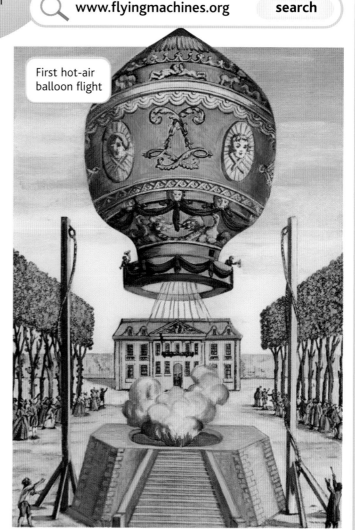

First hot-air balloon flight

First nonstop solo flight
U.S. adventurer Steve Fossett made the first nonstop solo and fastest around-the-world balloon flight, June 19 to July 3, 2002.

Shipwrecks

Shipping disasters as a result of collisions, storms, fires, explosions or military action are among the most famous of human tragedies. Some wrecks were carrying treasure that has since been recovered.

The *Mary Rose*, which sank in 1545

Mary Rose
This Tudor galleon sank in 1545 as Henry VIII watched from the shore. It was found in 1968, raised in 1982, and is exhibited in Portsmouth, UK.

Spanish Armada
Between August and October 1588, military action and storms combined to destroy the Spanish fleet off the British coast. About half the 130 ships that set out were wrecked, killing about 4,000 men.

Empress of Ireland
In the St. Lawrence River, Canada, on the night of May 29, 1914, the liner was struck by the Norwegian coal ship Storstad and quickly sank. Of 1,477 passengers and crew on board, 1,012 were killed; out of 318 children, only four were saved. The wreck is still at the bottom of the river.

Tek Sing
This Chinese junk carrying 2,000 passengers and 350,000 pieces of porcelain sank in 1822. It was found in 1999 and its treasures sold for high prices.

Sultana
On April 27, 1865, the *Sultana*, a steamboat on the Mississippi River near Memphis, Tennessee, was destroyed by a boiler explosion. This was the worst ever marine accident in the U.S. and a total of 1,547 people died.

Princess Alice
On September 3, 1878 the pleasure steamer *Princess Alice* was taking people down the Thames in London. It collided with the *Bywell Castle* and 786 people died.

Titanic
On the night of April 14, 1912, the "unsinkable" *Titanic* struck an iceberg on its maiden voyage and sank the next day, killing 1,517. The wreck was discovered and explored by Robert Ballard in 1986.

Lusitania
The British liner was torpedoed off the Irish coast by a German U-boat on May 7, 1915, with the loss of 1,198 lives.

Wilhelm Gustloff
The German liner, laden with refugees, was torpedoed off Gdansk, Poland, on January 30, 1945, by a Soviet submarine, S-13. Between 5,348 and 7,800 people died, making this the worst ever marine disaster.

Dona Paz
The *Donna Paz* sank off the Philippines on December 20, 1987, killing up to 3,000 people. This was the world's worst passenger ferry disaster.

Kursk
This Russian nuclear submarine sank in the Barents Sea on August 12, 2000, with the loss of all 118 crew.

Rail disasters

Rail travel is one of the safest ways of journeying from place to place, taking into account the large numbers of passengers carried and distances traveled. But there have been accidents.

World's worst
At Telwatta, Sri Lanka, on December 26, 2004, the *Queen of the Sea* train was struck by the Indian Ocean tsunami. The exact number killed is unknown, but is estimated to be between 1,700 and 2,000.

North America
On April 3, 1955, an express train was derailed and fell into a canyon near Guadalajara, Mexico, leaving about 300 people dead.

U.S.
Two U.S. accidents resulted in 101 deaths. On August 10, 1887, a bridge at Chatsworth, Illinois caught fire and collapsed as a train was passing over. As many as 372 people were injured and 101 died. The second accident happened on July 9, 1918, at Nashville, Tennessee, when two trains collided head-on.

Canada
At St. Hilaire, Quebec, on June 29, 1864, a train filled with German and Norwegian immigrants failed to stop at a swing bridge and plunged into the Richelieu River. About 99 people were killed and many seriously injured in Canada's worst rail disaster.

Subway
On October 28, 1995, at Baku, Azerbaijan, an underground train caught fire one evening, killing more than 300 people.

U.S. subway
America's worst subway accident was on November 1, 1918, in Brooklyn, New York. A train was derailed in the Malbone Street tunnel, leaving 97 dead.

Road disasters

Many people are killed and injured on the roads — more than 40,000 a year in the U.S. — but accidents involving more than a few drivers or pedestrians are rare.

Worst road disaster On November 3, 1982 an oil tanker collided with a Soviet army truck and exploded in the 1.7 mi. (2.7 km) Salang Tunnel in Afghanistan. At least 2,000, and perhaps as many as 3,000, people died as a result of the explosion, fire and fumes.

U.S. road disaster The worst U.S. road disaster took place on December 15, 1967. The Silver Bridge across the Ohio River from Kanauga, Ohio, to Point Pleasant, West Virginia, collapsed during heavy pre-Christmas rush-hour traffic. About 60 vehicles plunged into the river and 46 people died.

Canadian road accident On September 3, 1999, dense fog caused pileups near Windsor, Ontario, the worst of which killed eight people and left 33 injured.

The Ashtabula Bridge disaster

On December 29, 1876, a train traveling from New York to Chicago, and pulled by two locomotives, crossed the Ashtabula Bridge, Ohio, in a snowstorm. At 7:28 p.m., after the first locomotive, Socrates, had crossed, the bridge collapsed behind it.

The second engine, Columbia, broke away, and it and all 11 carriages plunged 75 ft. (23 m) into the ravine. About 92 people were killed and many injured in what at that time was the worst rail disaster in the U.S.

Two hijacked planes crash into the World Trade Center, New York

Air disasters

Worst ever
Two terrorist attacks on the twin towers of the World Trade Center, New York, on September 11, 2001, killed everybody on both hijacked planes (92 on one and 65 on the other). More than 2,000 people also died in the buildings.

On the ground
On March 27, 1977, two Boeing 747s collided on the runway of Los Rodeos airport in Tenerife in the Canary Islands. The aircraft were carrying 614 passengers and 30 crew between them. A total of 61 people managed to escape.

Single-aircraft disaster
On August 12, 1985 a JAL Boeing 747 on a domestic flight from Tokyo to Osaka crashed, killing 520.

Midair collision
At Charkhi Dadri, India, on November 12, 1996, a Saudi Airways Boeing 747 collided with a Kazakh Airlines Ilyushin IL-76 cargo aircraft. A total of 349 people died.

Miracle on the Hudson

On January 15, 2009, as a US Airways Airbus A320 took off from LaGuardia airport, New York, it struck a flock of geese and lost power to both engines. The aircraft's captain, Chesley Sullenberger, managed to ditch it in the Hudson River, where all 155 passengers and crew were rescued.

History of tourism

People have been traveling from place to place since ancient times. Nomadic people moved around to graze their livestock. Later people traveled to trade, or to seek their fortunes in gold rushes, and millions emigrated to other countries to escape persecution or to seek better lives.

Apart from a few historical examples, tourism — traveling for pleasure — is a relatively modern idea. Today, people spend more than $850 billion a year on tourism.

Taking the waters
The Romans placed great value on bathing. They settled in many places with natural springs and developed cities as spas (the name comes from Spa in Belgium). In the 18th century, it became fashionable to visit these spas to "take the waters" — drinking and bathing as cures for various illnesses. Bath, in England, is a well-known Roman spa.

Package tours
On July 5, 1841, British travel pioneer Thomas Cook took 570 members of the Temperance Society (an organization opposed to drinking alcohol) on the newly opened railway from Leicester to Loughborough. This was the first package tour, and the beginning of what was to become the world's best-known travel company. When the Paris Exhibition opened in 1851, Cook took "excursionists" abroad for the first time. By the time Thomas Cook died in 1892, he had made travel possible for the masses.

Exhibitions
During the 19th and 20th centuries, major exhibitions in the U.S. and Europe brought millions of people to the big cities of the world. Many had never traveled before. The Great Exhibition in London, England in 1851 had more than six million visitors. The Paris Exposition of 1889, for which the Eiffel Tower was built, had 28 million visitors, and more than 51 million visited the New York World's Fair of 1964–65.

Festivals

Sleeping Beauty's Castle, Disneyland, Paris

The world's major arts and music festivals receive millions of visitors. The annual Texas State Fair in the U.S. attracts as many as three million, and many other North American fairs receive one million or more. Festivals such as the carnival held in Rio de Janeiro, Brazil, and Mardi Gras in New Orleans, Louisiana, are attended by large crowds.

Sport tourism
Winter sports such as skiing, water sports and adventure sports such as white-water rafting have become very popular. When the Olympic Games are held, the host country can expect a huge boost to its tourist industry.

Amusement parks
The world's most-visited amusement park is Disney World, Florida, which attracts 17.06 million visitors a year. The total number of visitors at all Disney attractions around the world is 115 million a year.

See also
Countries of the World: pages 116-117

Space tourism

The first fare-paying space tourist was American millionaire Denis Tito. In 2001 he paid $20 million to spend a week on the *International Space Station*. Anglo-South African Mark Shuttleworth paid a similar amount for a trip in 2002. Several companies, such as Virgin Galactic, are planning to take passengers to a height of about 100 km (62 miles) in 2010.

The Roman baths in Bath, England

Serengeti National Park, Tanzania

Serengeti National Park

This vast park in Tanzania was founded in 1951 and covers 5,700 sq. mi. (14,760 sq km) Wildebeest, gazelles and zebras graze here, along with lions, elephants, giraffes and other animals. It is one of Africa's most popular tourist attractions.

National parks

National parks are established by governments to preserve areas of land and the plants and animals they contain. Yellowstone National Park, set up in 1872, was the first. There are more than 1,200 national parks in over 100 countries. Including protected places, a total of more than 6,500 such areas have been designated worldwide.

Banff National Park (founded 1885; 2,564 sq. mi./6,641 sq km) Canada's oldest national park, in the Canadian Rockies in Alberta. Its forests and glaciers attract about four million visitors a year.

Everglades (founded 1934; 2,289 sq. mi./ 5,929 sq km) The Everglades, Florida is the only subtropical park in North America. Many different types of creatures live in its swamps, including alligators.

Great Barrier Reef (founded 1979; 132,742 sq. mi./ 343,800 sq km) Australia's Great Barrier Reef, off the coast of Queensland, is the world's largest coral reef system, supporting many rare marine animals and plants.

Galápagos Islands (founded 1986; 2,678 sq. mi./6,937 sq km) These volcanic islands off the coast of Ecuador are home to birds, seals and unique creatures including giant turtles and marine iguanas.

Lake District (founded 1951; 885 sq. mi./ 2,292 sq km) The largest and most visited of Great Britain's national parks. The parks receive a total of 100 million visitors a year.

Wrangell-St. Elias (founded 1980; 13,057 sq. mi./ 33,820 sq km) This national park in Alaska is the largest in the U.S.. It contains the most glaciers and peaks higher than 16,010 ft.

(4,880 m) in North America, as well as many wild animals, including bears, wolves and moose.

Xingu (founded 1961; 8,500 sq. mi./22,000 sq km) This large area of Brazilian rainforest is teeming with tropical wildlife. It is also inhabited by tribes of indigenous peoples who have little contact with outsiders.

Yellowstone (founded 1872; 3,471 sq. mi./ 8,991 sq km) This area of the Rocky Mountains in the U.S. is famed for its hot springs and geysers. Most famous is the Old Faithful geyser which sprays steam and water up to 184 ft. (56 m) high.

Top tourist countries

In 2007, one in every seven people in the world traveled as tourists to another country — a total of 903.3 million. Of these, almost half visited the top ten destinations below. By the year 2020 the number of international tourists is likely to more than double to 1.5 billion.

Country	Visitors	% of world total
1 France	81,900,000	9.1
2 Spain	59,193,000	6.6
3 U.S.	55,986,000	6.2
4 China	54,720,000	6.1
5 Italy	43,654,000	4.8
6 UK	30,677,000	3.4
7 Germany	24,420,000	2.7
8 Ukraine	23,122,000	2.6
9 Turkey	22,248,000	2.5
10 Mexico	21,424,000	2.4
Top 10 total	417,344,000	46.2

Language & Literature

Languages under threat

In 2009, UNESCO published its online atlas of endangered languages, which aims to keep track of the languages that are in danger of dying out. Included in the atlas is Aymara, spoken in the Andean region of South America and under threat from the dominant language of the area — Spanish. There are more than 6,000 languages being spoken in the world today — it is estimated that half of these will have vanished in 100 years.

Most spoken languages

Chinese (Mandarin)
Approximately 885,000,000 speakers. Chinese has many dialects, but about two-thirds of the people speak Mandarin. Wu is the next most common dialect, with approximately 77 million speakers. At least 30 million people around the world are learning Mandarin Chinese because China is becoming an important economic power.

Spanish
Approximately 332,000,000 speakers. Spanish is one of the most widely used of all languages. It is spoken not only in Spain but also in the U.S., South America, and the west coast of Africa.

English
Approximately 322,000,000 speakers. Far fewer people have English as their main language than Chinese, but millions more know at least some English and it is spoken in every corner of the globe. The United States dominates film, television, pop music, technology (Internet) and business, and this has increased the importance of the English language. At least 800 million people use the Internet and about 35 percent of them communicate in English. There are probably more than one billion people worldwide learning English.

Arabic
Approximately 246,000,000 speakers. Arabic is the official language of 17 countries and it is also the language of the Muslim religion. As a result, many millions of Muslims in other countries have some knowledge of the language.

Hindustani
Approximately 182,000,000 speakers. Hindustani includes Hindi and Urdu, which are almost the same language. Hindustani is the official language of Pakistan, where it is written in modified Arabic script and called Urdu. It is also the official language of India, but there it is written in the Devanagari script and called Hindi.

Portuguese
Approximately 177,500,000 speakers. Portuguese is spoken as a first language by the people of Portugal and also by many of the inhabitants of Brazil, Angola and other former colonies in Africa and elsewhere. These stretch from the Caribbean to Macau, China.

Languages spoken in most countries

English: 57 countries
French: 33 countries
Arabic: 23 countries
Spanish: 21 countries
Portuguese: 7 countries

Other major languages

Bengali
Approximate number of speakers: 189,000,000

Russian
Approximate number of speakers: 170,000,000

Japanese
Approximate number of speakers: 125,000,000

German (standard)
Approximate number of speakers: 95,450,000

Chinese (Wu)
Approximate number of speakers: 77,200,000

French
Approximate number of speakers: 77,000,000

A stop sign in English and Inuktituk (the language of the Inuit people)

Disappearing languages
There are about 6,912 living languages but 516 of these are considered almost extinct as they are spoken only by a few elderly people.

Alphabets

An alphabet is the basis of a system of writing, using letters or characters to represent sounds or words. These are some of the oldest and most important alphabets.

Greek
The Greek alphabet is the oldest surviving European alphabet. The early Greek alphabet was written from right to left, but by about 500 BC it was written from left to right. The Greeks introduced an uppercase (capital letters) and a lowercase (small letters).

Cyrillic
The Cyrillic alphabet was invented in the 9th century by two Greek missionaries, St. Cyril and his brother St. Methodius. It is used for Slavonic languages such as Russian, Bulgarian and Ukrainian. The Russian Cyrillic alphabet originally had 43 letters, but the number was reduced to 33 after the Russian Revolution of 1917. Like the Greek alphabet, Cyrillic also has uppercase and lowercase versions of the alphabet.

Hebrew
Hebrew is written horizontally from right to left. Also, sometimes the letters are used as numerals.

Arabic
Arabic evolved from Aramaic in the 4th century, and is written from left to right. It consists of 28 consonants. Vowels are shown by marks placed above or below the consonants but are not always used. Arabic letters are

Writing in Braille

Braille

Braille is a system of raised dots that allows blind people to read by touch. It was invented in the 19th century by a blind French man named Louis Braille. The dots are embossed on to paper, either by hand or using a machine. They are read by moving the fingers across the top of the dots.

The reader uses both hands — the right works out the message while the left feels ahead for the beginning of the next line. A skilled Braille reader can understand up to 150 words a minute, which is about half the speed of a sighted person reading ordinary text.

Braille cell

The basic unit of Braille is called a cell. It is made up of six dots, which allows for 63 possible combinations to represent letters, numbers and punctuation marks.

written differently depending upon where they appear in a word. The positions of characters are known as final (end), medial (middle), initial (beginning) and isolated (on its own).

Chinese and Japanese

These are logographic writing systems. This means that each symbol represents a word, or part of a word, instead of a sound. The Chinese system has 40,000–50,000 characters and the Japanese system has 18,000, but you need to know only about 2,000 and 1,850, respectively, to get by in these languages. In 1966 the Chinese language changed quite dramatically, when books and newspapers were printed with the characters running horizontally from left to right rather than vertically from right to left. There is now a phonetic alphabet known as pin-yin, made up of 25 letters taken from the Roman alphabet.

Most Chinese characters are made up of eight basic strokes. These are all in the character for eternity. Words in a Chinese dictionary are in order of the number of strokes they contain. Chinese verbs and adjectives usually contain only one character or syllable, but nouns often consist of two characters or more. The examples below show how some compound words are made up.

| tree | woodland (2 trees) | forest (3 trees) |

Chinese symbol in the background means eternity

Phonetic alphabet

You may have heard pilots and soldiers on television and in films using the phonetic alphabet in radio messages. The alphabet is used to spell out parts of a message that might be difficult to recognize in unclear radio transmissions. The version generally used was developed in the 1950s.

It is known as the NATO (North Atlantic Treaty Organization) Phonetic Alphabet and was designed to be understood and easily pronounced by all NATO members. They chose words that were used in lots of different languages and could not be confused with other common words or those used for another letter. Aircraft and ship crews also use the phonetic alphabet. For example, in the phonetic alphabet "over and out" becomes Oscar Victor Echo Romeo Alpha November Delta Oscar Uniform Tango.

A Alpha	**K** Kilo	**U** Uniform
B Bravo	**L** Lima	**V** Victor
C Charlie	**M** Mike	**W** Whiskey
D Delta	**N** November	**X** X-ray
E Echo	**O** Oscar	**Y** Yankee
F Foxtrot	**P** Papa	**Z** Zulu
G Golf	**Q** Quebec	
H Hotel	**R** Romeo	
I India	**S** Sierra	
J Juliet	**T** Tango	

See also

Brainchildren: young inventors: page 81

Hieroglyphics on the pillars of Habu Temple in Luxor, Egypt

Hieroglyphics

The simplest of all writing systems use pictures. These are called pictograms and look like the things they describe — just like many road signs and computer icons today.

Writing or carving pictograms is very slow and a lot of work, so people began to use simpler versions of images, such as hieroglyphics. Ancient Egyptian hieroglyphics were used on obelisks, wall paintings, tombs and papyrus (documents on a type of paper made from reeds). They are symbols that represent an object, a sound or an idea. They are not a code: you cannot simply convert an Egyptian hieroglyph into a letter and read it as we read words in a book. People stopped using hieroglyphics in the 1st century AD. From then on, no one could understand them until 1822 when French scholar Jean François Champollion worked out how to translate the text of the Rosetta Stone in the British Museum.

Morse code

By using Morse code you can send a signal in a series of dots and dashes. The signal can be sent by sound or by flashing lights. There are five parts to the code: a dot, a dash, a short gap or pause (between letters), a medium gap (between words) and a long gap (between sentences).

Morse was created by and named after the U.S. artist and inventor Samuel Finley Breese Morse (1791–1872). He sent the first Morse code message from Washington D.C., to Baltimore, Maryland, on May 24, 1844. It read, "What hath God wrought!" An international version of Morse code became widely used to send telegrams by wire. Once people could send messages by radio transmissions they still used Morse code in situations such as warfare, when clear voice signals were not always possible.

A ·-	N -·	0 -----	5 ·····
B -···	O ---	1 ·----	6 -····
C -·-·	P ·--·	2 ··---	7 --···
D -··	Q --·-	3 ···--	8 ---··
E ·	R ·-·	4 ····-	9 ----·
F ··-·	S ···		
G --·	T -		
H ····	U ··-		
I ··	V ···-		
J ·---	W ·--		
K -·-	X -··-		
L ·-··	Y -·--		
M --	Z --··		

A Morse key for sending messages

Social networking websites

Social networking has become the Internet phenomenon of the 2000s, with over 200 sites worldwide attracting millions of visitors every day.

	Site	Visits*
1	facebook.com	1,191,373,339
2	myspace.com	810,153,536
3	twitter.com	54,218,731
4	flixter.com	53,389,974
5	linkedin.com	42,744,438
6	tagged.com	39,630,927
7	classmates.com	35,219,210
8	myyearbook.com	33,121,821
9	livejournal.com	25,221,354
10	imeem.com	22,993,608

* In January 2009

Communications milestones 3500 BC

A variety of ways of communicating between people without speaking have been devised, some dating back thousands of years. These are just some of the important steps in this history.

3500 BC First writing

1700–1450 BC Minoans of Crete use Linear A and Linear B scripts for writing

100 BC Roman alphabet with 23 letters

AD 105 Chinese make paper

150 Parchment books replace scrolls

400–1400 Monks produce copies of manuscripts

1034 First moveable type (made of clay) in China

1450 First printing presses in Europe

1476 William Caxton prints first books in London

1588 Beacons used in England to warn of invasion by Spanish Armada

1702 *The Daily Courant* was the first daily newspaper in the UK

1783 *The Pennsylvania Evening Post and Public Advertiser* was the first daily newspaper published in America

1791 Optical telegraph invented by Claude Chappe (France)

Postal factfile

First stamps
The first adhesive stamps were Penny Blacks, issued in the UK in 1840.

Largest stamps
In 1913, Chinese express delivery stamps were issued that measured 9.75 x 2.75 inches (248 x 70 mm).

Smallest stamps
In 1863 10 cent and 1 peso stamps of the Colombian State of Bolivar were ⁵/₁₆ x ³/₈ inch (9.5 x 8 mm).

Upside-down stamp
Because they are rare, stamps with printing mistakes are prized by collectors. In 2005 a block of four 1918 U.S. 24 cent stamps with a biplane upside-down was sold for $2.7 million.

Mail boxes
The first mail boxes in the UK date from 1852. India is the country with the most mail boxes, a total of 661,987. India also has the most post offices – 155,204.

Letters
Despite the increasing use of e-mail, people in the U.S. send and receive more letters than any country in the world, a total of more than 200 billion a year out of a worldwide total of 433 billion.

Oldest American post office
The Post Office and Customs House in Galena, Illinois, dates from 1858 and has been preserved as a perfect example of a working mid-19th century American post office.

Papal mail
The Vatican sends the most letters per person of any country: 6,973. This is because people in Rome use the Vatican's postal service as it is more reliable than the Italian post.

Pony Express
Started in the U.S. in 1860, the Pony Express carried mail by a network of riders galloping between towns on horses. The famous cowboy and showman Buffalo Bill was once a Pony Express rider. It closed in 1861 as the telegraph made it possible to send messages instantaneously.

Pigeon mail
Carrier pigeons have been used to carry messages since ancient times, especially in wartime: microfilm was first used to send messages out of Paris when it was under siege by the German army in 1870–71, and from the trenches in World War I.

Post office railway
A 6.5-mile (10-km) underground railway with driverless electric trains once carried four million letters and parcels a day across London. It ran from 1927 until it was closed in 2003.

Text messaging is one of the world's most widely used communication methods

Texting abbreviations

Texting is also known as SMS (Short Message service) as there is a limit to the number of characters. Because of this and to save time in composing messages, abbreviations are commonly used.

Word or Phrase	Abbreviation(s)
at the moment	atm
be right back	brb
by the way	btw
don't worry	dw
got to go	g2g, gtg
later	L8er
laugh out loud	lol
message	msg
no problem	np
see you/see you later	cya, cu, cya, cul8er, l8a
text (me) back	tb, tmb
to be honest	tbh
tomorrow	2moz, 2moro
whatever	wateva

Mail on stilts

In some countries, such as France and Holland, postmen used to walk on stilts to get across canals, ditches and marshy areas.

2000s

1839 First commercial telegraph (London)

1867 Sending messages by flashing signal lamps, invented by Philip Colomb, adopted by the British Navy

1867 The first commercially successful typewriter invented by Christopher Scholes (U.S.)

1876 The heliograph for signalling using sunlight reflected by a mirror patented by Sir Henry Mance (UK)

1888 The Telautograph, an early version of the fax machine, invented by Elisha Gray (U.S.) — the modern fax machine was developed in the 1970s

1943 *Colossus*, an early computer, was built in the UK to decode messages encoded by the German *Enigma* machine

1960 The first international telex service enabled electronic transmission of text messages

1971 The "@" sign became standard in e-mail addresses; email began to be used from 1972 onward

1972 Ceefax, the first TV text information service, was launched in the UK

1993 Although there are earlier claims, it is probable that the first SMS (text) messages were sent

2006 Twitter, a "micro-blog" service, was started in the U.S.

The main reading room at the Library of Congress in Washington, D.C.

Largest libraries

A library is a collection of books and other printed material. The word library can also be used to describe the building where a collection of books is kept, as well as manuscripts, maps, periodicals and photographs. Below are the world's largest libraries, each containing over 15 million books.

The Library of Congress, Washington, D.C., was founded in 1800 and holds 32,124,001 books.

The British Library*, London, England, was founded in 1753 and holds 29,000,000 books.

Library of the Russian Academy of Sciences, St. Petersburg, Russia was founded in 1714 and holds 22,500,000 books.

Deustche Bibliotek, Frankfurt, Germany was founded in 1990 and holds 22,200, 000 books.

National Library of Canada, Ottawa, Canada, was founded in 1953 and holds 19,500,000 books.

The Russian State Library, Moscow, Russia, was founded in 1862 and holds 17,000,000 books.

Harvard University Library, Cambridge, Massachusetts, was founded in 1636 and holds 15,826,570 books.

* Founded as part of the British Museum, 1753; became independent in 1973

Page from the Codex Hammer

Valuable books and manuscripts

● The Codex Hammer (previously called the Codex Leicester) was sold in New York, N.Y., in 1994 for $28,800,000. It was bought by Bill Gates, the billionaire founder of Microsoft. The Codex is one of Leonardo da Vinci's notebooks and includes many of his scientific drawings and diagrams.

● John James Audubon's *The Birds of America* (1827–38) was sold in New York, N.Y., in 2000 for $8,000,000, making it the most expensive printed book. Its giant pages feature more than 400 hand-colored engravings of birds.

● One of the first-ever printed books was Geoffrey Chaucer's *The Canterbury Tales* (c. 1477). A copy was sold in London, England, in 1998 for $7,570,941.

● A "first folio" (early edition) of the works of William Shakespeare dating from 1623 was sold in London, England, in 2001 for $6,166,000.

● A rare copy of the Gutenberg Bible, one of the first books ever printed, was sold in New York, N.Y., in 1987 for $5,390,000.

Types of book

Almanac
This is an annual calendar of dates and events. It originally contained astronomical facts and figures, but now includes useful statistics and other information. Almanac is sometimes spelled almanack.

Anthology
A collection of writings by one author or on a theme, such as an anthology of animal poems.

Atlas
A book of maps.

Autobiography
An account of a person's life written by himself or herself. Sometimes a "ghost" writer may help someone write an autobiography.

Bibliography
A list of books or sources on a particular subject.

Biography
A book about someone's life written by another person.

Chronology
A dictionary of dated events.

Dictionary
An alphabetical list of words and their meanings. There are also dictionaries on a single subject, for example *Dictionary of Art*.

Dictionary of quotations
A listing of interesting remarks or extracts from the writings of famous people.

Directory
An alphabetical list of names and addresses of people or organizations.

Encyclopedia
A book of articles on many subjects, arranged alphabetically. Encyclopedias are often published in many volumes or, today, on CD-ROM or on the Internet.

Gazetteer
A book that lists and describes places (countries, cities, etc).

Glossary
A list of words and phrases used in a particular subject area, for instance *A Glossary of Computer Terms*.

Language dictionary
A dictionary that gives translations of words and phrases to and from other languages, for example a *French-English/English-French Dictionary*.

Monograph
A book on a specialized subject, such as the work of a particular artist.

Novel
A work of fiction, usually involving imaginary people. A historical novel may be about real historical characters.

Novella
A short work of fiction.

Phrasebook
A book for travellers, with translations of words and phrases into and from a foreign language.

Pop-up book
A book, usually for children, made so that pictures stand up or move when the pages are opened.

Thesaurus
A book organized to show words with similar meanings.

Travel guide
A book of information about a particular country or area.

Who's who or biographical dictionary
Alphabetical summaries of the lives of famous people, living or dead, sometimes by their subjects (such as a *Dictionary of Scientists*).

Yearbook
An annual reference book with information about the events of the previous year. Yearbooks containing statistical information about a country are often called *Abstracts*.

Book firsts and records

First printed books
Books were printed in China in the 8th century using woodblocks, and in 14th-century China and Korea using movable type.

First books printed in English
In 1474 William Caxton printed the first book in English, *Recuyell of the Historyes of Troye*. It was printed in Bruges, Flanders. Chaucer's *Canterbury Tales* was probably the first book in English to be printed in England, in about 1477.

First books printed in America
Massachusetts Bay Colony: The Oath of a Free-Man (1638) and *An Almanack for the Year of Our Lord* (1639) are the first two books known to have been printed in the new American colonies.

Longest novel
A science-fiction novel by French writer Georges-Jean Arnaud, *La Compagne des Glaces* (1980–92), runs to 62 volumes and has about 11,000 pages.

First sequel
Daniel Defoe wrote *The Farther Adventures of Robinson Crusoe* in 1719, after the success of *Robinson Crusoe* earlier that year.

First American novel
The Power of Sympathy (1789) was the first novel published in America. It was published anonymously, but is believed to have been written by William Hill Brown.

First detective story
Murders in the Rue Morgue, by American author Edgar Allan Poe, was first published in *Grahame's Magazine* in 1841.

Smallest book
This was produced by a German typographer Josua Reichertand called *The World's Smallest Book*. It measures 2.4 x 2.9 mm (0.09 x 0.1 in) – the size of a match head.

Largest book
The largest book was published in 2003. It is a collection of photos called *Bhutan: A Visual Odyssey Across the Last Himalayan Kingdom*. When opened out it measures 2.1 x 1.5 m (7 x 5 ft) – almost the size of a table-tennis table! It costs $15,000 a copy.

Electronic books
The Amazon Kindle was launched in 2007. In 2009 the Kindle 2 offered improved features and better battery life. *UR*, a short novel by Stephen King, was available only for downloading to the Kindle 2.

Stephen King's *UR*, available exclusively for the Kindle 2

www.fireflybooks.com   search

Famous diaries

People have kept personal diaries for more than 500 years. Most were written as personal records about the times the writers lived through or events that happened to them, and they are often fascinating to read.

Samuel Pepys (1633–1703)

Pepys kept a diary for nearly 10 years from 1660. He lived in London and wrote about events such as the Great Plague and Great Fire of London. He wrote in a special code, which was not translated until the 19th century. Pepys' original diaries are kept in the library of Magdalene College, Cambridge.

Anne Frank (1929–1945)

Anne Frank was forced to hide with her family in Amsterdam, Netherlands, during World War II, when Jewish people were being persecuted by the Nazis. Anne kept her diary while she was in hiding, but left it behind when she and her family were found. She was deported and died in a German concentration camp. Her father survived and edited her diary, which was published after the war. *The Diary of Anne Frank* became a bestseller and was translated into more than 55 languages. It has also been made into an award-winning play and a film. The house in which the Frank family hid is now a museum.

Adolf Hitler (1889–1945)

In 1993, the German magazine *Stern* paid 10 million marks ($8 million) to journalist Gerd Heidemann to publish extracts from what were claimed to be the diaries of the German dictator Adolf Hitler. The diaries were soon discovered to have been forgeries written by Konrad Kujau. He and Heidemann were imprisoned for their deception.

Bestsellers

These are some of the bestselling books ever. But the Bible has outsold them all. It is believed to have sold more than six billion copies in hundreds of versions and translations.

● One of the bestselling books of all time is a collection of quotations by Chinese leader Mao Zedong, known as his *Little Red Book*. Between 1966 to 1971 every Chinese adult had to own a copy and 900 million were printed.

● J.R.R. Tolkien's *The Lord of the Rings* trilogy was first published in 1954–55. It has sold well over 100 million and its sales received a further boost when the films based on the books were released between 2001 and 2003.

● *The American Spelling Book* by Noah Webster (1783) was used in American schools for generations. It has sold nearly 100 million copies.

● *The Common Sense Book of Baby and Child Care* by American doctor Benjamin Spock came out in 1946. Since then more than 50 million copies have been sold.

● British crime writer Agatha Christie has sold at least one billion copies of her novels in English and another billion in 45 foreign languages. In 1935 her novel *The Mysterious Affair at Styles* was one of the first Penguin paperbacks ever published.

● American author Margaret Mitchell's only book, *Gone With the Wind* (1936), has sold around 30 million copies. It is one of the bestselling novels ever.

Covers for two *Harry Potter* books

J.K. Rowling

J.K. Rowling was born on July 31, 1965 as Joanne Rowling (she later borrowed the name Kathleen from her grandmother to create a middle initial). Her first Harry Potter book, *Harry Potter and the Philosopher's Stone*, was published in 1997. It has been followed by six more books with sales now over 400 million copies in 67 languages. If all Harry Potter books ever sold were placed end to end, they would stretch 49,710 miles (80,000 km) — twice the distance round the Equator! Earnings from the book sales and films have made J.K. Rowling the richest author ever, and the first to make more than $1 billion from writing. She has given large amounts to charities. The final book, *Harry Potter and the Deathly Hallows*, was published on 21 July 2007.

Translations

These are the ten most translated authors in the world, according to UNESCO's *Index Translationum* (1979–2009).

Author	Count	Author	Count
Agatha Christie	6,453	Barbara Cartland	3,403
Jules Verne	4,185	Danielle Steel	2,858
William Shakespeare	3,603	Hans Christian Andersen	2,811
V. I. Lenin	3,516	Stephen King	2,696
Enid Blyton	3,495	Jakob Grimm	2,448

Imaginary lands

Writers usually invent the characters in their books, but some have also created imaginary lands in which the action of the book takes place. These are some of the best known fictional worlds, and the books in which they first appeared. Some featured again in later books by their authors.

Thomas Moore – **Utopia** in *Utopia* (1516)

Jonathan Swift – **Lilliput** in *Gulliver's Travels* (1726)

Lewis Carroll – **Wonderland** in *Alice's Adventures in Wonderland* (1865)

L. Frank Baum – **Oz** in *The Wonderful Wizard of Oz* (1900)

J.M. Barrie – **Neverland** in *Peter and Wendy* (1911)

J.R.R. Tolkien – **Middle Earth** in *The Hobbit* (1937)

C.S. Lewis – **Narnia** in *The Lion, The Witch and The Wardrobe* (1950)

Terry Pratchett – **Discworld** in *The Colour of Magic* (1983)

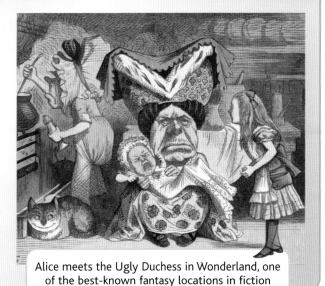

Alice meets the Ugly Duchess in Wonderland, one of the best-known fantasy locations in fiction

J.K. Rowling
Photograph
© Richard Young

Nobel Prize for Literature

Nobel prizes have been given every year since 1901 for achievements in different fields, including literature. Nobel Prize winners for literature include poets, playwrights and authors from all over the world. Below are some of the best known winners.

2008 J.M.G. Le Clézio (France, 1940–)
2007 Doris Lessing (UK, 1919–)
2006 Orhan Pamuk (Turkey, 1952–)
2005 Harold Pinter (UK, 1930–2008)
2003 J.M. Coetzee (South Africa, 1940–)
2001 V.S. Naipaul (UK, 1932–)
2000 Gao Xingjian (China, 1940–) first win by a Chinese writer
1999 Günter Grass (Germany, 1927–)
1995 Seamus Heaney (Ireland, 1939–)
1993 Toni Morrison (U.S., 1931–)
1991 Nadine Gordimer (South Africa, 1923–)
1983 William Golding (UK, 1911–93) author of *The Lord of the Flies*
1973 Patrick White (Australia, 1912–90)
1970 Alexander Solzhenitsyn (Russia, 1918–2008)
1962 John Steinbeck (U.S., 1902–68) author of *The Grapes of Wrath*
1958 Boris Pasternak (Russia, 1890–1960) author of *Doctor Zhivago*
1954 Ernest Hemingway (U.S., 1899–1961)
1953 Winston Churchill (UK, 1874–1965) British prime minister and writer
1948 T.S. Eliot (US-born, UK, 1888–1965) author of the book that inspired the musical *Cats*
1938 Pearl Buck (U.S., 1892–1973)
1932 John Galsworthy (UK, 1867–1933) author of *The Forsyte Saga*
1925 George Bernard Shaw (UK, 1856–1950)
1923 William Butler Yeats (Ireland, 1865–1939)
1907 Rudyard Kipling (UK, 1865–1936) author of *The Jungle Book*
1901 Sully Prudhomme (France, 1839–1907) the first winner

http//www.jkrowling.com   search

Children's firsts

First children's book
The first English children's book for entertainment (not a school book) was a collection of rhymes called *A Booke in Englyssh Metre, of the Great Merchante Man called Dives Pragmaticus, very preaty for Children to reade*. It was printed in London, England, in 1563.

First children's book printed in the U.S.
John Cotton's *Milk for Babies* was printed in Cambridge, Massachusetts, in 1641–45.

First children's encyclopedia
Pera Librorum Juvenilium (Collection of Juvenile Books) was compiled in Germany by Johann Christoph Wagenseil in 1695.

First story for children
The History of Little Goody Two-Shoes was published by John Newbery in London, England, in 1765. Some experts believe it was written by the famous British poet and playwright Oliver Goldsmith.

First nursery rhyme book
Tommy Thumb's Pretty Song Book was published in London, England, in 1744. It contained well-known rhymes such as "London Bridge is falling down," "Hickory, dickory dock" and "Sing a song of sixpence."

First children's library
The Bingham Library for Youth was set up in Salisbury, Connecticut, in January 1803 when Caleb Bingham, who came from the town, donated 150 books.

First winner of the Newbery Medal
The Newbery Medal is awarded by the American Library Association to the author of the outstanding American book for children. The first writer to receive it, in 1922, was Hendrik Willem van Loon for *The Story of Mankind*. In 2007 it was won by Susan Patron for *The Higher Power of Lucky*.

Fairy tale authors

Fairy tales are fantastic stories for children that do not always involve fairies. They are traditional tales that were retold from generation to generation. The writers below collected the stories and wrote or rewrote them in books that became hugely popular all over the world. Many fairy tales have been made into films—especially animated films by Disney.

Charles Perrault
French writer Charles Perrault (1628–1703) put together a collection of stories with the help of his son Pierre (1678–1700). Their collection contained *Cinderella*, *Little Red Riding-Hood*, *Sleeping Beauty* and *Puss in Boots*. The stories were translated into English in 1729. Later editions had the French title, *Contes de ma mère l'Oye*, or *Mother Goose's Tales*.

Brothers Grimm
German brothers Jacob Ludwig Carl Grimm (1785–1863) and Wilhelm Carl Grimm (1786–1859) were the authors of *Grimm's Fairy Tales*, which were first published for Christmas 1812. This was a collection of traditional stories, rewritten for a young audience. It included many famous fairy tales, such as *Hansel and Gretel*, *Rumpelstiltskin* and *Snow White and the Seven Dwarfs*. They were translated into English in 1823 and became a worldwide bestseller.

Hans Christian Andersen
Danish author Andersen (1805–75) wrote 156 fairy tales, including *The Little Mermaid*, *The Emperor's New Clothes* and *The Ugly Duckling*. His stories first appeared in English in 1846.

Glass slippers

In Perrault's re-telling of the story of Cinderella, he used the French phrase *pantoufle de verre*, which means glass slipper. However, it may be that he mistook *verre*, glass, for *vair*, an old French word for fur, and what Cinderella was actually wearing were furry slippers!

Illustration for *The Ugly Duckling*, a fairy tale by Hans Christian Andersen

Lucy Maud Montgomery

Lucy Maud Montgomery (1874–1942) is the Canadian author best known for Anne of Green Gables. The first book she wrote, it was published in 1908 and became a worldwide bestseller, along with Anne of Avonlea (1909) and other sequels. The original book has been made into a film, a television drama series and a stage musical.

Multi-million sellers

J.K. Rowling (UK, 1965–)
At the end of 2008, the seven Harry Potter books had sold more than 400 million copies worldwide. In 2007, *Harry Potter and the Deathly Hallows* sold 2,652,656 copies in the UK on its first day of release — the biggest one-day sale ever recorded.

Enid Blyton (UK, 1897–1968)
Enid Blyton wrote more than 700 children's books. Total sales of her works are more than 400 million. She was the bestselling English-language author until the arrival of J.K. Rowling.

René Goscinny (France, 1926–77) and Albert Uderzo (France, 1927–)
René Goscinny and Albert Uderzo created the comic-strip character

Astérix the Gaul in 1959. They jointly produced 24 books, and Uderzo went on to create 9 more after Goscinny's death. Their total worldwide sales are more than 330 million copies.

R.L. Stine (U.S., 1943–)
The 138 books in R.L. Stine's *Goosebumps* series and its sequels have sold over 330 million copies worldwide.

Goosebumps HorrorLand (2008–09) is Stine's latest series.

Hergé (Belgium, 1907–83)
Georges Rémi was the author-illustrator who wrote under the pen-name Hergé. He created the comic-strip character Tintin in 1929. The boy detective's adventures have appeared in book form since 1948 onwards and have been translated into about 45 languages and

The Cat in the Hat, a character from one of Dr. Seuss' most popular books

Famous illustrators

Below are some of the artists who have produced the best-loved illustrations for children's books. Some, such as Beatrix Potter, also wrote the books they illustrated.

Honor C. Appleton (American, 1879–1951) *Josephine and Her Dolls*
Quentin Blake (British, 1932–) Illustrated Roald Dahl's books and others
Raymond Briggs (British, 1934–) *The Snowman* and *Father Christmas*
Jean de Brunhoff (French, 1899–1937) *Babar the Elephant* series
Hergé (Belgian, 1907–83) the *Tintin* books
Tove Jansson (Finnish, 1914–2001) the *Moomin* series
Arnold Lobel (American, 1933–87) the *Frog and Toad* books
Henriette Willebeek Le Mair (Dutch, 1889–1966) *Our Old Nursery Rhymes*

© Hergé/Moulinsart 2005

Tintin by Hergé

Beatrix Potter (British, 1866–1943) the *Peter Rabbit* books and others
Arthur Rackham (British, 1867–1939) illustrated classics
William Heath Robinson (British, 1872–1944) illustrated classics
Maurice Sendak (American, 1928–) *Where the Wild Things Are* and others
Ernest Shepard (British, 1879–1976) *The Wind in the Willows, Winnie the Pooh*
Dr. Seuss (Theodor Seuss Geissel; American, 1904–91) *The Cat in the Hat* and many others
Jessie Willcox Smith (American, 1863–1935) *The Water Babies*
Albert Uderzo (French, 1927–) the *Astérix* books
Chris Van Allsburg (American, 1949–) *Jumanji, The Polar Express*

Children's bestsellers

A survey of the bestselling English-language children's books in the U.S. put four illustrated books at the top of the list. The top two are: Janette Sebring's *The Poky Little Puppy* (1942) with sales of 14.9 million and Beatrix Potter's *The Tale of Peter Rabbit* (1902) (9.4 million).

---

dialects. Total sales are over 200 million.
Beatrix Potter (UK, 1866–1943) *The Tale of Peter Rabbit* (1901) and her other books have sold more than 150 million copies in 30 languages.
Lewis Carroll (UK, 1832–98) There are no world figures for sales of Lewis Carroll's books, *Alice in Wonderland* and *Alice Through the Looking Glass*, but

these two books have never been out of print. They have appeared in hundreds of editions and in many languages.
Dr. Seuss (U.S., 1904–91) *Green Eggs and Ham*, one of Dr Seuss' most popular books, has sold more than 8 million in the USA alone. Worldwide, he has sold more than 100 million copies of his books.

Rev. W. Awdry (UK, 1911–97) Rev. Awdry began writing his *Thomas the Tank Engine* books in 1946. The books have sold more than 90 million copies.

Mark Twain (U.S., 1835–1910) Book sales in the **U.S.** were not accurately recorded before 1895. *The Adventures of Tom Sawyer* (1876) and *The Adventures of Huckleberry Finn* (1884) have probably each sold more than 20 million copies worldwide.

42explore.com/poetry.htm　　　search

Epic poem

An epic is an extended narrative poem, written in a grand style about the life of a heroic or mythological person. *The Mahabharata*, a famous Indian epic, is about four times longer than the Bible and seven times longer than Homer's great epics, the *Odyssey* and the *Iliad*.

Ancient poems

Before stories and poems were written down they were passed on orally. Some of the most famous long narrative, or story, poems were passed on this way for hundreds of years before being written down by the poet who is now known as the author.

The Iliad — Homer
This Greek poem dates from 850 BC and tells the story of the final year of the war between the Greeks and the Trojans. It describes the great battle and the story of how beautiful Helen left her husband Menelaus for the Trojan prince Paris. It also tells us about the interference of the gods and their quarrels about the action on the battlefield below them.

The Odyssey — Homer
This describes Odysseus' journey home from the Trojan war. Odysseus features briefly in *The Iliad*. Again, human characters work side by side with the gods, who are given

human characteristics. Although they are so powerful, the gods bear grudges, seek revenge and are very proud. The word odyssey has now come to mean any long, hard journey. The poem has strongly influenced other works of literature — most famously the novel *Ulysses* by the Irish writer James Joyce.

Rubáiyat
Omar Khayyám was a Persian writer, mathematician and astronomer who lived in the 11th and early 12th centuries. His *Rubáiyat* was introduced to the rest of the world in 1859, when it was translated by Edward Fitzgerald. Each verse contains a complete thought.

Beowulf
An epic poem of almost 3,200 lines written in Old English (or Anglo-Saxon). This is an early form of the English language that modern readers find hard to understand. The main theme is the struggle of the hero Beowulf with the water monster Grendel. Details of the poem's exact date and author are not known, but it may have been written in the 8th century by more than one person.

Sir Gawain and the Green Knight
This poem was written by a monk from the northwest of England during the second half of the 14th century. Its 2,530 lines describe events in King Arthur's court and the testing of Sir Gawain, a model knight. There are many opportunities for the character to fail, but he does not.

Famous poets and poems

Most poets write many poems. Below are some of the most famous poets and their best-known works.

Haiku

This is a traditional Japanese form of poetry which has 17 syllables, e.g.,

*Clouds appear
and bring to men a chance to rest
from looking at the moon.*

Matsuo Basho

Charles Baudelaire (1821–67), France, wrote *Les Fleurs du Mal*

William Blake (1757–1827), England, wrote *The Tyger; London*

Matsuo Basho (1644–94), Japan, wrote numerous haiku

Elizabeth Barrett Browning (1806–61), England, wrote *How Do I Love Thee?*

Robert Burns (1759–96), Scotland, wrote *Tam o' Shanter*

Lord Byron (1788–1824), England, wrote *Don Juan*

Geoffrey Chaucer (c. 1343–1400), England, wrote *The Canterbury Tales*

Samuel Taylor Coleridge (1772–1834), England, wrote *Kubla Khan; The Rime of the Ancient Mariner*

Dante Alighieri (1265–1321), Italy, wrote *The Divine Comedy*

Emily Dickinson (1830–86), U.S., wrote *Because I Could Not Stop for Death*

T.S. Eliot (1888–1965), U.S./England, wrote *The Waste Land*

Robert Frost (1874–1963), U.S., wrote *Stopping by Woods on a Snowy Evening; The Road Not Taken*

Allen Ginsberg (1926–97), U.S., wrote *Howl*

Homer (c. 8th century BC), Greece, wrote *The Iliad; The Odyssey*

John Keats (1795–1821), England, wrote *Ode to a Nightingale; La Belle Dame Sans Merci; To Autumn*

Rudyard Kipling (1865–1936), England, wrote *If*

Mikhail Lermontov (1814–41), Russia, wrote *The Novice*

Li Po (701–762), China, wrote *Drinking Alone Under the Moon*

John Milton (1608–74), England, wrote *Paradise Lost; Paradise Regained*

Pablo Neruda (1904–71), Chile, wrote *Canto General*

Nezami (1140–c. 1217), Iran, wrote *Khamseh* (or *The Quinary*)

Ovid (43 BC–AD 17), ancient Rome, wrote *Metamorphoses*

Sylvia Plath (1932–63), U.S., wrote *Ariel*

Edgar Allan Poe (1809–49), U.S., wrote *The Raven*

Arthur Rimbaud (1854–91), France, wrote *Une Saison en Enfer* (or *A Season in Hell*)

William Shakespeare (1564–1616), England, wrote *Sonnet 18* (or *Shall I Compare Thee to a Summer's Day*)

Percy Bysshe Shelley (1792–1822), England, wrote *Ozymandias*

Edmund Spenser (1552–99), England, wrote *The Faerie Queene*

Alfred Tennyson (1809–92), England, wrote *In Memoriam* and *The Lady of Shalott*

Dylan Thomas (1914–53), Wales, wrote *Fern Hill*

Virgil (70–19 BC), ancient Rome, wrote *The Aeneid*

Walt Whitman (1819–92), U.S., wrote *Song of Myself*

William Wordsworth (1770–1850), England, wrote *The Prelude* and *Daffodils*

William Butler Yeats (1865–1939), Ireland, wrote *Sailing to Byzantium; The Lake Isle of Innisfree*

An illustration by William McLaren for *Sir Gawain and the Green Knight*

U.S. 10¢
Robert Frost
AMERICAN POET

Antique U.S. stamp with a portrait of Robert Frost

Poets laureate

The word laureate means crowned with laurel. The expression dates back to ancient Rome, where a successful person was traditionally crowned with a wreath of laurel leaves.

In Great Britain, the position of poet laureate was created as a royal office in 1668 with the appointment of John Dryden by King Charles II. The position was traditionally held for life, but is now restricted to 10 years. When it becomes vacant the prime minister has a list of names drawn up and the monarch chooses a new laureate. The poet laureate's main task is to write odes to celebrate royal birthdays, marriages and important state occasions. Poets laureate receive a salary of $140 (£70) per year — the same as in the 17th century! Some famous poets laureate in the U.K. include William Wordsworth, Alfred Tennyson, Sir John Betjeman and Ted Hughes. The present laureate is Andrew Motion.

In the United States the first poet laureate (Joseph Auslander) was appointed in 1937. A new laureate is appointed every year. He or she serves from October to May and is paid $35,000.

Statue of Dante Alighieri in Florence, Italy

Most valuable comics

Copies of American comic books with the first appearances of superheroes Superman and Batman are the most valued by collectors. In perfect condition, an *Action Comics* No. 1, with the first Superman story, could be worth up to $5,800,000. *Detective Comics* No. 27, the first to feature Batman, is valued at up to $4,000,000.

All about comics

Captain America

Comic strips

A comic strip is a story told in a series of pictures published in a newspaper. The New York *Daily Graphic* was the first newspaper to feature a comic strip. It started on September 11, 1875, with *Professor Tigwissel's Burglar Alarm*. The first regular strip was The Yellow Kid, which began in a supplement of the *New York World* on May 5, 1895. A syndicated comic strip is one that appears in more than one newspaper. Some appear in hundreds of papers all over the world.

Comics

In the United States, series of cartoon strips began to appear in newspapers from the 1890s, and were syndicated nationwide. The *Katzenjammer Kids*, which was first published in *The American Humorist*, a Sunday supplement of the *New York Journal* on December 12, 1897, still appears in many newspapers and magazines.

Comic books

The first U.S. comic book was called *Funnies on Parade* and came out in 1933. The first to be published regularly was *Famous Funnies* in 1934. Many comic books were about the adventures of a single superhero, such as Batman or Superman, who used special powers to fight crime and defeat evil villains.

Top newspaper-reading countries*

1 Japan 551
2 Norway 517
3 Sweden 480
4 Finland 431
*daily copies per 1,000 people

See also

Book firsts and records: page 229

Newspaper fact file

First newspapers

From 59 BC onward Roman emperor Julius Caesar had handwritten reports on news posted in public places in Rome. China had newspapers from about AD 713. The first European printed newspapers appeared in Germany in 1609. The first daily newspaper, *Einkommende Zeitungen*, also started in Germany, in 1650. Great Britain's first daily paper was the *Perfect Diurnall*, published in London in 1660. America's first successful newspaper was the *Boston News-Letter*, which appeared in 1704.

Smallest

Newspaper publishers sometimes produce miniature editions for publicity purposes. The smallest regular publication was the *Daily Banner*, published in 1876 in Oregon. It measured just 3 x 3.75 in. (7.6 x 9.5 cm).

Largest

The edition of the Belgian newspaper *Het Volk* published on June 14, 1993, had pages measuring 39.2 x 55.9 in. (99.5 x 142 cm), which is more than six times the area of an ordinary broadsheet (large page size) newspaper.

First appearances

Some comic strip and comic book characters are older than you might think. Below is a list of some famous comic characters' first appearances.

Rupert Bear appeared as a strip in the *Daily Express* (UK) on November 8, 1920

Tintin *Le Vingtième Siècle* (Belgium) on January 10, 1929

Popeye appeared as a strip in *Thimble Theatre* (U.S.) on January 17, 1929

Dick Tracy appeared as a strip in the *Chicago Tribune* (U.S.) on October 4, 1931

Flash Gordon appeared as a syndicated strip (U.S.) on January 7, 1934

Desperate Dan *Dandy* (UK) on December 4, 1937

Superman *Action Comics* No. 1 (U.S.) in June 1938

Batman *Detective Comics* No. 27 (U.S.) in May 1939

Captain Marvel *Whiz Comics* No. 1 (U.S.) in February 1940

The Green Lantern *All American Comics* No. 16 (U.S.) in July 1940

The Flash *Flash Comics* No. 1 (U.S.) in January 1940

Robin (Batman's assistant) *Detective Comics* No. 38 (U.S.) in April 1940

Wonder Woman *All-Star Comics* No. 8 (U.S.) in December 1941

Captain America *Captain America Comics* No. 1 (U.S.) in March 1941

Dan Dare *Eagle* (UK) on April 14, 1950

Peanuts appeared as a syndicated strip (U.S.) on October 2, 1950

Dennis the Menace (U.S.) appeared as a syndicated strip (U.S.) on March 12, 1951

Dennis the Menace (UK) *Beano* (UK) on March 17, 1951

Astérix the Gaul *Pilote* (France) on October 29, 1959

Supergirl *Action Comics* No. 252 (U.S.) in May 1959

Spiderman *Amazing Fantasy* No. 15 (U.S.) in August 1962

The Incredible Hulk* *Hulk* (U.S.) in March 1962

X-Men *The X-Men* (U.S.) in September 1963

Daredevil *Daredevil* (U.S.) in June 1964

* The Hulk had gray skin in March 1962, but became The Incredible Hulk, with green skin, in the May issue two months later.

Magazine fact file

First-ever popular magazine
Mercure Galant, a gossip magazine, was first published in Paris, France, in March 1672.

First women's magazine
The Ladies' Mercury was first published in London, England, on June 27, 1693.

First American magazine
The American Magazine, published in Philadelphia, probably began on February 13, 1741.

First children's magazine
The *Lilliputian Magazine* appeared in the UK in June 1751 and ran for just over a year. The first in the U.S. was the *Children's Magazine*, published in January 1789.

First fashion magazine
The Paris magazine *Le Cabinet des Modes* was first published in 1785.

Longest-running U.S. magazine
Scientific American was launched on August 28, 1845, and is the longest continuously published magazine in the U.S. At first, it was a four-page newspaper and included features on science and technology as well as topics such as religion and poetry. Later it began to focus on science and is now the world's most popular scientific journal.

First photograph in a magazine
Each copy of the June 1846 issue of the *Art Union* (UK) contained a photograph by Henry Fox Talbot, one of the inventors of photography.

Heaviest
The Sunday edition of the *New York Times* for September 14, 1987, contained 1,612 pages and weighed 12 lb. (5.4 kg). At one time 314 acres (127 hectares) of forest containing almost 63,000 trees had to be chopped down to make one edition of the paper. Nowadays, much of the paper used for newspapers is recycled.

Top selling
The *Yomiuri Shimbun* (Japan) sells more than 14.2 million copies a day. *Bild-Zeitung* (Germany) is the highest circulation newspaper outside Japan, selling more than 4.2 million copies a day. *The Sun* (UK) sells 3.4 million copies, more than any other English-language newspaper in the world. The U.S.'s biggest-selling newspaper is *USA Today*, which sells 2.6 million a day.

First online newspapers
The *Mercury Center*, of San Jose, California, was the first online newspaper, made available to subscribers in May 1993. Britain's first online national newspaper was the *Electronic Telegraph*, launched in November 1994.

Education & the Arts

Underwater Archaeological Museum

In 2010, work starts on the construction of the world's first underwater museum. Visitors will be able to see the sunken ruins and statues of the ancient city of Alexandria where they lie under the Mediterranean Sea. Exhibits will include remains of Queen Cleopatra's palace and the Pharos of Alexandria, one of the Seven Wonders of the ancient world.

Students in higher education

The figures give the percentage of students enrolled in higher education. These countries have the highest number of students, but information is not available for all countries.

Country	%	Country	%	Country	%	Country	%
Greece	95	Ukraine	76	Estonia	65	France	56
Finland	93	Latvia	74	Argentina	64	Portugal	55
South Korea	93	Australia	73	Belgium	63		
Slovenia	83	Iceland	73	Canada	62	*World average*	*25*
U.S.	82	Russia	72	Cuba	61		
Denmark	80	Belarus	69	Netherlands	60		
New Zealand	80	Hungary	69	Ireland	59		
Sweden	79	Italy	67	UK	59		
Norway	78	Spain	67	Israel	58		
Lithuania	76	Poland	66	Japan	57		

U.S. grade system

American children have 12 years of schooling. They start at age 5 and the first year at school is called kindergarten. The grade system begins in the second year with 1st grade (6-year-olds) and continues to 12th grade (18-year-olds). In high schools, years have names instead of numbers: 9th grade is known as the freshman year, 10th as the sophomore year, 11th as the junior year and 12th as the senior year.

Harvard University, Cambridge

Education timeline 3000 BC

3000 BC The Sumerians pioneer the idea of teaching. Education available only to those who could afford to pay a teacher for each lesson

590 BC The city of Athens becomes the first to offer public education to all men for a small fee. Free education available to the sons of war veterans

597 King's School in Canterbury opens — the first school in the U.K.

859 The world's first university still in existence is founded in Fez, Morocco

1064 The first European university is founded in Parma, Italy

1160 Oxford University becomes the first university in England

1538 The first university of the New World opens in Santo Domingo (now the Dominican Republic)

1635 The first publicly funded high school in the U.S. opens in Boston

1636 Harvard University becomes the first university in the U.S.

1760 The first school for deaf children opens in Paris, France. Pupils are taught an early version of sign language

1781 The first nursery school is opened in Scotland for parents who have to go to work

Children at a Chinese boarding school doing their morning exercises

Countries with the most...

Primary school pupils
The country with the most primary school pupils is India, where there are 140,012,901 children in primary school. In China there are 112,739,964 primary school children.

Secondary school pupils
China has the most secondary pupils — 100,631,925 — although not all children go on from primary to secondary school. In India there are 89,461,794 secondary school children.

University students
In 2004 China overtook the U.S. for the number of students at university. By 2006 it had 23,361,000 compared with the U.S.'s 17,487,000. There are 12,853,000 at university in India and 9,167,000 in Russia.

Pupils per teacher at primary school
Primary school children in some African nations are taught in classes of more than 50: there are 72 pupils per teacher in Ethiopia and up to 83 in Congo. At the other end of the scale, there are only 10 per class in Italy, Norway and Sweden.

Pupils per teacher at secondary school
In secondary schools in Eritrea there are as many as 55 pupils for each teacher. The average class size in Malawi is 51. Schools in Azerbaijan, Belarus, Georgia, Greece, Montserrat, Norway and Portugal have only nine pupils, Lebanon eight and Andorra and Bermuda only seven.

See also
Largest countries: page 116

Schooling around the world

Time spent at school
● School children in China spend more time at school than children in any other country. They have 251 schooldays a year — 71 days more than American children.

● In the United States, Canada , the United Kingdom, France, Germany, Belgium, the Netherlands, Australia and New Zealand children have 10, 11 or 12 years of education. In most African countries and parts of South America children spend just five or six years at school. Only two African countries, Gabon and Tunisia, have 10 years of compulsory schooling.

● In Italy and China, children can legally finish school at the age of 14. In Myanmar (formerly Burma), Angola and Pakistan, children are allowed to finish at the age of 9, after only four or five years at school. In several European countries, including Croatia, Denmark, Sweden and Switzerland, parents don't have to send their children to school until they are 7 years old—two years later than in many other countries.

Largest school
The largest school in the world is the City Montessori school in Lucknow, northern India; it has more than 31,000 pupils.

2000s

1783 Poland becomes the first country to ban corporal punishment in schools
1784 The first school for blind children is started in Paris
1785 The University of New Brunswick, Canada's first English-language university, founded
1841 Oberlin College becomes the first university in the U.S.

to award degrees to women
1871 A school in New York introduces the first distance-learning courses for young people who live too far away from schools to travel to them
2001 No Child Left Behind Act passed in U.S. extends federal control over state schools and increases parental choice

2004 India launches EDUSAT, the first satellite dedicated to transmitting educational materials to remote places
2007 The National Education Budget in the United States is $1.14 trillion

Most remote school
The world's most remote school is Kiwirrkurra Remote Community School in Australia. It is a 25-hour road journey from the nearest major town. The 100 pupils and seven teachers at another school in the region, Oombulgurri Remote Community School, can only get to school by light aircraft or by barge. The aircraft takes just 35 minutes, but the barge can take up to 12 hours.

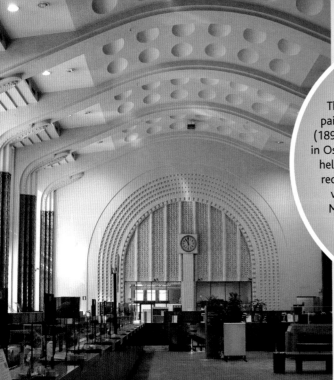

Art Deco interior of Helsinki railway station, Finland

Western art styles

Medieval
Paintings, mosaics and miniatures in manuscripts, mostly of religious subjects.

Renaissance
The word means rebirth — the Renaissance art of the 15th and 16th centuries replaced medieval styles and revived the art of the Greek and Roman period.

Mannerism
A style of 16th-century Italian art, which uses bright colors and distorts scale and perspective.

Baroque/rococo
An ornate style that was popular in Italy during the 17th and 18th centuries.

Neoclassicism
A style of the 18th century modeled on classical (Greek and Roman) art.

Romanticism
This late 18th/early 19th-century style explores emotion and shows nature in its untamed state.

Realism/naturalism
A 19th-century style that showed real life, including its unpleasant side such as poverty.

Pre-Raphaelitism
This short-lived style, inspired by medieval history and myths, was invented in 1848. The aim was to go back to the simplicity of painting before Raphael.

Impressionism
This style of painting developed in France and was named in 1874. The aim was to convey an impression of what the eye sees rather than what the mind knows is there.

Symbolism
An attempt by late 19th-century artists to link the real and the spiritual worlds in their work.

Post-Impressionism
A development from Impressionism, which includes the Pointillism (dot painting) of Seurat and others. In Pointillism, small dots of color are applied to the canvas. These appear to fuse when seen from a distance.

Art Nouveau
A flowing ornamental style of the late 19th/early 20th centuries that influenced architects, furniture makers and painters.

Expressionism/abstract expressionism
Early 20th-century styles in which the emotions of the painter are powerfully expressed.

Cubism
An abstract style which is mostly about shape and color.

Art Deco
An angular, decorative style popular in the 1920s and 1930s.

Surrealism
A style that emerged between the World Wars, in which artists explore dreams and fantasy.

Abstract art
Non-naturalistic art in which shapes, lines and color are more important than the objects they represent.

Action painting
Popular from the 1940s to 1960s, a style in which paint is splashed and smeared onto canvases.

Pop art
Style conceived in the 1950s, using images from popular culture such as comics and advertising.

Environmental art
Art in which the landscape is decorated or altered. The artists use natural objects such as stones to create their work.

Giant eggs decorate the Dali museum in Rosas, Spain.

Famous artists

Artist	Famous work
Fra Angelico (c. 1400–55) Italian	*Deposition of Christ*
Sandro Botticelli (1445–1510) Italian	*Birth of Venus*
Hieronymus Bosch (c. 1450–1516) Flemish	*Garden of Earthly Delights*
Leonardo da Vinci (1452–1519) Italian	*Mona Lisa*
Albrecht Dürer (1471–1528) German	*Four Apostles*
Michelangelo (1475–1564) Italian	Sistine Chapel ceiling
Raphael (1483–1520) Italian	*Madonna*
Hans Holbein (1497–1543) German	*Sir Thomas More*
El Greco (1541–1614) Greek	*Burial of Count Orgaz*
Sir Peter Paul Rubens (1577–1640) Flemish	*Descent from the Cross*
Rembrandt Van Rijn (1606–69) Dutch	*The Night Watch*
Jan Vermeer (1632–75) Dutch	*Girl with a Pearl Earring*
Antonio Canaletto (1697–1768) Italian	*The Grand Canal and the Church of the Salute, Venice*
Thomas Gainsborough (1727–88) British	*Blue Boy*
Francisco Goya (1746–1828) Spanish	*Maja Nude/Clothed*
J.M.W. Turner (1775–1851) British	*Rain, Steam, and Spee*
John Constable (1776–1837) British	*The Haywain*
Dante Gabriel Rossetti (1828–82) British	*Proserpine*
Sir John Everett Millais (1829–96) British	*Ophelia*
Sir Edward Burne-Jones (1833–98) British	*The Golden Stairs*
Edgar Degas (1834–1917) French	*The Rehearsal*
James McNeill Whistler (1834–1903) American	*Symphony in White*
Paul Cézanne (1839–1906) French	*Large Bathers*
Claude Monet (1840–1926) French	*Waterlilies*
Berthe Morisot (1841–95) French	*The Cradle*

Art terms

acrylic
Quick-drying plastic-based paint

cartoon
A preliminary sketch for a painting

chiaroscuro
Light and shade in painting

collage
A work made from pieces of paper and other materials stuck on to a background

composition
The arrangement of the elements and color within a work

fresco
A painting on a freshly plastered wall

gouache
Water-based paint

icon
A portrait of a religious subject, such as a saint

impasto
Thickly applied paint

landscape
A painting of the natural world

medium
The material used to create a work of art

montage
Cut-out objects mounted on a surface

palette
The surface used by an artist for mixing paints, but also used to refer to the selection of colors

pastel
Colored pigments in stick form used for drawing

still life
A painting of an object or a group of objects

tempera
Pigments mixed with egg yolk and oil or water

trompe l'oeil
A painting that plays tricks on the eye to look as if it is three-dimensional

watercolor
Colored pigments mixed with water

Record price for a photograph

German photographer Andreas Gurskey (1955–) broke the world record for a photograph at auction in London on February 7, 2007. His large double print *99 Cent*, which shows the interior of a supermarket, was sold for $3.3 million. The previous record holder was *The Pond – Moonlight* by Edward Steichen (U.S.), which was sold in 2006 for $2.9 million.

Portrait of Dr. Gachet (1890), by Vincent van Gogh

Most expensive paintings

Jackson Pollock's *No. 5, 1948*, was sold privately in New York in 2006 for a price believed to have been about $140 million, making it the most expensive painting not sold at auction. Among the highest prices paid at auction are:

- Pablo Picasso, *Boy with a pipe*, $104.2 million, May 2004

- Pablo Picasso, *Dora Maar with Cat*, $95.2 million, May 2006

- Gustav Klimt, *Portrait of Adele Bloch-Bauer II*, $87.9 million, November 2006

- Francis Bacon, *Triptych*, $86.3 million, May 2008

- ● Vincent van Gogh, *Portrait du Dr Gachet*, $82.5 million, May 1990

- Claude Monet, *Le bassin aux nymphéas* (water lilies), $80.4 million, June 2008

www.artcyclopedia.com   **search**

Artist	Famous work
Pierre Renoir (1841–1919) French	*Luncheon of the Boating Party*
Mary Cassatt (1844–1926) American	*The Bath*
Paul Gauguin (1848–1903) French	*Nevermore*
Vincent van Gogh (1853–90) Dutch	*Sunflowers*
Georges Seurat (1859–91) French	*Sunday Afternoon on the Island of La Grand Jatte*
Henri de Toulouse-Lautrec (1864–1901) French	*Aristide Bruant* (poster)
Henri Matisse (1869–1954) French	*The Dance*
Piet Mondrian (1872–1944) Dutch	*Broadway Boogie Woogie*
Pablo Picasso (1881–1973) Spanish	*Guernica*
Edward Hopper (1882–1967) American	*Nighthawks*
Georgia O'Keeffe (1887–1986) American	*Light Iris*

Artist	Famous work
Tom Thomson (1887–1917) Canadian	*The Jack Pine*
Grant Wood (1891–1942) American	*American Gothic*
Norman Rockwell (1894–1978) American	*Dr. and Doll*
Salvador Dali (1904–89) Spanish	*The Persistence of Memory*
Francis Bacon (1909–92) British	*Study after Velazquez's Portrait of Pope Innocent X*
Jackson Pollock (1912–56) American	*Number One 1948*
Lucien Freud (1922–) British	*Girl with Roses*
Roy Lichtenstein (1923–97) American	*Whaam!*
Jasper Johns (1930–) American	*Flag*
Andy Warhol (1930–89) American	*Marilyn Monroe*
David Hockney (1937–) British	*A Bigger Splash*
Tracey Emin (1963–) British	*My Bed*
Damien Hirst (1965–) British	*Golden Calf*

Art exhibitions and world fairs

Major art exhibitions and world fairs have been held for more than 200 years. Art exhibitions focus on a particular artist or style. World fairs promote the trade or image of a country and display new inventions.

Great Exhibition, London, UK, 1851

This was a showpiece of the arts and industries of the world and the first exhibition of its kind in the UK It was seen by 6,039,195 visitors.

First Impressionist Exhibition, Paris, France, 1874

Many Impressionist painters, including Claude Monet, first showed their work at this exhibition, which was shocking to many people.

Philadelphia Centennial Exposition, Philadelphia, Pennsylvania, 1876

This first major show in the U.S. was held to celebrate the 100th anniversary of the Declaration of Independence. It was seen by 9,910,966 people. Inventor Alexander Graham Bell first demonstrated the telephone at the Exposition.

Exposition Universelle, Paris, France, 1889

The Eiffel Tower was built as a temporary exhibit for this show, which commemorated 100 years since the French Revolution. It attracted 28,121,975 visitors.

World's Columbian Exposition, Chicago, Illinois, 1893

This show celebrated the 400th anniversary of Columbus' discovery of America and had more than 27.3 million visitors. Many Americans experienced electricity and handheld cameras for the first time.

Armory Show, New York, 1913

This was the first exhibition of modern art in the United States and included the work of Picasso. It influenced American artists, collectors and museums.

Exposition Internationale des Arts Décoratifs et Industriels Modernes, Paris, 1925

This exhibition of art marked the beginning of Art Deco style and attracted 5,852,783 visitors.

National Museum of the American Indian, in the Smithsonian Institution, Washington DC

World's Fair, Flushing Meadow Park, Queens, New York, 1939–40

The fair had 44,932,978 visitors and first introduced television to the public.

Festival of Britain, London, 1951

This was a celebration of post-war life, held 100 years after the Great Exhibition. It attracted 8.5 million visitors.

Treasures of Tutankhamen, British Museum, London, 1972–73

This was one of the most popular exhibitions of all time and attracted 1,694,117 visitors. The show went to New York in 1978–79, where it was seen by 1,226,467 people.

Expo 2005, Japan

22 million people visited the show, themed "Nature's Wisdom". All the exhibition pavilions were built from recycled materials.

Museum fact file

First museum open to the public
Uffizi Gallery, Florence, Italy, 1591.

First public museum in the U.S.
Charleston Museum, Charleston, South Carolina, opened 1773.

Oldest museum in Canada
The Niagara Falls Museum was opened by Thomas Barnett in 1827. It once displayed the mummy of Egyptian pharaoh Ramses I, but this was returned to Egypt on October 24, 2003.

Canada's oldest art museum
The Montreal Museum of Fine Arts (Musée des Beaux-Arts de Montreal) was founded as the Art Association of Montreal in 1860. The museum itself opened in 1912.

First open-air museum
Skansen, Stockholm, Sweden, opened in 1891.

First children's museum
The Brooklyn Children's Museum in New York City, opened in 1899 and was the first of more than 300 children's museums worldwide.

First interactive museum
The Exploratorium, San Francisco, California, U.S., opened in 1969 and has hundreds of hands-on exhibits.

Largest museum complex
The Smithsonian Institution in Washington, D.C., consists of 16 museums with a total of more than 140 million items in their collections.

The Buddhas of Bamian (Bamiyan)

Two giant buddhas 180 ft. (55 m) and 121 ft. (37 m) were carved into the side of a cliff in Afghanistan between the 5th and 9th centuries. They were listed as a UNESCO World Heritage site, but were blown up in 2001 by the Islamic fundamentalist Taliban who then ruled the country. A plan has been proposed to project laser images of the statues on the rock face where they once stood.

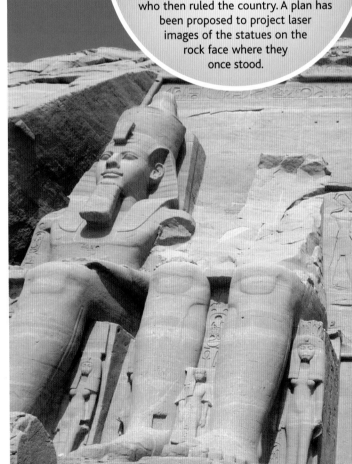

The world's tallest monuments

Many giant monuments around the world proudly celebrate the achievements of countries or their people. They also serve as memorials to — or the tombs of — their rulers and leaders.

Monument/location/year	ft	m
Gateway Arch, St Louis, Missouri (1965)	630	192
San Jacinto Monument, La Porte, Texas (1939)	570	174
Crazy Horse Memorial, Thunderhead Mountain, South Dakota (under construction)	563	172
Juche Tower, Pyongyang, North Korea (1982)	558	170
Washington Monument, Washington, DC (1884)	555	169
Cruz de los Caidos, San Lorenzo de El Escorial, Spain (1956)	492	150
Victory Monument, Moscow, Russia (1995)	465	142
Pyramid of Khufu, Giza, Egypt (2560BC)	455	139
National Monument, Jakarta, Indonesia (1975)	449	137
Pyramid of Khafre, Giza, Egypt (2532BC)	448	136

Gateway Arch
The Gateway Arch, St Louis, Missouri, is part of a national memorial commemorating the westward expansion of the United States. Visitors can travel up inside it in a specially-designed tram car and look out from an observation deck.

Abu Simbel, Egypt
The four huge statues, each standing 66 ft. (20 m) high, used to guard a temple. They were moved in 1966 when the Aswan High Dam was built and the area flooded.

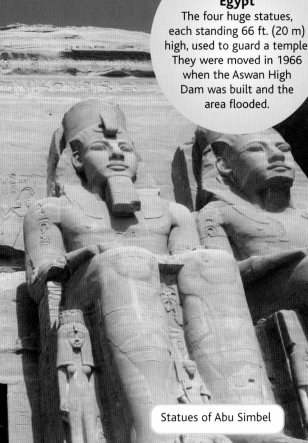

Statues of Abu Simbel

Unusual museums

Cockroach Hall of Fame, Plano, Texas
Record-breaking cockroaches, and insects dressed as famous people

Colman's Mustard Museum, Norwich, Norfolk.
Tells the fascinating history of mustard

The Prince Edward Island Potato Museum, O'Leary, PEI, Canada
Tells the story of potato cultivation and contains a large exhibit of potato artifacts

Gallery of Also-Rans, Norton, Kansas
A collection celebrating people who came second or lost political campaigns and other contests

The Lunch Box Museum, Columbus, Georgia
Over 2,500 lunch boxes from the 1950s to the present

The Medieval Crime Museum, Rothenburg, Germany
Medieval crime, punishment and torture implements

National Wool Museum, Geelong, Australia
The only museum devoted to wool, opened in 1988

Nut Museum, Old Lyme, Connecticut
Nut carvings, 7.9 ft (2.4 m) long nutcrackers and other nut-related exhibits

Philips Mushroom Museum, Kennett Square, Pennsylvania
A museum focusing on all types of mushrooms and other fungi

The Piggy Bank Museum, Amsterdam, Netherlands
Displays 12,000 piggy banks from all periods

Porter Thermometer Museum, Onset, Massachusetts
More than 3,000 devices for taking temperatures

Amazing collectors

Louis XIV

The French king owned a collection of 413 ornate beds. He kept them in different places all over France, so wherever he traveled, he could sleep in his own bed.

The Schlumpf brothers

French factory owners Hans and Fritz Schlumpf built up one of the world's largest car collections. They had 427 vehicles, including 120 rare Bugattis. These are now on public display at the National Auto Museum of France in Mulhouse.

Sir Thomas Phillips

Eccentric English book collector Sir Thomas Phillips (1792–1872) wanted to own a copy of every book ever printed — and he almost succeeded. He acquired more than 50,000 books and 100,000 manuscripts. His collection plunged his family into debt, but he rescued many priceless treasures from destruction. Sales from his collection have continued almost every year since his death.

George Gustav Heye

Heye (1874–1957) of New York built up the world's largest collection of Native American artifacts, which became the basis of the Smithsonian Institution's National Museum of the American Indian, Washington, D.C.

Harold LeMay

Millionaire LeMay (1919–2001) of Tacoma, Washington, collected more than 3,000 vehicles, which will become the core of the world's largest automobile display in America's Car Museum, opening in 2009.

In 2005, George Barris, the "King of Customizers," auctioned his film and television cars, including this one he made for Elvis Presley.

Unusual auction items

● The skull of the Swedish philosopher Emanuel Swedenborg was sold at Sotheby's, London, UK in 1978 for $2,900. Stockholm Royal Academy of Science bought the skull and reunited it with the rest of his body, which was buried in Uppsala Cathedral.

● A pair of Napoleon's socks was sold at Sotheby's, London, in 1996 for $4,660.

● A pair of Queen Victoria's underpants were sold at Sotheby's, London, in 1996 for $395. A pair of Victorian rollerblades dating from c. 1860 was sold at the same sale for $900.

● Several pairs of glasses belonging to John Lennon of the Beatles have sold for up to $1.5

● A dish containing a sample of penicillum mold prepared by penicillin inventor Alexander Fleming in 1935 was sold by Christie's, London, in 1997 for $23,770. At the same sale a box of 300 glass eyes was sold for $4,390.

● More than 2,000 items that had belonged to the singer Elvis Presley were sold at an auction in Las Vegas in 1999. These included clothing as well as letters, one of Elvis's school report cards and 29 dry-cleaning bills made out to Elvis.

● In 2007, Christie's auction house in Paris, France, sold a Siberian mammoth skeleton for 312,000 euros ($422,242) and a dinosaur egg for 1,800 euros ($2,436).

● The Texas Schoolbook Depository window from which President Kennedy was shot was sold on eBay in 2007 for $3,001,501.

Young enthusiasts sorting a collection of baseball cards

Who collects what?

As soon as someone starts to collect something a word is invented to describe the collector. Most end in -ist, which means a person who does something (as a motorist is someone who drives a car or a violinist someone who plays a violin). Another ending is -phile or -philist, which means a lover of something.

Collectable	Collector
airmail	**aerophilatelist**
autographs	**philographist**
badges and patches	**scutelliphilist**
banknotes	**notaphilist**
beer bottle labels	**labeorphilist**
beer mats	**tegestologist** or **tegetologist**
book plates	**ex-librist**
books	**bibliophile** or **bibliophilist**
butterflies and moths	**lepidopterist**
cigar bands	**brandophilist** or **cigrinophilist**
coins, money, medals	**numismatist**
corkscrews	**helixophile**
dolls	**plangonologist**
eggs	**oologist** (illegal in many countries)
egg-cups	**pocillovist**
flags and banners	**vexillologist**
gramophone records	**discophilist**
keyrings	**copoclephilist**
keys	**cagophilist**
maps	**cartomaniac**
match books	**phillumenist**
matchboxes	**cumyxaphilist**
money boxes	**argyrothecologist**
postcards	**deltiologist**
prints and book illustrations	**iconophilist**
shells	**conchologist**
stamps	**philatelist**
sugar packets	**sucrologist**
teddy bears	**arctophilists**
telephone cards	**fusilatelist**
transport tokens	**vecturist**

Stamp collection themes

Many philatelists (stamp collectors) follow topical philately, which means they collect stamps by theme.

They may acquire stamps from many different countries and periods. Here are some of the hundreds of popular themes.

aircraft	dinosaurs	medicine
animals	dogs	mountains
art and artists	dolls	mushrooms
authors	exploration	music
bicycles	famous people	Nobel Prize
birds	fish	Olympic Games
butterflies	flags	police
cars	flowers	railways
castles	food	religion
cats	heraldry	scouting
chess	horses	seashells
children	insects	ships
Christmas	lighthouses	space
cinema	literature	sports
costumes	maps	stamps
dance		theater
		uniforms

Postage stamps from around the world

www.smithsonianeducation.org.idealabs/collecting/index.html **search**

A collection of shells

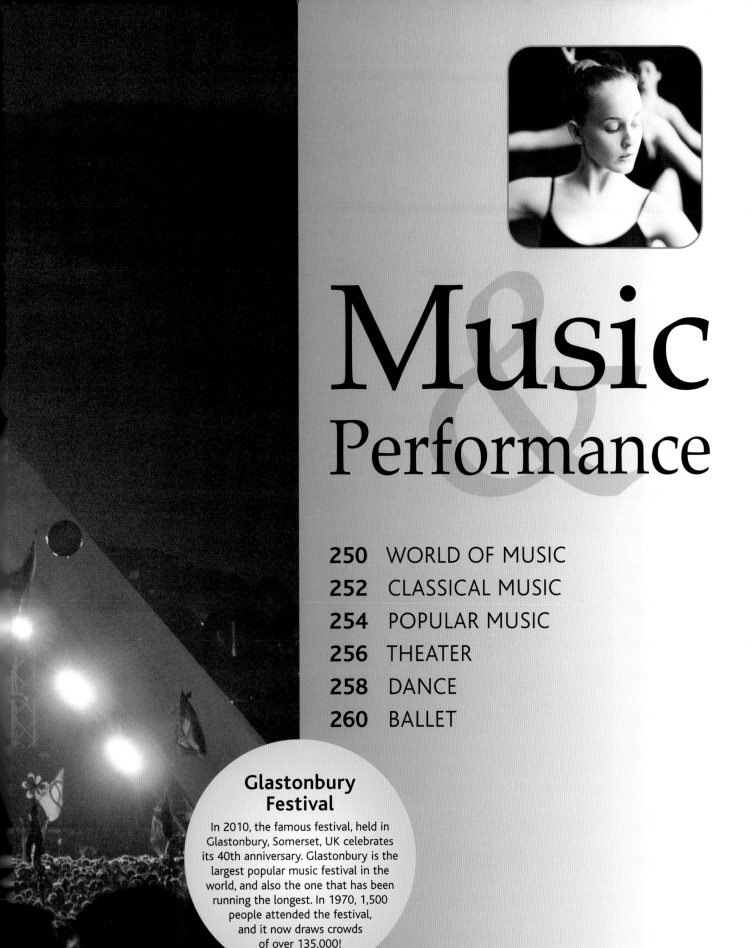

Music

& Performance

Glastonbury Festival

In 2010, the famous festival, held in Glastonbury, Somerset, UK celebrates its 40th anniversary. Glastonbury is the largest popular music festival in the world, and also the one that has been running the longest. In 1970, 1,500 people attended the festival, and it now draws crowds of over 135,000!

Musical instrument records

Double bass
A double bass 14 ft. (4.3 m) long and weighing 1,300 lb. (590 kg) was built by Arthur K. Ferris of Ironia, New Jersey, USA, in 1924.

Drum
The University of Texas Longhorn Band has a drum nicknamed Big Bertha which is 24.9 ft. (7.6 m) in circumference.

Guitar
A giant version of a Gibson guitar 38.2 ft. (11.63 m) long was made in 1991 by students at Shakamak High School, Jasonville, Indiana. Large stringed instruments that are bigger than the span of human hands are difficult or even impossible to play.

Pianos
In 1935 in London, England, Charles H. Challen built a piano which is probably the largest in the world. It weighs 1.4 tons (1.25 tonnes) and is 11.6 ft. (3.6 m) long. One of the lightest pianos ever made was a baby grand weighing just 397 lb. (180 kg). It was made mostly of aluminium covered in yellow pigskin. It was made by the Blüthner company of Germany for the airship *Hindenburg*, and was destroyed when the airship exploded in 1937.

Tuba
In 1896 John Philip Sousa, who is the American inventor of the sousaphone, played a 7.48 ft. (2.28 m) tuba on a world tour. This is the largest brass instrument ever made and had 38.7 ft. (11.8 m) of tubing.

Organs

The world's loudest instrument is the Auditorium Organ in Atlantic City, N.J. It was built in 1930 at a cost of $500,000, has more than 32,000 pipes and is powered by a 365 horsepower blower.

The world's largest cathedral organ was built in St. Stephen's Cathedral, Passau, Germany, in 1928. It has 17,774 pipes.

The world's largest church organ is in St. Stephen's Cathedral, Passau, Germany.

Valuable instruments

Guitars
In 2002 two guitars owned by Grateful Dead guitarist Jerry Garcia were sold in New York: "Tiger" for $957,500 and "Wolf" for $789,500. A Fender Stratocaster signed by over 20 famous rock guitarists has been sold twice at auctions in aid of a charity to help tsunami victims, raising a total of $3.7 million.

Violins
A Stradivarius violin made in 1707 and named "The Hammer" after its former owner, Christian Hammer, was sold at auction in New York in 2006 for a record $3,544,000.

Upright piano
John Lennon's Steinway Model Z upright piano, on which he wrote such songs as *Imagine*, was sold to George Michael in 2000 for $2,105,472.

See also
Inventions: pages 80–81

Recording timeline   1800s

1877 Thomas Alva Edison first recorded a human voice (singing "Mary Had a Little Lamb") on a tinfoil cylinder phonograph
1878 Edison is granted phonograph patent
1885 "Graphophone" with wax cylinders is invented by Alexander Graham Bell and Charles Tainter

1888 "Gramophone," with 7-inch (17.8 cm) flat disk, is patented by Emile Berliner
1895 First spring-driven phonograph is sold by Edison
1896 Improved gramophone produced by Eldridge Johnson
1897 Shellac disks introduced

1898 First magnetic recorder, with steel wire, patented by Valdemar Poulsen
1904 First mass-produced, double-sided disks are sold in Germany
1925 First electrically recorded disks make it possible to record entire orchestral works. Sound recordings for films are introduced

1927 First coin-operated juke box is produced
1931 Stereo recording introduced
1934 First hi-fi (high-fidelity sound) records are made
1935 "Magnetophone" (tape recorder) is demonstrated in Berlin, Germany

Musical terms

Many musical terms are derived from Italian words. Here are the meanings of some common ones.

Musical tempos

Tempo	Meaning
Larghissimo	As slow as possible
Largo	Very slow and solemn
Largementa	Slow, broad
Larghetto	Slightly less slow
Lento	Slow
Adagissimo	Very slow
Adagio	Slow (from the Italian for at ease)
Adagietto	Slightly faster
Andante	Moderately slow (from the Italian for walk)
Andantino	Slightly slower than andante
Moderato	At a brisk walking pace
Allegretto	Fairly lively
Allegramente	Lightly
Allegro	Lively, fast (from the Italian for cheerful)
Vivace	Fast
Vivacissimo	Very quick
Presto	Very fast
Prestissimo	Extremely fast

Other musical terms

Term	Meaning
Agitato	Agitated or excited
Brillante	Sparkling, brilliant
Brio	Spirit or vigor
Crescendo	Gradual increase in volume
Dolce	Sweet, soft and gentle
Dolente	Sad
Forte	Loud or strong
Fortissimo	Very loud
Grave	Slow and serious
Legato	Smoothly and evenly
Molto	Much or very
Pianissimo	Very soft
Piano	Soft
Ritenuto	Slowing in tempo
Scherzo	Lively
Sotto voce	Quiet and subdued
Tutti	All the players

National anthems

Most countries have a national anthem, a patriotic song, often based on a hymn or a poem about the country that is sung on special occasions.

The Dutch anthem *Het Wilhelmus*, which dates from the 1570s, is considered the world's oldest. Britain's anthem, *God Save The Queen*, which is also sung, with variations, in some British Commonwealth countries, has been sung to the same tune since 1744. The tune is also used for the anthems of other countries, including Liechtenstein and Norway. The French *Marseillaise* was officially adopted in 1795. In the *The Star-Spangled Banner*, although written in 1814, did not become the national anthem until 1931.

Happy Birthday to You

In 1893 two American sisters, who were teachers, wrote this song to sing in school assemblies. Mildred J. and Patty Smith Hill originally called the song "Good Morning to You." After the words were changed in 1924, it became known the world over. The song will be in copyright until 2030, but only for commercial purposes. Singing it at a birthday party does not infringe copyright!

Thomas Edison (1847–1931) with his first phonograph

2000s

1948 First 12-in. (30.5 cm) 33-1/3 rpm, microgroove LP vinylite record is produced, with 23-minute capacity per side
1949 First 7-in. (17.8 cm), 45 rpm, microgroove EP (Extended Play) vinylite record and player are introduced
1958 First stereo LPs are sold
1963 First compact audio cassette is produced

1969 Dolby Noise Reduction is introduced
1979 First Sony Walkman portable audio cassette players are sold
1980 First camcorders are sold
1982 First CDs are sold
1987 DAT (Digital Audio Tape) players are launched
1992 Mini-disks are introduced

1997 MP3 format is launched
1999 DVD-Audio format is introduced
2001 Apple Computer's iPod is launched
2005 Total U.S. recorded music sales (albums, singles, video and

downloads) top one billion for the first time.
2006 MSI launches the solar-powered MP3 player
2007 It is estimated that 200 billion CDs have been sold since the launch of the format 25 years ago.

www.recording-history.org   search

Strings

Violin   Viola

Cello

Double bass

Harp

The viola is larger and deeper-voiced than the violin, and is played in the same way.

The violin has a hollow wooden body which resonates when the violinist pulls a bow over the four strings. There may be 30 or more violins in a modern orchestra.

The cello's full name is the violoncello. It is the third-largest member of the violin family and is played sitting down.

The largest and deepest stringed instrument in an orchestra is the double bass. Double bass players usually stand to play, pulling a bow across the strings, or plucking them.

The orchestral harp has 48 strings of different lengths, attached to the top and side, and seven pedals at the base.

Opera terms

aria
A song for a single voice
comic opera
Opera with a comic plot
finale
The ending, when the whole cast often sing together
libretto
The text of an opera, from the Italian for little book

operetta
A light (rather than serious) opera, usually with an amusing story
prima donna
First lady (from the Italian) — the main female singer, or diva
recitative
A part in an opera that is spoken rather than sung

Instruments of the orchestra

The range and number of instruments in a modern orchestra varies enormously. There may be as many as 100 or more, and less familiar instruments are brought in for special performances. The ones illustrated here are the most common instruments.

Brass

Trumpet

The trombone is also made from coiled metal and has a section called the slide, which players move in and out to create different notes. The trombone plays lower notes than the trumpet.

Trombone

A trumpet is a tightly coiled metal tube with a cone called the bell at one end. Trumpets have three small buttons called valves which make different notes when pressed.

Flugelhorn

Tuba

French horn

French horn players make different notes by changing the shape of their lips as they blow into the mouthpiece of this coiled metal tube.

Euphonium

There is usually just one tuba in an orchestra. It plays the lowest notes of all the brass instruments.

Singing parts

Name	Female voices
Soprano	The highest female voice
Mezzo soprano	Between a soprano and a contralto
Contralto	The lowest female voice
	Male voices
Alto	The highest male voice, traditionally sung by choirboys
Tenor	A high male voice. A countertenor voice is very high
Baritone	A voice higher than a bass, but lower than a tenor
Bass	The lowest male voice. Basso profundo is the lowest possible voice
Falsetto	An unnaturally high voice sung by tenors and basses

Woodwind

Piccolo

Flute

The concert flute is played through a blow hole at one end. Alto and bass flutes are larger versions which play lower notes. The piccolo is half the size of the concert flute and plays the highest notes in the orchestra.

Oboe

Oboe players blow through a double reed made from two small slices of cane tied together and inserted into the mouthpiece of the instrument.

Clarinet

The clarinet is also played through a reed. There are several different types of clarinet. B flat and A are played most often.

Bass clarinet

The bassoon plays the lowest notes of the woodwind instruments. It is a doubled-up wooden tube with a curved metal crook at one end, which holds the reed.

Bassoon

English Horn

Opera facts

Most-performed operas

Puccini's *La Bohème* is the most-performed opera in London and New York. It has been staged 969 times since 1897 at London's Royal Opera House, and 1,200 times at the Metropolitan Opera House in New York. *Aïda* and *Carmen* are the closest runners-up in both places.

Longest operas

Richard Wagner's *Gotterdämmerung* is the longest regularly performed opera. The opera can last up to six hours, including intervals.

Largest opera venues

he two largest opera houses where operas are regularly performed are in Italy and the United States. They are the Arena di Verona in Verona, which holds 16,663 people, and the Municipal Opera Theater in St. Louis, Missouri, which holds 11,745. The Teatro alla Scala, Milan, Italy, which has 3,600 seats, is one of the world's largest indoor opera theaters, although several U.S. opera houses come close in size.

Nellie Melba

Poster advertising *Madama Butterfly* by Puccini

MADAMA BUTTERFLY

GIACOMO PUCCINI

Grandest grand opera

The opera *Aïda* has often been performed on a grand scale, with a huge cast including elephants and other animals. It has been staged at the pyramids, Egypt, and in the year 2000 was performed in a football stadium in Shanghai, China, with a cast of 3,000 and an audience of 45,000.

Dame Nellie Melba

The real name of Australian opera singer Dame Nellie Melba (1881–1931) was Helen Mitchell. She was a great food lover and inspired the famous chef Escoffier to create several new dishes for her at the Savoy Hotel, London, U.K. These included Peach Melba (a raspberry and redcurrant sauce poured over peaches and ice cream), Melba Toast (crisp dried bread) and Melba Garniture (chicken, truffles and mushrooms stuffed into tomatoes).

Percussion

Timpani/Kettledrums

Triangle

Cymbals   Side drum

Bass drum

Orchestras usually have three or four timpani or kettledrums. They are made of copper with a plastic skin stretched over the top.

Various other instruments are sometimes played in orchestras, including keyboards (piano, organ, celesta, etc.), bells, castanets, glockenspiels, gongs, marimbas, rattles, tambourines, wind machines, wood blocks, xylophones, guitars, mandolins and saxophones.

Top singles of all time*

The numbers of singles sold outside the U.S. and some other countries have only been recorded fairly recently, so world sales here are estimates.

"White Christmas" was the world's bestselling single for more than 50 years until it was overtaken by Elton John's tribute to Princess Diana in 1997.

*These figures are for singles sung in the English language.

Artist/single/year	Estimated sales (millions)	
	U.S.	World total
Elton John, "Candle in the Wind" (1997)/ "Something about the Way You Look Tonight" (1997)	11	37
Bing Crosby, "White Christmas" (1945)	n/a	30
Bill Haley and His Comets, "Rock Around the Clock" (1954)	n/a	17
Elvis Presley, "It's Now or Never" (1960)	1	12
The Beatles, "I Want to Hold Your Hand" (1963)	0.5	12
The Beatles, "Hey Jude" (1968)	4	10
Whitney Houston, "I Will Always Love You" (1992)	4	10

Downloads fact file

- Digital downloads have been included in the Billboard Hot 100 since 2005.

- In 2005 Gwen Stefani's "Hollaback Girl" became the first single to be downloaded more than one million times in the U.S.

- In January 2007, Fergie's single "Fergalicious" became the fastest-selling downloaded track when 295,000 digital downloads were sold in a single week in the U.S.

- In 2006, "Keep Tryin'" by Utada Hikaru (Japan) set a new record for 2.5 million downloads.

- Flo Rida's "Low" (2007) became the bestselling digital single in the U.S., with sales of more than 4 million. In 2009 Flo Rida's "Right Round" set a record of 636,000 downloads in a single week.

- Up to 2009, six years after its launch, Apple's iTune Store had sold 6 billion song downloads.

Apple's iPod

The Beatles, 1963

One and only

The Beatles had all top five positions in the U.S. singles chart on April 4, 1964, with:

1 "Can't Buy Me Love"
2 "Twist and Shout"
3 "She Loves You"
4 "I Want to Hold Your Hand"
5 "Please Please Me"

See also
Entertainment lasts: page 306

Popular music styles

Blues Blues music began in the U.S. in the 1860s, when it grew out of work songs (songs sung by people working to a rhythm, such as picking crops) and spirituals.

Country Country, country and western, bluegrass and related types of music began in the south-western states of the U.S. Nashville, Tennessee, is the home of the Country Music Hall of Fame. Its foremost male performer, Garth Brooks, is one of the bestselling artists of all time, having sold nearly 130 million albums.

Electronic Electronic music emerged in the 1950s as the technology to record and synthesize sounds became available to musicians. Electronic equipment is used to create both classical and popular music, with such branches as techno — a popular dance genre.

Folk Folk music includes the popular songs and dances that are passed from generation to generation in a country. In modern times, artists such as Bob Dylan have based many of their songs on their national folk tradition.

Hip hop Hip hop is a style of music that emerged in New York in the 1970s. It is often used to mean rap music, although rap is strictly a style of lyrics involving rhyming and wordplay to a rhythmic beat that originated earlier and remains one of the most widely popular styles today.

Jazz Jazz music originated in New Orleans, in the 1890s and became so popular in the 1920s that the period is sometimes known as the "Jazz Age."

Pop Pop music is the general name given to the type of music that became popular in the 1950s with the arrival of artists such as Elvis Presley. Its rebellious spirit, energy and volume were designed to appeal to a young audience.

Reggae Reggae is a style of music that grew out of 1950s Jamaican

Major rock events

The following are among the best-attended rock events ever. The Live Aid concerts (July 13, 1985) and Live 8 concerts (July 2, 2005) had smaller audiences split over several venues but were believed to have had the greatest TV audiences of all time.

About 1.5 billion people, or one quarter of the world's population, watched Live Aid on television. The figure for Live 8 was over 2 billion.

Event/date	Est. audience
Rod Stewart, Copacabana Beach, Rio de Janeiro, Brazil, December 31, 1994	3,500,000
Golden Jubilee Concert, Buckingham Palace, London, UK, June 3, 2002	over 1,000,000
Live 8: 10 free concerts in nine countries, July 2, 2005	over 1,000,000
(The largest single audience was 200,000 in Hyde Park, London, UK)	
Garth Brooks in Central Park, New York, N.Y., August 7 1997	750,000
U.S. Festival, San Bernardino, California, May 28–30, 1982	725,000
Summer Jam, Watkins Glen, New York, July 28, 1973	600,132
Third Isle of Wight Festival, UK, August 30, 1970	up to 600,000
Simon and Garfunkel in Central Park, New York, N.Y., September 19, 1981	500,000
Rolling Stones Free Concert, Hyde Park, London, UK, July 5, 1969	up to 500,000
Molson Canadian Rocks for Toronto, Toronto, Ontario, July 30, 2003	489,176
Woodstock Festival, Bethel, New York, August 15–17, 1969	over 400,000

Jimi Hendrix playing at Woodstock Festival, Bethel, New York, 1969

Top albums of all time worldwide

The U.S. has always led the world in album sales. Total worldwide sales are less easy to find, but using the best estimates available these albums can claim to be world-beaters.

Michael Jackson, *Thriller* (1982)
104 million copies (27 million U.S.)
Eagles, *Their Greatest Hits 1971–1975* (1976) 42 million copies (29 million U.S.)
AC/DC, *Back in Black* (1980)
42 million copies (21 million U.S.)
The Bodyguard (soundtrack) (1992)
42 million copies (17 million U.S.)
Backstreet Boys, *Millenium* (1999)
40 million copies (13 million U.S.)
Saturday Night Fever (soundtrack)
(1977) 40 million copies
(15 million U.S.)
Pink Floyd, *The Dark Side of The Moon* (1973) 40 million copies
(15 million U.S.)

Shania Twain, *Come On Over* (1997)
39 million copies (20 million U.S.)
Meatloaf, *Bat out of Hell* (1978)
37 million copies (14 million U.S.)
Led Zeppelin, *Led Zeppelin IV* (1971)
32 million copies (23 million U.S.)
The Beatles, *Sgt Pepper's Lonely Hearts Club Band* (1967) 32 million copies
(11 million U.S.)

John Lennon's Rolls-Royce

Treasures of rock

Fans of rock music often like to buy items that belonged to their favourite singers and bands. The more successful the artist, the higher the price.

● The bass drum skin that appears on the cover of The Beatles' *Sgt Pepper's Lonely Hearts Club Band* album (1967) was sold in London on July 10, 2008 for $1,068,000. At the same auction, John Lennon's handwritten lyrics for *Give Peace a Chance* (1969) were sold for $831,200. The record price for Beatles memorabilia is the $1,047,300 paid in London on July 28, 2005 for Lennon's handwritten lyrics for *All You Need is Love*.

● "Blackie" Fender Stratocaster guitar owned by Eric Clapton. Sold in New York, on June 25, 2004 for $959,500.

● Bernie Taupin's handwritten lyrics for the re-written "Candle in the Wind," sung by Sir Elton John in Westminster Abbey at the funeral of Diana, Princess of Wales. Sold in Los Angeles, on February 11, 1998 for $400,000.

● The 1965 Rolls-Royce Phantom V touring limousine, painted in psychedelic colors, owned by John Lennon of The Beatles. Sold at auction in New York, on June 29, 1985 for $2,299,000.

ska and in turn influenced British pop music. Its most famous performer was Bob Marley.

Rhythm and blues Rhythm and blues, or R&B, developed in the U.S. from blues and pop music, with Bo Diddley and Chuck Berry among its most famous performers.

Rock Recorded by Bill Hailey and His Comets, Rock Around the Clock (1954) was the first commercially successful rock and roll record. During the 1960s, many of the world's leading bands, including the Beatles and Rolling Stones, established rock music as the most popular of all musical styles.

Soul Combining gospel, blues and jazz, soul music is an often highly emotional style of music. It was especially popular in the 1960s when its leading exponent was Aretha Franklin.

 www.billboard.com   search

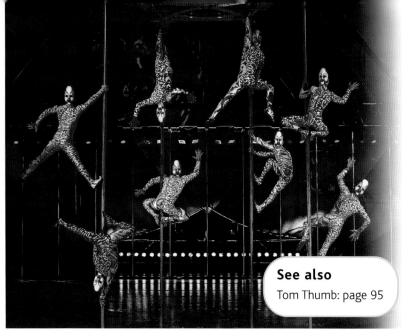

Canadian circus troupe Cirque du Soleil (French for "Circus of the Sun")

A quick history of circus

Open air-circuses with acrobats, chariot races, bareback riders and comedy acts were popular in ancient Rome. In the 18th century fixed buildings were used, and in the early 19th century traveling circuses appeared in Europe and the U.S. Troupes moved from place to place, setting up a large tent, or "big top." The most famous U.S. circus proprietor was Phineas T. Barnum (1810–91).

His shows were spectacular, with trick riding, juggling, trapeze acts, tightrope walking, strong men and wild-cat tamers. They also featured "human oddities," or freak shows, in which Siamese twins, giants or bearded ladies were often paraded before the curious crowd. Since the 20th century, all-human Chinese and Russian circus companies have toured the world, as well as alternative circus troupes such as Circus Oz, Ra Ra Zoo and Archaos, whose acts have included juggling with chainsaws and jumping over blazing motorbikes.

See also

Tom Thumb: page 95

Famous playwrights and their famous plays

Aeschylus (Greek, c. 525–546 BC) — *The Oresteia*
Edward Albee (American, 1928–) — *Who's Afraid of Virginia Woolf?*
J.M. Barrie (Scottish, 1860–1937) — *Peter Pan*
Samuel Beckett (Irish, 1906–89) — *Waiting for Godot*
Anton Chekhov (Russian, 1860–1904) — *The Cherry Orchard*
Noël Coward (English, 1899–1973) — *Private Lives*
Euripides (Greek, c. 484–406 BC) — *The Trojan Women*
Federico García Lorca (Spanish, 1898–1936)— *Blood Wedding*
Henrik Ibsen (Norwegian, 1828–1906) — *Hedda Gabler*
Ben Jonson (English, 1572–1637) — *The Alchemist*
David Mamet (American, 1947–) — *Glengarry Glen Ross*
Christopher Marlowe (English, 1564–93) — *Doctor Faustus*
Arthur Miller (American, 1915–2005) — *The Crucible*
Molière (French, 1622–73) — *Tartuffe*
Eugene O'Neill (American, 1888–1953) — *Long Day's Journey into Night*
Harold Pinter (English, 1930–) — *The Birthday Party*
Peter Shaffer (English, 1926–) — *Amadeus*
William Shakespeare (English, 1564–1616) — *Hamlet*
George Bernard Shaw (Irish, 1856–1950)— *Pygmalion*
Neil Simon (American, 1927–)— *Plaza Suite*
Sophocles (Greek, c. 496–405 BC)— *Antigone*
August Strindberg (Swedish, 1849–1912) — *Miss Julie*
Tom Stoppard (Czech, 1937–)— *Rosencrantz and Guildenstern are Dead*
J.M. Synge (Irish, 1871–1909)— *The Playboy of the Western World*
John Webster (English, 1580–1625)— *The Duchess of Malfi*
Oscar Wilde (Irish, 1854–1900)— *The Importance of Being Earnest*
Tennessee Williams (American, 1911–83)—*A Streetcar Named Desire*

Theater records

First actor
Thespis was the first performer ever recorded. He was an actor in Greece in 534 BC. At this time, Greek actors used masks, and Thespis was the first to use stage makeup.

World's oldest theaters
The oldest indoor theater in the world is the Teatro Olimpico, Vicenza, Italy, which opened on March 3, 1585. London's oldest theater, and one of the world's oldest still operating, is the Theatre Royal, Drury Lane, which opened on May 7, 1663. It burned down in 1672 and was rebuilt by Sir Christopher Wren. The oldest surviving theater in the U.S. is the Walnut Street Theater in Philadelphia, Pennsylvania, which opened in 1809.

World's biggest theaters
The National People's Congress Building Theatre, Beijing, China was built in 1959 and can hold audiences of 10,000. The Perth Entertainment Centre, Australia (1976) has up to 8,500 seats, the Chaplin (originally Blanquetta), Havana, Cuba (1949) has 6,500 and Radio City Music Hall, New York, U.S., has 6,200. The 3,483-seater Hammersmith Odeon is the largest theatre in Britain, but the Royal Albert Hall in London can hold up to 7,000, depending on the event and how the seating is organized.

The Teatro Olimpico in Vicenza, Italy

Worst disasters at a theater

Fires, in which people were burned or trampled to death, have caused the worst disasters at theaters. The worst ever was at Canton (now Guangzhou), China, in 1845 when 1,670 died. The worst in the U.S. was at the Iroquois Theater, Chicago, in 1903, which left 602 dead. Europe's worst was at the Ring Theatre, Vienna, Austria, in 1881, which killed at least 620 people. These are the worst single-building (rather than city or forest) fires in history.

Longest-running shows

The Golden Horseshoe Revue (Disneyland, California, 1955–86) 47,250 performances

The Mousetrap (London, 1952–) *23,440 p.

The Fantasticks (New York, 1960–2002) 17,162 p.

La Cantatrice Chauve (The Bald Soprano) (Paris, 1957–) *17,135 p.

Shear Madness (Boston, 1980–) *12,231 p.

Les Misérables (London, 1985–) *9,682 p.

The Mousetrap (Toronto, 1977–2004) 9,648 p.

The Drunkard (Los Angeles, 1933–59) 9,477 p.

Shear Madness (Washington DC, 1987–) *9,378 p.

The Phantom of the Opera (London, 1986–) *9,347 p.

Perfect Crime (New York, 1987–) *8,955 p.

Cats (London, 1981–2002) 8,949 p.

The Phantom of the Opera (New York, 1988–) *8,803 p.

Blood Brothers (London, 1988–) *8,587 p.

The Woman in Black (London, 15 Feb 1989–) *8,077 p.

Tubes (New York, 1991–2005) *8,006 p.

Shear Madness (Chicago, 1982–2007) 7,697 p.

* Still running, total as of March 31, 2009

Short runs

A play is expensive to stage, so everyone involved hopes that it will run for long enough to earn back the money spent on it. Shows that run for years earn back their initial investment many times over, but some fail on their first night — or even earlier!

● On December 18, 1816, the one and only performance of J.R. Ronden's *The Play Without an A* took place at the Paris Théâtre des Variétés. It was written with words without the letter "a," which made it very hard to perform and understand. The audience rioted and did not allow the play to finish.

● In 1888, at London, England's Shaftesbury Theatre, *The Lady of Lyons* failed to make its first night when the safety curtain jammed.

● The *Intimate Revue* opened and closed at the Duchess Theatre, London, on March 11, 1930. It was a disaster from start to finish. The scenery changes took so long that seven scenes were abandoned to allow the long-suffering audience to go home before midnight.

● *Little Johnny Jones*, a musical starring Donny Osmond, opened and closed at the Alvin Theater, New York, on March 21, 1982.

● *Carrie* closed in New York on May 17, 1988, after struggling through five performances. It is said to have cost the Royal Shakespeare Company, who performed it, $7 million.

Longest play

Neil Oram's *The Warp* was first performed at the ICA (Institute of Contemporary Art) in London, UK from January 18–20, 1979. It lasted 18 hours and 5 minutes.

Oberammergau

Oberammergau is a town in Bavaria, Germany, where a Passion play (a play dealing with the crucifixion of Christ) is performed. The first play was put on in 1634 after an outbreak of plague in the town. The people vowed to repeat the play every 10 years from then on. More than 2,000 people take part in the play, nearly all of them from Oberammergau, and the performance lasts six hours.

Scene from the Singapore production of *Les Misérables*

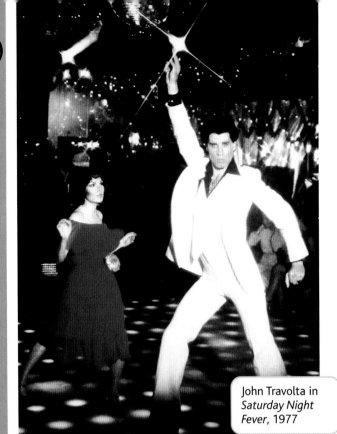

John Travolta in *Saturday Night Fever*, 1977

Highest-earning dance films

The most successful dance film of all time is *Saturday Night Fever*. It starred John Travolta as a talented disco dancer and has earned nearly $300 million around the world. Below are some of the other highest-earning dance films in the world.

1 *Saturday Night Fever* (1977) $285.4 million
2 *The Full Monty* (1997) $257.9 m.
3 *Dirty Dancing* (1987) $214.0 m.
4 *Shall We Dance* (2004) $170.1 m.
5 *Step Up 2 the Streets* (2008) $148.4 m.
6 *Save the Last Dance* (2001) $131.7 m.
7 *Staying Alive* (1983) $127.6 m.
8 *Step Up* (2006) $114.2 m.
9 *Coyote Ugly* (2000) $113.9 m.
10 *Billy Elliot* (2000) $109.3 m.

Girl breakdancing

Breakdancing

Breakdancing began in New York in the late 1970s and early 1980s. Some of its movements came from martial arts such as kung fu and from gymnastics. It became a feature of hip-hop culture.

Dance spectaculars

American choreographer Busby Berkeley (1895–1976) staged the most spectacular dance films ever made. He used his knowledge of organizing military parades during World War I to create dance numbers with casts of hundreds.

They were often photographed from cranes high above them, on huge sets and sometimes with giant mirrors so that they formed geometrical patterns apparently vanishing into infinity. His films included *42nd Street* (1933) and *Gold Diggers of 1933* (1933), which was hit by an earthquake during filming in Los Angeles. The quake cut all power and nearly collapsed the set.

Popular dances

Ballroom dancing
Ballroom dancing has a long history and gained an international following through the popularity of competitive dancing on television. In recent years, TV shows such as *Dancing with the Stars*, in which celebrities dance with professionals, have revived interest in this style of dancing.

Barn dances
These developed from traditional Scottish dancing. They were popular in the U.S. in the 1890s when they were held to celebrate the building of a barn on a farm. Barn dances are still held today in country areas.

Belly dance
The popular name of a style of dance that originated in the Middle East, especially Egypt. It was originally danced only by women, and men were not permitted to watch.

The Charleston
The Charleston was named after the city in South Carolina, and was one of the most popular dances of the 1920s.

The conga
People dance the conga in a line, each dancer holding on to the person in front. The conga began in Latin American carnivals and spread to the U.S. in the 1930s.

The hula
The hip-swaying hula is danced by Polynesian islanders who settled in Hawaii. It was banned by Christian missionaries for a while, but became popular again in the late 19th century.

The limbo
This competitive dance comes from Trinidad. Dancers lean back to pass under a bar, which is placed lower and lower. The winner is the dancer who passes under the lowest bar.

Lindy Hop
The Lindy Hop was a version of the Charleston and another dance called the Breakaway. It was named after U.S. aviator Charles Lindbergh (nicknamed Lindy).

Line dancing
Line dancing grew in popularity in the 1990s. Although often associated with Western or cowboy dances, it developed from various traditional dances in which people dance in lines.

The polka
The polka was originally a Czech peasant dance which developed in Bohemia in the 1830s. It became popular in Paris in the 1840s and eventually spread worldwide.

Salsa
Salsa derives from rhythmic dances such as the mambo, cha cha cha and rumba. It has its roots in Spanish-speaking communities in Cuba, Puerto Rico and parts of the U.S.

Dance marathons

Dance marathons began in New York in 1923, when Alma Cummings won a contest by dancing for 27 hours with six different partners. Marathons were popular during the Depression years of the 1930s, when unemployed people danced nonstop for many days to win money.

See also
Film winners:
pages 268–69

The last couple standing won. Dancers were allowed only very short breaks and partners pinched and kicked each other to stay awake or tied themselves together to prevent one from falling down. Dance marathons were banned in many places because they were so dangerous for people's health.

Mike Ritof and Edith Boudreaux danced from August 29, 1930, to April 1, 1931, at the Merry Garden Ballroom, Chicago, Illinois, to win a prize of $2,000. They danced for a total of 5,154 hours, 28 minutes, 30 seconds (215 days) with only short rest breaks.

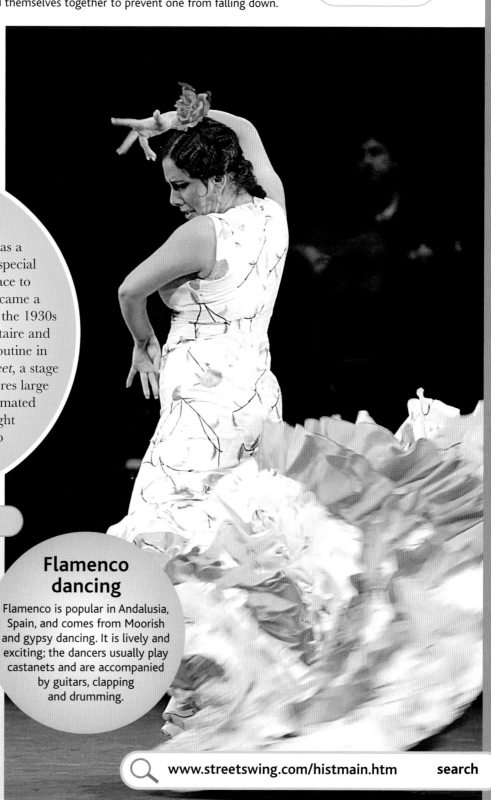

Tap dancing

Tap dancing became popular as a stage act in which dancers wear special shoes and dance on a hard surface to produce a distinctive sound. It became a feature of many popular musicals of the 1930s onwards with such stars as Fred Astaire and Gene Kelly, famed for his dance routine in *Singin' in the Rain* (1952). *42nd Street*, a stage show first performed in 1980, features large numbers of tap dancers. The animated film *Happy Feet* (2006) brought this style of dancing back to public attention.

The twist
The twist started when Hank Ballard recorded the song of this name in 1959. It became popular when Chubby Checker performed his cover version on U.S. television on October 22, 1961. A woman called Ra Denny holds the twist record. She twisted for 100 hours at Christchurch, New Zealand, in March 1962.

The waltz
The waltz began in Austria in the late 18th century. Its name comes from a German word meaning to revolve. Many people were shocked by the dance when it first came to England in 1812 because it involved men and women dancing close to each other. because it involved men and women dancing close to each other.

Flamenco dancing

Flamenco is popular in Andalusia, Spain, and comes from Moorish and gypsy dancing. It is lively and exciting; the dancers usually play castanets and are accompanied by guitars, clapping and drumming.

www.streetswing.com/histmain.htm   search

Most-performed ballets

These are the ballets most often performed by the Royal Ballet at the Royal Opera House, Covent Garden, from 1946 to 2008.

Ballet	Choreographer	First performance at ROH	Perfs.
Swan Lake	Marius Petipa, Lev Ivanov	Dec 19, 1946	917
The Sleeping Beauty	Marius Petipa	Feb 20, 1946	818
Giselle	Jules Perrot, Jean, Coralli, Marius Petipa	Jun 12, 1946	524
Romeo and Juliet	Kenneth MacMillan	Feb 9, 1965	418
Cinderella	Frederick Ashton	Dec 23, 1948	383
Les Sylphides	Michel Fokine	May 16, 1946	352
La Fille Mal Gardée	Frederick Ashton	Jan 28, 1960	323

Best-known ballet companies

Alvin Ailey American Dance Theater (New York), founded 1958
American Ballet Theater (New York), founded 1940
Australian Ballet (Melbourne, Australia), founded 1962
Ballet Rambert (London, U.K.), founded 1926
Ballets Russes* (Moscow, Russia), founded 1909
Bolshoi Ballet (Moscow, Russia), founded 1776
Dance Theater of Harlem (New York), founded 1961
English National Ballet (London, U.K.), founded 1950
Kirov/Marlinsky Ballet (St. Petersburg, Russia), founded 1935
Martha Graham Dance Company (New York), founded 1927
Merce Cunningham Dance Company (New York), founded 1953
National Ballet of Canada (Toronto, Canada), founded 1951
New York City Ballet (New York), founded 1948
Paris Opéra Company (Paris, France), founded 1669
Royal Ballet (London, U.K.), founded 1936
Royal Danish Ballet (Copenhagen, Denmark), founded 1748

* not in existence today

Ballet terms

arabesque
Position in which the dancer stands on one leg, with arms extended, the body bent forward and the other leg stretched back

ballerina
A female ballet dancer

barre
The bar dancers hold on to while they practice, to help them balance

choreographer
The person who works out the steps and movements in a ballet

corps de ballet
Chorus of dancers (not those dancing solo)

entrechat
Rapid crossing and uncrossing of the feet during a jump

fouetté
A turn in which one leg is whipped round

glissade
A gliding movement

jeté
A jump from one foot to the other

pas
A dance step

pas de deux
A dance for two (usually the principal male and female dancers in the company)

pas seule
A solo dance

pirouette
A complete turn on one leg

plié
A knee-bending movement

pointes
On the tips of the toes. Dancers wear special point shoes with blocks in the toes to help them stand on their toes

positions
A range of five positions that are the basis of ballet dancing

prima ballerina
The leading ballerina in a company

tutu
The stiff skirt worn by ballerinas performing classical ballet

Sleeping Beauty by the Royal Ballet

See also
Famous last words: page 305

Famous ballet dancers

Carlos Acosta (Cuban, 1973–)
Trained in Cuba and became a
principal dancer with the Royal
Ballet in London, UK. He has also
staged his own show.

George Balanchine (Georgian-
American, 1904–83) Dancer and
choreographer with the New York
City Ballet and other major
companies.

Mikhail Baryshnikov
(Russian, 1948–) One of the
greatest male dancers. He began
with the Kirov in Russia but later
joined the American Ballet Theater.

Darcey Bussell (British, 1969–)
Became a principal dancer with the
Royal Ballet at the age of 20. She is
one of their most popular soloists,
and in 1995 she was awarded an
OBE for her work in dance. She
retired in 2006.

Sir Anton Dolin
(British, 1904–83) Originally danced
with Diaghilev's Ballets Russes.
He founded the London Festival
Ballet (now English National Ballet).

Sir Anthony Dowell
(British, 1943–) He was principal
dancer with the Royal Ballet for
many years and was Director of the
Royal Ballet for 15 years from 1986.

Dame Margot Fonteyn
(British, 1919–91) Royal Ballet
prima ballerina, she is most famous
for her long-term partnership
with Rudolf Nureyev.

Dame Beryl Grey
(British, 1927–) Prima ballerina at
the Sadler's Wells Ballet, London, UK
and the first English ballerina to
perform with the Bolshoi.

Sylvie Guillem (French, 1965–)
Principal guest artist with the
Royal Ballet, she is a versatile and
athletic dancer, famous for her
extraordinarily high leg extensions.

Karen Kain
(Canadian, 1951–) Principal dancer
with the National Ballet of Canada
and later its artistic director.

Dame Alicia Markova
(British, 1910–2004) She danced
with Anton Dolin and they are most
famous for their *Giselle*. Dolin and
Markova formed a ballet company.

Rudolf Nureyev
(Russian, 1938–93) Former Kirov
star who defected to the West and
became the most popular male
dancer of his generation.

Anna Pavlova
(Russian, 1881–1931) Became the
most famous ballerina of her
generation through her world tours.

Dame Marie Rambert
(Polish/British, 1888–1982)
Dancer and teacher whose dance
company promoted many new
works.

Maria Taglioni
(Swedish/Italian, 1804–84) One of
the first ballet stars, famous for
her role in *La Sylphide*.

Vaslav Nijinsky

(Russian, 1890–1950)
One of most famous of all
male dancers. He was a leading
dancer with the Ballets Russes
and best known for his
performance in
Stravinsky's *Rite
of Spring*.

Darcey Bussell dancing with Igor Zelensky

Ballet firsts and records

First ballet
In the late 16th century, performances that included
dancing, music and acting were given at the French
court of Henri II and Catherine de Médici. The ballet
Comique de La Reine (1581) was the first recorded.

First professional ballerina
On January 21, 1681, Mademoiselle de La Fontaine
appeared in Jean Baptiste Lully's *The Triumph of Love*
at the Paris Opéra.

First ballet in the U.S.
On February 7, 1827, Francisquy Hutin performed a
ballet in the play *The Deserter* at the Bowery Theatre,
New York. The women in the audience
were so shocked by it that they
fled from the theater.

Most curtain calls for a ballet performance
In October 1964 Margot
Fonteyn and Rudolf
Nureyev received 89
curtain calls after their
performance in *Swan
Lake* at the Staatsoper,
in Vienna, Austria.

Most pirouettes
Delia Gray (15) performed
166 consecutive turns at
The Playhouse, Harlow,
Essex, UK, on June 2, 1991.

First tutu and first on points
Ballerina Maria Taglioni (1804–84) wore
a muslin dress known as a tutu when she
danced in *La Sylphide* at the Paris Opéra
on March 12, 1832. The dress allowed
more freedom of movement so became
popular in classical ballet. In the same
ballet she danced on points
without support — the first
time any dancer had
done so.

www.national.ballet.ca   search

Film, TV & Radio

Last *Lost*

One of the world's most popular cult television shows comes to an end in May 2010. *Lost* lasted six seasons and mystified millions of watchers worldwide. The show has been a critical and commercial success, making stars of many of the ensemble cast. Its creators are now considered among the most powerful people in film and television.

Feature films produced (2007)

● India	1,164		● South Korea	124
● USA	453		● Germany	122
● Japan	407		● Italy	121
● China	402		● Brazil	117
○ France	228		● UK	117
● Russia	200		○ Canada	111
● Spain	172		● Iran	105

No. of films

Latest available figures from each country

Countries

Top cinema-goers*

1 India 3,997,000,000
2 USA and Canada 1,360,000,000
3 France 177,520,000
4 China 176,200,000
5 Mexico 174,200,000
6 UK 164,200,000
7 Japan 163,200,000
8 South Korea 158,800,000
9 Germany 125,400,000
10 Italy 120,000,000
11 Spain 116,900,000

* per annum, latest available figures

Poster advertising the Indian film *Ek Kali Muskai* (1968)

Casts of thousands

About 200,000 of the extras in *Gandhi* were volunteers, but another 94,560 were paid a small fee. They appeared in the scene showing Gandhi's funeral, which lasted just two minutes and five seconds after editing.

In *Around the World in 80 Days* (1956), there were animal extras too – 3,800 sheep, 2,448 buffalos, 950 donkeys, 800 horses, 512 monkeys, 17 bulls, 15 elephants, 6 skunks and 4 ostriches. In recent films, such as the *Lord of the Rings* trilogy, scenes with thousands of people were computer-generated, so huge numbers of extras were not needed.

Film	Extras
Gandhi (UK, 1982)	294,560
Kolberg (Germany, 1945)	187,000
Monster Wangmagwi (South Korea, 1967)	157,000
War and Peace (USSR, 1968)	120,000
Ilya Muromets (*The Sword and the Dragon*) (USSR, 1956)	106,000
Dun-Huang (*Ton ko*) (Japan, 1988)	100,000
Razboiul Independentei (*The War of Independence*) (Romania, 1912)	80,000
Around the World in 80 Days (USA, 1956)	68,894
Intolerance (USA, 1916)	60,000
Dny Zrady (*Days of Betrayal*) (Czechoslovakia, 1973)	60,000

Who does what in a film?

Director The director controls everything, gives orders to the cast and crew and makes sure that the script is followed.

Producer(s) There can be more than one producer, who is responsible for raising the money to make the film and for other important activities, such as casting and controlling the costs.

Cast The actors and actresses who appear in the film.

Screenplay writer The person who writes the script. This gives the actors and actresses their lines and explains how the action takes place.

Extras The people who appear in crowd scenes but do not have speaking parts.

Animatronic engineer The person who makes the robotic creatures used in science-fiction and fantasy films.

Art director The art director coordinates the costumes, sets and make-up to set the overall style of the film.

Best boy The deputy electrician, assistant to the gaffer.

Casting director The person who chooses the actors for each role in the film.

Caterer The caterer supplies meals so that the cast and crew can work all day.

Cinematographer The person who directs the lighting and films the action, originally called the cameraman.

Clapper loader Details of each scene are written on a special board called a clapper board. The clapper loader snaps it shut in front of the camera as filming begins to record what is being filmed.

Film budgets

The production budgets of a film include the salaries paid to the director, writer(s), stars and crew, the designing and building of sets, costumes, the transport and location costs (filming away from the studio) and the cost of making and editing the film. Other costs include P & A (Prints and Advertising) – making thousands of copies of the film, distributing them to cinemas, and advertising the film in the press, on television and on the Internet.

An average Hollywood feature film takes eight weeks to film. It may cost $5 million or more a week, depending on how lavish the production is and how expensive the stars are. *Titanic* (1997) held the record for largest production budget ($200 million) until it was equalled by *Spider-Man 2* (2004), then broken by *King Kong* (2005) at $207 million. It has since been overtaken by *Superman Returns* (2006) at $270 million and *Spider-Man 3* (2007) at $258 million.

Most cinema screens

	Country	Estimated number of screens (2007)
1	USA	38,974
2	China	36,112
3	India	10,189
4	France	5,398
5	Germany	4,832
6	Spain	4,296
7	Italy	4,071
8	Mexico	3,936
9	UK	3,596
10	Japan	3,221

Costs and income of a typical big-budget Hollywood film, *Spider-Man 2* (2004)

COSTS

Estimated cost ($US million)

Actors	17
Toby Maguire	7
Kirsten Dunst	3
Alfred Molina	3
Rest of cast	10
Director (Sam Raimi)	20
Story rights	10
Screenplay	15
Producers	45
Production costs	65
Special effects	5
Music	
Total production budget	**200**
Prints and advertising	75
Income	
US box office	374
Rest of world	410
Home video/DVD sales and rentals	58.5
TV broadcast rights	15.0
Total	**784**
Profit	**509**

Video and DVD sales and rentals and TV broadcast rights would also add to the total income

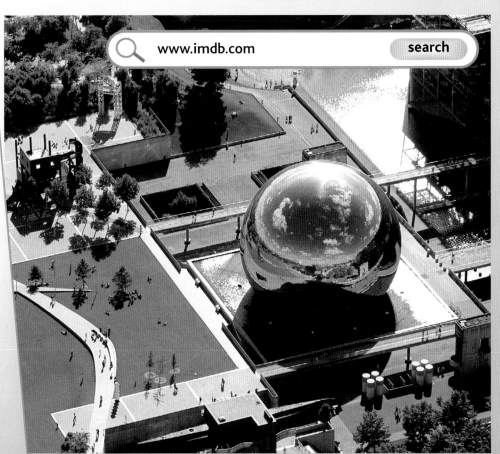

www.imdb.com   search

La Géode cinema stands in the Parc de la Villette, Paris. Inside the enormous dome is a giant screen measuring 1,000 sq m (10,764 sq ft).

Composer The composer writes the music or adapts an existing score as a backing track for the film.

Costume designer The costume designer is responsible for designing and supplying the clothing worn by the cast.

Editor The editor cuts and connects the best versions of each section of film to create the final version.

Gaffer The chief electrician, who is responsible for lighting the set. The word may come from slang for grandfather – a senior person respected by everyone. Gaffer tape is the heavy-duty tape used on sets to secure cables and almost anything else.

Key grip A grip is responsible for moving the sets and for laying the tracks on which the camera runs. The key grip is in charge of all the other grips.

Make-up artist He or she applies the cosmetics which alter or improve an actor's looks under the studio lights.

Sound engineer This engineer makes sure that the dialogue and other sounds heard on the film are properly recorded and synchronized with the action.

Special-effects coordinator This person is responsible for creating spectacular scenes with photographic, mechanical and computer methods.

Stunt man/woman Specialists who perform the actions that are too difficult or dangerous for an actor. Stunt doubles are stunt men or women made up to look like the actors so it looks as though the actors have performed a feat themselves.

Wardrobe mistress The wardrobe mistress (or master) is in charge of the costumes, making sure they fit, are in good condition and available when they are needed for a scene.

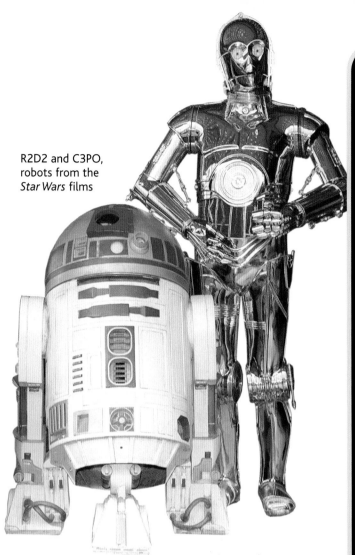

R2D2 and C3PO,
robots from the
Star Wars films

Musicals

Musicals – films in which songs sung by the characters are part of the story – date back 80 years.

Soon after the end of the silent era and the introduction of sound to films, one of the earliest musicals, *The Broadway Melody* (1929), featured eight songs and was the first sound film to win a Best Picture Oscar. The 1930s was regarded as the 'Golden Age' of film musicals, while those of the 1950s and 1960s, such as *The King and I* (1956) and *The Sound of Music* (1965) were often based on successful stage shows. After a decline in the 1980s and 1990s, the 2000s have seen a revival of musicals, with *Mamma Mia!* becoming the most successful musical and one of the 50 highest-earning films ever.

Film	World total ($US million)
Mamma Mia! (2008)	602.4
Grease (1978)	394.6
Chicago (2002)	306.8
Saturday Night Fever (1977)	285.4
High School Musical 3: Senior Year (2008)	251.0
Hairspray (2007)	200.6
Moulin Rouge! (2001)	177.7
The Sound of Music (1965)	163.2
The Phantom of the Opera (2004)	154.6
Sweeney Todd; The Demon Barber of Fleet Street (2007)	152.5
Evita (1996)	141.0
The Rocky Horror Picture Show (1975)	139.9
Staying Alive (1983)	127.6

Highest-earning films

These films have made the most money at the box office.

Film	World total ($US million)
Titanic (1997)	1,848.8
The Lord of the Rings: The Return of the King (2003)	1,133.0
Pirates of the Caribbean: Dead Man's Chest (2006)	1,066.2
The Dark Knight (2008)	1,001.9
Harry Potter and the Sorcerer's Stone (2001)	985.8
Pirates of the Caribbean: At World's End (2007)	961.0
Harry Potter and the Order of the Phoenix (2007)	938.5
The Lord of the Rings: The Two Towers (2002)	926.3
Star Wars: Episode I - The Phantom Menace (1999)	924.3
*Shrek 2** (2004)	920.7
Jurassic Park (1993)	914.7
Harry Potter and the Goblet of Fire (2005)	896.0
Spider-Man 3 (2007)	890.9
Harry Potter and the Chamber of Secrets (2002)	879.0
The Lord of the Rings: The Fellowship of the Ring (2001)	871.4
*Finding Nemo** (2003)	864.6
Star Wars: Episode III – Revenge of the Sith (2005)	850.0
Spider-Man (2002)	821.7
Independence Day (1996)	817.0
*Shrek the Third** (2007)	799.0
Star Wars: Episode IV - A New Hope (1977)	797.9
Harry Potter and the Prisoner of Azkaban (2004)	795.5
E.T. the Extra-Terrestrial (1982)	792.9
Indiana Jones and the Kingdom of the Crystal Skull (2008)	786.6
Spider-Man 2 (2004)	784.0
*The Lion King** (1994)	783.8
The Da Vinci Code (2006)	758.2
The Chronicles of Narnia: The Lion, The Witch and The Wardrobe (2005)	745.0
The Matrix Reloaded (2003)	738.6
Transformers (2007)	708.3
Forrest Gump (1994)	677.4
The Sixth Sense (1999)	672.8
Pirates of the Caribbean: The Curse of the Black Pearl (2003)	654.3
*Ice Age: The Meltdown** (2006)	651.6
Star Wars: Episode II - Attack of the Clones (2002)	649.4

* animated film

Computer games and films

Computer games are big business and a number of recent blockbuster films have been based on some of the most popular games.

These include *Max Payne* (video game 2001, film 2008), *Lara Croft: Tomb Raider* (game 1992, film 1995) and *Mortal Kombat* (game 1992, film 1995).

The link between films and games also works the other way, with games based on live-action and animated films – for example, *Quantum of Solace* (film and game 2008), *The Incredibles* (2004) and *The Lord of the Rings: Battle for Middle Earth* (2004) – a game based on *The Lord of the Rings* trilogy (2001–2003).

James Bond films

Including the latest, *Quantum of Solace*, Ian Fleming's 12 James Bond books have been made into 22 official and two unofficial films, the original *Casino Royale* (1967), a comedy starring David Niven, and *Never say Never Again* (1983), with Sean Connery as Bond, which was a remake of *Thunderball*.

Daniel Craig as James Bond in *Quantum of Solace*

Film	Bond actor	World total ($US million)
Casino Royale (2006)	Daniel Craig	594.2
Quantum of Solace (2008)	Daniel Craig	576.4
Die Another Day (2002)	Pierce Brosnan	432.0
The World is Not Enough (1999)	Pierce Brosnan	390.0
GoldenEye (1995)	Pierce Brosnan	352.2
Tomorrow Never Dies (1997)	Pierce Brosnan	339.3
Moonraker (1979)	Roger Moore	210.3
For Your Eyes Only (1981)	Roger Moore	195.3
The Living Daylights (1987)	Timothy Dalton	191.2
Octopussy (1983)	Roger Moore	187.5
The Spy Who Loved Me (1977)	Roger Moore	185.4
Licence to Kill (1989)	Timothy Dalton	156.2
A View to a Kill (1985)	Roger Moore	152.4
Thunderball (1965)	Sean Connery	141.2
Live and Let Die (1973)	Roger Moore	126.4
Goldfinger (1964)	Sean Connery	124.9
Diamonds Are Forever (1971)	Sean Connery	116.0
You Only Live Twice (1967)	Sean Connery	111.6
The Man with the Golden Gun (1974)	Roger Moore	97.6
From Russia with Love (1963)	Sean Connery	78.9
On Her Majesty's Secret Service (1969)	George Lazenby	64.6
Dr No (1963)	Sean Connery	59.6

Bond is back

Daniel Craig first appeared as James Bond in *Casino Royale* (2006) and again in *Quantum of Solace* (2008), the two highest-earning Bond films so far. He is contracted to star in at least two more sequels.

See also
All about comics: page 236

Top films based on comic books

Comic book characters have been popular subjects for film makers ever since the 1930s. The characters are already familiar, so are immediately appealing to audiences. The exploits of superheroes such as Superman and Batman are perfect for exciting action films, many of which have been hugely successful.

Film	Comic first published	Film released	World total ($US million)
The Dark Knight	1939	2008	1001.9
Spider-Man 3	1962	2007	890.9
Spider-Man	1962	2002	821.7
Spider-Man 2	1962	2004	784.0
Men in Black	1990	1997	589.4
Iron Man	1963	2008	582.0
X-Men: The Last Stand	1963	2006	459.3
300	1998	2007	456.1
Men in Black II	1990	2002	441.8
Batman	1939	1989	413.4
X2: X-Men United	1963	2003	407.6
Superman Returns	1938	2006	391.1

The American Film Institute's top films

The American Film Institute has listed greatest films in a number of categories, based on the views of a panel of 1,500 film experts.

Greatest American movies of all time

1 *Citizen Kane* (1941)
2 *Casablanca* (1942)
3 *The Godfather* (1972)
4 *Gone with the Wind* (1939)
5 *Lawrence of Arabia* (1962)
6 *The Wizard of Oz* (1939)
7 *The Graduate* (1967)
8 *On the Waterfront* (1954)
9 *Schindler's List* (1993)
10 *Singin' in the Rain* (1952)

Funniest films

1 *Some Like It Hot* (1959)
2 *Tootsie* (1982)
3 *Dr Strangelove, or: How I Learned to Stop Worrying and Love the Bomb* (1964)
4 *Annie Hall* (1977)
5 *Duck Soup* (1933)
6 *Blazing Saddles* (1974)
7 *M*A*S*H* (1970)
8 *It Happened One Night* (1934)
9 *The Graduate* (1967)
10 *Airplane!* (1980)

Love stories

1 *Casablanca* (1942)
2 *Gone With the Wind* (1939)
3 *West Side Story* (1961)
4 *Roman Holiday* (1953)
5 *An Affair to Remember* (1957)
6 *The Way We Were* (1973)
7 *Doctor Zhivago* (1965)
8 *It's a Wonderful Life* (1946)
9 *Love Story* (1970)
10 *City Lights* (1931)

Thrillers

1 *Psycho* (1960)
2 *Jaws* (1975)
3 *The Exorcist* (1973)
4 *North by Northwest* (1959)
5 *The Silence of the Lambs* (1991)
6 *Alien* (1979)
7 *The Birds* (1963)
8 *The French Connection* (1971)
9 *Rosemary's Baby* (1968)
10 *Raiders of the Lost Ark* (1981)

Science fiction film *Alien* was voted one of the greatest-ever thrillers

What is an Oscar?

The Academy Awards or "Oscars" have been presented since 1929. The award is a gold-plated statuette made of tin, copper and antimony. It is 34.3 cm (13.5 in) high and weighs 3.8 kg (8.4 lb). Winning an Oscar is important because it encourages more people to see the film and helps the individual winners' careers.

Why is it called an Oscar?

According to legend, Academy librarian Margaret Herrick named it when she declared that the statuette looked like her Uncle Oscar!

Who decides who wins?

Members of the US Academy of Motion Picture Arts & Science members, including previous nominees and winners, vote to create a shortlist of five nominees in each of 24 categories, other than special, honorary and technical awards.

Who can win an Oscar?

The main categories are Best Picture, Best Director, Best Actor, Best Actress, Best Supporting Actor and Best Supporting Actress. There are other awards eg screenplay, cinematography, soundtrack, documentary, animated feature, foreign film.

Oscar® winners

These are the Best Picture, Best Actor and Best Actress winners for the last 25 years. The date given is the date of release. Oscars are awarded the following year.

Year	Best Picture	Best Actor	Best Actress
2008	*Slumdog Millionaire*	Sean Penn	Kate Winslet
2007	*No Country for Old Men*	Daniel Day-Lewis	Marion Cotillard
2006	*The Departed*	Forest Whitaker	Helen Mirren
2005	*Crash*	Philip Seymour Hoffman	Reese Witherspoon
2004	*Million Dollar Baby*	Jamie Foxx	Hilary Swank
2003	*The Lord of the Rings: The Return of the King*	Sean Penn	Charlize Theron
2002	*Chicago*	Adrien Brody	Nicole Kidman
2001	*A Beautiful Mind*	Denzel Washington	Halle Berry
2000	*Gladiator*	Russell Crowe	Julia Roberts
1999	*American Beauty*	Kevin Spacey	Hilary Swank
1998	*Shakespeare in Love*	Roberto Benigni	Gwyneth Paltrow
1997	*Titanic*	Jack Nicholson	Helen Hunt
1996	*The English Patient*	Geoffrey Rush	Frances McDormand
1995	*Braveheart*	Nicholas Cage	Susan Sarandon
1994	*Forrest Gump*	Tom Hanks	Jessica Lange
1993	*Schindler's List*	Tom Hanks	Holly Hunter
1992	*Unforgiven*	Al Pacino	Emma Thompson
1991	*The Silence of the Lambs*	Anthony Hopkins	Jodie Foster
1990	*Dances With Wolves*	Jeremy Irons	Kathy Bates
1989	*Driving Miss Daisy*	Daniel Day-Lewis	Jessica Tandy
1988	*Rain Man*	Dustin Hoffman	Jodie Foster
1987	*The Last Emperor*	Michael Douglas	Cher
1986	*Platoon*	Paul Newman	Marlee Martin
1985	*Out of Africa*	William Hurt	Geraldine Page
1984	*Amadeus*	F. Murray Abraham	Sally Field
1983	*Terms of Endearment*	Robert Duvall	Shirley MacLaine

Highest-earning actors and actresses

	Estimated 2008 earnings ($US million)
Will Smith	80
Johnny Depp	72
Cameron Diaz	50
Leonardo DiCaprio	45
Bruce Willis	41
Ben Stiller	40
Nicolas Cage	38
Keira Knightley	32
Jennifer Aniston	27
Gwyneth Paltrow	25
Daniel Radcliffe	25
Reese Witherspoon	25

Kate Winslet won an Oscar for her role in *The Reader* (2008)

AFI's Top ten film songs

Song	Film
1 Over the Rainbow	*The Wizard of Oz* (1939)
2 As Time Goes By	*Casablanca* (1942)
3 Singin' in the Rain	*Singin' in the Rain* (1952)
4 Moon River	*Breakfast at Tiffany's* (1961)
5 White Christmas	*Holiday Inn* (1942)
6 Mrs Robinson	*The Graduate* (1967)
7 When You Wish Upon a Star	*Pinocchio* (1940)
8 The Way We Were	*The Way We Were* (1973)
9 Stayin' Alive	*Saturday Night Fever* (1977)
10 The Sound of Music	*The Sound Of Music* (1965)

See also
Awards: page 155

Most wins
These three films have each won 11 Oscars, including Best Picture: *Ben-Hur* (1959), *Titanic* (1997) and *The Lord of the Rings: The Return of the King* (2003).

A no-win situation
The Turning Point (1977) and *The Color Purple* (1985) had 11 nominations each but neither of them won a single Oscar. *Gangs of New York* (2002) received 10 nominations, also without winning anything.

Long and short
Gone with the Wind (1939) was the longest film (238 minutes) and the first colour film to win Best Picture. *Marty* (1955) was the shortest Best Picture winner at 91 minutes.

Black and white
Marty was also one of the last black and white films to win Best Picture. *The Apartment* (1960) and *Schindler's List* (1993) are the only black and white films to have won since.

First appearances

These are the films in which some of the most famous animated characters made their first appearances.

Mickey Mouse
Plane Crazy (1928)
Plane Crazy was Walt Disney's first Mickey Mouse cartoon and was silent. Two months later Mickey appeared in Disney's *Steamboat Willie*, the first Mickey Mouse cartoon with sound. Mickey starred in *Fantasia* (1940), and his *Lend a Paw* won an Oscar® in 1941.

Popeye *Popeye the Sailor with Betty Boop* (1933)
Popeye was born in 1929 as a newspaper comic strip by Elzie Crisler Segar. Animator Max Fleischer adapted it for the screen. Popeye cartoons were made for cinema and TV until the 1980s.

Donald Duck *The Wise Little Hen* (1934)
Clarence Nash was the voice of Donald Duck for 50 years. The Donald Duck anti-Hitler film *Der Fuehrer's Face* (1942) won an Oscar.

Bugs Bunny *Porky's Hare Hunt* (1938)
A Wild Hare (1940) was the first cartoon in which Bugs Bunny said "Eh, what's up, Doc?" but he was not named until *Elmer's Pet Rabbit* (1941). *Knighty-Knight Bugs* (1958) won an Oscar.

Tom and Jerry
Puss Gets The Boot (1940)
The very first Tom and Jerry cartoon was nominated for an Oscar. The characters also appeared in the 1992 film *Tom and Jerry: The Movie*. This full-length film is the only one in which they speak.

Casper the Ghost *The Friendly Ghost* (1945)
Casper starred in more than 50 cartoons and in a part live action/part computer animated feature film in 1995, which earned nearly $300 million around the world.

The Flintstones *The Flintstone Flyer* (1960)
This was the first episode of *The Flintstones* to be broadcast on TV. It went on to become the longest-running cartoon series until it was overtaken by *The Simpsons*. The live-action film *The Flintstones* (1994) was one of the top-earning films of the year.

Simpsons *Simpsons Roasting on an Open Fire* (1989)
Matt Groening's hugely successful animated series began in 1987 as short episodes screened on the Tracey Ullman Show. It was developed into longer weekly episodes and has become the longest-running and most successful cartoon series ever.

Walt Disney's first animated features

Walt Disney (1901–66) produced short animated films, including Mickey Mouse cartoons, before making main features. *Snow White* was Hollywood's first full-length animated feature film and earned Disney an honorary Oscar. The film made $188 million in the USA alone.

Film	First released in cinemas
1 *Snow White and the Seven Dwarfs*	21 December 1937
2 *Pinocchio*	7 February 1940
3 *Fantasia*	12 November 1940
4 *Dumbo*	23 October 1941
5 *Bambi*	9 August 1942

Walt Disney in his studio

Types of animation

The word animation comes from the Latin *animatus*, meaning filled with life. Even before the invention of cinema, people realized that if the human eye sees a series of images that change at a rate of at least 24 frames a second, the brain can be tricked into thinking it is seeing a live moving image. 19th-century optical toys such as zoetropes worked on this principle.

A zoetrope – when the viewer spins the zoetrope and looks through a slit, the pictures inside appear to be moving.

Traditional animation
Individual frames of a story are hand drawn on cels – transparent sheets of plastic. They are then photographed as a sequence against painted backgrounds.

Cut-out
In this type of animation, two-dimensional drawings are placed on a fixed background. These are moved and photographed to create the impression of movement.

CGI
CGI (Computer Generated Imagery) has been used since the 1970s, originally for short films. The 1989 film *The Abyss* used some CGI visual effects, but the hugely successful

WALL-E

WALL-E (2008) was the most expensive animated film ever made, but has earned almost three times as much as its $180-million production budget. It also won an Oscar for Best Animated Feature.

Most expensive animated films

Making animated films has become more and more expensive. In 1937 *Snow White and the Seven Dwarfs* cost $1.49 million – a record-breaking sum at the time. *WALL-E* (2008) and *The Polar Express* (2004) are the costliest films ever made and were more than 100 times as expensive as *Snow White*.

Film	Year	Budget ($US million)
WALL-E	2008	180
The Polar Express	2004	170
Shrek the Third	2007	160
Bee Movie	2007	150
Beowulf	2007	150
Madagascar: Escape 2 Africa	2008	150
Ratatouille	2007	150
Shrek 2	2004	150

Toy Story (1995), from the Disney and Pixar Animation Studio, was the first CGI feature film. Another development known as 3D motion capture has been used in films such as *Beowulf* (2007), a $150 million budget film with Ray Winstone in the title role, in which the movements of the actors are converted into computer images.

Stop motion
This type of animation is created by moving three-dimensional figures and other objects a tiny amount between shots. This method has been used since 1925, but the best-known modern examples of this technique are the *Wallace & Gromit* films by Aardman Animation.

Beowulf was filmed by the motion capture process

Highest-earning animated films

Film	Earnings ($US million)
Shrek 2 (2004)	920.7
Finding Nemo (2003)	864.6
Shrek the Third (2007)	799.0
The Lion King (1994)	783.8
Ice Age: The Meltdown (2006)	651.6
Kung Fu Panda (2008)	631.9
The Incredibles (2004)	631.4
Ratatouille (2007)	621.4
Madagascar: Escape 2 Africa (2008)	591.4
WALL-E (2008)	534.8
Madagascar (2005)	532.7
Monsters, Inc. (2001)	529.1
The Simpsons Movie (2007)	527.1
Aladdin (1992)	504.1
Toy Story 2 (1999)	485.0
Shrek (2001)	484.4
Cars (2006)	462.0

Casablanca (1942), in which screen legends Humphrey Bogart and Ingrid Bergman both starred

Top 10 screen legends

This is the Top 10 of the American Film Institute's list of the greatest American screen legends.

	Actor	Actress
1	Humphrey Bogart	Katharine Hepburn
2	Cary Grant	Bette Davis
3	James Stewart	Audrey Hepburn
4	Marlon Brando	Ingrid Bergman
5	Fred Astaire	Greta Garbo
6	Henry Fonda	Marilyn Monroe
7	Clark Gable	Elizabeth Taylor
8	James Cagney	Judy Garland
9	Spencer Tracy	Marlene Dietrich
10	Charlie Chaplin	Joan Crawford

Child stars

Shirley Temple
An American dancer and singer, Shirley Temple (born 1928) began appearing in films at the age of four and became the world's most famous child star. After retiring from show business, she became a diplomat, serving as US Ambassador to Ghana and Czechoslovakia.

Judy Garland
The American actress (1922–69) appeared in her first role at the age of seven. She is best known as Dorothy in *The Wizard of Oz* (1939).

Tatum O'Neal
Born in the USA in 1963, Tatum O'Neal became the youngest-ever Oscar winner for her role in *Paper Moon* (1973).

Georgie Henley
The British actress (born 9 July 1995) plays Lucy in *The Chronicles of Narnia* series. At the age of 10 she won a Phoenix Film Critics Award for her role in *The Lion, the Witch and the Wardrobe*.

Stars whose films have earned most

These are the stars who have appeared in the most films that have made more than $100 million at the US box office. A number of less well-known actors who have supplied their voices to animated films have made as many or even more high-earning films.

Star	$100 m+ films
Tom Hanks	17
Tom Cruise	16
Eddie Murphy	13
Morgan Freeman	13
Samuel L. Jackson	12
Harrison Ford	12
Robin Williams	11
Stan Lee	11
James Earl Jones	10
Bruce Willis	10

Will Smith

Top stars

Since the 1920s, cinemas across the USA have nominated the top stars of the year according to the number of people who pay to watch their films. These are the top stars of 2008.

1 Will Smith
2 Robert Downey Jr
2 Christian Bale
4 Shia LaBeouf
5 Harrison Ford
6 Adam Sandler
7 Reese Witherspoon
8 George Clooney
9 Angelina Jolie
10 Daniel Craig

Movie monsters

Ever since cinema began, film-makers have played on everyone's fear of monsters. These are some of the most popular monster films.

Aliens
Hundreds of films have been made about alien monsters attacking Earth. The most successful of these was *Independence Day* (1996).

Dinosaurs
One of the first cartoons was *Gertie* (1914). It featured a drawing of a brontosaurus that comes to life. Dinosaur films *Jurassic Park* (1993) and its two sequels, *The Lost World: Jurassic Park* (1997) and *Jurassic Park III* (2001), are among the biggest blockbusters of all time.

Egyptian mummies
The Mummy (1932) featured an Egyptian mummy that comes to life and attacks people. *The Mummy* was remade in 1999 and its sequel, the comedy-adventure *The Mummy Returns* (2001), has made more than $433 million.

Frankenstein's monster
Frankenstein is the name of the creator of the monster, not the monster itself. The original story was written in 1816 by English writer Mary Shelley. It was first made into a silent film in 1910 by the inventor Thomas Edison and has been remade many times since. *Mary Shelley's Frankenstein* (1994) is the highest-earning of all the versions.

Stage names

Actors and actresses choose stage names for a variety of reasons. Their real names may be the same as or similar to those of other people, or they may be difficult to spell or pronounce.

Here are some famous performers who decided to change their names.

Film name	Real name
Woody Allen	Allan Stewart Konigsberg
Jennifer Aniston	Jennifer Linn Anastassakis
Mel Brooks	Melvin Kaminsky
Nicolas Cage	Nicholas Kim Coppola
Michael Caine	Maurice Joseph Micklewhite
Jackie Chan	Chan Kong-sang
Tom Cruise	Thomas Cruise Mapother IV
Kirk Douglas	Issur Danielovitch Demsky
Whoopi Goldberg	Caryn Elaine Johnson
Cary Grant	Archibald Alexander Leach
Richard E. Grant	Richard Grant Esterhuysen
Goldie Hawn	Goldie Jean Studlendegehawn
Hulk Hogan	Terry Gene Bollea
Angelina Jolie	Angelina Jolie Voight
Ben Kingsley	Krishna Bhanji
Queen Latifah	Dana Elaine Owens
Jet Li	Li Lian Jie
Marilyn Monroe	Norma Jean Baker
Demi Moore	Demetria Gene Guynes
Natalie Portman	Natalie Hershlag
Winona Ryder	Winona Horowitz
Susan Sarandon	Susan Abigail Tomalin
Christian Slater	Christian Michael Leonard Hawkins
Sigourney Weaver	Susan Weaver

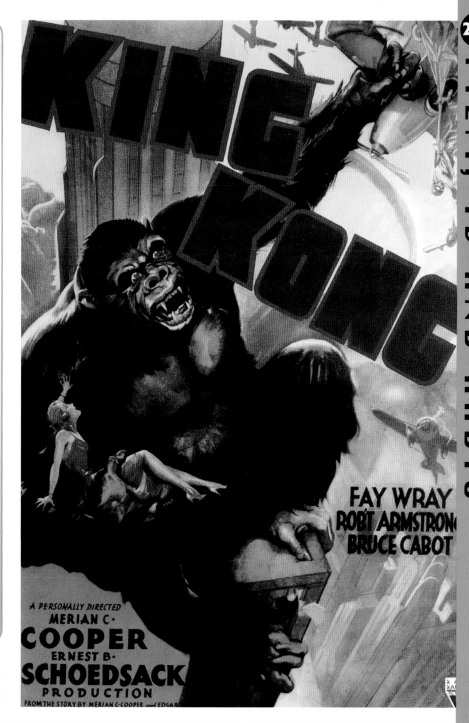

Poster for the original horror-adventure film *King Kong* (1933); the film has been remade twice, most recently in 2005

Funny monsters
Some of the most successful cartoon monsters are those in *Monsters, Inc.* (2001). The monsters are led by Sulley, whose secret is that the monsters are scared of children!

Killer creatures
Giant ape King Kong is one of the most famous animal monsters and the star of the film *King Kong* (1933, 1976 and 2005).

Giant spiders have featured in films such as *Arachnophobia* (1990) and *Eight Legged Freaks* (2002). Harry Potter also meets an army of huge spiders in *Harry Potter and the Chamber of Secrets* (2002). Other famous killer creatures include sharks (*Jaws*, 1977), alligators (*Lake Placid*, 1999) and snakes (*Anaconda*, 1997 and *Snakes on a Plane*, 2006).

Vampires
Irish writer Bram Stoker's vampire novel *Dracula* was first published in 1897. Since then it has been made into countless films. The version starring Bela Lugosi (1931) is one of the most famous. *Twilight* (2008), *Van Helsing* (2004) and *Interview with the Vampire* (1994) are the highest-earning vampire films.

Zombies
Zombies are the "undead" – bodies that come out of their graves and terrorize the living. They have been the subject of many films, including the most successful, *Dawn of the Dead* (2004) and comedy spoofs such as *Shaun of the Dead* (2004).

This was billed as the first "Rom-Com-Zom" (Romantic Comedy Zombie film).

See also

Mythical creatures: pages 170–71

www.afi.com   search

Video and DVD fact file

- The terms video recording and videotape were first used in the early 1950s, but only among TV professionals.

- The abbreviation VCR (video cassette recorder) was first used in the UK and USA in 1971.

- The first domestic video cassette recorders were sold in 1974, but both machines and tapes were very expensive and few people bought them.

- The VHS (video home system) was launched in 1976 in the US and 1978 in Europe.

- By 1980 about 7,687,000 homes had video recorders; by 1996 the global figure was put at 400,976,000.

- DVD (digital video disc or digital versatile disc) players and discs were launched in Japan and the USA in 1997.

- Worldwide, sales of DVDs overtook video sales in 2002.

- By 2003 almost one in three UK households had a DVD player. In 2007 the figure increased to over 83 per cent, with sales of discs over £2.3 billion.

- In 2007, most major film studios stopped releasing films on video. In 2008 Blu-Ray was adopted as the standard format for HD (High Definition) DVD.

TV-owning countries

Country	TVs households*	Country	TVs households*
China	380,559,800	Japan	49,396,100
India	133,891,800	Germany	39,041,400
USA	118,035,600	UK	26,819,500
Indonesia	55,665,400	Mexico	25,666,600
Russia	51,272,700		
Brazil	50,929,800		

* Households with colour TVs, 2010 forecast

A 1950s US magazine advertisement for TVs

First countries to have television*

The BBC's first broadcasts used Baird's mechanical television system. In this, spinning disks were used to scan images.

This was later dropped in favour of US inventor Philo Taylor Farnsworth's electronic system. Electronic television did not rely on moving parts, was more reliable and gave a better picture.

Country	Year
UK	1936
USA	1939
USSR	1939
France	1948
Brazil	1950

* High-definition regular public broadcasting service

TV viewing

- In the average US home, the TV is switched on for 7 hours 40 minutes a day.

- US children aged 2 to 17 watch an average of 19 hours 40 minutes' TV every week. That is 1,023 hours a year compared with 900 hours a year in school.

- In the UK children aged 8 to 15 spend an average of 2 hours 13 minutes a day watching TV and adults over 16 spend an average of 2 hours 23 minutes.

TV milestones   1900s

1922
18 October, BBC (British Broadcasting Company) founded

1929
First transmissions of Scottish inventor John Logie Baird's experimental mechanical television system and, in the USA, Philo T. Farnsworth's electronic TV system

1936
22 November, BBC opens the world's first regular high-definition television service, from Alexandra Palace, London

1937
21 June, Wimbledon Tennis Championships first broadcast

1938
30 April, television coverage of the FA Cup Final
31 May, first BBC TV panel game, *Spelling Bee*

1939
1 September, BBC television service is suspended throughout World War II
30 April, Franklin D. Roosevelt is the first president to appear on TV, opening the World's Fair in New York

10 June, the first king and queen on TV in the USA are King George VI and Queen Elizabeth, seen visiting the World's Fair

1941
1 July, the first ever TV commercial, for a Bulova clock, is broadcast by WNBT New York, during a game between the Brooklyn Dodgers and the Philadelphia Phillies

1946
1 June, first TV licences are issued in the UK (cost £2)
7 June, BBC television broadcasts resume

7 July, first British children's TV programme, *For the Children*, is broadcast

1947
21 February, America's first regular daytime serial, or soap opera, *A Woman to Remember*, begins its run

1948
29 July, London Olympic Games is televised

1951
24 December, in the USA *Amahl and The Night Visitors* becomes the world's first commercial colour broadcast

Radio milestones

1896
2 June, Italian inventor Guglielmo Marconi applies for first British "wireless" patent

1906
24 December, first radio programme (music and speech) broadcast by Professor Reginald Fessenden from the US coast and received by ships.

1920
15 June, Marconi broadcasts a concert by opera singer Dame Nellie Melba

1922
18 October, BBC (British Broadcasting Company) founded. The first BBC broadcast was made on 14 November – the six o'clock news read by Arthur Burrows

1923
26 April, first daily weather forecast by the BBC

1926
24 January, launch of *The Week's Good Cause*, the BBC's longest-running programme

1933
28 August, first BBC woman announcer, Sheila Borrett

1939–45
During World War II the BBC provides information and stirring speeches from Winston Churchill and other wartime leaders

1951
1 January, launch of *The Archers*, longest-running BBC radio serial

1964
Pirate radio stations broadcast from ships to UK, encouraging the BBC to launch a pop music station (Radio 1, 30 September 1967)

1993
First Internet radio broadcasts

1995
First experimental DAB (digital audio broadcasting) in UK. DAB gives listeners better quality reception, easy tuning and text information

2002
BBC launches five new DAB channels

2005
BBC radio begins to make programmes available as podcasts that can be downloaded to computers, MP3 and DAB players

2007
Internet radio becomes available to mobile phones

2009
More than 1,800 US radio stations use HD radio technology that allows high quality digital and analogue signals and text data to be broadcast simultaneously.

Why soap opera?

Radio (and later TV) serials about everyday life in the USA have been sponsored by soap manufacturers since the 1930s. They advertised their products during the shows. The name of these serials has been shortened to soaps since 1943.

www.bbc.co.uk   search

Portable radio from the 1950s

2000s

1953
2 June, the coronation of Queen Elizabeth II is watched live by about 20 million people in the UK and 200 million worldwide
21 November, current affairs programme Panorama is launched; goes on to become the longest-running programme on British TV

1954
1 January, the *Tournament of Roses* parade at Pasadena, California, USA, becomes the first programme ever broadcast coast-to-coast

11 January, first TV weather forecast in the UK
9 April, Britain's first TV soap opera, *The Grove Family*

1955
22 September, first TV advert in the UK, for Gibbs SR toothpaste

1957
13 May, first schools programmes broadcast in UK
25 December, the Queen's first TV Christmas message broadcast

1958
16 October, *Blue Peter* starts, and becomes the longest-running children's programme

1969
21 July, first live broadcasts from the Moon (*Apollo XI*)
15 November, BBC1 and ITV start broadcasting in colour

1981
1 August, MTV launched; The Buggles' *Video Killed the Radio Star* the first music video to be broadcast

1989
5 February, Sky begins satellite broadcasting in the UK

1997
9 November, BBC1 begins broadcasting 24 hours a day, seven days a week (previously, TV closed down at night)

2000
18 July, UK launch of *Big Brother* starts a fashion for reality TV

2006
High Definition television (HDTV) becomes available in the UK and other countries

2008
SED (Surface-conduction electron-emitter display) high definition televisions go on sale

Sports

Winter Olympics

2010 is the year of the XXI Olympic Winter Games. The event is being held in Vancouver, Canada, and more than 5,000 competitors, from over 80 countries, will be involved. More than 80 events will be contested.

Teams and competitors

Team sizes
These are the number of players allowed on a field at any one time. The full team can also include some substitutes. In football, for example, there are 45 full-time team members. Different players come on the field for defensive and offensive moves.

Sport	Team on pitch
Australian Rules football	18
Rugby Union	15
Rugby League	13
Canadian football, women's lacrosse	12
Football (American), cricket, field hockey, soccer, speedball (paint ball)	11
Men's lacrosse, slow-pitch softball	10
Baseball, fast-pitch softball	9
Tug-of-war	8
Team handball, netball, water polo	7
Ice hockey, volleyball	6
Basketball, roller hockey	5
Polo	4

Most competitors
● The Boston Marathon centenary race in 1996 attracted a record 38,706 competitors, the most ever for a marathon.

● The Athens Olympic Games (2004) had 11,099 competitors, the most of any Olympics.

● The world's biggest road race is the 7.5 mi. (12 km) Bay to Breakers race in San Francisco, California. It has been held every year since 1912. The 1988 race had a record 78,769 official entries, but the total number of people taking part was probably about 110,000, many of them in fancy dress.

● In 1929 the Grand National horse race had a record 66 runners, but only nine reached the finish line.

Most-watched sporting event
The 2008 Beijing Olympics was the most-watched sporting event ever with an estimated 4.7 billion watching on television. Approximately 7 million tickets, for watching events live, were sold.

Sporting sizes

	Dimensions and distances
Blade of an ice skate (width)	1.3 in. (3.3 cm)
Tenpin height	15 in. (38 cm)
Parallel bars in gymnastics (distance between)	16.5 in. (42 cm)
Dartboard diameter	17.7 in. (45 cm)
Basketball (diameter)	29.5–30.25 in. (34.9–76.8 cm)
Tennis net height (at center)	35.8 in. (91 cm)
Hurdles height (men's 400 m)	3 ft. (91.4 cm)
Water polo pool depth (minimum)	3.3 ft. (1 m)
Women's javelin length (minimum)	7.2 ft. (2.2 m)
Soccer goal height	8 ft. (2.44 m)
Men's javelin length (minimum)	8.5 ft. (2.6 m)
Basketball net rim (above floor)	10 ft. (3.05 m)
Table tennis table	5 x 9 ft. (1.5 x 2.7 m)
Snooker table (full size)	6.1 x 12 ft. (1.9 x 3.7 m)
Boxing ring	20 x 20 ft. (6.1 x 6.1 m)
Soccer goal width	24 ft. (7.32 m)
Basketball court (NBA)	50 x 94 ft. (15 x 29 m)
Hockey rink	85 x 200 ft. (26 x 61 m)
Football field (U.S.)	160 x 360 ft. (49 x 110 m)
Indianapolis Motor Speedway (oval track length)	2.5 mi. (4.023 km)
Marathon distance	26 mi., 385 yd. (42.2 km)
Longest hole in open golf (14th at St. Andrews)	1,853 ft. (565 m)
Iditarod dog sled race, Alaska north route (even-numbered years)	1,112 mi. (1,790 km)
south route (odd-numbered years)	1,131 mi. (1,820 km)
Le Mans 24 hour race (greatest distance covered in the time, 1971)	3,314.2 mi. (5,333.7 km)
Tour de France cycle race (record longest, 1926)	3,470 mi. (5,745 km)
Around alone (solo around-the-world yacht race)	28,754.6 mi. (46,276.7 km)

Marathon sprint!
If athletes could run a marathon at the same rate as a 100 m sprint, they would finish in 43 minutes. In reality, no one has run a marathon in under two hours.

Sport origins

Who invented baseball?

Baseball is a much older game than you might think. Medieval manuscripts show ball games with bats, while a game called "base-ball" appears in a picture published in London, England, in 1744. Baseball is also mentioned in Jane Austen's novel *Northanger Abbey*, which she began writing in 1798. The game of "rounders" was first described 30 years later, and this or a similar game was known among British settlers in the U.S. Abner Doubleday is sometimes said to have invented baseball in 1839, but Alexander Joy Cartwright Jr. wrote the game's rules in 1845. He founded the first team, the Knickerbocker Base Ball Club of New York.

When did basketball start?

The inspiration for basketball may have been the Aztec game *ollamalitzli* and other ball and hoop games played by South American peoples. The modern game was invented in 1891 by Canadian physical education teacher Dr. James A. Naismith at the International YMCA College at Springfield, Massachusetts. He wanted to find a game that could be played indoors during the winter. Peach baskets were originally used as goals — players had to climb a ladder to fetch the ball after scoring. Then someone hit on the idea of removing the bottom! The baskets were soon replaced by metal rings with netting.

Sport top speeds

Sport	mph	km/h
Competition rifle bullet	2,353	3,787
Longbow arrow	340	547
Drag racer (0.4 km [0.25 miles] from standing start)	332	535
Free-fall skydiver	330	531
Pelota (jai-alai) ball	188	302
Indy 500 racing car (record, 1990)	186	299
Golf ball (leaving tee)	170	273
Downhill skier (record)	154	248
Squash ball (record, 1988)	151	243
Tennis serve (record, 2004)	155	249
Racing car (Formula One)	148	238
Water skiing (record, 1983)	143	230
Isle of Man TT race (record, 2007)	130	209
Snowboarding (record)	126	202
Ski-bob (record, 2003)	125	201
Ice hockey puck	118	190
Table tennis ball	106	170
Baseball (pitched)	101	162
Cricket bowl (record, 2003)	100	161
Luge	85	137
Frisbee	74	119
Cyclist (record, 2008)	82	132
Skateboard (record, 1998)	63	101
4-man bobsleigh	56	90
Racehorse	45	72
Greyhound	42	67
100-m sprinter	37	59
Boxing punch	35	56
Karate chop	32	51

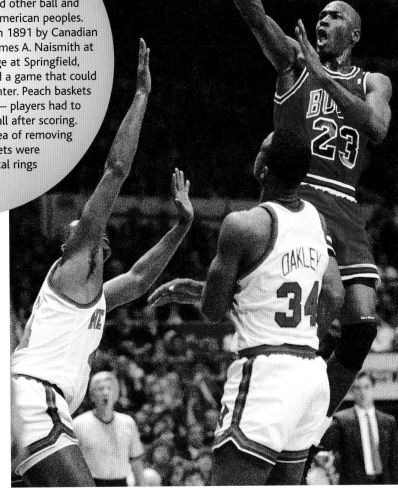

Famous U.S. basketball player Michael Jordan about to score

Longest events

● In Formula One motor racing, the 17-race season (2009) is spread over eight months.

● The Tour d'Afrique cycle race includes 100 days of cycling and 20 days of rest.

● The Tour de France lasts 22 days (with rest days).

● The Iditarod dog sled race, held in Alaska, lasts nine days.

● The 10th Volvo Ocean Race (formerly the Whitbread Round the World Race) started from Alicante (Spain) in October 2008 and ended eight and a half months later at St. Petersburg, Russia, after a total of 36,995 nautical miles.

● The longest boxing match with gloves was a 100-round bout between Andy Bowen and Jack Burke (both U.S.). It started at 9:15 p.m. on Thursday, April 6, 1893, and finished at 4:34 a.m. on Friday, April 7, — a total of 7 hours, 19 minutes.

Oldest sporting events

Doggett's Coat and Badge Race is the world's oldest continuous sporting event. It is a rowing contest held on the River Thames in England and has been held every year since 1715. The Newmarket Town Plate horse race is even older, but the race was discontinued for a while.

Event	First held	Event	First held
Newmarket Town Plate horse race	1665	Stanley Cup ice hockey competition	1893
Doggett's Coat and Badge Race (rowing)	1715	U.S. Open golf championship	1895
Real Tennis Championship	1740	Davis Cup tennis tournament	1900
St. Leger horse race	1776	Baseball World Series	1903
Epsom Derby horse race	1780	Tour de France cycle race	1903
County Cricket Championship	1827	Ryder Cup golf tournament	1927
Oxford and Cambridge Boat Race	1829	Commonwealth Games	1930
Grand National steeplechase	1836	FIFA Soccer World Cup	1930
Henley Regatta	1839	NASCAR racing	1949
British Open golf championship	1860	Formula One World Championship	1950
Melbourne Cup horse race	1861	Canadian Grand Prix (Formula One)	1967
America's Cup yachting series	1870	Super Bowl football championship	1967
Football Association Challenge Cup	1872	Athletics World Cup	1977
Kentucky Derby horse race	1875	World Athletics Championships	1983
Wimbledon Lawn Tennis Championships	1877	Breeders' Cup horse race series	1984

Grand National steeplechase (19th century)

Top sporting events

These are the leading events in the world's most popular sports, in addition to the Olympic Games.

Athletics IAAF (International Association of Athletic Federations)

Auto racing NASCAR Nextel Cup, Indianapolis 500, World Formula One Championship

Baseball World Series

Basketball NBA (National Basketball Association) Final

Cycling Tour de France

Football Super Bowl

Golf U.S. Open, U.S. Masters, U.S. PGA, British Open

Hockey Stanley Cup

Horse racing Kentucky Derby, Breeders' Cup, Epsom Derby, Grand National

Marathons New York City Marathon

Rallying (off-road race) Dakar Rally

Soccer FIFA World Cup (every four years)

Tennis U.S. Open, Wimbledon Championships

Motor cycling MotoGP world championship

See also
Major rock events: page 255

Sports timeline

Experts argue about the exact origins of many sports. The dates here are generally agreed to be when these sports were first played or contested on an organized basis.

Sport	Date	Sport	Date	Sport	Date
Athletics	3800 BC	Soccer	1848	Motor racing	1887
Horse racing	AD 1540	Tenpin bowling	1850	Basketball	1891
Boxing	1681	Show jumping	1864	Darts	1896
Rowing	1715	Cycling	1867	Motorcycling	1896
Ice skating	1742	Badminton	1873	Speedway	1902
Cricket	1744	Lawn tennis	1873		
Golf	1744	Football	1874		
Swimming	1791	Hockey (field)	1875		
Baseball	1839	Hockey (ice)	1887		

Bare-knuckle boxing match (1820)

Biggest soccer crowd

The biggest-ever crowd for a soccer match was at the 1950 World Cup Final. The match between Brazil and Uruguay at the Maracanã Stadium (now called the Journalista Mário Filho Stadium) in Brazil was watched by 199,854 people.

The Journalista Mário Filho Stadium in Rio de Janeiro, Brazil, was built for the 1950 World Cup and held almost 200,000 people.

Biggest crowds

In the past, more than 100,000 people at a time crammed into the Rose Bowl Stadium in Pasadena, California, and other venues to watch their favorite sports. Today, there are laws that limit the number of people allowed in a sports stadium. Outdoor events such as the New York City Marathon and the Tour de France now draw the biggest crowds. They are held over open roads and people don't have to pay to watch them.

- About 2.5 million people watch the New York Marathon — the biggest crowd for a single day at a sporting event.

- As many as 15 million people turn out to see the Tour de France during its three weeks.

- The record crowd for a golf tournament was set at the U.S. Open, Flushing Meadows, 2005, which was attended by 659,538 people.

- Some of the biggest crowds at U.S. and Canadian sporting events are for Indy car races. About 270,000 fans attend the Indianapolis 500 every year and as many as 332,000 attended the 2006 Canadian Grand Prix in Montreal.

- In horse racing, a record 163,628 saw Cannonade win the 100th Kentucky Derby in 1974. A total of 156,635 attended the Kentucky Derby in 2007.

Elephant polo

Elephant polo is the same as conventional polo but played on elephants rather than horses. The elephants are ridden by two players, one who steers and the other who hits the ball. The sport was first played by the English in India in the 19th century and a world championship has been staged since 1982.

Sports on TV

TV audiences for many sporting events were larger 30 years ago than they are today. Fewer people had televisions, but there were not as many channels and no video recorders, so more people watched events live.

UK event	Audience*
World Cup Final, England v West Germany, 1966	32,500,000
World Cup, Brazil v England, 1970	32,500,000
FA Cup Final replay, Chelsea v Leeds United, 1970	32,000,000
World Heavyweight boxing match, Muhammad Ali v Joe Frazier, 1970	27,000,000

U.S. event	Audience*
Super Bowl XLIII, Pittsburgh Steelers v Arizona Cardinals, 2009	151,600,000
Super Bowl XLII, New York Giants v New England Patriots, 2008	148,300,000
Super Bowl XXXVIII, New England Patriots v Carolina Panthers, 2004	143,600,000
Super Bowl XL, Pittsburgh Steelers v Seattle Seahawks, 2006	141,400,000
Super Bowl XLI, Indianapolis Colts v Chicago Bears, 2007	140,000,000
Super Bowl XXXVII, Tampa Bay Buccaneers v Oakland Raiders, 2003	138,900,000
Super Bowl XXX, Dallas Cowboys v Pittsburgh Steelers, 1996	138,488,000
Super Bowl XXVIII, Dallas Cowboys v Buffalo Bills, 1994	134,800,000

Summer Olympics

The modern Olympic Games have been held every four years since 1896, except during World Wars I and II. Over this time the numbers of competitors, events and nations taking part have all increased dramatically.

Winter Paralympic events for athletes with disabilities have been held since 1976. The Summer Paralympics began in 1960 and were first held in conjunction with the regular Summer Olympics in 1988.

Year/City/country	Competitors	No. of nations	Events	Most golds	Most medals
1896 Athens, Greece	245	14	43	U.S. 11	Greece 47
1900 Paris, France	1,225	26	95	France 26	France 95
1904 St Louis, U.S.	687	13	91	U.S. 79	U.S. 245
1906 Athens, Greece	884	20	76	France 15	France 40
1908 London, UK	2,035	22	110	UK 54	UK 138
1912 Stockholm, Sweden	2,547	28	102	U.S. 25	Sweden 64
1920 Antwerp, Belgium	2,669	29	154	U.S. 41	U.S. 95
1924 Paris, France	3,092	44	126	U.S. 45	U.S. 99
1928 Amsterdam, Netherlands	3,014	46	109	U.S. 22	U.S. 56
1932 Los Angeles, U.S.	1,408	37	117	U.S. 41	U.S. 103
1936 Berlin, Germany	4,066	49	129	Germany 33	Germany 89
1948 London, UK	4,099	59	136	U.S. 38	U.S. 84
1952 Helsinki, Finland	4,925	69	149	U.S. 40	U.S. 76
1956* Melbourne, Australia	3,342	72	145	USSR 37	USSR 98
1960 Rome, Italy	5,348	83	150	USSR 43	USSR 103
1964 Tokyo, Japan	5,140	93	163	U.S. 36	U.S. 90
1968 Mexico City, Mexico	5,531	112	172	U.S. 45	U.S. 107
1972 Munich, West Germany	7,123	121	195	USSR 50	USSR 99
1976 Montreal, Canada	6,028	92	198	USSR 49	USSR 125
1980 Moscow, USSR	5,217	80	203	USSR 80	USSR 195
1984 Los Angeles, U.S.	6,797	140	221	U.S. 83	U.S. 174
1988 Seoul, South Korea	8,465	159	237	USSR 55	USSR 132
1992 Barcelona, Spain	9,367	169	257	EUN† 45	EUN 112
1996 Atlanta, U.S.	10,744	197	271	U.S. 44	U.S. 101
2000 Sydney, Australia	10,651	199	300	U.S. 39	U.S. 97
2004 Athens, Greece	11,099	202	301	U.S. 35	U.S. 103
2008 Beijing, China	11,028	204	302	China 51	U.S. 110

* The equestrian events in 1956 were held in Stockholm, Sweden, from June 10–17, because of quarantine restrictions in Australia at the time.

† The Unified Team (EUN) was made up of the former Soviet republics of Russia, Ukraine, Kazakhstan and Uzbekistan.

Out of the Olympics

Various sports have been dropped from the Olympic Games over the years. These include croquet, underwater swimming, duelling pistol shooting, stone-throwing, lacrosse, archery with live birds, tug-of-war, club-swinging and rope climbing.

Beijing 2008 medal table

	Country	gold	silver	bronze	Total
			Medals		
1	China	51	21	28	100
2	U.S.	36	38	36	110
3	Russia	23	21	28	72
4	Great Britain	19	13	15	47
5	Germany	16	10	15	41
6	Australia	14	15	17	46
7	South Korea	13	10	8	31
8	Japan	9	6	11	26
9	Italy	8	10	10	28
10	France	7	16	17	40
11	Ukraine	7	5	15	27
12	Netherlands	7	5	4	16

The Olympic flag

The five-ring Olympic flag was first raised at the 1920 Antwerp Olympics. The rings on the flag represent the five major regions of the world: the Americas, Europe, Asia, Africa and Australasia. At least one of the colors on the flag (blue, yellow, black, green and red) can be found on the flags of every nation in the world.

Beijing records

At Beijing in 2008, 43 new world records were set and 132 new Olympic records established. A record 87 countries won a medal. Afghanistan, Bahrain, Mauritius, Sudan, Tajikistan and Togo all won their first ever Olympic medals.

Olympic firsts   1800s

1896 First modern Olympics. Doves released to symbolize peace

1896 First American gold medal winner, James Connolly (triple jump)

1900 First women competitors. First woman to win a gold medal, Charlotte Cooper from Great Britain for tennis

1908 First parade of athletes with national flags

1908 First athlete to win ten gold medals (in four Olympics, 1900, 1904, 1906 and 1908), Ray Ewry (U.S.)

1912 Electronic timing and photo-finish equipment first used

1920 Olympic oath, "We swear that we will take part in the Olympic Games in a spirit of chivalry, for the honor of our country and for the glory of sport," first taken, by Belgian fencer Victor Boin

1920 Olympic flag first raised

1924 First Olympics with more than 100 women competitors (there were 136 women and 2,956 men)

1924 First live radio transmissions of events

1928 First Olympic flame, large results display board first used

Michael Phelps

Michael Phelps created history at the Beijing Olympics when he won eight gold medals, beating the previous record of seven golds at one games by fellow American Mark Spitz in 1972. Having also won six at the 2004 Athens Olympics, Phelps took his Olympic total to 16, including a record 14 golds.

The spectacular opening ceremony at the 2008 Beijing Olympics

Top medal winners

These athletes have won the most medals in the history of the Summer Olympics from 1896–2008.

Athlete	Sport	Years	Gold	Silver	Bronze	Total
Larissa Latynina (USSR)	Gymnastics	1956–64	9	5	4	18
Michael Phelps (U.S.)	Swimming	2004-08	14	0	2	16
Nikolai Andrianov (USSR)	Gymnastics	1972–80	7	5	3	15
Boris Shakhlin (USSR)	Gymnastics	1956–64	7	4	2	13
Edoardo Mangiarotti (Italy)	Fencing	1936–60	6	5	2	13
Takashi Ono (Japan)	Gymnastics	1952–64	5	4	4	13
Paavo Nurmi (Finland)	Athletics	1920–28	9	3	0	12
Sawao Kato (Japan)	Gymnastics	1968–76	8	3	1	12
Alexei Nemov (Russia)	Gymnastics	1996–2000	4	2	6	12

Athlete Ray Ewry (U.S.) won only ten medals but they were all gold! He still holds the record for the most individual gold medals. Ewry won his medals between 1900 and 1908 in the standing jump events: high jump, long jump and triple jump. Amazingly, Ewry had suffered polio as a child, but overcame his illness to become one of the greatest athletes ever.

2000s

1928 First women competitors in track and field events
1932 First Olympic logo, three-tier victory stand, national anthem played and flag raised for winner
1936 Introduction of Olympic torch relay (from Olympia, Greece, to Berlin, Germany)

1936 Games televised for the first time
1956 Athletes enter closing ceremony together to symbolize unity
1956 First games in the southern hemisphere (Melbourne, Australia)
1960 First Summer Paralympics, held in Rome, Italy

1960 Worldwide TV coverage for the first time
1984 Professionals allowed to compete for the first time
2004 Women competed in freestyle wrestling for first time.

Ukraine, Japan and China all won gold medals
2004 First Olympics broadcast over the Internet
2008 BMX cycling events introduced

 www.olympic.org **search**

Cuban high jumper Javier Sotomayor

1 second improvement in 96 years!

The first official IAAF world record for the 100 meters was in 1912 when Don Lippincott (U.S.) registered a time of 10.6 seconds while running in a first round heat at the Stockholm Olympic Games. Nearly 100 years later, that record has been lowered by less than one second. In 1968 Jim Hines (U.S.) broke the 10 second barrier with a new world record of 9.9 seconds. Since the compulsory use of electronic timing in 1977, the 100 meters world record has come down by hundredths, rather than tenths of a second. Calvin Smith (U.S.) set a new mark of 9.93 seconds in 1983 and Carl Lewis (U.S.) then twice set new records of 9.92 and 9.86. Maurice Greene (U.S.) took the record down from 9.84 to 9.79 seconds in 1999 and the next significant drop in the record occurred at the Beijing Olympics in 2008 when Usain Bolt of Jamaica lowered his own world record from 9.72 seconds to a remarkable 9.69 seconds.

Running a mile

For decades, athletes struggled to run a mile in less than four minutes. At 6:07 p.m. on May 6, 1954, British runner Roger Bannister eventually broke the record. He ran a mile in 3 minutes, 59.4 seconds at the Iffley Road track in Oxford.

Since that historic day, Bannister's record has been beaten many times. The current record speed for running a mile is 3 minutes, 43.13 seconds.

Marathon

The race takes its name from a place called Marathon in Greece, which was the scene of a battle between Athenian and Persian troops in 490 BC.

The Athenians won and supposedly sent a messenger named Pheidippides from Marathon to Athens to spread the news — a distance of about 25 mi. (40.2 km). It is said that Pheidippides dropped dead after delivering his message! The current marathon distance of 26 mi., 385 yd. (42.2 km) was first used at the 1908 Olympics in London, England. It was worked out so that the race from Windsor would finish in front of the Royal Box at the White City Stadium. This distance has been the standard for all marathons since 1924.

Marathon fact file

Hundreds of marathon races are held all over the world every year. There is an Antarctica Marathon, a Sahara Marathon and even a nighttime marathon, run in Marburg, Germany. The following are some of the biggest and most popular events.

Boston Marathon
This race has been held since 1897 and is run on Patriots' Day every April. It is the oldest marathon in the United States and one of the world's most important road races. Kenya's Robert Kipkoech Cheruiyot won the race in 2003, 2006, 2007 and 2008.

New York City Marathon
First held in 1970, the race goes through all five boroughs of New York and finishes in Central Park. It is usually held on the first Sunday in November. In 2006 a world record 37,850 competitors finished the race.

Chicago Marathon
The Chicago Marathon began in 1977. It was originally called the Mayor Daley Marathon after Chicago mayor Richard J. Daley, who died in office in 1976. Khalid Khannouchi of Morocco won the men's race a record four times between 1997 and 2002.

Track and field records

These are the current world records for major track and field events as of January 1, 2008. Most events have both male and female record holders. A few events are contested by only men or women. (Country abbreviations are found on page 318.)

Event		Time (min:sec)	Record holder	Date
100 m	(m)	9.69	Usain Bolt (Jam)	2008
	(w)	10.49	Florence Griffith-Joyner (U.S.)	1988
200 m	(m)	19.30	Usain Bolt (Jam)	2008
	(w)	21.34	Florence Griffith-Joyner (U.S.)	1988
400 m	(m)	43.18	Michael Johnson (U.S.)	1999
	(w)	47.60	Marita Koch (GDR)	1985
800 m	(m)	1:41.11	Wilson Kipketer (Den)	1997
	(w)	1:53.28	Jarmila Kratochvílová (Cze)	1983
1500 m	(m)	3:26.00	Hicham El Guerrouj (Mar)	1998
	(w)	3:50.46	Qu Yunxia (Chn)	1993
1 mile	(m)	3:43.13	Hicham El Guerrouj (Mar)	1999
	(w)	4:12.56	Svetlana Masterkova (Rus)	1996
5,000 m	(m)	12:37.35	Kenenisa Bekele (Eth)	2004
	(w)	14:11.15	Tirunesh Dibaba (Eth)	2008
10,000 m	(m)	26:17.53	Kenenisa Bekele (Eth)	2005
	(w)	29:31.78	Wang Junxia (Chn)	1993
3,000 m steeplechase	(m)	7:53.63	Saaeed Shaheen (Qat)	2004
	(w)	8:58:81	Gulnara Galkina-Samitova (Rus)	2008
110 m hurdles	(m)	12.87	Dayron Robles (Cub)	2008
100 m hurdles	(w)	12.21	Yordanka Donkova (Bul)	1988
400 m hurdles	(m)	46.78	Kevin Young (U.S.)	1992
	(w)	52.34	Yuliya Pechonkina (Rus)	2003
4 x 100 m relay	(m)	37.10	Jamaica	2008
	(w)	41.37	GDR	1985
4 x 400 m relay	(m)	2:54.20	U.S.	1998
	(w)	3:15.17	USSR	1988

Event		Ht/lgth (m)	Record holder	Date
High jump	(m)	2.45	Javier Sotomayor (Cub)	1993
	(w)	2.09	Stefka Kostadinova (Bul)	1987
Pole vault	(m)	6.14	Sergey Bubka (Ukr)	1994
	(w)	5.05	Yelena Isinbayeva (Rus)	2008
Long jump	(m)	8.95	Mike Powell (U.S.)	1991
	(w)	7.52	Galina Chistyakova (USSR)	1988
Triple jump	(m)	18.29	Jonathan Edwards (GBR)	1995
	(w)	15.50	Inessa Kravets (Ukr)	1995
Shot	(m)	23.12	Randy Barnes (U.S.)	1990
	(w)	22.63	Natalya Lisovskaya (USSR)	1987
Discus	(m)	74.08	Jürgen Schult (GDR)	1986
	(w)	76.80	Gabriele Reinsch (GDR)	1988
Hammer	(m)	86.74	Yuriy Sedykh (USSR)	1986
	(w)	77.80	Tatyana Lysenko (Rus)	2006
Javelin	(m)	98.48	Jan Zelezny (Cze)	1996
	(w)	72.28	Barbara Spotakova (Cze)	2008

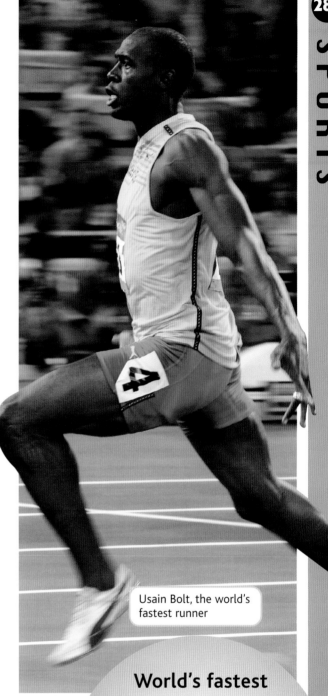

Usain Bolt, the world's fastest runner

World's fastest

The world's fastest man is Usain Bolt of Jamaica who ran the 100 meters in 9.69 seconds during the Beijing Olympics on August 16, 2008.

The world's fastest woman was Florence Griffith-Joyner (U.S.), who died in 1998. She ran the 100 m in 10.49 seconds in Indianapolis in 1988. The fastest living woman is Marion Jones (U.S.). She ran the 100 m in 10.65 seconds in Johannesburg in 1998.

London Marathon
Dionico Cerón (Mexico), António Pinto (Portugal) and Martin Lel (Kenya) have each won the men's race a record three times. Ingrid Kristiansen (Norway) won the women's race four times between 1984 and 1988.

Marathon record holders
The current male record holder, Haile Gebreselassie (Ethiopia), ran the Berlin Marathon in 2 hours 3 minutes 59 seconds on September 28, 2008. The female record is held by Paula Radcliffe (UK), who ran the London Marathon on April 13, 2003, in 2 hours, 15 minutes, 25 seconds.

See also

Ancient Greece: page 106

www.ingnycmarathon.org

search

Yankees All-Star Alex Rodriguez

Baseball

Baseball is one of the most popular sports in Canada and the U.S. and is also played in Japan, Mexico and a number of South American countries. It is played by two teams of nine players each.

Games that resemble baseball are shown in medieval manuscripts. In the United States, Alexander Joy Cartwright Jr. drew up baseball's first rules on September 23, 1845. He also founded the first organized team, the Knickerbocker Base Ball Club of New York. The first game of baseball played according to the Cartwright Rules took place at the Elysian Fields, Hoboken, New Jersey, on June 19, 1846 between the New York Nine and the Knickerbocker Club.

Golf majors

The four big competitions in golf are known as the majors. They are the U.S. Masters, British Open, U.S. Open and U.S. PGA Championship, and are played in that order every year.

The Masters, founded in 1934, is the only one of the four played on the same course each year, at Augusta National in Georgia. The oldest of the majors is the British Open, which was first held in 1860. It is also the only one played outside the U.S. The U.S. Open was first played in 1895 and the U.S. PGA in 1916.

Players with most professional major wins

Jack Nicklaus (U.S.) 18:
3 British Open; 4 U.S. Open;
5 U.S. PGA; 6 Masters
Tiger Woods (U.S.) 14:
3 British Open; 3 U.S. Open;
4 U.S. PGA; 4 Masters
Walter Hagen (U.S.) 11:
4 British Open; 2 U.S. Open;
5 U.S. PGA

Ben Hogan (U.S.) 9:
1 British Open; 4 U.S. Open; 2 U.S. PGA;
2 Masters
Gary Player (S. Africa) 9:
3 British Open; 1 U.S. Open; 2 U.S. PGA;
3 Masters
Tom Watson (U.S.) 8:
5 British Open; 1 U.S. Open; 2 U.S. Masters

Basketball

Basketball is hugely popular in the U.S. and is now played in other parts of the world, as well as at the Olympics. The game is played by two teams of five players each, usually on an indoor court.

Players score points by shooting the ball through the basket. The National Basketball Association (NBA) in the U.S. was formed in 1949. It contains 30 teams divided into two conferences, Eastern and Western. At the end of the season the two conference winners meet in a best-of-seven series for the NBA Championship.

Record breakers

Outstanding player Kareem Abdul-Jabbar (Milwaukee Bucks and Los Angeles Lakers) scored a record 38,387 points during his career.

Teams with most wins
Boston Celtics: 17
Minneapolis/Los Angeles Lakers: 14
Chicago Bulls: 6

Corliss Williamson (Sacramento Kings) drives for the basket

Rugby

The game of rugby probably started in 1823 at Rugby School in England, when William Webb Ellis picked up a football and ran with it. The first rules were drawn up in 1848 and the Rugby Football Union (RFU) was formed by Edwin Ash in 1871.

Today's game of Rugby Union is played between two teams of 15 players. The two biggest events are the International Championship and the World Cup. The International Championship began in 1884 and was originally played by four teams: England, Ireland, Scotland and Wales. France joined in 1910 and Italy in 2000, making it a six-nation tournament. The Rugby World Cup was launched in 1987 and has been held every four years since then. In 2003, 20 teams took part and more than 2.25 million people watched the 48 live matches at an average of 47,150 per game.

Rugby League

Rugby League dates from August 29, 1895, when 21 major clubs in the north of England formed a league outside the RFU. They were protesting against the RFU's refusal to pay players who had to take time off work. To make Rugby League less like Rugby Union they changed various rules, including reducing the team size from 15 to 13. Rugby League is now played in Australia, New Zealand, France, Russia and some Pacific nations, as well as in Britain. One of the major events in Rugby League is the Challenge Cup, open to British, French and Russian teams. There is also a Rugby League World Cup, which was last won by New Zealand in 2008.

Softball

Softball (fastpitch and slowpitch) is a form of baseball invented in 1887 as a form of "indoor baseball", although these days it is generally played outdoors.

Some major differences between baseball and softball include: the bat is smaller, and the ball in softball, which is pitched underhand, is bigger than a baseball ball, but not as dense. On the pitch, the base lines are only 60 ft. (18 m) apart in softball (90 ft. [27.4 m] in baseball), the outfield fence is a constant distance from the home plate, and there is no pitcher's mound. There are normally seven innings in softball as opposed to baseball's nine. Both games are played with nine players (slowpitch softball has ten players).

Little league baseball

Little League baseball was inaugurated in 1938 by Carl Stotz, a clerk from Williamsport, Pennsylvania, when, with the help of his nephews and their friends, they started playing their own form of baseball. He felt it would have an appeal to local children and, the following year he and two friends each managed a team in what became the first Little League. The three teams obtained local sponsorship, and the first Little League game was played on June 6, 1939.

From its humble beginnings, Little League baseball has now spread and is played in every state of the U.S. and in more than 100 countries worldwide. There are believed to be more than three million boys and girls between the ages of five and 18 playing either Little League baseball or softball.

Little League World Series

The first Little League World Series was held in Williamsport, Pennsylvania in 1947 when the home team beat Lock Haven, 16–7 in the final. Originally for teams from the United States only, teams from all over the world now take part and in 1960 Berlin (then in West Germany) became the first European team to participate. In that same year, the World Series was broadcast on National Television for the first time.

Children aged 11 to 13 can take part in the Little League World Series, and 16 teams take part each year in two brackets, or 'pools'. Each bracket is sub-divided into two brackets of four teams who play each other once. At the completion of the round robin matches, the top two in each bracket take part in semi-finals, with the eventual winners of the U.S. bracket meeting the International winners in the Little League World Series.

www.nba.com   search

The World Cup

The first soccer World Cup was played in 1930 in Uruguay. Thirteen teams took part and the hosts beat Argentina 4–2 in the final in Montevideo.

The Italian team that won the 2006 World Cup

They won the Jules Rimet trophy, named after the president of FIFA (Fédération Internationale de Football Association) when the competition began. Brazil were allowed to keep the trophy after winning it for the third time in 1970 and it was replaced by the FIFA World Cup trophy. The World Cup final takes place every four years.

Winning country	Year	Winning country	Year
Uruguay	1930	Brazil	1970
Italy	1934	West Germany	1974
Italy	1938	Argentina	1978
Not held	1942	Italy	1982
Not held	1946	Argentina	1986
Uruguay	1950	West Germany	1990
West Germany	1954	Brazil	1994
Brazil	1958	France	1998
Brazil	1962	Brazil	2002
England	1966	Italy	2006

World Cup facts

● The only man to captain and manage a World Cup winning team is Franz Beckenbauer of Germany.

● In the third-place play-off match in 2002, Turkey's Hakan Sükür scored the fastest goal in the competition's history against South Korea after a mere 10.8 seconds — even though the Korean team kicked off!

Most World Cup wins

Brazil	5
Italy	4
West Germany	3
Uruguay	2
Argentina	2

U.S. soccer

Organized soccer was first seen in the United States in 1862. It became a prominent collegiate sport in the 1870s, and on November 28, 1885, the U.S. played Canada in the first soccer international outside Britain.

The United States entered the first World Cup in 1930, losing 6–1 to Argentina in the semi-final, and 20 years later enjoyed their greatest World Cup moment when they beat a star-studded England team 1–0 in one of the biggest World Cup shocks.

The United States won its first major soccer tournament in 1991 beating Norway to win the FIFA Women's World Championship in China.

Most goals (as of January 1, 2008)

Player	Years	Goals
Landon Donovan	2000–2007	34
Eric Wynalda	1990–2000	34
Brian McBride	1993–2006	30
Joe–Max Moore	1992–2002	24
Bruce Murray	1985–1993	21
Earnie Stewart	1990–2004	17
DaMarcus Beasley	2001–2007	15
Cobi Jones	1992–2004	15
Marcelo Balboa	1988–2000	13
Hugo Perez	1984–1994	13
Clint Mathis	1998–2005	12
Frank Klopas	1987–1996	12
Peter Vermes	1988–1998	11
Eddie Johnson	2004–2007	10
William Roy	1965–1973	10

Soccer timeline   1800s

500 BC Football (*tsu chu,* meaning to kick a ball) played in China

1314 First reference to "football" in England when Edward II prohibited the game because "too many people were bustling over footballs on London streets"

1848 The first rules of soccer drawn up at Cambridge University, England

1852 First interschool scoccer game, Westminster vs. Harrow

1855 Sheffield football soccer club, the oldest still in existence, formed in England

1862 Notts County, the oldest current League club, formed

1863 Football Association (FA) formed in England

1870 First international game, England vs. Scotland, played at Kennington Oval

1871 FA Cup launched

1872 Corner kick introduced

1873 Scottish FA formed; Scottish Cup started

1874 Shin pads first worn

1875 The crossbar replaced a tape across the top of the goals

1876 Welsh FA formed

1878 Irish (now Northern Ireland) FA formed

1878 Referee's whistle first used

1885 Professional soccer legalized

1888 Football League of professional soccer clubs from England and Wales formed

1889 The term "soccer" first used in the world; may be an abbreviation of association football — the FA was formed to standardize the rules of the game

1890 Scottish League formed

1891 Goal nets first used

1891 Linesmen (now assistant referees) replace umpires

1891 Penalty kick adopted by the FA

Football records

Dallas Cowboys, Pittsburgh Steelers and San Francisco 49ers have all won the Super Bowl five times.

Morten Andersen is the NFL's record scorer with 2,544 points in regular season games between 1982 and 2007 with New Orleans Saints, Atlanta Falcons (twice), New York Giants, Kansas City Chiefs and Minnesota Vikings.

The New England Patriots (wearing blue and white) have won three Super Bowls this century.

Football

Football, know as American football in other parts of the world, is the number one sport in the United States. The National Football League (NFL) is split into two conferences, the American Football Conference (AFC) and National Football Conference (NFC). Each conference is split into four divisions — North, South, East and West — and each division has four teams.

Each team plays 16 games and the six teams with the best records in both the AFC and NFC take part in the playoffs with the winner of each conference then meeting for the Super Bowl early in February. The winning team receives the Vince Lombardi Trophy.

No.	Year	Winners	No.	Year	Winners	No.	Year	Winners	No.	Year	Winners
I	1967	Green Bay Packers	XII	1978	Dallas Cowboys	XXIII	1989	San Francisco 49ers	XXXIII	1999	Denver Broncos
II	1968	Green Bay Packers	XIII	1979	Pittsburgh Steelers	XXIV	1990	San Francisco 49ers	XXXIV	2000	St Louis Rams
III	1969	New York Jets	XIV	1980	Pittsburgh Steelers	XXV	1991	New York Giants	XXXV	2001	Baltimore Ravens
IV	1970	Kansas City Chiefs	XV	1981	Oakland Raiders	XXVI	1992	Washington	XXXVI	2002	New England Patriots
V	1971	Baltimore Colts	XVI	1982	San Francisco 49ers			Redskins	XXXVII	2003	Tampa Bay Buccaneers
VI	1972	Dallas Cowboys	XVII	1983	Washington Redskins	XXVII	1993	Dallas Cowboys	XXXVIII	2004	New England Patriots
VII	1973	Miami Dolphins	XVIII	1984	Los Angeles Raiders	XXVIII	1994	Dallas Cowboys	XXXIX	2005	New England Patriots
VIII	1974	Miami Dolphins	XIX	1985	San Francisco 49ers	XXIX	1995	San Francisco 49ers	XL	2006	Pittsburgh Steelers
IX	1975	Pittsburgh Steelers	XX	1986	Chicago Bears	XXX	1996	Dallas Cowboys	XLI	2007	Indianapolis Colts
X	1976	Pittsburgh Steelers	XXI	1987	New York Giants	XXXI	1997	Green Bay Packers	XLII	2008	New York Giants
XI	1977	Oakland Raiders	XXII	1988	Washington Redskins	XXXII	1998	Denver Broncos	XLIII	2009	Pittsburgh Stealers

1900s

1904 FIFA formed in Paris; first international game outside Great Britain — Belgium vs. France played near Brussels

1907 Professional Footballers' Association (PFA) formed in the UK (as the Football Players and Trainers Union)

1921 FA of Ireland (Republic of Ireland) formed

1923 First Wembley Cup Final (Bolton vs. West Ham)

1928 Players' numbers introduced

1930 First World Cup in Uruguay

1932 Substitutes formally agreed by FIFA

1954 Union of European Football Associations (UEFA) formed

1955 European Cup started

1960 Football League Cup started

1965 Football League agrees on use of substitutes

1968 Red cards introduced (at the Mexico Olympic Games)

1975 Scottish Premier Division (now Premier League) formed

1981 Football League changed the number of points for a win from two to three

1982 Professional foul rule introduced

1992 FA Premier League formed

2000s

1993 Ch League replaces the European Cup

2004 Greece are surprise winners of the European Championship

2007 David Beckham moves to Los Angeles Galaxy for $150 million over five years

2008 Spain beat Germany to win the European Championship, its first major trophy for 44 years.

 www.fifa.com   search

Badminton

Badminton probably came from an old children's game called "battledore and shuttlecock." The battledore is a small wooden bat that the player uses to hit the shuttlecock. The game was popular in India and other Asian countries, and the aim was to keep the shuttlecock in the air as long as possible. British army officers played the game in India in the 1860s and they added a net to hit the shuttlecock over. They called the game "poona."

When the officers returned to England they continued enjoying poona. The game was renamed badminton at a garden party at the home of the Duke of Beaufort in 1873. His home was called Badminton House. By 1877 the first official rules of the game were drawn up and in 1893 the first governing body, The Badminton Association of England, was set up. The Badminton Club of New York began in 1878, although the game did not become popular until the 1930s.

Badminton's greatest player

American-born Judy Hashman (née Devlin) is the greatest player Badminton has seen, winning a total of 83 major titles including the coveted All-England singles title a record 10 times between 1954 and 1965, five of them in succession. She also won seven doubles titles (four with her sister Susan) making her total of 17 an All-England record.

Pelota

Pelota is the name given to a variety of sports that are played by hitting a ball with the hand, a racquet, or a basket attached to the hand. Pelota and its variations were first played during the 13th century in the Basque region of Spain. There are variations of the game depending upon the equipment used.

- Played with the hand it is called *pelota mano*, or just pelota.

- Played with a racquet, it is called *frontenis*.

- Played with a hand basket, it is called *jai-alai*.

The game is similar to squash — players hit the ball against the end wall of a three-sided court, if possible, out of reach of their opponent. Pelota is popular in Spain, Mexico, South America, Cuba, Italy and many U.S. states, including Florida.

The origin of table tennis

Table tennis is believed to have been first played as an after-dinner game in country houses and army messes in Victorian England. Manufacturers J. Jacques & Son patented the name Ping-Pong in 1901, so other manufacturers used the name table tennis instead. The introduction of celluloid balls and the rubber-faced bat led to table tennis becoming one of the most popular indoor games.

Pelota player in action

Lawn tennis timeline   1800s   2000s

1877 First Wimbledon Championship

1881 First U.S. Championship

1891 First French Championship — until 1925 for French nationals

1896 Tennis played at the first Modern Olympics in Athens

1900 Davis Cup began after Dwight F. Davis donated a trophy

1905 First Australian Open

1913 International Lawn Tennis Federation founded in Paris with 12 member countries

1922 Seeding (method of ranking players) first used, at the U.S. National Championships

1923 Women's tennis became international with the launch of the Wightman Cup (named after U.S. team captain Hazel Wightman)

1938 Donald Budge (U.S.) became the first player to complete the Grand Slam

1950 Louise Brough (U.S.) became the first woman to complete the Grand Slam

1963 The Federation Cup, the women's equivalent of the Davis Cup, began

1968 Tennis tournaments were opened to professional players, effectively ending the amateur game

1971 The tie-break was introduced by the British LTA as an experiment

1972 Davis Cup changed from being run on a challenge basis to a knockout tournament involving all competing nations

1973 Introduction of official world rankings by the ATP and LTA

1988 Tennis revived as an Olympic sport after 64 years

2004 World ranking points first allocated to competitors in the Olympic Games

2008 On 17 August Roger Federer's record run of 237 consecutive weeks at No.1 in the ATP rankings came to an end when he was deposed by Rafael Nadal.

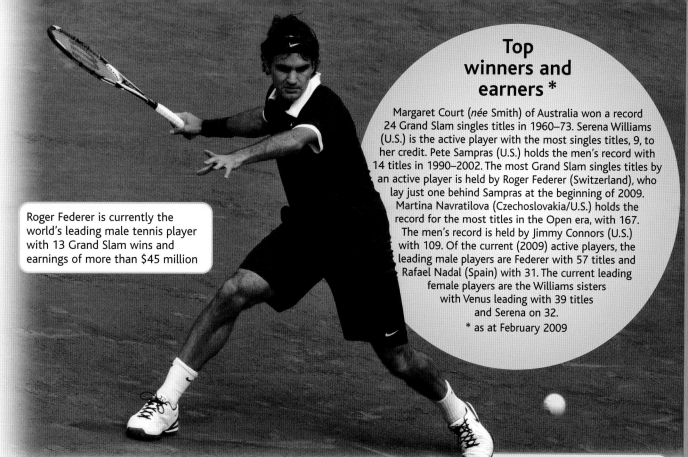

Roger Federer is currently the world's leading male tennis player with 13 Grand Slam wins and earnings of more than $45 million

Top winners and earners *

Margaret Court (*née* Smith) of Australia won a record 24 Grand Slam singles titles in 1960–73. Serena Williams (U.S.) is the active player with the most singles titles, 9, to her credit. Pete Sampras (U.S.) holds the men's record with 14 titles in 1990–2002. The most Grand Slam singles titles by an active player is held by Roger Federer (Switzerland), who lay just one behind Sampras at the beginning of 2009. Martina Navratilova (Czechoslovakia/U.S.) holds the record for the most titles in the Open era, with 167. The men's record is held by Jimmy Connors (U.S.) with 109. Of the current (2009) active players, the leading male players are Federer with 57 titles and Rafael Nadal (Spain) with 31. The current leading female players are the Williams sisters with Venus leading with 39 titles and Serena on 32.

* as at February 2009

Lawn tennis Grand Slam events

The Grand Slam consists of the Australian, French, Wimbledon and U.S. Championships. A player is said to have completed the Grand Slam if he or she holds all four titles simultaneously, although not necessarily in the same year. These events were originally for amateur players but are now open to all, including professionals.

Wimbledon Championships

First held in 1877, Wimbledon is the world's most famous tennis championship. From 1877 to 1921 it was a challenge event with the defending champion qualifying for the next year's final. Women first took part in 1884. Since 1968 Wimbledon has been an open event. This means it is open to all players, including professionals.

U.S. Open

This was first held in 1881. Until 1911, the U.S. tournament operated as a challenge system, with the defending champion automatically going through to the following year's final. Women first competed in 1887. Two championships were held in 1968 and 1969, one for amateurs and an open championship. It became completely open in 1970.

French Open

The French Open was first held in 1891 and until 1925 it was only for French nationals. It became the French Open in 1968 and has been played at the Stade Roland Garros (named after a famous French aviator) since 1928. Women have competed since 1897.

Australian Open

This competition was first held in 1905 as the Australasian Tennis Championship. Women first competed in 1922. The competition became the Australian Championship in 1927, and since 1969 has been the Australian Open. It is played at Melbourne every January.

Most titles in Grand Slams

Australian Roy Emerson won 28 Grand Slam titles between 1961 and 1967. He is the only male player to win singles and doubles titles at all four Grand Slam events. Margaret Court (née Smith), also from Australia, won a record 62 Grand Slam titles, between 1960 and 1973.

Squash champions

Jahangir Khan

Jahangir Khan is the greatest male squash player of all time. He has won six World Open titles, three World Amateur titles, four World Masters and 10 consecutive British Open titles. Khan was born in Karachi in 1963. His father, Roshan, was a British champion, as were Roshan's cousins Hashan and Azam. At one point in his career, Jahangir competed for an amazing five years and eight months without defeat, playing more than 800 games. He was voted Pakistan's Sportsman of the Millennium and elected President of the World Squash Federation in 2002.

Heather McKay

Heather McKay (née Blundell) dominated ladies' squash during the 1960s and 1970s. She was born in New South Wales, Australia, in 1942, the eighth of 11 children. Between 1962 and 1977 she won 16 consecutive British Open titles and remained undefeated for 17 years before her retirement. She lost just two games in her career. In 1999 Heather McKay became a founder member of the WISPA Hall of Fame, and was awarded the Australian Sports Medal in 2000.

Boxing weights

Boxing matches are held between two contestants of similar weight. The weight classes were first used in the 19th century and more were added during the 20th century.

Weight class	Max lb.	(kg)
Strawweight/Mini flyweight	106	(48)
Junior flyweight/ Light flyweight	108	(49)
Flyweight	112	(51)
Junior bantam/ Super flyweight	115	(52)
Bantamweight	119	(54)
Junior featherweight/ Super bantamweight	121	(55)
Featherweight	126	(57)
Junior lightweight/ Super featherweight	130	(59)
Lightweight	134	(61)
Junior welterweight/ Super lightweight	143	(65)
Welterweight	148	(67)
Junior middleweight/ Super welterweight	154	(70)
Middleweight	161	(73)
Super middleweight	168	(76)
Light heavyweight	174	(79)
Cruiserweight	201	(91)
Heavyweight	201	(>91)

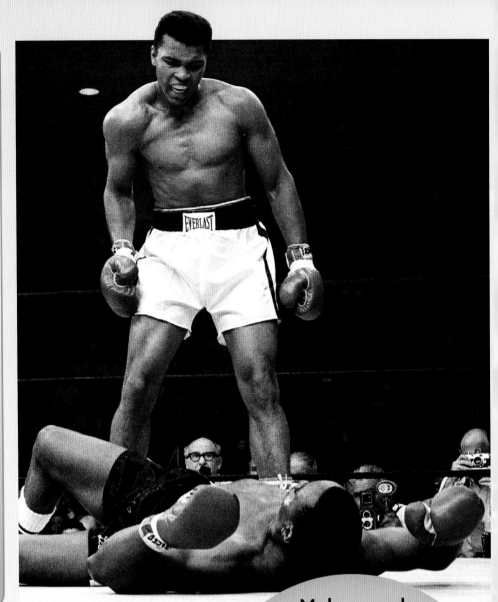

Muhammad Ali defeating Sonny Liston in 1965 to retain his world title.

Boxing's greatest champions

● "Sugar" Ray Robinson was one of the best boxers in any weight division. His first world title was at welterweight in 1946. Moving up a division, he beat Jake La Motta in 1951 to capture the middleweight title. He even had a crack at the light heavyweight title, but failed after a 14th-round knockout. Robinson was born in Detroit in 1920 and turned professional in 1940. He went on to have 201 fights and won 174 of them, 109 with knockouts.

● Oscar de la Hoya from Los Angeles, California, first became famous at the 1992 Barcelona Olympics — he won the U.S.'s only boxing gold that year. La Hoya turned professional after the Olympics. He went on to become only the third man to capture world titles at five different weights, from junior lightweight to junior middleweight. His greatest win was beating his idol Julio Cesar Chavez in four rounds at Caesar's Palace, Las Vegas, in 1996.

● When he beat Oscar de la Hoya in 2007, Floyd Mayweather Jr. joined the ranks of all time greats when he won a world title at a fifth weight. He was regarded as the greatest pound-for-pound fighter by Ring magazine from 2005 until his retirement in June 2008. The son of a former boxer, Mayweather won a bronze medal at the Atlanta Olympics and his first world title in 1998, when he captured the WBC Super-featherweight title. He retired in 2008 undefeated after 39 bouts.

Muhammad Ali

Muhammad Ali was born Cassius Clay in Louisville, Kentucky, in 1942. He burst on to the boxing scene at the 1960 Rome Olympics where he took the light heavyweight gold medal. In 1964, aged 22, he won his first world heavyweight title by beating Sonny Liston. He beat George Foreman 10 years later to become only the second man to regain his title. In 1978, at the age of 36, he beat Leon Spinks to become the first man to win the title a third time. He lost his last world title fight to Larry Holmes in 1980.

Snooker and pool

Snooker was first played by British army officers in India and later became popular in Great Britain, while pool began in the U.S. One of pool's top events is the Mosconi Cup, named after the great American pool player and 14 times world champion Willie Mosconi.

It is now an annual contest in the U.K. and pits the best pool players from the U.S. against those from Europe.

Pool champion

Earl Strickland from Greensboro, North Carolina has won three world Nine-ball titles (1990, 1991, 2002). He has also been the U.S. Open Nine-ball champion five times. Nicknamed "The Pearl," he has appeared in 13 Mosconi Cups, winning 42 matches out of 65.

Snooker champions

The first great champion was Joe Davis who won the professional world title every year from 1927–46. In the modern era the most world titles have been won by:

7 wins Stephen Hendry, Scotland (1990, 1992-96, 1999)

6 wins Ray Reardon, Wales (1970, 1973-76, 1978)

6 wins Steve Davis, England (1981, 1983-84, 1987-89).

Wrestling

The World Wrestling Federation was started in the 1960s as the WorldWide Wrestling Federation (WWWF) by Vince McMahon. In the early 1980s Vince's son, Vince McMahon Jr., renamed it WWF.

The sport changed and became widely popular. Characters such as Hulk Hogan became household names, attracting huge crowds to live matches and millions of followers via TV. The WWF is now known as WWE, World Wrestling Entertainment, Inc. The two biggest events in the WWE calendar are Wrestle Mania, which decides the world champions, and the Royal Rumble. The first WWF Wrestle Mania was at Madison Square Garden on March 31, 1985.

Top wrestlers

● Texan Shawn Michaels is one of the most popular of all wrestlers. He weighs in at about 256 lb. (116 kg). Michaels has won the WWE title, WWE World Heavyweight title, the WWE World Tag Team title and twice won the Royal Rumble, among many other top honors and titles.

● The Rock (real name Dwayne Johnson) is 6.36 ft. (1.94 m) tall and weighs 260 lb. (118 kg). He has been the WWE Champion, the WWE World Tag Team Champion and was the winner of Royal Rumble 2000. He took to the sport after a brief professional football career, and has also appeared in several films, including *The Mummy Returns* (2001), *The Scorpion King* (2002), *The Game Plan* (2007), *Be Cool* (2005), and *Get Smart* (2008).

● Triple H, or "The Game," made his WWE debut in 1995 as Hunter Hearst Helmsley. He weighs about 260 lb. (118 kg). He has been WWE Champion, WWE World Heavyweight Champion, WWE World Tag Team Champion, King of the Ring and Royal Rumble. He is the only man to win the Grand Slam, King of the Ring and Royal Rumble.

"The Undertaker"

Mark William Calaway, known as "The Undertaker," started his wrestling career in 1984 under the name "Texas Red," and is one of WWE's senior fighters. He has won six world titles and the world heavyweight title twice. He won the 2007 Royal Rumble at the age of 42. He has also fought under other names including "Mean" Mark Callous.

Hossein Rezazadeh

Hossein Rezazadeh (Iran) holds the men's weightlifting record. He lifted 1,041.7 lb. (472.5 kg) at the Sydney Olympics in September 2000. This is heavier than a cow!

Weightlifting records

In an Olympic weightlifting competition, contestants perform two types of lifts, the snatch, and the clean and jerk. They have three attempts at each. The score is the total of the best of each type of lift.

In the snatch the contestant lifts the bar from the floor directly above the head and holds it for two seconds. In the clean and jerk the contestant first takes the bar from the floor to the shoulders and then above the head.

The women's world record stands at 723.1 lb (326 kg), set by Jang Mi Ran of South Korea in Beijing on August 16, 2008.

Iranian weightlifter Hossein Rezazadeh

WATER SPORTS

Olympic water sports

Sailing
The first Modern Olympics in 1896 should have included sailing, but the races could not be held because of bad weather. Sailing was included for the first time four years later in Paris and has been a full Olympic sport since 1908. Boardsailing made its debut in 1988. Men and women have competed together in sailing events over the years, but in 1988 women had events of their own. Until the 2000 Olympics, sailing was known as yachting.

Top gold-medal winning nations (1900–2008)
UK 28
U.S. 20
Norway 17

Rowing
Rowing was to have been part of the 1896 Olympics, but the events were canceled. It was first included in Paris four years later, and has appeared at every Olympics since. Women first competed in 1976.

Top gold-medal winning nations (1900–2008)
East Germany 33
U.S. 31
Great Britain 24
Germany/United Germany 23

Canoeing
Canoeing was first included as a demonstration sport in 1924, and did not become a full Olympic sport until 1936. Women took part for the first time in 1948.

Top gold-medal winning nations (1936–2008)
USSR/Unified Team 31
Germany/United Germany 29
Hungary 19
Sweden 15
East Germany 14

Michael Phelps swimming in the 2004 Olympic Games

Michael Phelps

Before he went to Beijing for the 2008 Olympics, American swimmer Michael Phelps was already one of the great Olympians with six gold medals and two bronzes to his credit from the 2004 Athens Games. Phelps also had seven golds from the previous year's world championships and had his sights firmly set on equalling the great achievement of Mark Spitz in winning seven golds at one Olympics — but went one better with eight gold medals.

Michael Phelps' gold medals at the 2008 Olympics

Event	Time (min:sec)
400 m individual medley	4:03.34 (WR)
4 x 100 m freestyle relay	3:08.24 (WR)
200 m freestyle	1:42.96 (WR)
200 m butterfly	1:52.03 (WR)
4 x 200 m freestyle relay	6:58.56 (WR)
200 m individual medley	1:54.23 (WR)
100 m butterfly	50.58 (OR)
4 x 100 m medley relay	3:29.34 (WR)

(WR) = World Record, (OR) = Olympic Record

Start of the men's coxless fours rowing final at the 2004 Olympic Games.

Rowing knights
British rower Steve Redgrave won gold medals at five consecutive Olympic Games (1984–2000), while Matthew Pinsent won gold medals at four consecutive Games — in coxless pairs (with Steve Redgrave) in 1992 and 1996 and coxless fours in 2000 and 2004. Pinsent and Redgrave were knighted for their rowing achievements.

Olympic swimming

These are the top medal-winning Olympic swimmers. Totals include medals won in relays.

Swimmer	Gold	Silver	Bronze	Total
Men				
Michael Phelps (U.S.)	14	0	2	16
Mark Spitz (U.S.)	9	1	1	11
Matt Biondi (U.S.)	8	2	1	11
Gary Hall Jr. (U.S.)	5	3	2	10
Women				
Jenny Thompson (U.S.)	8	3	1	12
Dara Torres (U.S.)	4	4	4	12
Natalie Coughlin U.S.)	3	4	4	11
Dawn Fraser (Australia)	4	4	0	8
Kornelia Ender (GDR)	4	4	0	8
Shirley Babashoff (U.S.)	2	6	0	8
Inge de Bruijn (Netherlands)	4	2	2	8
Petria Thomas (Australia)	3	4	1	8

Olympic Tarzans

Johnny Weissmuller won the 100 m freestyle at the 1924 Paris Olympics. He went on to win a total of five golds and one bronze medal during his Olympic career. While training for the 1932 Olympics, he was offered a $500-a-week contract to advertise swimwear. A Hollywood executive saw the ads and offered Weissmuller the role of Tarzan. In 1932 he made his debut in the film *Tarzan the Ape Man*. He played the character in 11 more films over the next 16 years. He was the first of four Olympic medalists to play the film role. The others were Buster Crabbe (freestyle swimmer), Herman Brix (shot put) and Glenn Morris (decathlon).

The America's Cup

The America's Cup is the top sailing trophy and one of the best known trophies in the sporting world. It began in 1851 when the English Royal Yacht Squadron organized a 6-mi. (10 km) regatta of 17 boats around the Isle of Wight. The 102-ft. (31 m) American schooner *America* entered and won the trophy, then called the One Hundred Guinea Cup.

Swimming strokes

Breaststroke
The breaststroke was the first stroke used in competitive and recreational swimming. It is also the stroke that many people learn when they first take up swimming. The first reference to the breaststroke was in a French book in 1696. The sidestroke, with a scissor leg action, developed from breaststroke. Top swimmers can swim the breaststroke at 4.5 ft. (1.37 m) a second.

Backstroke
The backstroke is the only stroke in which the swimmers start in the water, rather than diving in. The stroke, in which swimmers lie on their backs and use their arms in a windmill motion, was first made popular in the U.S. by Harry Hebner in 1912. An earlier form of the backstroke was first seen at the 1900 Olympics. For this fast stroke, top speed is about 5 ft. (1.52 m) a second.

Butterfly
In this stroke, both arms enter and leave the water at the same time, while the legs perform a dolphin kick. It was developed in the 1930s and evolved from the breaststroke. Swimming coach David Armbruster developed the arm movement of the stroke at the University of Iowa in 1934 and the following year one of his swimmers, Jack Sieg, developed the foot and leg movements. The two combined produced the butterfly. The stroke was not officially approved until 1953 and became an Olympic event in 1956. Maximum speed is 5.5 ft. (1.67 m) a second.

Front crawl/freestyle
In 1844 two Native Americans competing in a swimming regatta in London, England, introduced their new revolutionary overarm stroke. Flying Gull beat Tobacco to take the winner's medal. The stroke was later developed by Englishman John Trudgen, and then by Australian Richard Cavill, who realized the importance of kicking the feet at the same time as moving the arms. Front crawl is the fastest swimming stroke and has a maximum speed of 5.6 ft. (1.71 m) a second.

Competitors in the America's Cup, 2003

After *America*'s win, the trophy was renamed the America's Cup and given to the New York Yacht Club. There it remained unless won by a challenger. Over the next 132 years the New York Yacht Club successfully defended the trophy against 25 challengers, until in 1983 it was won by Australia. In 2003 the trophy returned to Europe when Russell Coutts in *Alinghi* won for Switzerland — a landlocked country! The latest Cup was held at Valencia, Spain, in 2007, and was once again won by *Alinghi* for Switzerland.

WHEEL SPORTS

Tour de France

The oldest and best-known of the world's great cycling tours is the Tour de France. The others are the Vuelta (Tour of Spain) and Giro (Tour of Italy).

- The Tour de France was first staged in 1903 when the course was made up of six stages over 1,509 mi. (2,428 km). Now the race is 3,000 mi. (4,830 km) or more and the course takes in more than 20 stages, often going into neighboring countries.

- The famous yellow jersey (*maillot jaune*) is worn by the current overall time leader in a race. It was first worn in 1919.

- The longest race was in 1926 when Lucien Buysse of Belgium won after 3,570 mi. (5,745 km).

- Around 15 million people every year line the streets to watch the Tour de France over its three weeks.

- The first U.S. winner of the Tour de France was Greg LeMond who won it in 1986, and again in 1989 and 1990. He was also the first English-speaking winner of the race.

- Eddie Merckx has won more of the big three tours than any other man. He has won the Tour de France five times, the Giro five times and the Vuelta once.

Olympic cycling

Cycling was included in the first Modern Olympics in 1896. Léon Flameng (France) won the first cycling gold in the 100 km race. Only two men competed — Flameng and Georgios Kolettis of Greece — and they had to race around a 1,093.5 ft. (333.3 m) track 300 times! During the race, Kolettis's bicycle needed repairing, so Flameng waited for him while the repairs were carried out. Cycling has been included in every Olympics since then. Below are the current Olympic events (BMX racing will be introduced in 2008).

Men
Track
  Sprint (1,000 m)
  Time trial (1,000 m)
  Individual pursuit (4,000 m)
  Team pursuit (4,000 m)
  Points race (40 km)
  Madison (60 km)
  Keirin (2,000 m)
Road
  Road race (individual)
  Time trial (individual)
  BMX (individual)
Mountain bike
  Cross-country

Women
Track
  Sprint (1,000 m)
  Time trial (500 m)
  Individual pursuit (3,000 m)
  Points race (25 km)
Road
  Road race (individual)
  Time trial (individual)
  BMX (individual)
Mountain bike
  Cross-country

Chris Hoy

In winning three gold medals at the Beijing Olympics in 2008, Chris Hoy of Scotland became the first Brit to win three golds at one Games since swimmer Henry Taylor in 1908. He was knighted in 2009.

Mountain biking

Mountain biking, or off-road biking, was started in 1974 by a group of Californian enthusiasts, who modified their bikes. By 1977, there was so much interest in the sport that manufacturers started to produce mountain bikes, and in 1983 the National Off-Road Bicycle Association (NORBA) was formed.

There are two principle types of mountain bike competitions — downhill riding and cross-country — and the first world championships were held in 1990. Cross-country mountain biking was first held at the Olympics in 1996. Competitors ride over a hilly, sometimes mountainous, natural course. Men race 25 to 30 mi. (40 to 50 km), and women 19 to 25 mi. (30 to 40 km).

The top male and female riders are both French. Nicolas Vouilloz won seven men's downhill world titles between 1995 and 2002. Anne-Caroline Chausson (France) has won 16 World Championship titles. She won the downhill event every year from 1996 to 2003 and again in 2005.

Olympic women's mountain bike race

Formula One

The Formula One World Championship usually lasts from March to October/November. In 2009 the schedule consisted of 17 races.

Since 2003 the points system has been that the winner of each race was awarded 10 points, the second 8, third 6, down to one point for 8th place, with the leading points-scorer becoming World Champion. From 2010 the system will change so that the World Champion will be the driver with the most wins. The points system will still be used in the event of a tie.

In 2007, his first season in Formula One, Lewis Hamilton finished second behind Kimi Räikkönen. Even though he finished fifth in the Brazilian Grand Prix, the final race of the 2008 season, he won the World Championship on points.

Best ever

German Michael Schumacher is the world's most successful Formula One driver. He has won a record seven world titles (1994, 1995, 2000, 2001, 2002, 2003, 2004) and also has the most race wins in a season — 13 in 2004.

Motor cycle racing: champions by class

World Championship motor cycle racing is competed by class (engine size — currently 125 cc, 250 cc and 500 cc/Moto GP), with titles awarded to riders and manufacturers.

500 cc/MotoGP
Most world titles – rider:
8 Giacomo Agostini (Italy)
6 Valentino Rossi (Italy)
5 Michael Doohan (Australia)

Most world titles – manufacturer:
18 Honda (Japan)
15 MV Agusta (Italy)
11 Yamaha (Japan)

350 cc (last contested 1982)
Most world titles – rider:
7 Giacomo Agostini (Italy)
4 Jim Redman (Rhodesia)
3 John Surtees (UK)

Most world titles – manufacturer:
9 MV Agusta (Italy)
6 Honda (Japan)
5 Yamaha (Japan)

250 cc
Most world titles – rider:
4 'Max' Biaggi (Italy)
4 Phil Read (UK)

Most world titles – manufacturer:
19 Honda (Japan)
14 Yamaha (Japan)
8 Aprilia (Italy)

125 cc
Most world titles – rider:

7 Angel Nieto (Spain)
6 Carlo Ubbiali (Italy)

Most world titles – manufacturer:
15 Honda (Japan)
8 Aprilia (Italy)
7 MV Agusta (Italy)

50/80 cc (last contested 1989)
Most world titles – rider:
6 Angel Nieto (Spain)
4 Stefan Dörflinger (Switzerland)

Most world titles – manufacturer:
8 Kreidler (Germany)
5 Suzuki (Japan)
5 Derbi (Spain)

Andretti dynasty

The Andretti family is one of the best known in auto car racing. Mario Andretti is an ex-Formula One world champion. Twin brother Aldo also raced before a severe crash ended his career. Mario's sons Michael and Jeff followed the family tradition, as did Aldo's sons John and Adam. The third generation, Michael's son Marco, was the 2006 Indy Rookie of the Year.

Young winners

● In 2008, Britain's Lewis Hamilton became the youngest Formula One World Champion at the age of 23 years 8 months 26 days.
● Also in 2008, Sebastien Vettel of Germany became the youngest race winner when he won the Italian Grand Prix at 21 years 2 months 12 days.
● The youngest driver to start a race is Mike Thackwell (New Zealand) who was aged 19 years 5 months 29 days when he started the 1980 Canadian Grand Prix.
● Other young Formula One World Champions are: Fernando Alonso (Spain), aged 24 years 1 month 18 days in 2005 and Emerson Fittipaldi (Brazil), aged 25 years 8 months 29 days in 1972.

Indianapolis 500

The biggest single auto racing event in the United States is the Indianapolis 500, which is not just a race but a day-long festival. The race is part of the Memorial Day celebrations at the end of May, and crowds of 250,0000 flock to Indianapolis Motor Speedway from all over the U.S.

The course, which opened in 1909, is known as the Brickyard because the original circuit was made out of thousands of bricks. The first Indy 500 was held in 1911 and was won by Ray Harroun in his Marmon Wasp. Contestants race over 200 laps of the 2.5-mi. (4 km) oval track.

🔍 www.formula1.com   **search**

Winter Olympics

The Winter Games (officially the International Winter Sports Week, but later recognized as the first Winter Olympics) was first held in 1924. It included five events: Nordic skiing, figure skating, speed skating, bobsledding and hockey.

Winter Olympics were held in the same years as the Summer Olympics until 1992, but since 1994 they have taken place every four years between the Summer Games. The sports being contested at the 2010 Vancouver Games are:

- Alpine skiing
- Biathlon
- Bobsled
- Cross-country skiing
- Curling
- Figure skating
- Freestyle skiing
- Ice hockey
- Ice sledge hockey
- Luge
- Nordic combined
- Short-track speed skating
- Skeleton
- Ski-jumping
- Snowboarding
- Speed skating
- Wheelchair curling

Summer and Winter Olympians

Eddie Eagan (U.S.) is the only person who has won gold medals at both Olympics. He won the light-heavyweight boxing gold in 1920 and in 1932 was a member of the gold medal-winning U.S. four-man bob team.

Top medal winners at the Winter Olympics (1924–2006)

Athlete — Men	Sport	Gold	Silver	Bronze	Total
Bjorn Dählie (Norway)	Cross-country	8	4	0	12
Sixten Jernberg (Sweden)	Cross-country	4	3	2	9
Ole Einar Bjoerndalen (Norway)	Biathlon	5	3	1	9
Ricco Gross (Germany)	Biathlon	4	3	1	8
Kjetil André Aamodt (Norway)	Alpine skiing	4	2	2	8
Sven Fischer (Germany)	Biathlon	4	2	2	8

Athlete — Women	Sport	Gold	Silver	Bronze	Total
Raisa Smetanina (USSR/Unified Team)	Cross-country	4	5	1	10
Stefania Belmondo (Italy)	Cross-country	2	3	5	10
Lyubov Egorova (Unified Team/Russia)	Cross-country	6	3	0	9
Uschi Disl (Germany)	Biathlon	2	4	3	9
Claudia Pechstein (Germany)	Speed skating	5	2	2	9

Top medal-winning nations at the Winter Olympics (1924–2006)

Country	Gold	Silver	Bronze	Total
USSR/Unified Team/ Russia	122	89	86	297
Norway	96	102	84	282
U.S.	78	81	59	218
Germany/ West Germany	76	78	57	211
Austria	50	64	71	185

🔍 www.vancouver2010.org   search

Winter Olympic facts and figures   1900s

1924 Chamonix, France
There were 294 competitors from 16 nations. Norway won the most medals (17) and tied with Finland for gold medals (4).

1928 St. Moritz, Switzerland
Twenty-five nations and 495 competitors took part. Norway won the most medals (15) and the most golds (6).

1932 Lake Placid, U.S.
A total of 306 competitors from 17 nations competed. The U.S. won the most medals (12) and the most golds (6).

1936 Garmisch-Partenkirchen, Germany
There were 755 competitors from 28 nations. Norway won the most medals (15) and most gold medals (7).

1948 St. Moritz, Switzerland
A total of 28 nations and 713 competitors took part. Norway, Sweden and Switzerland tied for top medal position (10). Norway and Sweden tied for most golds (4).

1952 Oslo, Norway
A total of 732 competitors from 30 nations took part. Norway held both top medal (16) and top gold (7) position.

1956 Cortina D'Ampezzo, Italy
Thirty-two nations and 818 competitors took part. USSR were top medal winners (16) with the most gold wins (7).

1960 Squaw Valley, U.S.
Thirty nations took part with 665 athletes. USSR again won the most medals (21) and most golds (7).

1964 Innsbruck, Austria
Thirty-six nations and 1,186 athletes took part. The USSR won the most medals (25) and most golds (11) for the third time.

1968 Grenoble, France
A total of 1,293 athletes competed from 37 nations. Norway won the most medals (14) and most gold medals (6).

1972 Sapporo, Japan
There were 1,232 competitors from 35 nations. USSR were top of the overall medal table (16) and won most gold medals (8).

Competitors in the Men's Snowboard Cross final at the Turin 2006 Winter Olympics

The Stanley Cup

Every player on the winning team takes the Stanley Cup home for 24 hours to show off to family and friends. New York Islander Clark Gillies used it in 1980 to feed his dog, and in 1996 Colorado Avalanche defenceman Sylvain Lefebvre baptized his daughter in it.

Hockey

Hockey probably developed from a game called bandy that was played on ice-covered fields. The modern game is played over three 20-minute periods between two teams. Each team has six players on the ice at any one time. The object is to move the puck (a hard rubber disk) across the ice with a stick (maximum length 63 in. [160 cm]) and put it into the opponent's goal.

The National Hockey League (NHL) was formed in 1917. Today the NHL is made up of 30 teams split into two conferences. The Eastern Conference has 15 teams divided into three divisions: Atlantic, North-East and South-East. The Western Conference is also divided into three divisions: Central, North-West and Pacific. At the end of season the leading teams in each conference play each other. The winner of each plays for the Stanley Cup.

NHL's top points-scorers

Player	Points
Wayne Gretzky	2,857
Mark Messier	1,887
Gordie Howe	1,850
Ron Francis	1,798
Marcel Dionne	1,771
Steve Yzerman	1,755

Top teams Stanley Cup wins

Montreal Canadiens	24
Toronto Maple Leafs	13
Detroit Red Wings	11
Boston Bruins	5
Edmonton Oilers	5

Ice skating

Famous skaters
● Ulrich Salchow, born in Sweden in 1877, was the greatest men's figure skater of all time. He won the first Olympic skating title at the 1908 London Olympics and between 1901 and 1911 he was the world champion on 10 occasions.

● Norway's Sonja Henie won Olympic golds in 1928, 1932 and 1936. She also won 10 world titles. She won nearly 1,500 cups and medals during her career. After leaving the sport in 1936 she became a film star and appeared in 11 films.

Fastest speed skaters
● Finland's Pekka Koskela set a new men's world record at Salt Lake City, Utah, on November 10, 2007 when he covered 1000m in 1 minute 7 seconds, knocking 3/100ths of a second off the old record.

● Cindy Klassen of Canada set a women's world record of 1 minute, 13.46 seconds for the 1,000 m at Calgary on March 24, 2006. The next day, she lowered the record further to 1 minute, 13.11 seconds.

Great sportsmanship

At the 1964 Winter Olympics, Italian Eugenio Monti loaned British bobsleigh pair Tony Nash and Robin Dixon an axle bolt from his own sled. They came first; Monti finished third.

Ski-jumping

In 2005 the world ski-jumping record was broken three times within 75 minutes! At the final meeting of the 2004–2005 Ski Jumping World Cup Bjørn Einar Romøren (Norway) set a new mark at 769.3 ft. (234.5 m). Then Matti Hautamaeki (Finland) put the record up to 772.6 ft. (235.5 m) before Romøren retook the record with a leap of 784.1 ft. (239 m).

2000s

1976 Innsbruck, Austria
Thirty-seven nations and 1,128 athletes took part. USSR won the most medals (27) and most gold medals (13).

1980 Lake Placid, U.S.
There were 1,067 competitors from 37 nations. USSR won the most medals overall (22) and most golds (10).

1984 Sarajevo, Yugoslavia
A total of 1,278 competitors from 49 nations took part. USSR won the most medals (25) but East Germany won the most golds (9).

1988 Calgary, Canada
Fifty-seven nations fielded 1,423 athletes. USSR won the most medals (29) and most golds (11).

1992 Albertville, France
Sixty-three nations with 1,801 competitors took part. Germany won the most medals (26) and most gold medals (10).

1994 Lillehammer, Norway
A total of 1,739 athletes from 67 nations took part. Norway won the most medals (26) but Russia won most golds (11).

1998 Nagano, Japan
There were 72 nations taking part and 2,302 athletes. Germany won the most medals (29) and most gold medals (12).

2002 Salt Lake City, U.S.
Seventy-eight nations fielded 2,399 athletes. Germany again won the most medals (35) and most golds (12).

2006 Turin, Italy
A record 2,663 athletes from 82 nations took part. Germany was the top medal winner for the third time in a row (29)

and also won the most gold medals (11).

2010 Vancouver, Canada
The 21st Winter Olympics will be held in Vancouver between 12 and 28 February 2010.

See also
The Olympics: pages 282–83

Greyhound racing

Dog racing has been popular since ancient times, when dogs were used for hunting. Modern greyhound racing takes place on an oval-shaped track over distances from 690 ft. (210 m) to 3,600 ft. (1,100 m). An electric "rabbit" goes around the track, and the dogs are released from traps to chase it.

In the United States, greyhound races are run with eight dogs. There is a draw before the race to decide which trap each dog starts from. Each dog wears a colored jacket that matches its starting trap.

Harness racing

In harness racing the horses pull the drivers who sit in a two-wheeled cart called a sulky. There are two forms of harness racing — pacing and trotting.

The difference between pacing and trotting is in the way the horse moves. A pacing horse moves its right front and back legs together, then its left front and back legs. A trotter moves its left front leg and right back leg at the same time, followed by its right front leg and left back leg.

Hambletonian harness race

Main races

The leading race for trotters is the Hambletonian. This race was first held at Syracuse, New York, in 1926 and is now run every year at The Meadowlands, East Rutherford, New Jersey. It is named after a trotter called Hambletonian. The leading race for pacers is The Little Brown Jug, named after a 19th-century horse. It has been held at Delaware, Ohio, every year since 1946.

Top drivers

Herve Filion, born in Quebec, Canada, is the most famous driver in harness-racing history and set many records in his 35-year career. In 1968 he became the first driver to win 400 races in a season. He went on to achieve 400 or more wins per season in 14 other years. He was forced to retire in 1995 but made a comeback in 2002. He achieved his goal of reaching 15,000 wins before finally retiring in 2003 with 15,086 wins.

John Campbell, from Ontario, Canada, is the top money-winning jockey in the sport. He started driving in 1972 at the age of 17 and was the first man to pass the $100 million and $200 million milestones in career earnings. He won the Hambletonian six times and the 10,000th race of his career in 2008 at the age of 53.

Top horse

Moni Maker was the first horse to pass the $5 million mark. Remarkably, she achieved this during a four-year career between 1997–2000. She won 60 of her 91 trotting races and won the Horse of the Year Award in 1998 and 1999. In 2003, the Italian-bred horse Varenne surpassed Moni Maker's career winning record. He won 63 of 74 starts to amass career earnings of $5,651,061.

Rodeo

Professional rodeo developed from the early days of ranching, when bull riding and calf roping were common activities. The first known rodeo with prize money was held at Deer Trail, Colorado, in 1869. The All-Round Cowboy World Champion is decided each year — the champion is the cowboy who wins the most money over a series of events. Top cowboys win more than $250,000 a year.

The Triple Crowns

● The Triple Crowns of the U.S. and the UK are the most prestigious of all Triple Crowns in thoroughbred racing. The U.S. Triple Crown consists of the Kentucky Derby, Preakness Stakes and Belmont Stakes, while the UK Triple Crown consist of the 2000 Guineas, Derby and St. Leger.

● Only 11 horses have completed the famous treble, the last being Affirmed, ridden by Steve Cauthen in 1978.

● Fifteen horses have won the English version, the first being West Australian, ridden by Frank Butler in 1853. There were seven winners in the 20th century and none since Nijinsky, ridden by Lester Piggott, in 1970. Steve Donoghue is the only man to ride two English Triple Crown winners, Pommern (1915) and Gay Crusader (1917).

The Breeders' Cup

The Breeders' Cup Limited was started in 1982 to encourage thoroughbred racing throughout the U.S. The first Breeders' Cup day was held on November 10, 1984, at Hollywood Park, Inglewood, California. Between 1984 and 2006 the championship was a single day event, but since 2007 has been spread over two days. It is held at a different course each year.

There are eight races on Breeders' Cup Day, which is held at a different course each year in October or November. The total prize money for the 2008 Breeders' Cup is $25.5 million. The top race is the Breeders' Cup Classic which runs over 1 mile, two furlongs. The prize money for this race in 2008 is $5 million with the winner receiving more than $2.7 million.

Winner of the Breeders' Cup Classic 2002

Most successful jockey

In 2008, Canadian Russell Baze became the first jockey to ride 10,000 winners, and at the beginning of 2009 his total was approaching 10,400. Baze was ten times U.S. Champion Jockey (for wins) yet, despite all his wins, Baze has never won a Triple Crown or Breeders' Cup race.

Top horse races

England
● The Epsom Derby was first held in 1780 and is now run over 1.5 mi. (2.4 km) at Epsom Downs each June. The first winner was a horse named Diomed. Jockey Lester Piggott won the Derby a record nine times.

● The Grand National is the world's best-known steeplechase, a horse race over a course with obstacles to be jumped. It was first run as the Grand Liverpool Steeplechase in 1839. The race now takes place every spring over 4.5 mi. (7.2 km) at Aintree in England and the winning horse has to clear 30 challenging fences. The famous horse Red Rum won the race a record three times between 1972–76.

France
● The Prix de L'Arc de Triomphe was first run in 1920. It takes place on the first Sunday in October every year and covers 1.5 mi. (2,400 m) over the Longchamps race course, Paris. Alleged, ridden by Lester Piggott, won the race in 1977 and 1978 and was the last horse to win two years in a row.

Australia
● The most important horse race in Australia is the Melbourne Cup which dates from 1861. It is run on the first Tuesday in November at the Flemington Park race track in Victoria. Trainer Bart Cummings won the race a record 12 times between 1965 and 2008.

United States
● The Kentucky Derby was first held in 1875. It is run over 1 mile, 2 furlongs at Churchill Downs, Kentucky, on the first Saturday in May and is the most famous of all U.S. horse races. Eddie Arcaro and Bill Hartack have been the most successful jockeys with five wins each.

Breeders' Cup records

Most wins (jockey)	15 (Jerry Bailey)
Most prize money (jockey)	$23,033,360 (Pat Day)
Most wins (trainer)	18 (D. Wayne Lukas)
Most prize money (trainer)	$19,645,520 (D. Wayne Lukas)
Most used track	Churchill Downs, Kentucky, used in 1988, 1991, 1994, 1998, 2000, 2006

Breeders' Cup record payout
When the 5-year-old Arcangues won the 1993 Breeders' Cup Classic it was the biggest upset in the history of the race. His victory paid out a record $269.20 for a $2 wager. It was the horse's first race on a dirt track.

 www.usef.org   search

Last
Lists

The Last Space Shuttles

NASA is planning to retire the surviving shuttles in its Space Shuttle programme — *Atlantic, Endeavour* and *Discovery* — in 2010, nearly 30 years after the program started. A replacement space shuttle, *Orion*, is being developed to launch in 2014. The *Orion* will be able to travel beyond Earth's orbit, carrying passengers and cargo.

Unusual deaths

Aeschylus
Aeschylus was a famous Greek dramatist who died in 456 BC. A prediction that he would be killed by a blow from heaven came true when an eagle carrying a tortoise dropped it on his head.

King Alexander of Greece
He died after being bitten by his pet monkey in 1920.

Francis Bacon
This Elizabethan philosopher caught a chill while trying to deep-freeze a chicken by stuffing it with snow. He died in 1626.

Hilaire Belloc
Although born in France, Hilaire Belloc was an English writer and member of parliament. He died in 1953 after a burning coal fell out of his fire and set him ablaze.

Madéleine-Sophie Blanchard
Madame Blanchard was the widow of pioneer balloonist Jean-Pierre Blanchard. She was killed in Paris, France, in 1819, when fireworks set fire to her balloon.

Jerome Cardan
Cardan was an Italian physician, mathematician and astrologer. He starved himself to death in 1576 to make sure that his own prediction of his death would come true.

Lord Carnarvon
Carnarvon was an amateur Egyptologist who financed the excavation of Tutankhamun's tomb in 1922. Several months after opening the tomb, Carnarvon died suddenly from a mosquito bite. This began the legend of the curse of Tutankhamun.

Isadora Duncan
This American dancer was strangled in 1927 by her scarf. It became caught in the wheel of a Bugatti sports car in which she was a passenger.

Anton Dvorák
The Czech composer died in 1904 of a chill which he caught while trainspotting.

Frederick, Prince of Wales
Frederick was the son of George II and heir to the British throne. He died in 1751 after being hit by a cricket ball.

Harry Houdini (Erich Weiss)
Houdini was a famous escapologist who claimed he could withstand being punched in the stomach. He died in 1926 — after being punched in the stomach.

William Huskisson
Huskisson was a British member of parliament. He was run down by a train during the opening of the first railway in 1830.

Jean-Baptiste Lully
This Italian-French composer died in 1687 after accidentally stabbing his foot with a stick while beating time. The short conductor's baton came into use soon afterward.

Thomas Midgley
Midgley was an American inventor who was strangled in 1944 by a machine he had invented to help him move after contracting polio. He invented three products that have since been found to be environmentally harmful: lead in gasoline, CFCs in fridges and aerosols, and the insecticide DDT.

Forever young

The following are some of the most famous people who died early and so remain forever young in our minds.

Name/cause/year	Age at death
King Edward V of England, murdered, 1483	12
King Edward VI of England, natural causes, 1553	15
Anne Frank German diarist, in concentration camp, 1945	15
Lady Jane Grey Queen of England, executed, 1554	16
Thomas Chatterton English poet, took poison, 1770	22
Anastasia Grand Duchess of Russia, assassinated, 1918	17
Ritchie Valens American rock singer, plane crash, 1959	17
King Tutankhamun Egyptian pharaoh, c. 1340 BC	18
Joan of Arc French heroine, burned at the stake, 1431	19
Catherine Howard Queen of Henry VIII, beheaded, 1542	20
Billy the Kid (William H. Bonney) American outlaw, shot, 1881	21
Eddie Cochran American rock singer, car accident, 1960	21

Name/cause/year	Age at death
Pocahontas Native American Indian princess, smallpox, 1617	22
Buddy Holly American rock singer, plane crash, 1959	22
Aaliyah (Aaliyah Haughton) singer, plane crash, 2001	22
River Phoenix actor, drug overdose, 1993	23
Clyde Barrow U.S. outlaw, shot by Texas Rangers, 1934	24
James Dean American film actor, car crash, 1955	24
Lee Harvey Oswald assassin of John F. Kennedy, murdered, 1963	24
John Keats English poet, tuberculosis, 1821	25
"Red Baron" Manfred von Richthofen German flying ace, shot down, 1918	25
Jean Harlow film actress, illness, 1937	26
Brian Jones Rolling Stones guitarist, drowned, 1969	26
Jimi Hendrix rock guitarist, drugs, 1970	27
Kurt Cobain Nirvana lead singer, shooting suicide, 1994	27
Heath Ledger Australian actor, accidental drug overdose, 2008	28
Anne Brontë British writer, tuberculosis, 1849	29

Famous last words

Julius Caesar, 44 BC
Roman emperor, who was assassinated by conspirators, including Brutus, a man he thought was his friend. According to legend and Shakespeare, Caesar said: "Et tu Brute?" (You as well, Brutus?)

Caligula, AD 41
Roman emperor who was assassinated: "I am still alive!"

Catherine de Medici, 1589
Queen of France: "Ah, my God, I am dead!"

Joseph Henry Green, 1863
British doctor, after checking his own pulse: "Stopped."

General John Sedgwick, 1864
In the American Civil War, Sedgwick was shot by a sniper as he remarked: "They couldn't hit an elephant at this distance."

Viscount Palmerston, 1865
British Prime Minister: "Die, my dear doctor? That's the last thing I shall do."

Billy the Kid (aka William Bonney, Henry McCarty), 1881
American outlaw, before being shot by Sheriff Pat Garrett: "Who is it?"

Marie Antoinette, 1893
French queen, who accidentally trod on her executioner's foot as she went to the guillotine: "Pardonnez-moi, monsieur." (Pardon me, sir.)

Oscar Wilde, 1900
Opinions differ about the Irish writer's last words. Some people claim he said: "Either these curtains go/that wallpaper goes, or I do."

Prince Philippe
Prince Philippe, heir to the French throne, was killed when his horse tripped over a pig in the streets of Paris in 1131.

Pliny the Elder
Roman writer Pliny was choked by the fumes of the erupting volcano Vesuvius in AD 79.

Sir Thomas Urquhart
Urquhart was the Scottish author of books with extraordinary titles such as *Logopandecteision*. He died laughing when told of the Restoration of Charles II in 1660.

William III
This British king died in 1701, after a fall from his horse when it stumbled over a molehill. His opponents drank a toast to the mole, calling it "The little gentleman in black velvet."

See also

Volcanic eruptions: page 46

Joan of Arc, 15th-century French heroine who was burned at the stake aged 19

Poster for Houdini show

Queen Victoria, 1901
British queen: "Oh, that peace may come" (a reference to the war at the time in South Africa). "Bertie!" (her husband, Prince Albert).

Captain Lawrence Oates, 1912
Oates was a member of Scott's expedition to the South Pole. He was terribly injured from frostbite and went to his death rather than hold up his companions. When he left the tent he said, "I am going outside and may be some time."

Anna Pavlova, 1931
Ballerina: "Get my swan costume ready!"

Lytton Strachey, 1932
English writer: "If this is dying, then I don't think much of it."

Douglas Fairbanks Sr., 1939
American film actor: "I've never felt better."

Heinrich Himmler, 1945
Nazi leader, as he committed suicide by taking poison: "I am Heinrich Himmler!"

H.G. Wells, 1946
English novelist, author of *The Time Machine*: "I'm all right."

John F. Kennedy, 1963
Moments before he was shot, Kennedy replied to "You certainly can't say that the people of Dallas haven't given you a nice welcome, Mr. President" with his final words, "No, you certainly can't."

 www.findagrave.com   search

Entertainment lasts

Shakespeare's last play
Most people agree that *The Tempest* (1611), is the last play Shakespeare wrote, although some think he may have written a later play that has been lost. Shakespeare died in 1616, and *The Tempest* was first published in 1623.

Charles Dickens' last story
The Mystery of Edwin Drood was Charles Dickens' last novel. It was published in monthly episodes, but ended, unfinished, when Dickens died in 1870.

The last silent film
The Four Feathers (1929) was the last silent film released by a major studio. The 1976 film *Silent Movie* does contain one word, "Non!" (French for no), which is spoken by Marcel Marceau, a mime artist.

The last Beatles concert
The Beatles last played together in public at Candlestick Park, San Francisco, on August 29, 1966. Their last publicly performed song was "Long Tall Sally."

The sixth and last Star Wars film
Star Wars: Episode III — Revenge of the Sith was released in 2005. It made almost $850 million worldwide, bringing the total for the series to $4.3 billion.

Last *Harry Potter*
The last Harry Potter novel, *Harry Potter and the Deathly Hallows*, was published on July 21, 2007, 10 years after the first. It sold 11 million copies in the first 24 hours and has gone on to sell over four times as many. The film version will be released in two parts in 2010 and 2011.

Crime and punishment lasts

Last executions for witchcraft in the U.S.
On September 22, 1692, seven women and one man were hanged for witchcraft at Salem and other places in New England.

Last stagecoach robbery in the U.S.
On May 29, 1899, Canadian-born Pearl Hart, with her partner Joe Boot, held up a stagecoach near Globe, Arizona, robbing the passengers of $421. They were caught and Hart was sentenced to five and Boot to 30 years in Yuma Prison.

Last public hanging in the U.S.
On August 14, 1936, in Owensboro, Kentucky, Rainey Bethea was hanged for murder in front of a crowd of 20,000 people. Public hanging was banned in the U.S. soon afterward.

Last executions in Canada
Murderers Ronald Turpin (Canada) and Arthur Lucas (U.S.) were hanged at Toronto's Don Jail on December 11, 1962. Capital punishment was officially abolished in Canada on July 14, 1976.

Last witness to the assassination of Abraham Lincoln
Samuel James Seymour, who died on April 13, 1956, was the last surviving witness to the assassination of the American president. Seymour was only 5 years old when he saw John Wilkes Booth shoot Abraham Lincoln at Ford's Theatre, Washington D.C., on April 14, 1865.

Last person executed by guillotine
The last person to be executed in public was the murderer Eugene Weidmann who had his head cut off at Versailles, France, on June 17 ,1939. The last official use of the guillotine in France was on September 10, 1977, when Hamida Djandoubi was executed for murder.

Last prisoner of Alcatraz
Alcatraz Island, in the Bay of San Francisco, was a prison for over 100 years. Surrounded by freezing water, it was considered impossible to escape. Armed robber Frank Clay Weatherman was its last prisoner. He left the island on March 21, 1963, after which Alcatraz closed.

Last Aztec emperor
Montezuma II was removed from power by Spanish invaders and killed in June 1520.

Montezuma II, the last Aztec emperor

Last men on the Moon
U.S. *Apollo 17* astronauts Eugene A. Cernan and Harrison H. Schmitt spent three days on the Moon, blasting off to return to Earth on December 14, 1972. This was the last day on which any human walked on the surface of the Moon.

Royal lasts

The last Egyptian pharaoh
Cleopatra VII ruled from 69 BC, when she was 17 years old, until 30 BC, when Egypt became a province of the Roman empire.

The last Roman emperor
Romulus Augustus was about 14 when he was removed from power in AD 476. The Roman empire split into western and eastern divisions.

The last British king killed in battle
Richard III was killed at the battle of Bosworth on August 22, 1485.

The last British king born abroad
George II was born in Hanover, Germany, on November 10, 1683.

The last king of France
Louis-Philippe (1773–1850) reigned from 1830 until February 24, 1848, when he gave up his throne. Disguised as "Mr. Smith," he traveled to England where he lived until his death.

The last emperor of China
Hsüan T'ung gave up his throne on February 12, 1912, and later took the name Henry Pu-yi. The film *The Last Emperor* (1987) is about his life.

The last tsar of Russia
Nicholas II was removed from power by the Russian Revolution of 1917, and murdered with his family at Ekaterinburg in July 1918. Their remains were reburied in St. Petersburg in July 1998.

Transportation lasts

Last Pony Express
The Pony Express service carried urgent mail by horse in the United States, but died out when coast-to-coast telegraph lines were connected near Salt Lake City, Utah, on October 26, 1861.

Last horse car in New York
The last horse car — a horse-drawn bus — operated on the Bleecker Street Line, New York City, on July 26, 1917.

The last Model T Ford
The Model T, first produced in 1908, was one of the most popular cars of all time. The last U.S.-made Model T (number 15,007,033) rolled off the production line on Thursday May 26, 1927.

Last transatlantic airships
The giant German airship Hindenburg exploded in Lakehurst, New Jersey, on May 6, 1937. At the same time, the Graf Zeppelin flew from Brazil to Germany — it was the last to cross the Atlantic and made its final flight on June 19, 1937.

Last flight of Concorde
Concorde was the world's only supersonic airliner. It was in service for 34 years until it made its last commercial flight, from New York to London, on October 24, 2003.

Pharos of Alexandria

Last of the Seven Wonders

The last of the Seven Wonders of the world to be built was the 406.9 ft. (124 m) Pharos (lighthouse) of Alexandria, Egypt, which was completed in 279 BC. It was partly knocked down by invaders and later destroyed by an earthquake. The only one of the Seven Wonders that survives today is the Great Pyramid at Giza in Egypt.

Last voyage of the Titanic

The last voyage of the *Titanic* was also its first. It sank on April 15, 1912, after striking an iceberg, killing 1,517 people.

See also
The Seven Wonders of the ancient world: pages 206–7

Prow of the wreck of the *Titanic*

See also
Shipwrecks: page 218

Q

Qatar 137
quasars 20
Queen Mary 2 (ship) 211
queens and kings 108, 109, 306
Quimby, Harriet 216

R

racquet sports 290–1
Radcliffe, Daniel 156
radio 275
rail transport 214–15, 218
rail tunnels 205
rain gauges 45
Rainforest Pyramid 201
Rambert, Dame Marie 261
Realism 242
recession (2008) 186, 187
recording timeline 250, 251
recycling and rubbish 72–3
Red Crescent Movement 111
Reformation 102
refrigerators 189
religions 160–9
religious buildings 162, 200
Renaissance 102, 198, 242
reptiles and amphibians 62–3
Rezazadeh, Hossein 293
Richter Scale 47
rivers and lakes 38–9
road disasters 218
road tunnels 205
roadkill recipes 98
robberies 184
Robin Hood 171
robots 74, 75
rock music 254–5

rockets, space 29
rocks and minerals 34–5
rococo style 198, 242
rodeo 300
Rogers Centre 201
Rolls Royce 212
Roman building style 198
Roman empire 106
Roman gods 161
Roman numerals 82
Romanesque building style 198
Romania 129
Romanticism 242
Rome, foundation of 104
roofs and domes 201
Roosevelt's Four Freedoms 111
Routemaster bus 307
rowing 294
Rowling, J.K. 230, 232
royal "lasts" 306
Royal Observatory, Greenwich 26
Rubáiyat of Omar Khayyám 234
rubbish and recycling 72–3
rugby league 287
rugby union 287
rulers and leaders 108–9
running (athletics) 284
Russia 137
Russian Revolution 105
Rwanda 134

S

sacred texts 164–5
Sagrada Familia Cathedral 200
sailing 294, 295
saints 167
Salt Lake City 163
Samoa 143

San Marino 126
Santiago de Compostela 163
Santorini volcano 46
São Tomé and Príncipe 133
satellites 29
Saturn 23, 24
Saudi Arabia 137
Scarlatti, Domenico 67
Schlumpf brothers 246
schools 240, 241
Schulz, Charles 67
Schumacher, Michael 297
science and technology 74–89
science of life 48–73
scientific crime detection 185
Scott, Sheila 152
Scottish law 182
scouts and cub scouts 157
Scrabble 191
Scream, The (painting) 242
screen legends 272
sea battles 181
sea life 56–7
sea water elements 79
seas and oceans 40–1, 56–7
seconds (of time) 14, 15
security uses of animals 65
sedimentary rocks 35
Senegal 131
Serbia 129
Serengeti national park 221
Seuss, Dr 233
Seychelles 141
Shakespeare, William 150, 306
sharks 56, 57
Shaw, George Bernard 155
sheep 64
ships 210–11
shipwrecks 218
shrapnel 178
Sidis, William James 156

Sierra Leone 132
signs and symbols 226–7
Sikhism 164
silk 65
Simpsons 270
Sing Sing Prison 185
Singapore 140
singing and songs 251, 252
singles, top-selling 254
Sir Gawain and the Green Knight (poem) 234
skeleton (of humans) 93
ski-jumping 299
skin, human 93
skins of animals 65
skyscrapers (buildings) 202–3
skyscrapers (flags) 210
Slovakia 128
Slovenia 129
snakes 62, 63
snooker 293
snowboarding 298
soap operas 275
soccer 288–9
sodium 79
solar energy 195
Solar System 22–5
solids (mathematical shapes) 83
Solomon Islands 142
Somalia 131
songs and singing 251, 252
sound barrier 217
sound levels 77
South Africa 135
South America 122–3
South Korea 139
space 18–31
space exploration 28–31
space toilets 29
space tourism **31**, 220
space walks 31
spacecraft 28, 29, 31, 302, 303
Spain 126

Author's acknowledgments

The author would like to thank the following people, organizations and publications for kindly supplying information for this book.

Whitaker's Almanack 2009

Academy of Motion Picture Arts and Sciences (AMPAS)*
Alexa
American Film Institute
American Forests
Artnet
Association of Leading Visitor Attractions
Alexander Ash
Caroline Ash
Nicholas Ash
Audit Bureau of Circulations Ltd (ABC)
Bloomsbury Publishing
Box Office Mojo
BP Statistical Review of World Energy 2008
Richard Braddish
Thomas Brinkhoff
The British Council
British Film Institute
British Library
British Museum
British Phonographic Industry (BPI)
Carbon Dioxide Information Analysis Center
Central Intelligence Agency, *The World Factbook 2008*
Christie's
Computer Industry Almanac
Department for Environment, Food and Rural Affairs (DEFRA)
Earth Impact Database
The Economist
Emporis
Energy Information Administration
Ethnologue
Euromonitor
Federal Bureau of Investigation
Food and Agriculture Organization of the United Nations (FAO)
Forbes magazine
Ross Fulton
Global Education Digest (UNESCO)
Global Forest Resources Assessment (FAO)

Golden Raspberry Award Foundation
Russell E. Gough
Monica Grady
Robert Grant
Greyhound Racing Association of America
Hollywood Reporter
Home Accident Surveillance System (HASS)
Home Office
Human Development Report (United Nations)
Imperial War Museum
Index Translationum (UNESCO)
Intellectual Property Office
International Centre for Prison Studies
International Federation of Audit Bureaux of Circulations
The International Institute for Strategic Studies, *The Military Balance 2009*
International Labour Organization
International Olympic Committee (IOC)
International Shark Attack File, Florida Museum of Natural History
International Telecommunication Union (ITU)
International Union for the Conservation of Nature (IUCN)
Internet Movie Database (IMDb)
Internet World Stats
Inter-Parliamentary Union
Julien's Auctions
Dr. Benjamin Lucas
Mattel, Inc
Chris Mead
National Aeronautics and Space Administration, USA (NASA)
National Basketball Association, USA (NBA)
National Football League, USA (NFL)
National Statistics
Natural History Museum, London
AC Nielsen
The Nobel Foundation
Organisation for Economic Co-operation and Development (OECD)
Organisation Internationale des Constructeurs d'Automobiles (OICA)
Felicity Page

Parker Brothers
Periodical Publishers Association
Quigley's Motion Picture Almanac
Recording Industry Association of America (RIAA)
Dafydd Rees
Louise Reip
Royal Astronomical Society
Royal Observatory, Greenwich
Royal Opera House, Covent Garden
Screen Digest
Robert Senior
Sotheby's
Time magazine
Tree Register of the British Isles
United Nations (UN)
United Nations Children's Fund (UNICEF)
United Nations Educational, Scientific and Cultural Organization (UNESCO)
United Nations Environment Programme
United Nations Population Division (UNPD)
Universal Postal Union
U.S. Census Bureau International Data Base
U.S. Geological Survey
U.S. Mint
U.S. Patent and Trademark Office
Variety
Lucy T. Verma
Ward's Motor Vehicle Facts & Figures 2008
WebElements
World Association of Girl Guides and Girl Scouts
World Association of Newspapers
World Bank
World Christian Database
World Gazetteer
World Health Organization (WHO)
World Organization of the Scout Movement
World Tourism Organization (WTO)
World Nuclear Association

Population data
© by Stefan Helders
www.world-gazetteer.com

Country names
The following abbreviations are used for country names on page 285
BUL: Bulgaria
CHN: China
CUB: Cuba
CZE: Czech Republic
DEN: Denmark
ETH: Ethiopia
FRA: France
GBR: Great Britain
GDR: German Democratic Republic (1955–90)
MAR: Morocco (Maroc)
QAT: Qatar
ROM: Romania
RUS: Russian Federation
UKR: Ukraine
U.S.: United States of America
USSR: Union of Soviet Socialist Republics (1922–91)

ACKNOWLEDGMENTS

Picture acknowledgments

L = left, R = right, C = center, T = top, B = bottom

Page **2** Colin Mead/Photolibrary; **4** Photolibrary; **8** Jose Fuste Raga/Photolibrary; **10** Mark Pink/Alamy; **11T** Jeremy Swinborne/iStockphoto; **12C** Jeremy Horner/Corbis; **14TL** Eileen Tweedy/The Art Archive; **15B** David Taylor/Getty Images; **16C** Charles & Josette Lenars/Corbis; **17TR** REGIS MADEC/Thaiworldview.com; **18** Dennis di Cicco/Corbis; **19B** NASA; **19T** NASA; **20TR** NASA; **20BR** NASA; **20C** NASA; **20CR** NASA; **22BL** NASA; **22CL** NASA; **22CR** NASA; **22C** NASA; **22TR** NASA; **23BL** NASA; **23BC** NASA; **23BR** NASA; **23TL** NASA; **24CR** Gianni Dagli Orti/Corbis; **24C** NASA; **24TR** NASA; **24TC** NASA; **25CL** NASA; **25C** NASA; **26CL** Roger Ressmeyer/Corbis; **26TR** Bettmann/Corbis; **27C** NASA; **28R** NASA; **29TL** NASA; **30CL** NASA; **30C** NASA; **31TR** NASA; **32** Andrew Brownbill/EPA/Corbis; **34C** Charles & Josette Lenars/Corbis; **35T** Timothy Ball/iStockphoto; **36BL** Theo Allofs/ ZEFA/Corbis; **36TL** iStockphoto; **37CR** Robyn Glover/iStockphoto; **38B** Andre Klaassen/iStockphoto; **38T** Frank Leung/iStockphoto; **40T** Daniel Leclair/Reuters/Corbis; **41C** Stewart Westmorland/Corbis; **41BR** UPPA/Photoshot; **44TR** Shaun Lowe/iStockphoto; **45T** Clint Spencer/iStockphoto; **46B** Gary Braasch/Corbis; **47T** Koch Valerie/iStockphoto; **48** Frans Lanting/Corbis; **50TC** Cristi Bastian/Shutterstock; **50BL** Dr. Morley Read/Shutterstock; **51BR** Frans Lanting/Corbis; **51C** Jon Rasmussen/iStockphoto; **52BL** Condor 36/Shutterstock; **53TR** Brad Thompson/iStockphoto; **53BR** Summer/Shutterstock; **54TL** Jim Jurica/iStockphoto; **55R** iStockphoto; **55BL** iStockphoto; **56CL** Amos Nachoum/Corbis; **57TR** Will Burgees/Reuters/Corbis; **57CL** Don Bayley/iStockphoto; **58TR** Tim Davis/Corbis; **58BL** Anastasiya Maksymenko/iStockphoto; **59B** Tim Davis/Corbis; **60TL** Thomas Bedenk/iStockphoto; **61CL** Dave Marsden/Alamy; **61TR** Will Schmitz/iStockphoto; **62B** Jeremy Edwards/iStockphoto; **63TR** Steve Geer/iStockphoto; **64CR** Jose Carlos Pires Pereira/iStockphoto; **64BL** David Scharf/Science Photo Library; **65TR** Wolfgang Kaehler/Corbis; **66B** Nico Smit/iStockphoto; **66TR** Callalloo Canis/Fotolia; **67TR** Mark Hamblin/OSF/Photolibrary; **68T** Christoph Ermel/iStockphoto; **69BR** Jameson Weaton/iStockphoto; **70TR** Wayne Lawler/Ecoscene/Corbis; **70B** Loic Bernard/iStockphoto; **72B** Roger Milley/iStockphoto; **73BC** Marcelo Wain/iStockphoto; **73CR** Nathan Watkins/iStockphoto; **74** Nils Jorgensen/Rex Features; **75TR** Les Cunliffe/iStockphoto; **78CL** Donall O Cleirigh/iStockphoto; **79BL** Bettmann/Corbis; **81T** Phil Walter/Getty Images; **84L** Hulton-Deutsch Collection/Corbis; **84R** Carole Gomez/iStockphoto; **86CL** Courtesy of Apple; **86CR** One Laptop Per Child; **87T** Dean Mitchell/Shutterstock; **89TL** Bettmann/Corbis; **89TR** Courtesy of Apple; **90** Professor Miodrag Stojkovic/Science Photo Library; **91TR** Carol Munoz/iStockphoto; **92TR** Stephen Sweet/iStockphoto; **93C** Maria Boytunoa/iStockphoto; **94CL** Bettmann/Corbis; **95R** Bettmann/Corbis; **95BL** Corbis; **96TL** Maria Bibikova/iStockphoto; **97TR** Serghei Starus/Shutterstock; **97BL** Shutterstock; **98TL** Andresr/Shutterstock; **98CR** Joe Gough/Shutterstock; **99BL** Coca-Cola; **99BR** Elena Moiseeva/Shutterstock; **99TL** Olivier Samson Arcand/Dinner In The Sky; **99TR** Olivier Samson Arcand/Dinner In The Sky; **100** Chuck Kennedy/Pool/Corbis; **102CR** iStockphoto; **102TR** Jose Marafona/iStockphoto; **103R** David Lewis/iStockphoto; **104TL** Falk Kienas/iStockphoto; **104C** Eliza Snow/iStockphoto; **105T** Bettmann/Corbis; **106B** Karim Hesham/iStockphoto; **107TR** Jivko Kazakov/iStockphoto; **107TL** Francisco Orellana/iStockphoto; **108TR** Jack Tzekov/iStockphoto; **108CL** John Woodworth/iStockphoto; **109L** Palazzo Baberini. Rome/Dagli Orti/The Art Archive; **109R** John Steele/iStockphoto; **110TR** Corbis; **110BL** Wally McNamee/Corbis; **111TR** Natalia Bratslavsky/iStockphoto; **112** Warrick Page/Corbis; **116BR** Bob Krist/Corbis; **116T** Arne Thaysen/iStockphoto; **117BR** Ivan Mateev/iStockphoto; **118B** James Rabinowitz/Corbis; **119T** Yann Arthus-Bertrand/Corbis; **120T** Randy Mayes/iStockphoto; **121B** Steven Miric/iStockphoto; **122T** Dennis Sabo/iStockphoto; **123BL** Fabian Guignard/iStockphoto; **124TC** Mike Morley/iStockphoto; **124BR** Emilia Kun/iStockphoto; **125T** Rob Broek/iStockphoto; **126TL** iStockphoto; **126B** Stephen Hoerold/iStockphoto; **127TR** Ekatrina Fribus/iStockphoto; **128TL** Klemen Demsar/iStockphoto; **128BR** Marisa Allegra/iStockphoto; **129TR** Mark Weiss/iStockphoto; **130T** John Woodworth/iStockphoto; **131BR** Alan Toby/iStockphoto; **132BL** Paul Almasy/Corbis; **133TL** Andrew Cribb/iStockphoto; **133BR** Steven Tilson/iStockphoto; **134BR** Torleif Svensson/Corbis; **134TL** iStockphoto; **135TR** Michel de Nijs/iStockphoto; **136TL** iStockphoto; **136R** John Sigler/iStockphoto; **137TR** iStockphoto; **138B** iStockphoto; **139TR** iStockphoto; **140TL** Stefan Tordenmalm/iStockphoto; **140B** Ondrej Cech/iStockphoto; **141R** Andy Green-AGMIT/iStockphoto; **142B** Lisa Kyle Young/iStockphoto; **142TR** Felix Mockel/iStockphoto; **143C** Matthew Scholey/iStockphoto; **144** Angelo Cavalli/Getty Images; **145TR** Sandra O'Claire/iStockphoto; **146TL** Frank May/DPA/Corbis; **147CR** Bettmann/Corbis; **148TR** Gianni Dagli Orti/Corbis; **148BL** Nik Wheeler/Corbis; **149BL** Dave Wirtzfeld/iStockphoto; **149CL** Alan Collins/Alamy; **150TL** Historical Picture Archive/Corbis; **150CR** Bettmann/Corbis; **150CL** Peter Spiro/iStockphoto; **151B** Jeff Christensen/AFP/Getty Images; **152TL** Bettmann/Corbis; **153C** Jim Sugar/Corbis; **154TL** NASA; **154BR** The Scotsman/ Corbis/Sygma; **155C** Shannon Stapleton/Corbis; **156T** Alison Wright/Corbis; **156BL** Mario Anzuoni/Reuters/Corbis; **157B** Edward Parsons/UN/EPA/Corbis; **158** Rodrigo Buendia/AFP/Getty Images; **160B** Sandro Vannini/Corbis; **161C** Richard A. Cooke/Corbis; **162C** Bennett Dean/Eye Ubiquitous/Corbis; **163CR** Jeremy Horner/Corbis; **164TR** Corbis; **164L** Nancy Louie/iStockphoto; **165C** Elio Clol/Corbis; **166C** Fred de Noyelle/Godong/Corbis; **167TR** Mary Evans Picture Library; **168BL** Earl & Nazima Kowall/Corbis; **169TR** Reuters/Corbis; **169C** Nikhil Gangavane/iStockphoto; **170L** iStockphoto; **170TR** Pam Wardlaw/iStockphoto; **171C** Geoffrey Hammond/iStockphoto; **172C** Christine Balderas/iStockphoto; **172L** iStockphoto; **173B** Sharon Dominick/iStockphoto; **174B** Jiri Vatka/iStockphoto; **175L** Joza Pojbic/iStockphoto; **176** Brennan Linsley/AFP/Getty Images; **177TR** Lise Gagne/iStockphoto; **178C** Owen Franklen/Corbis; **180C** Christie's Images/The Bridgeman Art Library; **181T** Fine Art Photography Library/Corbis;

ACKNOWLEDGMENTS

182R Jeff Gynane/iStockphoto; **183CL** Gianni Dagli Orti/Corbis; **183BR** Katrina Leigh/Shutterstock; **184T** Gerald French/Corbis; **184C** Dusty Cline/iStockphoto; **185B** Reuters/Corbis; **186** Frank Rumpenhorst/epa/Corbis; **187T** Joel Blitt/iStockphoto; **188CL** Sandro Vannini/Corbis; **188TR** Bettmann/Corbis; **190B** Reuters/Corbis; **190TR** Neema Frederic/Corbis Sygma; **191TR** David L. Moore/Alamy; **192C** Arko Datta/Reuters/Corbis; **193TL** South West News/Rex Features; **193CR** WpN/UPPA/Photoshot; **194B** Tonylady/Shutterstock; **195B** Otto Rogge/Corbis; **196** Bryan Sinclaire/Alamy; **198C** Asier Villafranca Valasco/iStockphoto; **198B** Jim Jurica/iStockphoto; **199TC** Andrea Jemolo/Corbis; **199TR** Paul Hardy/ Corbis; **200B** Roger Antrobus/Corbis; **201T** Pawel Libea/Corbis; **202L** Jose Fuste Rag/Corbis; **203T** Paul Cheyne/iStockphoto; **204T** Jean-Philippe/Corbis ; **205CR** Richard T. Nowitz/Corbis; **206B** Liu Liqun/Corbis; **208** Terrafugia.com/Solent/Rex Features; **210B** Tony Arruza/Corbis; **212C** Aston Martin; **213T** Bill Nation/ Corbis Sygma; **214C** Tim Wimborne/Reuters/Corbis; **214TR** Thomas Hottner/iStockphoto; **215R** Robert Churchill/iStockphoto; **216B** Underwood & Underwood/Corbis; **216T** Bettmann/Corbis; **217R** Bettmann/Corbis; **218TL** Eileen Tweedy/Magdalene College, Cambridge/The Art Archive; **219B** Justin Lane/epa/Corbis; **219T** Reuters/Corbis; **220B** Jaques Langevin/Corbis; **220CL** Allison Marles/iStockphoto; **221T** Duncan Gilbert/iStockphoto; **222** David Sanger/Getty Images; **223T** Catherine dée Auvil/ iStockphoto; **224BL** Alison Wright/Corbis; **225T** Andres Balcazar/iStockphoto; **226BR** Ian Poole/iStockphoto; **226TL** Robert Dawson/ iStockphoto; **227T** Philip Date/Shuttertock; **228CR** Seth Joel/Corbis; **228T** iStockphoto; **229B** Amazon.com; **231TR** Mary Evans Picture Library; **232C** Blue Lantern Studio/Corbis; **234T** Blue Lantern Studio/Corbis; **235CL** Marisa Allegra Williams/ iStockphoto; **235BR** Rey Rojo/iStockphoto; **236R** Marvel Characters Inc./Corbis; **238** © Jacques Rougerie Architect; **239TR** iStockphoto; **240C** Joseph Sohm; ChromoSohm Inc./Corbis; **241T** Michael S Yamashita/Corbis; **242CR** Gillet Luc/iStockphoto; **242TL** Adrian Beesley/ iStockphoto; **243TR** Archivo Iconografico, SA/Corbis; **244C** Laryn Bakker/iStockphoto; **244BR** Matej Michelizza/iStockphoto; **245TR** Mitch Aunger/Shutterstock; **247TL** Gabe Palmer/Corbis; **247CR** iStockphoto; **247BR** Olga Shelego/iStockphoto; **248** Nils Jorgensen/Rex Features; **250TR** Dave Bartruff/Corbis; **251C** Bettmann/Corbis; **253TR** David Lees/ Corbis; **253C** Corbis; **254CL** Bettmann/Corbis; **254CR** Courtesy of Apple; **255C** Bettmann/Corbis; **255TR** Henry Dilz/Corbis; **257B** Jonathan Drake/Reuters/Corbis; **256BR** Luke Daniek/iStockphoto; **258TL** Sunset Boulevard/Corbis; **258C** Josef Philipp/iStockphoto; **259R** Fernando Mañoso/EFE/Corbis; **260B** Robbie Jack/Corbis; **261TL** Robbie Jack/Corbis; **262** Touchstone/ABC/ The Kobal Collection; **264TL** Swim Ink 2/LLC/Corbis; **265CR** Yann Arthus-Bertrand/Corbis; **266TL** Trapper Frank/Corbis Sygma; **267TR** Starstock/Photoshot; **267BL** Starstock/Photoshot; **268C** 20th Century Fox/ Album/AKG-Images; **269R** Moloshok/Reuters/Corbis; **270CR** Disney/The Kobal Collection; **271T** Pixar Animation Studios/ Walt Disney/AKG-Images; **271B** Warner Bros. Pictures/Image Move/AKG-Images; **272C** Andrew Gombert/epa/Corbis; **272TL** Sunset Boulevard/Corbis; **273TR** RKO/The Kobal Collection; **275C** Dan Herrick/iStockphoto; **276** Bob Frid/Corbis; **277TR** Tracy Hebden/iStockphoto; **278B** Duomo/Corbis; **279TR** Bettmann/Corbis; **280BR** Historical Picture Archive/Corbis; **280CL** Historical Picture Archive/Corbis; **281T** iStockphoto; **282BR** Karl Weatherly/Corbis; **283C** Everett/Photoshot; **284TL** Tim de Waele/Isosport/Corbis; **284C** Jorge Delgado/iStockphoto; **285R** Kay Nietfeld/epa/Corbis; **286TL** Tomasso DeRosa/Corbis; **286BR** Leo Mason/Corbis; **287TR** Jeff Lewis/Icon SMI/Corbis; **288TR** AFP/Getty Images; **289CR** Matt A. Brown/Newsport/Corbis; **290CR** Jim Sugar/Corbis; **291T** Stephane Reix/For Picture/Corbis; **292TR** Bettmann/Corbis; **293BL** Duomo/Corbis; **294BL** Andy Clark/Reuters/Corbis; **294TR** David Gray/ Reuters/Corbis; **295BR** Maggie Hallahan/Corbis; **296BL** Pichon P/Corbis/Sygma; **296TC** Jamie Squire/Corbis; **297T** Bryn Lennon/ Getty Images; **298TR** Olivier Marie/EPA/Corbis; **300BL** Kevin R Morris/Corbis; **300TR** Kelly-Mooney Photography/Corbis; **301CR** Steve Boyle/Newsport/Corbis; **302** Justin Dernier/epa/Corbis **305CL** Gianni Dagli Orti/Corbis; **305TR** Corbis; **306CR** Archivo Iconografico, SA/Corbis; **307B** Ralph White/Corbis; **307TL** Bettmann/Corbis